Contemporary Jewish Ethics and Morality

5-99
29/12

D0144158

Contemporary Jewish Ethics and Morality

A READER

Edited by

Elliot N. Dorff
Louis E. Newman

New York   Oxford
OXFORD UNIVERSITY PRESS
1995

Oxford University Press

Oxford   New York   Toronto
Delhi   Bombay   Calcutta   Madras   Karachi
Kuala Lumpur   Singapore   Hong Kong   Tokyo
Nairobi   Dar es Salaam   Cape Town
Melbourne   Auckland   Madrid

and associated companies in
Berlin   Ibadan

Copyright © 1995 by Oxford University Press, Inc.

Published by Oxford University Press, Inc.
198 Madison Avenue, New York, New York 10016-4314

Library of Congress Cataloging-in-Publication Data
Contemporary Jewish ethics and morality : a reader / edited by
Elliot N. Dorff, Louis E. Newman.
    p.   cm.   Includes bibliographical references.
    ISBN 0-19-509065-9. — ISBN 0-19-509066-7 (pbk.)
  1. Ethics, Jewish   2. Jewish law—Moral and ethical aspects.
3. Judaism and social problems.   4. Medicine—Religious aspects—
  Judaism.   5. Judaism—20th century.   I. Dorff, Elliot N.
          II. Newman, Louis E.
            BJ1285.C65   1995
        296.3′85—dc20   94-12180

4 6 8 9 7 5

Printed in the United States of America
on acid-free paper

For our children

Tammy, Michael, Dana, Havi, and Jonathan Dorff
and Etan and Jonah Newman

May God make you like Efraim and Menashe
May God make you like Sarah, Rebekah, Rachel, and Leah

May the Lord bless you and guard you.
May the Lord show you favor and be gracious to you.
May the Lord show you kindness and grant you peace.

PREFACE

This collection of essays grew out of a perceived need for a single volume which accurately reflects the developments within contemporary Jewish ethics over the past twenty years. During this period a substantial literature has developed, triggered partly by a renewed interest in ethics generally, partly by the dramatic developments in the area of medical technology in particular, and partly by the trend within the American Jewish community to reevaluate and reappropriate important aspects of Jewish tradition. In all, there are today numerous Jewish scholars and rabbis investigating issues in Jewish ethics and morality from a wide range of perspectives. But, until now, this work has not been collected in a single place and made accessible to a wide audience.

No reader of this sort can include everything that deserves to be read in this field, and we readily acknowledge that many other important and useful essays are not to be found here. Our goal has been to make this collection representative, not exhaustive. In the process of selecting and organizing these materials we have learned a good deal from one another and from many other colleagues as well. We are grateful to all those who provided guidance along the way. We wish to acknowledge two colleagues in particular whose comments were especially helpful in the early stages of our work. Peter Ochs made suggestions which resulted in a more diverse and representative collection of essays. Paul Lauritzen offered valuable advice about how to organize the articles in the most logical way. Their contributions helped make this reader more useful that it otherwise would have been.

We have chosen to dedicate this book to our children. Our offspring represent our faith in the future and our desire to preserve the best of what we have inherited. Our teaching of Jewish ethics—and our efforts to live morally in a Jewish way—have been influenced by our experiences as fathers. We hope that they, like their parents, will continue to find within their tradition "a tree of life to them that hold fast to it."

Los Angeles   E. N. D.
Northfield, Minn.   L. E. N.
May 1994

ACKNOWLEDGMENTS

The editors and publisher of this volume would like to thank the following authors, publishers, and executors for permission to reprint:

Menachem Kellner, "The Structure of Jewish Ethics," in *Contemporary Jewish Ethics,* Menachem Kellner, ed. (New York: Sanhedrin Press, 1978), pp. 3–18.

Louis Newman, "Ethics as Law, Law as Religion: Reflections on the Problem of Law and Ethics in Judaism," *Shofar,* vol. 9, no. 1 (Fall 1990), pp. 13–31. *Shofar,* Copyright © 1990, by Purdue Research Foundation, West Lafayette, Indiana 47907.

David Novak, "Natural Law, Halakhah, and the Covenant," in his *Jewish Social Ethics* (New York: Oxford University Press, 1992), pp. 22–44.

Harold M. Schulweis, "The Single Mirror of Jewish Images: The Pluralistic Character of Jewish Ethics," *University Papers* (January 1982) (Los Angeles: University of Judaism, 1982), pp. 1–16.

Elliot N. Dorff, "The Covenant: The Transcendent Thrust in Jewish Law," *Jewish Law Annual,* vol. 7 (1988), pp. 68–96.

S. Daniel Breslauer, "Modernizing American Jewish Ethics: The Liberal Dilemma," *Encounter,* vol. 43 (1982), pp. 143–56.

Eugene Borowitz, "The Jewish Self," in his *Renewing the Covenant* (Philadelphia: Jewish Publication Society, 1991), pp. 284–99.

Richard J. Israel, "Jewish Tradition and Political Action," in A. Jospe, ed., *Tradition and Contemporary Experience* (Washington, D.C.: B'nai Brith Hillel Foundations, 1970), pp. 189–204.

David H. Ellenson, "How to Draw Guidance from a Heritage: Jewish Approaches to Mortal Choices," in *A Time to Be Born and a Time to Die: The Ethics of Choice,* Barry Kogan, ed. (New York: Aldine de Gruyter), pp. 219–32. Copyright © 1990 Walter de Gruyter, Inc., New York.

Louis E. Newman, "Woodchoppers and Respirators: The Problem of Interpretation in Contemporary Jewish Ethics," *Modern Judaism* 10:2 (February 1990):17–42. Reprinted by permission of the John Hopkins University Press.

Elliot N. Dorff, "A Methodology for Jewish Medical Ethics," *Jewish Law Association Studies* Vol 7 (1991): 35–57.

Michael L. Morgan, "Jewish Ethics after the Holocaust," *Journal of Religious Ethics,* vol. 12, no. 2 (Fall 1984), pp. 256–77. Reprinted by permission of Religious Ethics, Inc.

Alfred Jospe, "The Meaning of Jewish Existence," in *Jewish Heritage Reader,* Lily Edelman, ed. (New York: B'nai Brith, 1965), pp. 87–97. Reprinted with permission from B'nai B'rith International Commission on Continuing Jewish Education.

Sol Roth, "Toward a Definition of Humility," *Tradition,* vol. 14 (1973–74), pp. 5–22. Copyright © Rabbinical Council of America. Reprinted with permission from Rabbi Sol Roth and the Rabbinical Council of America.

David Novak, "Some Aspects of Sex, Society, and God in Judaism," in his *Jewish Social Ethics* (New York: Oxford University Press, 1992), pp. 84–103.

Arthur Waskow, "Down-to-Earth Judaism: Sexuality," *Tikkun,* vol. 3, no. 2 (March/April 1988), pp. 46–49, 88–91. Copyright © 1988 by Arthur Waskow.

Martha A. Ackelsberg, "Jewish Family Ethics in a Post-*halakhic* Age," in David Teutsch, ed., *Imagining the Jewish Future,* (New York: State University of New York Press, 1992), pp. 149–64. Reprinted by permission of the State University of New York Press. Copyright © 1992.

Blu Greenberg, "The Theoretical Basis of Women's Equality in Judaism," in her *On Women and Judaism* (Philadelphia: Jewish Publication Society, 1981), pp. 39–55.

Robert Gordis, "Ecology and the Judaic Tradition," in his *Judaic Ethics for a Lawless World* (New York: Jewish Theological Seminary, 1986), pp. 13–22. Reprinted by permission of David Gordis, executor of the estate of Robert Gordis.

Seymour Siegel, "A Jewish View of Economic Justice," in Donald G. Jones, ed., *Business, Religion, and Ethics* (Cambridge, Mass.: Oelgeschlager, Gunn and Hain, 1982), pp. 89–98; reprinted by permission of Allen Siegel, executor of the estate of Seymour Siegel.

Elie Spitz, "The Jewish Tradition and Capital Punishment," in David M. Gordis, ed., *Crime, Punishment, and Deterrence: An American-Jewish Exploration* (Los Angeles: The Wilstein Institute of Jewish Policy Studies, 1991), pp. 49–55.

Fred Rosner, "Euthanasia," in Fred Rosner and J. David Bleich, eds., *Jewish Bioethics* (New York: Hebrew Publishing Co., 1979), pp. 253–65.

Byron Sherwin, "A View of Euthanasia," *Journal of Aging and Judaism,* vol. 2, no. 1 (1987), pp. 35–57. Copyright © Byron L. Sherwin.

David M. Feldman, "This Matter of Abortion," in his *Health and Medicine in the Jewish Tradition: L'Hayyim—To Life* (New York: Crossroad, 1986), pp. 79–90. Copyright © 1986 by Lutheran Institute of Human Ecology.

Sandra Lubarsky, "Judaism and the Justification of Abortion for Nonmedical Reasons," *Journal of Reform Judaism,* vol. 31 (1984), pp. 1–13.

Irving Greenberg, "The Ethics of Jewish Power," in Marc H. Ellis and Rosemary Radford Ruether, eds., *Beyond Occupation* (Boston: Beacon, 1990), pp. 22–36, 64–74. Copyright © Irving Greenberg.

Judith Plaskow, "Israel: Toward a New Concept of Community," in her in *Standing Again at Sinai* (San Francisco and New York: Harper Collins, 1991), pp. 107–20.

David Hartman, "Living with Conflicting Values," in his *Conflicting Visions: Spiritual Possibilities of Modern Israel* (New York: Schocken, 1990), pp. 231–42.

We would especially like to thank the following authors who wrote new articles for this volume:

Aaron L. Mackler, "Cases and Principles in Jewish Bioethics: Toward a Holistic Model."

Laurie Zoloth-Dorfman, "An Ethics of Encounter: Public Choices and Private Acts."

Annette Aronowitz, "Emmanuel Levinas's Talmudic Commentaries: The Relation of the Jewish Tradition to the Non-Jewish World."

Einat Ramon, "The Ethics of Ruling a Jewish State with a Large Non-Jewish Minority."

CONTENTS

Introduction   3

I Jewish Ethics   9

A. *The Literature and Context of Jewish Ethics*   *12*

1 The Structure of Jewish Ethics   12
Menachem Marc Kellner

B. *Theoretical Issues in Traditional Jewish Ethics*   *25*

2 Judaism: From Either/Or to Both/And   25
Harold M. Schulweis

3 Natural Law, *Halakhah,* and the Covenant   38
David Novak

4 The Covenant: The Transcendent Thrust in Jewish Law   59
Elliot N. Dorff

5 Ethics as Law, Law as Religion: Reflections on the Problem of Law and Ethics in Judaism   79
Louis E. Newman

C. *Reconceptualizing Jewish Ethics in Modern Times*   *94*

6 Modernizing American Jewish Ethics: The Liberal Dilemma   94
S. Daniel Breslauer

7 The Jewish Self   106
Eugene B. Borowitz

8 Jewish Tradition and Political Action   118
Richard J. Israel

D. *Methodological Problems: The Case of Jewish Medical Ethics*   *129*

9 How to Draw Guidance from a Heritage: Jewish Approaches to Mortal Choices   129
David H. Ellenson

10 Woodchoppers and Respirators: The Problem of Interpretation in Contemporary Jewish Ethics   140
Louis E. Newman

11 A Methodology for Jewish Medical Ethics   161
        Elliot N. Dorff

12 Cases and Principles in Jewish Bioethics: Toward a Holistic
        Model   177
        Aaron L. Mackler

E. Alternative Visions of Jewish Ethics   **194**

13 Jewish Ethics after the Holocaust   194
        Michael L. Morgan

14 Emmanuel Lévinas's Talmudic Commentaries: The Relation of
        the Jewish Tradition to the Non-Jewish World   212
        Annette Aronowicz

15 An Ethics of Encounter: Public Choices and Private Acts   219
        Laurie Zoloth-Dorfman

II Jewish Morality   **247**

A. Traditional Jewish Values and Virtues   **249**

16 The Meaning of Jewish Existence   259
        Alfred Jospe

17 Toward a Definition of Humility   284
        Sol Roth

B. Jewish Perspectives on Sex and Family   **271**

18 Some Aspects of Sex, Society, and God in Judaism   271
        David Novak

19 Down-to-Earth Judaism: Sexuality   289
        Arthur Waskow

20 Jewish Family Ethics in a Post-*halakhic* Age   300
        Martha A. Ackelsberg

21 The Theoretical Basis of Women's Equality in Judaism   315
        Blu Greenberg

C. Jewish Perspectives on Social Problems   **327**

22 Ecology and the Judaic Tradition   327
        Robert Gordis

23 A Jewish View of Economic Justice   336
        Seymour Siegel

24 The Jewish Tradition and Capital Punishment   344
        Elie Spitz

D. Jewish Perspectives on Medical Ethics **350**

    25 Euthanasia 350
        Fred Rosner

    26 A View of Euthanasia 363
        Byron Sherwin

    27 This Matter of Abortion 382
        David M. Feldman

    28 Judaism and the Justification of Abortion for
        Nonmedical Reasons 392
        Sandra B. Lubarsky

E. Jewish Perspectives on Politics and Power: The State of Israel **403**

    29 The Ethics of Jewish Power 403
        Irving Greenberg

    30 Israel: Toward a New Concept of Community 422
        Judith Plaskow

    31 Living with Conflicting Values 432
        David Hartman

    32 The Ethics of Ruling a Jewish State with a Large
        Non-Jewish Minority 441
        Einat Ramon

Epilogue: The Future of Jewish Ethics and Morals 455

Contributors 463

Suggestions for Further Reading 467

Contemporary Jewish
Ethics and Morality

INTRODUCTION

Basic Definitions and Presuppositions

Contemporary Jewish ethics addresses both perennial and distinctly modern moral problems using the resources of the classical Judaic tradition. Doing so requires Jewish ethicists to grapple with the relationship between tradition and modernity. On the one hand, the ethicists represented here believe that the moral insights found in classical Jewish literature—both Scripture and the voluminous rabbinic sources—constitute the primary resource for contemporary Jewish reflection on moral matters. Indeed, these ethicists stand apart from their secular counterparts by virtue of their commitment to think and act morally in ways essentially continuous with their religious-cultural heritage. On the other hand, contemporary Jewish ethicists are acutely aware that they work in an intellectual and social context which bears little resemblance to that of their ancestors. Modernity has radically altered the context of Jewish life and the scope of Jewish thought. Contemporary Jewish ethicists differ from one another, then, in the ways they balance the competing claims of tradition and modernity, in their understandings of how to maintain and interpret Jewish tradition, and in their responses to modern technology and philosophy. It is the purpose of this volume to orient readers to the breadth and diversity of contemporary Jewish ethical reflection on these matters.

Although all three Western religious traditions—Judaism, Christianity, and Islam—have come into conflict with the beliefs, methods, and morals of the modern secular world, certain special aspects of the Jewish case deserve some attention. To Jews, living as an oppressed (or, at best, tolerated) minority throughout Christian Europe, the Enlightenment ideas of people like John Locke, Jean-Jacques Rousseau, and Charles-Louis Montesquieu brought far-reaching changes in the social as well as the intellectual context of Jewish life. The resulting political emancipation during the late eighteenth and early nineteenth centuries enabled Jews to enter European society—by attending universities, owning land, engaging in all forms of commerce, holding public office—all of which had been restricted or prohibited in earlier centuries. The vast majority of Jews welcomed these social and political changes, and the subsequent transformation of Europe's Jews from a culturally (and in many cases physically) isolated people into a cosmopolitan group was extraordinarily rapid.

The intellectual revolution that followed was no less dramatic. Prior to this time most Jews had accepted as authoritative both Scripture and the body of rabbinic teaching contained in the Talmud and related literature. It represented the primary, if not exclusive, source of metaphysical truths, moral teaching, and spiritual guidance. In the aftermath of the Enlightenment, however, Jews found these traditional teachings problematic in numerous ways. Following traditional Jewish law (halakhah) was no longer convenient in a pluralistic society, nor did communal sanctions carry their traditional weight. Moreover, traditional teachings were based on religious beliefs and assumed a social world neither of which could any longer be taken for granted. The religiously based ethical teachings of the past could be embraced only insofar as they continued to seem relevant to the radically new intellectual and social context of Jewish life.

Thus modern Jewish thinkers have been forced to reassess their relationship to their own religious tradition, including that portion of their tradition which concerns specifically ethical matters. As one might expect, various thinkers have done this in a wide variety of ways. Some have preserved as much as possible the categories and concepts embedded in traditional Jewish teaching, drawing on the vast body of Jewish law as they seek precedents for contemporary moral problems. Others have been far more willing to overlook or reject the "letter" of traditional teaching in their search for its "spirit," which they believe can still be instructive. Despite their differences, however, traditionalists and liberals share two fundamental perspectives: that Jewish ethics must draw substantively on traditional Jewish teaching, since this is what ultimately distinguishes it from other systems of ethical thought and practice, and that traditional Jewish teaching is not self-evidently relevant to modern circumstances but must be appropriated and interpreted if it is to provide authentic moral guidance to modern Jews. Each of these assumptions merits further consideration.

Jewish ethics is Jewish insofar as it derives from the values of those religious authorities of the past whose teachings are preserved in classical Jewish religious literature. This presupposition, shared by all the contributors to this volume, is not self-evident. Many Jewish thinkers in the nineteenth century who were influenced by Kantian philosophy regarded ethics as inherently "universal," since all moral obligations derived from the very nature of human beings. For them, ethics could be "Jewish" only in the very limited sense that there could be particular Jewish expressions of universal values and obligations. By contrast, in this century the tendency toward "universalism" has been undermined first by the rise of existentialism with its emphasis on the particularity of experience and later by the development of Zionism with its focus on Jewish values as an expression of national identity. Thus, contemporary Jewish ethicists see themselves engaged in an endeavor which is distinctively Jewish because it is continuous with the religious experience and ethical perspectives of previous generations of Jews.*

This brings us directly to the second major presupposition of contemporary Jewish ethicists. It is apparent to all but the very most traditional contemporary writers (who are not represented here) that Jewish tradition can be made to address modern moral issues only with some difficulty. Plainly, in the late twentieth century we are faced with a great number of moral issues which, due to rapidly advancing technology and changing social conditions, are genuinely unprecedented. Even questions that have been with us for centuries, such as how much to respect fetal life and how to deal fairly with others in business, have taken on new dimensions as medical technology and commercial transactions have become more sophisticated. To draw from this religious-moral tradition, even to speak on its behalf, about contemporary moral issues thus requires a process of translation and interpretation.

---

*Of course, this in now way precludes Jewish ethicists from drawing upon other sources of ethics—especially philosophical and/or Christian ethics—which, in fact, many in this volume have done.

Again, not all thinkers "read" the tradition's values and apply them in the same way. But all are aware that it is their responsibility as Jewish ethicists to engage in this process of creative interpretation, making the tradition "live" by demonstrating its capacity to enlighten and inform our moral choices.

From all that has been said, it should be clear that contemporary Jewish ethics and morality are, of necessity, closely related to Jewish theology. How one understands and applies traditional Jewish moral teachings will depend, at least partly, on how one interprets basic theological concepts, such as revelation and redemption. Contemporary Jewish ethics is thus an extension of Jewish theology, indicating how certain religious understandings of the world have influenced moral insight and can continue to do so. As the essays in this volume amply attest, theological considerations influence the treatment of both theoretical and practical questions, both how Jews conceive of the ethical contours of their tradition and how they believe they ought to make specific moral decisions. In the concluding essay in this volume, we will have more to say about the theological ambiguities that characterize this field and that account for its distinctive tensions.

Finally, though for the sake of simplicity we sometimes refer to "Jewish ethics" in an inclusive sense, we have chosen to divide the subject matter according to the often-utilized distinction between "ethics" and "morality." Ethics (sometimes called "metaethics") refers to a theoretical enterprise, an effort to discover and critically assess the foundations of the good life. Thus, ethics concerns questions such as, what is the source of moral principles, how do we come to know them, and (in a religious system such as Judaism) what is the relationship between moral norms and other religious concepts. Morality, by contrast, concerns practical problems of determining what is the right thing to do in specific settings. Morality is also concerned with determining the best course of action in cases where there are competing goods and evils. So, discontinuing life support for terminally ill patients, establishing respectful relationships between men and women, and determining the just use of political power are all questions of morality or, as it is sometimes called, "applied ethics." While it is clear that ethics and morality are closely interrelated, for purposes of this book it has seemed advantageous to organize this material into these two separate categories of ethics and morals.

Criteria of Selection

In any volume such as this, significant choices must be made about which topics to cover and which essays to include. Many important essays, including some pieces that could be regarded as "classics," are not found here. In making the hard choices about what to present and what to exclude, we have been guided by several considerations.

First, we have sought to include authors whose work reveals significant attention to methodological issues. The best work in any field is that which engages foundational questions in the discipline as a whole. In the case of Jewish ethics, as we noted earlier, this means a willingness to recognize the ways in which one has chosen to appropriate and interpret the moral values and principles of the Jewish tradition. Unfortunately, many Jewish scholars working in this field present particular moral positions without explaining either the principles that guide their interpretation of classical sources, or why one interpretation may be preferable to others. This tendency has been especially prevalent among those Orthodox rabbis who feel that traditional texts speak directly to modern moral problems and so devote little attention to methodological issues. Hence, the selection of essays included here is heavily weighted toward non-Orthodox ethicists whose work is more theoretically oriented and who are more explicit (and self-critical) about their orientation.

Second, we have chosen essays that we believe accurately represent the diversity of perspectives in the field. In some cases, such as the essays on family, abortion, and euthanasia, we have deliberately juxtaposed essays that highlight sharply contrasting views. But we have also made a concerted effort to see that diverse voices have been included. Though few Jewish feminists have written on ethics per se, we believe their distinctive perspective is an integral component of the current Jewish intellectual landscape. Similarly, we have made a special effort to incorporate essays by less well-known figures, as well as some articles by the most prominent scholars in Jewish ethics whose work by and large is already recognized. By being inclusive in these ways, we hope to give readers a feel for the breadth and diversity of contemporary Jewish ethics and morality.

Third, we have attempted to find articles which are accessible to a general audience. Since it is our hope that this volume will be of use to both non-Jews and Jews, scholars and students, clergy and laypeople, we have chosen not to include essays which we felt were too techinical for this purpose. By the same token, in the opening section especially, we have tried to include several essays which orient readers in a general way to the world of Jewish ethics and law, thereby providing a context for what follows.

Finally, we have given preference to essays published in the last fifteen years. In fact, much new and exciting work has been done in this field in recent years, prompted in part by a resurgence of interest in ethics generally (especially in issues of biomedical ethics). At the same time, we have avoided as much as possible including articles which seemed so timely that they would quickly become dated. While the rapid pace of social and scientific developments seems destined to force ethicists continually into uncharted territory, it is our hope that the issues and views discussed in these pages will continue to be worthwhile reading for at least another fifteen years.

Organization

The organization of these materials is meant to reflect our sense of how Jewish ethics and morality can be approached most readily. Of course, anthologies are rarely read in their entirety, and each entry is intelligible independent of its placement in this volume. Still, it may be useful pedagogically to indicate why these materials may be best approached in the order presented.

We have chosen to place the section on ethics (theory) before morality (practice) so that readers will become acquainted with how and why Jewish ethics is distinctive before they are confronted with the specifics of Jewish moral norms. Arguably, the opposite order conforms more closely to traditional Jewish modes of thought, which tend to work from specific cases to generalizations. It seems, however, that for general readers the debates among Jewish ethicists over proper action will be more intelligible if they already understand the general foundations of Jewish ethical discourse. Thus, the volume opens with an essay designed to introduce readers to the history and literature of Jewish ethics, followed by several essays which take up core questions about the basic nature of Jewish ethics, especially its relationship to law and covenant. The section which follows directly addresses the place of religious tradition for contemporary Jewish ethicists. This issue, as we indicated, concerns the ways in which traditional values and texts should be interpreted and applied to modern problems. We use medical ethics as our example here. The concluding section of Part I presents several fresh approaches to Jewish ethics and offers some significant challenges to the orientation represented by most of the preceding essays.

The second half of this volume is devoted to contemporary Jewish morality. We open with two essays that explore the religious dimensions of classical Jewish moral values and virtues. In the two sections that follow we offer articles on issues that relate primarily to individual behavior (family and sexuality) and to social behavior (ecology, economic justice, and capital punishment). Questions of medical ethics, because they figure so prominently in current ethical discourse, seemed to warrant a section of their own. We conclude the book with reflections on ethics and politics in the Israeli context. We have placed these essays last since the issues raised here are in some ways the most unprecedented and so the problem of drawing upon the resources of the tradition is most acute.

Notwithstanding the breadth we have tried to achieve here, there is much else that could, and perhaps should, have been included. Overall, it is our hope that readers find that these essays provide entrée into the world of contemporary Jewish ethics and morality. If we have been successful, readers should feel after concluding this survey that they have acquired a general framework for understanding Jewish ethics and morality, including those aspects of the topic not specifically included in this volume. We thus include suggestions for further reading at the conclusion of the book in the hope that readers will realize, as Hillel once said, "The rest is commentary. Go and study."

I

JEWISH ETHICS

Jewish ethics—the theories underlying Jewish moral norms and ideals—comes out of the full richness of the Jewish tradition, its stories, laws, values, literature, customs, songs, poetry, and so forth. That is only to be expected: the theories which try to explain how Judaism and Jews make moral decisions and determine moral ideals are actually latter-day attempts of scholars to describe the methods and concepts implicit in the tradition itself. In other words, the tradition developed first, following its own inherent logic and history; the theories explaining how the tradition deals with morality come much later, after the tradition has had an opportunity to do its moral work for some time. At that point, if the tradition has made significant moral contributions and continues to do so, as Judaism has and does, philosophers and others begin to look for the underlying assumptions and methods of the tradition. They do so to understand its past performance better and to help those currently involved in the tradition to apply it to the present and the future.

Since Jewish moral theory, or Jewish ethics, then, is based upon the Jewish tradition, the first essay in this section describes the literature and development of many of the relevant texts of the Jewish tradition. It is not intended to be exhaustive; given the vastness of the Jewish tradition, no such essay could be. It probably pays too much attention to the legal manifestations of Jewish ethics and not enough to its theological and literary contexts. Still, it provides the reader with an overview of some of the most important texts and historical developments in Jewish ethics and morals up to the modern period.

The second section in Part I includes four essays on some of the most important theoretical points in traditional Jewish ethics. Harold Schulweis points out the pluralistic character of Jewish ethics, warning us against any facile (and perhaps self-serving) summary of its values as being, for example, this-wordly and not other-worldly. Instead, to understand Jewish ethics correctly, we must appreciate its many voices—and then ask how all of these voices are nevertheless part of a coherent tradition. David Novak's essay probes the complex relationship between Jewish ethics and natural law. Elliot Dorff asks a very modern question of the traditional understanding of things—namely, exactly what difference does it make that the Jewish tradition conceives of Jewish values in terms of the Jewish covenant with God? By posing that question Dorff reveals some of the salient ways in which Jewish ethics, as a religious approach to ethics, is both like and unlike secular systems of ethics. Finally, Louis Newman's article explores the relationship between Jewish ethics and Jewish law in light of the ambiguities inherent in the covenantal relationship.

The third section in Part I includes some contemporary attempts to reconceptualize Jewish ethics, veering from the traditional concepts described in the preceding section in response to one or another facet of modernity. Both S. Daniel Breslauer and Eugene Borowitz ask how a liberal Jew committed to the modern value of autonomy can nevertheless be committed also to Jewish values. If one has the right and perhaps even the obligation to make one's own moral decisions and to take responsibility for them, how can Judaism play a role in that process? Can a liberal Jew ever feel *commanded* to abide by the dictates of Jewish morals? If so, how can autonomy be reconciled with such normative qualities of Jewish ethics? Richard J. Israel does not ask those questions directly, as Breslauer and Borowitz do, but he assumes them as he explores how a contemporary Jew—in particular, he himself—can use the Jewish tradition and the realities and concerns of contemporary Jewish life to make what is both his own and yet a Jewish decision.

The fourth section applies these questions to a specific field, that of medical ethics. Hopefully, the essays in this part will make the questions embodied in the two preceding sections clearer and more compelling as these articles apply those questions to the concrete issues of bioethics. Because of the revolutionary changes in medicine in the twentieth century, people in Western countries live close to twice as long now as they did in 1900. While that is a blessing in most ways, it raises some sticky moral questions which our ancestors either never had to face, or confronted under very different medical realities. When we could not extend a person's life, we simply did our best to make dying as comfortable as possible; but now that we often *can* help people to live longer, we have to ask—at least in some circumstances— whether we *should*. Similarly, at the other end of life, we are now faced with difficult moral questions about new artificial methods to generate life, genetic engineering, and the termination of pregnancies where the rationale is not the life or health of the mother but the health status of the fetus.

The readings in the fourth section do not seek to answer such questions directly, although some of the essays in Part II will. Instead, the four articles of this section seek to delineate the methods by which the Jewish tradition can serve as a resource in answering such questions. Since the contexts, if not the questions themselves, involved in contemporary bioethics are so very new, are traditional Jewish sources from centuries and even millenia ago at all relevant to making contemporary decisions in this area? If so, how are Jewish sources to be used? David Ellenson, Louis Newman, Elliot Dorff, and Aaron Mackler discuss the difficulties in using the tradition for these purposes and develop some suggestions as to how it can nevertheless be helpful and perhaps even normative on this most contemporary topic of Jewish and general moral discourse.

The final section of Part I includes some new, alternative visions of Jewish ethics. The Holocaust was a historic event whose implications for Jewish life and thought are only now being developed, and Michael Morgan explores its relevance to contemporary Jewish ethics. Laurie Zoloth-Dorfman presents a feminist reading of the biblical Book of Ruth as a model for doing Jewish ethics in a different mode than hitherto practiced, and Annette Aronowicz explains how the insights of the French Jewish theologian, Emmanuel Levinas, point us in the direction of a Jewish ethic consciously and markedly different from one based on common Western assumptions.

If Part I does its job, it should alert the reader to the inextricable bond between the methodological questions it discusses and the specific moral questions which we all face. Only if we know *why* and *how* to use the Jewish tradition is it possible to speak sensibly of Jewish values and Jewish moral norms for our time. Therefore, even if we cannot come to a settled and universally agreed upon rationale and method for applying the Jewish tradition to our current moral concerns, we need ever to be cognizant of those issues so that we can better understand the status of any claims to be "the Jewish view" of any moral question.

A. The Literature and Context of Jewish Ethics

1

The Structure of Jewish Ethics

MENACHEM MARC KELLNER

The word *ethics* may be used and understood in many different ways. It is important, therefore, to define what ethics is in general before an attempt can be made to describe Jewish ethics in particular. Questions of ethics are, broadly speaking, questions of value. The province of ethics within the commonwealth of evaluative issues is determined by the particular values it seeks to understand, define, and elucidate. These are generally accepted to be good and evil, right and wrong. Ethics, that is, deals with (1) the ends which truly fulfill human personality, (2) the character of moral agents, and (3) the nature of moral obligation.

Generally speaking, statements of or about ethics are divided into three groups: descriptive, normative, and metaethical. *Descriptive ethics* simply describes actual moral behavior (i.e., behavior which may appropriately be described as good or evil, right or wrong) and actual moral reasoning. It does not attempt to prescribe or to judge such behavior.[1] *Normative ethics* purports to evaluate moral behavior or to determine moral principles. It seeks to determine the *norm* or *norms* of moral behavior. *Metaethics* takes the judgments of normative ethics as its subject. Thus it seeks not to make moral judgments but to analyze their nature. Judgments of metaethics describe and analyze words (such as "good" or "bad") and judgments (such as "murder is wrong" or "one ought always seek to maximize the greatest good for the greatest number").

Traditionally, philosophers concerned with ethics sought to give general moral guidance. Such philosophers were not usually concerned with the details of moral behavior so much as with its basic principles and their justification. Since World War II, however, and until the early 1970s, moral philosophers have increasingly given up the task of normative ethics in favor of pursuing the more purely philosophical questions of metaethics. The field of normative ethics was largely left to religious thinkers (often called "ethicists") who had always been active in it.[2]

The field of religious ethics is rather more difficult to define and describe than is that of philosophical ethics. Broadly speaking, it may be construed as the study of the ethical teachings of the various religious traditions.[3] In this sense it is purely descriptive. In the United States, however, in most academic contexts, "religious ethics" really means "Christian ethics," and is most definitely normative (or sometimes metaethical) as opposed to descriptive. To characterize Christian ethics thus construed, we may say that it is primarily concerned with translating the general moral-religious teachings of the Christian faith into general principles of moral conduct and into specific moral injunctions. It is further characterized by the fact that almost all systems of Christian ethics seem to presuppose some single overarching norm (often agape, or love). There is frequently disagreement over what the norm is or how to interpret it, but there is usually agreement that some such norm exists.

The situation in Christian ethics is conditioned by the fact that Christianity and its basic texts are fundamentally concerned with questions of faith. Thus, while no one can deny that the Christian religion is concerned with moral behavior, its specific teachings with respect to such behavior must be derived from the basic teachings of faith and are often a matter of dispute.[4]

Jewish ethical teaching, on the other hand, is conditioned by the fact that Judaism is a religion which emphasizes human behavior over general claims of theology and faith—a religion of pots and pans in the eyes of those who derogate its concern with actions.[5] Jewish tradition contains minutely detailed teachings regulating that behavior. The problem facing the Jewish ethicist, therefore, is not so much to derive moral obligations from general theological teachings but rather to justify his own undertaking in the face of the fact that the all-embracing character of Jewish law (*halakhah*) would seem to leave no room for supralegal Jewish ethics as such.[6] To characterize Jewish ethics simply, we may say that it attempts to show what Judaism, either in the guise of *halakhah* or in some other form, teaches about moral issues.[7]

We may conveniently divide the literature of what has been called Jewish ethics into four main periods: biblical, talmudic, medieval, and modern. Strictly speaking, the Bible and Talmud do not fall under our view here: they are the sources of Jewish ethics but do not in any systematic sense devote themselves to that subject. Permeated as they are with moral concern, they contain almost no texts specifically given over to ethics.[8] Furthermore, in an important sense all Jewish ethics which takes *halakhah* seriously is Talmudic not only because the Talmud is the source of *halakhah* but because any attempt to determine a *halakhic* position on virtually any issue must begin with an analysis of the relevant talmudic data. It is thus doubly difficult to talk of talmudic ethics as such.[9]

The situation changes radically in the medieval period with the rise of a distinct Jewish ethical literature seeking systematically to expound upon morals and human conduct. The literature of the period seems to fall rather naturally into four different and widely recognized categories: philosophic, rabbinic, pietistic, and kabbalistic. Joseph Dan points out[10] that medieval Jewish ethics appeared in many literary forms beyond what might be called the classical ethical literature of books and treatises on specific ethical issues. Among the many forms which ethical literature took, we find homiletical works, ethical wills[11] and letters, moralistic storybooks and collections of ethical fables, poetry, and commentaries on the biblical book of

Proverbs and on Tractate Avot. There were also concrete and specific manuals of behavior, the so-called *hanhagot*.

Jewish philosophy in the medieval period was deeply concerned with the question of the proper relationship between faith and reason. The literature of the Jewish philosophical ethics of the period reflects this concern in its emphasis on the problem of the proper relationship between religious and ethical perfection. The earliest of the Jewish philosophers to write on ethics, Saadia Gaon[12] and Solomon ben Judah ibn Gabirol,[13] simply took over systems of secular philosophical ethics whole and made no serious attempt to root them in Judaism. The situation was considerably changed by the appearance of *Duties of the Heart* (*Ḥovot haLevavot*) by Baḥya ben Joseph ibn Paquda, a Spanish thinker of the eleventh century.[14] Baḥya sought not only to instruct the Jew in religious and moral behavior but to develop an ethical system rooted in Judaism. In his book, Baḥya distinguishes between the (*halakhic*) obligations of the body, which directly involve behavior, and inner obligations, the "duties of the heart" of his book's title. There are many *halakhic* works, he says, devoted to an elucidation of the outward duties of the Jew, but none devoted to his inward obligations, and it is this gap that he seeks to fill. Baḥya's emphasis on inward disposition (*kavanah*) was perhaps the first expression of a motif which was to characterize and even dominate much of Jewish ethical literature and which was to blossom forth much later in the *Musar* movement. This is the idea that proper moral behavior could best be attained through the religious perfection of the individual. This may possibly reflect the fact that the availability of *halakhic* guidelines for most moral problems made their analysis by ethicists superfluous. Whatever the reason, however, it is certainly the case that Jewish ethical texts tend to emphasize character, development and personal virtues over social ethics. The latter is seen as dependent on the former.[15]

The greatest medieval Jewish philosophical ethicist was the most outstanding of the medieval Jewish philosophers, Moses Maimonides (1135–1204).[16] It was Maimonides' general position that faith and reason do not conflict,[17] and this attitude is reflected in his ethics. He adopts the basic outline of Aristotle's golden mean, rooting it, however, in Judaism and modifying it to meet the exigencies of the tradition as he understood it.[18]

Maimonides is the author, among other things, of three major works: *Commentary on the Mishnah*, the *Mishneh Torah* (or *Yad haḤazakah*), and the *Guide of the Perplexed* (*Morah Nevukhim*). The first two of these contain material directly relevant to Jewish philosophical ethics, while the *Guide* can be read as a work of which the ultimate end is ethical. The introduction to Maimonides' commentary to Tractate Avot is a self-contained ethical treatise, called *Eight Chapters* (*Shemonah Perakim*).[19] It is in this text in particular that he develops his ideas on the golden mean. The commentary to *Avot* itself is obviously also important here.[20] Maimonides' code of Jewish law, the *Mishneh Torah,* contains a number of texts in which ethics plays an important role. In particular, two parts of the first section of the book, the *Book of Knowledge* (*Sefer haMada*), are important: "Laws of Ethics" and "Laws of Repentance."[21] Maimonides' discussion of messianism at the end of the *Mishneh Torah* contains material which played an important role in Jewish ethics in the modern period.[22]

Mention should be made here also of the philosophical commentary to the Pentateuch of Levi ben Gerson (Gersonides, 1288–1344). At the end of each Torah portion, Gersonides listed those *to'aliyot* or advantages to be derived from the portion. Many of these are explicitly mentioned as being part of an ethical character.[23]

The tradition of medieval Jewish philosophy reached its apogee with the work of Maimonides; its descent thereafter was quick and precipitous. Certainly none of the philosophers who followed Maimonides, Gersonides included, had anything significant to add to his philosophical analysis of Jewish ethics. Indeed, given the general opposition to Jewish philosophy which followed upon the apostasy of so many Jews in Spain and Portugal in the fourteenth and fifteenth centuries (which was blamed, in part, on their devotion to philosophical pursuits), it is hardly surprising that there arose a trend in Jewish ethics in direct opposition to philosophical ethics. Writers identified with this category of Jewish ethical literature sought to demonstrate that rabbinic Judaism and its texts provided all that one required in order to generate a full-fledged ethical system. There was no need, they felt, to turn to the Greeks for ethical instruction. This literature contains little innovation, and seeks rather to apply rabbinic ethics directly to the conditions of the medieval world. The two most influential texts in this genre are Jonah ben Abraham Gerondi's *Gates of Repentance* (*Sha'arei Teshuvah*) (thirteenth century) and Isaac Aboab's *Candelabrum of Illumination* (*Menorat haMa'or*) (fourteenth century).[24]

The third generally recognized category of medieval Jewish ethical literature is that associated with the Hasidei Ashkenaz, a pietistic movement in twelfth- to thirteenth-century Germany. The major work in this category is the *Book of the Pious* (*Sefer Ḥasidim*), an extensive compilation attributed to Judah ben Samuel heḤasid of Regensburg (d. 1217).[25] German pietistic literature is concerned largely with specific problems and actual situations. It is marked by deep piety and superstition, and by an emphasis on the effort involved in a deed; the more difficult an action, the more praiseworthy it is. The *Book of the Pious* introduces the distinction between the law of the Torah and the much stricter law of Heaven. The pietist is marked by his adherence to the law of Heaven, which demands greater devotion and involves more difficulty than the law of the Torah which applied to all. This general attitude was to have tremendous influence on the development of European Jewry, and its effects are still felt strongly today.

Two other works in the tradition of German pietism deserve mention. These are the anonymous *Ways of the Righteous* (*Orḥot Ẓaddikim*)[26] and Rabbi Asher ben Jehiel's *Ways of Life* (*Orḥot Ḥayyim*).[27] *The Ways of the Righteous* was probably composed in Germany in the fifteenth century. It has had great influence and has been published over eighty times. Although its author was clearly influenced by Jewish philosophical ethics, there is no doubt that the book was written by one of the German pietists as it is permeated with the attitudes and values of that movement.

Rabbi Asher ben Jehiel (Asheri or Rosh: c. 1250—1327) was one of the leading *halakhists* of his generation. A refugee from Germany (where his father, his first teacher, was active in the pietist movement and was himself a student of Judah ben Samuel), R. Asher settled in Spain. His *Ways of Life,* often called *Ethical Manual of the Rosh* (*Hanhagot haRosh*) or *Testament of the Rosh* (*Ẓavva'at haRosh*), consists of ethical sayings arranged for daily recitation.

One of the major developments in the history of medieval Judaism was the rise of Kabbalah (Jewish mysticism).[28] This had definite impact on Jewish ethics, stimulating the development of a fairly well-defined class of kabbalistic-ethical texts. This literature is permeated with the kabbalistic idea that the actions of human beings have a profound impact on the very structure of the universe. There is a definite interdependence between the deeds of human beings and the mystical development of the world.

Of the many works in this category two of the most important are *Palm Tree of Deborah* (*Tomer Devorah*) by Moses ben Jacob Cordovero (1522–70)[29] and *Beginning of Wisdom* (*Reshit Ḥokhmah*) by Elijah ben Moses de Vidas (sixteenth century), a student of Cordovero's.[30] Cordovero's work is a detailed guide to ethical behavior, relating moral perfection on the one hand to mystical union with aspects of the deity on the other. He seeks to unfold the mystical and ethical significance of God's thirteen attributes of mercy (enumerated in Exod. 34:6–7 and Mic. 7:18–20) and to explain how it is possible to imitate them, as the *halakhah* demands. De Vidas makes explicit use of kabbalistic texts and develops the idea that the cosmic struggle between good and evil is affected by the moral behavior of individual human beings.

What may be the most important work in the field of kabbalistic ethics, *The Path of the Upright* (*Mesillat Yesharim*), is rarely considered to be in that category at all. This may simply reflect the fact that by the close of the Jewish middle ages (mid-eighteenth century), Kabbalah had so permeated all aspects of Jewish life that no one took special notice of a kabbalistic-ethical work. In addition to this, and more importantly, this work of Moses Ḥayyim Luzzatto made relatively little use of explicit kabbalistic texts, while still being overwhelmingly kabbalistic in tone.[31] Luzzato (1707–46), an Italian mystic, playwright, and ethicist, leads the reader of his book along the way or path of the upright, which begins with the forsaking of sin and culminates in mystical contact with God. *The Path of the Upright* develops the Mishnaic concept of the world as a corridor leading to the world to come; human life must be devoted to preparation for the ultimate end.[32] Luzzatto's book became enormously influential and popular; to this very day it is considered by many traditionalistic Jews to be the Jewish ethical text par excellence.

Before turning to a discussion of contemporary developments in Jewish ethics, we must consider one important and still-influential outgrowth of medieval Jewish ethics, the *Musar* movement. Jewish life in eastern Europe (specifically Poland and Russia) at the end of the Jewish middle ages was characterized by a marked religious, cultural, and social decline. Eastern European Jewry suffered what can only be called a "failure of nerve" as a consequence of the Chmielnicki massacres of 1648, the collapse of effective government in Poland which followed shortly thereafter in the face of the Ukrainian and Swedish wars, and the remarkable and pervasive despair and degradation of spirit engendered by the apostasy of the false Messiah, Shabbetai Zevi (1666).[33] In the face of these calamities, Jewish education suffered terribly; Talmud study became cold, rigid, and formalistic; the democracy and sense of mutual responsibility which had formerly characterized the Jewish communal organizations degenerated; and there arose a huge mass of ignorant and only nominally observant Jews.[34]

The most well-known reaction to this situation is to be found in the Hasidic movement, which sought to regenerate Jewish life and spirit. The Hasidic teachers, evangelical and charismatic religious leaders, tried to inject mysticism into everyday life and emphasized, as did the earlier pietists of medieval Germany, the importance of inwardness and intention as opposed to the formalistic obedience to law. The *Musar* (ethical reproof) movement may be seen as a non-Hasidic response to the same degradation of spirit which engendered Hasidism. The *musarniks* sought to bridge the gap between rabbinic training on the one hand and religious-ethical fervor on the other. The *Musar* movement was founded for the training of Jews in strict ethical-religious behavior. It emphasized character development (echoing one of the earliest and most consistent themes in medieval Jewish ethics) and concerned itself strongly with the psychological health of the individual. Followers of the *Musar* movement often organized themselves into small groups which met regularly to read ethical texts and to engage in mutual criticism and spiritual strengthening. By the early years of the present century, the *Musar* ideal had been adopted by most of the great European rabbinical academies (*yeshivot*), almost all of which set aside a portion of each day for the study of ethical texts and many of which had individuals on their staffs specifically devoted to the ethical guidance of the students.[35]

The distinction between contemporary and medieval Jewish ethics reflects the great difference that obtains between premodern and contemporary Judaism. Up until the end of the eighteenth century there was no country in Europe (and, outside of the United States, no country in the world at all) which recognized its Jews as full-fledged citizens possessed of normal civil rights. The spread of Enlightenment ideals, however, led to the gradual emancipation of European Jewry. But the call of emancipation was often couched in terms such as: "To the Jew as Frenchman, everything; to the Jew as Jew, nothing!" Emancipation was predicated in almost every case on assimilation. The Jews of western Europe were faced with a situation unique in their experience and were confronted with a wholly new problem: how to remain Jewish while simultaneously participating in Western civilization. It was largely by way of response to that problem that the various religious movements of contemporary Judaism—Orthodoxy, Conservatism, Reform—developed and defined themselves.

Contemporary Judaism is distinguished from medieval Judaism, therefore, in that it is faced with an entirely new problematic and in that it presents a multiplicity of answers to that complex of problems. With respect to the subject at hand, we may say that contemporary Jewish ethics is distinguished from medievel Jewish ethics in that the problems it faces are largely those it shares with the surrounding culture (e.g., the problem of relating morality and religion, and specific questions like political obedience and medical ethics). In short, Jews and Judaism have become part of the modern world and, to a significant degree, the modern world has become a factor which cannot be ignored by both Jews and Judaism. Contemporary Jewish ethics is further distinguished from its medieval counterpart by the fact that it speaks with a divided voice. One must not ask today, "What is the Jewish position on such and such?" but rather, "What is the Orthodox, Conservative, or Reform interpretation of the Jewish position on such and such?" Although many writers persist in presenting the Jewish position on various subjects, it very often ought more correctly to be characterized as *a* Jewish position.

In order to understand fully the differences between Orthodox, Conservative, and Reform Judaism one ought to examine them in terms of their historical development.[36] For our purposes, however, it should be sufficient to sketch out their basic theological differences. This can be done conveniently by examining their varying conceptions of revelation. Briefly put, Orthodoxy follows the traditional rabbinic claim that the Torah represents the direct, conclusive revelation of God's will. *Halakhah,* which derives directly from that revelation, is the will of God. It is normative for all Jews in all places and at all times. Although Orthodoxy recognizes the fact of *halakhic* change, it insists that such change has come about and may come about only within the context of well-recognized *halakhic* mechanisms. The basic Orthodox contention with respect to the *halakhah* is that it is a divine, not a human, system and that as such it is not subject, in essence, to the sort of historical development which is characteristic of human institutions.

Reform Judaism, on the other hand, in both its classic and modern positions, entirely rejects the claim that the *halakhah* represents the revealed will of God. Revelation, it maintains, is progressive, akin to inspiration, and is ultimately concerned with ethics. This emphasis is summed up in the famous motto of early Reform, that Judaism is nothing more than ethical monotheism. While contemporary Reform thinkers have largely given up the classic Reform claim that Judaism took a quantum leap from the time of the Prophets (in whose call for social morality early Reform thinkers saw God's revelation most clearly embodied) to the nineteenth century and the rise of Reform, it is still the case that Reform Judaism rejects the *halakhah* as a norm and still looks to the prophetic tradition for the "essence" of Judaism.

The Conservative[37] position is roughly midway between that of Orthodoxy and Reform. Conservative Judaism does not view revelation as God "talking" to the Jewish people, as it were, revealing to them exactly what it is he wants them to do. Rather, Conservative Judaism maintains that the Jewish people have had what may be called "revelatory" experiences of God, to which they responded by creating the Torah. *Halakhah,* then, is the way in which Jews have sought to preserve their experiences of God. Although taking its source in the Jews' experience of God, it is basically a human institution and undergoes change and historical development like all human institutions. It is normative in the conditional sense that one ought to obey the *halakhah* if one wants to preserve the insights and experiences of the Jewish people as a whole and of those Jews in particular who have confronted God directly in their own lives. Conservative Judaism thus sees the *halakhah* as the Jewish vocabulary for approaching God. It does not see the *halakhah* as normative in the absolute sense, however, which would imply that obedience to *halakhah* is explicitly demanded of every Jew by God.[38]

These three different interpretations of revelation and *halakhah* give rise to different emphases within Jewish ethics. Generally speaking, Orthodox thinkers will approach questions of ethics by seeking to determine the teachings of the *halakhah* on the issues at hand. That is not to say that they do not recognize a super-*halakhic* realm of Jewish ethical teaching. Aharon Lichtenstein, for example, has shown the extent to which an Orthodox thinker can recognize such a realm. But no Orthodox thinker will admit the possibility of there being a Jewish ethical teaching which might contradict *halakhah*.[39] That possibility, however, is explicitly stated by at least one important Conservative thinker, Seymour Siegel. "It is my thesis," he writes, "that according to our interpretation of Judaism, the ethical values of our tradition should have power to judge the particulars of Jewish law. If any law in our tradition does not fulfill our ethical values, then the law should be abolished or revised."[40] This position would most likely be rejected by Orthodox thinkers on the grounds that it sets human beings up as judges of God's law.

Generally speaking, at least until the 1970s, the Reform approach to ethics has been to identify Jewish ethics with prophetic teachings which, in turn, were usually interpreted in terms of contemporary liberalism. Of late, however, Reform thinkers have shown new sensitivity to the teachings of the postbiblical Jewish tradition and generally seek to ground their ethical judgments in the Jewish tradition as a whole.[41]

Summing up, we may say that the contemporary Jewish approach to ethical problems is distinguished from the medieval approach in at least two important ways. It is no longer informed by the basic unanimity of spirit which underlay medieval Jewish ethics in all its various styles and forms. Further, and as a result of the Jew's unprecedented level of integration into the surrounding world, Jewish ethics today faces an entirely new complex of problems. Although there are elements of continuity between medieval and modern Jewish ethics, the discontinuities are more important. This is one of the many ways in which the wrenching changes which accompanied the Jewish entry into the modern world are reflected. It is basically the confrontation with that world which sets the theme for the essays collected in this volume, exploring the new problems facing contemporary Judaism and the novel approaches taken to solve them.

Notes

1. I am using the terms "ethics" and "morals" interchangeably here even though there are some differences in usage between them. The term "ethics" seems to have more of a practical, actional connotation than does "morals" (we say "medical ethics," for example, not "medical morals").

2. Good, brief descriptions of philosophical ethics may be found in William K. Frankena, *Ethics,* 2nd ed. (Englewood Cliffs, N.J., 1973), pp. 1–11, and in P. H. Nowell-Smith, *Ethics* (London, 1954), pp. 11–35. In the last few decades, it should be noted, philosophers have once again been devoting attention to normative ethics. The appearance of John Rawls's *A Theory of Justice* and of such journals as *Social Theory and Practice* and *Philosophy and Public Affairs* are indicative of this renewed interest.

3. For a fuller, and very important, discussion of the nature of religious ethics, see David Little and Sumner B. Twiss, "Basic Terms in the Study of Religious Ethics," in Outka and Reeder (eds.), *Religion and Morality* (New York, 1973), pp. 35–77. On the general question of the relationship between religion and morality, see the essays in the Outka and Reeder volume and the essays by Fackenheim, Samuelson, Jacobs, and Leiman in Menachem Kellner, ed., *Contemporary Jewish Ethics* (New York: Sanhedrin Press, 1978), pp. 61–83, 84–100, 41–57, and 58–60, respectively.

4. James Gustafson has devoted much attention to the delineation of the scope and content of Christian ethics. In particular, one ought to consult his *Christ and the Moral Life* (New York, 1968), chaps. 1 and 7; "What Is the Contemporary Problematic of Ethics in Christianity?" *CCAR Journal* (January, 1968), pp. 14–26; and "Theology and Ethics," in his *Christian Ethics and the Community* (Philadelphia, 1971), pp. 83–100. Further relevant readings include Bernard Häring, "Essential Concepts of Moral Theology," in Gustafson and Laney (eds.), *On Being Responsible* (New York, 1968), pp. 86–108; Clyde A. Holbrook, "The Problem of Authority in Christian Ethics," *Journal of the American Academy of Religion* 37 (1969), pp. 26–48; Roger Mehl, *Catholic Ethics and Protestant Ethics* (Philadelphia, 1971), pp. 15–42; and Paul Ramsey, *Basic Christian Ethics* (New York, 1950), chaps. 3–6.

5. Among the comparative studies of Jewish and Christian ethics which may be consulted with profit are: Elie Benamozegh, *Jewish and Christian Ethics* (San Francisco, 1873); I. M. Blank, "Is There a Common Judeo-Christian Ethical Tradition?" in D. J. Silver (ed.),

Judaism and Ethics (New York, 1970), pp. 95–108; Aḥad Ha'am (Asher Ginzberg) in Leon Simon (ed.), *Philosophia Judaica: Ahad Ha'am* (London, 1946), pp. 127–37; Joseph Klausner, "Jewish and Christian Ethics," *Judaism* 2 (1953), pp. 16–30; Kaufman Kohler, "Synagogue and Church in Their Mutual Relations, Particularly in Reference to the Ethical Teachings," in *Judaism at the World Parliament of Religions* (Cincinnati, 1894), pp. 114–26; and H. F. Rall and Samuel S. Cohon, *Christianity and Judaism Compare Notes* (New York, 1927). Two chapters of Benamozegh's work were separately translated into English by William Wolf and published in *Judaism* 13 (1964), pp. 220–27 and 346–50.

6. General studies of Jewish ethics as a whole include two works by Jacob Bernard Agus, *The Vision and the Way: An Interpretation of Jewish Ethics* (New York, 1960), and "Jewish Ethics," in his *Dialogue and Tradition* (New York, 1971). pp. 442–49. Other works include Simon Bernfeld (ed.), *The Foundations of Jewish Ethics* (New York, 1929 and 1968); Mordecai M. Kaplan, "A Philosophy of Jewish Ethics," in Louis Finkelstein (ed.), *The Jews: Their Role in Civilization* (New York, 1949 and 1971), pp. 32–64; Moritz Lazarus, *The Ethics of Judaism* (Philadelphia, 1900); and Mordecai Waxman, *Judaism: Religion and Ethics* (New York, 1958).

7. "*Halakhah*" means Jewish law and practice.

8. The one notable exception to this generalization is the Mishnaic tractate *Avot* ("Fathers"), a compilation of rabbinic moral maxims and homilies, and its related literature. Of the many translations of this text two are of particular importance: R. Travers Herford's *Ethics of the Talmud* (New York, 1962) presents a critical edition of the text, an accurate translation, and valuable historical notes. His introduction is particularly helpful: among other things, he explains how a work like *Avot* came to be included in the Mishnah. In his *Living Talmud* (New York, 1957), Judah Goldin presents the reader with a brilliant and elegant translation of the text coupled with a representative sampling of medieval Jewish commentaries on it. This makes his edition of great value for the study of medieval Jewish ethics as well. Goldin is also the editor and translator of *The Fathers according to Rabbi Nathan* (New Haven, 1955, and New York, 1974), another text from the period of the Mishnah which parallels *Avot*. The translation is distinguished, the notes scholarly and helpful. For a selection of other talmudic texts on moral subjects, one may consult Montefiore and Loewe (eds.), *A Rabbinic Anthology* (New York, 1974), pp. 382–99. The secondary literature on rabbinic ethics per se (as opposed to studies of contemporary ethical problems which draw upon rabbinic materials) is not large. Among the most accessible and helpful studies are the following: A. Cohen, *Everyman's Talmud* (New York, 1949), pp. 210–37; David Daube, *Collaboration with Tyranny in Rabbinic Law* (London, 1965); Max Kadushin, "Introduction to Rabbinic Ethics," *Yehezkel Kaufman Jubilee Volume* (Jerusalem, 1960), pp. 88–114; Max Kadushin, *Worship and Ethics: A Study in Rabbinic Judaism* (Chicago, 1964); and George Foot Moore, *Judaism in the First Centuries of the Christian Era*, vol. 2 (Cambridge, 1927, and New York, 1971), pp. 79–197. On biblical ethics generally, see I. Efros, *Ancient Jewish Philosophy* (New York, 1964 and 1976), part 2, "The Philosophy of Biblical Ethics."

9. See David Feldman, "The Structure of Jewish Law," in his *Birth Control in Jewish Law* (New York: New York University Press, 1968), ch. 1, for a discussion of what Mishnah and Talmud are.

10. In his excellent article on "Ethical Literature" in the *Encyclopaedia Judaica* (Jerusalem, 1972), vol. 6, cols. 922–32. Dan is also the author of many of the other articles in the *Encyclopaedia* relating to Jewish ethical literature. See Vol. 1 (Index), p. 438, s.v. "Ethical Literature" and "Ethics." There are two histories of Jewish literature which contain material relevant to medieval Jewish ethics. These are Meyer Waxman, *A History of Jewish Literature*, 4 vols. (New York, 1938–41) and Israel Zinberg, *A History of Jewish Literature*, vols. 1–3 (Cleveland, 1972–73), Vols. 4–9 (New York, 1974–76). Two anthologies which contain selections from medieval Jewish ethical texts are Curt Leviant, *Masterpieces of Hebrew*

Literature (New York, 1969), and Louis Jacobs, *Jewish Ethics, Philosophy, and Mysticism* (New York, 1969).

11. See Israel Abrahams' collection, *Hebrew Ethical Wills* (Philadelphia, 1948 and 1976).

12. Saadia ben Joseph (892–942) initiated the tradition of medieval Jewish philosophy. He was a *Gaon*, head of one of the talmudic academies in Babylonia. His major work, the *Book of Beliefs and Opinions* (*Emunot veDeot*), is available in two English translations. The first, under the title just given, is by Samuel Rosenblatt (New Haven, 1948). The second, a partial translation, was published by Alexander Altmann under the title *Book of Doctrines and Beliefs* (Oxford, 1956). This translation was republished together with selections from Philo and Judah Halevi under the title *Three Jewish Philosophers* (New York, 1960). Saadia's views on ethics are included in Treatise Ten of his book, on "proper conduct." The standard study of Saadia is Henry Malter's *Saadia Gaon: His Life and Works* (Philadelphia, 1921). On his philosophy generally, see Isaac Husik, *A History of Medieval Jewish Philosophy* (New York, 1930 and 1969), pp. 23–47, and Julius Guttmann, *Philosophies of Judaism* (New York, 1973), pp. 69–83. On Saadia's ethics, see I. Efros, "Saadia's General Ethical Theory and Its Relation to Sufism," *JQR 75th Anniversary Volume*, pp. 166–77, and Marvin Fox, "On the Rational Commandments in Saadia's Philosophy: A Reexamination," in M. Fox (ed.), *Modern Jewish Ethics* (Columbus, Ohio, 1976), pp. 174–87.

13. Solomon ben Judah ibn Gabirol (c. 1021–1058) was a neoplatonist philosopher and poet. On Gabirol generally, see Husik, pp. 59–79, and Guttmann, pp. 101–16. Gabirol is the author of an ethico-psychological work (*Tikkun Middot haNefesh*) called, in I. M. Wise's translation, *On the Improvement of the Moral Qualities* (New York, 1901). This is analyzed in D. Rosin, "The Ethics of Solomon ibn Gabirol," *Jewish Quarterly Review* (Old Series), vol. 3 (1891), pp. 159–81. *Choice of Pearls* (*Mivḥar haPeninim*), a collection of ethical maxims and proverbs heavily influenced by Arabic literature, is also attributed to Gabirol, although that attribution is doubted by many scholars. It was translated by B. Ascher (London, 1859) and A. Cohen (New York, 1925). Alexander Marx analyzes the problem of Gabirol's authorship of this work in "Gabirol's Authorship of the 'Choice of Pearls' and Two Versions of Joseph Kimchi's *Shekel HaKodesh*," *Hebrew Union College Annual* 4 (1927), pp. 433–48.

14. Baḥya's work has appeared in two English versions. Moses Hyamson translated the book from a medieval Hebrew version of the Arabic original (Jerusalem, 1965), Menahem Mansoor's version, translated directly from the original Arabic, is called *The Book of Direction to the Duties of the Heart* (London, 1973). On Baḥya generally, see Husik, pp. 80–105, and Guttman, pp. 117–23.

15. Mention ought to be made here also of the work of Abraham bar Ḥiyya of Barcelona (twelfth cent.), author of the *Meditation of the Sad Soul* (*Hegyon haNefesh haAẓuvah*), translated by Geoffrey Wigoder (London, 1969). Leon Stitskin analyzed bar Ḥiyya's contribution to Jewish philosophical ethics in his *Judaism as a Philosophy: The Philosophy of Abraham bar Hiyya* (New York, 1960).

16. For a general introduction to his life and works see Isadore Twersky (ed.), *A Maimonides Reader* (New York, 1972), and the literature cited in the bibliography there. On his thought generally, see also Husik, pp. 236–311, and Guttman, pp. 172–206.

17. For the necessary qualifications on this otherwise hopelessly broad generalization, see Norbert Samuelson, "Philosophic and Religious Authority in the Thought of Maimonides and Gersonides," *CCAR Journal* (October 1969), pp. 31–43.

18. For a very valuable study of Maimonides' modifications of the doctrine of the mean, see Steven Scharzschild's "Moral Radicalism and Middlingness in Medieval Jewish Ethics," *Studies in Medieval Culture* 11 (1977), pp. 65–94.

19. This was translated by J. Gorfinkle under the title *The Eight Chapters of Maimonides on Ethics* (New York, 1912 and 1966). Herbert Davidson subjects this work to close textual

study in "Maimonides' 'Shmonah Perakim' and Al-Farabi's *Fusul al Madani*," *PAAJR* 31 (1963), pp. 33–50. See also Harry S. Lewis, "The Golden Mean in Judaism," *Jewish Studies in Memory of Israel Abrahams* (New York, 1927), pp. 283–95, and Eliezer Schweid, *Studies in Maimonides' "Eight Chapters,"* 2nd ed. (Jerusalem, 1969).

20. *Commentary to Aboth,* translated by Arthur David (New York, 1968).

21. Volume 1 of the *Mishneh Torah,* the *Book of Knowledge,* was translated into English by Moses Hyamson (New York, 1974). In referring to "*Hilkhot Deot*" as the "Laws of Ethics" I am following the suggestion of R. L. Weiss, "Language and Ethics: Reflections on Maimonides' 'Ethics'." *Journal of the History of Philosophy* 9 (1971), pp. 425–33. On the ethical teaching of the *Book of Knowledge,* see Leo Strauss, "Notes on Maimonides' Book of Knowledge," in E. E. Urbach, R. J. Zwi Werblowsky, and Chaim Wirszubski, eds., *Studies in Mysticism and Religion Presented to Gershom Scholem* (Jerusalem: Magnes Press [Hebrew University], 1967), pp. 269–83; R. L. Weiss, *Wisdom and Piety: The Ethics of Maimonides* (Chicago, 1966); A. Cronbach, "The Maimonidean Code of Benevolence," *HUCA* 20 (1947), pp. 471–540; and H. I. Levine, "The Experience of Repentance: The Views of Maimonides and William James," *Tradition* 1 (1958), pp. 40–63. On the *Mishneh Torah* generally, see David Feldman, *Birth Control* [at n. 8], ch. 1.

22. Maimonides' most important statements about the Messiah are found at the very end of his *Mishneh Torah,* in his "Laws of Kings" (*Hilkhot Melakhim*), the last section of the *Book of Judges,* translated by A. M. Hershman (New Haven, 1949), and in his commentary to the tenth chapter of Mishnah *Sanhedrin.* This commentary was translated by A. J. Wolf in *Judaism* 15 (1966), pp. 95–101, 211–16, and 337–42. This translation is included in Twersky's *A Maimonides Reader,* pp. 401–23.

Many of Maimonides' ethical writings are collected conveniently in Raymond L. Weiss and Charles E. Butterworth (eds.), *Ethical Writings of Maimonides* (New York, 1976), as well as in Twersky's anthology. Further studies on the subject include B. Z. Bokser, "Morality and Religion in the Theology of Maimonides," in J. L. Blau (ed.), *Essays on Jewish Life and Thought* (S. W. Baron Festschrift) (New York, 1959), pp. 139–58; Marvin Fox, "Maimonides and Aquinas on Natural Law," *Dine Yisrael* 3 (1972), pp. 5–36 and reprinted in J. Dienstag (ed.), *Studies in Maimonides and St. Thomas Aquinas* (New York, 1975); and Steven S. Schwarzschild, "Do Noachites Have to Believe in Revelation?" *JQR* 52 (1961–62), pp. 297–308 and 53 (1962–63), pp. 30–65.

23. Although a seventeenth-century Yiddish translation of the *To'aliyot* exists, they were never translated into any other language. Published independently of the Bible commentary in their original Hebrew, they achieved widespread popularity. Further on the *To'aliyot* see Zinberg, vol. 3, pp. 138–39. On Gersonides generally, see Husik, pp. 328–61, Guttman, pp. 236–53.

24. Gerondi's *Gates of Repentance* was and is a book of wide influence and has been published repeatedly in the centuries since it was written. It was translated by S. Silverstein (Jerusalem, 1967). On Gerondi see Waxman, vol. 2, pp. 273–74.

The *Candelabrum of Illumination* is actually the name of two fourteenth-century ethical compilations. Aboab's book became one of the standard Jewish religious texts of the Middle Ages, going through over seventy editions. It has been translated into Spanish, Ladino, Yiddish, and German. See Waxman, vol. 2, pp. 282–87, and I. Efros, "The Menorat Ha-Maor," *JQR* 9 (1918–19), pp. 337–57. The other book of the same name, which remained in manuscript until the present century, was written by Israel ben Joseph al-Nakawa of Toledo (d. 1391). On this book see Waxman vol. 2, pp. 279–80, and Israel Davidson, "Enelow's Edition of Al-Nakawa's Menorat HaMeor," *JQR* 21 (1930–31), pp. 461–68.

25. Portions of the *Book of the Pious* were published in English translation by S. Singer under the title *Medieval Jewish Mysticism—Book of the Pious* (Northbrook, Ill., 1971), and by A. Cronbach, "Social Ethics of 'Sefer Hasidism,' " *HUCA* 22 (1949), pp. 1–148. On the Ḥasidei Ashkenaz see Waxman, vol. 1, pp. 360–64; Zinberg, Vol. 2, pp. 35–56; Gershom

Scholem, *Major Trends in Jewish Mysticism* (New York, 1961), pp. 80–118; S. Kramer, *God and Man in the Sefer Hasidim* (New York, 1966); A. Rubin, "Concept of Repentance among Hasidei Ashkenaz," *Journal of Jewish Studies* 16 (1965), pp. 161–76; and Haym Soloveitchik, "Three Themes in the *Sefer Hasidim*," *AJS Review* 1 (1976), pp. 311–58.

26. Translated under that title by S. J. Cohen (New York and Jerusalem, 1974).

27. Published as *Orchos Chayim LehawRaush or The Pathways of Eternal Life* by K. S. Orbach (Israel, 1968).

28. On the Kabbalah, see Scholem's *Major Trends,* the standard work in the field. His articles on the major figures, works, and issues of the Kabbalah from the *Encyclopaedia Judaica* have been collected and published under the title *Kabbalah* (New York, 1974). He is also the author of *On the Kabbalah and Its Symbolism* (New York, 1969).

29. Translated by Raphael Ben Zion (Jacob Cohn) in *The Way of the Faithful: An Anthology of Jewish Mysticism* (Los Angeles, 1945), pp. 11–80, and by Louis Jacobs (London, 1960).

30. On de Vidas, see Waxman, vol. 2, pp. 288–89, and Zinberg, Vol. 4, pp. 56–62.

31. Luzzatto's book was translated by Mordecai M. Kaplan under the title *Mesillat Yesharim: The Path of the Upright* (Philadelphia, 1936 and 1964). On Luzzatto, see Simon Ginzberg, *The Life and Works of M. H. Luzzatto* (Philadelphia, 1931), and Zinberg, vol. 6, pp. 186–87.

32. *Avot* 4:16.

33. On Sabbateanism, see Gershom Scholem's *Sabbatei Sebi* (Princeton, 1973).

34. For the historical background, see Howard M. Sachar, *The Course of Modern Jewish History* (New York, 1958), pp. 25–35.

35. The literature on the *Musar* movement in English is extensive. Two general works which ought to be consulted are Zalman F. Ury, *The Musar Movement* (New York, 1970), and Lester S. Eckman, *The History of the Musar Movement* (New York, 1975). The notes in Hillel Goldberg, "Toward an Understanding of Rabbi Israel Salanter," *Tradition* 16 (1976), pp. 83–119, constitute an annotated bibliography of some writings on the subject. At least one *musar* text is available in English: Rabbi Joseph Hurwitz of Nevardok's *Mezake HaRabim: To Turn the Many to Righteousness,* translated by S. Silverstein (New York and Jerusalem, 1972). Mention ought to be made here of the work of Rabbi Israel Meir haKohen (Kahan, Kahana, Kagan), 1838–1933. Universally known as the "Hafez Hayyim," he is the most distinguished modern expositor of traditional rabbinic ethics. Many of his writings have appeared in English translation. Among them are: Leonard Oschry (trans.), *Ahavath Hessed: Kindness as Required by God* (Jerusalem, 1967); A. Kagan (trans.), *The Dispersed Hand of Israel* (New York, 1951); S. E. Brog (trans.), *Fortress of Faith* (New York, 1964); and I. Aryeh and J. Dvorkes (eds. and trans.), *Hafetz Hayyim on the Siddur* (Jerusalem and New York, 1974). Mendel Weinbach has collated and translated some of the Hafez Hayyim's ethical teachings in *Who Wants to Live* (Jerusalem, 1968), and *Give Us Life* (Jerusalem, 1969). Biographical studies include M. M. Yosher, *Saint and Sage* (New York, 1935), and Lester Eckman, *Revered by All* (New York, 1974).

36. This is admirably done in David Rudavsky, *Modern Jewish Religious Movements* (New York, 1967).

37. The reader should be careful to differentiate our use of the word "Conservative," denoting the movement, and "conservative," in its usual adjectival meaning.

38. On the contemporary situation with respect to the three main interpretations of Judaism, see Eugene B. Borowitz, "The Prospects for Jewish Denominationalism," *Conservative Judaism* 30 (1976), pp. 64–74.

39. For an Orthodox perspective on this problem see Emanuel Rackman, "Jewish Law in the State of Israel: Reflections from History," *Dine Yisrael* 6 (1976), pp. vii–xxiv, esp. pp. xxi–xxiv. The essay by Eliezer Berkovits in Kellner, ed., *Contemporary Jewish Ethics* (New York: Sanhedrin, 1978), pp. 335–74, however, shows how far a thinker of impeccably Ortho-

dox credentials is willing to go in judging *halakhah* by ethical norms (which norms, however, he assimilates into *halakhah* itself). See also Aharon Lichtenstein, "Does Jewish Tradition Recognize an Ethic Independent of Halakha?" in Kellner, *Contemporary Jewish Ethics,* pp. 102–24.

40. Seymour Siegel, "Ethics and the Halakhah," *Conservative Judaism* 25 (1971), pp. 33–40, see pp. 33–34.

41. For a general view of Reform ethical thinking today, see the various essays in D. J. Silver (ed.), *Judaism and Ethics* (New York, 1970).

B. Theoretical Issues in Traditional Jewish Ethics

2

Judaism: From Either/Or to Both/And

HAROLD M. SCHULWEIS

Jewish thinkers feel compelled to get at the "essence of Judaism." What character-izes the distinctiveness of the Jewish belief system? What is the Jewish position on the Messiah, resurrection, immortality, revelation, redemption? How does Judaism decide such issues as capital punishment, birth control legislation, pacifism, nuclear testing? And what, after four thousand years, is the answer to the question, "Who is a Jew?"

Those thinkers who know the character of Judaism find it difficult to present essences or definitive Jewish positions on these issues without qualifications. Many of the questioners, however, have little tolerance for the real universe of ambigu-ities and ambivalences. They want "yes" or "no" answers without "however" and "on the other hand" qualifications. It is tempting to surrender to the call for simple answers, and some yield to the pressure and pronounce positions in the name of "Torah-true Judaism," the "authentic tradition," or "normative" Judaism. They claim that while they articulate mainstream Judaism, the other dissenting voices are minor rivulets of little consequence or, worse, deviant paths to apostasy. Closer examination of the course of Jewish history and thought, however, reveals the windings of a broad river with multiple branches running into the sea. Another's tributary is my mainstream and vice versa. Open to the rich diversity of Jewish ideas, ideals, and practices, we observe that the streams of Jewish mysticism mingle with the waters of Jewish rationalism, Hasidism and Kabbalah alongside Maimo-nides and the Haskalah, the analytic temper of the Vilna Gaon joined with the ecstatic passion of the Baal Shem Tov. That which yesterday was excommunicated as an aberration from Judaism is tomorrow celebrated as the vital undercurrent of Jewish faith.

To be faithful to the multidimensional character of Judaism is to make it difficult to respond simplistically, to offer answers with apodictic certainty and finality. To be open to the evolutionary character of the tradition presents an obstacle to those who would settle for doctrinaire denominational definitions. Judaism is an old-new religious civilization reflecting the ideologies, beliefs, and practices of a world people whose career extends across many continents and centuries. It mirrors a variety of responses to the challenges of different environments. Beside the still waters of Spain's Golden Age breathes the calm spirit of rationalism; with the catastrophe of the Inquisition and expulsion, the waters rage with expectations of messianic redemption and the fantasies of mystic salvation. Jewish theologies and philosophies respond to the different moods of a people lonely in the desert, joyous in the vineyards, frightened in the valley, exultant on the plains. Portions of Judaism are consequently this-worldly and otherworldly, ascetic and materialistic, ethnocentric and universalistic.

In this essay we have sought to avoid the hard disjunctions that cast Judaism into forced either/or options. We direct attention to some of the biases which split reason from emotion, law from spirit, ethnicity from religion, nationalism from universalism, ritual from morality. The polemical arguments between liberal and conservative viewpoints, and Jewish and Christian perspectives, have distorted the intriguing dialectical interplay in Jewish thought which allows seemingly contradictory elements to complement each other. We touch lightly upon some of the more celebrated illustrations of prima facie internal conflicts which, seen with a wider lens, are revealed as elements of the civilizational whole of Judaism.

Either/Or Polemics

Liberal authors characterize Jewish ethics as idealistic, universal, this-worldly, optimistic, rational, antiascetic, humanistic.[1] Writers of the Orthodox school depict the same subject matter quite differently. To them it appears otherworldly, particularistic, largely concerned with ritual, law, and obedience to the divine will. With notable exceptions, Christian theologians find Judaism abounding in ceremonialism, legalistic, parochial, formalistic.[2]

These conflicting presentations of Jewish ethics spawn an array of polemics and apologetics. Each polemicist, hiding his own vulnerability, searches for the Achilles heel of the other. The apologist, defending his position through artful theological gerrymandering, assigns the best portions to his own jurisdiction while projecting the worst onto the lot of his adversary. Such battles have led to convenient but misleading dualisms: law versus spirit, nationalism versus universalism, formalism versus inwardness, materialism versus idealism, justice versus love. Corroborative evidence is carved from the huge and manifold tradition, some citations exaggeratedly pronounced, others chipped away to fall unnoticed by the side. To the uninitiated, Jewish ethics then appears as an unrelieved paragon of virtue or a monstrous anachronism. He is either amazed by its contemporaneity or repelled by its primitive crudeness.[3]

Upon closer scrutiny, the student will discover that each interpretation is capable of producing an array of scriptural and talmudic quotations and utterances vindicating either position. As Professor Louis Ginzberg once noted, "The Devil can quote scripture and were he more knowledgeable he would quote the Talmud as well." Supporting quotations are easy to produce. For one thing, there is little apparent concern in the tradition for a systematic treatment of ethics or theology. Yet another factor militating against neatly packaged catechisms of ethics is the long and varied history of an old-new people.[4] It should not be surprising that different levels of civilization and divergent social and economic situations produce a diversity of ethical response. To seize upon one period or one disposition toward ethics as "typical" or "dominant" invariably misrepresents the organic whole.

To appreciate the holistic character of Jewish ethics, it is better to abandon these partisan, single-stranded characterizations which lay exclusive claim to represent the authentic tradition. We have before us two principal sources to draw upon in portraying the nature of Jewish ethics: the maxims and epigrams aphoristically strewn throughout the entire body of the literature; and the ethics, both implied and articulated, in the codes of law and ritual practice. We cannot produce without distortion an undiversified Jewish system of ethics out of this civilizational complexity. A truer picture will portray a gamut of pluralistic moods and dialectical exchanges reflecting the richness of the Jewish experience.

Liberal and Conservative Viewpoints

The Humanistic Bias

Most modern liberal ethicists attempt to demonstrate that Jewish ethics is optimistic, this-worldly, and peculiarly congenial to a naturalistic approach.[5] This version of Jewish ethics is bolstered by selecting such cheerful citations as follows:

BIBLICAL

> Be fruitful, and multiply, and replenish the earth, and subdue it. [Gen. 1:28]
>
> And God created man in His own image, in the image of God created He him. [Gen. 1:27]
>
> Ye shall therefore keep My statutes and My ordinances which, if a man do, he shall *live* by them. [Lev. 18:5]

RABBINIC

> Every man will be held accountable before God for all the permitted things he beheld in life and did not enjoy. [Yerushalmi, *Kiddushin,* end]
>
> God's commandments are intended to enhance the value and enjoyment of life, but not to mar it and make it gloomy. [*Yoma* 85a]
>
> The spirit of God rests upon man neither in a state of gloom nor in a state of indolence, but solely in the joy of performing a duty. [*Shabbat* 30b]
>
> Rabbi Samuel declared: "He that fasts is called a sinner," basing this on an interpretation of Numbers 6:11. [*Ta'anit* 11a]

The liberal, humanistic strain is as unmistakable as it is one-sided. To cite but a few illustrations of what has been omitted by the liberal view:

BIBLICAL

> Cursed is the ground for thy sake; in toil shalt thou eat of it all the days of thy life. Thorns also and thistles shall it bring forth to thee. . . . In the sweat of thy face shalt thou eat bread. [Gen. 3:17–19]

> . . .for the imagination of man's heart is evil from his youth. [Gen. 8:21]

RABBINIC

> Rabbi Jacob said: "This world is like a vestibule before the world-to-come." [*Ethics of the Fathers* (*Pirke Avot*) 4:21–22]

> In order to be holy it is necessary to abstain even from things that are permitted. [*Yevamot* 20a]

> This is the way of Torah: a morsel of bread with salt must thou eat, and water by measure must thou drink, thou must sleep upon the ground and live a life of anguish the while thou toilest in the Torah. [*Pirke Avot* 6:4[6]]

> For two and a-half years, debate between the two rabbinic schools of Shammai and Hillel raged as to the merit of life. A vote was finally taken and it was decided that "it were better for man not to have been created than to be created, but now that he has been created let him investigate his past deeds or, as others say, let him examine his future actions." [*Eruvin* 13b[7]]

> Rabbi Eleazer declared: "He that fasts is called holy," interpreting Numbers 6:5 for his support. [*Ta'anit* 11a]

> Rabbi Judah the Prince said: "He who accepts the pleasures of this world is deprived of the pleasures of the world to come, and vice versa." [*Avot de-Rabbi Nathan* 1:28, 43a]

When confronted by such illustrations contrary to the humanistic mood, liberal theoreticians invoke quantitative and/or qualitative criteria for determining their true weight. Typically, the nineteenth-century Jewish philosopher Moritz Lazarus explained, "But in all the controversies, the party of energetic action and joyous living is represented by the best names and outnumbers by far its antagonists."[8] This optimistic bias sets aside the ascetic traditions of the Rechabites, Essenes and Nazirites, and the talmudic record which cites prominent and compelling rabbinic personalities who not only advocated but practiced a quite severe asceticism. Among the latter are Mar, son of Rabina, who sat in fast the entire year excepting a few festivals (*Pesaḥim* 68b),[9] and Rabbi Judah, the compiler of the Mishnah, who proudly practiced asceticism as evidence of his piety.[10]

The mystic saints in Jewish posttalmudic life who advocated asceticism, and the writings of a number of eminent Jewish theologians and moralists cannot be so readily dismissed. The eleventh century Ibn Paquda includes "renunciation of luxuries and love of the world" as the ninth fundamental principle of the religious "duties of the heart" in his influential work of the same name.[11] Moses Hayyim Luzzatto, the eighteenth-century author of *The Path of the Upright, Messilat Yesharim*, demonstrates that "abstinence is the beginning of saintliness," that man should therefore "avoid contact with worldly affairs as much as possible."[12]

The preceding illustrates how blinded we are to the half-conscious selection of sentiments and heroes we prefer. It was the philosopher Schopenhauer who cavalierly labeled Judaism as optimistic. But much of the optimism is the creation of thinkers who have absorbed the values of the Enlightenment. The age of confidence in human progress which experienced the joy of this-worldly life understandably found little interest in the talmudic heeding that there be "no unrestrained laughter in this world" (*Berachot* 31a). The essays composed and sermons preached in that hopeful era filtered the scriptural and talmudic sea for corroborative texts congenial to the spirit of their own age. Given the absence of structured ethical theory in Judaism and the casual and unsystematic form of ethics in traditional literature, these constructions selected from the classics were readily woven together to form an ethics claiming "major tendencies." By virtue of repetition and the acceptance of this-worldly humanism by the contemporary Jewish audience, these interpretations were presented as the sole authoritative version of the authentic Jewish tradition. We know, however, that in the insulation of the ghetto and in moments of medieval catastrophe, for example, quite contrary versions were acknowledged as authentic.[13]

Ethical Absolutes versus Contextual Relativism

Conservative interpreters of the tradition tend to stress the absolute character of revealed law. Liberal interpreters of the tradition point to the qualifications which beset the abstract law once it is contextually applied. On closer examination, the tradition appears as a "relative absolutism" wherein the general principles remain constant but are softened by consideration of the particular situations to which they are applied. Jewish ethics allows itself few immutable absolutes. The notable exceptions are the three absolutes which prohibit murder, incest, and idolatry. Whereas ritual ordinances of the highest importance may be transgressed in the interest of the conservation of health and life, the aforementioned cardinal sins are excluded. "We may cure ourselves with all [forbidden] things except idolatry, incest and murder."[14] Yet, in the face of the brutal Hadrianic persecutions, the rabbinic sense of realism attenuated even these absolutes. Consideration of the public or private character of the transgression, distinctions as to who decreed the transgression, the motivation of the transgressor, the number and nature of the public witnessing the prohibited act were introduced to qualify these absolutes.[15] In these ways, the rabbinic exercise of the law encouraged reason and experience to free men from blind obedience to unyielding categorical imperatives.

Religious and Autonomous Ethics

Jewish ethics belongs to the category of religious or theistic ethics. In philosophical literature, this category is contrasted with that of natural or secular ethics. The genesis of and sanction for secular ethics is said to lie in experience, intuition, human reason, and appeal to natural consequences, individual and social, physical and psychological.[16] Secular humanistic ethics prides itself on its autonomous and therefore uncoerced manner of arriving at the ethical decision. Secular morality declares that it does not cringe before the voice thundering from above. It is not bound to the external constraints of the Other's Will. By contrast, theistic ethics legitimizes its moral philosophy by appealing to its Divine Source, by claims of revelatory experiences, or by virtue of the logic which derives ethical principles from those of theology. For its part, secular humanistic ethics dismisses theistic ethics as either arguing in circular fashion or as "pseudo-heteronomous morality" (Von Hartmann), that is, unreflected obedience to an external Divine Imperative. In response, theistic ethics maintains that the secular effort in ethics leads to the conceit of anthropocentrism and unbridled subjectivism.

Is Jewish ethics, then, autonomous or heteronomous, a product of human reason or divine fiat? The answer will not feed into the either/or framework. The hard-and-fast distinctions of heteronomy (subjection to the law of another) and autonomy are largely unknown in Jewish ethics despite the efforts of Moritz Lazarus and others to read the Kantian ethics of autonomy into the rabbinic tradition.[17] While Jewish ethics is traditionally believed to be derived from God's revealed will, its claimed origin does not contradict the free exercise of man's moral reason. The human intellect is a divine gift, and man's autonomous conscience is a manifestation of his divine image. Human moral discoveries may be seen as one side of the coin of revelation. If God's voice is to be distinguished from the ventriloquism of Satan, revelation must be examined by moral reason and adapted into moral law. If fidelity to the covenant is not servile acquiescence to supernatural power, reason and moral sensibility must be elevated to sacred status.

The instance of the universal Noahide laws is instructive. How do the rabbis understand the character of the seven Noahide laws which apply to mankind in general, that is, the prohibitions against shedding blood, robbery, idolatry, adultery, blasphemy, and eating flesh from live animals, and the injunction to set up courts of justice? Are these laws autonomous, inasmuch as their origin is pre-Sinaitic and no special revelation of these natural principles is explicitly recorded in the Bible, or are they heteronomous, derived from God's will? The rabbis and the medieval Jewish philosophers insisted that these natural laws were derived from the biblical verse in Gen. 2:16 and are thus divinely ordained.[18] Maimonides insists that only those who believe that these seven Noahide laws are revealed by God in the Torah will merit a share in the world-to-come, the desserts of the righteous gentiles of the world. Moritz Lazarus, however, argued that Jewish ethics is autonomous and was determined to show that "reason [as opposed to revelation] was the source of his [Abraham's] ethical instruction."[19] To support his Kantian bias, Lazarus quotes an oft-cited mishnaic passage: "Abraham observed the whole Torah before it was given." Heteronomists quote another mishnah, one which maintains that Abraham's practice was divinely ordained, on the basis of the scriptural verse "because that Abraham obeyed My voice and kept My charge, My commandments, My statutes and My laws" (Gen. 26:5).[20]

The rabbis appear to be oblivious to the bifurcated realms of nature and the supernatural in the sense that contemporary theologians employ them, just as they did not see autonomous and heteronomous ethics as contraries. Natural law is congenial to divinity because "the earth is the Lord's." Chastity could be learned from the dove, modesty from the cat, not to rob from the ant, propriety from the cock, and "if they had not been written [in Scripture] they should have been written."[21] Man's discoveries in nature are no blasphemy to God but to his glory. The issues which are presented as hard disjunctives, either/or, are reconciled by viewing them as different aspects of the same thing. After all, the reason and ethics of man flow from a being created in the image of God. In the relationship between man and God, nothing divine is untouched by nature, and nothing natural is untouched by the divine. In the realm of ethics, that which God wills is good and that which is good is the will of God.

The Christian-Jewish Polemic

Polemics introduce invidious distinctions. Apologetics return the compliment in kind. Christian theologians, from Paul onward, have for the most part felt the need to loosen Christianity from its antecedent anchorage, to prove its independence and its advancement over the "old" tradition. Ancient Israel is forever portrayed as obsolescent, "concerned with rites and ceremonies, with the maintenance of obsolete, useless and even harmless customs; it has been narrowly nationalistic; it has been socially and intellectually unprogressive";[22] "The principle of love . . . and the principle of moral inwardness" are distinctive Christian contributions.[23] In defense of these harsh critiques, many apologists fall into the very either/or trap set by the polemicists and seek to deny the nationalistic, ritualistic, legalistic character of Jewish ethics. In such a debate, both extremes err. The distortion, common both to those who overrate and to those who berate Judaism, is the assumption that love of people and mankind, law and spirit, ceremony and inwardness, cultus and social consciousness are inherently incompatible. Both defenders and detractors tend to split what is organically whole in Judaism, each taking one or the other part of the disjunction as the essence of Judaism. To worship the part as if it were the whole is to sacrifice at the arena of idolatry. Within Jewish religious civilization, these segregated features strain and struggle but coexist. The following sections touch briefly upon the alleged contradictions within Judaism.

Nation and Humanity

The rabbinic mind sensed no contradiction in holding that Israel stands in special relation to God and holding that "the pious and virtuous of all nations participate in eternal bliss" (*Sifra* on Leviticus 19:18). The prophet who spoke lovingly of God's interest in raising the fallen tabernacle of David could still rebuke the "chosen." "Are ye not as children of the Ethiopians unto Me, O children of Israel?" (Amos 9:7). For the rabbis, the same prophet who conceived of Israel as the Suffering Servant persecuted by the nations could still speak of God's blessing "Egypt, My people, and Assyria, the work of My hands" (Isa. 19:25). The evident particularism in Judaic literature does not preclude the High Holy Day prayers that God impose his awe upon all mankind and that "all Thy works may revere Thee . . . that they may form a single band to do Thy will with a perfect heart." So, too, rabbinic law ordains that giving charity to the poor, burying the dead, attending funerals, eulogizing the deceased, consoling the bereaved are to be extended to the non-Jew as well as to the Jew.[24] The particularistic rabbinic imagination is capable of spinning a legend of ethics in which God chastizes the ministering angels singing a hymn of praise over the destruction of the Egyptians in the Red Sea: "My children lie drowned in the sea and you would sing hymns of triumph?" (*Megillah* 10b). To be sure, the danger looms that love of peoplehood may gain the ascendancy and degenerate into zealous ethnocentrism; but the risk is no more real than that universalism may turn into religious imperialism.

Ritual and Ethics

In the relationship between ritual and ethics, something of the polemicist's assumption seeps into the defense walls of the apologists. Theologians on the defense are found interpreting Jewish religion as "essentially . . . the emergence of ethical ideals out of a background of purely ritual and ceremonial observances."[25] The apology thereby accepts the strange logic which sets up ethics in opposition to ritual by placing each in a separate stage, one primitive (ritualistic), the other emergent (ethical). In truth, however, the hard disjunctives separating rite and righteousness, cult and conscience, are not so pronounced in biblical and talmudic literature. Within the breadth of the same biblical chapter, arational and amoral ritual law prohibiting the wearing of wool and linen together is coupled with the moral concern which enjoins the removal of young ones or eggs from the nest in the presence of the mother bird.[26]

The prophets condemn the hypocrisy and mechanism of ritual, but their vision aspires to sacrifice *with* mercy, adoration *with* charity, rite *with* justice, form *with* inwardness. Statute and ordinance of both ethical and ritual significance lay equal claim to divine sanction. The rabbis admonish man to be "heedful of a light precept as of a grave one" (*Pirke Avot* 2:1).

Ritual observance itself was invested with so great a degree of ethical purpose that the two were regarded as inseparable. "For indeed, what difference does it make to God how we slaughter an animal or of what kind of food we partake, except that he desires by such laws and regulations to benefit his creatures, to purify our hearts and to ennoble our characters."[27] Ritual observance is variously taken as a pedagogic means to instruct man in self-control, as obedience to divine law, as hygienic principles, as repudiation of idolatry, and so on.[28]

While ritual frequently serves an indispensable function as an active reminder intensifying ethical resolutions, it is dispensable when its observance would violate ethical principle. "Even the entire body of Biblical precepts and rituals are not equal to one ethical principle."[29] Respect for the personal dignity of a human being supersedes a negative biblical injunction.[30]

The obduracy with which ritual observance is often maintained strongly suggests that there is more here than ritual law for its own sake. Observance or abandonment of ritual is not solely an issue of religious ideology. Many a ritual came to be associated with the supreme virtue of loyalty, and often a history of martyrdom added emotive value to the ritual far beyond the initial intention. The rabbis wisely observed that "every commandment for which the Israelites gave their lives in times of persecution they now observe openly; the others have grown effete among them."[31] The religious struggle in the Hanukkah story was initiated by ritual struggles whose symbolic meaning was intertwined with the issue of loyalty to one's own people. To have the flesh of swine forced down one's throat was experienced as defilement of one's fidelity to people and covenant. In moments of religious persecution, "even to change one's shoe strap" may demand martyrdom.[32]

In much the same way, Pauline antinomianism and anticeremonialism may have given additional impetus to the conservation of rituals. The retention of many ceremonial laws, following the destruction of the Temple, was invested with a nation's survival value. The early Christian opposition to dietary laws and circumcision was considered a double-pronged attack upon the efforts to preserve the peoplehood of Judaism and the relevance of the tradition and rabbinic law. Ceremonial laws, more than the more abstract universal laws of ethics, were focused upon because they possessed indigenous national symbolism. Their importance reached unparalleled heights as unifying and stabilizing factors, especially after political sovereignty was lost or, as in the Diaspora, where both territorial and political integrity were absent. The value of Jewish rituals was not only significant as a response to religious imperatives, but as an expression of the ethics of loyalty as well. It became important for the rabbis to insist that Abraham, though living ages before the Sinaitic revelation, had observed all the precepts and regulations of the law,[33] though earlier tradition assured his justification by faith alone.[34] For the Pauline principle, setting up the justification of faith over that of works, sought its sanction from the merit of the pre-Sinaitic religious heroes of the Bible such as Abraham. "Therefore it is of faith, that it might be by grace . . . not to that only which is of the law but to that also which is of the faith of Abraham, who is the father of us all."[35] So the cleavage between ritual and ethical law was introduced to polemics over the issue of the justification by faith or by works. In this manner, ritual works may have been catapulted to a level of importance nearly eclipsing the sphere of ethics.[36]

Law and Theology

Partly because of this historical pitting of Christian creed and faith against Jewish deed and act, and partly because of Judaism's inherent distrust of abstract theory, it is law which identifies the dominant trait in the Jewish ethic. The Christian antithesis of faith and works finds its Jewish analogue in the debate over which is more important in the pursuit of the religious life: the study of the law or the practice of good deeds.[37] In the talmudic controversy over which is more important, study or doing, Rabbi Tarfon emphasizes study while Rabbi Akiva insists upon doing. But then "they all agreed that study was greater, for it led to doing."[38]

It seems more accurate, then, to speak of Jewish ethics as rooted in religious law than of its modern formulation as essentially "theologic."[39] Judaism's religious ethics is not theological in the sense that Aquinas's systematization of Christian ethics is theological. The problems surrounding evil, atonement, sin, and free will in Judaism developed less as metaphysical or theological issues than as issues of moral law. The medieval endeavors to theologize Judaism, to extrapolate a system of belief, were mainly abortive.

The legal character of Jewish ethics does not lessen its implicit theocentric source. But while the legitimization of *halaçhah*, or law, was viewed as dependent upon the wisdom of a divine ruler who revealed his will, the theological implications were taken for granted and not made into dogma. The law was Judaism's applied theology. The aspirations of the Bible and ideals of the prophets were there; there was no question of enduring legitimacy. The law sought to rescue the ethical insights of the prophets from the mistiness of generalized goodwill and utopian imagination. The excitement and drama of prophetic denunciation and vision were translated into prescribed, detailed, concrete, daily activity. Goodness and virtue required more than the good intentions with which the road to moral laxity is so liberally paved. If ideals were not to go up in the smoke of pious verbiage, fences must be erected to guide the wayward, and transgressors made to sense the reality of this-worldly punishment. "The task of prophecy," declares a talmudic passage, "was taken from the prophets and given to the wise men," to promulgate and enforce regulatory law.[40]

Such guiding principles of ethics as the conservation of health, life, and property and their use for the ennoblement of man and society were concretized into legal precepts. The issue of philanthropy, for example, was not left solely to the whim and caprice of the individual. Laws of tithing and restrictions even as to the generosity of the charity given were articulated. Man should not "squander more than one-fifth of his wealth, lest he himself becomes indebted to society."[41] The Levitical formula "to love one's neighbor as oneself" was not allowed to waste away into pious declaration. The rights of adjoining neighbors were spelled out pragmatically in the Talmud. A property owner has a prior claim over any other person to purchase property adjoining his. If the owner, lacking neighborly feeling, ignores his neighbor's rights by selling the property to a third person, the latter may be compelled to turn over the bought property to the adjacent neighbor for the purchasing price.[42] Theological ethics embraced reality through the implementation of law in the daily activities between man and man.

It is undeniable that there are dangers of a law-abiding ethic turning into a monument of inflexible injunctions and prohibitions. The spirit may turn into an empty word and the law may congeal into an impersonal letter. Spontaneity and inwardness in ethical decision may shrivel into a deadening conformity to the book of statutes. Law as instrument can, with imposing power, turn into the end itself; the noble search for God's will may deteriorate to a prosaic casuistry. The Talmud itself cautions, "For those who make a right use of the law, it is a medicine for life; for those who make a wrong use, it is a drug for death."[43]

Many of these dangers have indeed engulfed the consecrated end of Jewish law. The further removed from the sovereignty of natural community, the more stringent grows the conservative impulse, the more timid the initiation of changes and amendments. Dependence upon the past for authentic rendition of the law and reliance upon the talmudic rabbis "greater in number and wisdom than we" increased. The liberating character of classic rabbinic law was threatened.

The Word of God and the Commentary of Man

The Christian characterization of the Jewish law as oppressive, and of the Pharisaic rabbis as narrow-minded legalists, distorted the liberating and democratizing character of the *halakhah*. One of the consequences of the Pharisaic approach to Bible study was its popularization among the people. The democratization of learning weakened the influence of miracle men and their charismatic magnetism. The text, not the prophet, was called holy, perfect, divine, and the text was open to all. Neither voices from heaven moving carob trees nor falling walls held still could detract from the law based on verse and chapter, and applied contextually by human intelligence.[44] Interpreters of the text, often locked in conflicting judgments, were equally regarded: "These and these are both the words of the living God."[45]

The law, in the hands of the rabbinic scholars, humanized revelation, allowed it growth, continuity, and change. God's wisdom was not exhausted with the theophany at Sinai. "Things not revealed to Moses were revealed to Akiva."[46] This, the rabbis explained, was due to the omniscience of his word. Divine truth, if given at once, would overwhelm a generation and congeal the hearts of a nation with fear.[47]

With such a concept of progressive revelation, the rabbis could free the people from priestly and patrician bibliolatry.[48] They could transform the pentateuchal *lex talionis* (the so-called eye-for-an-eye law of retaliation) into a complex code entailing monetary compensation in consideration for the pain, unemployment, medical expenditures, and humiliation suffered by the victim. They could, through the subtleties of hermeneutics, so qualify the conditions under which the biblical "stubborn and rebellious son," "idolatrous city," and "leprous house" were to be condemned that they became de facto unenforceable.[49] These laws, it was explained, were made to function for the benefit of jurisprudential theory. The cited biblical instances themselves "never were nor will be." The reason for their preserve was purely theoretical. Their purpose was for "you to study and receive thereby reward."[50] In this manner, *halakhah* was able to circumvent the Deuteronomic law (15:1–2) which canceled all debts in the sabbatical year by the imaginative institution of Hillel's *prosbul* that authorizes a rabbinic tribunal to collect the debts. A verse from the Book of Psalms (119:126), "It is time for Thee, Lord, to work; for they have made void Thy law," was audaciously mistranslated to mean that for the sake of God there are times when it is permissible to set aside or amend the commandments of God enjoined in his law.[51]

Both/And

There are scholarly as well as pragmatic reasons to resist a characterization of Jewish ethics neatly tailored to our particular bias. The rabbis, judges, and philosophers whose spirit is reflected in Judaism did not consciously sit down to create a uniform and unambiguous code of ethics. The civilizational character of Jewish ethics cannot be simply located. It is better apprehended when viewed as an indispensable part of an organic totality which weaves jurisprudence and theology, legend and philosophy into a religious civilizational fabric. Such a schema exhibits the generalized aim of Jewish ethical life: *kiddush ha-Shem,* the sanctification of God's name, binding heaven with earth, countenancing no rupture in God's universe, transforming the secular into the holy, knitting together the torn fragments of what was originally whole, praying toward the day when his name shall be One. Sanctification uses every means at its command: prayer and charity, piety and social action, body and soul, heart and mind.

The ethics of Judaism clings therefore to both prophet and priest; holds both the love of Israel and that of mankind; believes both in the world-to-come and in the imperatives to labor in this world; remembers the power of human freedom and recalls its frustrating limitations; is both God-centered and aware of the centrality of the self. These conjunctions are not taken by the tradition as paralyzing paradoxes throwing man into despair. They are complementary values, expressions of a healthy tradition, rooted in the twin principles of reality and ideality, in what is and what ought to be. They manifest the dialectic of love and wisdom which reflects the complexity and maturity of life. Mature living and mature religion are not either/or. Polarities need not turn into polarizations, nor dualities into dualisms, nor ideologies into segregating sects.

Notes

1. See Samuel Schulman's popular essay "Jewish Ethics," reflecting the liberal Reform approach to the subject, in *Popular Studies in Judaism.*

2. Notable among these exceptions are G. F. Moore and R. T. Herford.

3. Illustrations of the Kantian formulation of Jewish ethics are conspicuous in Lazarus's *The Ethics of Judaism,* Kaufmann Kohler's *Jewish Theology* ("The Ethics of Judaism and the Kingdom of God"), and Emil Hirsch's "Ethics" in the *Jewish Encyclopedia.*

4. Biblical ethics alone includes a period ranging from primitive times to the second century of the common era. Not all of this is of one coherent mood. It contains period ethics of the priestly theocracy with those of the Prophets and Wisdom series. To this must be added the centuries of the talmudic era (ending about 500 c.e.), the philosophical efforts of the Middle Ages, the mysticism of Kabbalah, the romance of Hasidism, the period of Enlightenment, Reform, and the contemporary religious and secular philosophies. For the sake of economy and because works on Jewish ethics usually restrict themselves to the major sources of the Bible and Talmud, we have concentrated on these classic periods.

5. See Van Meter Ames's review of Israel Mattuck's *Jewish Ethics* for such a version. The review may be found in the *Menorah Journal,* Spring–Summer 1955.

6. Israel Mattuck's apology for this dictum seeks to soften its ascetic tone by asserting, "This should probably be interpreted not absolutely but relatively." *Jewish Ethics,* p. 139.

7. C. Montefiore, commenting on this pessimistic note, apologetically assures the reader that "the passage is clearly a record of some famous dialectical discussion, without any true bearing upon the arguer's *real* views about actual life," *A Rabbinic Anthology* (London, 1938), p. 539.

8. M. Lazarus. *The Ethics of Judaism,* vol. 2, p. 120.

9. *Berakhot* 30b, where Rabbi Johanan, Rabbi Ashi, and others assent to this mournful attitude.

10. *Ketubot* 104a.

11. Baḥya Ibn Paquda, *Duties of the Heart,* p. 17.

12. *Messilat Yesharim,* p. 122.

13. Gershom G. Scholem's *Major Trends in Jewish Mysticism,* pp. 244ff., illustrates the wide influence of these moods in critical times.

14. *Pesaḥim* 25a.

15. *Sanhedrin* 74a–b.

16. Mordecai M. Kaplan, in his introduction to the English translation of *Messilat Yesharim,* pp. xiv–xxx, discusses the basic traits and divergent methods of approach to the problem of human conduct.

17. For a discussion of this issue in Jewish philosophy, see Felix Perles Königsberg's "Die Autonomie der Sittlichkeit in jüdischen Schriften," in *Judaica Festschrift in Honor of Hermann Cohen* (Berlin: Verlag Bruno Cassirer, 1912).

18. *Sanhedrin* 56a, end.

19. Lazarus, *Ethics of Judaism,* vol. 1, p. 118.

20. *Kiddushin* 4:14.

21. *Yoma* 67b.

22. Albert C. Knudson, *The Principles of Christian Ethics* (New York, 1943), p. 285.

23. Ibid., p. 39; see the New Testament critique of Pharisaic morality in such sections as John 7:22–24, Matt. 23:23–26, Acts 15:24–29, Rom. 3:28–29.

24. Mishnah *Gittin* 5:8; Tosefta 5:4–5.

25. *Universal Jewish Encyclopedia* (1941), s.v. "Ethics," vol. 4, p. 175.

26. Deuteronomy 22:11, 22:6.

27. *Genesis Rabbah* 44.1; *Tanḥuma, Shemini* 15b; ed. Buber.

28. See Moses Maimonides, *Guide to the Perplexed,* 3:43–49, for such ethical interpretations of the Sabbath, festivals, and the dietary laws, among others.

29. Jerusalem Talmud, *Peah* 16a, as cited by J. Z. Lauterbach in his essay on the "Ethics of Halakah." He quotes similar talmudic passages, *Sukkot* 30a, *Nazir* 23b, in his notes on p. 271.

30. *Shabbat* 81b.

31. *Sifre Deuteronomy, Re'eh* 90b.

32. *Sanhedrin* 74b.

33. *Yoma* 28b.

34. *Mechilta, Be-Shallach* 6; ed. Weiss, 40b.

35. Romans 4:16.

36. For additional illustrations, see Lauterbach's and Kohler's articles on nomism in the *Jewish Encyclopedia.*

37. See *Pirke Avot* 1:17, 3:12, 3:22, 4:6, for consistent emphasis, giving primary value to works over wisdom and erudition.

38. *Kiddushin* 40b.

39. Lazarus. *Ethics of Judaism*, vol. 1, pp. 109f. Emil Hirsch, s.v. "Ethics," *Jewish Encyclopedia,* passim. Kohler, *Jewish Theology,* p. 477.

40. *Bava Bathra* 12a.

41. *Ketubot* 50a.

42. See Lauterbach. *The Ethics of the Halakah,* p. 283.

43. *Shabbat* 88b.

44. *Bava Metzia* 59b.

45. *Eruvin* 13b.

46. *Numbers Rabbah* 19:6.

47. *Tanhuma, Devarim* 1a.

48. For illustrations of the democratic "plebeian" character of the Pharisaic reforms through law, read Louis Finkelstein's suggestive chapter, "The Oral Law," in his two-volume *The Pharisees* (Philadelphia: Jewish Publication Society, 1946).

49. Deut. 13:17, 21:18; Lev. 14:34ff.

50. *Sanhedrin* 71a. The rabbis' humanitarian employment of law and exegesis allows them to boast that a Sanhedrin (religious supreme court) that executes a person once in seven years is called murderous. Rabbi Eliezer ben Azzariah corrected, "once in seventy years."

51. Mishnah *Berachot* 9:5.

Bibliography

Moritz Lazarus, *The Ethics of Judaism,* translated by Henrietta Szold (Philadelphia: Jewish Publication Society 1900).

Israel Mattuck, *Jewish Ethics* (London: Hutchinson's University Library, 1953).

Leo Baeck, *The Essence of Judaism* (New York, 1936).

Mordecai M. Kaplan, "The Contribution of Judaism to World Ethics," in *The Jews,* edited by Louis Finkelstein, vol. 1 (New York, 1949).

C. G. Montefiore and H. Loewe, *A Rabbinic Anthology* (Philadelphia: Jewish Publication Society, 1960).

Emil Hirsch, "Ethics," in *The Jewish Encyclopedia,* Vol. 5, pp. 245–58.

J. Z. Lauterbach, "The Ethics of Halakah," in *Rabbinical Essays* (Cincinnati: Hebrew Union College Press, 1951).

M. Mielzinger, "Ethics of the Talmud," in *Judaism at the World's Parliament of Religions, Proceedings of the Union of American Hebrew Congregations* (Cincinnati: Clarke and Co., 1894), pp. 107–13: Reprinted in his *Introduction to the Talmud* (Cincinnati: Hebrew Union College Press, 1894), pp. 265–80.

3

Natural Law, *Halakhah,* and the Covenant

DAVID NOVAK

Natural Law or Legal Positivism

Philosophers of law, certainly in modern times, can be divided into two main groups: legal positivists and natural law theorists. In essence, the difference between the two groups can be seen in their understanding of the relation of authority and right within a legal system. For legal positivists, authority is prior to right, that is, a legal system is grounded in the power of *the* political authority to make laws, which then determine what is right and wrong. For natural law theorists, right is prior to authority, that is, *a* political authority is ordained to make laws because such power is conceived to be right. For both schools of thought, legal authority is a manifestation of political power. For both, "right" means "that which is allowed" and "wrong" means "that which is not allowed." The point of difference, then, is whether there is a trans-political validation for political power manifest as legal authority. Legal positivists would say that society itself (either collectively or in the person of its sovereign) is the *terminus a quo* and the *terminus ad quem* of its own authority. Natural law theorists would say that the political power qua legal authority of a society is derivative from something else and contained by it—traditionally called "nature."[1]

Into which school of thought a modern philosopher of law fits can be ascertained by looking at his or her answer to the challenge made by an outstanding contemporary legal philosopher, Ronald Dworkin, that one constitute rights as "the one feature that distinguishes law from ordered brutality."[2] A legal positivist would say that this distinction lies in *how* a legal system is ordered. If a legal system's commands are norms, that is, clearly defined rules consistent with an overall normative structure, then there is a sufficient distinction between these prescriptions and the arbitrary, erratic commands associated with "ordered brutality."[3] Natural law theorists would say that this distinction lies in the purpose, the *why,* of a legal system. If a legal system's prescriptions are rational norms, that is, ordered toward objective human goods qua ends, which themselves transcend the system, then there is a sufficient distinction between these prescriptions and the commands associated with "ordered brutality," commands that serve no end other than the exercise of political power as an end in itself.[4]

In times such as these, when rival political claims are so pronounced and have such staggering global consequences, it is easy to see why philosophy of law is of such current intellectual interest. Aside from the fact that Jewish theologians have always been interested in perennial philosophical problems (and, indeed, the philosophical problem of legal positivism versus natural law theory can be traced back to the time of Socrates, at least), and aside from the fact that Jews are part of the current international scene, there are two more particular historical factors that make this issue the point of considerable discussion among contemporary Jewish thinkers. These two factors are the most overriding events of modern Jewish history: the Holocaust and the establishment of the state of Israel. Both of these events call for discussion by Jews of the differences between legal positivism and natural law theory as a pressing practical need and not just as a speculative pastime (*pilpula b'alma*).

In the Holocaust Jews were the most cruelly ravaged victims of the most ordered brutality in history. They were victims not just of random acts of violence but of a system legally structured and aimed at their annihilation. The immediate Jewish reaction of "never again!" leads either consciously or unconsciously, I believe, to a concern with defining for all humanity the difference between law, which Judaism has always affirmed as being international in scope, and ordered brutality as an aberrational imitation of legal order. However, if Jews are interested in law on an international level, they cannot avoid asking the same philosophical questions about their own system of law, *halakhah.* One cannot speak to the conscience of humanity without simultaneously speaking to his or her own conscience.[5] These philosophical questions, as we have just seen, concern the relation of right and authority.

The establishment of the State of Israel has given the Jewish people for the first time in over two thousand years sovereign political power. The political issues that concern the State of Israel, and along with it the overwhelming number of Jews throughout the world who have accepted Zionism as integral to their Judaism, practically involve the philosophical question of the relation of right and authority. Thus, for example, how *halakhah* is used to determine a legal approach to non-Jews living under Israeli rule will probably be decided differently depending on whether the particular *halakhist* is an advocate of legal positivism or natural law theory.[6]

One can see an antinomy between legal positivism and natural law theory, and the Jewish theologian must bear it in mind in his or her attempt to define the essential character of *halakhah.* The antinomy is as follows:

Natural law is a body of norms, rationally apprehended, universally applicable, independent of the promulgation of any authority.	Positive law is a body of norms, given for application in a particular society (and whomever it controls), dependent on promulgation by a particular authority.

It is clear that the natural law theorist can resolve this antinomy, that is, incorporate the two extremes into one coherent position, whereas the legal positivist cannot. Traditionally, natural law theorists have resolved the antinomy by asserting that positive law is the historical specification of the general principles of natural law, that is, whereas right is in principle changeless, authority is the temporal application of right by *an* authority conscious of both the general principles of natural law and the particular circumstances of a historical society.[7] Legal positivists, on the other hand, regard the natural law position as little more than an illusion, not required by the cogent operation of any system of positive law.[8] Like all positivists, they define a finite range of meaning and simply dismiss any issues outside that finite range as meaningless "pseudoquestions." However, as in all suppressions of perennial human concerns—and certainly natural law is such a perennial human concern—the suppressed keeps returning and raising its questions over and over again. Positivism does not seem to understand that rational response to hard questions requires that they be answered, not dismissed, that our criteria of meaning strive to be adequate to truth rather than continually reducing truth to our range of meaning.

It seems that this position of legal positivism is the one that Jewish theologians would adopt in their essential characterization of *halakhah,* for one can easily translate the positivist position into the following proposition:

> *Halakhah* is a body of norms, given for application among the Jewish people (and whomever they control), promulgated by God and subsequently by the Rabbis authorized by God in the revealed sources: the Written Torah and the Oral Torah.[9]

It seems that the adoption of a natural law position would require the authority of God's will as the prime authority of the *halakhic* system to be subordinated to a higher order of right. This seems to go directly against the transcendent theocentricity of Judaism, and hence it is not difficult to see why many Jewish theologians have willingly included themselves in the positivist school and have rejected the claim that *halakhah* can be essentially characterized using natural law theory.

In this chapter, I propose that natural law theory is necessary for an adequate essential characterization of *halakhah.* I will specifically argue against the claims of two contemporary Jewish theologians, Marvin Fox and José Faur, who have rejected natural law theory in their discussions of the character of *halakhah.* I will also argue against the assertion of the late Jewish philosopher Leo Strauss (d. 1973) that there is no idea of nature in the Hebrew Bible (and, by extension, in normative Judaism per se). In developing my proposal, I will present the idea of covenant as one that correlates natural law and positive aspects of *halakhah* in such a way as to avoid the attempt of positivists to deny natural law claims altogether, and the attempt of some natural law theorists to assume that an acceptance of natural law necessarily requires that all positive laws, in our case the mitzvoth, be subordinated to it.

Marvin Fox: Law as Commandment

One of the most consistent advocates of legal positivism in contemporary Jewish thought is the American Orthodox theologian Marvin Fox. In a number of papers devoted to the legal philosophy of Maimonides, he has argued against other Jewish thinkers (one gets the impression that he is arguing in particular against Jewish neo-Kantians who follow Hermann Cohen) who have maintainted that Maimonides is a natural law theorist. In presenting what he considers Maimonides' true position, Fox has generalized that Judaism itself is antithetical to any natural law position. "In Judaism there is no natural law doctrine, and, in principle, there cannot be. . . ."[10] Commenting on the famous passage in B. Yoma 67b that if the laws prohibiting idolatry, sexual immorality, murder, robbery, and blasphemy had not been written in the Torah "reason would have required that they be written" (*din hu sheyikatevu*), Fox writes, "What is asserted is only that, having been commanded to avoid these prohibited acts, we can now see after the fact, that these prohibitions are useful and desirable."[11] He goes on to say, "Seen this way, we can say of them that though they are not rational, in the sense of being demonstrable, they are reasonable in the sense that we can give good reasons for them."[12] Finally, he notes, "Just as the commandments are reasonable without being rationally demonstrable, so are they in accord with man's nature without being natural."[13]

Elsewhere I have criticized the positivist interpretation of Maimonides advocated by Fox and others.[14] It would take us too far afield to repeat those criticisms here. Let me, therefore, confine myself to Fox's rejection of a natural law position within Judaism per se. I would suggest that Fox's position is untenable on three grounds: (1) the theological sources he ignores; (2) the classical sources he interprets; and (3) the philosophical questions he does not discuss.

In denying a place for natural law theory in Judaism, Fox has ignored evidence to the contrary in Saadyah, R. Judah Halevi, Nahmanides, and R. Joseph Albo.[15] Even Maimonides, who Fox goes to such great lengths to show rejected natural law theory in the area of morality, nevertheless speaks of laws that "reason persuades" (*hekhrea ha-da'at*) and to which "reason inclines" (*ha-da'at noteh*), even though he denies such prudential reasoning alone transcendent validity.[16] Now, one certainly has the option of arguing against the position of the five theologians cited above (let alone the position of someone as unorthodox as Hermann Cohen).[17] However, unless one is prepared to eliminate their thought from Judaism, one cannot, therefore, say, "In Judaism there is no natural law doctrine."

In the much-quoted rabbinic source Fox explicates, one could well contend that what is rational before the fact can indeed be logically separated from what is only perceived as useful and desirable after the fact. One could say, taking an example of what the rabbis clearly considered a nonrational commandment, that having been commanded to refrain from eating pork, I can subsequently consider this act to be "useful" (it reduced the amount of saturated fat in my diet, thus lessening the buildup of cholesterol in my blood vessels)[18] and "desirable" (it helps curb my gluttony).[19] These subsequent explanations are not rational in the sense that I could not have invented the exact prohibition by being aware of its "uses" and "benefits" before my actual obedience of the commandment "and the pig . . . from its flesh you shall not eat" (Lev. 11:7–8). However, this is the case because the needs fulfilled by ordinary eating do not lead one directly to the conclusion that eating pork will contradict them. Refraining from pork, then, introduces one to a level of cultural experience that is not universal. Thus the meaning of this experience can be inferred only ex post facto, that is, after the commandment has already been fulfilled.

Nevertheless, this type of explanation will not suffice when dealing with the first category of commandments with which the celebrated rabbinic source deals. First of all, they are all prohibitions dealing with what the rabbis considered ordinary, universal experience. Let us take the most indisputable of these prohibitions, the prohibition of murder (*shefikhut damim*). Does not our experience of society and our need for society indicate to us *in advance* of any promulgated prohibition that murder is the most fundamentally antisocial act, that the permission of murder would destroy social intercourse? In other words, this commandment does not introduce us to a new experience whose meaning is only subsequently inferred; rather, it itself is inferred from an experience the rabbis considered to be universal. Thus Maimonides, Fox's prime example of an anti–natural law Jewish theologian, writes about the prohibition of murder, "Even though there are transgressions more serious than murder, none of them involves the destruction of society [*yishuvo shel olam*], as does murder."[20] The difference, then, between these two types of commandments, which the rabbis so clearly separated, is that in the nonrational commandments the phenomenological sequence is (1) the commandment, (2) the experience, and (3) the inference of secondary meaning. In the rational commandments, conversely, the phenomenological sequence is (1) the experience, (2) the inference of primary meaning, and (3) the commandment, whose reason is the continued duration of that which the experience showed to be good. In our example of the prohibition of murder, the phenomenological sequence is as follows: (1) the experience of human society; (2) the inference from this experience that human society is a good that is required for satisfactory human life; and (3) that acts that counteract this good and prevent its duration in any situation are wrong and thus not to be done. The fact that a prohibition like that of murder is also a divine commandment indicates that it has covenantal meaning *over and above* its ordinary human meaning.[21] The nonrational commandments, on the other hand, have only covenantal meaning, at least for us in this world.

It is clear, then, that explanations after the fact apply to only nonrational commandments. To give such an explanation after the fact when dealing with a rational commandment such as the prohibition of murder, when there is a perfectly obvious reason or primary meaning for it, is to give a *rationalization*. A rationalization is the substitution of a secondary meaning or effect when a primary meaning or cause is available.[22] This is theoretically intolerable because it is a distortion of what we know to be true. In the case of the nonrational commandments, conversely, such as the prohibition of eating pork, we admit that the primary meaning, reason, or cause is unknown to us. Hence any secondary meaning we infer subsequent to our acceptance and observance of the prohibition is clearly only secondary and does not in any way masquerade as the primary meaning. Thus Fox's attempt to see the category of commandments universally practiced as having meaning only after the fact is untenable precisely because it ignores the clear distinction between the two types of commandments made by the Rabbis. Because some of the commandments have only secondary meanings known to us does not necessitate our looking at all the commandments this way. By making a serious confusion between "reasons" for these commandments and "rationalizations" for them, Fox has misinterpreted the famous rabbinic passage whose main point is that at least some of the commandments have reasons clearly evident even *before* the actual promulgation of the law. By not recognizing this distinction, I think, Fox has seriously underestimated this aspect of the "reasons for the commandments" (*ta'amay ha-mitsvot*) tradition in Judaism.

Fox's characterization of *halakhah* as only positive law does not answer two basic philosophical questions: (1) Why did God command the people of Israel? and (2) Why did the people of Israel accept God's commandments? Now the first question can be considered unanswerable in the sense of "My thoughts are not your thoughts" (Isa. 55:8), although the kabbalists, especially, devoted considerable effort to formulating an answer to it.[23] Nevertheless, this question is one more for metaphysics than philosophy of law. Therefore, let us deal with the second question. It is especially pertinent in our day when the majority of the Jewish people do not seem to consider themselves obligated by divine commandments.

It seems that there are three possible answers to why the people of Israel accepted God's commandments: (1) fear of immediate negative consequences if they did not, (2) total caprice, and (3) faith in God's goodness. These alternatives are treated in several important aggadic [homiletical] sources. Indeed, such questions cannot be the subject of strictly *halakhic* [legal] answers because they deal with the foundations of the whole *halakhic* system itself.

Concerning acceptance of the Torah because of fear of immediate negative consequences if it were to be refused, we read the following:

> "And they stood at the foot [*be-tahtit*] of the mountain" [Exod. 19:17]. R. Avdimi bar Hama bar Hasa said that this teaches us that the Holy-One-blessed-be-he turned the mountain over them like a tub and said to them that if you accept the Torah, it will be well and good [*mutav*]; if not, this will be your grave. R. Aha bar Jacob said that this constitutes a great indictment [*mod'a rabba*] of the Torah.[24]

According to Rashi, this means that such acceptance of the Torah out of fear of immediate death implies compulsion (*ones*).[25] Rabbenu Tam says that such divine compulsion implies lack of a sufficiently free human response (*b'al korham*).[26] Both commentators, no doubt, had in mind the *halakhic* rule that "one is not liable for acts done under compulsion" (*ones Rahamana patrayh*).[27] Indeed, the term *moda'a* ("indictment") is a *halakhic* term used to denote the nullification of a contract because it was made under coercion.[28]

Concerning acceptance of the Torah capriciously, the continuation of the Talmud's discussion above notes that a certain nonbeliever accused the Jews of being an impetuous people (*ama peziza*) because they accepted the Torah without first inquiring about its contents and judging whether or not to accept them.[29] The Babylonian sage Rava answered him that this is a sign of Jewish perfection. About this Rashi notes, "Because of our love [*me'ahavah*] we relied on God that he would not burden us with anything we could not stand."[30] This answer states that there is a fundamental difference between a capricious and a loving response.

A loving response to God's revelation provides an adequate reason for the acceptance of the Torah by the people of Israel. This is brought out by the following midrash:

> "I am the lord your God who brought you out of the land of Egypt. . . ." [Exod. 20:2] . . . So did the All-Present One [*Ha-Maqom*] bring Israel out of Egypt, split the sea for them. . . . He said to them, "May I rule over you?" They said, "Yes, yes!"[31]

Later this same midrashic text continues:

> He said to them, "Am I he whose kingship you accepted in Egypt?" They said to him, "Yes." [He said to them] "As you have accepted my kingship upon yourself, so accept my decrees [*gezerotay*] too."[32]

In the Talmud text we examined earlier, the same sage, Rava, who answered the nonbeliever's accusation of Jewish impetuousness with the retort that the Jewish response to revelation was one of love, answered that in the days of Ahasuerus the

Jews willingly upheld what had been forced upon them at Sinai.[33] As Rabbenu Tam interpreted this answer, "They accepted willingly [*me-da'atam*] because of the love of the miracle," namely, the deliverance from the extermination plot of Haman recorded in the Book of Esther.[34]

It is the understanding of this reason for Jewish acceptance of the Torah, a motif having considerable development in the Aggadah [lore] and later theological writing, that enables one to see how the giving and the acceptance of the Torah is so helpful for our insight. The point underlying this whole discussion is that the Jews experienced God as good and thus judged it right to respond to his commandments. Before they responded to his specific commandments, they responded to his presence in Egypt. In accepting God's offer of liberation, they judged freedom to be good and, therefore rejected Pharaoh's enslavement of them as wrong.[35] In other words, their response to God's presence presupposed that they had general criteria of good and evil, thus judging what acts are right and what acts are wrong. This is what made their response rational and not capricious. Their response to God's presence involved their admission that God's knowledge of their needs was greater than Pharaoh's and even greater than their own, and they were willing to accept the commandments of such a loving and knowing God even before understanding their meaning in detail. "And God saw the Israelites and God knew" (Exod. 2:25).[36]

Finally, the famous legend that describes God's offering the Torah to all the nations of the world, and its acceptance by Israel alone, implies prior standards of right and wrong that enable the Jewish people to accept the Torah rationally. The interesting thing about this legend, in all its versions, is that the nations of the world reject the Torah because they cannot accept the prohibitions of murder, sexual immorality, and robbery.[37] Why are they not told about the Sabbath or the dietary and clothing restrictions, which are themselves unique to the Mosaic Torah? The legend answers that the former, more universal, prohibitions are some of the Noahide laws incumbent upon all humankind, laws that the nations have already thrown off.[38] If, then, they cannot uphold these seven laws, how can they uphold the 613 commandments of the Mosaic Torah? It should be recalled that these three prohibitions are most of the ones that the Talmud text from B. Yoma 67b, brought by Fox, stated, "Had they not been written, reason would have required that they be written." Therefore, one can see how the rabbis regarded these prohibitions as the necessary rational preconditions required by the free acceptance of the Torah based on cognitive criteria. The point made by Fox and other Jewish positivists is that all standards of right and wrong are a posteriori, that is, subsequent to the promulgation of the specific commandments of the Torah. The aggadic passages we have been examining seem to assume otherwise. They seem to assume that at least some standards of right and wrong are a priori, that is, they are presupposed by the promulgation of the specific commandments of the Torah.

Leo Strauss: Philosophy and Law

On the question of whether or not there is any natural law doctrine in Judaism, there is at least specific agreement between Fox and the German-then-American Jewish philosopher Leo Strauss. Both answer the question in the negative. Thus Strauss wrote in his major work on natural law:

> The idea of natural right must be unknown as long as the idea of nature is unknown. . . . The Old Testament, whose basic premise may be said to be the implicit rejection of philosophy, does not know "nature." The Hebrew term for "nature" is unknown to the Hebrew Bible. It goes without saying that "heaven and earth," for example, is not the same thing as "nature."[39]

Fox quotes this same statement with approval.[40]

One could even assume, to a certain extent, that Fox is the mirror image of Strauss.[41] That is, whereas Fox argues against natural law in Judaism in order to maximally emphasize the superiority of revelation over reason, Strauss seems to argue against natural law in Judaism in order to maximally emphasize the superiority of reason over revelation.[42] I now propose to show why Strauss is wrong about the Hebrew Bible (and, by extension, about Judaism per se) on factual grounds and, more important, on conceptual grounds.

It is true that the Hebrew word for "nature," *teva* is not used in postbiblical or even in postrabbinic Hebrew. It does, of course, show the introduction into Jewish nomenclature of a term deriving from the Arabic *tab'a,* which is itself a translation of the Greek *physis* (as is the Latin *natura,* too).[43] Nevertheless, in what might well be his most important statement on religion and philosophy, Strauss argues for philosophy's unique ability to transcend "a particular or contingent event" (like that of revelation).[44] Hence, he cannot be taken to limit his understanding of philosophy, which is the means to the discovery of nature's truth, to its *particular* enunciation by the ancient Greeks. If that were so, philosophy would have no more theoretical value than scriptural revelation, by Strauss's own criteria, that is. But Strauss indicates that "Philosophy is the quest for . . . 'first things,' "[45] that is, nature. Therefore, philosophy's proper object must be defined, not simply named. Strauss, to be sure, does define nature, following Plato and Aristotle:

> The purport of the discovery of nature cannot be grasped if one understands by nature "the totality of phenomena." For the discovery of nature consists precisely in the splitting-up of that totality into phenomena which are natural and phenomena which are not natural: "nature" is a term of distinction.[46]

Nature is thus to be seen as an intelligible order to be discovered by the intellect. It encompasses less than "the totality of phenomena," which are capable of being experienced. Being a term of distinction, "nature" functions as a transcendent criterion of judgment. In regard to moral questions, it is used to distinguish between "good and bad," and in the more specifically legal sense, to judge between "right and wrong" or "innocence and guilt."

However, if this is how the idea of nature functions in moral judgment, then Strauss has missed its functional (if not terminological) equivalent in the Hebrew Bible. That functional equivalent is the idea expressed in the word *mishpat,* which is the hypostatization of the verb *shafot,* "to judge" or "judging." *Mishpat* denotes (1) "judgment" (the act of judging), or (2) "verdict" (the result of judging), or (3) "rule" (the specific criterion of judging), or (4) "justice" (the general criterion of judging).[47] In its first appearance in Scripture it means *justice.* That is in Abraham's dialogue with God concerning God's proposal to destroy the cities of Sodom and Gomorrah because of the wickedness of their inhabitants.

In his narrative God informs Abraham of how he plans to judge the cities so that Abraham "might command his children and household after him to keep the ways [*derekh*] of the Lord to do righteousness [*tsedaqah*] and justice [*mishpat*]" (Gen. 18:19). Although one could certainly interpret "righteousness" and "justice" as two separate things, one could also interpret them, with at least as much plausibility, as "righteous judgment" or *correct justice,* as in the verse "They shall judge the people justly [*mishpat tsedeq*]" (Deut. 16:18).[48] The question is: How is Abraham to learn what he is authoritatively to teach thereafter? He is not just to reiterate precepts; he is to teach a "way," a *method* of acting in general.[49] Now, if Abraham did not have a prior notion of justice, he could only follow God's example. But, as the text dramatically shows, he did not follow it before questioning its very intelligibility: "Shall the Judge [*ha-shofet*] of the whole earth not do justice [*mishpat*]?!" (Gen. 18:25). Thus it seems that Abraham already had some idea of what justice is to be; hence the basis of his question.[50] The basis of his question seems to be that correct judgment, *by definition,* requires making a consistent distinction between the innocent (*tsadiqim*) and the guilty (*resha'im*).[51] If God chooses to be a judge, and expects morally cogent imitation by his human creatures, his judging must be just.

The idea of *mishpat* as what might be termed "created order" is found in a number of places in the Hebrew Bible, and it is invoked for clearly normative reasons.[52] It also functions the same way in rabbinic teaching. Let it be recalled that the "rational commandments" are seen as the scriptural *mishpatim.*[53] Moreover, for the Rabbis, this idea of created order was expressed in such terms as *nivra ha'olam* ("as the world was created") and *beriyyato shel olam* ("the created structure of the world"), and these terms are invoked for normative reasons.[54] All these terms function as general moral principles, distinct from specific moral rules.[55]

The theological problem that now faces this line of argument, however, is that it seems to subject God, as it were, to a standard of judgment that transcends him. As such, it seems to deny that "I am the first and I am the last, and there is no God other than Me" (Isa. 44:6). A natural law doctrine seems to subordinate God to some*thing* higher. Fox, especially, is quite aware of this problem. Denial of the doctrine of natural law altogether seems to him the only way out of it.[56]

The opponents of the doctrine of natural law in Judaism, for whatever philosophical reason, seem to accept the definition of natural law proposed by Cicero, a definition consistent with Stoic philosophy and having its roots in Plato. Cicero writes:

> Therefore, since there is nothing better than reason, and since it exists both in man and God, the first common possession of man and God is reason [*prima homini cum deo rationis societas*]. But those who have reason in common must also have right reason in common. And since right reason is Law, we must believe that men have Law in common with gods. . . . Hence we must now conceive of this whole universe as one commonwealth [*una civitas communis*] of which both gods and men are members.[57]

In this definition of natural law, both God and humankind are included in a whole called *nature,* a whole that subsumes them and governs them.

However, if one adopts a more modest and limited definition of natural law, understanding it as the body of elementary norms without which a society of interpersonal communion would not be possible, then one can see these norms being presupposed in a covenanted community. Although this natural order is the minimal *form* of such communion, personal-historical relationship with God and Israel is its maximal *substance.* The formal structure is the background, not the ground, of this reality; its *conditio sine qua non,* not its *conditio per quam.* In Platonic-Stoic metaphysics, conversely, form and substance are ultimately one.[58]

In this regard, the more modest natural law theory of the twentieth-century Italian neo-Kantian philosopher of law Giorgio Del Vecchio might be helpful. He writes:

> Moreover, even when we distinguish . . . the various types of equality, there remains always the consideration that they have nothing to do with justice except in so far as they refer to subjects or persons; an equality or proportion of things . . . is not, properly speaking, either just or unjust. Only by beginning with the value of the person, and considering in some way its identity in different individuals, can one arrive at the basis of the concept of justice, which . . . is essentially a coordination and intersubjective relation.[59]

Del Vecchio clearly and persuasively puts forth a theory of natural law that does not subsume the norms of interpersonal relationship under some impersonal, eternal, and substantial cosmic order. Rather, he presents these norms as formal requirements of any genuine field of interpersonal relationships. In this formalism he is very much indebted to Kant. I think by seeing the relevance of this formalism for our understanding of the covenant and *halakhah,* we can successfully avoid the type of natural law theory that many have seen as being incompatible with Judaism.[60]

In Kantian formalism, the data of experience, its "matter," manifest themselves singularly. The structure of experience, its "form," manifests itself conceptually, that is, by general categories.[61] However, because conceptual form structures perceptual matter, this does not mean that form has any substantial priority over matter. It is simply an intellectual precondition for matter's intelligibility. This is why Kant (as opposed to many later idealists) insisted on positing the *Ding an sich,* that is, that the particularities that experience intends themselves ontologically transcend our general categories of understanding.[62] What neo-Kantians like Del Vecchio have done is to apply Kant's formalism to the area of our social experience and its law, whereas Kant himself seemed to have limited his theory of experience to experience of sense data. (In his moral theory autonomous humans qua *homo noumenon* seem to create their own social experience.)[63] In other words, the Kantian formalism of someone like Del Vecchio saves the social meaning of natural law theory from being reduced to Platonic-Stoic metaphysics, which is so incompatible with the Jewish doctrines of creation and covenant.[64]

José Faur: Covenantal Law

The contemporary Sephardic theologian José Faur, like Fox and Strauss, rejects the idea of natural law as "totally foreign to Jewish thought."[65] However, unlike Fox and Strauss, he does see a necessary precondition to the acceptance of the commandments of the Torah. This precondition is the covenant, which Faur contrasts with the classical philosophical idea of nature, as the foundation of law.

> The effect of this conception of religion is the establishment of a bilateral pact, a *berit,* between God and man by which both parties freely agree to maintain a relationship between themselves. Thus conceived, religion for Judaism is a relation-

ship between God and man, the sole ground of which is the free and mutual election of God and man.[66]

In dealing with Faur's theory I propose three questions: (1) Are covenant and natural law in truth mutually exclusive ideas? (2) Is the *berit* in truth a "bilateral pact"? and (3) Is the human choice of God the same as God's choice of humans?

I certainly agree with Faur that the authority of the Torah's law could be understood more primarily on the basis of covenant than on the basis of divine will alone (heteronomy) or divine wisdom in nature alone (natural law). Covenant also involves these two other factors in a way that they, either separately or alone, do not involve covenant.[67]

But minimal natural law must not be excluded from one's understanding of the covenant. Indeed, it seems that Faur's covenantal theology requires natural law theory even more evidently than Fox's legal positivism, for Faur is basically taking the philosophical idea of social contract and placing it in a theological context. (As for Strauss, he does not deny natural law; he denies only its locus in Judaism.) Now, historically speaking, social contract theorists have themselves been proponents of natural law theory, some in a wider and some in a narrower sense. All of them posit some "state of nature" as the background of the social contract. One can see this in the theories of Hobbes, Locke, Rousseau, and most recently, John Rawls (whose theory is admittedly indebted to Kantian formalism).[68] Furthermore, two perennial philosophical questions must be dealt with in any cogent social contract theory: (1) Why do the parties choose to enter into the social contract? and (2) What enables the contract to endure?

In the context of the covenant the first question breaks into two subquestions: (1a) Why does God choose to covenant with humans? and (1b) Why do humans choose to covenant with God? As we saw before, the first subquestion might well be unanswerable, although the kabbalists did speculate about it. The second subquestion, however, must be answered because if it is not, then the ancient charge of Jewish capriciousness in entering the covenant is true.[69] If this is the case, then how can people who stood at Mount Sinai be considered to be bound by a totally irrational, blind choice—much less their descendants? Rational choice presupposes intelligent judgment (*nihil volitum nisi praecognitum*).[70] Therefore, it seems to me that the best reason for the choice of the Jewish people to enter into the covenant with God, as we saw before, was their judgment that God's knowledge of their needs and his concern for them was sufficient reason for them to choose to accept his authority, to accept his laws as continually binding obligations, for the keeping of these laws itself is man's active participation in the same divine concern first manifest in Egypt. "And it will be right [*tsedaqah*] for us when we observe and do this commandment before the Lord our God as he has commanded us" (Deut. 6:25).[71] In order for the people to know that God's commandments are right for them, they obviously have to possess some knowledge of what is right in general. This precondition is simply unavoidable.

The second question, namely, what enables the contract to endure, also involves natural law theory, for a contract presupposes the norm that promises are to be kept (*pacta sunt servanda*).[72] Without this presupposition, a contract would have no duration and would be, therefore, meaningless. This natural law precondition seems to be an integral part of the covenantal theory in Scripture. Israel is frequently (and rightly) accused by the prophets of being unfaithful to the covenant, that is, of not keeping its word. "Instead you have broken faith [*begadatem*] with me, as a woman breaks faith with a paramour, O' house of Israel . . ." (Jer. 3:20). And this unfaithfulness is the same as breaking a covenant between two persons. "Thus says the Lord, for three sins of Tyre, for four I will not forgive . . . for they did not remember the covenant [*berit*] of brothers" (Amos 1:9). If the covenant is the foundation of the Law, as Faur rightly maintains, then covenantal faithfulness cannot be commanded by the Law inasmuch as it is already presupposed by the Law itself.[73]

Before we can analyze the covenant as that which cogently correlates natural law and positive aspects of *halakhah,* I must seriously question Faur's definition of the covenant between God and Israel as a "bilateral pact." It is bilateral, of course, in the sense that both God and Israel are bound by it. However, it is not bilateral in terms of its initiation or its enduring authority. In a bilateral pact, a social contract, both parties enter the agreement as legal equals and the requirements of the contract are based on *their* mutual authority to obligate themselves and each other. In the *berit,* on the other hand, God initiates the covenant as sovereign, the goals of the covenant are set down by God, and the authority of the covenantal requirements is the will of God alone when there is human resistance to it.[74] This does not mean that humans cannot freely accept or reject the covenant. If they could not do that, they would not be morally responsible for it. The covenant and its commandments make no sense without this presupposition, as Maimonides most persuasively argued.[75] In constituting what is involved in this freedom to accept or reject the covenant and its norms, we have seen that natural law theory cannot be avoided. However, there is an essential difference between freedom of response and freedom of initiation. This is a crucial point overlooked by Faur.

This leads us into our last question about Faur's position, namely, is human choice of God the same as God's choice of humans? It seems, viewed from the scriptural and rabbinic sources of Jewish theology, that God's choice is fundamentally different from human choice. Covenantal theory must be seen in the context of creation theory.[76] Creation theory always emphasizes the absolute freedom of God. There are no causes for his creative acts and, therefore, there is no necessity for them. "For He spoke and it came to be" (Ps. 33:9). Just as nothing required God to create the world, nothing required God to make a covenant with Israel. His was always the option not to make the covenant, or to make one with some other people. When the Israelites assume God is obligated to tolerate anything they do out of necessity, the prophet reminds them, "To Me O' Israelites you are just like the Ethiopians" (Amos 9:7). Thus from God's perspective the covenant is like a contract in that *a party cannot be bound unless he or she chooses to be bound by obligating himself or herself.*[77]

The choice of humans, however, seems to be much more limited in that it is only the freedom to respond or not. The prime obligation already exists; humans in no way create or even cocreate it. (Cocreation pertains only to secondary obligation, as we shall see in the next section.) It is this point that makes the *berit* for humans unlike a contract. In a contract, one in essence obligates oneself in general *beforehand,* and then participates with the contractual partner in the creation of mutual obligations *thereafter.* In the *berit,* conversely, humans are called by God to respond to a relationship that God has already initiated and structured.[78] In a contract, written or tacit, there is always the assumption that the agreement is initiated in mutual freedom and maintained in mutual freedom. Thus, it is always assumed that the contractual partners have other good options both before initiation of the contract and after its expiration.[79] But in the *berit,* these other options are only God's; for humans, the covenant is coeval with life. "To love the Lord your God and to listen to his voice and to cleave unto him: that is your life and the length of your days. . . ." (Deut. 30:20). "If these statutes pass away from before me, says the Lord, so also will the seed of Israel cease to be a nation before me all the days" (Jer. 31:35).[80] Humans can accept the covenant or reject it, but cannot escape it because the covenant is the most immediately normative aspect of God's everlasting presence. "The corrupt one [*naval*] says in his heart 'there is no God' [*ayn Elohim*]. . . . God looks down from heaven on all humankind . . ." (Ps. 54:2–3).[81] "Where can I go away from your spirit, and where can I flee from your presence?" (Psalms 139:7). But whereas humans are obligated to enter the covenant, God alone binds himself to it with no prior obligation. "This is my covenant with them, says the Lord . . . from this time forth and forever" (Isa. 59:21).

In this sense, then, the covenant is like natural law in that it is unavoidable. Accordingly, just as the fact of human sociality makes such norms as the prohibition of murder necessary, so does the covenant make the prohibition of adopting the religious practices of the Gentiles (Lev. 18:3) necessary. Without the former, society disintegrates; without the latter, the covenantal community disintegrates.[82]

This inescapable element of the covenant, which is God's everlasting commitment to Israel, is what makes the covenant binding transgenerationally. However, according to Faur's definition of the *berit* as a contract, why are the descendants of the Israelites who stood at Sinai and on the plains of Moab morally bound by a covenant accepted by their ancestors? It seems to be a rational norm, one certainly accepted by the *halakhah,* that personal obligation requires consent.[83] Faur states that "the nation of Israel of the future participates in the pact by their solidarity with Israel of Sinai-Moab."[84] That is well and good if future Jews *themselves* choose this solidarity, but what if they do not? (In an age of such widespread Jewish secularity this is more than an academic question.) Does that mean that they are not, therefore, bound by the covenant? Although such people might very well believe just that and act accordingly, the *halakhah* itself refuses to accept this in that it rules that "even when he sins, a Jew is still a Jew."[85] This applies even to one who becomes an apostate (*mumar*). Thus, the explanation of why the covenant is binding on all generations of Jews is that God never stops offering it to them.[86] It is divine offering, not human acceptance, that creates the obligation. This seems to be the meaning of the well-known rabbinic doctrine that all Jews were present at Sinai for the giving of the Torah.[87] In this context human agreement is confirmation after the fact. Surely, this is the only cogent position Jewish traditionalists can assert in an age when the majority of Jews do not regard themselves bound by the covenant and its law in any consistent way.

The Human Side of the Covenant

We have seen heretofore that the covenant presupposes natural law and human freedom of choice, that is, human freedom to respond or not to God's covenant, based on rational judgment. It does not, however, presuppose human freedom of will, that is, the freedom either to initiate the covenant or to terminate it. Both decisions are God's alone. Indeed, both are based on grace: "For the mountains will depart and the hills will be moved, but My kindness will not depart from you and My covenant of peace will not be moved, says the Lord who loves you" (Isa. 54:10).

Nevertheless, the *halakhah* and its development seem to manifest a role for human freedom over and above the choice to respond or not to what God has commanded. In this sense, the covenant seems to call forth not only a human response but, moreover, human initiative, even autonomy of sorts. This greater human freedom within the covenant is best seen in the role assigned to human implementation of the covenant. The Torah states, "According to the instruction [*torah*] which they will instruct you and the verdict [*mishpat*] they will render shall you act; you shall not depart from the ruling they will declare to you . . ." (Deut. 17:11). According to the prima facie meaning (*peshat*) of the text, this verse is authorizing judicial application of the norms of the Written Torah by the duly constituted authorities of the Jewish people. Surely, the Law itself requires judicial authority to be operative. But this verse was used by the rabbis to justify rabbinic innovation, that is, the rabbinic creation of positive law.[88] The Law itself, strictly speaking, does not require any such innovations, and this was the ancient Sadducee position. Nonetheless, the covenant does require these innovations lest new areas of Jewish experience (for example, Hanukkah as a response to the Hasmonean restoration of the Temple) be constituted outside its context and compete with it.[89] This freedom of innovation is broader than the freedom of choice presupposed by the covenant and its revealed law.

This power of human innovation entails the limitation of revelation to make room for this essentially human contribution to the covenant. Thus, the rabbinic doctrine that although the Torah is "from Heaven" (min ha-shamayim), it is no longer "in Heaven" (lo ba-shamayim hi), which means that its interpretation and application are now a human responsibility, performs this function of limitation.[90] The Written Torah as the repository of the direct divine revelation is now limited to the five books of the Mosaic Torah to which no new normative revelation can be added.[91] Indeed, even the prophetic books and the Hagiographa function only as either illustrations of the norms of the Mosaic Torah or as admonitions to be faithful to them. In themselves these latter two-thirds of Scripture are not normative.[92] Rabbinic law, although seen as authorized by scriptural law (*Oraita*) is, however, essentially different in that human beings now have the power of initiation of law and repeal of law. In rabbinic law the humanly appointed authorities can make either positive enactments (*taqqanot*) or restrictions (*gezerot*), and they have the power to repeal this legislation (*bittul*)—at least in principle.[93] In fact, the greater bulk of the *halakhic* system is not *from* direct scriptural revelation but from human reason, ultimately operating *for* the sake of the covenant.[94]

In considering the covenant in its aspect of divine revelation, we saw how natural law and positive factors are correlated. The so-called nonrational commandments are indeed experienced as *jus divinum positivum.* However, even if they do not seem to have rational grounds, they do have rational conditions. Without them human assent to this law would be nothing more than caprice itself, having no binding moral force. Furthermore, if the hallmark of natural law is that its norms are part of an intelligible order, then the assumption that divine positive law too has its reasons (*ta'amay ha-mitsvot*) is the point these two types of law have in common.[95] Both are aspects of the Torah as God's cosmic law. Their point of difference is that the norms of natural law, by virtue of their very generality, are more easily known, whereas the norms of the divine positive law, by virtue of their greater specific obscurity, are assumed to be intelligible even if that intelligibility is only partially perceived by us.

In considering the covenant in its aspect of human institutions (*mitsvot de-rabbanan*), we can see how natural law and positive factors are again correlated, for the interpretation of the divine law and, even more, the legislation of the rabbis, requires natural law factors in order to be rationally convincing. Thus a number of important rabbinic institutions were justified on the basis of their being "for the benefit of society" (*mipnay tiqqun ha'olam*).[96] Here we see the natural law principle of the common good, namely, that which enhances the life of the human community.[97] The common good, moreover, can be served only when the dignity of the individual members of the community is mandated. Accordingly, the enhancement of human dignity (*kevod ha-beriyot*) finds important applications in rabbinic interpretations of scriptural law, and even more so in independent rabbinic legislation.[98] The covenantal element in this type of legislation is that the relationship with God is considered to be the highest human good. Therefore, the composition of the liturgy is seen as a positive human contribution to the covenant.[99] On the other hand, negatively speaking, any compromise with idolatry, even if in the interest of human goodwill, is to be rejected as countercovenantal, that is, contrary to the highest human good.[100]

Positive rabbinic law, precisely because it is humanly ordained, involves natural law factors in its very initiation, in the setting forth of its grounds. In divinely revealed positive law, natural factors are immediately present only in the conditions for human response to the commandments of God. However, even here, we assume that the reasons for the divine decrees are far better than those we see more readily in humanly instituted law because of the greater wisdom of God. Indeed, part of the messianic hope is that we will fully understand God's law so that it will immediately persuade us and require no external coercion. At this time we will fully and immediately understand the law of God in all its manifestations. "It will not be like the covenant which I made with their fathers on the day I forced them [*hehiziqi be-yadam*] to leave Egypt. . . . For this is the covenant which I will make with the house of Israel after these days, says the Lord: I will place my Torah in their innermost parts and I will write it upon their hearts; I will be for them God and they will be for me a people" (Jer. 31:31–32).[101]

Notes

1. This discussion comes out as early as Plato's contraposition of the views of Thrasymachus and Socrates. Thus when Thrasymachus states, "The right [*dikaion*] for subjects [*tois archomenois*] is that which is to the rulers' advantage [*ksympheron*] and whoever deviates from it they call a lawbreaker and unjust" (*Republic*, 2 vols., 338E, trans. P. Shorey [Cambridge, Mass., 1937], 1:48–49), Socrates asks, "Do you not hold that it is right to obey those in authority [*mentoi tois archousi*]?" (ibid., 339C, Shorey, 1:50–51). In other words,

Socrates argues that political authority can function only because those following it have judged it (however inadequately) to be right. (See *Theatetus,* 177D; *Gorgias,* 483C.) This distinction comes out in modern times in Leo Strauss's polemic against Hans Kelsen. Whereas Kelsen wrote, "Vollends sinnlos ist die Behauptung, dass in der Despoten herrsche . . . stellt doch auch der despotisch regierte Staat irgendeine Ordnung menschilichen Verhalten dar. . . . Diese Ordnung ist eben die Rechtsordnung" (*Algemeine Staatslehre* [Berlin, 1925], 335, quoted in Strauss's *Natural Right and History* [Chicago, 1953], 4 n. 2), Strauss wrote contrarily, "To reject natural right is tantamount to saying that all right is positive right, and this means that what is right is determined exclusively by the legislators and the courts of various countries. Now it is obviously meaningful, and sometimes even necessary, to speak of 'unjust' laws or 'unjust' decisions. In passing such judgments we imply that there is a standard of right and wrong independent of positive right and higher than positive right . . ." (ibid., 2). See *infra,* 234f.

2. *Taking Rights Seriously* (Cambridge, Mass., 1978), 205.

3. See Hans Kelsen, *The Pure Theory of Law,* trans. M. Knight (Berkeley, 1970), 44ff.

4. See Thomas Aquinas, *Summa Theologiae,* 2-1, q. 90, a. 1 and a. 2; also, my teacher Germain G. Grisez, "The First Principle of Practical Reason," *Natural Law Forum* 10 (1965):168–201.

5. For the necessary personal involvement in all moral questions, see R. M. Hare, *Freedom and Reason* (New York, 1963), 73.

6. See infra, 187ff.

7. See Aquinas, *Summa Theologiae,* q. 91, a. 3.

8. See Kelsen, *Pure Theory of Law,* 217ff.

9. See M. Elon, *The Principles of Jewish Law* (Jerusalem, 1975), 10.

10. "Maimonides and Aquinas on Natural Law," *Dinē Israel* 3 (1972):v. Also see Fox's prolegomenon to A. Cohen, *The Teachings of Maimonides* (New York, 1968), xii–xlii; "On the Rational Commandments in Saadia's Philosophy: A Reexamination," in *Modern Jewish Ethics,* ed. M. Fox (Columbus, Ohio, 1975), 174ff.; *Interpreting Maimonides: Studies in Methodology, Metaphysics, and Moral Philosophy* (Chicago, 1990), pt. 2, passim. For other rejections of natural law in Judaism generally along similar lines, see M. Kadushin, *Worship and Ethics: A Study in Rabbinic Judaism* (Evanston, Ill., 1964), 39ff.; E. E. Urbach, *Hazal: Emunot Ve-De'ot* (Jerusalem, 1971), 283ff.; Y. Leibowitz, *Yahadut, Am Yehudi U-Medinat Yisrael* (Jerusalem, 1976), 26–27.

11. Fox, "Maimonides and Aquinas," viii. See the parallel to B. Yoma 67b in *Sifra: Aharay Mot,* ed. Weiss, 86a.

12. Fox, "Maimonides and Aquinas," xxvi.

13. Ibid., xxvii.

14. *The Image of the Non-Jew in Judaism: An Historical and Constructive Study of the Noahide Laws* (New York and Toronto, 1983), chap. 10. For another critique of Fox on the specific question of natural law, which explicitly agrees with mine mutatis mutandis, see M. P. Levine, "The Role of Reason in the Ethics of Maimonides," *Journal of Religious Ethics* 14 (1986):279ff., esp. 290–94; "Maimonides: A Natural Law Theorist?" *Vera Lex* 10 (1990):11–15, 26, esp. 26 n. 3. Also, for a critique of Fox's view of Maimonides on this point that influenced my own, see D. Hartman, *Maimonides: Torah and Philosophic Quest* (Philadelphia, 1976), 260–61 n. 38.

15. See Saadyah, *Emunot Ve-de'ot,* 9.2; Halevi, *Kuzari,* 1.48; Nahmanides, *Commentary on the Torah:* Gen. 6:2 and Deut. 6:20; Albo, *Iqqarim,* 1.5.

16. See Maimonides, *Hilkhot Melakhim,* 8.11 and 9.1; also *Hilkhot Yesoday Ha-Torah,* 5.7; *Hilkhot Gezelah,* 4.16; *Shemonah Peraqim,* chap. 6; *Commentary on the Mishnah:* Peah, 1.1.

17. See, e.g., *Religion of Reason out of the Sources of Judaism,* trans. S. Kaplan (New York, 1972), 123ff.

18. See Maimonides, *Moreh Nevukhim*, 3.48; *Hilkhot De'ot*, 3.3 re M. Avot 2.2; *Hilkhot Ma'akhalot Asurot*, 17.29–31. Cf. *Sifra:* Qedoshim, ed. Weiss, 93b, and David Novak, *Law and Theology in Judaism*, 2 vols. (New York, 1976), 2:38ff.

19. See Nahmanides, *Commentary on the Torah:* Lev. 19:2.

20. *Hilkhot Retishah*, 4.9. See B. Ta'anit 23a. Cf. Aristotle, *Nicomachean Ethics*, 1155alff.; *Politics*, 1263alff.

21. See Emil Fackenheim, *Quest for Past and Future* (Bloomington, Ind., 1968), 208ff.

22. See Plato, *Euthyphro*, 10A–E.

23. See Gershom Scholem, *Kabbalah and Its Symbolism*, trans. R. Manheim (New York, 1969), 115–17.

24. B. Shabbat 88a. See B. Avodah Zarah 3a re Gen. 1:31.

25. Rashi, s.v. "moda'a rabba."

26. Tos., s.v. 'moda'a rabba." See also B. Yevamot 48a, Tos., s.v. "ella."

27. Baba Kama 28b re Deut. 22:26.

28. See Baba Batra 39b–40a and Rashbam, s.v. "ve-khen" and Tos., s.v. "meha'ah."

29. The Talmud text interprets Exod. 24:7 to mean that they agreed to perform the commandments before understanding their specific meanings.

30. Shabbat 88b, s.v. "de-saginan."

31. *Mekhilta:* Yitro, ed. Horovitz-Rabin, 219.

32. Ibid., 222. See M. Berakhot 2.2.

33. B. Shabbat 88a re Esther 9:27. Re rabbinic debate over whether future generations, who accepted the Torah voluntarily, were not actually more meritorious than the "generation of the wilderness," upon whom it was forced, see M. Sanhedrin 10.3; T. Sanhedrin 13.10–11; Y. Sanhedrin 10.4/29c; B. Sanhedrin 110b re Ps. 50:5, also Y. Shevi'it 6.1/36a re Neh. 10:1. Cf. B. Avodah Zarah 3a and parallels.

34. Tos., s.v. "moda'a rabba."

35. Later on, of course, some of them had a change of heart. See Num. 11:4–5. For the notion that they were rejecting moral responsibility, see B. Yoma 75a and Rashi, s.v. "hanakh."

36. See Novak, *Law and Theology in Judaism*, 2:22.

37. *Sifre:* Ve-z'ot Ha-Berakhah, no. 343, ed. Finkelstein, 395–97, and B. Avodah Zarah 2b re Deut. 33:2.

38. See Novak, *The Image of the Non-Jew in Judaism*, chap. 9.

39. *Natural Right and History*, 81.

40. Interpreting Maimonides, 126.

41. See, e.g., ibid., 150–51, 225.

42. Note: ". . . a philosopher . . . refuses assent to anything which is not evident to him, and revelation is for him not more than an unevident,, uproven possibility." "The Mutual Influence of Theology and Philosophy," *Independent Journal of Philosophy* 3 (1979):113. (The original version of this essay was published in *Iyyun: Hebrew Philosophical Quarterly* 5 [1954]:110–26.)

43. See José Faur, *Iyunim Be-Mishneh Torah Le-Ha-Rambam* (Jerusalem, 1978), 64–65. For modern philosophical problems with the concept of "nature," see *infra*, 70ff., 141ff.

44. "The Mutual Influence of Theology and Philosophy," 111.

45. *Natural Right and History*, 82.

46. Ibid.

47. For *mishpat* (a) qua "judgment," see, e.g., Lev. 19:5, Isa. 28:6; (b) qua "verdict," see, e.g., Deut. 17:9, Jer. 4:12; (c) qua "rule," see, e.g., Exod. 21:1, Ps. 119:102; (d) qua "justice," see, e.g., Deut. 32:4, Isa. 1:27. Also, *mishpat* can mean a "characteristic," e.g., Gen. 40:13, Jud. 13:12. See *infra*, 163f. Strauss only wanted, it seems, to understand *mishpat* in this philosophically weakest sense. See his "Progress or Return? The Contemporary Crisis in Western Civilization," *Modern Judaism* 1(1981): 1:4.

48. LXX translates *tsedaqah u-mishpat* as *dikaiosynen kai krisin,* "righteousness and judgment," which seems to mean general benevolence *and* specific punishment of wrongdoers. A modern commentator, A. S. Hartom, in his *Commentary on Genesis* (Tel Aviv, 1972), *ad locum,* interprets *tsedaqah* as the positive command to practice benevolence to others, and *mishpat* as the negative command to avoid harming others (p. 70). However, virtually all of the other commentators, ancient, medieval, and modern, see *tsedaqah u-mishpat* as one concept. For a homiletical use of *tsedaqah u-mishpat* as different concepts, see *Beresheet Rabbah,* 49.4, ed. Theodor-Albeck, 2:502.

49. For the use of *derekh* as a "method" more general than specific rules (*mitsvot*), see *Sifre:* Devarim, no. 49 re Deut. 11:22, ed. Finkelstein, 114.

50. In the same sense, God can question Cain about the murder of Abel (Gen. 4:9), based on the assumption that Cain already has some idea of what justice is to be (see ibid., 4:7).

51. See *infra,* 168f.

52. See, e.g., Jer. 8:7; Amos 3:3–6; Job 28:23–28 and 38:1ff.

53. *Sifra:* Aharay Mot, 86a; B. Yoma 67b.

54. M. Gittin 4.4; B. Yevamot 61b. See *infra,* 84f.

55. See John Finnis, *Natural Law and Natural Rights* (Oxford, 1980), 63–64, for the distinction between moral principles and moral rules.

56. See, e.g., *Interpreting Maimonides,* 141.

57. *De Legibus,* trans. C. W. Keynes (Cambridge, Mass., 1928), 320–23. For Plato's notion that the gods are subject to higher law or forms, see *Timaeus,* 29A–C; also, David Novak, *Suicide and Morality* (New York, 1975), 33–35. Cf. Aristotle, *Metaphysics,* 1015a15.

58. See David Novak, *Jewish-Christian Dialogue: A Jewish Justification* (New York, 1989), 152–54, where an answer to the "Eurthyphro" problem (viz., if God is subject to a standard, then the standard is greater than God) is proposed from a covenantal perspective.

59. *Justice: An Historical and Philosophical Essay,* trans. Lady Guthrie (Edinburgh, 1952), 87 n. 3. See Aristotle, *Politics,* 1282b5ff. Even such a supposed legal positivist as H. L. A. Hart acknowledges a certain minimal natural law, in content not too different from what I am advocating here as a theological context. See *The Concept of Law* (New York, 1961), 188–89; also Novak, *The Image of the Non-Jew in Judaism,* 345–46.

60. This adoption of Kantian formalism regarding law per se does not, for me, entail adopting Kantian autonomy as the ultimate ground of law. See Jewish-Christian Dialogue, 135–37, 148–51.

61. *Critique of Pure Reason,* B34.

62. Ibid., B164, A249.

63. Ibid., B575ff.

64. See T. Bowman, *Hebrew Thought Compared with Greek,* trans. J. L. Moreau (New York and London, 1970), 172ff.

65. "Understanding the Covenant," *Tradition* 9 (1968):41. Faur also writes, "It is pertinent to add that the term and notion 'nature' are absent in the entire Biblical and rabbinical literature, and they are introduced into Jewish thought and vocabulary in the Arabic period" (ibid.). For Faur's sustained critique of Jewish natural law theory, see his *Iyunim Be-Mishneh Torah Le-Ha-Rambam,* 61ff. Cf. my late revered teacher Boaz Cohen, *Jewish and Roman Law* (New York, 1966), 2 vols., 2:28 n. 97; also Moshe Silberg, *Ba'in K'Ehad* (Jerusalem, 1981), 166.

66. "Understanding the Covenant," 42. See Otto Gierke, *Natural Law and the Theory of Society,* trans. E. Barker (Boston, 1957), 108–9; also S. Federbush, *Mishpat Ha-Melukhah Be-Yisrael,* 2d rev. ed. (Jerusalem, 1973), 33.

67. See David Novak, "The End of the Law: The Difference between Judaism and Christianity" (unpublished paper).

68. See C. J. Friedrich, *The Philosophy of Law in Historical Perspective,* 2d rev. ed.

(Chicago, 1963), 88–91, 101–3, 127. For Rawls's Kantianism, see his *Theory of Justice* (Cambridge, Mass., 1971), 179ff., 251–57.

69. B. Shabbat 88a.

70. See Thomas Aquinas, *Summa Theologiae,* 2-1, q. 9, a. 1; q. 13, a. 1.

71. For *tsedaqah* as "right" rather than "merit," see Gen. 18:19 and B. Yoma 38b; also Nahmanides, *Commentary on the Torah:* Gen. 15:6 (contra LXX; 1 Macc. 2:52; *Targumim* and Rom. 4:3).

72. See Charles Fried, *Contract as Promise: A Theory of Contractual Obligation* (Cambridge, Mass., 1981), 8–13.

73. For the notion that the Torah itself presupposes obligation, see, e.g., B. Kiddushin 13b and Rashi, s.v. "de-l'av" and Tos., s.v. "malveh." In the same logical sense, belief in the existence of God cannot be commanded by divine law because such a belief is itself presupposed by the acceptance of that very law. See David Novak, *Law and Theology in Judaism,* 2 vols. (New York, 1974), 1:138ff.

74. Thus the Hebrew word *berit* is rendered by LXX (e.g., Exod. 24:7) *diathēkē* in the sense of the Latin *testamentum, rather than synthēkē* in the sense of the Latin *pactio.* See W. F. Arndt and F. W. Gingrich, *A Greek-English Lexicon of the New Testament* (Chicago, 1957), 182. This also is the sense of *diathēkē* in rabbinic nomenclature. See, e.g., M. Baba Batra 8.6; *Bemidbar Rabbath,* 2.7; Y. Sanhedrin 2.6/20c. See Philo, *De Mutatione Nominum,* 5.52–53; my late revered teacher Abraham J. Heschel, *The Prophets* (Philadelphia, 1962), 229–30; Novak, *Law and Theology in Judaism,* 2:18ff.

75. *Hilkhot Teshuvah,* 5.1–4. For the difference between the ancient idea of freedom of choice (*liberum arbitrium*) and the modern idea of freedom of the will (*Willensfreiheit*), see Hannah Arendt, *The Life of the Mind: Willing,* 2 vols. (New York, 1978), 2:28–29.

76. See Jon D. Levenson, *Creation and the Persistence of Evil: The Jewish Drama of Divine Omnipotence* (San Francisco, 1988), 131ff.

77. Re God's binding himself to covenantal norms, not just the enforcement of covenantal sanctions, see Y. Rosh Hashanah 1.3/57a–b re Lev. 22:9; B. Berakhot 6a re I Chron. 17:21; also see David Novak, *Halakhah in a Theological Dimension* (Chico, Calif., 1985), chap. 9.

78. Re the historical background of *berit,* see D. R. Hillers, *Covenant: The History of a Biblical Idea* (Baltimore, 1969), 49.

79. Thus Socrates, who conceives of man's relation to a historical community as founded on tacit agreement (*homologia*) and contract (*synthēkē*), presents the policy of Athens in these words, "Anyone who is not pleased with us may take his property and go wherever he pleases. And none of us prevents or prohibits any of you to take his property and go away whenever he wants . . ." (*Crito,* 51D, trans. H. N. Fowler [Cambridge, Mass., 1914], 180–81). This rejection of a real possibility to do otherwise with impunity rather than remain an Athenian citizen convinces Socrates that he is morally bound to obey the laws of Athens (see ibid., 52D–E). See Strauss, *Natural Right and History,* 119. The *berit,* on the other hand, does not allow any such "checkout" clause. See L. E. Goodman, *On Justice: An Essay in Jewish Philosophy* (New Haven, 1991), 13–14, 41–42.

80. See B. Pesahim 68b.

81. The *naval* is not one who is a "fool" (as in the Vulgate's rendition of *naval* as *insipiens*) but, rather, one who acts with morally culpable, self-willed blindness to the provident and judging presence of God (see Isa. 40:27–31). Being a *naval* is to lack *yir'at Elohim* ("the fear of God"—see Gen. 20:11, Ps. 111:10; Prov. 1:7), which is a moral characteristic. See Job 2:9–10.

82. See *Encyclopedia Talmudit,* 17:305ff., s.v. "huqqot ha-goyyim."

83. See R. Isaac Abrabanel, *Commentary on the Torah:* Nitsavim, no. 1 re M. Eruvin 7.11; B. Ketubot 11a. Abrabanel argues that the acceptance of the covenant by ancestors thereby bound their descendants into perpetual slavery (*me-din avdut*). Aside from the

irrelevance of this explosion today, when slavery is regarded as morally repugnant by *consensus gentium,* even children's involvement in parental obligation or responsibility is seen as contingent on their own choice. See, e.g., B. Berakhot 7a re Exod. 20:5. For the noncontractual character of the *berit,* see R. Isaiah Halevi Horowitz, *Shenay Luhot Ha-Berit: B'Assarah Ma'amarot* (Amsterdam, 1648), pt. 1, 31b–32a.

84. "Understanding the Covenant," 42. For the notion of the original power of a community to bind individuals perpetually, even transgenerationally, see R. Solomon ibn Adret, *Responsa Rashba Attributed to Nahmanides* (Warsaw, 1883), nos. 280 and 285 (end).

85. See B. Sanhedrin 44a re Josh. 7:11; T. Demai 2.4; Bekhorot 30b; *Tur:* Yoreh De'ah, 266 (end) and Karo, *Bet Yosef, ad locum.* See also B. Shabbat 87a and Tos., s.v. "ummah;" B. Yevamot 62a and Tos., s.v., "Ha-Torah." Cf. *Mekhilta:* Bo, ed. Horovitz-Rabin, 53 and Zevahim 22b re Exod. 12:43.

86. See B. Shevu'ot 29a–b and Tos., s.v., "ki," and *Hiddushay Ha-Ramban, ad locum,* ed. Lichtenstein (Jerusalem, 1976), 132–33; Maimonides, *Hilkhot Shevu'ot,* 6.8–9. Many statements about the obligation to obey divine law seem to imply that acceptance of this law creates the obligation to obey it (see, e.g., B. Shabbat 88a; B. Avodah Zarah 2b). However, we have seen that such is not the case. (Re the primordial character of the covenant, see Niddah 30b and R. Hanokh Zundel, *Ets Yosef ad locum* in *Ayn Ya'aqov;* cf. Plato, *Meno,* 81Cff.) Perhaps such statements, which imply acceptance as a ground of the Law rather than a subjective condition for its observance, can be illuminated by Maimonides' solution to the conflict between the law that a man can divorce his wife only of his own free choice (M. Yevamot 14.1) and the law that enables the Jewish court and even its agents to force him to do so against his choice in certain cases (M. Gittin 9.8; M. Arakhin 5.6; M. Ketubot 7.1ff). Is not the use of such judicial force invalid coercion (*me'ones*)? Maimonides writes, "We do not say that one is coerced unless he is forced and pressured to do something for which he is not commanded in the Torah . . . but when he is overcome by passion (*she-toqfo yitsro ha-ra*) . . . his own bad character (*be-da'ato ha-ra'a*) coerced him. . . . [H]e really wants to perform all the commandments and to separate himself from sin, but his passions overcame him" (*Hilkhot Gerushin,* 2.10). In other words, we assume that if fully cognizant, one would have internalized the divine law *as if it were their own free choice.* See M. Avot 2.4; also *Bemidbar Rabbah,* 2.16 re Ezek. 20:32–33; B. Kiddushin 50a.

87. *Tanhuma:* Nitsavim (end), ed. Buber, 25b and Y. Nedarim 1.3/37d re Deut. 29:14. See *Sifre:* Devarim, no 33, ed. Finkelstein, 59 re Deut. 6:6; *Responsa Ribash* (Constantinople, 1507), no. 511.

88. B. Berkahot 20b; B. Shabbat 23a.

89. See Novak, *Law and Theology in Judaism,* 2:129–32.

90. M. Sanhedrin 10.1; B. Baba Metsia 59b re Deut. 30:12. See Temurah 16a.

91. The commandment "You shall not add [*lo tosifu*] onto the word [*davar*] which I command you" (Deut. 4:2) was interpreted by the rabbis using *davar* in its specific rather than its general sense (cf. Isaiah 40:8) viz., new details cannot be introduced into the commandments accepted as *d'Oraita.* See *Sifre:* Devarim, no. 82. However, by freeing the general sense of *davar* from this restriction, rabbinic exegesis justified all the rabbinic additions to the corpus of the Law as a whole.

92. See B. Baba Kama 2b; also Chaim Tchernowitz, *Toldot Ha-Halakhah,* 2d rev. ed., 4 vols. (New York, 1945), 1:19.

93. M. Eduyot 1.5; Maimonides, *Hilkhot Mamrim,* 2.2–7.

94. It was Maimonides, more than any other *halakhist,* who emphasized the human contribution to the covenant and its law, but without eliminating its ground in revelation. See *Sefer ha-Mitsvot,* shoresh 1–2; also David Novak, "Maimonides and the Science of the Law," *Jewish Law Association Studies* 6 (1990):94–134. For a modern attempt to eliminate the ground in revelation, cf. Haim H. Cohn, "Secularization of Divine Law," in his *Jewish Law in Ancient and Modern Israel* (New York, 1971), chap. 1.

95. See Isaak Heinemann, *Ta'amay Ha-Mitsvot Be-Sifrut Yisrael,* 2 vols. (Jerusalem, 1959), 1:29; Novak, *Law and Theology in Judaism,* 1:136–38.

96. M. Gittin 4.2ff.

97. See Aristotle, *Nicomachean Ethics,* 1129b15; *Politics,* 1252a1; Thomas Aquinas, *Summa Theologiae,* 2-1, q. 90, a. 2; *infra,* 98, n. 1.

98. See B. Berakhot 19b; Y. Kilayim 9.1/32a. For the idea of *imago Dei* as a more sufficient ground for human dignitiy than either rationality or political freedom, see Novak, *Halakhah in a Theological Dimension,* 96ff.

99. B. Berakhot 28b–29a; Maimonides, *Hilkhot Tefillah,* 1.1–2.

100. See M. Gittin 5.8; Y. Demai 4.3/24a; Y. Gittin 5.9/47c; Y. Avodah Zarah 1.3/39c. Cf. B. Avodah Zarah Ba re Exod. 34:15.

101. See Menahot 45a for the notion that all obscurity regarding the *mitsvot* will be removed during the days of the Messiah by Elijah.

4

The Covenant: The Transcendent Thrust in Jewish Law

ELLIOT N. DORFF

Jewish Law presents an intriguing set of issues for legal philosophers. In some respects it resembles secular legal systems very closely: it prescribes rules which range across the whole gamut of human concerns, and it uses familiar legal mechanisms to apply and change the law and to adjudicate disputes under it. On the other hand, there are elements within Jewish law which make it a distinctly religious legal system. These include its claims that God acts as its ultimate author, executor, and judge as well as more subtle religious influences on the scope of its content and the motivations for obeying it.[1]

To explain the secular and religious features of Jewish law, writers have invoked several models from non-Jewish legal theories. There are philosophical and educational reasons for such analogies. Since Jewish law functions in large measure as other legal systems do, one would expect that a legal theory worth its salt would be applicable to Jewish law as well. If the theory is philosophically correct, the areas where it fails to fit Jewish law should be directly attributable to the special religious character of Jewish law. The attempt to apply a general legal theory to Jewish law is therefore potentially enlightening about both the legal theory and Jewish law: the application should test the validity of the legal theory on a somewhat unusual legal system, and it should reveal the extent to which Jewish law is indeed unusual as a legal system—and, perhaps, why. This philosophical goal coalesces with an educational one: a common educational technique is to compare an unknown quantity with something known, and so explication of Jewish law through analogy with other legal systems is a natural method to gain better understanding of the nature and functioning of Jewish law.

In three previous articles[2] I have suggested that conceiving Jewish law as a covenant can help to illuminate its nature and operation. In those articles I did not address the underlying jurisprudential difficulties involved in using that concept. I welcome this opportunity to take up that challenge because I remain convinced that the covenant analogy, while not perfect, is the best available: it is genuinely helpful in understanding the phenomena of Jewish law, and to the extent that it is misleading, it is not seriously so.

What the Covenant Theory Explains

Since any analogy must ultimately be evaluated in terms of its strengths and weaknesses as an explanation, it is important that we first delineate the reasons why anyone would be tempted to use the covenant analogy in the first place.

The most obvious rationale for its use is that the Jewish tradition itself describes Jewish law in covenantal terms. *Covenant* is not a word or concept that is imported from the outside to explain Jewish law: it comes from the very roots of the Jewish tradition. It is the original and natural language in which the tradition expressed and understood itself.

Self-perceptions may be mistaken, however, and so it is important to spell out the ways in which the covenantal terminology reports the facts about Jewish law. To do that we must first clarify what understanding of *covenant* we mean to apply to Jewish law, for even in the Bible the word *covenant* is used for a wide variety of relationships. When it denotes a bond among human beings, it sometimes describes ties of friendship, with no legal dimensions whatsoever (e.g., 1 Sam. 18:3, 20:8, 23:18), or the deeper bond of marriage (Mal. 2:14, Prov. 2:17). It is more commonly used, however, to designate a legal tie, and then, while it can refer to a contract between two individuals (e.g., Gen. 14:13, 21:22ff., 31:44ff.), it is used more often to describe a pact between nations (e.g., Exod. 23:32; 34:12, 15; Deut. 7:2; Josh. 9:6, 7, etc.; 1 Sam. 11:1; 1 Kings 5:26; Ezek. 17:13–19; Ps. 83:6). The political connotations of the term are also evident in its use as a constitution between a monarch and his subject (2 Sam. 5:3 = 1 Chron. 11:3; Jer. 34:8–18), similar to ancient Near Eastern suzerainty treaties between kings and their vassals.[3] Such agreements are probably the model for the biblical covenants that God contracts with Noah (Gen. 9:9–17, Isa. 54:10, Jer. 33:20, 25), the patriarchs (Gen. 15:18, 17:2–21, Exod. 2:24, 6:4, 5, etc.), Joshua and the people (Josh. 24:25), David (Ps. 89:4, 29, 34, 39; 132:12; Jer. 33:21), Jehoiada and the people (2 Kings 11:17 = 2 Chron. 23:3), Hezekiah and the people (2 Chron. 29:10), Josiah and the people (2 Kings 23:3), Ezra and the people (Ezra 10:3), and, especially, Moses and the people at Sinai (Exod. 19:5; 24:7, 8; 34:10, 27, 28; etc.). In a number of these cases the "covenant" is not strictly a contract in the common law sense of the term since God only promises something without a clear specification of the consideration that he is to receive from human beings in compensation, but whatever is missing in one context is unambiguously supplied in others: God demands obedience for the protections and blessings that he will bestow, and failure to obey will result in punishment (e.g., Lev. 26; Deut. 28, 29). It is this suzerainty treaty, or Covenant,[4] between God and the people of Israel at Sinai that is the foundation of Jewish law, and it is that Covenant on which we will concentrate in this study.

The Covenant theme pinpoints and clarifies at least these facts about the nature and practice of Jewish law:

1. God as Legislator and Judge

The Covenant is between God and the Jewish people, and therefore it clearly expresses the Jewish belief in the divine authorship of Jewish law. Jewish philosophers interpret the process by which God commands Jewish law in a variety of ways,[5] but most are at pains to retain God's legislative role, even if they must explain it in untraditional ways. Jewish law must be construed as God-given not only because the Torah portrays it as such; as Professor Simon Greenberg has pointed out,[6] several phenomena of the ongoing practice of Jewish law can only be adequately understood if we presume divine authorship. The Jews' "sense of overwhelming awe when they contemplated the grandeur and majesty of the Law"[7] is certainly part of the religious feeling motivating those who observe it. Another element in the Jews' commitment to Jewish law is their conviction that through it they perform a cosmic role in helping God complete creation. The strength of these perceptions of God's role in creating Jewish law is especially evident in the numerous sacrifices which Jews have made to uphold it; only their belief that Jewish law expresses the will of God can explain their persistence. They also, of course, were motivated by their faith in divine reward for those who obey Jewish law and divine punishment for those who disobey it. That tenet is so central to Judaism that the rabbis defined a heretic as one who claims that "there is no justice and no Judge."[8] God is legislator, judge, and enforcer, and any adequate philosophy of Jewish law must articulate that pivotal doctrine clearly. The Covenant does just that: God announces his Covenant amid thunder and lightning at Sinai (Exod. 19–24), and he will avenge breaches of the Covenant with vigor (Lev. 26, Deut. 28).

2. Love of God as a Motivation for Obedience

The Covenant theme not only declares God's authorship and enforcement of Jewish law; it also articulates the relationships which underlie the law. Although we commonly think of elaborate governmental agencies when we think about law, those institutions really only account for a small percentage of the operations of a legal system. A legal system works only when the vast majority of those bound by it abide by its rules automatically. Then legal authorities can handle the conflicts that arise and the small minority of the society that seriously disobeys the law. To procure consistent and largely voluntary obedience, societies must create feelings of pride, respect, and even love for their community and its laws. That is hard because government and law are abstract and inanimate. It is much easier to relate to people. Therefore secular societies typically teach the history of the group, its songs, stories, and exemplary personalities in order to instill strong commitments to social institutions, and they reinforce those commitments through recurring rituals.

Jews do that too: Jewish education usually includes a study of the same subjects, and Jewish ritual patterns provide ample opportunity to renew national ties. But there is a difference. Jewish law is obeyed not only out of a sense of kinship and loyalty to other Jews, but to God himself. God is the King and Judge, but he is also the covenanted partner, and that provides the context for covenantal obligations.

The Bible develops the personal implications of the Covenant fully. It speaks of God having chosen the people of Israel as his special people out of an act of love, and Jews should observe the commandments because of that love and not spurn their divine lover through disobedience (Deut. 7:6–11):

> For you are a people consecrated to the LORD your GOD; of all the peoples on earth the LORD your GOD chose you to be His treasured people. It is not because you are the most numerous of peoples that the LORD set His heart on you and chose you—indeed,

you are the smallest of peoples; but it was because the LORD loved you and kept the oath He made to your fathers that the LORD freed you with a mighty hand and rescued you from the house of bondage, from the power of Pharaoh king of Egypt.

Know, therefore, that only the LORD your GOD is GOD, the steadfast GOD who keeps His gracious covenant to the thousandth generation of those who love Him and keep His commandments, but who instantly requites with destruction those who reject Him—never slow with those who reject Him, but requiting them instantly. Therefore, observe faithfully the Instruction, the laws, and the norms, with which I charge you today.

Conversely, just as God loves Israel, so should Israel love God. God will reward those who obey him and punish those who do not, but that should not be the exclusive motivation for obedience. Beyond pragmatics, Israel should obey God as an act of love; "Love the Lord your God, and always keep His charge, His laws, His norms, and His commandments" (Deut. 11:1). The Prophets picture God and Israel as husband and wife, joined in a covenant of marriage (e.g., Jer. 2:2, 3:20; Ezek. 16:8; Hos. 2). Obedience out of love of God is thus deeply rooted in the Jewish tradition. While that may seem natural to Jews, it should be remembered that most legal systems do not describe themselves as the fruit of a relationship between the lawgiver and the people, and so most legal theories do not speak to this important element in Jewish law. The covenant model does.[9]

3. *Promise Keeping as the Source of Obligation*

There is another aspect of the personal relationship between God and Israel that affects Jewish law significantly. Legal systems commonly hold native-born citizens liable for obeying the law (once they achieve the age of majority) without ever asking them for their consent. Enjoying the benefits of a society is generally taken to be sufficient justification for imposing its obligations on the grounds of fairness and also on the basis of the "tacit consent" that is implied by continuing to live within it. Judaism goes much further. It claims that Jews at all times and places *explicitly* promised to obey the law because they all stood at Sinai. The Bible expresses this with regard to the generation after the Exodus:

> It was not with our fathers that the Lord made this covenant, but with us, the living, every one of us who is here today. Face to face the Lord spoke to you on the mountain out of the fire. (Deut. 5:3–4)

> I make this covenant, with its sanctions, not with you alone, but both with those who are standing here with us this day before the LORD our GOD and with those who are not with us here this day. (Deut. 29:13–14)

And the rabbis expand the theme to cover all subsequent generations, as this famous passage from the Haggadah of Passover declares:

> In every generation one must look upon himself as if he personally had come out of Egypt, as the Bible says: "And you shall explain to your child on that day, 'It is because of what the Lord did for *me* when *I* went free from Egypt' " (Exod. 13:8). For it was not alone our forefathers whom the Holy One, praised be He, redeemed, but He redeemed us together with them, as it is said: "He freed *us* from there to bring us to, and give us, the land that He promised on oath to our forefathers." (Deut. 6:23)

Moreover, the people promised God to obey the law not out of fear alone but for ample consideration: God made His will known to the people of Israel, redeemed them, and gave them the land of Israel, and therefore the promise that they made is clearly valid (Exod. 19:2–8, cf. Deut. 4:32–40):

> Israel encamped there in front of the mountain, and Moses went up to God. The LORD called to him from the mountain, saying, "Thus shall you say to the house of Jacob and declare to the children of Israel: 'You have seen what I did to the Egyptians, how I bore you on eagles' wings and brought you to Me. Now then, if you will obey Me faithfully and keep My covenant, you shall be My treasured possession among all the peoples. Indeed, all the earth is Mine, but you shall be to Me a kingdom of priests and a holy nation.' These are the words that you shall speak to the children of Israel."
>
> Moses came and summoned the elders of the people and put before them all the words that the LORD had commanded him. All the people answered as one, saying, "All that the LORD has spoken we will do!" And Moses brought back the people's words to the LORD.

This justification of obligation through the explicit promise of the people is a major element of Jewish legal theory, and it is best explicated through the concept of two contracting parties, each of whom promises something to the other to form the agreement.

4. The National Domain of Jewish Law

The Covenant is specifically between God and the Jewish people; its terms do not apply to others. The rabbis make this explicit by claiming that non-Jews are subject to only the Seven Commandments of the Children of Noah,[10] but the Bible is also quite clear in restricting the jurisdiction of its commandments to Israelites.[11] While positivist theories could account for this, theories which base Jewish law on universal phenomena like natural law or reason would be hard-pressed. The Covenant clearly expresses the national character of Jewish law since it is specifically a Covenant between God and the people Israel.

During the nineteenth and the first third of the twentieth centuries, some Jews tried to minimize the national character of Jewish law because of the danger of producing a narrow, chauvinistic outlook, thus undermining the universal, messianic goals of Judaism. Those who have taken that view have found the Covenant problematic precisely because of its nationalism. Hermann Cohen, for example, bitterly attacked the cliquish consequences of a national Covenant and stressed that its restriction to Israel was to be temporary in the messianic sweep of biblical historiography;[12] Franz Rosenzweig was more comfortable with Israel's special Covenant with God but claimed that Christians had one too (albeit an inferior one) in his famous "dual-covenant" theory.[13] Since the 1930s the value of ethnic roots has been recognized even by those who would deny that the Jewish people are specially chosen, and so the Covenant has been reinterpreted but reasserted. Probably the best example of this is Mordecai Kaplan, who conscientiously denies that God chose the Jewish people for both theological and moral reasons but who affirms the Covenant equally strongly because it is only through national affiliation that one can contribute creatively to mankind. Jews are not chosen to serve God over and above any other nation of the world, according to Kaplan, but they do have a unique calling to serve God in their own specific circumstances and their own unique way:

> If we regard God as the Life of the universe, the Power that evokes personality in men and nations, then the sense of the nation's responsibility for contributing creatively to human welfare and progress in the light of its own best experience becomes the modern equivalent of the covenant idea. In it is implied that reciprocity between God and the nation that the term covenant denotes.[14]

The ability of the Covenant theme to express the national character of Jewish law is thus increasingly being recognized as an advantage for both historical and philosophical reasons.

5. *The Relationship of Jewish Law to Nature*

While Jewish law is specifically the law of the Jewish people, it is not only that: the classical Jewish texts picture it as rooted in nature. Psalm 19, for example, describes God's ordering of nature and then easily shifts to God's ordering of human life through the Torah in order to make the point that the two acts of God are parallel. Similarly, the Prophets complain that animals know and follow the rules that God has set for them, but Israel does not know or obey the Torah, which should be equally as obvious to them (e.g., Isa. 1:3; Jer. 8:7). Moses invokes heaven and earth as witnesses to the Covenant (Deut. 4:26; 32:1), and Jeremiah proclaims that the heavens are astounded when Israel flagrantly breaks the Covenant (Jer. 2:12; cf. 4:22–8, 6:19). Nature itself, in fact, takes vengeance on Israel when it breaks some provisions of the Covenant (e.g., Lev. 18:26–30). Israel's Covenant is thus rooted in nature in ways that no other legal system is, and that is part of the reason why Israel is warned not to follow other nations' laws (Lev. 20:22–26; Jer. 10:1–5). The rabbis, in fact, claimed that the very existence of the world is dependent upon Israel's acceptance of the Torah (*Shabbat* 88a):

> What is the meaning of the words, "The earth feared and was still" (Ps. 76:9)? . . . Before Israel accepted the Torah, the earth was afraid; after they accepted the Torah, it was still. . . . For the Holy One, blessed be He, stipulated a condition with the earth: If Israel accepts the Torah, you may exist, but if not, I will return you to the state of being unformed and void.

In direct contrast to the previous section, natural law theories (and perhaps other absolutist approaches) can account for this element of Jewish law, while positivist views cannot. The Covenant expresses both the particular, national character of Jewish law and also its universal, natural roots: God, who created the world, enters into a covenantal relationship with Israel so that the law of at least one human society may reflect divine purpose just as natural law does.

6. *The Scope and Specifics of the Law*

Because God gave the law, it can speak to every area of life, including many that fall outside of the jurisdiction of other legal systems. Jewish law sets an order not only for society but also for the private lives of an individual and a family, and it assumes competence to regulate even the speech patterns and thoughts of Jews. So, for example, it includes rules which detemine even the shoe that you are to tie first when getting dressed and the position in which you are to sleep, and it specifies with remarkable particularity the duties incumbent upon spouses to each other, including even the number of times that a man must offer to have sex with his wife.[15] The Talmud forbids oppressing one's neighbor in speech and gives a number of examples of that, and it also commands that one who intends to give a gift to a needy person should consider himself bound by that thought even if he never promised verbally or in writing.[16] These are all areas which legal systems do not dare to touch, let alone regulate, but Jewish law exercises jurisdiction on these subjects because its author is God (however that authorship is understood), and God has the power, the right, and perhaps even the obligation to address these crucial areas of life.

Since human beings are all a part of nature, natural law theories could presumably have an equally expansive scope and detail. In practice, however, they vary widely when it comes to specifying exactly what natural law demands, ranging from a few general rules to Maritain's rather specific list.[17] Positivist theories would probably find it easier to account for the specificity of Jewish law, but they would have to be substantially modified to explain its scope through providing for a divine legislator and enforcer; human positive law is severely limited in these areas. The Covenant model nicely describes both the wide range of concerns treated by Jewish law and the specificity of its rules: a covenant has specific clauses, and when God is the author, they can cover the whole gamut of human experience.

7. The Legal Techniques Used in Jewish Law

The biblical picture of God giving the law amid thunder and lightning at Sinai (Exod. 19:20) misleads many into thinking that Jewish law does not operate as other legal systems do. The Bible not only implies but explicitly states that its rules are never to be amended (Deut. 4:2; 13:1), and human legal systems do not include such prohibitions, even in regard to their constitutions. The rabbis, however, interpreted their biblical mandate to judge very broadly, with the result that Jewish law in fact has changed over the centuries through differentiation of cases and other normal legal techniques. That is a surprising development for a God-given law. After all, God's rules *should* be constant, and if they are to be changed at all, it should be by new revelations from God himself, as fundamentalist Protestants claim. The Covenant model, however, provides the basis for Jewish legal development, for God not only commands but enters into a legal relationship through the Covenant. Therefore, such legal techniques as interpretation, usage, and recourse to course of dealings became appropriate legal techniques to give meaning to the parties' original relationship. That would not be true if Jewish law were God's commands or natural laws outside the framework of a covenant—at least not as clearly so—for then God's rules would not be explicitly legal in character and would not be part of an ongoing development in time. The Covenant makes them law and thereby makes them amenable to human legal reasoning.

8. The Messianic Goal of Jewish Law

Preambles to constitutions commonly spell out noble purposes for the law, but they do not aspire to transform both human and animal nature. The Covenant does, at least as it was developed by the Prophets and rabbis. The ultimate aim is that all people worship God (e.g., Isa. 2:2–4, Zeph. 2:11; 3:8) with the result that there will be universal peace among people and in nature to the extent that the lion will lie down with the lamb (e.g., Isa. 2:2–4; 11–12). Toward that end Israel is to be "a light unto the nations" (Isa. 49:1–6, 51:4). Jeremiah experienced the failure of Israel to perform its role of moral leadership and the consequent destruction wrought by God, but he promises that God will not destroy Israel completely (5:18; 30:11; 46:28) and looks forward to a time when the law will be abrogated because there will be no need for it: it will be written in the heart and thus totally internalized (Jer. 31:31–34; cf. 3:14–18):

> See, a time is coming—declares the Lord—when I will make a new covenant with the House of Israel and the House of Judah. It will not be like the covenant I made with their fathers, when I took them by the hand to lead them out of the land of Egypt, a covenant which they broke, so that I rejected them—declares the Lord. But such is the covenant I will make with the House of Israel after these days— declares the Lord: I will put My Teaching into their inmost being and inscribe it upon their hearts. Then I will be their God, and they shall be My people. No longer will they need to teach one another and say to one another, "Heed the Lord": for all of them, from the least of them to the greatest, shall heed Me—declares the Lord.

The Bible and most rabbinic opinion assume that the Torah is immutable and eternal and that in messianic times it will be better understood and better fulfilled than ever before, but some rabbinic sources envisage a world so changed that the Law itself will be radically altered.[18] The following midrash clearly illustrates this dispute (*Midrash Psalms* 146, par. 4):

> "The Lord permits forbidden things" (Ps. 146:7, usually rendered, "The Lord sets the bound loose"): what does "permits forbidden things" mean? Some say: Every beast declared forbidden [to eat] in this world the Holy One, blessed be He, will one day allow. . . . And why has He forbidden them? In order to see who would accept His words and who would not. In the time to come, however, He will allow everything which He has forbidden. But others say, He will not permit forbidden animals in the hereafter.

In later Jewish history the doctrine of a radically new Torah was popular in those times and places where the Messiah seemed to be coming soon or already here; the more conservative notion of a more complete observance of the present Torah held sway when the messianic idea was a distant abstraction.

The Covenant theme accommodates both the anticipated changes in animal and human nature and the possible revision of the Law: since God is Creator of our present world, he can presumably change the nature of creation; and since Jewish law is based on a contract with God, it can be amended or even totally rewritten in a new age—although it would not necessarily have to be. In contrast, a realist approach that would interpret Jewish law as simply the policies practiced in Jewish courts and society now would ignore the messianic orientation of Jewish law, its hope not only to regulate what is but to produce what ought to be. And it is not only the psychological context of Jewish law which realism distorts, but its very operation, for the long-term goals embedded in Jewish law affect it in concrete ways. Traditional Jewish jurists sometimes override present desires and practices in an effort to realize Judaism's long-term goals, and that goal-directedness is absent in realist accounts. On the other hand, Jewish law is not to be identified with the law of nature along the lines of natural law theories. God has established law for mankind as he has established law for nature, and the one fits the other to the extent that nature even enforces some Jewish laws according to the Bible, as we have seen; but God can change both the laws of nature and the laws of mankind. Natural law theory is rooted in nature as it now is; the Covenant provides for the present tie of Jewish law to nature as we know it as well as the possibility of a future in which both natural law and Jewish law would be significantly changed. The Covenant theory therefore has the advantage of accommodating the future, messianic thrust of Jewish law in ways that competing theories do not.

The Problems with the Covenant Theory

An analogy by its very nature must compare two different things: if the objects of comparison were the same, we would have not an analogy but an equivalence. Analogies are useful for the philosophical and educational purposes described at the beginning of this essay, but they inevitably involve the danger of drawing false comparisons on the basis of the analogy. The only way to prevent that is constantly to keep in mind that the analogy is just that—a comparison that may illuminate certain features of an object or phenomenon but may be downright misleading in regard to others.

Both the advantages and the problems with using analogies are heightened when speaking about God. On the one hand, the only language available to us is derived from human experience, and so to talk about God it would seem that we must use symbols and analogies. On the other hand, if such metaphors can never be translated without remainder to words used literally, how can we ever be sure what the symbols and analogies mean—let alone whether they make true claims. Those philosophical problems have been discussed by a number of medieval and modern philosophers,[19] and theologians constantly warn us that any speech about God is inevitably limited by the constraints of our human abilities.

With that general background in mind, we should not be surprised that the problems with analogical thinking in general and the extra problems in using analogies with reference to God are all very much in evidence when we try to talk about a set of laws given by God. No analogy to human legal practice is going to be totally satisfying, and yet we must find some way to capture the idea of God's legislative activity if we are ever going to make sense of the fundamental assumptions of Jewish law, and we must also find a way to explain how this God-given law can be interpreted and applied openly and aggressively by human beings if we are ever to capture the methodology that has actually been used in the development of Jewish law. The real question, then, is the extent to which a given theory illuminates the axioms and methods of Jewish law and the extent to which it is misleading.

My contention is that the covenant analogy is the least misleading of the available theories and that, in fact, it is not very misleading at all because the places where the Covenant deviates from human covenants are rather obvious. To demonstrate the latter part of this claim, I shall consider nine arguments against describing Jewish law in covenantal terms. The first three raise questions about whether the sense of "covenant" is at all preserved in God's Covenant with Israel; the remaining six are theological objections to the model based upon what the model says about God and man.

1. How can God's Authority be Independent of, and Antecedent to, the Contract?

Social contracts are usually understood to be agreements among the inhabitants of a region to abide by certain rules. Authority to define and enforce those rules is created through the contract: before the contract is concluded people live in a "state of nature" in which nobody has moral or legal authority over anyone else, except as the laws of nature provide (however that is interpreted). In Judaism, however, God's authority precedes the Covenant and is independent of it. That is why, despite all of the talk of a "covenant" in the Bible, God ultimately *commands* the law unilaterally rather than negotiating its terms with his covenanted partner, Israel. In what sense, then, is this a covenant?

The question assumes that the model for the biblical Covenant is the social contract that we know from the world of philosophy, but it is not: it is rather the suzerainty agreements of the ancient Near East. Monarchs concluded covenants with their subjects in which they spelled out the history of their relationship to the nation, the commands of the monarch, and the blessings and curses that would accrue to those who obeyed and disobeyed respectively. As in the biblical Covenant, the suzerainty compacts did not create the sovereign power; that existed antecedently.

The importance of remembering the historical origins of the biblical idea of Covenant is underscored by the fact that the rabbis use that common biblical theme very little. By their time it was not the practice of kings to write covenants with their subjects; they simply insisted that those whom they ruled accept the yoke of their reign. Consequently, the rabbis expressed the Covenant idea in language appropriate to their times, that is, as "giving the Torah" (*Mattan Torah*) and "accepting the yoke of the Kingdom of Heaven" (*Kabalat ol Malkhut Shamayim*), parallel to, but also in contrast with, accepting the Roman yoke.[20] The idea, however, remained the same: Jewish law was to be seen as the product of God's command and Israel's acceptance, acts which created a special relationship between them, but God existed and held sway over the world before he entered into that special relationship.

2. If the Covenant is not a Social Contract in the Modern Sense, How Does it Provide an Explicatory Model For Us At All?

As indicated above, there are at least two goals in suggesting a philosophical model for a legal system, one philosophical and one educational. This question casts doubt on the effectiveness of the Covenant as an educational tool. After all, the didactic purpose of suggesting an analogy is to enhance understanding of Jewish law by reference to other, better-known phenomena, but if the Covenant model is based on ancient suzerainty treaties and not modern social contracts, how does it help to communicate the essence of Jewish law? The point could be taken even further: is not the term "covenant" downright misleading to modern people since they would most likely understand it as a social contract similar to other "covenants" which establish legal systems?

Theories are always subject to misunderstanding, of course, but the question is whether the Covenant promotes that. If people not expert in Judaica were asked to think about Jewish law, their first associations might well be the scene at Sinai. That would prevent them from making the mistake in Question 1 above since God's commanding authority is certainly in evidence at Sinai. The very assertion that the Covenant is with God should alert people to the fact that the Covenant is not a social contract. If anything, it is the opposite error that is more likely: people may conclude from the Sinai event that Jewish law is not a legal system in any normal sense at all, that it is entirely composed of immutable, apodictic commands spoken in awesome circumstances. That is a real danger, but any further study of the subject will quickly dispel the misconception. The chapters immediately following the description of Sinai in Exod. 19 and 20 already speak in a very different tone and beg for normal legal analysis. Consequently, while the Covenant theme may be somewhat misleading, it is not seriously so.

There may be no absolute monarchs who engage in formal covenants with their nations any more, but it is not difficult to imagine how one could. The scene, in fact, would probably be not so different from Sinai, with due allowance, of course, for the different degrees of awe inspired by human kings and God. The model, therefore, can be educationally availing. Indeed, if the first part of this essay is right, it should be pedagogically quite productive.

3. Did Jewish Law Ever Operate Like a Suzerainty Treaty?

This question probes the philosophical status of the Covenant theory: Is it a description of how Jewish law operated historically, either consciously or unconsciously? Is it a justification for observing Jewish law? Is it an analysis of some of the fundamental assumptions of Jewish law? Is it an explanatory analogy to elucidate some features of Jewish law?

It is certainly an educational device, as we have developed in the previous section. It may also serve as a way of justifying obedience to the law by reminding us that God legislated it, enforces it, and judges under it, that we owe obedience to Him as an expression of our love for Him, and that we made a covenantal promise to obey.[21] Its success in that role would clearly vary from listener to listener, but the very assertion of a close bond between the individual Jew, the Jewish people, and God through the Covenant can be a powerful motivation for new and continuing adherence to its terms.

The Covenant model may even serve as a description of the historical functioning of Jewish law if we understand that Jewish tradition modified the role of the receiver of the Covenant considerably. Specifically, it is the case that Jews have continually seen themselves bound to God through Jewish law; that even God is understood to be bound by his promises (hence the liturgical and literary complaints to God that are produced in times of distress); and that, for the Jewish tradition, God sets the rules. These are all features of a relationship based on the Covenant: complaints to God in particular are hard to reconcile with either natural law theory or positivism. It is also the case that the Jewish tradition created ways to repeatedly celebrate the Covenant. The talmudic rabbis, for example, connected the festival of Shavuot with the Sinai revelation (Pes. 68b), and medieval Jewish tradition initiated the festival of Simhat Torah and utilized all of the symbolism of a couple (in this case Israel and God) entering into a marital relationship. The verses from Hosea that are prescribed for putting on tefillin each morning (Hos. 2:21–22) are explicitly reaffirmations of the Covenant, as the context indicates (cf. Hos. 2:20). It is therefore probable that Jews not only acted but consciously thought in covenantal terms throughout Jewish history. The operation of Jewish law, however, did not follow the model of ancient suzerainty treaties (at least as far as we know them), for Jewish law provided for ample room for the rabbis of each generation to interpret and apply Jewish law in new ways, and in some periods it even recognized the customs of the laity to be legally authoritative under specific conditions. That active role for the receivers of the treaty seems to be absent in the monarchical covenants of yore, but other features of those covenants do in fact fit the historical functioning of Jewish law.

For our purposes, however, the most important contribution of the covenantal model is strictly philosophical: it reveals some of the fundamental assumptions of Jewish law, specifically, all of those mentioned in the first part of this essay. Consequently, while it may be useful in the educational, motivational, and historical contexts that we have discussed, it is the philosophical strengths and weaknesses of the model that most concern us here. Aside from the assertion of a relationship between God and Israel, covenantal legal theory has a number of implications for the nature of God and mankind, some of which are quite problematic. It is to those that we now turn.

4. How Can the Covenant Bind God?

Even if the Covenant does not create sovereignty, it does establish obligations upon God as well as man. It must do that if it is to be a "covenant"—even on the model of the monarchical compacts of the ancient Near East—but how can that be? How can any obligations of God's be enforced? And if they cannot be enforced, in what sense are they obligations?

God does, of course, take upon himself a number of specific obligations in the Bible, including the duties to give the people Israel posterity and the land of Israel and the responsibility to reward those who obey the commandments and punish those who do not. God's justice extends to other nations as well as Israel (e.g., Amos chaps. 1–3; Isa. 2:4; Jer. chaps. 46–51), and both Abraham (Gen. 18:25) and Job assume that small groups and even individuals should be rewarded and punished by God according to their merits. That sets the stage for raising Question 4 in the piercing way that Job does:

9.1 Then Job answered and said,
2   I surely know that it is so,
    when you say, "How can a man be just before God?"
3   If one wished to contend with Him,
    .He would not answer once in a thousand times.
4   However wise and stouthearted a man might be,
    has he ever argued with God and emerged
    unscathed?

10 Yes, He does great things beyond understanding,
    and wonders without number.
11 Lo, He passes by me, and I do not see Him,
    He moves on, and I do not perceive Him.

12 Behold, when He robs, who can make Him return it?
    Who can say to Him, "What are you doing?"
13 God will not restrain His wrath,
    before which Rahab's helpers were brought low.
14 How then can I answer Him,
    choosing my words with Him?
15 For even if I am right, I cannot respond,
    but must make supplication to my opponent.
16 If I called Him, would He answer me?
    I cannot believe that He would hear my voice.
17 For He crushes me for a trifle,
    and increases my wounds without cause.
18 He does not let me catch my breath,
    but fills me with bitterness.
19 If it be a matter of power, here He is!
    But if of justice who will arraign Him?
20 Though I am in the right, my mouth would condemn me;
    though I am blameless, it would prove me perverse.

32 For God is not a man like me, whom I could answer
    when we came to trial together.
33 If only there were an arbiter between us
    who would lay his hand upon us both,
34 who would remove God's rod from me
    so that my dread of Him would not terrify me.
35 Then I would speak, and not fear Him,
    for He is far from just to me.[22]

Job dares to speak for several reasons. There may not be a third party who can adjudicate disputes between God and Israel or enforce the rules against God, but God's personality is such that he keeps his promises. Nobody can force him to do so, of course, but there is no need for that: God does so automatically. Even after an enraging incident like the Golden Calf God forgoes his desire to destroy the people Israel when Moses reminds him that he promised the patriarchs not to do so (Exod. 32:13–14). Moreover, God has chosen Israel in love and therefore will not deceive or disappoint Israel in carrying out his part of the bargain (Exod. 20:6; 34:6–7; Deut. 7:1–16; etc.). Proof of his good intentions are his past acts of loyalty to the Covenant and love of Israel (e.g., Deut. 4:1–14, 32–40). Consequently, while God cannot be coerced into abiding by the Covenant, he can be trusted to do so.

Once again, the situation is similar to a covenant with an absolute monarch: there can be no suits against him to force him to carry out his responsibilities, but he is generally trusted to do so, at least as long as his reign lasts. It is also similar to a child-parent relationship in that the child assumes that he has no recourse against his parent if the parent fails to fulfill his duties, but the child nevertheless expects the parents to act responsibly and honorably. And indeed, two of the most common appellations of God in the tradition are King and Father.

5. Does the Covenant Limit God?

Even if the Covenant cannot be enforced by a third party, it does impose obligations on God. Does that not limit God?

The truth is that it does, but the Jewish tradition has generally not found such limitations theologically opprobrious because they were voluntarily assumed by God and because they are ultimately unenforceable.

6. Can God Revoke the Covenant Unilaterally?

Just as human beings would be left without recourse if God failed to fulfill his responsibilities under the Covenant, so there is no way to prevent God from abrogating the Covenant entirely if he so chooses. But God's nature is such that he can be generally trusted not to renege on his commitments under the Covenant, and he similarly is to be trusted not to rescind the Covenant completely.

The Covenant is thus crucially dependent upon man's faith in God. As we have seen, trust also plays a key role in human king-subject and parent-child relationships, and so we should not be surprised about this feature of the covenantal relationship with God. These human analogues will also be helpful in understanding man's rights under the Covenant, to which we now turn.

7. Was Man's Acquiescence Necessary to Validate the Covenant?

The biblical and rabbinic traditions were both ambivalent on this. The Bible clearly records Israel's agreement to the Covenant both at Sinai (Exod. 19:8; 24:3, 7) and during the reaffirmation in Ezra's time (Neh. chap. 10), and it asserts that the Covenant was made with the people Israel of all generations (Deut. 5:3; 29:13–14, 28), who presumably agreed to it. The Bible also speaks, however, of God's "commanding" the clauses of the Torah amid thunder and lightning, it describes the people's fear at the time (e.g., Deut. 5:19ff.), it expresses God's wish that the people fear him enough to obey the commandments (e.g., Deut. 5:26), and it confirms the Covenant in a ceremony that is designed to inspire awe in the people (Deut. 11:26–32; 27:11–26). All of that certainly does not sound like voluntary acceptance of the Covenant! The rabbis continue this: one popular midrash describes God's fruitless search for a people to accept the Torah until he asked the people Israel, who said, "We shall do and we shall hear" (Exod. 24:7) (*Sifre Deut* par. 343; *Num.R.* 14:10), while another equally popular midrash pictures God overturning Mount Sinai over the people and telling them that he will bury them with the mountain unless they accept the Torah (*Shab.* 88a, *A.Zar.* 2b, etc.).

The situation is not as strange as it sounds. In both king-subject relationships and parent-child relationships there is an element of voluntary acceptance, and both the king and parent would like to maximize that for both practical and moral reasons: practically, it is simply easier to gain adherence to the rules if there is willing obedience; morally, it is easier to justify the authority of the rules if they are accepted voluntarily. Free acceptance is not only a nice adornment for a legal system: it is absolutely crucial to its viability because enforcement procedures can never be totally effective. Thus the Bible contemplates the possibility of disobedience even to God, the perfect Enforcer. But neither Jewish law nor any other legal system is totally dependent upon uncompelled obedience: there must be means of enforcement. Moreover, there are situations in life in which there are no choices about accepting a set of rules in the first place. Subjects of an absolute monarchy are one good example of this, and children's duty to obey their parents' rules are another. The Jewish tradition depicts Israel's special status and even her existence as being dependent upon her obedience of the Torah because that was the mission God assigned her. Israel's acceptance of the Torah was therefore good and proper, but the authority of its laws is not dependent upon that: God, even more than a human king or father, can dictate the rules.

8. Can Man Change the Terms of the Covenant?

The immediate answer to that question is "no," and the Torah says as much: "You shall not add anything to what I command you or take anything from it" (Deut. 4:2; 13:1). That is perfectly understandable when we remember that it is God, the Creator, who commands, but that does make the Covenant a very peculiar covenant indeed: all other covenants are subject to continual embellishment and emendation.

Upon closer examination, however, it becomes clear that the Covenant is also subject to change because by its own terms human beings are given interpretive powers in Deut. 17. The rabbis expanded this judicial mandate significantly—so much so that they took it to include asserting human judicial authority despite a new, conflicting revelation (*B.M.* 59b), narrowing biblical institutions like capital punishment to virtual nonexistence (cf. *Makk.* 1:10), instituting a long list of new rules to the extent that they themselves recognized the Sabbath legislation to be like a mountain of rabbinic rules hanging on a hair of biblical law (*Hag.* 1:8), and actually legislating emendations in the law on occasion (*takanot,* e.g., *R.H.* 4:1, 3; *R.H.* 31b). They clearly did all of this to make Jewish law viable in new historical circumstances and not to undermine or annul it, but it is important to realize that this was done: despite the special character of Jewish law as divine legislation, many of the normal legal techniques used to apply nonreligious law have also been extensively used in Jewish law. Outright legislation is still uncommon in Jewish law, but rabbis use interpretation to produce judge-made law to fill the legislative vacuum. Consequently, the Covenant is methodologically a covenant in the full sense of the word.

Do Human Beings Have the Power and/or the Right to Revoke the Covenant Unilaterally?

This question arises in a variety of different contexts, and it has a different meaning in each one of them. We shall consider three:

a. Since human beings can change provisions of the law, does not that ultimately amount to the power and/or right to revoke the Covenant entirely? When the question is put that way, the answer is definitely no. The interpretive mandate was always to be used to further the observance and objectives of the law, not to abrogate it. A man might even be permitted to violate all the laws of the Sabbath in order to save his life, but the purpose of setting aside the law in this way was explicitly so that he might observe many future Sabbaths (*Mekhilta Ki Tissa* on Exod. 31:12). Interpretation of the law for the purpose of abolishing it would be a gross abuse of the legal methodology of the system. It also would be a highly questionable exercise in the first place: if one wants to abandon Jewish law, why bother to try to justify that through exegesis of its provisions? There comes a point at which one simply has to decide whether one takes Jewish law seriously or not, and those who do not would best leave it in place. This brings us to the second formulation of Question 9:

b. Since no country in the world requires Jews to live by Jewish law (except Israel in matters of personal status), what prevents Jews from abandoning it completely? A traditional believer would answer that God does, and observance of Jewish law is thus mandatory regardless of what governments do and do not require. Those who do not believe that God enforces Jewish law certainly do have the power in the post-Enlightenment world to invalidate the Covenant for themselves, and many in fact do. Whether they have a *right* to do so depends upon one's understanding of the authority of the Covenant in the first place. The situation is thus directly parallel to civil legal systems: a citizen of Israel, for example, has the power to avoid army service if he lives outside of Israel, beyond the power of Israel to enforce its law; whether he has a right to evade the law in that way depends upon how one construes the basis of authority of Israeli law on him in the first place. Is it only a matter of enforcement? Are there moral obligations to abide by the law? If so, to what extent, and why? The exact same questions apply to Jewish law for those who have doubts about its divine enforcement.

c. After the Holocaust do Jews have the right to abandon the Covenant since God seems to have reneged on his part of the bargain? The answer to that troubling question depends, in the first place, upon how one construes the relationship of God to the Holocaust. Was it only a man-made atrocity for which God shares no blame? Was God actively involved in creating it as the "Creator of good and evil" (Isa. 45:7)? Was he at least passively implicated for not stopping it sooner? Can we know? Even if God is to blame, does that free us of the covenantal obligations? There are those that claim that it does. Rabbi Yitshak (Irving) Greenberg,[23] for example, argues that after the Holocaust Jews must voluntarily choose to obey the Covenant if they are to obey at all. In part this is because, for Greenberg, no divine punishment could be worse than the Holocaust was, and so Lev. 26 and Deut. 28 have lost their punch, as it were. In part, though, it is not a matter of power but of right: did not God lose the right to demand obedience when he let so many innocent people suffer so?

There are no clear-cut answers to these questions. Some will in fact construe the Holocaust as a justification to abandon Jewish law. Those who continue to obey it, however, may well find the Covenant to be a good expression of their commitment for all of the reasons listed in the first part of this essay. They may admit that the Holocaust is a major problem for their faith, but in that they are in no worse position than those who understand Jewish law through other analogies. On the contrary: the degree to which the Holocaust is problematic for a continued dedication to Jewish law is best understood when we see the law as the product of a Covenant between a benevolent, loving God and Israel; if the law is simply the practice of the people (realists), or the specific legislation of a sovereign power (positivists), or even natural law, the problem that the Holocaust poses is not nearly as poignant as it in fact is and as the Covenant theory portrays it.

This brings us to the second part of my claim: whatever the weaknesses in the above arguments in defense of the Covenant model, I would claim that the alternatives are no better and, often, are worse. We cannot reasonably expect an absolutely adequate analogy, but we can rank-order the ones available, and when we do, we find the Covenant to be the best of the lot.

A complete analysis to prove this point would take us well beyond the confines of a paper such as this, for it would require a full critique of each of the alternatives in addition to a comparison of their relative strengths and weaknesses. I would, however, make two more observations to provide sufficient proof of the point. Both of them call attention to the transcendent thrust of Jewish law which is at the root of many of the strengths of the Covenant model discussed in the first part of this essay.

The fact that the authority of the law is derivative from, and dependent upon, God's antecedent authority is central to Jewish law. The fact is clearly expressed by the Covenant, modeled as it is after the suzerainty compacts of biblical times, but other theories have difficulty with this feature of Jewish law. Contrary to positivism, the subjects may not overturn Jewish law as they may annul the constitution in positivist theory precisely because of God's antecedent authority; and the legal and judicial discretion built into Jewish law is based upon the fact that God has granted those powers, and he could do that because of his dominion prior to, and independent of, the law. The Covenant also more clearly captures the element of revelation which is so crucial to Jewish law and which is absent in natural law theories: God establishes the Covenant in a direct, public act just as monarchs did in the ancient world, not just indirectly through his reign over nature. The historical school cannot explain why we ought to obey the law that developed from before Sinai to our own day, but the Covenant does: God commanded obedience to both the form of the law at Sinai and new forms that it would take in succeeding generations. It is for that reason that the rabbis were so careful to establish the authority of the judges of each generation (e.g., *R.H.* 25a–25b) and to claim even that the process of judicial interpretation represented a new and continuing revelation of God (*B.B.* 12a; *Num. Rabb.* 19:6; *Tanḥuma,* ed. Buber, *Devarim,* 1a):[24] only under those circumstances would the later developments of Jewish law have juridical authority. A similar point can be made in preference of the Covenant over realist interpretations of Jewish law: the Covenant establishes the transcendent authority and context of Jewish law, in contrast to the ethical relativism inherent in legal realism.

But it is not just a matter of authority. Probably the most important advantage of the Covenant theory over the alternatives is that it clearly expresses the *relationship* between God and the Jewish people on which Jewish law is built. The ultimate attraction of Judaism in general and Jewish law in particular is that it enables the Jewish people to relate to God as they understand him. Through Judaism they aspire to incorporate holiness in their lives, to capture the divine element which gives direction to life and makes it worth living. Judaism has historically claimed that the relationship with God is best expressed through observance of the terms of the Covenant as detailed in Jewish law, but even non-*halakhic* approaches to Judaism like those of Buber[25] and Borowitz[26] have used the Covenant model because of its powerful affirmation of the bond between God and Israel. People vary widely in their understanding of how and what God communicates to us, but some link to God is necessary if many of the phenomena mentioned in the first part of this essay are going to make sense. It is that transcendent thrust which the Covenant conveys: it is that relationship with God which provides much of the raison d'être of Jewish law.[27]

Notes

1. I have explored the ways in which Jewish law is both a legal system in the secular sense of the term and also a distinctly religious phonomenon in "Judaism as a Religious Legal System," *The Hastings Law Journal* 29 (1978), 1331–60.

2. Specifically, the essay listed in note 1; "The Meaning of Covenant: A Contemporary Understanding," in *Issues in the Jewish-Christian Dialogue: Jewish Perspectives on Covenant, Mission, and Witness,* ed. Helga Croner and Leon Klenicki (New York: Paulist Press, 1979), 38–61; and "The Covenant: How Jews Understand Themselves and Others," *Anglican Theological Review* 64:4 (1982), 481–501.

3. For examples of such documents, cf. James B. Pritchard, ed., *Ancient Near Eastern Texts Relating to the Old Testament* (Princeton, N.J.: Princeton University Press, 1950), 159–61 (Lipit-Ishtar Lawcode) and at 163ff. (The Code of Hammurabi—cf. esp. the prologue on pp. 164–65 and epilogue on pp. 177–80). Good secondary reading on this includes D. J. McCarthy, *Old Testament Covenant: A Survey of Current Opinions* (Oxford: Basil Blackwell, 1973) and Delbert R. Hillers, *Covenant: The History of a Biblical Idea* (Baltimore: Johns Hopkins Press, 1969).

Moshe Weinfeld has noted ("Covenant," *Encyclopedia Judaica,* vol. 5, p. 1021) that the idea of a covenant between a god and a people is unknown in other religions and cultures; it was a special feature of the religion of Israel. That makes sense when we remember that it was only the religion of Israel that demanded exclusive loyalty to its deity, and hence it was only in Israel that the covenant model was appropriate, for suzerainty covenants also demanded exclusive loyalty to the sovereign.

4. From here on I shall adopt the usual convention of using *Covenant* (with a capital *C*) to denote God's Covenant with Israel at Sinai and a small letter *c* for all other covenants.

5. For a summary of the range of modern interpretations of God's legislative role, cf. my *Conservative Judaism: Our Ancestors to Our Descendants* (New York: United Synagogue Youth, 1977), chap. 3, sec. D.

6. Simon Greenberg, "A Revealed Law," *Conservative Judaism* 19 (1946), 36–50; reprinted in Seymour Siegel, ed., *Conservative Judaism and Jewish Law* [hereinafter cited as Siegel] (New York: Rabbinical Assembly, 1977), 175–94, and discussed in E. Dorff, "Judaism as a Religious Legal System", *supra* note 1, at 1348–49.

7. Ibid., at 41 (in Siegel, ed., at 182).

8. *Gen. Rabb.* 26:6.

9. William Moran has argued in "Ancient Near Eastern Background of the Love of God in Deuteronomy," *Catholic Biblical Quarterly* 25 (1963), 77–87, that the root "*ahv*" is a technical, political term in the Bible denoting obedience and loyalty rather than love. Even if he is right, later generations of Jews understood it to designate the full gamut of emotions that we call "love." Thus the rabbis accepted Rabbi Akiva's interpretations of Song of Songs as love poetry between God and Israel (*M. Yad.* 3:5; cf. *M. Eduy.* 5:3 and *Tos. Sanh.* 12:10, *Yad.* 2:14), and Rabbi Akiva said: "Beloved is Israel, for they are called the children of God, and it was a special token of love that they became conscious of it" (*M. Avot* 3:18).

10. Cf. *Sanh.* 56–60, *A.Zar.* 64b, *Gen. Rabb.* 34:4. The Bible (Gen. 9:8–17) speaks about a covenant between God and all living beings; but the rabbis do not connect their doctrine of the Seven Noahide Laws to that covenant. They derive it instead from Gen. 2:16 (R. Yohanan on *Sanh.* 56b) or seven separate verses from Gen. 6 and 9 (The School of Menashe on *Sanh.* 56b–57a). The *Book of Jubilees* (Chapter 7), which has a slightly different list, derives it from Gen. 9 on the death of Noah.

11. For example, cf. Exod. 19:5–6; 34:10; Lev. 20:22–26; 25:39–46; Deut. 7:1–11; 10:12–22; 33:4; Jer. 11:1–13.

12. Hermann Cohen, *Religion of Reason out of the Sources of Judaism,* trans. Simon Kaplan (New York: Frederick Ungar, 1972), chap. 13, paras. 35, 38, 40, at 252–54; chap. 14,

para. 4, 271; Chapter 16, 353; *Religion and Hope: Selections from the Jewish Writings of Hermann Cohen,* ed. and trans. Eva Jospe (New York: W. W. Norton, 1971), 46–50, 168ff., and chap. 6; cf. also my discussion of his doctrine of Covenant in the second article cited in note 2, *supra,* at 46–50.

13. Franz Rosenzweig, *The Star of Redemption,* trans. William W. Hallo (New York: Holt, Rinehart and Winston, 1970, 1971), pt. 3, bks. 1 and 2. The Bible is *a* revelation of God but not the only one since revelation is to the *individual;* cf. pt. 2, bk. 1, 309, and bk. 2, esp. 167–88. Consequently, other claims to revelation might well be true: "Did God wait for Mount Sinai or, perhaps, Golgotha? No paths that lead from Sinai and Golgotha are guaranteed to lead to Him, but neither can He possibly have failed to come to one who sought Him on the trails skirting Olympus. There is no temple built so close to Him as to give man reassurance in its closeness, and none is so far from Him as to make it too difficult for man's hand to reach. There is no direction from which it would not be possible for Him to come, and none from which He must come; no block of wood in which He may not take up His dwelling, and no psalm of David that will always reach His ear" (from Nahum N. Glatzer, *Franz Rosenzweig: His Life and Thought* [New York: Schocken Books, 1953, 1961], 29).

14. Mordecai M. Kaplan, *The Meaning of God in Modern Jewish Religion* (New York: The Jewish Reconstructionist Foundation, 1947), 102; cf. also his *Judaism as a Civilization* (New York: The Reconstructionist Press, 1934, 1957), 258f. Cf. also my discussion of Kaplan's doctrine of Covenant in the second article cited in note 2, *supra,* and, in general, the third article cited there.

15. On shoes cf. *Shulḥan Arukh, Oraḥ Ḥayyim* 2:4, 5; on sleeping positions cf. *M.T., Hilkhot Déot* 4:5; on the duties incumbent on spouses to each other cf. *M.Ket.* 5:5–7, 9 and *Mishneh Torah, Laws of Marriage* 12:10,11,14,15; 13:3–6; on sexual obligations cf. *M.Ket.* 5:6.

16. On oppression through speech cf. *Mishnah B.M.* 4:10 and *B.M.* 58b–59b; on carrying through with an intended gift cf. *Kitsur Shulḥan Arukh* 62:17.

17. Jacques Maritain, *The Rights of Man and Natural Law* (New York: Charles Scribner's Sons, 1949), 111–14.

18. Cf. Joseph Klausner, *The Messianic Idea in Israel* (London: George Allen and Unwin, 1956), 444–50; Raphael Patai, *The Messiah Texts* (Detroit: Wayne State University Press, 1979), 247–57 (a convenient selection of primary texts in translation); W. D. Davies, *Torah in the Messianic Age* (Philadelphia: Society of Biblical Literature, 1952); G. Scholem, *The Messianic Idea in Judaism* (New York: Schocken Books, 1971), 49–77.

19. E.g., Maimonides, *Guide of the Perplexed,* Part I, chaps. 51–61; David Hume, *Dialogues Concerning Natural Religion,* pt. 2; Paul Tillich, *Dynamics of Faith* (New York: Harper and Row, 1957), 41–54; Paul Edwards, "Being-Itself and Irreducible Metaphors," *Mind* 74 (1965), 197–206; Eric L. Mascall, *Existence and Analogy* (London: Longman's, Green, 1949; Anchor Books, 1967), 97–121. The last three articles are reprinted in Ronald E. Santoni, ed., *Religious Language and the Problem of Religious Knowledge* (Bloomington and London: Indiana University Press, 1968), chaps. 7–9.

20. I am indebted to Mr. Seymour Rosenberg, an M.A. student at the University of Judaism and a member of its board of directors, for pointing this out to me.

21. Cf. the first three sections of the first part of this essay.

22. Job 9:1–4, 10–20, 32–35, as translated by R. Gordis, *The Book of God and Man: A Study of Job* (London and Chicago: University of Chicago Press, 1965), 248–49.

23. Irving Greenberg, *Guide to Shavuot* (New York: National Jewish Resource Center, 1976).

24. For a presentation and discussion of the sources on this point, cf. my *Conservative Judaism: Our Ancestors to our Descendants, supra* note 5, at chap. 3, sec. C.

25. Martin Buber, *On Judaism,* trld. Eva Jospe (New York: Schocken Books, 1937, 1967), 112–13; *Israel and the World* (New York: Schocken Books, 1948), 170–71. Buber is

not a complete antinomian: every I-Thou experience with God involves a demand upon the individual having the experience, but those demands are specific to the individual and not necessarily the requirements of Jewish law; cf. *Israel and the World,* 209, and Rosenzweig's response to him in "The Builders," in N. Glatzer, ed., *On Jewish Learning* (New York: Schocken, 1965), 72–92.

26. Eugene Borowitz, *Renewing the Covenant* (Philadelphia: Jewish Publication Society, 1991), pp. 284–99 [reprinted as chapter 7 of this volume].

27. I would like to thank Professors Arnold Band, Stanley Gewirtz, Henry Fisher, Steven Lowenstein, and Joel Rembaum for their helpful comments on a previous draft of this paper presented to the Los Angeles members of the Association of Jewish Studies.

5

Ethics as Law, Law as Religion: Reflections on the Problem of Law and Ethics in Judaism

LOUIS E. NEWMAN

For some years now, scholars have been engaged in a lively debate concerning the relationship between law and ethics in Judaism.[1] Numerous talmudic texts which appear to suggest that rabbinic authorities of the past indeed recognized a distinction between law and ethics have occupied a central place in these debates. Much of this discussion accordingly turns on how to understand certain key terms and the texts in which they appear, and how to construe the difference between "law" and "ethics." Different answers to the question, "What is the relationship between law and ethics in Judaism," then, rest on the ways in which scholars have addressed prior questions of both hermeneutics and conceptual definition.

The thesis of this paper is that both the hermeneutical and conceptual dimensions of this issue have been muddled by those engaged in this debate. As a result, one finds that scholars invariably cite the same body of texts but draw from them radically different conclusions about the relationship between law and ethics. Each claims simply to report what the tradition says on these matters, but none seems willing or able to explain why others, drawing on the very same evidence, have reached different positions. In order to clarify this confusing and, as yet, intractable problem, it will be necessary first to review briefly the sorts of evidence that play a central role in the debate about law and ethics, then to clarify the nature of the question itself, and finally to explain why the question cannot be answered, at least in the terms in which it has been framed by all those engaged in the debate.

The Evidence

The rabbinic sources that bear on the problem of law and ethics fall into two categories. First, there are texts which identify a type of moral behavior that is "extralegal," that is, morally commendable but (apparently) not legally required. Second, there are texts which suggest that in certain instances the formulation of the law itself was influenced by moral considerations, instances in which a rabbi interprets or applies a law in a particular way because this yields a more morally acceptable result. While it is impossible here to examine all the sources pertinent to this debate, it will suffice to look at representative texts and to sketch the spectrum of interpretation surrounding them.

One phrase often cited as evidence of an "extralegal" morality in Judaism is *ruah hachamim noha heimenu,* "the spirit of the sages is pleased with him." Consider the following passage from *Mishnah Shebiit* (10:9):

> [As regards] one who repays a debt during the Sabbatical year [even though he has no legal obligation to do so; see Deut. 15:1–2]—the sages are pleased with him. . . .
>
> All chattels are acquired through drawing [them into one's possession. That is, only when the buyer draws the item that he purchases toward him is the transaction formally concluded]. But [as regards] anyone who stands by his word [and does not withdraw from a sales agreement before the buyer has drawn the items toward him, even though either party to the transaction has the legal right to do so]—the sages are pleased with him.

The point would seem to be that certain actions may be legally permitted yet morally objectionable. The law may not require conformity to these standards of behavior, but the sages highly commend it. We do not know the exact force of the phrase "the sages are pleased with him," whether this indicates simply moral approval, or whether some social pressure was applied to encourage such commendable actions. It should be noted that there are cases of the reverse, that is, actions that are legally permitted, but if performed, "the sages are *not* pleased."

Another instance of the same sort is *kofin al midat s'dom,* "we coerce a person not to act in the manner of the Sodomites." This term presupposes the notion that the Sodomites' moral failing was their extreme selfishness, their refusal to do favors for others, even when this would cost them nothing. Hence, the rabbinic dictum that, in such cases, we should force people to perform acts of generosity, even if they are not legally required to do so. By way of example, consider the following case from the Talmud (*Baba Batra* 12b):

> A certain man bought a field adjacent to the estate of his father-in-law. When they came to divide the latter's estates, he said: "Give me my share [actually, my wife's share] next to my own field." Rabbah said: This is a case where a man can be compelled not to act after the matter of Sodom.

Since the two beneficiaries of this estate must divide the field equally, there is no reason why the one man should not be permitted to take the portion of his father-in-law's field which is contiguous with his own. This would be a great convenience to him and entails no loss to the other beneficiary. The point, then, would seem to be that, even in the absence of a specific legal requirement to act in a certain way, some rabbis were prepared to enforce what they regarded as morally appropriate behavior. It should be noted that in every instance in the Talmud where one rabbi invokes this principle, *kofin al midat s'dom,* another disputes the appropriateness of compelling such behavior.

In still other cases, the rabbis refer to *middat hasidut,* "the trait or quality of piety." This seems to denote an especially high moral standard which is characteristic of, or expected of, certain individuals. The following talmudic discussion (*Hullin* 130b) is illustrative.

> If a householder was traveling from place to place and needs to take gleanings, the forgotten sheaf, the corners of the field, or the Poorman's Tithe [all of these being agricultural gifts which, according to Scripture, must be left for the poor], he may take them. But when he returns to his house he must make restitution [by paying the value of the food he had eaten to the first poor man who claims it.]—so Rabbi Eliezer. Rabbi Hisda said, "They taught this only as a rule of conduct for the pious." [Since he was in fact temporarily poor at the time, he was entitled to consume this food and has no obligation to make restitution to the poor for it.]

We have here a dispute between rabbis Eliezer and Hisda. The former would insist upon restitution to the poor. The latter, however, regards this not as obligatory, but rather as an act characteristic of those truly righteous people who are more generous than the law requires them to be. At least in Hisda's view, then, there is a distinction between what the law requires and what the most righteous element in society would do.

But perhaps the most often cited example of a so-called extralegal morality in Judaism is that of *lifnim mishurat hadin*.[2] The term, which appears a number of times in rabbinic literature, translates "beyond the line of the law," and refers to instances in which an individual waives a legal right in order to benefit the other party. Examples include choosing to forgo one's legal rights in a sales contract or refusing to avail oneself of a special exemption to which one is legally entitled. In cases of *lifnim mishurat hadin,* then, one does more than the law requires (or, what amounts to the same thing, presses one's rights less strictly than the law permits). Against this background consider the following quotation (*Baba Metzia* 30b):

> "That they shall do"—that means *lifnim mishurat hadin.* [Commenting on this explication of Exod. 18:20,] Rabbi Yohanan said, "Jerusalem was destroyed only because they gave judgments therein in accordance with biblical law (*din Torah*)." [How can this be?] Were they then to have judged in accordance with untrained arbitrators? [Surely not. So what can be the meaning of Rabbi Yohanan's statement?] Rather say this: [Jerusalem was destroyed] because they based their judgments on biblical law [alone], and did not act *lifnim mishurat hadin.*

Failure to measure up to this high standard of behavior is cited as grounds for the most catastrophic sort of punishment which God brought upon the people of Israel. This strongly suggests that actions designated *lifnim mishurat hadin,* even if "extralegal" in some sense, are nonetheless part of what God expects of Israel.

In addition to these sources we find texts which suggest that moral considerations sometimes entered into the development of the law itself. In other words, at times the sages appear to construe legal duty in a particular way precisely because this accords with their moral judgments. A number of cases of this sort are frequently cited by contemporary Jewish scholars.

Every seventh year, in addition to allowing the land to remain fallow, all debts were to be forgiven, in accordance with Deut. 15:1–2: "At the end of every seven years you shall make a release. . . . Every creditor shall release that which he has lent to his neighbor." This rule had the consequence (not surprisingly) of making it very difficult to borrow money in the years immediately preceding the year of release. According to the Mishnah, the sage Hillel addressed this problem by creating a legal fiction known as a *prosbul* which authorized a court to collect an outstanding debt on the creditor's behalf during or after the Sabbatical year. This technically did not violate the scriptural rule which specifies only that the *creditor* cannot collect the debt after the seventh year. By establishing this legal fiction, it is often suggested, Hillel merely interpreted the law very narrowly so that one could observe the law (after all, one can never abrogate a divinely ordained scriptural rule) while at the same time fulfilling one's apparent moral duty.

In other cases, it is often claimed, the rabbis would deliberately misinterpret a biblical verse or rule if they found it morally objectionable. Perhaps the classical example of this is the rabbinic understanding of Exod. 21:24, "an eye for an eye and a tooth for a tooth." The sages interpret this to mean that one must pay monetary compensation to the victim equal to the value of an eye or tooth, not that one engaged in physical retribution. The plain meaning of the biblical rule presumably came to be regarded as barbaric in light of the moral standards of a later age. As a result, the application of the law had to be changed to accord with accepted principles of ethical conduct.

In yet another sort of case, it is argued that the rabbis, when faced with a conflict between a biblical law and their moral principles, would limit the application of the law so severely that, in effect, it became inoperative. Examples here would include the way in which biblical laws sanctioning capital punishment were reinterpreted by later rabbinic authorities. The rabbis introduced extraordinarily stringent conditions which had to be met before a person could be convicted of a capital offense. Since these conditions could never be met, no one could be convicted of a capital offense and the death sentence could not be carried out. Again, it seems that the rabbis were morally opposed to capital punishment and then interpreted the law accordingly.[3]

The Parameters of the Debate

Most contemporary scholars argue that these sources (and others like them) establish definitively that Judaism does indeed recognize a distinction between law and ethics. Moreover, they claim that the sources reviewed above demonstrate that traditional rabbis employed this distinction quite consciously, though they may not have been explicit about what they were doing. Elliot Dorff's assessment of this "extralegal" ethic is typical of one commonly held position. He writes, "Here we see a clear recognition of moral obligation beyond the scope of responsibility as set by the law and two means, short of actual coercion, to prompt people to act in accordance with those moral obligations, i.e., the opprobrium of being formally cursed in court, and the lesser, but important, stimulus of informing one who breaks his promise that he is a source of shame to the Jewish community."[4] Robert Gordis articulates a similar position with respect to the cases in which ethical considerations appear to have influenced the development of the law itself: "Here we see the genius of Rabbinic Judaism at work. In one case, the law is modified to meet the demands of justice as the Sages understood it. In the other, the law is completely set aside because the Rabbis could not reconcile it with their ethical stance and their fundamental faith that the Torah was designed to teach men to practice justice and mercy. In both instances, and in many others in the Mishnah and the Talmud, this ethical dynamism is clearly evident."[5]

Examining the same evidence, David Weiss Halivni has reached a rather different conclusion. He maintains that the rabbis did not, indeed could not, acknowledge a conflict of any sort between law and ethics. In his words, "The notion that the Rabbis of the Talmud were aware of a possible conflict between morality and religious law, and consciously resolved in favor of morality, cannot be defended historically. Historically, they gave other reasons for their interpretation." And in reference to the rabbis' treatment of capital punishment, he writes, "By retaining capital punishment in principle, and by not overtly saying that capital punishment is offensive to morality, the Rabbis tell us that their opposition to capital punishment was not based on moral grounds. . . . How could it be morally offensive if the Bible sanctions it? They objected to capital punishment because of lack of confidence in human justice."[6] Halivni concedes that, on a subconscious level, moral considerations were almost certainly at work in these cases. Yet, he insists, the traditional authorities could never have acknowledged such a distinction, much less employed it explicitly, insofar as this would imply that the received law, and the divine authority behind it, were morally flawed.[7] The rabbis were not deceiving themselves, they simply operated within a framework of assumptions which precluded them from recognizing and articulating the sorts of distinction between law and ethics that we employ. They were unable to do so because the very sorts of distinctions which we employ were meaningless in the context of their views about the divine nature of Torah, which encompasses without distinction both law and ethics.[8] Shubert Spero and Aharon Lichtenstein have adopted positions somewhere between those of Dorff/Gordis and Halivni. Both acknowledge that Judaism recognizes a distinction of sorts between strictly legal duties and other kinds of morally appropriate behavior. The question is how to characterize the distinctions and whether, indeed, it conforms in any sense to the sorts of distinctions we have in mind when we differentiate law and ethics. In Lichtenstein's words, ". . . traditional halakhic Judaism demands of the Jew both adherence to Halakha and commitment to an ethical moment that, though different from Halakha, is nevertheless of a piece with it and in its own way fully imperative."[9] The difference, as Lichtenstein sees it, between *halakhah* proper and this other ethical moment is that the latter is contextual or situational. Because no legal system can ever prescribe the appropriate response to every imaginable fact pattern, there arises the need to apply the values and principles implicit within the system to situations where no established law exists. But, following Nachmanides, Lichtenstein finds this ethical demand within the Torah itself, as it says, "And you shall do the right and the good" (Deut. 6:18). So the Torah contains both specific demands, which are the realm of *halakhah* proper, and more open-ended demands, which must be sought out and applied contextually.

For Spero, the difference between *halakhah* and these other ethical demands turns on the conflict between strict justice and benevolence. The legal system, by its nature, is concerned with enforcing justice and equity. Yet, the tradition also acknowledges that these values do not exhaust the whole of the moral life. Acts of selflessness and loving-kindness which do not fall within the domain of administrative justice are nonetheless morally, indeed divinely, mandated. These additional demands arise not, as Lichtenstein would have it, because legal systems are imperfect but because they are, quite appropriately, limited in purpose. They are in the business of ensuring social justice, not compelling benevolence.[10]

Reframing the Issues

The inconclusive nature of this debate points toward two distinct methodological problems, neither of which has been adequately addressed by those concerned to sort out the relationship between law and ethics in Judaism. First, the sources out of which answers to this question have been constructed are themselves ambiguous. Second, the key terms in the question, "law" and "ethics," have not been subjected to rigorous conceptual analysis, and so the question itself remains unclear.

Anyone who examines the texts cited above cannot help noticing that the evidence does not speak with a single voice. Some voices within the tradition openly contradict others. To take just one example, let us return to that category of *lifnim mishurat hadin,* "going beyond the line of the law." According to some medieval authorities these acts were morally praiseworthy but not legally required. Others, however, regarded such actions as backed by the full coercive authority of the law.[11] Likewise, some endorse the principle of compelling people "with respect to a trait of Sodom," while others do not. Again, what Eliezer sees as legally required, Hisda regards as an act of special piety. Those who write about this material, of course, note the existence of these controversies among traditional authorities. But they fail to see that the very existence of such controversies within the tradition invalidates the whole question as they have framed it. To ask "what is *the* relationship between law and ethics in Judaism" is to assume that there is only one relationship and, so to speak, one Judaism. It is to assume that the tradition is not rich and subtle enough to permit more than one legitimate answer to such a question. But the evidence itself belies this assumption. These texts do not answer our questions about the relationship between law and ethics in Judaism. Rather, they are themselves a reflection of the problem, a problem to which traditional authorities responded in divergent ways.

In short, this entire discussion of the relationship between law and ethics in Judaism has been conducted in a completely ahistorical framework. As a result, when the evidence points in more than one direction, contemporary scholars have felt the need to resolve the tensions. After all, if it is assumed at the outset that there is only one correct answer to the question, then all the opposing views within the tradition must be shown to converge at some point into an internally consistent position.[12]

But even if we were to take a more historically critical perspective on this material, other difficulties would remain. The fact is that, as regards distinctions between law and ethics, the sources are simply ambiguous. The problem is not just that different texts say contradictory things. Many sources do not say one thing very clearly. This explains why the same sources can be cited by contemporary scholars in support of such different conclusions about the relationship between law and ethics.

So, for example, it may be clear that certain actions—designated as "pleasing to the sages," or as "a trait of the pious," or as "going beyond the line of the law"—are morally praiseworthy. But do these represent moral duties incumbent upon all, or only upon those who strive to be exemplary; are they imperatives in force every-where and at all times, or only in special circumscribed instances? The sources simply do not speak directly to these questions. As a result, it is difficult, if not impossible, to determine what sorts of distinctions were, in fact, at work in these cases.

This brings us to the second main problem with the debate as it has been framed, namely, the lack of clarity about what sort of distinction we are looking for in the first place. Historically, a great many definitions of "law" and "ethics" have been proposed and defended by philosophers and social scientists of all sorts. For the question about law and ethics in Judaism to have any clear meaning, one must first adopt some view of the nature of law and ethics in general. A brief overview of some of the classic options in this respect will suffice to indicate the nature of the problem.

In the first place, it is acknowledged by all concerned that law and ethics are closely related. Both are prescriptive or normative in nature.[13] Both involve attempts to regulate human behavior and, to some extent, attitudes. Implicit in both law and morality is the appeal to some authority taken to be the source of the norms in question. We may leave aside for the moment the exact nature of that authority, whether divine or human, the state, the church, the individual's conscience, or whatever. Likewise, law and morality have what some have called a "claim of superiority."[14] That is, in cases of conflict, legal and moral norms, by their very nature, have priority over other sorts of (nonlegal and nonmoral) norms. For example, legal and moral rules take precedence over other cultural rules, such as those concerning proper ways to dress, eat, and so forth. Given these broad areas of overlap between law and morality, how can they be distinguished from one another?

In general, several types of differences have been proposed. First, it is often noted that law is enforceable while morality generally is not. One can be forced (by judicial order and, if necessary, by the coercive force of the sovereign authority) to comply with a legal duty. This is not true of moral duties (unless, of course, they also happen to be legal duties).[15] This difference is related to another often-cited distinction between law and morality. The function of law is relatively limited to preserving social order and promoting social cohesiveness.[16] The scope and purpose of morality, by contrast, is wider and encompasses potentially every sort of interpersonal interaction. For example, one may have a moral duty to take one's child to the park if one has promised to do so, but most societies will not treat this as a legal duty insofar as keeping such a promise (or breaking it) has few if any social ramifications. Thus, law is strictly social, while morality may govern personal as well as social behavior. Law and morality may also be distinguished from one another in that the former is relatively circumscribed, while the latter is relatively open-ended. That is, the set of laws operative in any given society is finite and capable of being formulated in some determinate way. Indeed, any effective mechanism for enforcement presupposes that this is so. Moral rules, on the other hand, are less susceptible to specific, definitive formulation, because they are less closely linked to social enforcement and because they encompass broader spheres of life.

At present, we need not enter into the debates about the relative strengths and weaknesses of any of these characterizations. We need only note that, unless and until Jewish scholars specify which definitions of law and ethics they have chosen to employ, the question they ask is inherently ambiguous. To ask how Jewish tradition understands the relationship between law and ethics is to ask whether any of the distinctions just noted or others like them play any role in the thinking of Jewish authorities over the centuries. Indeed, at this juncture it is possible to reformulate in clearer terms the issue at the heart of this debate. Specifically, (1) is there evidence that traditional Jewish religious authorities recognized any distinction whatsoever between what we identify as law and as ethics, and (2) if they did, did they identify the similarities and differences between them (either implicitly or explicitly) in any of the ways that we have? When the question is posed in this form, it becomes clear that each of the interpretations of the relationship between law and ethics sketched above is both partially true and partially false. It also becomes apparent that Judaism by its very nature does not permit a clear, unambiguous answer to the question.

Law and Ethics in the Context of Judaism as a Religious System

The source of the confusion about law and ethics in Judaism lies at the very heart of Judaism as a religious system. To understand the nature of Jewish ethics and its relationship to law, we must begin with a clearer conception of the religious character of the whole tradition. It is in the context of a particular religious worldview, a distinctive understanding of the relationship between God and the world, that all Jewish ethical reflection takes place. The essence of this relationship, as it has been understood from biblical times on, is the covenant that God established with Israel. This covenant was created through God's revelation of Torah to Israel. Through this gift of Torah, Israel became a "holy nation," set apart from others by its divine mandate to live in accordance with God's will as revealed in Torah. And that revelation took the form of law, first the biblical law dictated directly by God, then (so the rabbis tell us) through the proper interpretation and development of that law, which is an expression of God's ongoing revelation to Israel. These facts about the tradition are well known and uncontroversial. Yet, their import for the problem of law and ethics in Judaism has not been sufficiently appreciated.

This covenant between God and Israel establishes a communal way of life dedicated to *kedushah,* "holiness." By giving them the law, God makes Israel holy; by observing God's law, Israel affirms and realizes this holiness. All of the demands embodied in these commandments, whether they concern the sacrificial cult or agricultural gifts to the poor, whether they relate to the Sabbath and festivals or to the administration of justice and civil damages, together these define the content of a life of holiness lived in accordance with God's revealed will. As concerns this life of holiness, there are no distinctions between ritual and ethical imperatives. More to the point of this paper, there are no distinctions between moral offenses that destroy the fabric of society (such as murder and theft) and those that undermine personal relationships (such as cursing parents or hating a neighbor in one's heart).[17] Moral failings in both spheres constitute offenses against God, for the whole of Israel's life is to be permeated with holiness, consecrated to God, an expression of God's will. At this level, then, the sorts of distinctions that we make between social ethics and personal ethics or, as some would have it, between law and ethics, are meaningless.

Similarly, this covenant establishes a framework within which Israel strives to be godlike. As many theologians and biblical scholars have noted, the central underlying commandment is that of imitatio Dei, the imitation of God.[18] Just as God embodies moral perfection, Israel must strive to do likewise. As the rabbis interpreted the biblical injunction " 'You shall walk in His ways' (Deut. 28:9)—What are His ways? Just as it is God's way to be merciful and forgiving to sinners . . . so do you be merciful one to another. Just as God is gracious and gives gifts gratis both to those who know Him and to those who know Him not, so do you give gifts freely to another. Just as God is longsuffering to sinners, so be you longsuffering one to another."[19] The covenant and the commandments which it embodies provide Israel with the means of achieving this end. But if the goal of this holy way of life is the quest for moral perfection, then God demands far more than mere compliance with the provisions of biblical law interpreted narrowly. Every act of generosity, of forgiveness, of compassion, in short, every virtuous act is part and parcel of the holy life which God commands Israel to live. Israel is bound both by the letter of the law and by its spirit, or as others would put it, both by a divine law and by a divine ethic which at one and the same time is embodied in that law and transcends it.

Finally, the provisions of biblical law, being divine in origin, are also backed by divine sanctions. Scripture is replete with God's promises to reward the righteous and punish those who stray from obedience to the law. To be sure, some of the civil and criminal statutes found in the Pentateuch include human sanctions, such as capital punishment, the payment of specific damages, and so forth. Others are not backed by specific sanctions. But from God's perspective, the distinction hardly matters. Israel knows that ultimately it is accountable for its behavior before God. Whether or not humans are authorized to take action against those who violate God's laws, God certainly is. So, once again, the line between moral norms which are enforceable and those which are not, or between law and ethics in this sense, marks a distinction without a difference.

Each of the distinctions which we tend to make between law and ethics, then, is undermined at the most fundamental level by the religious worldview of Judaism. At every point, that worldview blurs the lines between the social and the private spheres, between the written law and the unwritten moral imperative, between moral imperatives backed by human sanctions and those that are not. It should be noted, too, that in this very fundamental respect, the religious worldview of Judaism has remained essentially unchanged from biblical times to the present, at least for those Jews today who continue to live their lives within the context of *halakhah*.

It would appear, then, that we have reached the answer to our question. "What is the relationship between law and ethics in Judaism?" It seems that there is no distinction, they are one and the same, both are part of one seamless body of divine instruction which as a whole constitutes God's revelation to Israel. But this is not the whole story. Indeed, we know this from the sources examined above. For even if it is not possible to pin down with certainty what the sources meant when they referred to actions as "pleasing to the sages," or as "going beyond the line of the law," they certainly were trying to mark some category of actions as distinctive. By the same token, while divine sanctions stand behind all commandments of the Torah, it remains true that some also carry human sanctions and some do not. The fact is that within the realm of ethical action distinctions are made both in biblical and in rabbinic texts. The lines between law and ethics are *blurred* by notions of holiness, covenant, and *imitatio Dei* but never entirely *obliterated*. To understand why this is so, we must understand the dual nature of Jewish law.

The *halakhah*'s unique character derives from the fact that it fulfills a social as well as a religious function.[20] *Halakhah* in large part and for most of Jewish history has regulated the daily life of Jewish communities. Like every other functioning legal system, then, it has faced a variety of social and jurisprudential issues, among them, the problems of legislating both conduct and attitude, emending prior rulings, enforcing its injunctions, and so on. In this sense, *halakhah* is subject to a whole range of social forces, even as it attempts to regulate and channel those forces.

Nonetheless, *halakhah* never loses its character as a system of religious instruction. And insofar as *halakhah* attempts to bring the Jew closer to God, the cultivation of certain godlike qualities will be central to its purpose. Of particular importance are those qualities of compassion and mercy which Scripture defines as the essential attributes of God and so too the hallmarks of the righteous person. Viewed from this perspective, *halakhah* represents what we might call an "open-ended" moral system. Within this system, as we noted above, Israel's moral obligations are potentially limitless, for ultimately they are required to see moral perfection through a process of *imitatio Dei*. It is not surprising to discover, then, that the tradition tends to blur any distinction between righteous behavior and fully actionable legal duties. But it is no less surprising that they could not do away with these distinctions altogether.

The same point can be made with respect to the rabbi, who serves both a jurisprudential and a religious role. Insofar as rabbis were lawyers and judges, their task did not include promoting exceptional piety. They mandated only that behavior which they saw as necessary for maintaining a just society. For the purpose of protecting individual rights and enforcing basic social responsibilities, it was not necesary to mandate special acts of selflessness or generosity. Moreover, as a practical matter, rabbis were understandably hesistant to legislate pious behavior which the average person could not be expected to emulate.[21] Thus, for both theoretical and practical reasons, rabbis refrained from giving legal sanction to acts of special generosity which, in any case, were not required to ensure a basically just society. From this standpoint, those who are more generous or selfless than the law requires may be praised for their righteousness and piety but will not be made the standard for the community at large.

In short, the religious character of Judaism necessarily blurs the line separating law and ethics. Each way of delineating law and ethics examined above is challenged by the most fundamental theological presuppositions upon which the whole tradition is based. Yet, the social reality within which this body of divine law functions tends to reintroduce and reinforce the differences between law and ethics. So, when we attempt to generalize about the tradition as a whole, we discover that the distinctions between law and ethics are never hard-and-fast, but they are also never obliterated. There are forces at work breaking them down and others, equally persistent and powerful, that serve to build them up again.

We are now in a position to understand the truth of the assertions that both Spero and Lichtenstein make. They want to acknowledge that there are different spheres of ethics, different sorts of ethical imperatives in Judaism. Some are more akin to our conception of law, some are closer to what we would consider a nonlegal ethic. And they are right to assert that, notwithstanding these differences, all ethics are in a certain sense "of a piece," all encompassed within God's revelation to Israel. What they fail to appreciate is just how fluid the boundaries between these categories really are. For the very same actions that, at one period in history, are clearly "extralegal," at another may become fully part of the legal system. What for one rabbi is merely virtuous, for another is fully compulsory and legally binding.

But the boundary between law and ethics is blurred for yet another reason. Apart from the tensions that exist as a result of the special character of *halakhah*, there is an ambiguity within the religious worldview of Judaism itself concerning the nature of the covenant between God and Israel. And, like the tensions discussed above, it too is rooted in the very foundations of Judaism. Perhaps the best way to get a handle on this ambiguity is to look closely for a moment at one biblical passage which, like so many others, describes the covenantal relationship between God and Israel. Deut. 26:16–19 reads:

> This day the Lord your God commands you to do these statutes and ordinances; you shall therefore be careful to do them with all your heart and with all your soul. You have declared this day concerning the Lord that he is your God, and that you will walk in his ways, and will obey his voice; and the Lord has declared this day concerning you that you are a people for his own possession, as he has promised you, and that you are to keep all his commandments, that he will set you high above all the nations that he has made, in praise and in fame and in honor, and that you shall be a people holy to the Lord your God, as he has spoken.

What does this passage tell us about the covenant? First, that God has a unique relationship with Israel and that this relationship defines Israel's distinctiveness among the nations of the world. That relationship is based on Israel's willingness to obey God faithfully, to dedicate its communal life to God. Moreover, that relationship is mutual. If Israel does its part, God will reward the people; they will be praised and honored above all others. So the covenant defines a relationship between God and Israel. But the covenant is also defined by the specific laws which God has given Israel and which they are to obey. It is, in effect, a legal contract, albeit one of a very unusual sort. It defines legal rights and responsibilities between the two parties to the agreement.

Covenant, then, refers both to a relationship and to laws which define the terms of that relationship. One might say that the goal or purpose of the covenant is to create a unique relationship, while its content is the body of law which to a large extent fills the Torah. But precisely here is the root of the ambiguity. On the one hand, the covenant, like all relationships, is open-ended and flexible. On the other, it is fixed in black and white, unchanging and formal. Insofar as the covenant is a legal contract, its demands are finite and self-contained. It is complete in itself. But insofar as the covenant is a relationship, like all human relationships it must be dynamic, and the demands that it makes cannot be fixed in advance or set in stone once and for all time. When we read about "keeping God's commandments, statutes and ordinances," we are in the realm of covenant as contract. When we read about "walking in God's ways" and "being a people holy to the Lord," we are in the realm of covenant as relationship.

The difference between these two notions of covenant comes into sharp relief when we turn back to the sources examined earlier about the way in which ethics operates within the legal system, influencing the way rabbis interpret and apply Jewish law. There are two ways of understanding what is going on in these cases. Dorff regards them as clear evidence that the rabbis recognized the difference between law and ethics, indeed, consciously struggled whenever they felt the tension between the two. Though Dorff does not put it in these terms, he ascribes to the rabbis a view of covenant primarily as an ever-changing relationship. Given this conception of covenant, the relationship is primary and the legal content is secondary. Because he attributes to the rabbis this perspective on covenant, he reads the sources as evidence of a tension between the demands of the law and the demands of this divine relationship. For, on this view, the established law will sometimes clash with what one perceives that God expects. And when this happens, the demands of the relationship as they are perceived at the moment will take precedence over the received legal tradition. Seymour Seigel articulates this position at the very outset of one of his many articles on Jewish ethics: "It is my thesis that according to our interpretation of Judaism, the ethical values of our tradition should have the power to judge the particulars of Jewish law. If any law in our tradition does not fulfill our ethical values, then the law should be abolished or revised. This point of view can be supported historically and theologically."[22] From this theological perspective, it is inevitable that there be conflicts between the perceived legal rules and what our covenantal relationship with God demands of us, between Jewish law and Jewish ethics. And it is equally inevitable that, when these conflicts occur, they be resolved in favor of ethics.

The other theology of covenant is represented by Halivni and, by now, its implications for Jewish law and ethics are predictable. If the covenant is the law, if fulfilling the covenant means nothing more and nothing less than fulfilling the dictates of the law, then there can be no conflict between law and ethics. For, after all, this law is divine and therefore, by definition, perfect. As Ps. 19:8–10 states, "The law of the Lord is perfect, restoring the soul; the testimony of the Lord is sure, making wise the simple; the precepts of the Lord are right, rejoicing the heart; the commandment of the Lord is clear, enlightening the eyes; the fear of the Lord is pure, enduring forever; the judgments of the Lord are true, they are righteous altogether." From this theological perspective, if any established law ever appears less than perfect, the only conceivable conclusion is that we have not understood it properly. Any apparent conflict between law and ethics is only apparent, for God cannot have meant for us to apply a revealed law in a way which is blatantly unjust or unethical. Again, without articulating this view in theological terms, Halivni has attributed to the rabbis a concept of covenant which leads inexorably to the view that law and ethics are one and the same.

Both views of covenant, with their corresponding implications for law and ethics, are equally well rooted in Judaism. So we dare not ask whose interpretation of the sources is correct or which theology of covenant best accounts for the evidence. The answer is that both are correct. There is no way to choose between them and, more to the point, no need to do so.[23] Once it is acknowledged that both theologies of covenant are legitimate options within the tradition, and that they lead to different conclusions about the relationship between law and ethics, then it becomes clear that every solution which contemporary scholars have offered is correct. And it is equally clear that every solution, offered as the whole truth, is incorrect.

To conclude, then, the problem of the relationship between law and ethics in Judaism is genuinely irresolvable in the terms in which it has been formulated. It is not a problem which can be defined by postulating firm distinctions where none exist. Neither can it be swept under the rug, as though the problem were entirely illusory, a product of our collective misunderstanding. The problem is rooted in the very foundations of Judaism as a system of religious truth and as a functioning legal system. And the situation is further complicated by the fact that the tradition embraces more than one theory of covenant. Thus, the whole enterprise of lawmaking and norm setting can be understood from within the system in two quite different ways. Given these facts—that the law is both divine instruction and functioning legal system, that covenant can be defined both by its specific content and by the relationship which it creates—the paradox is in place. And that paradox is that Judaism both does and does not acknowledge a distinction between law and ethics as we tend to use those terms. Indeed, on one level it must recognize such a distinction and yet just as surely it must refuse to recognize it. Once we have discovered the paradoxical quality of the situation, and once we have recognized that it is inherent in the tradition, then we have said as much as there is to say about the relationship between law and ethics in Judaism.

I wish to conclude this analytical discussion with a metaphor that expresses somewhat poetically much of the argument of the paper. The relationship between law and ethics in Judaism is rather like that between the sea and the shoreline. The boundary between them is constantly shifting, and necessarily so. The forces of the sea eat away at the shore, washing away the sand. But the land is equally powerful; it holds back the sea, and sets limits to its movement. The one force is dynamic and fluid, the other is stable and solid. From one perspective, we might think of them as opposing forces, working against one another, deadlocked in a fight in which neither can totally prevail. But from another perspective, the ebb and flow between them is a model of complementarity. Neither could exist without the other. There is no question but that there is an absolute difference between the land and the sea—any child can see that. But just as surely there is no way to fix, even at a single moment in time, the precise point where one ends and the other begins. And, viewed from the perspective of a religious believer, these two are really one. They are not two forces working against, or even with, one another. To the religious believer, both are part of a single world, both are expressions of God's creative power, and finally, both have their assigned roles to play in a cosmic order that God has ordained. So too with the relationship between law and ethics in Judaism.[24]

Notes

1. See J. David Bleich, "Is There an Ethic beyond Halakhah?" in ed. Norbert M. Samuelson, *Studies in Jewish Philosophy* (Lanham, MD, 1987), pp. 527–46; Eugene B. Borowitz, "The Authority of the Ethical Impulse in Halakhah," in ed. Samuelson, op. cit., pp. 489–505; Boaz Cohen, "Letter and Spirit in Jewish and Roman Law," in his *Law and*

Tradition in Judaism (New York, 1969); Elliot N. Dorff, "The Interaction of Jewish Law with Morality," *Judaism* 26:455–66; José Faur, "Law and Justice in Rabbinic Jurisprudence," in ed. Gersion Appel, Morris Epstein, and Hayim Leaf, *Samuel K. Mirsky Memorial Volume* (New York, 1970); Simon Federbush, *"Al hamusar v'hamishpat"* [Hebrew], *Bitzaron* 6:525–32; Robert Gordis, "The Ethical Dimensions of the Halakhah," *Conservative Judaism* 26:70–74; Alexander Guttmann, "The Role of Equity in the History of the Halakhah," in his *Studies in Rabbinic Judaism* (New York, 1976); David Weiss Halivni, "Can a Religious Law Be Immoral?" in ed. Arthur A. Chiel, *Perspectives on Jews and Judaism: Essays in Honor of Wolfe Kelman* (New York, 1978); Milton Konvitz, "Law and Morals: In the Hebrew Scriptures, Plato and Aristotle," *Conservative Judaism* 23:44–71; Eugene B. Korn, "Ethics and Jewish Law," *Judaism* 26:455–66; Leo Landman, "Law and Conscience: The Jewish View," *Judaism* 18:17–29; Jacob Lauterbach, "The Ethics of the Halakhah," in his *Rabbinic Essays* (Cincinnati, 1951); Aharon Lichtenstein, "Does Jewish Tradition Recognize an Ethic Independent of Halakha?" in ed. Marvin Fox, *Modern Jewish Ethics* (Columbus, 1975); Jacob J. Ross, "Morality and the Law," *Tradition* 10:5–16; Seymour Siegel, "Ethics and the Halakhah," *Conservative Judaism* 25:33–40; Moshe Silberg, "Law and Morals in Jewish Jurisprudence," *Harvard Law Review* 75:306–31; Shubert Spero, *Morality, Halakha and the Jewish Tradition* (New York, 1975), esp. chap. 6, "Morality and Halakhah."

2. See, for example, Eliezer Bashan, *"Lifnim mishurat hadin besifrut hahalakha"* [Hebrew], *Deot* 39:236–43; Saul Berman, *"Lifnim Mishurat Hadin,"* *Journal of Jewish Studies* 26:86–104, 28:181–93; Shear-Yeshuv Cohen, *"Lifnim mishurat hadin"* [Hebrew], *Adam-Noah Baron Memorial Volume* (Jerusalem, 1970), pp. 165–88; Tzvee Yehuda Meltzer, *"Megadray lifnim mishurat hadin"* [Hebrew] *Hadarom* 12:33–36. I have analyzed the controversy surrounding this term in my "Law, Virtue and Supererogation in the Halakha: The Problem of 'Lifnim mishurat hadin' Reconsidered," *Journal of Jewish Studies* 40: 61–88.

3. For other examples, see Siegel, op. cit., pp. 35–36, who writes, "From these and many other examples it is clear that the sages modified the law when they saw that following another norm would result in unfavorable results. Ethical considerations and public policy were sufficient to change the decision."

4. Dorff, op. cit., p. 458.

5. Gordis, op. cit., p. 73. A similar interpretation of these sources can be found in Guttmann, op. cit.

6. Weiss Halivni, op. cit., pp. 165, 168.

7. For a more extensive treatment of the traditional view that Jewish law is divine and its implications for Jewish jurisprudence, see Haim Cohn, "Prolegomena to the Theory and History of Jewish Law," in ed. Ralph A. Newman, *Essays in Jurisprudence in Honor of Roscoe Pound* (Westport, CT, 1973), pp. 44–81.

8. The same view has been defended by Konvitz, op. cit., p. 46, whose judgment about the biblical view of law and ethics could apply to the whole of Jewish tradition: "In the Hebrew Scriptures, the distinction between law and morals does not exist; or at least, it is not articulated. Neither is there a difference between religion and morals, nor any separation between religion and law. There is a single order of values which make a total claim on the people of Israel. By covenant, they became God's people. Their rights are all subordinate to God's rights; their duties are all subordinate to their duties to him; and these duties are all commanded by God, who made the law and whose will and nature fixed what is good and what is evil."

9. Lichtenstein, op. cit., pp. 62–88.

10. Spero, op. cit., pp. 166–200.

11. For a complete history of the treatment of this term by legalists over the centuries, see Menachem Elon, *Ha-mishpat ha-ivri* (Jerusalem, 1978), pp. 176–80.

12. An example of such harmonizing of diverse texts and viewpoints can be found in Louis Jacobs, *A Tree of Life: Diversity, Flexibility and Creativity in Jewish Law* (Oxford, 1984), pp. 182–92.

13. See D. Don Welch, ed., *Law and Morality* (Philadelphia, 1987), pp. 1–2.

14. See David Little and Sumner B. Twiss, *Comparative Religious Ethics* (San Francisco, 1978) pp. 28–31, 80–82. For a more extensive discussion of the interrelationship of law and morality, see H. L. A. Hart, *The Concept of Law* (Oxford, 1961), pp. 151–207.

15. E. Adamson Hoebel makes this point when he notes that a social norm is legal if infraction is met by physical force of a recognized authority; *The Law of Primitive Man* (Cambridge, 1954), p. 28. For a more recent discussion of the intimate connection between law and violence, see Robert Cover, "Violence and the World," *Yale Law Journal* 95 (1986):1601–29.

16. Roscoe Pound, for example, notes that the specific purpose of law is to preserve social order and maintain general security; *An Introduction to the Philosophy of Law* (New Haven, 1922). In his famous essay "On Liberty," J. S. Mill similarly defended the view that the law should not regulate the private lives of citizens, except insofar as it prevents people from harming one another.

17. This point is nicely developed by Elliot Dorff, "The Covenant: The Transcendent Thrust in Jewish Law," *The Jewish Law Annual* 7:78–79. This article provides an extremely thoughtful and clear exposition of the concept of covenant and its implications for Jewish law. [It is reprinted in this volume.]

18. See David S. Shapiro, "The Doctrine of the Image of God and *Imitatio Dei*," and Martin Buber, "Imitatio Dei," both in ed. Menachem Marc Kellner, *Contemporary Jewish Ethics* (New York, 1978).

19. *Tanna d'bei Eliyahu,* as cited in C. G. Montefiore and H. Loewe, *A Rabbinic Anthology* (New York, 1974), pp. 468–69.

20. For a fuller discussion of the ways in which the religious nature of *halakha* shapes its character as a legal system, see Dorff, "Judaism as a Religious Legal System," *Hastings Law Journal* 29 (1978): 1331–60.

21. This view is reflected in the talmudic principle that "they do not impose an injunction upon the community unless the majority of the community are capable of enduring it"; Baba Batra 60b.

22. Siegel, op. cit., pp. 33–34.

23. This is true only with regard to an analysis, like the present one, which is descriptive rather than normative. Clearly, theologians and others who claim to speak on behalf of the tradition will need and want to articulate a position on this crucial question. In doing so, however, they would do well to acknowledge the existence historically of positions other than the one they themselves have adopted.

24. An earlier version of this paper was given at the University of Washington in May 1989. I am grateful for the comments I received on that occasion. In addition, I wish to acknowledge the specific suggestions for revisions that I received from Howard Eilberg-Schwartz, Martin Jaffee, Barry Kogan, Paul Lauritzen, Robert Levy, Mark Verman, and Howard Vogel.

C. Reconceptualizing Jewish Ethics in Modern Times

6

Modernizing American Jewish Ethics: The Liberal Dilemma

S. DANIEL BRESLAUER

Changing ethical and moral theories often reflect important changes in religious self-perceptions. Moral arguments have more than intellectual interest since they "reflect a feeling on the part of important groups of a population that something is right and therefore will work, or something is wrong and therefore will not work."[1] When a religious ideology holds up as a model of what is right and will work a system of living which pragmatic experience says will not work and is therefore wrong, a crisis in belief, or a state of cognitive dissonance, is created. The modern consciousness experiences the world in radically different ways from traditional consciousness; the radically altered sense of what will and will not work has challenged the claim of traditional religion and religious values. Modern ethics has become problematic and this situation may well have "something to do with the ripening general affluence of Western industrialized society, with the pace of social change, with the erosion of traditional authoritarian religion."[2] The last mentioned element in this list should not be taken lightly. Religious authority and religious values have often been so closely linked as to be identified with each other. One of the challenges facing modern religion is that of defending its values without recourse to the argument from authority. The modern world has challenged religious ethics by offering a nonauthoritarian ethics as an alternative to religious ethics. Religion is challenged to offer a more flexible and humanistic ethical system if it is to meet the demands of contemporary society.[3]

Jewish ethics, like those of other religious systems in the modern world, faces the difficult task of reconceiving its message and reshaping its self-image. The resources for this task can be found in the Jewish tradition itself which was never univocal or unambivalent. Even scholars are divided: some suggest that classical

Jewish ethics is merely a by-product of Jewish law; others find an independent Jewish ethic which pervades the legal and nonlegal tradition alike; still others identify a responsive, personalistic ethic which manifests itself in the legal and nonlegal tradition but which uses traditional Jewish forms merely as vehicles for a basically individualistic ethic of personal choice.[4] The challenge of modernity has increased the problematic diversity of Jewish ethics. Philip Sigal notes that the dilemma facing Jewish ethics lies in the inappropriateness of traditional forms of Judaism in the modern age coupled with the indispensability of those forms for Jewish survival. Writing of the Jewish legal tradition, the *halakhah,* he comments that "Judaism cannot survive in a free Western environment with its present halakhah and . . . without a discipline of halakhah it cannot survive at all."[5]

The Conservative Jewish thinker Robert Gordis finds the modern world and its atmosphere clearly contradictory to Jewish values. The modern world makes Jewish ethics problematic because it cultivates a life in diametric opposition to the life envisioned by Jewish ideals. The emphasis on personal gratification, the alluring variety of moral options competing for the individual's attention, and a radical uncertainty about present and future existence have, in his view, "undermined the authority of religious teaching, particularly in the area of personal morality."[6]

Modernity as a challenge to tradition or as a set of competing values is only part of the problem. Were the threat of modernism to be limited to these specific issues Judaism could meet that threat with traditional techniques. In the past Judaism coped with diversity, innovation, and changing social mores by interpreting traditional texts; it remained "true to itself while absorbing, or at least fruitfully confronting, various aspects of non-Jewish thought."[7] The most acute problem created by modernity is a change in consciousness. The world as perceived by the modern Jew is radically different from the one assumed by traditional Jewish ethics. The classical trilogy of Judaism—God, Torah, and Israel—are problematic entities in the modern world. God's existence no longer justifies blind obedience to traditional law; Torah as a God-given set of commands is no longer accepted as self-evidently beneficial to human beings; Israel as a political and spiritual community has been obscured by the twin realities of the Nazi Holocaust and the State of Israel. With these three elements in Judaism in doubt the foundations of Jewish ethics have been brought into question.

God and a Modern Jewish Ethics

The task of the modern Jewish ethicist, therefore, is a unique one. The thinker must confront more than changing values—the problem is a transformed world. Menachem Kellner is surely correct to note that the contemporary Jewish ethicist has the unusual task of justifying the very undertaking of constructing a Jewish ethics. The usefulness and viability of the ethicist's profession has been questioned.[8] The Jewish thinker must legitimate the search for a parochial Jewish ethics in an age when the presuppositions of that ethics are no longer self-evident.

Perhaps the primary issue not only for Jewish ethics but for any religious ethics concerns the nature of God. What role does the divine play in a religious ethical system? Can modern humanism accept the divine as an active element in any relevant human ethics? Classical Judaism conceives God as the creator of the world and lawgiver whose laws provide creatures with a clear guide to their actions. Not only Jews but all human beings have been given laws by God; these laws are self-evidently right and good since the author of nature knows best how creation can function. The ethical precepts of Judaism are sanctioned by their source of origin—nature's God. Without that sanction they would lose much of their power. As Jacob Agus expresses it, "Ethical values are obligatory for us because they are willed by a Supreme Will. They could not appear to us as objective, if they did not exist apart from human minds."[9]

One role the divine plays is that of supplying the sanction and authority for a religious ethics. That ethics is claimed to be most natural and beneficial because of its grounding in the divine will. This approach is clearly authoritarian. God's power and knowledge imposes upon human beings a system of ethics which is for their own good. Humanity receives an ethic by divine fiat and follows it because of God's supreme power. The basic ethical injunction is obedience to an external code, a code which finds its justification and legitimation by an appeal to authority.

The authoritarian basis for Jewish ethics has been undermined in contemporary life. Modern philosophy from Kant onward has attacked the legitimacy of a heteronomous—or if you will a theonomous—ethic. Some philosophers claim that only an autonomous act, an act performed by a free agent choosing to follow a self-legislated morality, has true moral worth. Jewish thinkers have responded to this challenge and sought by various means to undermine the force of its criticism. From the point of view of philosophy the tension between authoritarian ethics and the moral worth of the individual agent has produced a creative discussion among Jewish thinkers.[10]

Another aspect of the modern restlessness with authoritarian ethics is less philosophical than psychological. The modern Jew rejects a heteronomous ethic because of personal, not philosophical, reasons. The modern Jew seeks maturity and independence. While remaining interested in the Jewish past and willing to experiment with Jewish ethics, this modern Jew will refuse to be dominated by authoritarian tradition. Maturity for such a Jew includes being flexible, open to new possibilities, able to see the various aspects of each situation. This Jew "seeks a religious moral imperative, but wants to remain open to the demands of each new situation," declares one Reform Jewish analyst.[11] Not only the Reform Jew but all modern American Jews recognize the force of this argument. Moral and personal growth is stunted if the individual gives up freedom of response for the sake of obedience to external commands. Maturity in our culture demands moral as well as legal independence. To become a self means to develop a value system independently of, even if informed by, traditional teachings and moral codes.

The moral problem involved is more Freudian than Kantian: how do I solve my Oedipal ambivalence toward the Jewish ethical system without lapsing into a passive acceptance of it (an eternal childhood) on the one hand, or rejecting it completely on the other, becoming a free, but rootless adult (symbolically burying my paternal tradition)? Richard Rubenstein uses this Freudian formulation when he characterizes his own personal dilemma as being forced "to choose between trusting my own insights and experience and what had been handed down to me. . . . The psychological posture of the believer before his God within the Law is always that of sonship."[12] Choosing against the tradition is no longer an unambiguously evil act; it is also an affirmation of maturity. From a Freudian standpoint it is seen as the necessary murder of the father by which the child gains salvation and independence. Jewish ethics is problematic because it represents an arrested childhood.

Eugene Borowitz, perhaps the leading exponent of Reform Judaism's "covenant" theology, is less explicitly Freudian but equally perceptive in analyzing the problem of modernity. He is caught between a recognition that "Jewish faith increasingly cannot be the passive continuation of a social heritage" and a realistic appraisal of the modern situation in which "the high value attached to autonomy is no longer self-explanatory."[13] Borowitz expresses the Jewish ethicist's task—to affirm both autonomy and heteronomy, independence and traditionalism. An unambiguous affirmation of independence is as impossible as an unambiguous affirmation of authority. Returning to the Freudian image we might say that the child becomes an adult both by rebelling against the parent and by incorporating elements of that parent into the emerging mature self.

Borowitz's "covenant theology" suggests that this is possible by maintaining a dynamic tension between independence and tradition; one swings between the past and the present allowing each a voice in decision making. The God of this theology provides guidance but not authority. Borowitz presents an attractive theology but its tension with the tradition requires more investigation. Why should God's will be for inner conflict? Why should God place individuals in such a tense situation? Often Conservative Jewish thinkers rather than Reform theologians are the best analysts of this situation since their commitment to the traditional elements in Jewish theology makes their sense of tension even more acute than that of thinkers like Borowitz. His merit, however, is that of clarity—his analysis makes it plain that the Jewish ethicist must wrestle with a new image of God—a God who rejoices in disobedience as well as obedience, whose will is for tension rather than stasis.

Classical Jewish Anthropology and Its Problems

Theology strictly understood is not the sole stumbling block in the path of a credible Jewish ethics. The demand raised against authoritarian religion reflects a certain view of humanity. Human beings are presupposed as able to make use of freedom. Classical Judaism agrees with that view; human beings have the potential to become autonomous ethical beings. While the theologian Leo Baeck wrote from a modern liberal perspective when he called Judaism a religion of "heroic optimism," his conclusions are consistent with classical Jewish thought. Even traditionalists can agree when he comments that "every belief implies a responsibility; this is a distinctly Jewish idea . . . God placed the good in the world as a moral demand which man is able to fulfill."[14] Torah as traditionally understood is a set of commandments, mitzvoth which are known to be capable of fulfillment just because they were commanded. All human beings are by nature law-abiders since God has addressed laws to them; the laws given to Noah apply to all humanity—those given to Moses only to Jews. Classical Jewish ethics is constructed on the foundation of a religious anthropology: human beings possess the capability of moral decision making since God has directed moral demands toward them. The content of Torah is good for humanity not merely because it comes from the God of nature but because it is addressed to human beings and takes note of their basic nature—that of being law-observers.

The major thrust of this view is that human beings live in and exemplify a moral universe. The story of Sodom and Gomorrah illustrates this belief. The biblical tale is laconic—the cities are identified as "evil," one example of their sexual perversity and violent nature is given, and God destroys them. Jewish commentators elaborated upon the story. A variety of sins were attributed to the Sodomites. They are shown to have been cruel, uncharitable, greedy, and materialistic. A characteristic view stated in *The Fathers according to Rabbi Nathan,* chapter 12, suggests that Sodom was destroyed because its inhabitants hated one another. Such groundless hatred, the comment implies, is self-destructive and leads to disaster.

The story and its commentaries suggest the two major implications of the Jewish anthropology upon which exaltation of the Torah depends. The first is that human beings are culpable for their actions—they can do good if they will good. The second is that disaster is the natural consequence of evil. To choose the unethical is to court destruction; to choose the ethical is to gain benefit. Both these assumptions are challenged by contemporary experience. We live in a world of chaos, a world at the brink of disaster, and are impotent to save ourselves. American Jews see America heading toward disaster, lost in a confusion of events seemingly out of control. At the same time they are reluctant to point the finger of blame at any one person or group of people. Psychology and sociology have revealed how we are victimized by our circumstances. Moral expectations are too weak to counteract the reality of contextual pressures moving the world inexorably toward disaster.

The American Jew lives in a post-Auschwitz world in which the unthinkable is credible. Political destructiveness is a live possibility—even with a well-meaning citizenry. Auschwitz and Hiroshima demonstrate the impotence of moral theory over political reality. Despite good intentions we face "possible nothingness" in the future.[15] The Nazi Holocaust is a reminder of how painfully powerless moral sanctions are in the face of the impersonal forces of social and political life. While most Jews agree that we live "on the knife-edge of history," they also feel unable to act either to prevent disaster or to change it.[16]

Some thinkers like Eugene Borowitz find in this reassessment of human potential a hopeful sign. Jews have become disillusioned with American promises; they have learned to distrust liberal thinking; they have returned to traditional ideals out of their rejection of Americanism.[17] Yet the psychological dimension of this new sense of impotence is as important as its social manifestation. The Jew may espouse a new social ethic and still despair of controlling personal actions. The psychological paradigm of human behavior has undermined belief in personal ethics no less than in public ethics. Borowitz admits this and notes that we must rethink our view of human beings.[18] Hans Jonas, however, has caught the actual dilemma facing the modern ethicist: "The paradox of the modern condition is that this reduction of man's stature, the utter humbling of his metaphysical pride, goes hand in hand with his promotion to quasi-God-like privilege and power."[19] On the one hand we must admit that human beings do not control their own lives. We are conditioned by the world in which we live. Richard Rubenstein is right to insist that human actions are "the resultant of vast non-personal forces."[20] On the other hand human destructiveness has never been more potent. Human beings destroy one another in war; they destroy the very ecological basis which makes living possible. Human beings have the awesome power to "destroy all life on the planet" and to misuse the environment so that "the conditions for human life may disappear within forty, thirty, or even twenty years"; human beings possess the demonic potential of creating "vast death-cultures as instruments of national policy."[21]

A simple substitution of traditional Jewish values for an outmoded and bankrupt American liberalism will not solve the problem. Jewish ethics assumes human beings to be capable of responsible choosing. The ideal person is the responsible agent. If a slave is ordered to set fire to someone's barn he is culpable since all human beings are assumed to be moral agents. Yet the modern individual finds such an assumption problematic. We are impotent actors—impotent because we are caught up in forces beyond our control, actors because of our powerful effect—often destructive—on others.

The response to this new situation requires realistic acceptance of the findings of sociology and psychology. We cannot just revert to an older view of human responsibility. Yet this realism must be tempered with an acceptance of blame for our destructiveness. That we too are victims does not excuse our also being victimizers. A new Jewish ethics must recognize both human vulnerability and human culpability. The new ethics appropriate to the modern situation will reflect the ambiguity of human nature and be responsive to the person as victim while demanding accountability for acts of destruction. Torah must be understood as addressing both aspects of human nature. The mitzvoth must be set in the context of human impotency and human power if they are to be taken seriously.

The State of Israel as an Ethical Dilemma

The experience of Auschwitz, Hiroshima, and Viet Nam means that more than just human nature is problematic. Richard Rubenstein has been exemplary in pointing out that the Holocaust is the final culmination of Western culture; it represents the political ideal of modern life. Faith in human relationships in general and political relations in particular has been undermined by these experiences of political domination and power. Auschwitz has taught us, he comments, "that membership in a political community is no longer a guarantee of the most elemental human rights."[22]

For Jewish ethics this issue is crucial because of the third element in classical Judaism: Israel. Even before the State of Israel an important component in Jewish thinking was an emphasis upon group loyalty—all Jews are responsible for each other. Jewish ethics is based upon a covenantal understanding of group identity. God entered into a covenant with Israel because of certain divine needs—among them the need for an exemplary political unit which Israel was to provide. David Bleich, an Orthodox Jewish spokesman, maintains that "to live in Israel is clearly a religious ideal" and that "residence in Israel constitutes fulfillment of a *mizvah* [sic] in our own day."[23] He goes on to argue that while "putting one's life in danger" is a prohibition in Jewish law it is more dangerous for the Jew to live in the Diaspora and face the threat of assimilation than to stay in Israel and face the threat of Muslim tanks. The Jewish ethicist must confront the political and nationalistic elements within Jewish tradition. The Jew is called upon to support the Jewish group, even the Jewish nation. In the face of Auschwitz and Viet Nam can such support of any nation be ethically justified?

The Christian thinker John Roth has reflected on the lessons of the Holocaust and suggested an answer to this dilemma. He insists that "after Auschwitz the only way in which it can make good sense to say that a group or an individual is 'chosen' is if that conviction leads men to empty themselves in service that meets human need."[24] Such a criterion for judging any group or nationalist loyalty seems useful, but can it be applied to modern Jewish nationalism? Hannah Arendt implies that Israeli nationalism is intrinsically at odds with humanism. She claims that "Jewish interests will clash with those of all other Mediterranean peoples" and lead to inevitable social, political, and human conflict.[25] She suggests that the problem lies not in group pride but in nationalism—that is, in the political dimension of Jewish group loyalty. Were "nationalism nothing worse than a people's pride in its outstanding or unique achievement," she comments, then all Zionism should desire is a spiritual center with schools and model economic conclaves like the kibbutzim. Instead Zionism mobilized armies, sought political and territorial power, and thereby inevitably instigated human suffering.[26] The confusion of cultural and political goals makes the classical stand of Jewish ethics on Israel as a spiritual and territorial homeland particularly problematic.

The modern Jewish ethicist must insist that no position toward Zionism can be unambiguous. John Roth's view of chosenness is applicable to Israel no less than to any other nation. The Jew must do more than explain apologetically that Jews were chosen for tasks not privileges, that other national groups were invited to accept God's commands but refused them, or that chosenness is merely another term for uniqueness. A modern Jewish ethics needs to find a way of affirming the viability of the State of Israel without affirming unconditionally its right to national aggrandizement. Jewish nationalism needs to be placed in the context of human existence as a whole; its liabilities and advantages to that total context need to be weighed objectively. The situation requires that the Jewish ethicist approach the question without an a priori position toward Jewish nationalism; only a flexible approach and an ambivalent attitude toward the State of Israel is adequate in a world which has seen the destructive power of nation-states.

The Liberal Dilemma in Modernizing Jewish Ethics

Modernizing Jewish ethics is problematic because the Jewish liberal has found the basic assumptions of a modern liberal ethics undermined by Jewish experience. The self-consciously Jewish thinkers we have cited here—Eugene Borowitz, Richard Rubenstein, Robert Gordis, and Jacob Agus—have undergone important changes in their thinking. They all began with optimistic views of American and Jewish options in the modern world. They all confronted modernity certain that the Jewish tradition could offer insights into the modern predicament and that the modern emphasis upon autonomy and progress would help evolve a new and more progressive Judaism.

In every case disillusionment replaced optimism. For some like Richard Rubenstein the Nazi Holocaust stimulated a rethinking of human potential, of social organization, and of the status of the Jew. For others like Eugene Borowitz and Robert Gordis the decay of modern morality, the failure of the American dream, and the chaos of modern political life led to a retreat from liberal stances. Orthodox

Jewish leaders, of whom Bleich is a leading representative, have undergone a similar retreat. The ecumenical embracing of colleagues from the Reform and Conservative movements popular in the 1940s and even in the 1950s has been supplanted by a more strident exclusivism and a narrowed concern with parochial issues. Whether the issue is a ritualistic one—should Jews drive to synagogue on the Sabbath—or a political one—what is the relationship of the American Jew to the State of Israel—or one of personal morality—what is the status of the homosexual in Judaism—Orthodox, Reform, and Conservative Jews who once took liberal stands are now becoming more and more wary of traditional liberal answers.

American liberalism upon which Jewish thinkers of an earlier age optimistically constructed their ethics has been undermined by the empirical experiences of the modern Jew. The political vulnerability of the Jew in Germany—not only a vulnerability to looting, murder, and pogroms but more dramatically a vulnerability to being declassed, declared excess population—has undermined confidence in any political system. Politics has been shown to be arbitrary. Human beings construct their politics in terms of pragmatic, expediential goals; the absolute ideals which were believed to govern American politics have been demonstrably flouted. Viet Nam has warned the Jew that American politics is as pragmatically hypocritical as was Germany's under Hitler. Without trust in the political system American Jewish thinkers have retreated into a self-interested parochialism.

The explosion of options for personal self-expression in the 1960s and 1970s made liberals pause to reevaluate an ethics of self-realization. The chaotic variety of possible paths to selfhood meant that the liberal could no longer trust human nature to develop those values affirmed by tradition. The liberal had no ally in the world of experience to confirm a trust in the Jewish goals and aims inherited from past tradition. The balance between receiving a heritage from the past and maturely taking an independent stance became a tension and competition. In the face of this competition liberals who at one time argued from the premise that self-realization and adherence to Jewish tradition were complementary reversed their views.

Not only maturity but ethical self-control seemed at one time part of both Judaism and modernity. Liberals could believe that following Jewish law made one a better American, provided training in a universal ethics. As Eugene Borowitz suggests, the modern experience disconfirmed that belief. Being a Jew often implied opposing the ethics and morality of American life. Human actions are so destructive and yet so uncontrolled that they either contradict Jewish values or are contradicted by them. The liberal trust in modern consciousness has been betrayed, and the Jewish thinker has rejected that consciousness out of loyalty to the ethics of tradition.

The dilemma facing the modern Jewish ethicist can be stated in terms of both its consequences and its causes. The threefold consequences of the dilemma are first an ambivalence toward God's role in legitimizing a religious ethics, secondly a rejection of the identification of Jewish ethics and American ideals, and finally an affirmation of Jewish particularism and Zionism. The causes are an affirmation of an authoritarian ethics in the face of the modern chaos of values, a rejection of American ideals in favor of traditional Jewish commandments (*mitzvoth*) despite the recognition of the problematic nature of human freedom, and a sense of intense political vulnerability based upon the expediential and arbitrary uses to which political power is put.

Toward Resolving the Liberal Dilemma

The basis of the liberal dilemma lies in the challenge of empirical experience. The basic issue is the one cited in the beginning of this paper: what can be considered right and *therefore workable*. The Jewish liberal had attempted to create a synthetic ethics which took as its criteria for workability the assumptions of classical Judaism—God is the lawgiver who provides the means by which human beings learn their true tasks, Torah is the blueprint of human activity and by commanding an action it enables its fulfillment, Israel is a holy nation with a divine mission in the world of nations—and as its raw material the experiences of modernity. Those experiences, however, remained unmalleable and recalcitrant. Their challenge to classical Judaism refused to give way before the liberal's attempted synthesis. Is there a way in which that synthesis might still be made? Is there a potential resolution to the liberal's dilemma?

The only resolution seems to be one that is unapologetically ambivalent. Both tradition and independence are to be affirmed; both vulnerability and culpability are appropriate ways of analyzing human behavior; both nationalism and spiritual identity are legitimate responses for the modern Jew. The basis for such a duality of affirmations is the ambiguity of human nature itself. The human being is not one unified essence but a field of conflicting urges and energies. A liberal approach to Jewish ethics would confront modernity by acknowledging the complexity of all human activities.

Given that complexity we can ask the value of religious ethics, that is to say an ethics which owes its structure and content to a particular cultural tradition with a historic legacy of ideals and values. More specifically we can raise the question of why the Jew should seek a peculiarly Jewish ethics. Part of the ethical task is to sort out, organize, categorize, and thereby understand the various conflicting elements within any human situation. Decision making involves recognizing the problematic ambiguities of any particular choice. The construction and presentation of a traditional ethic provides such an ordering and categorizing of at least part of the elements within a situation. A religious ethics has a clarifying function—it provides one perspective on our choices.

The liberal who seeks to unite modernity and classical Judaism, who emphasizes human choice even while advocating loyalty to traditional mores, who does not allow human vulnerability to negate human culpability, and who advocates a realistic nationalism tempered by spiritual ideals may accept religious ethics as one element in human decision making. The role of such an ethics, however, would not be determinative. Religious ethics would retain its claim to divine sanction—Jewish ethics does represent a revealed perspective on human action. It would, however, share this claim with our empirical experiences of the world. Neither a revealed tradition nor our personal experience of life can encompass the infinity of the divine. Divinity is as ambiguous as human life. A modern Jewish ethics would enable both a liberal affirmation of modernity and tradition and a realistic response to living experience. A religious ethics provides the ideals and values which express one valid perspective; our experience provides an equally valid alternative.

Since neither experience alone nor religious tradition alone has determinative power, the dilemma of authority can be resolved. The relationship between mature acceptance of independence and an equally mature acceptance of tradition is not one of incompatibility. Rather, maturity consists of keeping the tension between the two alive and living in that tension. The liberal need not seek a synthetic truth made up of both; the mature person lives in the perpetual dynamism of the tension between tradition and independence.

This dynamic relationship is close to what Eugene Borowitz means by "covenant theology." He claims that his daily experiences generate predicaments which can be solved neither by traditional Judaism alone nor by independent action. Borowitz, however, is reluctant to make this tension an ethical as well as a religious or ritualistic one. He insists on the primacy of Jewish ethics. A liberal approach would emphasize that in our expectations of human beings we make use of a similar model. The vulnerability of human beings, their victimization by other people and circumstances must be kept in balance with their culpability, their responsibility for the destruction which they bring on others. The liberal would use a religious ethics to establish the upper limits of expectations. The Jewish code of living becomes a model of ideal standards. But this code is not to be the definitive standard of human behavior. A realistic understanding of human helplessness will temper the demands made by this code. Neither the existence of Torah nor the reality of victimization should be allowed veto power over the other. The ethicist will approach each ethical choice aware that neither source provides a clear answer to the problems human beings face.

Finally nationalism must be seen as both a potential danger and as a present and future necessity. The theology of Zion which Judaism espouses can be taken as an ideal projection for all nationalisms. That theology demands an exalted idealism and a spiritualized national vision. That vision, however, must be tempered by an awareness of the grim realities of national life. The ethicist must accept the theology of Zion as a sincere belief and vital motivation of Jewish nationalism. At the same time the vision does not represent the reality and no ethicist should confuse the two. Any particular decision about the State of Israel—even its right to exist in the modern political world—must be based on a balance between ideal theories of Zion and the cruel realities of a modern nation-state. By keeping the ideal and the reality in tension and by not allowing one an authoritative power over the other a Jewish thinker can retain a liberal's trust in ideals while recognizing the failure of those ideals to transform the realities facing us at present.

The dilemmas facing the Jewish thinker have been described here in their broad outline. The general areas of authoritarian ethics, of human capabilities to perform the commandments, and the problematics of Zionism have been sketched as particularly crucial for the modern Jewish ethicist, particularly one whose commitment is also to a liberal tradition. Within those areas specific issues are of profound importance. The status of women, the observance of the holidays, the question of conversion are some issues within the sphere of Jewish ethics and are problematic because of tradition's authoritarian stance. Support of a military establishment, abortion, sexual mores, and medical ethics become acute questions in Judaism when the realities of human potential are examined. The responsibility of Jews outside of Israel for Israel's policies toward Arabs, Russian Jews, and other minorities, the social and economic problems inside Israel, and the justification for Israel's war with the Arabs, must be faced by those who take both the theology of Zion and the contemporary situation seriously. A fully developed Jewish ethics would address these questions. Here the intent was to show why a modern Jewish ethics is problematic, particularly for the Jewish liberal, and to point out a general resolution to that problem. On the basis of this suggested resolution an analysis of the specific issues may be begun.

Notes

1. Franz Schurmann, "Systems, Contradictions, and Revolution in America," in Roderick Aya and Norma Miller, editors, *The New American Revolution* (New York: Macmillan, 1971), 42.

2. M. Brewster Smith, *Social Psychology and Human Values* (Chicago: Aldine Publishing Company, 1969), pp. 325–26.

3. Idem., *Humanizing Social Psychology* (San Francisco: Jossey-Bass Publishing Company, 1974), p. 92.

4. See Marvin Fox, editor, *Modern Jewish Ethics: Theory and Practice* (Athens, Ohio: Ohio State University Press, 1975), particularly part 2, pp. 29–101.

5. Philip Sigal, *New Dimensions in Judaism: A Creative Analysis of Rabbinic Concepts* (New York: Exposition Press, 1972), p. 9.

6. Robert Gordis, *Love and Sex: A Modern Jewish Perspective* (New York: Farrar, Straus and Giroux, 1978), p. 32.

7. Marvin Fox, "Judaism, Secularism, and Textual Interpretation," in Fox, *Modern Jewish Ethics,* pp. 3–26.

8. See Menachem Marc Kellner, *Contemporary Jewish Ethics* (New York: Sanhedrin Press, 1978), p. 5.

9. Jacob Agus, *Modern Philosophies of Judaism: A Study of Recent Jewish Philosophers of Religion* (New York: Behrman House, 1941), p. 343.

10. See Fox, *Modern Jewish Ethics,* pp. 166–73, and Emil L. Fackenheim, *Encounters between Judaism and Modern Philosophy: A Preface to Future Jewish Thought* (New York: Basic Books, 1973), pp. 3–77.

11. Michael Meyer, "Problematics of Jewish Ethics," in Daniel Jeremy Silver, editor, *Judaism and Ethics* (New York: KTAV, 1970), p. 113.

12. Richard L. Rubenstein, *My Brother Paul* (New York: Harper and Row, 1972), pp. 6, 16.

13. Eugene B. Borowitz, *A New Jewish Theology in the Making* (Philadelphia: Westminster Press, 1968), p. 213.

14. Leo Baeck, *The Essence of Judaism* (New York: Schocken, 1948), p. 88.

15. Arthur Waskow, *Godwrestling* (New York: Schocken, 1978), p. 164.

16. Ibid., pp. 136–37.

17. Eugene B. Borowitz, *The Masks Jews Wear: The Self-Deception of American Jewry* (New York: Simon and Schuster, 1973). pp. 15, 75.

18. Idem., *Reform Judaism Today: How We Live, Book III* (New York: Behrman House, 1978), p. 160; the entire discussion, "Rethinking Our Estimate of Human Beings," pp. 151–67, is of interest for this point.

19. Hans Jonas, "Contemporary Problems in Ethics from a Jewish Perspective," in Silver, *Judaism and Ethics,* p. 36.

20. Richard L. Rubenstein, *Morality and Eros* (New York: McGraw-Hill, 1970), p. 87.

21. Maurice Friedman, *The Hidden Human Image: A Heartening Answer to the Dehumanizing Threats to Our Age* (New York: Dell Publishing, 1974), p. 154.

22. See Richard L. Rubenstein, *The Cunning of History: The Holocaust and the American Future* (New York: Harper and Row, 1975), p. 87 and passim.

23. J. David Bleich, *Contemporary Halakhic Problems* (New York: KTAV, 1977), pp. 5, 6, 8–9.

24. John K. Roth, *A Consuming Fire: Encounters with Elie Wiesel and the Holocaust* (Atlanta: John Knox Press, 1979), p. 117.

25. Hannah Arendt, *The Jew as Pariah: Jewish Identity and Politics in the Modern Age,* edited and with an introduction by Ron H. Feldman (New York: Grove Press, 1978), p. 133.

26. Ibid., p. 214.

7

The Jewish Self

EUGENE B. BOROWITZ

Modern and postmodern non-Orthodox Jewish theologies diverge decisively in their views of the self's Jewishness. All the great modern systematizers considered it axiomatic that contemporary Jewish thought must be constructed on the basis of universal selfhood. To accommodate this concept, they willingly redefined Jewish responsibility in terms of the hierarchy of value it entailed: self first, Jewishness second. I rather see Jewish truth—the Covenant—as the primal, elemental ground of the Jew's existence. Without denying the spiritual validity of universal selfhood, I assert the need to rethink its meaning in Jewish terms. Jewish selfhood arises within the people of Israel and its covenant with God. Put in this unqualified form, the definition not only includes Orthodox as well as non-Orthodox Jews but could be used by thinkers of either group, lending it an inclusiveness that helps persuade me of the conceptual value of this approach.

I detect something of this personalism when some contemporary *poskim* (*halakhic* decisors) claim the right to issue directives to the community simply on the basis of *daas Torah*. In these cases they assert their authority in terms of their general "knowledge/sense" of Torah, though they cannot validate their stand on this specific issue by citing direct *halakhic* precedents. I interpret this as pointing to the legislative authority of their personal intuition of our Jewish duty, one growing out of their learning and piety but finally valid as the insight of a Torah personality. I have in mind something similar, a non-Orthodox self that is autonomous yet so fundamentally shaped by the Covenant that whatever issues from its depths will have authentic Jewish character. The secular conception of autonomy must be transformed in terms of its Covenantal context. We will best understand what this means by tracing the cumulative threefold progression of self (secular) to self-God (universal religion) and thence to self/Israel/God (Judaism). I will briefly state the foundation of the first two ideas and give the bulk of my attention to their culmination in the theory of the Jewish identity that mandates postmodern Jewish duty.

The Truth and the Limits of Secular Selfhood

The notion of the self-determining individual occasionally occurs in classic Jewish texts, but modern Western democracy so embellished the notion that it gained utterly new spiritual power. The resulting ideals of person and society it projected so enlarged the Jewish soul that they made the pains of emancipation well worth bearing. We contemporary Jews may have jettisoned the optimism that once sacralized modernization, but the very experience that has made us more realistic has reinforced our steadfast devotion to self-determination. Witnessing the moral failures of orthodoxies, institutions, and collectives has reconfirmed our trust in the self as the best critic of iniquity and our indispensable defense against social tyranny.

Emancipated Jewry imported the notion of the self into Judaism primarily under the rubric of ethics, which commended itself for uniquely integrating freedom, duty, Jewish change, and social responsibility. The irresistible interpretive appeal of an ethical framework may be estimated from the unanimity with which our thinkers made it central to their theories of Judaism. Mordecai Kaplan's naturalism provides even stronger testimony to the sovereign power of ethics than does Hermann Cohen's neo-Kantianism, which identified ethics with reason. Kaplan, who made folk culture the effective creator of human value and thus always open to revision, insisted on one exception to this rule: moral law. In Martin Buber's shift of thought to personalism, the interhuman experience becomes the paradigm not merely for duty but for the whole of the religious life. Abraham Heschel, despite making God's revelation, not human experience, the fulcrum of his theology, intimately identifies the prophetic experience of God's reality with the imperative to reach out to every human being. On no other theme—not God, nor the people of Israel, nor revelation, nor messianism, nor law, nor theological method—do these thinkers so completely agree.

This key concern of modernism remains vital today as postmodern non-Orthodox Jews continue to feel issues of interhuman obligation addressing them with an unparalleled imperative quality. Though they envision their Jewish duty as extending far beyond universal ethics, no other realm of Jewish obligation regularly outranks it.

Though the thinkers to whom I referred echoed the Enlightenment notion of the self, they significantly changed its meaning and that of its corollary terms by organically fixing them in a religious context. In various ways, they all declared that the autonomous self makes sense only in terms of each person's ineluctable bond with God, the source of our dignity and the criterion of its correct use. Our tradition spoke of this as the (Noahide) covenant, a term whose legal origin conveyed a sense of seriously contracted specific obligations. Opposing a heteronomic understanding of it, I reinterpret the term through the metaphor of personal relationship, which communicates duty without depriving either participant of selfhood and autonomy—an experience as characteristic of direct relationship with God as with persons through whom we know God indirectly.

Martin Buber, who taught us this self-God paradigm, also believed that single selves could join in common encounter, turning, for example, ethnic groups into nations whose formative experiences still exercised normative power over their descendants. He therefore believed that Zionism made certain inescapable national-spiritual demands of contemporary Jews. Yet he insisted that the independent self remained the judge of the legitimacy of group injunctions and he never clarified how one could integrate group authority with such rigorous individualism. This interpretation of his thought does not enable us to take the step from self-God to self-Israel-

God that would explain the postmodern intuition of the absoluteness attaching to Jewish identity.

Can the Noahide Self Take Jewish Particularity Seriously?

Because of Buber's continued liberal confidence in the single self (and despite the fact that he shifted its reference point from reason to relationship) I consider him more a transitional modern than a postmodern Jewish thinker. Rosenzweig sought to move Buber from this individualism and thus make possible a more authentic Jewish existence, but because Rosenzweig agreed that a postrationalist theory of Jewish duty needed to be grounded in the self, he faced the same difficulty. He finally integrated thought and intuition by dogmatically asserting that Jews must, in principle, accept the authority of the law, allowing practice to produce its personal confirmation. So to speak, he is the existentialist equivalent of what later emerged as the postmodern flight to Orthodoxy.

Rosenzweig's effort to add the law to the self-God relationship has a contemporary counterpart. Some thinkers suggest that if we derived our rulings on specific contemporary issues by classic *halakhic* methods utilized with non-Orthodox flexibility, we then would produce fully authentic *halakhah*. They variously argue that many factors might make such rulings authoritative to many despite the loss of the *halakhic* process's theological foundations: our continuing esteem of Jewish law; our respect for time-hallowed Jewish forms; our regard for Jewish scholars; our desire for non-Orthodox Jewish communal structure; and our willingness to accept an authentic Jewish discipline. Yet, to date, only a small minority of the non-Orthodox regularly subordinates its own good judgment to such rulings.

Autonomy lies at the heart of the decision about this suggestion. Why should thinking Jews consider giving up their self-determination to follow the rulings of decisors who have Jewish learning but otherwise no greater access to God's present will than the rest of us possess? The answer cannot be simply the cogency of their rulings, for these inevitably raise the question of the criteria they employ in reaching their decisions. Sometimes they are lenient, sometimes stringent, sometimes they insist on specific textual warrants, sometimes they substantially rely on interpretation. How do non-Orthodox decisors determine when a historical or ethical development requires us to change the law or resist changing it? For that matter, how can "history" require anything since it has no objective reality but depends entirely on the historian's theory of how we ought to structure events? (As applied to theology, this problem of the unknown criteria by which it is determined what traditional beliefs remain valid or must be discarded has been the chief criticism of the historical theologies of thinkers as diverse as Kaufmann Kohler and Louis Jacobs.) Judges have always manifested such methodological vagaries and have been enfranchised to do so by the authority vested in them. When God stood behind the operation of the *halakhah,* the self had no basis upon which to question given rulings. But without a non-Orthodox theology of *halakhic* process, what validates the old processes or simple learning in the face of conscientious Jewish doubt?

We cannot expect formal similarity to the past to empower even a responsive Jewish legal system without a convincing theory of authority to persuade us we ought to sacrifice our autonomy to it—and if we do not, it is merely wise counsel, not law. A modernized *halakhic* process could have considerable Jewish value, but we shall know what constitutes authentic "flexibility" only when we have theologically established its meta-*halakhah*. And only when we have been personally persuaded of the validity of its theory of Jewish decision making are we likely to make its rulings our law.

I think it unlikely that a non-Orthodox relegitimation of Jewish law would have either theoretical success or practical effect. I therefore turn first to the theological task and only then inquire what kind of Jewish discipline it engenders. I suggest we, whose Jewishness is primary to our existence, should reverse Buber's strategy. Instead of positing an axiomatic universal selfhood in whose terms we then seek to validate Jewishness, we seek to interpret our elemental Jewishness by the culturally compelling metaphor of selfhood, that is, by explicating the nature of a Jewish self.

Five Premises for Jewish Duty

Like all humankind (the *benei noah*), Jewish selves (the *benei yisrael*) have a grounding personal relationship with God; but where the *benei noah* relate to God as part of a universal covenant, the *benei yisrael* have a particular, ethnic Covenant with God. Being a Jew may then be described in this metaphor as having an individuality that is elementally structured by participation in the Jewish people's historical relationship with God. In the ideal Jewish self one can detect no depth, no matter how intensely one searches, where the old liberal rift between general self and particular Jew still occurs. Jewish selfhood arises as ethnic existentiality while remaining an individuality dignified by autonomy; in this case autonomy is properly exercised in terms of its ultimate situation in the Jewish people's corporate, historic relationship with God.

In contrast to contemporary privatistic notions of selfhood, the Jewish self, responding to God in Covenant, acknowledges its essential historicity and sociality. One did not begin the Covenant and one remains its conduit only as part of the ongoing people of Israel. Here, tradition and ethnicity round out the universal solidarity of humankind which this particularity grounds in its myth of the Noahide covenant. With heritage and folk essential to Jewishness, with the Jewish service of God directed to historic continuity lasting until messianic days, the Covenanted self knows that Jewish existence must be structured. Yet as long as we honor each Jew's selfhood with a contextually delimited measure of autonomy, this need for communal forms cannot lead us back to law as a required, corporately determined regimen. Instead, we must think in terms of a *self-discipline* that, because of the sociality of the Jewish self, becomes communally focused and shaped. The result is a dialectical autonomy, a life of freedom-exercised-in-Covenant. It differs so-from older non-Orthodox theories of folk discipline—Zionism or Kaplanian ethnnicity—or personal freedom—Cohenian ethical monotheism or Buberian relationship—that I wish to analyze in some detail its five major themes.

First, the Jewish self lives personally and primarily in involvement with the one God of the universe. Whereas the biblical-rabbinic Jew was almost entirely theocentric, the contemporary Jewish self claims a more active role in the relationship with God.

In the days of buoyant liberalism this self-assertion overreached to the point of diminishing God's active role, sometimes countenancing supplanting God with humanity writ large. Postmodernity begins with a more realistic view of our human capacities and a determination not to confuse the junior with the senior partner. Knowing Who calls and keeps us as allies endows each self with a value it could never give itself even by extraordinary achievement. To believe we bestow meaning on ourselves by our deeds inevitably destroys us, for no one can successfully keep filling up the relentless now of personhood with estimable accomplishment. When we live in covenantal closeness with God—asked only to be God's helpmeet, not God's equal in goodness—we acquire unique dignity and power and can hope to remain whole even when burdened by the world's injustice and our own heavy sins.

This consciousness of ongoing intimacy with God precedes, undergirds, and interfuses all the Jewish self's other relationships. It ties us to God's other partners for more than pragmatic or utilitarian reasons and gives us an ineradicable stake in humanity's welfare and destiny. It binds us with particular intensity to other Jews with whom we share a special dedication to God.

Yet the Covenant that affirms us also subjects us to judgment in terms of the quality learned through our personal involvement with God. What we do as persons, lovers, friends, citizens, humans, Jews, must live up to it or be found wanting. Wherever the Jewish self sees faithfulness to God imperiled, covenanthood requires it to be critical as well as supportive, perhaps even temporarily withdrawing from others in order to remain true to what once made them close. This applies with particular force to the people of the Covenant. Pledged to live most intensively with God, this people and its communities must always stand under special scrutiny even as they also deserve our special love.

Community, Tradition, and Messianic Hope

Second, a Jewish relationship with God inextricably binds selfhood and ethnicity, with its multiple ties of land, language, history, traditions, fate, and faith. By this folk rootedness covenantal Jewish identity negates the illusion that one can be loyal to humanity as a whole but not to any single people, and it rescues the messianic hope from being so abstract as to be inhuman. Ethnic particularity commits the Jewish self to the spirituality of sanctifying history through gritty social and political struggles. Internally as well, each Jew becomes implicated in this people's never-ending struggle to hallow grim social circumstances or the temptations of affluence and show itself another faithful Covenant generation.

Nowhere can Jews hope to better fulfill the multilayered responsibilities enjoined on them by the Covenant than in the land of Israel organized as a politically sovereign, self-determining nation, the State of Israel. Every Jewish self must face the covenantal challenge of the desirability of moving there to join the Jewish people in working out its uniquely full response to God's demand that we sanctify social existence. Jews who do not find themselves able to fulfill this behest must nonetheless live by a particularly intense tie to the land of Israel and measure their Diaspora fulfillment of the ethnic obligations of Jewish selfhood by the standard of the State of Israel's Covenant accomplishments.

Ethnicity also has a certain normative force. As the Jewish self ponders a decision, it must attend seriously to the attitudes and practices of other Jews in this matter. They share the same Covenant, serve the same God, and reflect the same folk experience and aspiration. Often, what Jews have been told to do and what they now value will commend itself as covenantal wisdom. When the Jewish self has some ambivalence about its accepted path, loyalty to the folk will often cause the Jewish self to sacrifice personal predilection for folk unity. That most easily takes place when a community standard makes possible common ethnic activity—for example, a folk, not a personal, Jewish calendar—or makes demands that hardly can be called onerous or defiling—for example, kiddush over wine or grape juice and not the whiskey or spring water one might prefer. For the Jewish self, then, Covenant means Covenant-with-all-other-Jews, past and present.

For all the inalienable ethnicity of the Jewish self, it surrenders nothing of its individual personhood. In a given matter, the Covenant people may be inattentive to its present duty to God or, in a given situation, an individual Jew of certain talents and limitations may find it covenantally more responsible to go an individual way. Now covenanted selfhood requires conscientious self-examination in the light of community standards to determine whether this dissent of the Jewish self is willfulness or an idiosyncratic sensitivity to God. I shall return to this theme later in this chapter.

Third, against the common self's concentration on immediacy, the Covenant renders the Jewish self radically historical. Our Jewish relationship with God did not begin with this generation, and its working out in Jewish lives has been going on for millennia. Social circumstances and Jewish self-perception have changed greatly in this time yet the Jews we encounter in our old books sound very much like us. Different social circumstances aside, the underlying relationship between God and the people of Israel has remained substantially the same. For one thing, the same religious moments decisively shape our Covenant sensibility—Exodus, Sinai, settlement, Temple, exile, return, destruction of the Second Temple, Diaspora, the rise of the rabbis, medieval triumph and trial, which we extend by emancipation, Holocaust, and Third Commonwealth. We too live by Jewish memory. For another thing, reading our classic texts inevitably points up the constancy of human nature with its swings between folly and saintliness. Jews then behaved very much as Jews do today. Hence, much of what they did as their covenant duty will likely still lay a living claim on us. For the Jewish self, then, Covenant means Covenant-with-prior-Jewish-generations.

Many modern Jewish thinkers deprecated the idea of such a spiritual continuity. They thought our vastly increased general knowledge made us more religiously advanced than our forebears and optimistically taught that each generation knew God's will better than the prior one, a notion they called progressive revelation. Postmodern thinkers, such as myself, reverse the hierarchy. On most critical religious issues, no one writing today can hope to command the respect the authors of the Bible rightly continue to elicit. Moreover, since their life of Covenant was comparatively fresh, strong, and steadfast, where ours is often uncertain, weak, and faltering, we should substantially rely on their delineation of proper covenantal existence. The biblical and rabbinic texts have every Jewish right to exert a higher criticism of the lives of each new generation of Jews, so classic Jewish learning must ground Jewish selfhood as firmly as does personal religious experience.

In one critical religious respect, however, we stand apart from prior generations:

our conviction that we must exercise considerable self-determination. If some re-spect for Jewish individuality had not always characterized Jewish spirituality, we would be astonished at the luxuriant display of change and innovation we find in Jewish religious expression over the centuries. Our radically transformed social and intellectual situation elicits a corollary reinterpretation of Covenant obligation. In particular, our sense of linkage with God prompts us to identify spiritual maturity with the responsible exercise of agency. Hence, we find it necessary to take initia-tive in untraditional fashion in order to be true to what our Jewish self discovers in Covenant. Here, too, our sacred books make their authority felt by challenging us to ask whether our deviance has grown out of covenantal faithfulness or trendy impulse.

Fourth, though the Jewish self lives the present out of the past, it necessarily orients itself to the future. All the generations of Jews who have ever been, including us, seek the culmination of the covenant in the days of the Messiah. The glories of the Jewish past and the rewards of the Jewish present cannot nearly vindicate Israel's millennial service of God as will that era of universal peace, justice, love, and knowledge of God. A Jewishness satisfied merely to meet the needs of the present but not radically to project covenantal existence into the far future betrays the hopes of the centuries of dedication that made our spirituality possible. The Jewish self, by contrast, will substantially gauge the covenantal worthiness of acts by their contribution to our continuing redemptive purpose. For the Jewish self, then, Covenant means Covenant-with-Jews-yet-to-be, especially the Messiah.

I can provide a personal analogy to the manner in which a vision of the far future limits the self in the immediate exercise of its freedom: the attainment of personal integrity. One can hope to accomplish that only over the years, for though the self constantly reconstitutes itself in the present, it also persists through time. Living detached from previous experience and with minimal concern for the future denies the chronological character of creatureliness and ignores our most creative individ-ual challenge, to shape an entire life into humane coherence. The responsible self will cultivate the forms, habits, and institutions indispensable to long-range fulfill-ment. And when, in our frailty or indecisiveness, our autonomy falters before life's demands, we can hope these structures will carry our fragile self through the dark times with integrity unimpaired. All this is true of every human being but, I suggest, more intensively so for the Jewish self, whose integrity involves messianic steadfast-ness to God as part of the Covenant between God and the Jewish people.

Nonetheless, our covenantal future-directedness may also compel us to break with an old, once valuable but now empty Jewish practice. For Jewish selfhood also requires us to assure the Jewish future by making our way to it through the pres-ently appropriate covenantal act. Even then, the awesome endurance of Jewish traditions will dialectically confront us with its question as to the staying power of the innovation we find so necessary.

The Compelling Selfhood of the Jewish Self

Fifth, yet despite the others with whom it is so intimately intertwined—God and the Jewish people, present, past, and future—it is as a single soul in its full individuality that the Jewish self exists in Covenant. I can illustrate my meaning best by using myself as an example. I must not hide from the fact that it is I, personally, who am making all these assertions. I believe God has objective reality—but I also do not know how anyone today can objectively make that assertion. I likewise believe that what I have been saying about Judaism is true regardless of my accepting it or not, that it would still be true and make rightful claims upon Jews even were I to come to deny all or any part of it. I proclaim the truth of the covenant between God and the Jewish people, but I know I can only speak from my own premises and perspective even as other people must do from theirs. None of us can escape from radical finitude to a conceptual realm of unconditional truth. The self, free and self-determining, must then be given its independent due even though, as a Jewish self, its autonomy will be exercised in covenantal context. At any given moment it is ultimately I who must determine what to make of God's demands and Israel's practice, tradition, and aspiration as I, personally, seek to live the life of Torah in covenantal faithfulness. For the Jewish self, then, Covenant means Covenant-with-one's self.

Before I turn to the issue of how Jewish selfhood could lead to a new sense of corporate Jewish duty, I want to say something about the gap between the ideal of the Jewish self and the realities of being an individual Jew. I have been describing more a spiritual goal than a present condition, my version of what Rosenzweig called our need to move from the periphery of Jewish living back to its center. By the standards of this ideal, fragmentariness and alienation characterize most Jewish lives today; our lives commonly reflect more the brokenness of humanhood in our civilization than any integrating Jewish vision. This diagnosis leads to a therapeutic goal: bringing Jews to the greater wholeness of Jewish selfhood, a reconstruction of Jewish life that begins with helping individual Jews find greater personal integration, one that ineluctably involves them in community as with God. This constitutes the obverse of Kaplan's emphasis on changing our pattern of Jewish community organization so as to foster a healthy Jewish life.

How might this ideal, so individualistically based, bring a critical mass of Jews to communal patterns of covenantal observance? It cannot be created by a contemporary version of heteronomous law as long as we continue to accept the personal and spiritual validity of self-determination. But if Jews could confront their Judaism as Jewish selves and not as autonomous persons-in-general, I contend that they would find Jewish law and lore the single best source of guidance as to how they ought to live. Rooted in Israel's corporate faithfulness to God, they would want their lives substantially structured by their people's understanding of how its past, present, and future should shape daily existence. But as autonomous Jewish selves, they would personally establish the validity of every *halakhic* and communal prescription by their own conscientious deliberation. We would then judge their Jewish authenticity less by the extent of their observance than by the genuineness of their efforts to ground their lives, especially their actions, in Israel's ongoing Covenant with God. The more fully they integrate their Jewish selves, the more fully will every act of theirs demonstrate their Jewishness.

With autonomy then an integral part of Jewishness, some subjectivity will inevitably enter our Jewish practice, leading to a greatly expanded range of covenantally acceptable ways of living as an authentic Jew. Moreover, our simultaneous responsibilities—to self, to God, to the Jewish past, present, and future, and to humankind as a whole (through our continuing participation in the covenant of Noah) will frequently clash with one another, leading to different views as to which should have greater weight. For these reasons I avidly espouse Jewish pluralism in thought and action. In our contemporary cultural situation I am more anxious about the corporate than the personal aspect of Jewish selfhood and therefore eagerly await the day when enough Jewish selves choose to live in ways sufficiently similar that we can create common patterns among us. A communal lifestyle, richly personal yet Jewishly grounded, would be the Jewish self's equivalent of *halakhah*.

Does my call for a community openness so tolerant of individuality destroy our character as a distinct people? Has not autonomy escaped from its covenantal containment and again manifested its anarchic and therefore ultimately un-Jewish character?

I cannot deny the risks involved in the path I am suggesting, but any theory that makes democracy a spiritual principle of our Judaism will face something of the same risks—and I do not believe any large number of Jews today will accept a nondemocratic theory of Jewish duty. Moreover, the act of passing substantial power from the rabbis to the community has, for all its weakening of community discipline also produced unique human benefit. The demand that everyone in our community tolerate other Jews' radically differing views has produced a harmony among us unprecedented in Jewish history; our contemporary distress at Jewish interreligious conflict testifies to our ideals and to our distance from the Jewish past, when surly antagonism often reigned among us. Though covenantally contextual individualism will surely amplify Jewish diversity and threaten communal solidarity, there will never be any question about its directly authorizing and commending Jewish democracy.

An Odd but Instructive Case

I can make my meaning clearer by providing some concrete examples of how I apply this standard (though I acknowledge that others might utilize the same theory to reach other conclusions). I begin with a somewhat unusual matter: how an Orthodox Jew should face the issues created by the medical treatment of dwarfism. The *halakhah* imposes no special disabilities upon Jewish dwarfs, and while the condition is troublesome to those who have it and often a heavy burden for their relatives, it does not constitute a threat to life deserving of exceptional *halakhic* consideration. Some *halakhic* urgency for the treatment of dwarfism arises from the greater than usual difficulty dwarfs have in conceiving children.

The special *halakhic* difficulty once raised by dwarfism arose from the hormone with which it was treated. Before it had been synthesized, the hormone had to be collected from human corpses, bringing the laws of respect for the corpse into conflict with the desirability of curing a non-life-threatening condition. Various decisors discussed how the incisions should be made in the corpses so as to create the least disfigurement, wishing to be as respectful as possible while fulfilling the law's higher concern with a significant human need.

The non-Orthodox Jewish self would think about this issue in somewhat different fashion. A corpse, the physical remains of the self, surely deserves respectful treatment. Indeed, with lessening concern for the dead—fewer people saying kaddish and visiting graves—Jews need to be reminded that we do not know disembodied persons. However, when one thinks primarily in terms of selfhood, there will be little doubt that the needs of a living person override respect for a corpse. One can surely be a Jewish self as a dwarf, yet the selfsame psychosomatic view of the self that authorizes honoring corpses makes us appreciate the trials of dwarfism. Hence I would rule with little hesitation that the suffering of the dwarf, not respect for the corpse, would be our primary Covenantal concern here.

Fortunately, we find little difference in the practical outcome of applying Orthodox and Covenantal procedures. But, hypothetically, had rigorous *poskim* imposed such stringent conditions on cutting into the corpse as to have impeded the collection of the hormone, I would have demurred. I do not believe our tradition implies, our community wants, or God requires our giving the corpse such precedence over the living—and in this theoretical solution I could not accept the *halakhah*.

The classic cases of the *agunah* (deserted wife) and *mamzer* ("bastard") trouble us very much more than does dwarfism because they can create a radical distinction between what the *halakhah* can allow and what non-Orthodox Jews perceive as our Jewish duty. If required, observant Jews will repress whatever stirrings of autonomous rebellion they may feel in these cases so as to faithfully follow God's law. The Jewish self I have described will far more likely react indignantly at the inability of Jewish legal authorities to respond to what they too know to be clear-cut human and Jewish values. To maintain proper legal procedure an *agunah* can be debarred from remarrying and establishing a fully ramified Jewish home. Or, in consequence of a parental sin, someone ruled a *mamzer* cannot contract a marriage with a kosher Jew. These disabilities contravene some of our most primary covenantal responsibilities. The Jewish pain attached to them intensifies when we think of the Holocaust. Is there much in our hierarchy of Jewish duty that takes priority today over contracting a Jewish marriage and creating a Jewish family?

The covenantal trauma created by these laws cannot be assuaged by mitigation, by suggesting that compassionate decisors will limit the number affected or that accepting the few unresolved cases will allow us to maintain familial unity among Jews. In fact, Orthodox decisors continue to declare some people *agunot* and *mamzerim* and apply the consequent Jewish legal disabilities to them. As I understand the range of my obligations under the Covenant, I do not believe God wants some Jews to relate to other Jews by categorizing and treating them as *agunot* and *mamzerim*. Thus I will abet Jews seeking to fulfill their covenantal responsibilities outside these laws. As a pluralist, I oppose any suggestion by the non-Orthodox that Orthodox Jews should be asked to compromise their understanding of God's law for the sake of communal unity. I do, however, find it troubling that while the *halakhah* has kept some laws such as "an eye for an eye" in force but practically inoperable, contemporary *poskim* have not yet demonstrated such creativity in this area.

The issue of women's rights in traditional Jewish marriage and divorce law disturbs Jews like me far more because, committed so fundamentally to the concept of personhood, I consider women's equality a critical matter for contemporary Judaism. Again the mitigations do not persuade. But I cannot usefully say more. Non-Orthodox Jewish women have reminded us that they must be allowed to speak for themselves and they increasingly do so to those who will listen.

Exercising Responsibility as a Jewish Self: Four Instances

I can now make some generalizations about covenantal decision making. Should our various covenantal obligations appear to conflict, our duty to God—most compellingly seen in the treatment of persons—takes priority over our responsibilities to the Jewish people or the dictates of Jewish tradition. I acknowledge only one regular exception to this rule, namely, those cases that clearly involve the survival of the Jewish people. Without Jews there can be no continuing Covenant relationship, and it is the Covenant, not universal ethics, that grounds the autonomous Jewish self.

What should an autonomous Jew do when confronted by a conflict between a divinely based responsibility to persons and another one that directly contributes to the survival of the Jewish people? I cannot generalize about how the Jewish self should proceed when it must compromise one of two values that have shaped it fundamentally, but I can compensate by indicating how I respond to four such situations.

Many years ago, as I was struggling with the old liberal identification of Judaism with universal ethics, I realized the ethical unsupportability of the Jewish duty to procreate. Bringing a child into the world to bear the name Jew potentially subjects that child to special danger. All the joys and advantages of being a Jew cannot ethically compensate for loading this ineradicable disability on another. Yet the Covenant absolutely depends on Jewish biological/historic continuity until the Messianic Days. For all its ethical difficulty, then, I believe I have a clear covenantal responsibility to proclaim the duty to have Jewish children.

Since many Jews believe that anything that limits the marriageability of all Jews critically affects Jewish survival, why do I then resist establishing one community standard for Jewish marriages and divorces? I do so because I believe our people will survive without a uniform marriage and divorce law. I base this conclusion on the fact that, despite their abandonment of the *halakhah,* the overwhelming majority of Jews worldwide still manifest a will to Jewish continuity. Without a relatively uniform standard of practice in family matters, Jewish life will not continue as it did when it had reasonable consensus in this area; but our people, as such, will survive. Reserving the supererogatory survival category for exceptional situations, I therefore cannot invoke it to override my covenantal sense of human obligation in this matter.

Then why will I not perform intermarriages when by some accounts more than half of the resulting families raise their children as Jews? Why do I not accept their will to be Jewish as a viable means of Jewish survival and thus remove the Jewish bar to my simple human responsibility, uniting in marriage two people well suited to one another though of different religions? I am moved by such arguments and acknowledge that my "Yes, but . . ." response may appear even more subjective than usual. My positive response to such people's Jewish concerns leads me to reach out to them with warmth and gladly accept their children as Jews when they manifest Covenant loyalty through education and participation. But I cannot be so approving as to officiate at their weddings, for it falsely symbolizes and communicates to them and others my understanding of covenantal obligation. The relation between God and the Jewish people is mirrored, articulated, and continued largely through family Judaism. Jews like me must then necessarily prefer a family structure fully espousing the Covenant to one that seeks to do so but with inherent ambiguity. Moreover, I understand myself as a rabbi authorized to function religiously within the Covenant community only on behalf of the Covenant.

My rabbinic colleagues who differ with me on this issue do so because they read the balance between human and Jewish obligation differently than I do. They believe, erroneously in my opinion, that performing intermarriages will help win and bind these families to the Jewish people. Because I may well be wrong and because I respect their reading of their Covenant responsibility, my pluralism makes itself felt here and I associate myself with them in full collegiality.

But it does not extend to those rabbis who now not only officiate at intermarriages but do so as co-officiants with Christian or other clergy. In so doing, they symbolize and communicate that it makes no difference what religion one espouses. They thus dissolve the Covenant of the *benei yisrael* into that of the *benei noah*. That clearly constitutes a threat to the survival of the Jewish people and its Covenant, and exceeds my liberally capacious pluralism. My Jewish self may not be able to state just where the boundaries of its openness lie, but in this instance it has no difficulty in identifying their transgressors.

Because I know myself to be related to God as part of the people of Israel's historic Covenant with God, I can be true to myself only as I, in my specific individuality, am true to God, to other Jews, to the Jewish tradition, and to the Jewish messianic dream. And while that truth is found more in the doing than in the thinking, it is by reflection on what constitutes true Jewish doing that Jews in every age have kept themselves alive to their responsibility as partners in the Covenant.

8

Jewish Tradition and Political Action

RICHARD J. ISRAEL

In the morning, if I can summon up the courage, I glance at the newspaper. I usually find it a deeply disturbing experience. First, I ask myself a question: Am I ever going to read another morning newspaper before the world goes up in smoke? Then I wonder whether there is anything I can do that may help forestall doomsday. But I don't know what makes sense. I suppose I can make gut-level decisions without any greater difficulty than anyone else; but I don't want to speak or act out of private feelings alone: I want some guidance. One of the areas I want some guidance from is my Jewish tradition. What kind of resources are available to me as, in the words of Maurice Pekarsky, "a human-being-born-Jew"? In what sense does my being a Jew give me help, direction, or purpose?

I

First of all, what kind of a resource is the Bible for me? Some people believe the Bible is full of solutions to the most contemporary kinds of problems. All we need to do is search the Book, and its words will tell us how to behave and what is right. But one can prove so much from the Bible, that one can prove very little. Is the Bible in favor of peace? Of course: "And they shall beat their swords into plowshares, and their spears into pruning hooks. Nation shall not lift up sword against nation, neither shall they learn war any more" (Isa. 2:4). But what of the Bible on war? It is in favor of that, too. We read: "Prepare war . . . let the men of war draw near, let them come up. Beat your plowshares into swords, and your pruning hooks into spears! Let the weak say: 'I am strong' " (Joel 4:9–10).

I am not attempting to suggest that the Bible does not say anything at all, but only that it is a very difficult book to use today. There is a clear message in the Bible that God is near, the he cares, and that he reacts to reward or to punish when something he cares about happens. God cares that man fulfill his ritual and ethical obligations. These obligations are very specific. Thus, it is wrong to muzzle an ox when he is threshing. One must not eat shellfish. It is wrong to gather wood on the Sabbath. One must leave the corners of the fields for the poor to gather. One must return a lost ox to its owner.

Yet, if there is any overriding religious theme in our own age, it is that God is far and that God is silent. Moreover, because we have lost the feeling that we know what God wants, we have lost our sense of sin. The Bible thus is not a readily available source of social or religious values for us today. It contains many passages whose tremendous force we can still feel, but it cannot be easily used as if it were a contemporary document. Any book is great, among other reasons, because its words have resonances which reach far beyond themselves and their simple meaning. That does not give us the right, however, to make the Bible say whatever we want it to say. Its contemporary use is too often that of a literary flourish. We know what we are trying to prove, and handily quote a first-rate verse which works out beautifully in the last paragraph. The Bible, unless used with great caution, is not so much a source of values as it is a decoration to give apparent substance to values we already have.

II

There is another source of Jewish social values that ought to be more promising: the *halakhah,* the legal system of the rabbinic tradition which had to respond to the continuing needs of the communitiy as it confronted day-to-day problems. *Halakhah* is supposed to embrace all the Jew's life, from the first moment of his waking when he washes his hands as an act of purification, until he says the Shema just before he goes to sleep. During the day, the *halakhic* Jew is reminded of his obligation to God and his fellowmen in countless ways. He has to recite at least a hundred blessings a day. There are foods which he may and may not eat. How he may conduct his business is clearly prescribed. His sexual relations with his spouse and his conduct toward his children are designated.

People argue that religion should not deal with all these trivial details. But generalities are a very dangerous guide for anything. A well-known story tells of a preacher whose congregation, overwhelmed with the beauty of his sermon on the subject "Thou shalt not steal," became angry and indignant the following week when he preached on the subject "Thou shalt not steal chickens." I do not know what others may need; but I need sermons on not stealing chickens. To give an example of another sort: even though the United States Constitution is a splendid document, which I endorse with enthusiasm, it is only because the city of New Haven (where I live) has a law against parking in front of fire hydrants that I manage with some reasonable degree of consistency to do what I know I ought to do. A law educates with a force that a publicity campaign or a general moral pronouncement alone does not possess.

I speak thus of the *halakhah* to describe some of the enormous appeal it has for me. I can take its authority seriously as far as it goes. The problem is that it does not go far enough. I do not think that it is adequate to deal with the really important problems of our day, the problems which may determine whether or not we are here tomorrow to *daven shaḥarit,* properly slaughter another chicken, or give to the United Jewish Appeal. For, while the *halakhah* is a comprehensive and sophisticated code of law that deals impressively with the interpersonal, aids in the development of the inner life of the individual, and promotes harmony in the Jewish community, its main concern with the world at large is, How we can minimize damage to the Jewish community from the non-Jewish community? It is almost totally apolitical in any sense in which we know modern politics.

The *halakhah* can tell me in great detail how I should conduct myself personally with fellow pacifists, vegetarians, or United States Marines. It cannot tell me which group, if any, I have an obligation to join, except perhaps to say, "Don't do anything dangerous for yourself or the Jews."

To extend my position event further: if the religious parties of Israel suddenly found themselves with an electoral majority and had to assume full responsibility for the direction of the government with all its modern problems, they would undoubtedly want to govern in a way which could assume that responsibility and, at the same time, would be consistent with Jewish law. Yet the body of law that would permit them to do so does not presently exist.

One of the most salient features of contemporary Jewish life is that this is the first time that the large Jewish communities have existed without any form of legally recognized self-government. Though there were variations, the basic pattern until the breakup of the ghettos was that the Jewish community was responsible for its own tax collections, its own internal civil litigation, and its own criminal litigation aside from capital crimes and some crimes affecting the crown. The *individual* Jew had no *rights* in a given place. The *Jewish community* had a number of *privileges* that were generally granted directly by the reigning monarch and in which individual Jews participated. When rabbis throughout the Middle Ages cited the verse in *Pirkei Avot* that one should pray for the peace of the government, for without it men would swallow each other alive, they were describing their own situation accurately. They felt they were continually living on the verge of a disaster. Any sudden change in government or governor was likely to have serious implications for the Jew. Governments were viewed as frail, temporary structures which could not be relied upon. Not only were they empirically unstable; theologically they were trivial as well. No institution that was not divinely authorized in the Torah could make any truly serious claim upon the Jew. Furthermore, all governments would be overturned at the coming of the Messiah. The only important law was Jewish law, *halakhah,* which they could take with them wherever they fled. It was a law not attached to any land.

It strikes me as noteworthy that the discussion in the Shulhan Arukh concerning the fact that the Jew is obligated to pay taxes is part of the discussion of thievery. Its context is the question whether or not taxes are theft and, thus, whether or not we are obligated to pay them. If they are theft, we are not obligated. It is concluded that taxes are not theft if they are parceled out in nondiscriminatory fashion. If a man's primary concern about the state is whether or not it is an honest and justifiable institution, he is certainly not going to pay much attention to its general welfare and still less to the problems between states. Within such a context it is not surprising that we have no theology of the state that would parallel the literature of the Roman Catholic church. Once, two thousand years ago, we began to develop such a theology; but since we have seldom been close to the sources of power, we have not continued to develop an adequate rationale for dealing with it.

Thus, if we want to find out what to do about communism, air pollution, or urban renewal, we are not going to find out from Jewish law. I am not saying that this material cannot be developed. I am making a plea that it should be. It should be developed quickly, too, before *halakhah* is relegated, even by those who care, to the realm of the unimaginably trivial. Whether or not swordfish have scales, whether marshmallows are kosher, and how high a *mehitzah* should be are not questions which will save either Judaism or the world. To relegate the totality of a glorious tradition to these kinds of questions, as most of the *halakhic* literature and intersynagogue warfare does, is to commit a very serious *hilul hashem*, a profanation of God's name.

III

Another source for Jewish values in addition to the biblical and the *halakhic* is the expediential, the Jewishly expediential. Its yardstick is a simple question: Is it good for the Jews? Let me give some examples. Even though the non-Jewish world, by and large, is quite certain that the Jewish community is monolithic and of one mind on almost every issue, we know that the real truth lies in Stephen Wise's old saw that the only thing two Jews can agree upon is what a third Jew should give to charity. How much more startling, then, when we come across an issue upon which Jews in the United States really were unified: namely, that there should not be prayers, denominational or otherwise, in the public schools, and that we really are not very enthusiastic about Christmas celebrations sponsored by public institutions. The Supreme Court seems to have agreed with the Jewish community. Of interest to me, however, is the nature of the Jewish community's argument: that we must maintain the wall of separation between church and state which alone permits a pluralistic American people to dwell together in harmony.

Where did we get this argument? Not from Jewish tradition, which would hold that the complete permeation of learning with religious values is the ideal. Jews never believed in the separation of religion and state. Traditionally, a state in which all the laws and lawgivers would be religious would be the best kind. If there is any idea that is remote from Judaism, it is that religion and law should be separate.

The real argument behind all the other arguments was very clear, though never explicitly stated. We did not want Christianity taught to Jewish children if we could possibly help it. This kind of sensitivity is a real source of Jewish values, values which may or may not be present in the Jewish tradition, but which are very much present in Jews. Why were Jews, in far greater numbers than any other religious group in the United States, against Senator Joseph McCarthy? He was no anti-Semite. He carefully covered himself by using Jewish assistants, Cohn and Schine, to make that point very clear. But most members of the Jewish community assumed that if full due process were not available to everyone all the time and if people were found guilty outside the courts, it would not be long before it would not be good for Jews. (I do not take this to be a cynical motivation, by the way. Enlightened self-interest is a motivation I can trust. I know how to deal with it—and cultivate it—in ways that are impossible with either altruism or avarice.)

I think a major factor motivating Jewish interest in the civil rights movement is related to this kind of enlightened self-interest. It is not the only motive, but it cannot be discounted. At the height of the civil rights movement, I received a letter which cost me more than one night's sleep. It was a short letter which said, "Dear Rabbi Israel: Congratulations for your civil rights efforts. You have come to our town, marched on our streets, prayed on our court-house steps and been imprisoned in our jail. Now you have returned to New Haven from your mission of justice to the warmth of your home. It may interest you to know that thanks to you and your colleagues' splendid efforts, last evening our city hosted the largest Klan meeting in southwestern Georgia in the past twenty years. As a Jewish merchant whose customers have already expressed their warm interest in your prayers, I thought you would want to know how much peace and comfort your spiritual efforts produced for those of us who find in the South a home and not a place to make headlines. Sincerely. . . ." What do I answer a man like this? Here I was, a cheap hero, while he had to suffer for my conscience. One thing that I cannot do is write him off as a bigot and forget him.

My only answer to this man—and it is not a short-range answer and will be of no consolation if his customers stop coming or if someone puts a match to his stock—is to recall the words of the German pastor Niemoeller: "When they arrested the labor leaders, I was not a labor leader. When they arrested the communists, I was not a communist. When they arrested the Jews, I was not a Jew. And when they arrested me, it was too late." Freedom is indivisible. If your freedom is in danger, then so is mine. When the blacks in southwest Georgia are full participants in American democracy, then my correspondent will not have to live in fear for the welfare of his family and his business. Injustice never stops with someone else. When it is bad for others, the Jew will soon feel it, too. From our concern for Jewish self-preservation, we have come to care for the virtue of society as a whole.

IV

There is yet another source of our values: our marginal status, the fact that we live in two cultures at once. We are Jews because we have a unique law, a unique past, and a curious contemporary history. In short, we are a peculiar people. There is the story of the Hasid from a New York yeshiva who went to gather funds in a little southern town. When he got off the train, the children of the town took one look at his beard and earlocks, his broad-brimmed hat, and his long, dark coat and began to follow him down the street with curiosity. The Hasid turned around in annoyance and said to them, "What's the matter? You've never seen a Yankee?"

Let us analyze this story. First of all, the Hasid really does feel like a Yankee. He is much more at home in his own New York environment than he is in the little town. If, like many Hasidim, he was born in this country, he is distinctly different from his fellow Hasidim, say, in Jerusalem, and they would look upon him in a sense as a Yankee, as affected by the American environment. But tell that to the children of the town and their response would surely be, "Man, you're the funniest Yankee we have ever seen."

Yet I am that Yankee. I feel like an American, and my Americanism is an important part of me. When I visit other countries, people look upon me primarily as an American; but, to my fellow Americans, I am a very special sort of American.

If anyone thinks that Jews in America are viewed just like everyone else, he ought to pause for a moment and consider the following question: What if the assassin of President John F. Kennedy had been a Jew? Would this have affected the Jewish community in exactly the same way Protestants were affected by the accusation of Lee Harvey Oswald? Perhaps I am an alarmist. I am sure we would all have survived. Nevertheless, the thought sends shivers down my spine.

I would assert that a unique aspect of Jewish community life outside Israel (and I am not altogether sure about Israel, either) is that we are marginal. We are almost, but not quite, full citizens of the countries in which we live. Though our legal rights are full, we still feel a sense of "we" and "they." Young people feel this less than their parents, and the parents less than their parents, but the feeling is there. From this feeling of marginality emerge many attitudes of the Jewish community.

Why does such a large percentage of Jews go to college as compared with non-Jews? There are two ways in this world to achieve status. One is to *be* someone important, the other is to *do* something important. Since we do not have the pedigree to be important, we have to do important things, and one of the best ways to do important things is to be a professional. Education is the quickest way up.

Do so many Jewish students go into medicine because of the Jewish insistence upon learning? What Jews used to study were traditional texts. If learning for its own sake were the goal, one might assume that as many Jewish students would study to be rabbis as doctors; but, as the old story goes, being a rabbi is no profession for a nice Jewish boy. Is it a question of healing and social welfare? Why, then, are Jewish girls as underrepresented in nursing as Jewish men are overrepresented in medicine? I would submit that medicine is viewed as offering quick social status, a good living with security, and the independence from the non-Jewish community which comes from self-employment. In short, Jewish marginality conditions our educational aspirations.

But it is not only Jewish doctors who are the products of Jewish marginality. The entire structure of the American Jewish community has, by and large, been created to provide uniquely American organizations to help us feel comfortable as Jews. The defense organizations, using the stated values of American democracy as a justification, that is, that all Americans should have an equal chance, have organized to protect the lot of the Jew in America.

Since all good Americans must belong to some kind of church, Jews who have very little concern for the religious values of Judaism join the synagogue, which then serves as their locus of secular Jewish identity. We have taken an American institution, the Protestant church, and utilized it so that we can feel at home in America and comfortable with our Jewishness. The synagogue is probably the oldest institution functioning continuously in Western civilization. But to show that, for most of its members, it is still a continuation of that ancient religious institution, one would have to explain the discrepancy between the number of Jews who join the synagogue and the number who worship there.

Our Jewish marginality is a source of values for us, values that I view as positive, like our concern for education and our ability to criticize our culture because we are not quite of it. At the same time, there are less positive aspects of the same phenomenon, e.g., mandatory Sunday morning trips to the delicatessen, and Jewish golf and bridge as essential aspects of community life.

V

Thus far I have attempted to indicate a number of sources of Jewish values. I have tried to show some of the kinds of values we have derived from each of these sources as well as some of the problems each of them presents. I have suggested that I find that I can use none of them exclusively. Let me now say that the only resolution I have found to the problems I have posed is a resolution that creates as many problems as it solves. It is, however, the only one available to me—that of personal synthesis: facing the world and attempting to deal with it as best I can as a modern Western man and as a concerned Jew. I use the tradition as a check on and a source of social values. It cannot present me with a rule book, much as my temperament tells me that I want one. If the tradition does not or cannot tell me explicitly whether I may endorse the use of atomic weapons or nerve gas, I might still find in it ideas that will give me help so that I am not left altogether to my own devices. One author put it rather well when he said that we could use the tradition in these areas of social concern as a goad, a guide, and a goal: a goad, in that it prods us into caring; a guide, in that it presents us with some limitations and suggested lines of action; a goal, in that it gives us a vision of the ideal future for which we are working.

I realize that I am proposing a very dangerous method. I run an enormous risk of tendentiousness, of being biased and deceitful, and of presenting my own vision of the truth as the tradition's vision. Moreover, to use such a method legitimately, I am obligated to be more Jewishly literate than I am ever likely to become.

In spite of all these qualifications, it must be this way for me. I have no alternative but to live a life of commitment plagued by great doubts. I must act without hesitancy out of information that is questionable. I know that I shall never have definite answers or even very good answers to most of the questions I am asking—not even to the important questions; but there is too much to do in the world to wait for all the answers to be in. All major decisions of my life—whether choosing a school, a wife, or an occupation—were made upon insufficient information. Yet, since someone is going to be making the major decisions of my life, it might as well be me.

Let me detail some of my attempts at synthesis. I shall begin with some of the social attitudes I have derived from my tradition. I present them as truths and as traditional Jewish values, subject to the qualifications I have already stated.

I am a Jew and I am living in the twentieth century. I cannot deny either my modernity or my Jewishness. The form of government which I warmly support is Western democracy. I am a liberal and a civil libertarian. I am strongly affected by the claims of my conscience, and I believe that others ought to have the right to respond to the claims of theirs. These attitudes do not make me a better Jew. They do not emerge from the Jewish tradition, yet they are part and parcel of me.

Democracy has never been a Jewish value. The messianic state was envisioned as a kind of constitutional monarchy. That people should vote regularly on important issues when the Messiah comes is unthinkable and silly. Not only in an ultimate messianic state but in the self-contained Jewish communities throughout history, democracy was the exception rather than the rule. There was voting within the governing bodies, but the representatives were rarely elected on a truly popular basis.

In the realm of civil liberties, due process and the rights of the accused are wonderfully protected by Jewish law, but freedom of speech or the press was unknown. The unconventional mind had difficulties in surviving within the community.

The appeal to conscience was irrelevant. If one is dealing with absolute truth, as the classical literature does, dissent has no place. There might be disagreement as to what the law should be or what ritual should be observed. But once the decision was made, one did exactly what the rest of the community did except within the narrowest of limitations. For example, the claim of a nonreligious person in Israel who says, "I do not believe in religious marriage, and I demand the freedom to be civilly married in accord with my own beliefs," would carry absolutely no weight in most religious circles. One should force a man to do the "right" thing even against his will.

I have grave difficulties in identifying with these aspects of my tradition because of those values of mine which I previously enumerated. But I am not only a twentieth-century American liberal. I am also a Jew, and that is also very much a part of the core of my being. So I engage myself seriously with the Jewish tradition, its texts and teachers, and in this engagement I find other positions, supplementing and challenging my Western values.

It is true that Judaism is not greatly interested in democracy, but it is passionately concerned with justice. I can respond to that. The tradition does not care what kind of government there is. But it does care that people be treated fairly and equally. This forces me to pause before I try to export my form of government to another culture and another continent. It may be that two houses of Congress, a president, and a Supreme Court are the best way to govern my particular land justly, but it is by no means clear to me that it is the best or the only way to govern other lands.

I know that my own country is important to me, but I know, too, that no state is of ultimate value. The rules governing the relations between people are important, but no nation-state really is, except insofar as it promotes justice in the relationships between men. I am in favor of social legislation which will promote a more equitable distribution of the good things of this world for all men, because the welfare of the community is far more important than the right of private property. After all, "the earth is the Lord's and the fullness thereof, the world and they that dwell therein" (Ps. 24). It is not mine. It is the Lord's world, and he wants justice.

It is not only my life that belongs to the Lord, but the lives of all the other people in this world as well. They are not mine to take at will. The earth of my nation belongs to the Lord, and so does the earth of my nation's enemies. I find it difficult to believe that my tradition, which would not sanction the cutting down of an enemy's fruit trees at a time of siege, on the grounds that they are the Lord's, would allow the burning of wheat stores, the defoliation of jungles, or the bombing of irrigation dams; or that a tradition which insists that noncombatants be allowed to leave the scene of battle would countenance imprecise high-altitude bombing in civilian areas.

Given my tradition's reservations about nation-states, I find it hard to understand some attitudes about other nations that seem to be among my nation's patriotic requirements. During World War II, all Japanese had buckteeth, wore heavy glassses, and were hideous, fanatical fiends. Now they arrange flowers, drink tea in charming rituals, and are the bulwark of democracy in Asia. The Nazis were murderers to a man. A good German did not exist. Teutonic viciousness was a national trait. Suddenly I discover that all that Germans want to do in this world is to clink beer glasses, sing joyous songs, and hurry about, being efficient; indeed, they are the only efficient nation in Europe, and thus are responsible for the miraculous economic recovery of the continent. The Chinese, of course, have gone in the other direction, and the French should be forewarned that unless they begin to treat us with proper deference, we shall shortly begin to discover just how effete they are and that their grand manner is merely a cover-up for an inner core of rottenness.

Nowhere in this nonsense is there any assumption that the citizens of all countries are people. The common humanity that we share is the uniqueness of each man, each with his own particular combination of strengths and weaknesses which can lead him to do terrible things or lead him to do wondrously virtuous ones, regardless of whether his government and ours happen to be allies at this particular moment.

But though I do not believe that my government or nation necessarily finds more favor in God's eyes than does my neighbor's, neither do I believe that his finds more favor than mine. I have every right to defend myself. (I must be exceedingly cautious about how I utilize the notion of defense, for in the rhetoric of modern nations, both sides engaged in a war are somehow always defending themselves. No one is ever an aggressor.) If I am honestly defending myself, defense is a religious obligation. This means that I would not only be foolish but immoral to lay down my arms before an enemy. Thus I would hold that, as I understand the Jewish tradition, any kind of total unilateral disarmament without careful and tight inspection that would be enforceable is wrong. Not only would the Russians or the Chinese exploit me were I to disarm; I quite believe that we would exploit them were they to do so. The *yetzer hara,* the "evil inclination," is present in all of us. I am intrigued by the notion of peace initiatives, in which each side agrees to reduce its armaments by a significant but not all-important unit, waiting until the other side responds with a comparable act. This, I think, would be in accord with what I understand to be the Jewish view.

Again, I know that every man is created in the image of God and that to despise my fellowman is to despise the living God. The midrash tells me to cast myself in a fiery furnace before I consent to embarrass or humiliate my neighbor. I find that I am daily complying in the humiliation of our Negro neighbors by denying them access to the housing, education, and employment that people with white skins and the same ability are able to obtain. Thus, I must enter into the maelstrom of the demonstration with all its hazards, if it is the most effective means to gain speedy public recognition of critical issues. I know I am descended from slaves and can hardly afford to disparage others who are descended from slaves.

I am not stopped by a call for civil disobedience, for civil law has for me no metaphysical or ultimate status. Its only function is to promote peace in the land. Peace, however, is not the absence of tension but the presence of justice. If the law does not promote justice, it is not a law which I have an obligation to follow. But if I disobey, I must do so in such a way that I show my respect for what the law ought to represent. I must submit to its punishments in order to recall it to its own intentions, purposes, and obligations: the promotion of justice.

What I have attempted to suggest is that the biblical and *halakhic* traditions are no longer generating the kind of continuous guidance that we need for the world in which we live. The contemporary Jewish community is more likely to derive its answers to these kinds of questions from its own sociological status. We can, however, let the tradition challenge us, and we can try to respond to that challenge honestly and fully. Jewish tradition still possesses great vitality, even though it does not always provide us with complete answers. It gives us a chance to stand back from our totally contemporary perspective and view our problem through other eyes.

VI

These considerations represent a context within which one can act. What about the process of action itself? For those who are ready to act, general ground rules can be spelled out.

First of all, fight for things that matter. Second, choose areas in which you can be effective; that is, every problem can be reduced to a size that you can comprehend and do something about. I would hold that the structure can still be repaired and does not need to be thrown out. Occasionally, pick areas where you have some chance of success. They will support you through many long, lean periods. In 1950 I was with a group of students who picketed two segregated music schools in Cincinnati. After one week apiece of picketing, each of the schools capitulated, and Negro students were admitted. We were then ready to take on the world. For a starter, we went to the local amusement park to protest the fact that swimming privileges were segregated. We barely escaped with our lives. (I will always remember my indignation when they began calling the whites in the group "dirty Jews." After all, we didn't look Jewish. How did they know we all were? Later on, I became more sophisticated.) Without the earlier experience, I think the sheer physical fright induced by the second would have kept me away from the barricades for a very long time.

Next, understand your opponents. Recognize that each is a man like you with virtues and vices along with strengths and vanities. Try to imagine how you would behave if you owned his property, held his political office, or had his job. If you can do this, you stand a much better chance of being able to communicate effectively. If you treat a man as if he were a living personification of evil, the chances are that he is going to behave that way. If you treat him like a man, with motivations no less complex than your own, he may respond to you like a man. In Georgia, I found that it was much easier to be arrested than it was to confront face-to-face the people who opposed what I was trying to stand for. It was probably safer, too. I suspect that it was also less effective. But then I was there trying to fight the system. I now think that I should have been there trying to talk to people.

Your greatest opposition may come from your families. They are worried about the implications your actions may have for your future. They will be worried about your life and safety. Be gentle with them. Recognize that their concerns and worries are real and cannot be dismissed as trivial.

Even outside your family circle, you are not going to find sympathy in all quarters. Most infuriating of all will not be those who oppose you, but those who write you off as an immature idealist. I am personally very much in favor of clean-shaven demonstrations. But remember, whatever you do, you are going to be labeled. I was in jail with an Episcopal priest who had an ulcer and who, after twenty-four hours of fasting, just had to have Maalox and requested some from the jailer. One of the local papers reported the next day that among those arrested were junkies who couldn't live without their stuff.

To the timid I must say that though there will be those who will both fight you and ignore you, there will also be some marvelous people whom you will be very proud to know, who will support you. There will be many more who will think you are a bit extreme, but on the side of the angels anyway.

Remember that the people who express themselves have more power than the people who do not. The activists constantly worry the Establishment because it is always concerned about new trends and public opinion.

The biggest changes that will result from any action you take will take place within you. You will change your own life in ways which you may not expect. If you are not very careful, some of the changes may be for the worse. The demonstrator and direct actionist is in grave danger of feeling like a hero with nothing but contempt for those who do not at once follow his one right way. Such a person does a rather poor job of sanctifying the name of the Lord among the multitudes. He becomes an ineffective leader and, worse, he serves as a very poor model for those who might be interested in his cause.

Rabbi Yitshak of Vorki once took his sons to see his teacher, Rabbi Bunam, who gave each of them a glass of bock beer and asked them what it was. The older boy said, "I don't know." Menahem Mendel, the younger, was asked and said, "It is bitter and good." Rabbi Bunam then turned to Menahem Mendel and said, "This one will become a great leader in Israel." If you have the stamina and the stomach, if you can take tradition and challenge it, if you can look at the world about you and force it to face up to the tradition, you will find the draught bitter and good.

D. Methodological Problems: The Case of Jewish Medical Ethics

9

How to Draw Guidance from a Heritage: Jewish Approaches to Mortal Choices

DAVID H. ELLENSON

The progress made by medical science over the last half century has been astounding. In the area of therapeutic medicine alone, developments have been nothing short of miraculous. Heart transplants give life to people who otherwise would have died. Artificial insemination by a donor (A.I.D.) and in vitro fertilization offer infertile couples the possibility of conception and birth. Advances in genetic research raise the prospect that potentially fatal diseases or physical defects might be eliminated while the embryo is still in utero. Life-support systems are now capable of maintaining the respiratory and circulatory functions of terminally ill patients indefinitely, while the invention of the electroencephalogram (EEG), combined with radionuclide cerebral angiography at the patient's bedside, permits doctors to confirm that irreversible, total brain death has occurred. These are among the almost countless advances made by medical researchers in our day.

Each of these discoveries, in addition to others not enumerated here, has presented doctors, nurses, patients, their families, and society with serious and often excruciating moral dilemmas. Are organs taken from animals permissible for use in human beings? Does A.I.D. constitute adultery? What does in vitro fertilization say about the meaning of parenthood? Does genetic engineering represent an unwarranted act of hubris on the part of human beings? If life is being maintained artificially through the use of a machine, is it morally acceptable to terminate life supports that will allow the patient to die? If brain death can now be determined, are the traditional criteria generally used to define death—the cessation of circulatory and respiratory functions within the body—outmoded and irrelevant?

Questions such as these and others are now so commonplace that they frequently occupy the headlines in our daily newspapers and often constitute the lead essays and articles in our most thoughtful magazines and journals. Moreover, increasing numbers of medical professionals, patients, and their families stand dazed and overwhelmed in physicians' offices, medical clinics, and hospitals throughout our country agonizingly confronting and desperately seeking just solutions to the life-and-death choices that lie before them. Faced with the often harrowing nature of this reality, many turn to religious tradition for direction and guidance. They ask the ethical authorities of their tradition to put forth principles that will guide judgments and to articulate reasons that will provide warrants for legitimating action.

Of course, making such determinations on the basis of a specific tradition is seldom a simple or an easy task. Modern literary criticism and theories of hermeneutics make clear that the reading of a religious tradition involves a nuanced and multilayered process. History teaches that values and principles evolve over time and indicates how deeply embedded such ideals and rules are in cultural and temporal contexts. Most significantly, anthropology reveals that a tradition's view of the nature of humanity and of humanity's relationship with God significantly informs the interpretive process. It is with these cautions and caveats in mind that I go on now to describe and analyze the dominant ways that Jewish ethicists have approached the sources and have characterized the ethos and traditions of Judaism in hope of guidance and direction on these mortal matters. Through an exploration and description of the major ways in which Jewish ethicists have in fact read the Jewish tradition to arrive at decisions on these questions, the essay is meant to highlight the critical role that methodology plays in rendering such judgments. It will argue that the different ways Jews approach their religious heritage are of significance in determining how Jewish medical ethics is to be done or, to put it in other terms, in determining what medical ethics is. These methodologies not only define who is competent to make such decisions, but, in doing so, show themselves possessed of profound implications for the normative judgment that might be rendered in a specific case.

Jewish medical ethics has been predominantly characterized by a methodology that one commentator has labeled "*halakhic* formalism." This classical mode of doing Jewish ethics seeks to identify precedents from the rich literature of rabbinic Judaism in order to extrapolate principles and norms that would yield authentic Jewish prescriptions on specific issues. Such an approach is hardly startling. After all, Judaism has preeminently grounded its authority in law and in the rabbinic interpretation of that law throughout its postbiblical history.[1] For over a millennium rabbis have employed responsa to apply the ideas and guides derived from the sacred texts of Judaism to the problems of a contemporary situation. Viewed in this way, Jewish medical ethics evidence the same methodological concerns and qualities that one would discover in any legal process.

This process, as David A. J. Richards has observed, displays two major characteristics. The first is that the judge, or the rabbi in our case, "infers the legal standards applicable to a particular situation from a body of so-called primary authority."[2] In Jewish law, this "body of so-called primary authority" includes both the Bible and the Talmud, which assumes a "statutory" role in the Jewish legal system, and an ongoing process of judicial opinions contained in responsa and codes that function in a "precedential" way. Here the interpretation of the law offered in the previous case (its holding) is seen to have a bearing on the adjudication of a contemporary case that deals, in the rabbi's opinion, with the same issue of law. A second feature of legal reasoning, related to but not identical with the first, is that of "reasoning by analogy." Rabbis, in this instance, not only take prior holdings on a comparable issue into account when rendering their decisions, but extend "principles of law found applicable to one set of fact patterns . . . to other fact patterns which are in relevant respects similar."[3]

Such an approach seems and, in many senses, is relatively straightforward. One simply plumbs the depths of Jewish law and discovers there the resources to resolve a perplexing moral issue. However, noting the method employed in such a moral exploration should not obscure the fact that genuine differences of opinion arise among diverse authorities as to the prescriptions the law yields on virtually every specific topic. Adherence to a common methodology does not preclude pluralism within the system. Authorities within any system of law can read precedents either stringently or leniently. They can assert that one set of precedents or values contained in the canon of a tradition is relevant to the matter at hand, while another group may assert that such precedents either have no bearing or have been completely misread. Affirmation of a common methodology in no way ensures a single substantive outcome.

An illustration of these points can easily be seen through an examination of several articles written by leading exemplars of "*halakhic* formalism" on the issue of the Jewish definition of death. Debate on this issue centers around whether Judaism considers what modern medicine terms "brain death" to be a sufficient criterion for establishing an individual as dead. All these writings cite an important talmudic text in tractate Yoma 85a as the locus classicus for the Jewish definition of death. Here the absence or cessation of breathing is regarded as the critical determinant of death. This definition is reinforced by passages in Maimonides' great code, the *Mishneh Torah*, Hilkhot Shabbat 2:19, and the subsequent, authoritative code of Joseph Karo, the *Shulḥan Arukh, Oraḥ Ḥayyim* 329:4. Furthermore, some later rabbinic authorities such as the Ḥatam Sofer, Rabbi Moses Schreiber of nineteenth-century Hungary, and Rabbi Eliezer Yehuda Waldenberg (Tzitz Eliezer) of twentieth-century Jerusalem comment on this ruling in the Talmud and codes and expand the talmudic definition of death to include the cessation of cardiac activity. Thus, the classical rabbinic understanding of death, based as it is on the statutory and precedential sources of the Jewish legal tradition, involves the cessation of both cardiac and respiratory activities in the individual. Only then, when resuscitation is impossible, is the person considered deceased.

Virtually every single position advanced by leading traditionalist rabbis and doctors on the subject of the Jewish definition of death cites these passages and others in offering views of the Jewish definition of death. In so doing, the authors, in the words of Rabbi Herschel Schachter of Yeshiva University in New York, are doing what Jewish legal decisors (*poskim*) have done for centuries. They are juxtaposing "the particulars of [their] own case and various halakhic precedents and principles, thereby decid[ing] into which category [their] own case falls. Then [they] must apply these precedents and principles to the situation at hand."[4]

The problem in the case at hand, in Rabbi Schachter's opinion, is that "the situation of a brain-dead individual is unique to our generation."[5] Only in our day has medical technology been so advanced that brain death—the determination that there is no connection between the brain and the circulation of blood in the rest of the body—could be ascertained. How does such a development affect the rabbinic understanding and application of traditional Jewish sources on the issue of the definition of death? Can principles be extrapolated from them that will allow contemporary authorities to state whether brain death in fact constitutes death? The answers, as we shall see, are varied.

Rabbi J. David Bleich rules that, even if there is brain death and irreversible coma, these are not sufficient to establish a person as dead in Jewish law. Jewish sources on the subject, in Rabbi Bleich's opinion, clearly define death as the complete cessation of cardiac and respiratory activities with no hope for resuscitation. No advance in modern medical technology can alter these criteria as the decisive ones in offering a Jewish definition of death. Rabbi Bleich obviously reads and applies the sources of traditional Judaism quite literally on this matter.[6]

Dr. Fred Rosner and Rabbi Dr. Moshe David Tendler understand the issue somewhat differently. Although they cite the same classical sources that Rabbi Bleich does in approaching this question, they also employ a responsum by the late Rabbi Moshe Feinstein, perhaps the foremost Orthodox *halakhic* authority in twentieth-century America, as a warrant for their contention that "Jewish writings provide considerable evidence for the thesis that the brain and the brain stem control all bodily functions, including respiration and cardiac activity. It, therefore, follows that if there is irreversible and total cessation of all brain function, including that of the brain stem, the person is dead, even though there may still be some transient spontaneous cardiac activity."[7]

Dr. Rosner and Rabbi Tendler, in disagreeing with Rabbi Bleich, do not, in a certain sense, dispute his reading of the sources. Rather, they question whether the Yoma passage on which Rabbi Bleich and others in part construct their definition of death is relevant to the matter at hand. The Yoma passage, in their opinion, focuses on the absence of breathing and movement as a confirmation that death has occurred. It looks to the cessation of respiratory activity as a sign that death has taken place. In light of contemporary medical advances that allow an intensive care unit patient's every function to be monitored, more sophisticated standards for determining whether these activities have ceased can be established. However, even when such cessation has been established by the finest and most accurate tests medical science has to offer, they still do not provide a definition of death. They confirm only that death has occurred. In other words, Dr. Rosner and Rabbi Tendler assert, against Rabbi Bleich, that the Yoma passage is in effect irrelevant for providing criteria for establishing a Jewish definition of death. My interest here is not to judge whose reading of the source is correct. Instead it is to point out that even when authorities employ the same methodology, they may read the sources of a tradition in quite dissimilar ways.[8]

What, then, are the criteria that Rabbi Tendler and Dr. Rosner utilize to establish a Jewish definition of death? An understanding of how they do this will be crucial in illuminating the nature of how "*halakhic* formalists" go about the business of Jewish medical ethics and will reveal the pluralism inherent in this approach. Returning to Rabbi Feinstein's responsum, they report his contention that, if it can be medically determined that there is no circulation to the brain, the patient is equivalent to a decapitated person whose heart may still momentarily be beating. Such a person, according to Jewish law, is dead.[9] In other words, not all organs need cease functioning for death to be said to occur. "Physiologic decapitation," to quote Rabbi Tendler, "is sufficient to provide a definition of death." In our day, according to Dr. Rosner and Rabbi Tendler, such "physiologic decapitation" can be determined through testing for brain death.

Dr. Rosner and Rabbi Tendler, on the basis of the talmudic principle *shinnui ha-ittim*, "a changed reality," are able, in effect, to assert that talmudic texts must be read in accord with the judicial principle of "purposive interpretation." Scientific evidence and advances possess the right to guide and inform Jewish legal interpretation. In an era when sophisticated medical tests that could measure brain death were not available, Jewish law naturally employed the criteria of its day—the observation that breathing had ceased and that all external bodily movement had completely stopped—to confirm that death had occurred. However, in our day, when medical tests do exist that can determine that all brain-related functions have completely ceased, it is possible to contend that the classical definition of "respiratory and circulatory death" as constituting the crucial criteria in determining an individual's death must be understood in a broader way. "The classic 'respiratory and circulatory death' is," write Dr. Rosner and Rabbi Tendler, "in reality brain death."[10]

Other authorities, notably Rabbi Aharon Soloveichik, sharply disagree with Dr. Rosner and Rabbi Tendler on this, just as the latter dissented from Rabbi Bleich.[11] Once more, the point here is not to suggest what a normative reading of Jewish law on this topic might be. Instead, in the context of our discussion, it is apparent that this approach to Jewish medical ethics, while text-centered, is hardly univocal. Different authorities read the same texts in diverse ways. They offer different opinions as to which texts provide appropriate analogues for understanding a contemporary situation. Rabbi Tendler and Dr. Rosner believe that the concept of "physiologic decapitation" is germane to this discussion and warranted by a reading of the sources. Rabbi Soloveichik sharply disagrees. Rabbi Bleich asserts that the traditional *halakhic* criteria for defining death must be narrowly and literally understood. Dr. Rosner and Rabbi Tendler contend that such texts must be comprehended in light of their "true intent," and that this intent is best captured in view of contemporary medical advances. A common methodological approach should not obscure the fact that the interpretive process is nuanced and variegated. Although the methodology of "*halakhic* formalism" may be text-centered, the judgments that emerge from such an approach are often multivalent.

"*Halakhic* formalism" is characterized by more that its attention to classical texts. It is also transdenominational, that is, not only Orthodox authorities have adopted this methodology in approaching the complex issues of medical ethics. It has also been the predominant manner in which non-Orthodox rabbis have attempted to deal with questions in this area. A glance at Jewish writings on the issue of euthanasia is illustrative of this. Addressing the question of whether a terminally ill patient suffering from excruciating pain can request a medicine that will simultaneously relieve his agony and hasten his death, Rabbi Solomon Freehof, the leading Reform rabbinic author of modern responsa, responds that "for a man to ask that his life be ended sooner is the equivalent of his committing suicide. Suicide is definitely forbidden by Jewish law."[12] Rabbi Elliot Dorff, a leading Conservative theologian and ethicist, writes on the same issues in an identical way. As Dorff phrases it, "Judaism prohibits murder in all circumstances, and it views all forms of active euthanasia as the equivalent of murder. That is true even if the patient asks to be killed."[13]

Orthodox Rabbi Immanuel Jakobovits also arrives at the same conclusion. Chief Rabbi of Great Britain and author of the definitive *Jewish Medical Ethics,* Jakobovits observes, "There is no question . . . to Judaism, of absolute and unconditional opposition to any form of direct or active euthanasia. . . . Any physician deliberately causing a patient to die, under whatever conditions of debility or suffering, is regarded as committing an act of first degree murder. Nor would any account whatsoever be taken of the wishes of the patient. We are no more masters of our own lives than we are masters of anyone else's. . . . We have no right . . . to forego our absolute claim to life by giving consent to its destruction."[14] Finally, Rabbi Bleich, already cited above, concurs with these sentiments and issues the following opinion:

> Elimination of pain is certainly a legitimate and laudable goal. According to some authorities it is encompassed within the general obligation to heal. . . . Yet when the dual goals of avoidance of pain and preservation of life come into conflict with one another, Judaism recognizes the paramount value and sanctity of life and, accordingly, assigns priority to preservation of life. Thus, a number of authorities have expressly stated that non-treatment or withdrawal of treatment in order for the patient to be freed from pain by death constitutes euthanasia and is not countenanced by Judaism. This remains the case even if the patient himself pleads to be permitted to die.[15]

The issue for us here is not whether the tradition could or should have been construed by these authorities in a different manner. As Rabbi Bleich has observed, and as Rabbi Jakobovits and others have noted, the commandment to relieve the pain of a suffering patient is mandated by Jewish law. Rabbi Freehof, in fact, expands on a view of this mandate and, in the end, issues a lenient ruling on this matter. He submits, on the basis of talmudic passages in Avodah Zarah 27a and b and Ketubot 104a, that "we may take definite action to relieve pain, even if it is of some risk to the last hours. . . . It is possible to reason as follows: It is true that the medicine to relieve the pain may weaken his heart, but does not the great pain itself weaken his heart? May it not be that relieving the pain may strengthen him more than the medicine might weaken him? At all events, it is a matter of judgment."[16] Rabbi Freehof, informed by the commandment to relieve suffering, offers the possibility that the fulfillment of this mandate does not abrogate the traditional directive to lengthen life in this instance. In so doing, he obviously departs from the ruling put forth by other *halakhic* authorities on this question. Furthermore, in his view of the revelatory character of Jewish law, he and Rabbi Dorff, too, will undoubtedly differ from the Orthodox rabbis cited here. However, once Freehof employs the same methodology that they do and elects to ground his judgments in the statutes and precedents of the Jewish legal tradition, any difference between him and them is incidental to the methodology he employs. In theory, other authorities could rule as he did.

Freehof's reading of the texts of the rabbinic tradition here is certainly informed by extralegal considerations such as personality and disposition. These cause him to apply precedents from the tradition that the others do not affirm. However, this has nothing to do with the methodology that is employed. His manner of making a decision is identical to the others. The pluralism evidenced here has nothing to do with Jewish denominationalism. It is qualitatively, from a methodological standpoint, no different than the difference of opinion we saw above between Rabbi Bleich and Rabbi Tendler on the matter of a Jewish definition of death. Furthermore, while Rabbi Freehof's own inclinations may have caused him to read the sources and cite the precedents for his decision in the manner that he did, this in no way distinguishes him methodologically from Orthodox *halakhists* who also admit extralegal considerations as factors that influence their own reading of the tradition. For example, Rabbi Faitel Levin of Melbourne, Australia, another prominent Orthodox authority in this area, cites the degradation of human life evidenced in the Holocaust as a factor, albeit not the decisive one, in his contention that Jewish law cannot countenance active euthanasia in any form, even to alleviate the suffering of a dying patient. Such a policy, he feels, would relativize the value of life.[17] In short, the methodological direction provided by "*halakhic* formalism" does not preclude lenient or demand stringent decisions. Tremendous discretion in how the sources are read remains with the rabbi who is issuing the decision. Rather, the methodology simply demands that the decision be warranted by a text taken from the tradition. The writings of Freehof, Dorff, and all the Orthodox authorities discussed here reveal the same text-centeredness, the same methodological grounding of their decisions in warrants derived from the literary canon of Judaism.

One final point about the nature of "*halakhic* formalism" must be made if a full appreciation of the character of this methodology is to result. Simply put, individual autonomy is not prized as an independent variable in this approach to Jewish medical ethics. Great concern for the individual is clearly present here. The suffering of persons and the nature of their lives are often taken into compassionate account. However, judgments are ultimately made, as Rabbi Jakobovits phrases it, by "competent moral authorities—rabbis in the case of those who submit to Jewish law."[18] Rabbis might decide, in a given case, that the law can be interpreted in such a way as to provide a coherent exception to the rule that Jewish law prohibits active euthanasia. This, as we saw, is precisely what Rabbi Freehof did. Nevertheless, the decision must ultimately be made, according to Rabbi Bleich, not by the patient nor by his or her family, but by "a qualified rabbinic authority for adjudication on a case-by-case basis."[19] This is because, as Conservative Rabbi Joel Roth, professor of Talmud at the Jewish Theological Seminary of America, observes in a strong, but accurate, description of this position, the "meaning of the Torah," the source for competent Jewish ethical judgment on these matters, is in the hands of the rabbis. "Rabbinic authority," Roth writes, "is, in theory, unbounded. . . . Rabbinic interpretation of the law is, as it were, the never-ending revelation of the will of God."[20]

The writings of every authority cited on the issue of active euthanasia reveal a refusal to recognize the ultimate right of individuals to make autonomous decisions concerning the nature of the treatment they will receive. Even when a terminally ill patient suffering unbearable agony requests that his or her life be ended or be permitted to expire, it is the rabbi, informed by considerations for the patient and by competent medical advice, who makes, in theory, the final decision. Such matters, from the standpoint of "*halakhic* formalism," are not left to individuals, their families, or physicians, but to rabbinic authority. "*Halakhic* formalism," precisely because it is textually centered, can grant supreme authority only to those who have

studied and mastered the texts—the rabbis. Again, this does not preclude a pluralism of views. It does not mean that decisions cannot be kindly and merciful. It does
indicate that individual autonomy is not a paramount, not perhaps even a secondary, value in the system.

A trend toward developing an alternative approach to the dominant one of
"*halakhic* formalism" has begun to emerge in recent years. The reasons for this
have been suggested in an insightful article written recently by Rabbi Daniel
Gordis, a member of the faculty at the (Conservative) University of Judaism in Los
Angeles. In an article entitled "Wanted—The Ethical in Jewish Bio-Ethics," Rabbi
Gordis suggests that developments in medical technology have been so dazzling in
recent years that a precedent-based classical approach to issues of Jewish bioethics
is simply inadequate to address contemporary realities. Gordis, for example, points
to the fact that A.I.D. has been labeled adultery by many Jewish ethicists if the
donor's semen is other than the husband's. "In an age in which adultery is a serious
societal issue," writes Rabbi Gordis, "employing *it* as the precendent for A.I.D. both
minimizes the moral claim against 'real' adultery, and lessens the seriousness with
which objective observers will view legitimate claims that *halakhah* has potential
relevance in other realms."[21]

Gordis goes on to provide examples of what he considers unwarranted extrapola-
tion of principles and norms from Jewish *halakhic* and aggadic writings on other
modern medical moral dilemmas. Although his contentions about the relevance of
precedents drawn from the sources of Judaism to modern medical ethics may be
somewhat exaggerated, the significant point is that this belief leads Gordis to assert
that "*halakhic* formalism" provides an inadequate methodology for doing Jewish
medical ethics. It is wrong or, at best, foolish to search the precedents of the Jewish
tradition in such a narrow, case-law fashion to find answers to matters of contemporary bioethics. Instead he turns to what can be identified as theological anthropology for a solution to his methodological dilemma; that is, Rabbi Gordis states that
the texts of Judaism must be examined to see what they have to say about the
nature of what it means to be human. Furthermore, in seeking an answer to such a
question, the ancillary issue of humanity's relationship with God arises. If one were
to receive answers to these broader questions, then it might well be that Jewish
medical ethics would draw normative conclusions in a far different way than it does
with a methodology based on precedent.[22]

Such a methodology, though nascent and somewhat inchoate—reminding one at
times of a theory of moral intuitionism—already has its champions. The maverick
Orthodox Rabbi Irving Greenberg, one of the most prominent interpreters of Jewish
tradition in North America, labels such a methodological approach "covenantal."
This "covenantal" approach to Jewish medical ethics, like its precedent-oriented
counterpart of "*halakhic* formalism," is transdenominational. Representatives from
both the Orthodox and liberal Jewish communities have championed this mode of
doing Jewish ethics. Among its most prominent representatives have been Rabbi
David Hartman of Jerusalem and Rabbi Eugene Borowitz of the Hebrew Union
College–Jewish Institute of Religion in New York. This approach is marked by the
dialectical, personal model of relationship between God and humanity found in the
Bible. It affirms the belief that "humankind is created so as to be God's partner in
completing creation."[23] This means that God's covenant with Israel does not restrict
human freedom, but presupposes it. As Rabbi Borowitz avers, "Though God's

sovereign rule of the universe is utterly unimpeachable, people under the covenant need not surrender their selfhood to God. If anything, to participate properly in the alliance they must affirm their freedom, for they are called to acceptance and resolve, not servility."[24] Or, as Rabbi Hartman phrases it, "The freedom of the beloved [humanity] precludes the possibility of absolute control [by God] and self-sufficiency [by persons]."[25] A covenantal mode of doing Jewish ethics calls for a balance between the belief in and reliance on God on the one hand and the affirmation of human autonomy on the other.

An authentic Jewish moral theory, from this covenantal perspective, must neglect neither God nor persons. "For Jewish ethics," as Rabbi Michael Morgan, professor of philosophy at Indiana University, has stated, "is by its very nature rooted in a Divine Command that is imposed and yet freely accepted."[26] Jewish medical ethics must involve a dialectic in which both God and humanity play an active role. This means that one must search out the tradition for those precedents relevant to the making of an ethical decision. Not to do so would provide an unwarranted break with a huge dimension of the tradition and would deny Jews the continuity and wisdom such precedents have to offer. However, this theory also affirms that since human beings are created in the image of God, they share in God's power. Human life and human wisdom, seen from this perspective, are reflections of the power of God. Such an approach, as the covenantal ethicists perceive it, does not usurp the power of God. Rather, it reflects the innate dignity inherent in both God and God's creation. In short, human autonomy—the ability of individual persons to make and to act on their own ethical decisions—derives from the freedom that God has given persons.[27] The affirmation of human autonomy seen in this dialectic is not the product of enlightenment thought. Rather, it receives a divine, religious warrant.

The implications of this methodology for Jewish decision making in the area of bioethics can be seen in an article entitled "Toward a Covenantal Ethic of Medicine," written by Rabbi Greenberg. In this paper, Rabbi Greenberg argues that the dialectical interplay between "power and partnership" that is the mark of the relationship between God and humanity in the Bible provides the proper model for Jewish medical ethics as well. This means, in part, that people are empowered to become more and more like God. They are charged by God with responsibility for their lives and are given permission to seek mastery and control over their environment. If someone asks, "What are the limits?" Rabbi Greenberg contends the covenantal response "is that the limit is nonexistent."[28]

Interestingly, Rabbi Greenberg, like Rabbi Levin above, cites the Holocaust in support of his position. However, instead of drawing the lesson from it that the Holocaust simply cheapened the value of human life, Greenberg states that the proper lesson to be derived from this horrific event is that bureaucracy, when left unchecked, can totally deprive people of power and lead to excesses of evil behavior. The Holocaust demonstrates what can occur when an "ethic of powerlessness" dominates. Greenberg desires to assert an ethic of power, an ethic of human beings charged with responsibility and control for their own decisions, as the proper Jewish model to be employed in our time. Autonomy within the covenantal dialectic, so understood, would mean not only that people frame actions and rules for their own lives in concert with the tradition, it also involves an affirmation of the person's right to act upon that determination. The covenantal model is one of partnership in which human beings have the legitimate right to exercise a high degree of control over their own lives.

This means that individuals have the right to ask quality-of-life, not only quantity-of-life questions. Greenberg states:

> The original birth control prohibition in Jewish law reflects the fear that human control over who shall be created, who shall be given life, is somehow robbing God of his power. What is really involved . . . is an ethical trade-off: the quality of life versus the quantity of life. It is necessary to know that quantity is important. It is also essential to know that quality matters. If the marriage needs more time, if the mother . . . cannot handle the number of children, then it is ethical *not* to have the child rather than have it. This is the balancing act that has to be undertaken.[29]

It is clear that this covenantal approach to Jewish medical ethics possesses implications that radically distinguish it from the precedent-oriented approach of the "*halakhic* formalists.*"* If we look at the issue of active euthanasia posed above, the covenantal ethicist, following Greenberg's methodology, might well reach a different conclusion than the classical Jewish ethicist concerning the decision to terminate life. Quality-of-life concerns could certainly enter the picture.

Far more significantly, it is impossible to imagine that the rabbi would be designated by the "covenantal ethicist" as the ultimate arbiter of what was moral in a case such as this. The rabbi could certainly occupy a legitimate role as a consultant and could provide the patient, the family, and the physician with information drawn from the precedents of Jewish tradition on this matter. The patient, in the end, might well choose to follow them. However, and this is the crucial point, it is the patient who would be empowered to make this decision—not the doctor, not the rabbi, not his or her family. The person's autonomy as a covenantal creature standing in relationship with God would ultimately be affirmed as the highest value in the system. All this is not to maintain that an individual is necessarily any better equipped to make an ethical decision than an institution or an outsider. It is also not to assert that a decision to terminate the life of a hopelessly ill patient suffering horrible pain is necessarily a more worthy moral choice than another one. For purposes of this paper, the substantive decision that might be made is beside the point. What is critical is that human autonomy, seen from this methodological perspective, is one pole on which Jewish medical ethics rests. Although a great deal of more rigorous work on the nature of this approach must be done, the direction already charted by its advocates clearly distinguishes it from the approach of the "*halakhic* formalists" and has far-reaching implications for the normative conclusions that Jewish medical ethics might ultimately draw.

The questions posed to humanity today by advances in medical science are truly frightening. There are no easy answers. Moreover, even when persons affirm a common approach to a religious tradition, the conclusions for normative practice can be many. However, I hope that this presentation has sensitized us not only to the way in which Jewish medical ethics has been done in our day, but to the important role that methodology occupies in the way that rabbis and individual Jews read their tradition for ethical guidance on the mortal issues. We Jews like to think of ourselves as *raḥmanim b'nei raḥmanim,* merciful people who are the children of merciful people. May our reading of our tradition on these mortal matters be, in view of these methodologies, a fulfillment of this vision as we deal with the realities of human suffering and human healing in our lives.

Notes and References

I would like to express my gratitude to Lee Bycel, Michael Signer, and Stanley Chyet for having discussed issues in this paper with me. I would especially like to thank my colleague William Cutter, who gave me extensive bibliographical assistance and who provoked me to think about many of the issues discussed in this presentation.

1. Daniel H. Gordis, "Wanted—The Ethical in Jewish Bioethics," *Judaism* 38 (1989): 29.

2. David A. J. Richards, *The Moral Criticism of the Law* (Encino and Belmont, CA: Dickenson Publishing Co., 1977), 26.

3. Ibid., 28.

4. Herschel Schachter, "Determining the Time of Death," *The Journal of Halacha and Contemporary Society* 17(1989): 32.

5. Ibid.

6. J. David Bleich, *Contemporary Halakhic Problems* (New York: KTAV, 1977), 372–93.

7. Fred Rosner and Moshe David Tendler, "Determining the Time of Death," *The Journal of Halacha and Contemporary Society* 17 (1989): 17.

8. Ibid., 24.

9. Ibid.

10. Ibid., 27.

11. Aharon Soloveichik, "Determining the Time of Death," *The Journal of Halacha and Contemporary Society* 17 (1989): 41–48.

12. Walter Jacob, ed. *American Reform Responsa* (New York: Central Conference of American Rabbis, 1983), 254.

13. Elliot N. Dorff, "Choose Life: A Jewish Perspective on Medical Ethics," University Papers, 4, 1 (Los Angeles: University of Judaism, 1985), 17.

14. Immanuel Jakobovits, "Ethical Problems Regarding the Termination of Life," in *Jewish Values in Bioethics*, Levi Meier, ed. (New York: Human Sciences Press, 1986), 90.

15. J. David Bleich, *Judaism and Healing: Halakhic Perspectives* (New York: KTAV, 1981), 137.

16. Jacob, op. cit., 256–57.

17. Faitel Levin, *Halacha, Medical Science, and Technology: Perspectives on Contemporary Halacha Issues* (New York and Jerusalem: Maznaim Publishing Corporation, 1987), 64–65.

18. Jakobovits, op. cit., 91.

19. Bleich, *Judaism and Healing*, 144.

20. Joel Roth, *The Halakhic Process* (New York: KTAV, 1987), 133.

21. Gordis, op. cit., 29.

22. Ibid., 28–40.

23. Irving Greenberg, "Toward a Covenantal Ethic of Medicine," in *Jewish Values in Bioethics*, Levi Meier, ed. (New York: Human Sciences Press, 1986), 124–49.

24. Eugene B. Borowitz, *Choices in Modern Jewish Thought* (New York: Behrman House, 1983), 367–68.

25. David Hartman, "Moral Uncertainties in the Practice of Medicine," *The Journal of Medicine and Philosophy* 4 (1979): 100.

26. Michael Morgan, "Jewish Ethics after the Holocaust," *The Journal of Religious Ethics* 12 (1984): 259.

27. Eugene B. Borowitz, "The Autonomous Self and the Commanding Community," *Theological Studies* 45 (1984): 48–49.

28. Greenberg, op. cit., 137.

29. Ibid., 145.

10

Woodchoppers and Respirators: The Problem of Interpretation in Contemporary Jewish Ethics

LOUIS E. NEWMAN

The central problem of constructing a contemporary Jewish ethic has been expressed succinctly by Immanuel Jakobovits, whose work on Jewish medical ethics is widely published and quoted.

> How does *Jewish law* go to work in relating to very modern issues, many of which obviously are the result of spectacular advances in medicine that are of very recent times? How can we apply to contemporary perplexities insights that have their origin in the timeless traditions of our faith and are imbedded in virtually all the layers of our *literature* going back to earliest biblical times? How we can [*sic*] find principles enshrined in those early *sources* that have relevance and application to the highly complex questions that arise from these dramatic advances in medicine?[1] (emphasis added)

Constructing a contemporary Jewish ethic, as Jakobovits and many others conceive it, involves interpreting traditional Jewish texts and applying their norms to complex, often unprecedented, contemporary issues. Textual interpretation, it seems, provides the foundation for contemporary Jewish ethics.

The purpose of this study is to explore the ways in which Jewish ethicists derive answers to contemporary moral problems from traditional texts.[2] I do this by examining the modes of interpretation which they employ, the ways in which they read traditional Jewish texts and use them to articulate Jewish views on contemporary moral problems. To illustrate this process and the hermeneutical issues to which it gives rise, I will focus on the contemporary Jewish ethical debate surrounding euthanasia. The issue of euthanasia is particularly well suited for this purpose in several respects. First, euthanasia has received a good deal of attention in recent years by Jewish ethicists of both traditional and liberal orientations. Thus there is a wealth of literature on the topic.[3] Moreover, the situations in which questions of euthanasia arise in our time are largely unprecedented, owing to recent dramatic advances in medical technology. As a result, the problem of applying traditional sources to contemporary cases in this instance is especially acute. At the same time, I want to emphasize that the interpretive problems raised here are in no way limited to this specific moral issue, or indeed to bio-medical ethics generally. To the extent that this process of textual interpretation is central to all contemporary Jewish ethical discourse, so too are the methodological problems which accompany it.

I will proceed by exposing, then challenging, the assumptions that underlie the process of textual interpretation as it is practiced by most contemporary Jewish ethicists. Specifically, I will argue that virtually all exegetes employ a model of textual interpretation which assumes first, that texts themselves contain some single determinate meaning and second, that the exegete's role is to extract this meaning from the text and apply it to contemporary problems. I suggest, however, based on the work of current literary and legal theorists, that these two assumptions regarding the character of the text and the role of the interpreter are questionable, if not altogether untenable. If, as these critics claim, the meaning of a text lies less in the words themselves than in the interpretive framework which the exegete brings to them, then most contemporary Jewish ethicists employ a very problematic methodology. In the concluding section of this paper I will suggest one way in which this methodological problem might be overcome, though not without altering significantly the way in which most people currently conceive of doing Jewish ethics.

Interpretation in Contemporary Jewish Ethics: Description and Analysis

Translating traditional Jewish values into specific norms for ethical conduct in the modern world involves three steps: (1) identifying precedents from classical Jewish literature, (2) adducing principles from these texts, and (3) applying these principles to new sets of facts. Though the interpretive process is rarely delineated so clearly, these basic steps are implicit in the work of virtually all contemporary Jewish ethicists. Thus, while Jewish authorities differ sharply both in the ways they approach these basic interpretive tasks and in the specific conclusions they reach, the process of interpretation and the problems that it entails are shared by all. It should be noted that these three steps are in some respect closely related. Determining whether a certain text is pertinent to the issue at hand (step 1) and applying the message of that text to a contemporary situation (step 3), for example, both involve identifying the ways in which traditional cases and contemporary ones are analogous and/or disanalogous.[4] In the contemporary discussions summarized below which illustrate this interpretive process we will note that these steps are not followed in a strict, chronological sequence. Nonetheless, it is helpful for analytical purposes to examine each step separately.

Let us begin by considering the difficulty of identifying precedents within the tradition for cases involving euthanasia. Traditional sources which permit people to pray for the speedy death of a dying individual who is in great pain are one striking case in point. These texts do not directly concern questions of euthanasia at all, but, in the view of some authorities, may nonetheless provide the basis for a Jewish position on such questions.

> On the day that Rabbi Judah was dying, the rabbis decreed a public fast and offered prayer for heavenly mercy [so that he would not die]. Rabbi Judah's handmaid

ascended to the roof and prayed [for Judah to die]. The rabbis meanwhile continued their prayers for heavenly mercy. She took a jar and threw it down from the roof to the ground. They stopped praying [for a moment] and the soul of Rabbi Judah departed.[5]

Sometimes one must request mercy on behalf of the ill so that he might die, as in the case of a patient who is terminal and who is in great pain.[6]

It happened that a woman who had aged considerably appeared before Rabbi Yose ben Halafta. She said: "Rabbi, I am much too old, life has become a burden for me. I can no longer taste food or drink, and I wish to die." Rabbi Yose answered her: "To what do you ascribe your longevity?" She answered that it was her habit to pray in the synagogue every morning, and despite occasional more pressing needs she never had missed a service. Rabbi Yose advised her to refrain from attending services for three consecutive days. She heeded his advice and on the third day she took ill and died.[7]

"There is a . . . time to die" (Eccles. 3:2) Why did Koheleth say this? With respect to one who is dying (*goses*),[8] we do not cry out on his behalf [in the hope] that his soul will return; he can at best live only a few days, and in those days will suffer greatly. Thus it says, "a time to die."[9]

Citing these sources, Solomon Freehof concludes that Jewish law sanctions passive euthanasia, at least in those cases in which the dying individual is incurable and/or in great pain. Noting that Rabbi Judah's handmaid is praised in the Talmud for her action, he writes,

Is it the physician's duty to keep this hopeless patient (who is also in all likelihood suffering great pain) alive a little longer, maybe a day or two? Jewish law is quite clear on this question. He is not in duty bound to force him to live a few more days or hours. . . . In other words, according to the spirit of Jewish tradition, just as a man has a right to live, so there comes a time when he has a right to die. Thus, there is no duty incumbent upon the physician to force a terminal patient to live a little longer.[10]

In short, if one may pray for the death of the hopelessly ill and dying patient, one may, it is argued, take other steps which will tend to promote the inevitable end. This same argument is stated more explicitly, and carried to a more radical conclusion, by Byron Sherwin, who argues that these texts, among others, might provide the basis for sanctioning certain forms of *active* as well as passive euthanasia. As Sherwin reads these texts,

The woman's withholding of her prayers removed the cause of the extension of her life. Similarly, the removal of "life-support" systems from a patient to whom—like this woman—life has become a burden, would be permissible. Nevertheless, it may be argued that this case underscores the inability always to make a clear-cut distinction between passive and active euthanasia. Her withholding of her prayers, or a physician or nurse's 'pulling the plug' may be considered a deliberate action aimed at precipitating an accelerated death. Once the line between passive and active euthanasia becomes so blurred, one may attempt to cross the line with care and with caution. For if the woman's withholding of her prayers is a sanctioned action deliberately designed to accelerate her own death, then other actions designed to accelerate the death of those to whom life has become an unbearable burden might also be eligible for the sanction of Jewish tradition.[11]

To others, however, such conclusions about euthanasia may not legitimately be derived from these texts. Asher Bar-Zev, for example, considers this argument but ultimately rejects it on the grounds that there is a qualitative difference between praying to God for death to come (or refraining from those prayers which presumably serve to sustain life) and taking active medical steps to hasten death.

> On the basis that prayer and medicine are considered equally efficacious in Jewish tradition, one might argue that medicinal means of hastening death would also be permitted. However, a fine distinction can be made in this case. Since one has asked God to kill oneself, it is God rather than man who is the active agent in bringing about the death. . . . We conclude, therefore, that there *is* a difference between prayers for a person to die and use of a physical act in order to cause death to come.[12]

Thus, there is considerable disagreement on the extent to which those sources which permit prayers for the death of an incurable person can be "translated" into permissive attitudes toward euthanasia. As Alan Weisbard astutely notes in this connection,

> Only a limited conclusion can be drawn from these materials on prayer. Clearly the rabbis were sympathetic to efforts to deliver incurables from their agony. They looked favourably upon and authorized behaviour inconsistent with a maximal effort to prolong life. Yet, in each instance, the process was mediated by and, presumably, consistent with, the divine will. Thus, to the extent prayer's nexus with the divine will is unique, lessons drawn from Jewish attitudes toward prayer for the dying provide only uncertain guidance with respect to medical interventions.[13]

Do texts about praying for death to come have precedential value for matters of euthanasia? The fundamental problem in answering such a question—and it is a question which must be asked by anyone who wishes to develop a position consistent with Jewish tradition—is simply that traditional sources do not come to us prelabeled to indicate which are relevant to the particular contemporary dilemma we happen to be facing. As a result, there is considerable room for contemporary authorities to differ in their choices of precedents for modern cases involving euthanasia.[14] Moreover, it is a matter of dispute among contemporary Jewish ethicists whether aggadic (nonlegal) texts can serve as valid precedents for contemporary decisions at all. This point emerges most clearly in contemporary discussions of the talmudic text describing the martyrdom of Rabbi Haninah ben Tradyon, on which some rely heavily and which others dismiss as entirely irrelevant.

> They took R. Haninah b. Tradyon and wrapped a Torah scroll around him, and encompassed him with faggots of vine branches, to which they set fire. They brought woolen tufts, soaked them with water, and laid them on his heart, so that his soul should not depart quickly. . . . His disciples said to him: "Open your mouth that the fire may penetrate." He replied: "Better is it that He who gave the soul should take it, and that a man should do himself no injury." Then the executioner said to him: "Master, if I increase the flame and remove the woolen tufts from off the heart, will you bring me to the life of the world-to-come?" "Yes," said Haninah. "Swear it," demanded the executioner. Haninah took the oath. Forthwith the officer increased the flame and removed the woolen tufts from over Haninah's heart, and his soul departed quickly.[15]

It is suggested by many authors that the story provides the basis for drawing a distinction between active euthanasia which is forbidden (insofar as Haninah would take no direct action to hasten his own death) and passive euthanasia which is permitted (for Haninah would allow the executioner to remove the obstacles which prolonged his death). As Byron Sherwin indicates,

> The Talmudic case of Hananiah ben Teradion is also used by post-Talmudic sources as a precedent for the permissibility of passive euthanasia. The rabbi permitted the tufts of wool which were "artificially" sustaining his life to be removed. This would seem to permit both voluntary and involuntary passive euthanasia. . . . To be sure, Jewish law would not permit the removal of any and all life-support mechanisms. . . . The text of the story of Haninah ben Teradion clearly relates to an individual who has no chance of survival in any case, i.e., to a terminal patient.[16]

Yet, Novak argues, such stories are not in general intended to serve as legal precedents. Presumably, they are meant rather to illustrate the rabbi's piety and willingness to die *al kiddush hashem,* for the sanctification of God's name.[17] Moreover, Nissan Telushkin notes that we have an obligation to preserve life by any medical means available, whereas there is no such necessity when the continuation of the status quo serves merely to perpetuate pain and suffering inflicted in order to torture (as in the case of R. Haninah ben Tradyon).[18] Thus, the case of Haninah ben Tradyon may be irrelevant either because it is not a legal precedent at all, as Novak argues, or because it concerns a situation of torture and so is not pertinent to matters of medical care for the dying, as Telushkin maintains. Needless to say, one's decision to accept or reject one or more texts as precedential will greatly affect one's ultimate conclusion about what constitutes a Jewish view on issues such as euthanasia.

Yet, even if all modern interpreters could agree on the body of traditional texts that constitute valid precedents, a second interpretive hurdle would remain, namely, how to articulate the general legal or moral principles embodied in these rules. Again, contemporary discussions of euthanasia illustrate this problem nicely. Certain traditional texts, for example, recognize a category of individual who is on the verge of death (*goses*) and specify what may and may not be done on that person's behalf. These rules about the treatment of the *goses,* however, do not readily lend themselves to generalization and so the way in which they should be applied to modern cases of euthanasia remains a matter of considerable debate.

> One may not close the eyes of a dying person (*goses*); one who touches him so as to move him is a murderer. R. Meir would say: "It is to be compared to a sputtering candle which is extinguished as soon as a person touches it—so too, whoever closes the eyes of a dying person is considered to have taken his soul."[19]

> A dying person (*goses*) is considered to be alive in every respect. . . . To what may he be compared? To a flickering flame, which is extinguished as soon as one touches it. Whoever closes the eyes of the dying while the soul is about to depart is shedding blood. One should wait a while; perhaps he is only in a swoon.[20]

> One may not prevent a person from dying quickly. For example, if there are factors preventing a speedy demise—such as a man chopping wood in the vicinity of a dying man's home, and the noise of the chopping prevents the soul from escaping—we remove the chopper from there. Likewise we do not place salt on his tongue to prevent his death. But if he is dying and he says, "I cannot die until you put me in a different place," they may not move him from there.[21]

It is forbidden to cause the dying to die quickly, such as one who is moribund (*goses*) over a long time and who cannot die, it is forbidden to remove the pillow from under him on the assumption that certain birdfeathers prevent his death. So too one may not move him from his place. Similarly, one cannot place the keys of the synagogue beneath his head [on the assumption that their presence hastens death], or move him so that he may die. But if there is something that delays his death, such as a nearby woodchopper making a noise, or there is salt on his tongue, and these prevent his speedy death, one can remove them, for this does not involve any action at all, but rather the removal of the preventive agent.[22]

It should be noted first that these texts regarding the *goses* raise some of the same issues noted above with respect to texts of prayer. Do these texts provide appropriate analogies, and so precedents, for contemporary cases of euthanasia? As defined by traditional sources[23] the term refers to an individual whose death is imminent and certain to come within seventy-two hours. Some contemporary authorities, following this definition strictly, have therefore held that terminally ill patients being kept alive on respirators do not fall within the category of *goses* at all, for it is clear that they can be kept alive for considerably longer than three days. As J. David Bleich argues,

. . . any patient who may reasonably be deemed capable of potential survival for a period of seventy-two hours cannot be considered a *goses*. . . . It would appear that *Halakhah* assumes axiomatically that the death process or the "act of dying" cannot be longer than seventy-two hours in duration. . . . The implication is that a *goses* is one who cannot, under any circumstances, be maintained alive for a period of seventy-two hours.[24]

On this view, the texts cited above are simply irrelevant to any case in which patients could be kept alive with the help of artificial life support systems for months and even years.

Ronald Green, however, has challenged Bleich's unwillingness to apply the category of *goses* to many contemporary cases.

Can it not be said, however, in view of the capabilities of modern medicine, that the category of the *goses,* as it was formerly understood, no longer exists? When the patient today begins choking on secretions, a tracheotomy is performed or the breathing passage is cleared out. When the 'last breath' is drawn, the ventilator is turned on. One conclusion, of course, is that very few patients any longer are *goses* so that whatever permission existed in such cases for the cessation of efforts no longer applies: everything must be done to extend life. This seems to be Bleich's conclusion. But it is equally open to the *halakhic* scholar to conclude that medical advance forces a radical reconsideration of the classical sources in order to discern the intent of rulings that mandated life-saving efforts or that created the special category of the *goses*. It may be that temporal limits no longer suffice to identify the imminently dying patient, for example, and that some consideration of the hopelessness of the patient's condition or continued quality of life are more relevant to the determination of this status.[25]

Others, consistent with Green's suggestion, have been inclined to interpret the category of *goses* more liberally. Marc Gellman, for example, argues

When therapeutic hope failed in the world of our ancestors, death was certain to come shortly, and so the category of *gessisah* was that short time (72 hours or less)

before death when therapy failed. What has happened in our time is that a new category applies. Medical science can fail to cure and yet continue to treat for far longer than 72 hours. Is this *gessisah?* . . . Just as the rabbis used a time limit to define *gessisah,* so must we recognize that life expectancy is a crucial factor in determining whether or not to treat. This is not a quality of life argument, it is a quantity of life argument and it counts.[26]

While Gellman does not argue here that the category of *goses* must be revised in response to changing medical technology, his observation that it could be so revised is very suggestive. At very least, the way in which one interprets this traditional term could radically alter one's application of these texts to a contemporary bio-medical issue. Indeed, a number of authors writing on the issue of euthanasia simply assume that the foregoing texts are applicable to any individual who is judged to be "in the process of dying" and who, without artificial assistance, would not survive for any substantial length of time. Seymour Siegel, in line with Gellman's suggestion, believes that the term should be applied to anyone who cannot be saved by medical science, for whom treatment is futile, actually a prolongation of death rather than a prolongation of life.[27] But as Weisbard notes in this connection, "Extension of that concept [*goses*] from the traditional three day period to a metaphoric understanding which would encompass the almost indefinite maintenance of a patient 'one moment from death' (made possible by modern medical technology) is far from universally accepted."[28]

Yet, even if all authorities could agree that traditional laws regarding the *goses* were applicable to contemporary cases of euthanasia, the principle underlying these cases is subject to several alternative interpretations. It is clear that the wood-chopper is an impediment to the patient's death. But how are we to construe the nature of this impediment—as something physically removed from the person, as something which has no therapeutic value, as something not placed there by the patient or those caring for that person, or simply as anything whatsoever that prevents a person from dying. Similar questions can be raised about the circumstances under which an impediment to death, of whatever sort, can be removed. Shall we restrict the principle that impediments may be removed to individuals who are in severe pain, to those who are irreversibly comatose and so feel no pain at all, or to those in neither of these categories who are terminally ill for whom medical technology can offer only palliative care but no cure?

Answers to these questions vary widely. Jakobovits, for one, concludes from these sources that "Jewish law sanctions, and perhaps even demands, the withdrawal of any factor—whether extraneous to the patient himself or not—which may artificially delay his demise in the final phase."[29] This view was also shared by Moshe Feinstein.[30] So too, Freehof has argued that a life-sustaining apparatus which prevents a terminal patient from dying is the sort of impediment which the text from *Sefer Hasidim* cited above would permit us gently to remove.[31]

Other authorities, however, question whether the impediments spoken of in these texts are of the same character as the modern life-support equipment often in place when decisions involving passive euthanasia need to be made. Rosner, for example, is somewhat more cautious in his application of these sources to the discontinuation of life-supporting equipment or therapy.

The impediments spoken of in the code of Jewish law, whether far removed from the patient as exemplified by the noise of wood chopping, or in physical contact with him such as the case of salt on the patient's tongue, do not constitute any part of the therapeutic armamentarium employed in the medical management of this patient. For this reason, these impediments may be removed. However, the discontinuation of instrumentation and machinery which is specifically designed and utilized in the treatment of incurably ill patients might only be permissible if one is certain that in doing so one is shortening the act of dying and not interrupting life.[32]

Consistent with the thrust of Rosner's view, Marc Gellman suggests that "modern medicine can become a woodchopper when its invasive procedures have lost their therapeutic rationale."[33] Presumably, though Gellman does not state this explicitly, a life supporting procedure which did have some therapeutic value would not be subject to the rule of the woodchopper.

David Novak proposes still another reading of the case of the woodchopper's noise and so questions its applicability to cases of euthanasia on other grounds. Perhaps the author of this text wanted to distinguish between obstacles to death which were physically removed from the patient (e.g., the woodchopper) and those which were in contact with the person (e.g., the keys of the synagogue). But, Novak argues, our understanding of modern physics may not permit us to maintain this clear distinction.

> . . . just as removing salt from the tongue was eliminated as an acceptable act because it involves the physiological result of moving the mouth, so I would argue that if one could possibly show that the sound waves caused by the woodchopper were actually life-sustaining in any way, then this folk remedy [that the woodchopper should be silenced], now having an etiology, would also be eliminated as an acceptable act.[34]

Thus, the way in which we adduce the principle embodied in a text may depend, in part, on our assessment of the scientific and medical knowledge on which those traditional judgments were based.

We have seen, then, that while these traditional texts concerning treatment of the *goses* both proscribe taking any action which would hasten death and permit removing certain obstacles which forestall death, it is not apparent how such rules can be translated into general principles applicable to contemporary situations. How broadly or narrowly should we construe these cases and the (unarticulated) general principles that underlie them? The sources themselves offer no guidance in this crucial respect. As Karl Llewellyn has noted, every legal precedent has not one value, but two; it can be interpreted either broadly, so as to encompass many new cases, or narrowly, thus restructuring its impact on future decisions. Both options are always open and both are equally valid.[35] In short, we have seen that quite distinct principles may be deduced logically from a single case insofar as this material is "rather opaque in terms of its underlying values."[36] As a result, these texts can be applied to contemporary situations in a number of ways and, in any event, only with considerable reservation.[37]

This same methodological problem arises when authorities turn from specific cases as precedents to general principles which, it is claimed, underlie the tradition as a whole. Many authorities, for example, base their opposition to euthanasia on the principle, derived from Scripture, that all life is a gift from God and thus sacred. This basic presupposition is most clearly articulated by J. David Bleich, who writes,

> In Jewish law and moral teaching the value of human life is supreme and takes
> precedence over virtually all other considerations. . . . Human life is not a good to be
> preserved as a condition of other values but as an absolute basic and precious good in
> its own stead. The obligation to preserve life is commensurately all-encompassing.[38]

It follows that the value of life is not quantifiable, for, having infinite value, even
the smallest fraction of life is precious.[39] On this view, the limited "quality of life"
which a dying patient enjoys, and even the limited quantity of life which such a
person can anticipate, are irrelevant where questions of euthanasia are concerned.

Others, however, would articulate the tradition's view of the sacredness of life
and apply it to cases of euthanasia quite differently. Sherwin, for example, writes:

> . . . exceptions to the prohibition against killing and self-killing were condoned by
> classical Jewish tradition, such as cases of martyrdom and cases of "justifiable homi-
> cide." These exceptions to the rule lead one to the conclusion that the value of life
> itself is not *always* considered absolute. The permissibility and even the desirability
> of martyrdom assumes that there are occasions where life itself may be set aside
> because the preservation of life itself is not always an absolute moral imperative.[40]

If the value of life is conceived as relative rather than absolute, then it may be
permissible to take life in the interests of furthering some other goal, for example, the
alleviation of the patient's suffering. In a similar vein, it has been argued that "the
principle of sanctity of life proscribes weakening of natural vital forces, but does not
prohibit removal of unnatural life-prolonging factors."[41] Indeed, some authors cite
the "sanctity of life" principle, but appear unable or unwilling to spell out just what
this principle requires in specific cases.[42] In short, it is not immediately obvious how
these broad principles about the value of life should be applied to questions of
euthanasia, insofar as the principles, in context, make no reference to such questions
at all.

The third and final step in the interpretive process involves the application of
general principles to contemporary situations. To do this the interpreter, once
again, must determine the extent to which a new fact pattern does or does not
correspond to the facts underlying previous rulings. The problem is, as lawyers and
journalists alike are well aware, that facts can always be construed in more than one
way. To state a set of facts is already to employ categories which shape perception,
thought, and judgment. And if the "facts themselves" do not fall neatly into established categories (which they very often do not), then the very nature of the matter
at hand will be difficult to determine. Indeed, much litigation in American courts
involves precisely a dispute over which rule or principle should govern this particular case, that is, whether this case is more like one sort of previously decided case or
another.

This, of course, is precisely the situation in many areas of bio-medical ethics
where unprecedented circumstances arise with the advance of medical technology.
When a person pulls out a pistol and shoots someone point blank, we all recognize
that as an act of murder (though, of course, the penalties imposed, if any, may vary
significantly depending on the circumstances). But when a person pulls a plug on an
artificial respirator, or refuses to resuscitate a terminally ill patient, or to give
nutrition to a person in an irretrievably comatose state—is this murder or something else? Is letting a dying person die, even gently speeding up the inevitable end,
the same as actively taking life? And to what extent, if at all, should it change our

description of the situation if that individual has expressed his or her wish in advance to be allowed to die (or if that person's representative does so later)? In all these cases, the very way in which we describe the facts will influence the way in which we apply a principle to the situation at hand.[43]

Contemporary Jewish discussion of euthanasia, like all other treatments of the issue, reflect this problem. What distinguishes the Jewish discussion from others is the pool of texts and analogies from which contemporary authors draw. As we have seen, some view an artificial life-support device as analogous to a woodchopper, or to salt on a dying person's tongue, or to the woolen tufts which prolonged Haninah b. Teradyon's tortured death. Some regard disconnecting a patient from such equipment as analogous to prayers offered for the death of those suffering or terminally ill. Others, as we have seen, call these analogies into question. My only point here is that all determinations of this sort entail judgments not only about the principle embodied in the case (which in many instances is difficult enough to discern), but also about the character of the act of euthanasia itself.

The Interpretation of Texts in a Legal Tradition

Thus far I have attempted to illustrate the problems inherent in the process of applying traditional texts, and the principles which they embody, to contemporary moral problems such as euthanasia. We have seen that contemporary authorities have cited traditional Jewish texts to support a wide range of positions on questions of euthanasia. The permissibility of passive euthanasia has evoked the greatest diversity of response, some appearing to prohibit it in any form,[44] some arguing that only when a patient no longer responds to therapeutic treatments are we permitted to cease further lifesaving efforts,[45] some permitting the removal of irreversibly comatose patients from a respirator,[46] and some inclining to permit passive euthanasia in any situation of extreme or needless suffering.[47] With respect to active euthanasia, the generally accepted view that this is "absolutely forbidden" has been challenged by Byron Sherwin, who argues for a minority view within the tradition which would permit even active intervention to cause death in certain circumstances.

But my point in exploring the interpretive process and the difficulties to which it gives rise is not primarily to note the fact that contemporary authorities, like their traditional predecessors, disagree about the meaning of specific texts. Rather, I want to stress that these differences arise within a framework of shared assumptions about the nature of the entire interpretive enterprise. Whatever other differences divide them, virtually all modern Jewish ethicists are united in their perspective on both the meaning of texts and the role of the ethicist as an exegete.

The two working assumptions that govern the entire enterprise can be stated simply as follows. First, the source of contemporary Jewish values lies within the texts and, second, the job of the modern ethicist/exegete is to extract this meaning from the texts and apply it to contemporary moral problems. The texts themselves contain meaning and the interpreter merely retrieves this meaning and draws our attention to the inherent connection between the text and the contemporary world. On this view, the interpreter's role appears to be rather limited, for it is really the texts themselves which yield fruit while the exegete is only, so to speak, the midwife. It is precisely because all the authorities cited in this study understand interpretation in this same way that they encounter similar problems in the process, though, as we have seen, they address these problems differently.[48]

But in the view of many contemporary legal and literary theorists, this represents a serious misunderstanding of the interpretive process, of the meaning of texts and of the role of the interpreter in creating that meaning. To illustrate this alternative theory of exegesis and its application to Jewish ethics, I will draw on recent discussions of the nature of textual (especially constitutional) interpretation by legal theorists.

The relationship between a text and its meaning is often discussed by legal scholars in terms of the extent to which the text (of a statute, or a constitutional clause) dictates or even constrains the meaning which later interpreters can attribute to it. The question is whether the author's words, and ultimately the intentions which the author meant those words to convey, set the limits of acceptable interpretation. In constitutional interpretation, at least, some have argued that they do not. As Terrance Sandalow has claimed, the document's language plays a role in the development of constitutional law, but does not itself dictate the meaning which subsequent generations of justices see in it.

> The "goals" and "ideals" that Judge Wright sees "embedded in the constitutional language" are those that subsequent generations have found there, which is not quite the same as saying that they were put there by the framers. Contemporary constitutional law does, to be sure, rest upon a conceptual framework and employ a vocabulary that is in large measure derived from the framers. . . . Decisions continue to be justified by an analysis which begins with the proposition that the exercise of power must be referable to the 'commerce' clause or one of the other heads of federal power. . . . In making these decisions, however, the past to which we turn is the sum of our history, not merely the choices made by those who drafted and ratified the Constitution. The entirety of that history, together with current aspirations that are both shaped by it and shape the meaning derived from it, far more than the intentions of the framers, determine what each generation finds in the Constitution.[49]

On this view, the meaning of a constitutional clause is not contained in its language, but rather emerges as it is applied over time by justices whose reading of the document is shaped by aspirations some of which the framers would not have shared or even understood.

By the same token, Paul Brest has noted that many constitutional provisions are inherently "open-textured," meaning that their language requires elucidation in ways which the document itself does not provide. The clause prohibiting "cruel and unusual punishment," for example, does not define the specific meaning of those terms. What we today consider "cruel" may differ significantly from the accepted definition in the eighteenth century. So the meaning of that clause is not contained in its language, but is supplied by us as we determine the perameters of what those words permit and prohibit.[50] In this way, an existing rule actually gains new meaning each time it is applied to a new set of facts.[51]

But if meaning is not fully embedded in the text itself, it follows that interpreters do not simply retrieve something which exists independent of their efforts. Indeed, many legal (and literary) theorists have argued that meaning is a product of the interaction between text and reader. James Boyd White, in an insightful comparison of legal and literary interpretation, writes,

... reading literature is an interaction between mind and text that is like an interaction between people—it is in fact a species of that—and the expectations we bring to a text should be similar to those we bring to people we know in our lives. . . .

"The reader, both of texts and of people, changes as he or she reads: one is always learning to see more clearly what is there and to respond to it more fully— or at least differently—and in the process one is always changing in relation to text or to friend. It is in this process of learning and changing that much of the meaning of a text or of a friendship resides; the text is in fact partly about the ways in which its reader will change in reading it.[52]

White asks us to see both law and literature as sharing a common goal of challenging the reader to become a different person, to respond to the ideals and expectations which the text articulates. The meaning of a text, then, is a function of the reaction of a reader, or a community of readers, to this challenge at a given moment. Its meaning will differ from one reader to another and even for a single reader at different points in his or her life. In sum, White argues, interpreting a text is a dialectical process; each of us plays a vital role in creating the meaning which we find in the texts we read.

These views of interpretation challenge Jewish ethicists to look at textual study and exegesis in a new light. Many of those engaged in contemporary Jewish ethics are inclined to treat the provisions of talmudic and medieval texts as if they were less open-textured than in fact they are. The Jewish legal tradition does not really constitute a body of views and precedents which "speak for themselves" to contemporary issues. Rather, it offers us categories, concepts (of life, of death, of suffering, etc.), and notions of the relationships that obtain among moral agents. It provides a rich resource of values and principles which Jewish ethicists, if they are committed to remaining within the tradition, must utilize. But the texts do not, either individually or collectively, dictate how to use or apply these resources. That is up to the interpreters, whose knowledge of the texts, of the culture which produced them, and of the history of previous exegesis, enable them to respond most fully and authentically to the textual tradition. But, as White has noted, the meaning which the interpreter finds in the text will change over time and will not be consistent from one interpreter to another.

It might appear that this hermeneutical theory turns all interpretation into pure subjectivity. If the meaning of a text is imputed to it by the interpreter, there would seem to be no limits to the possibilities, no way to distinguish legitimate from illegitimate, good from bad, readings of a text. Indeed, the deconstructionists and "reader-response" critics have adopted exactly this position.[53] But, as Owen Fiss has argued, we need not abandon all notions of objectivity in interpretation in order to acknowledge the subjective role of the reader. He writes,

> The idea of objective interpretation accommodates the creative role of the reader. It recognizes that the meaning of a text does not reside in the text, as an object might reside in physical space or as an element might be said to be present in a chemical compound, ready to be extracted if only one knows the correct process; it recognizes a role for the subjective. . . . At the same time, the freedom of the interpreter is not absolute. The interpreter is not free to assign any meaning he wishes to the text. He is disciplined by a set of rules that specify the relevance and weight to be assigned to the material (e.g., words, history, intention, consequence),

as well as by those that define basic concepts and that established the procedural
circumstances under which the interpretation must occur. . . .

   Rules are not rules unless they are authoritative, and that authority can only be
conferred by a community. Accordingly, the disciplining rules that govern an interpretive activity must be seen as defining or demarcating an interpretive community
consisting of those who recognize the rules as authoritative. This means, above all
else, that the objective quality of interpretation is bounded, limited, or relative. . . . Bounded objectivity is the only kind of objectivity to which the law—or
any interpretive activity—ever aspires and the only one about which we care.[54]

Objectivity in interpretation, according to Fiss, exists whenever there are constraints acknowledged and observed by a community of interpreters. These constraints, which both are generated by communities of readers and serve to define
those communities, provide the perameters within which interpretive activity takes
place. But these constraints are never wholly determinative; they never dictate in a
mechanistic fashion the result of any act of interpretation. And as Fiss goes on to
suggest, the nature and extent of these constraints or "rules of the game," may
themselves be the subject of some disagreement within an interpretive community.
This will not undermine the objectivity of the enterprise so long as there is general
consensus on the framework within which interpretation takes place.

   The interpretation of traditional Jewish legal texts by contemporary authorities,
I would argue, proceeds in accord with Fiss's model. Here, too, as we have seen,
there is latitude for considerable diversity of legitimate interpretation. Diversity
results from the inescapable subjectivity of individual interpreters. The differences
are legitimate because there is considerable consensus on the rules that place
contraints upon the interpretive process, and so ensure that the result is objective.[55]
All contemporary Jewish authorities look to the same body of literature as a source
of precedents, that is, they are committed to the same cannon. All would acknowledge that the history of previous interpretation of the sources must be given some
weight and that the principles embodied in these sources (and not merely the words
of the texts themselves) must be interpreted. It is within these parameters that each
interpreter works, rendering a personal, but constrained and therefore objective,
judgment as to the meaning of these texts when applied to a contemporary moral
problem.

   This account of the nature of interpretation demands that contemporary Jewish
ethicists reexamine the sort of enterprise in which they are engaged. Let me illustrate my point once again using a passage on euthanasia. This one is taken from a
handbook on Jewish bio-ethics and is typical of statements found throughout the
literature.

   The Jewish attitude towards euthanasia as well as towards suicide, is based on the
   premise that "Only He Who gives life may take it away." . . . Any deliberate
   induction of death, even if the patient requests it, is an act of homicide.
      "For Judaism, human life is "created in the image of God." . . . It may thus not
   be terminated or shortened because of considerations of the patient's convenience
   or usefulness, or even our sympathy with the suffering of the patient. Thus euthanasia may not be performed either in the interest of the patient or of anyone else.
   Even individual autonomy is secondary to the sanctity of human life. . . . In Judaism suicide and euthanasia are both forms of prohibited homicide.[56]

Rosner, like so many other scholars, writes as if the tradition relates directly to contemporary moral issues. But clearly this is not the case. For if by "Judaism" we mean that body of traditional Jewish literature which Jews cite to support their claims that some view or other is sanctioned by the tradition, then it must be acknowledged that Judaism says *nothing directly at all* about disconnecting artificial respirators, or about withholding antibiotics from a patient dying of cancer, or treating an anencephalic infant, or any of the other problems of euthanasia which contemporary medical science has forced upon us.[57] As we have seen, given a properly selected set of interpretive assumptions, the text can be invoked to support a whole range of positions on such questions. We should be wary, then, of exegetes who announce that they merely discover and report what the texts say. The very process of interpretation necessitates acts of judgment on the part of the interpreter—decisions about which cases constitute precedents, what the principles of those cases are, and how they should be applied to the case at hand. And these decisions can be made responsibly and authentically in a variety of ways. It follows that the interpretive assumptions that readers bring to the literature play a decisive role in creating the very meaning that they attribute to the text. And if this is true generally, it is especially true for interpreters of classical Jewish texts, which are notoriously terse and ambiguous. Then too the creative role of the interpreter will be still more pronounced when the task at hand is to apply these classical texts to complex, wholly unprecedented dilemmas created by rapidly advancing biomedical technology.

But, it will be objected, if we view the interpretive process in this way, do we not undermine the entire enterprise of contemporary Jewish ethics? How can contemporary authorities claim to render normative Jewish judgments, in Jakobovits's words, "apply[ing] to contemporary perplexities insights that . . . are imbedded in virtually all the layers of our literature going back to earliest biblical times?" To the extent that the meaning of a text lies as much in the activity of the interpreter as in the text itself, contemporary Jewish ethics becomes at least partly a matter of reading our values into the texts rather than deriving authentically Jewish views from them. And if eisegesis replaces exegesis, what is the point of doing Jewish ethics, or rather, what makes Jewish ethics Jewish and not just the subjective judgment of an individual reader?

In attempting to answer these questions, let me turn to a model of jurisprudence suggested by Ronald Dworkin. His work, which has received considerable attention among legal theorists, addresses the very problem which faces contemporary Jewish ethicists—the interplay between the constraints imposed by the textual tradition and the freedom inherent in the personal judgment of the interpreter. Dworkin suggests that judges who interpret a legal tradition are doing much the same thing as authors who interpret the literary creativity of their predecessors. Indeed, he asks us to imagine a series of authors who write a novel one chapter at a time. Each author (after the first) inherits the work of earlier writers in the series and so is given a kind of limited creative license, for the author's literary imagination must work within boundaries (however fluid) which have been established by previous writers. The need to preserve a sense of coherence within the novel will provide a general framework within which successive novelists will do their work. Building upon this example, Dworkin proceeds to argue that,

Deciding hard cases at law is rather like this strange literary exercise. The similarity is most evident when judges consider and decide common law cases; that is, when no statute figures centrally in the legal issue, and the argument turns on which rules or principles of law "underlie" the related decisions of other judges in the past. Each judge is then like a novelist in the chain. He or she must read through what other judges in the past have written, not only to discover what these judges have said, or their state of mind when they said it, but to reach an opinion about what these judges have collectively *done,* in the way that each of our novelists formed an opinion about the collective novel so far written. Any judge forced to decide a lawsuit will find, if he looks in the approriate books, records of many arguably similar cases decided over decades or even centuries past by many other judges of different styles and judicial and political philosophies, in periods of different ortho-doxies of procedure and judicial convention. Each judge must regard himself, in deciding the new case before him, as a partner in a complex chain enterprise of which these innumerable decisions, structures, conventions, and practices are the history; it is his job to continue that history into the future through what he does on the day. He *must* interpret what has gone before because he has a responsibility to advance the enterprise in hand rather than strike out in some new direction of his own. So he must determine, according to his own judgment, what the earlier decisions come to, what the point or theme of the practice so far, taken as a whole, really is.[58]

Dworkin's conception of legal interpretation enables us to account both for the latitude and the constraints which judges in all legal traditions inevitably confront. He goes on to suggest,

This flexibility may seem to erode the difference on which I insist, between interpre-tation and a fresh, clean-slate decision about what the law ought to be. But there is nevertheless this overriding constraint. Any judge's sense of the point or function of law, on which every aspect of his approach to interpretation will depend, will include or imply some conception of the integrity and coherence of law as an institution, and this conception will both tutor and constrain his working theory of fit—that is, his convictions about how much of the prior law an interpretation must fit, and which of it and how.[59]

The function of the judge, or of the contemporary Jewish ethicist, then, is not to filter out his or her own interpretive framework, but rather to use that framework to create a coherent tradition, encompassing both the body of legal precedents and the case at hand.[60] It follows that when contemporary Jewish authorities, armed with a body of traditional Jewish sources, confront a contemporary moral problem, the decision that they reach, through interpretation and application of those sources, will be guided by a sense of what "fits" the tradition. And this sense of "fit," in turn, will be shaped by a particular way of construing the coherence of the tradition as a whole, as it relates both to the particular question at hand and, no doubt, to other aspects of the tradition as well. This is precisely what makes contem-porary Jewish ethics Jewish, the commitment of those engaged in the exercise to render a judgment which accords with their own sense of the thrust of the tradition as it has evolved. Among contemporary Jewish ethicists, of course, there are many diverse conceptions of the coherence of the tradition as a whole and it would take us too far afield to sketch them here and trace their implications for the question of euthanasia in particular. Nonetheless, Dworkin's discussion enables us to see more clearly what interpreting a tradition entails and how this activity by its nature imposes certain constraints upon the interpreter while necessitating a certain degree of "interpretive license."

Contemporary Jewish Ethics—A Reassessment

I want now to explore the implications of the hermeneutical theory sketched here for the practice of contemporary Jewish ethics. In my judgment, contemporary Jewish ethics can absorb this understanding of the interpretive process without losing its raison d'être, though the fundamental questions raised above will need to be answered in a new way. Given this understanding of the interpretive process, we need to rethink the way that we conceive of Jewish ethics. A number of semantic, methodological and conceptual adjustments appear to be in order.

On the level of semantics, Jewish ethicists should avoid talking about what specific positions "Judaism" sanctions on contemporary issues. To do so, as I have argued, is seriously to misrepresent the nature of the enterprise in which one in engaged. Accordingly, the rhetoric of Jewish ethics should change from "what Judaism teaches" to "what we, given our particular interpretive assumptions and our particular way of constructing the coherence of the tradition as a whole, find within the traditional sources."[61] The difference is hardly a trivial one, nor is it only a matter of insisting upon a kind of "truth in advertising." I do not suppose that contemporary Jewish ethicists have deliberately set out to deceive their readers, or that they themselves are unaware of the spectrum of opinion which the foregoing analysis has highlighted. Yet, if contemporary Jewish ethicists presented their views in the more precise, qualified way that I have suggested, they would be forced to confront more self-consciously than they have their own role in the interpretive process.[62]

Because this fact has been obscured by the language of contemporary Jewish ethicists, a further important problem in this field has gone largely unaddressed. It is the working assumption of most of the authors cited in this study that to develop an authentic Jewish position on some contemporary moral problem one need only cite texts and draw conclusions from them. With rare exceptions (Novak, Weisbard), these authors have not attempted to defend their particular way of selecting and reading the sources against other possible or actual readings. Much less have they found it necessary to articulate a view of the coherence of the Jewish tradition as a whole in terms of which they have chosen to make interpretive decisions in one way as against another. As a result, it could be said that much contemporary Jewish discourse resembles a conversation in which the participants are talking past, rather than to, one another. If the foregoing analysis is substantially correct, it follows that any contemporary Jewish position is only as compelling as the interpretive assumptions on which it rests. To defend cogently any particular ethical position, then, requires that one offer reasons for adopting the interpretive stance that one has. Of course, these reasons may or may not be compelling to those who approach the texts with other interpretive theories. But, if interpretation is to be more than ad hoc decision-making, it must rest upon a theoretical foundation. And if one wishes to urge others to adopt a particular interpretation, that theory must be stated explicitly and defended. In American jurisprudence, producing, a "reasoned opinion" and defending it against competing opinions is standard procedure. Contemporary Jewish ethicists should do no less.

Moreover, given the obvious parallels between Jewish ethics as it is practiced by most contemporary authorities and Anglo-American jurisprudence, it is most unfortunate that Jewish ethicists have largely ignored developments in American legal theory. As I have noted throughout this paper, contemporary Jewish ethics as practiced by all the authorities discussed above is based on a kind of judicial model. This is most obvious when Jewish discussions of issues like euthanasia are juxtaposed with those of philosophers and of Christian ethicists who approach the topic from an entirely nonlegal perspective.[63] Of course, the Orthodox authorities cited here self-consciously do Jewish ethics within the framework of *halakhah*. Yet, even for those who do not view themselves as operating within a strictly *halakhic* framework,[64] the tradition of *halakhic* texts is the primary resource upon which they base their views. Virtually without exception, they formulate their own contemporary Jewish position in response to and in the attempt to maintain an essential continuity with *halakhic* precedent. But for this very reason, theories of judicial interpretation and of legal reasoning in general have much to offer those doing contemporary Jewish ethics. If more attention were given to the literature in general jurisprudence, Jewish authorities might gain both a fuller understanding of the nature of legal interpretation and useful models for thinking about the interplay between the authority of a textual tradition and the freedom inherent in the exercise of judicial discretion.

Finally, in no sense do I wish to suggest, given the subjective nature of interpretation as I have described it, that Jewish ethicists should quit reading traditional texts. Rather, it has been my assumption throughout this paper that what makes contemporary Jewish ethics Jewish is its attempt to develop positions which carry forward the views contained within that long textual tradition. I simply wish to spell out what is actually involved when contemporary Jewish ethicists engage in such exegesis and to suggest that, if this description is accurate, the ways in which people currently conceptualize the field need to be reexamined. I would propose that contemporary Jewish ethics be conceived, not as an attempt to determine what past authorities would say about contemporary problems if they were alive today, but as a dialectical relationship in which finally no sharp distinction can be make between our voices and theirs. What we discover through this relationship with sages of the past certainly will not be less valid just because it cannot finally be attributed solely to the authorities of past generations. Any reading of the texts that we produce, and any conclusions we draw from them, are as much our work as theirs. Those engaged in contemporary Jewish ethics surely need not quit reading texts, but just as surely they need to make more modest claims on their behalf.[65]

Notes

1. Immanuel Jakobovits, "Ethical Problems Regarding the Termination of Life," in Rabbi Levi Meier (ed.), *Jewish Values in Bioethics* (New York, 1986), p. 84.

2. I say "derive," for virtually all contemporary Jewish ethicists cite biblical and rabbinic texts as the basis for what they present as the "Jewish view" on a given ethical issue. Yet one must be cautious about taking these contemporary discussions at face value. It could be

the case that these views have not really been derived from the texts but developed quite independently and then "validated" by citing traditional Jewish sources. Notwithstanding this potential problem, we are in a position to analyze only the arguments which these authors have committed to writing. My analysis proceeds, then, on the assumption that these writers sincerely believe that the texts they cite support the conclusions they reach.

3. For a bibliography of articles in English, see S. Daniel Breslauer, *Modern Jewish Morality* (New York, 1986), pp. 67–76.

4. For a discussion of legal reasoning as "analogical," see Edward H. Levi, "The Nature of Judicial Reasoning," in Sidney Hook (ed.), *Law and Philosophy* (New York: New York University Press, 1964), pp. 263–81.). David Novak, writing about identifying precedents within traditional sources for contemporary problems, agrees that halakhic reasoning is based on analogizing and suggests that the theological or philosophical views of the decisor will shape the way an authority selects analogies from within the tradition. "Judaism and Contemporary Bioethics," *Journal of Medicine and Philosophy*, vol. 4, no. 4(1979), p. 358.

5. B.T. *Ketubot* 104a.

6. Rabbenu Nissim, commentary to B.T. *Nedarim* 40a.

7. *Yalkut Shimoni, Proverbs,* # 943.

8. The definition of the *goses* and the problems of applying such rules to cases involving euthanasia will be discussed in greater detail below.

9. *Sefer Hasidim* 234 [ed. Margaliot].

10. Solomon B. Freehof, "Allowing the Terminal Patient to Die," in Walter Jacobs (ed), *American Reform Responsa* (New York, 1983), pp. 258–59.

11. Byron Sherwin, "Euthanasia: A Jewish View," *Journal of Aging and Judaism*, vol. 2, no. 1 (Fall 1987), p. 47.

12. Asher Bar-Zev, "Euthanasia: A Classical Ethical Problem in a Modern Context," *Reconstructionist,* vol. 44, no. 9 (1979), pp. 13–14.

13. Alan Weisbard, "On the Bioethics of Jewish Law: The Case of Karen Quinlan," *Israel Law Review,* vol. 14(1979), p. 353.

14. See, for example, Barry D. Cytron and Earl Schwartz, *When Life Is in the Balance* (New York, 1986), who cite and discuss some sources (notably B.T. *Sanhedrin* 78a and *Mishneh Torah, Hilchot Rotze'ah* 2:7), which are discussed by none of the other authors cited in this study.

15. B.T. *Avodah Zarah* 18a. The text goes on to indicate that the executioner then committed suicide by leaping into the fire. A voice from Heaven announced that both Haninah and the executioner had been assigned a place in the world-to-come, whereupon Rabbi wept at the thought that one individual was granted immortality in a single hour, while another only after many years. The conclusion of the story, while curious in a number of respects, appears to add nothing to the discussion of euthanasia and so is generally not cited in contemporary treatments of the issue.

16. Sherwin, "Euthanasia: A Jewish View," pp. 42–43. So too Asher Bar-Zev argues on the basis of this text that one may remove life-support systems which are maintaining the life of a terminal patient. "Euthanasia: A Classical Ethical Problem in a Modern Context," pp. 14–15. Moshe D. Tendler cites the case of Hanina ben Tradyon in support of the proposition that, "if he [the patient] requests the discontinuance of therapy, emphasizing his inability to cope with his pain-filled existence, the absence of any real hope for cure makes this request binding on all who minister to him." "Torah Ethics Prohibit Natural Death," *Sh'ma,* vol. 7, no. 132(April 15, 1977), p. 98.

17. It seems that Novak needs to defend this position more fully, insofar as legal authorities not uncommonly refer to biblical and talmudic narratives in their opinions. In legal discussions concerning suicide, for example, the story of Saul's death (1 Sam. 31) figures prominently; see *Shulchan Aruch, Yoreh Deah*, 345:3 and several later sources as cited and

discussed in Basil Herring, *Jewish Ethics and Halakhah for Our Time* (New York, 1984), pp. 75–76.

18. Cited in Herring, *Jewish Ethics and Halakhah for our Time*, pp. 83–84.

19. *Mishnah Semahot* 1:4.

20. Maimonides, *Mishneh Torah,* Laws of Mourning, 4:5.

21. *Sefer Hasidim* 723 [ed. Margaliot].

22. R. Moses Isserles (*Rema*) on *Shulchan Aruch, Yoreh Deah* 339:1.

23. See *Shulchan Aruch, Yoreh Deah,* 339:2 and *Even ha-Ezer* 121:7.

24. Cited in Amos Shapira "The Human Right to Die—Some Israeli and Jewish Legal Perspectives," in Andre de Vries and Amnon Carmi (eds.), *The Dying Human,* (Ramat Gan, 1979) p. 268.

25. Ronald Green, "Contemporary Jewish Bioethics: A Critical Assessment," in E. E. Shelp (ed.), *Theology and Bioethics* (New York, 1985), pp. 254–55.

26. Marc Gellman, "Babies Doe, an Analysis and Response," *Sh'ma,* vol. 14, no. 274 (May 11, 1984), p. 108.

27. Seymour Siegel, "Biomedical Ethics," *Sh'ma,* vol. 14, no. 274 (May 11, 1984), p. 110.

28. Weisbard, "On the Bioethics of Jewish Law: The Case of Karen Quinlan," p. 357.

29. Immanuel Jakobovits, *Jewish Medical Ethics* (New York, 1975), p. 124.

30. Cited in Herring, *Jewish Ethics and Halakhah for our Time,* p. 84.

31. Freehof, "Allowing the Terminal Patient to Die," pp. 259–60.

32. Fred Rosner, *Modern Medicine and Jewish Ethics* (Hoboken, 1986), p. 200. Rosner goes on to question the possibility of making such a distinction between shortening the process of death and interrupting life. It seems that the use of the texts cited as the basis for passive euthanasia is problematic in this view.

33. Gellman, "Babies Doe: An Analysis and Response," p. 108.

34. David Novak, *Law and Theology in Judaism.* Second Series. (New York, 1976), p. 105.

35. Karl Llewellyn, *The Bramble Bush* (New York, 1960), p. 76.

36. Weisbard, "On the Bioethics of Jewish Law," p. 347.

37. The question of how to apply the values imbedded in these sources to contemporary cases becomes even more complex when we consider those individuals who are not technically in the category of *goses.* How, for example, should these sources be applied to cases of initiating life-support systems for anencephalic infants who have no hope of surviving, or of treating infections in terminal cancer patients who are not in the final throes of death, but who, without such measures, will die much sooner. The answers are not at all apparent.

38. Cited in Shapira, "The Human Right to Die: Some Israeli and Jewish Legal Perspectives," p. 366.

39. Jakobovits, "Ethical Problems Regarding the Termination of Life," pp. 88–89.

40. Sherwin, "Euthanasia: A Jewish View," p. 45.

41. Shapira, "The Human Right to Die—Some Israeli and Jewish Legal Perspectives," p. 368.

42. Sid Leiman, "The Karen Ann Quinlan Case: A Jewish Perspective," *Gratz College Annual of Jewish Studies,* vol. 6 (1977), pp. 43–50.

43. Consider, for example, the diametrically opposed ways in which antiabortion and abortion rights advocates describe the very same act—as "killing innocent life," or as "terminating an unwanted pregnancy."

44. In addition to the views of Novak cited above, see Simon Federbush, "The Problem of Euthanasia in the Jewish Tradition," *Judaism,* vol. 1 (1952), pp. 64–68, and Yaakov Weinberger, "Euthanasia in Jewish Religious Law," *Dine Yisrael,* vol. 7 (1976) pp. 99–127 [in Hebrew].

45. This position, as noted above, is adopted by Rosner. See also David Feldman, *Health and Medicine in Jewish Tradition* (New York, 1986), pp. 91–96.

46. This view is endorsed by Siegel, Jakobovits, and Feinstein.

47. In addition to the views of Freehof discussed above, see Hillel Cohn, "Natural Death—Humane, Just and Jewish," *Sh'ma,* vol. 7, no. 132 (April 15, 1979), pp. 99–101, and G. B. Halibard, "Euthanasia," *Jewish Law Annual,* vol. 1 (1968), pp. 196–99.

48. These differences are attributable to a whole range of differences among contemporary Jewish ethicists, most notably, their divergent views of the very authority of the *halakhah.* Yet, non-*halakhic* perspectives may also influence a rabbi's view of euthanasia. One case in point might be Novak's essay cited above which incorporates a thorough review of *halakhic* sources and of philosophical positions bearing on euthanasia, but then ends by connecting the practice of euthanasia with the spectre of Nazi genocide. He concludes his essay with the words, "if Judaism is not convincing, perhaps the modern Jewish experience is." *Law and Theology in Judaism,* p. 117. As Theodoro Forcht Dagi notes, "the spectre of genocide surrounds the entire question of euthanasia." "The Paradox of Euthanasia," *Judaism,* vol. 24 (1975), p. 163. The extent to which such considerations influence an author's reading of the sources is impossible to know. See also Green, "Contemporary Jewish Bioethics: A Critical Assessment," pp. 262–64, for an analysis of some sociological factors which, he argues, account for the conservative drift of much contemporary Jewish literature in the area of bioethics.

49. Terrance Sandalow, "Constitutional Interpretation," *Michigan Law Review,* vol. 79 (1981), pp. 1049–50.

50. Brest relies here on Ronald Dworkin, *Taking Rights Seriously,* (Cambridge, 1978), pp. 134–36, who notes that the Constitution supplies us with a *concept* ("cruel"), but not with a specific *conception* of cruelty or a set of criteria for applying that concept.

51. As Paul A. Freund has written, "The meaning of a rule . . . is . . . shaped in its application, which is a dialectical process that sharpens our appreciation of the rule and the facts alike." "An Analysis of Legal Reasoning," in Sidney Hook (ed.), *Law and Philosophy* (New York, 1964), p. 285.

52. James Boyd White, *Heracles' Bow* (Madison, 1985), pp. 90–91.

53. Stanley Fish, *Is There a Text in This Class?* (Cambridge, 1980) is among the most prominent exponents of this radical view of interpretation.

54. Owen Fiss, "Objectivity and Interpretation," *Stanford University Law Review,* vol. 34 (1982), pp. 744–45.

55. It could be argued that among contemporary Jewish authorities there is far less consensus on these matters than, say, within the American legal community. Perhaps liberal Jews, who have little if any commitment to the halachic process, constitute, in Fiss's terms, a different interpretive community with its own rules. Still, I would suggest that, at least those liberals such as Freehof who have written responsa on contemporary problems do in fact share with more traditional authorities a common framework of interpretive assumptions. It should be remembered that the American legal community encompasses a wide spectrum of views about the rules that govern (or should govern) constitutional interpretation; for a summary of current theories, see Paul Brest, "The Misconceived Quest for the Original Understanding," *Boston University Law Review,* vol. 60 (1980), pp. 204–38.

56. Fred Rosner (with David M. Feldman), *Compendium on Medical Ethics* (New York, 1984), p. 106.

57. Philip A. Bardfelt acknowledges this implicitly when he comments, "In some cases, there may be no precedent [for contemporary cases] in Jewish law or history. . . . " "Jewish Medical Ethics," *Reconstructionist,* vol. 42, no. 6 (1976), p. 7.

58. Ronald Dworkin, *A Matter of Principle* (Cambridge, 1985), p. 159. Dworkin's distinction between advancing the current enterprise and striking out in a new direction has been challenged by Fish who regards meaning as wholly a function of the reader's activity

("Working on the Chain Gang: Interpretation in the Law and in Literary Criticism," *Critical Inquiry,* vol. 9 (Sept. 1982), pp. 207–8.) Dworkin has responded to these criticisms, much as Fiss has, in terms of a limited notion of objectivity (*A Matter of Principle,* pp. 167–77). For a critical review of the Fish-Dworkin controversy, see R.V. Young, "Constitutional Interpretation and Literary Theory." *The Intercollegiate Review,* vol. 23, no. 1 (1987), pp. 49–60.

59. Dworkin, *A Matter of Principle,* p. 161.

60. This view is consistent with the following passages taken from Joel Roth's discussion of the role of judicial discretion in *halakha.* He writes, ". . . widespread agreement with one position in a matter of judicial discretion puts the full weight of precedent behind that position, and, as a general rule, dictates that the arbiter abide by it. . . . Yet it must be stressed again that even the full weight of precedent does not elevate the position it favors to an absolutely definitive matter of law. . . . The right of the judge to exercise his discretion in favor of the nonprecedented position is restricted only if he is unable to offer any cogent reason or evidence for his rejection of the precedented position. If he can offer them, his right to exercise his judicial discretion as he sees fit is, in fact, undeniable." *The Halakhic Process: A Systemic Analysis* (New York, 1986), p. 93.

61. A similar point has been made by Menachem Kellner, who writes, "Although many writers persist in presenting the Jewish position on various subjects, it very often ought more correctly to be characterized as *a* Jewish position." *Contemporary Jewish Ethics* (New York, 1978), p. 15.

62. It is striking that none of the major works in contemporary Jewish bioethics by Jakobovits, Bleich, Feldman, or Rosner addresses the methodological or hermeneutical issues outlined in this paper.

63. For some philosophical and Christian discussions of the ethics of euthanasia, see Marvin Kohl (ed.), *Beneficent Euthanasia* (Buffalo, 1975); Charles Curran, *Politics, Medicine and Christian Ethics* (Philadelphia, 1973); Paul Ramsey, *The Patient as Person* (New Haven 1970), esp. chap. 3, "On (Only) Caring for the Dying"; and John Ladd, (ed.), *Ethical Issues Relating to Life and Death* (Oxford, 1979).

64. In the words of Hillel Cohn, "But the conscious choice not to be bound by the *halacha* does not exempt me from examining as thoroughly as possible what the Jewish legal tradition says. . . . We are concerned about what the past says. We hold with Mordecai Kaplan that the past (the *halacha* in this case) has a vote but not a veto—or, as Solomon Freehof puts it, 'Rabbinic law is our guidance but not our governance; it is advisory but not directive.' " "Natural Death: Humane, Jewish and Just," pp. 99–100. See also Bardfelt, "Jewish Medical Ethics," p. 7, who suggests that the heritage of biblical and talmudic law should be supplemented with considerations of scientific knowledge, civil law and our conception of individual rights when we seek to develop guidelines in the area of Jewish medical ethics.

65. An earlier draft of this paper was read at the 1988 meeting of the Academy for Jewish Philosophy. I wish to express my appreciation for the helpful suggestions which I received from colleagues on that occasion. I would also like to acknowledge the many friends and colleagues whose critical comments on earlier drafts of this paper were extremely beneficial: Sheldon Berkowitz, David Blumenthal, Barry Cytron, Howard Eilberg-Schwartz, Martin Jaffee, Paul Lauritzen, Daniel Mandil, Riv-Ellen Prell, Mark Rotenberg, Earl Schwartz and Michael Zuckert.

11

A Methodology for Jewish
Medical Ethics

ELLIOT N. DORFF

The Problem

Every legal system seeks to provide for both constancy and change. Without legal constancy, individuals can never know what can be legitimately expected of them or what they can expect of others. This robs a legal system of some of its chief assets—namely, its ability to impart a measure of stability to the society it serves and to adjudicate disputes within that society with fairness. On the other hand, without the ability to accommodate change, a legal system can soon become irrelevant to the ongoing life of the community. It may thereby preserve its theoretical purity, but it simultaneously loses its ability to articulate the rules by which society actually operates. It thus forfeits its very rationale, for that was the whole reason people were interested in it in the first place.

This tension between continuity and change is probably most acutely felt in our day in the area of medical ethics, for truly revolutionary changes have occurred in the medical landscape. In the United States, for example, life expectancy at the turn of the century was between forty and forty-five years of age for both men and women, and now it is almost double that. Public health measures, like indoor plumbing, pervasive education to wash one's hands and to bathe frequently, and mass inoculation against some of the most common diseases have statistically been the most significant factor in this change. Antibiotics, a discovery barely fifty years old, has been the second most important element in this change. The new machinery, drug therapies, and methods of surgery of the last several decades, although undoubtedly the most widely publicized element in the new medical picture, are still only responsible for a statistically small increment in life expectancy, and the promise of genetic engineering to alter this situation is still to be realized in the future.

Now, of course, most of these developments are a blessing; otherwise, medical researchers would not have sought to achieve them! They raise, however, new and difficult moral questions. When medical science could only cut out a problem surgically or relieve its pain, there was no decision to be made, for human beings simply could not do much to lengthen life or improve its quality. Now, however, we can. Kant pointed out that moral responsibility only properly devolves upon a person who can act; we are now experiencing the converse of that, namely, that an increase in our ability to act raises new questions as to how we *should* act and imposes new obligations to act responsibly in areas which we never had to confront before. In other words, if "ought" logically entails "can," "can" may or may not morally entail "ought."

When we look to our legal systems to provide guidance in these matters in a straightforward way, however, we find them wanting. The combined effect of all of these medical developments is that statutes and precedents from not so long ago often seem remarkably out of place in addressing contemporary medical dilemmas. As a result, every legal system in our time finds itself stretching to the limit to accommodate the difficult questions raised by our new ability to affect the length and quality of life.

Jewish law is no exception. Although Jews have had a veritable love affair with medicine through the last millennium and even before, Jews were no more able than non-Jews to extend or significantly improve a person's medical history. It is, therefore, surprising that there are *any* precedents whatsoever on many of the subjects which currently concern us. As soon as we look at them, however, we see the difficulties in applying them to contemporary circumstances. If we examine the precedents which have been widely used to shed light on issues at the end of life, for example, we find that some of them are not properly medical; they speak, for instance, of Rabbi Hananya ben Tradeyon's responses to his students who were trying to relieve his suffering while he was being burned at the stake, and Rabbi Yehudah Hanasi's handmaiden interrupting the prayers of her master's students so that the rabbi could die. Others, while medical, bear little resemblance to contemporary medical contexts. They speak, for example, of the efficacy of salt on the tongue or a knocking noise coming through an open window to extend life. That is hardly the world of respirators and gastrointestinal tubes.

As a result, to address contemporary medical issues Jewish law will indeed have to extend itself considerably. It *must* do so if it is going to be at all relevant to some of the most critical issues of modernity. This, however, will require it to face some deeply rooted philosophical questions regarding the way it accommodates constancy and change—and, indeed, the way people interpret and apply texts in the first place. What *should* the methodology of Jewish law be in addressing these radically new realities?

Legal versus Nonlegal Models

Almost all Jews who have written about biomedical issues in our day have primarily, if not exclusively, used Jewish legal sources and methods. Conservative and Reform authors differ, of course, from Orthodox writers in the ways they identify the meaning of classical texts, the former adding historical and cross-cultural considerations to the traditional commentaries used by the latter. Authors from the three streams of American Judaism, and their counterparts elsewhere, differ even more in the ways they apply those sources to contemporary circumstances and the degrees to which they and their intended audiences feel obligated to follow the tradition, however it is interpreted. What unites them, however, is their assumption that policies in biomedical areas, as in all others, must be determined through interpreting and applying the *legal* precedents and statutes of the Jewish tradition. While this methodology comes naturally to Jews, it is by no means the only way to approach these matters, as even a cursory comparison to Catholic, Protestant, and secular treatments of these issues will clearly demonstrate.[1]

In a recent paper, Rabbi David Ellenson, an important Reform ideologue at Hebrew Union College in Los Angeles, has pointed out that, largely because of the wide disparity between contemporary medical conditions and those of times past, but also for some other reasons, some rabbis in all three of the major movements of American Judaism have suggested abandoning legal methodology altogether. They claim that applying legal methods to earlier sources is playing fast and loose with the sources and is simultaneously not doing justice to the issues at hand now. Instead, these writers are individually developing an alternative, nonlegal approach which Ellenson, following Rabbi Irving Greenberg, calls "covenantal."

> This approach is marked by the dialectical, personal model of relationship between God and humanity found in the Bible. It affirms the belief that "humankind is created so as to be God's partner in completing creation." This means that God's covenant with Israel does not restrict human freedom, but presupposes it. . . . This means that one must search out the tradition for those precedents relevant to the making of an ethical decision. Not to do so would provide an unwarranted break with a huge dimension of the tradition and would deny Jews the wisdom such precedents have to offer. However, this theory also affirms that since human beings are created in the image of God, they share in God's power. . . . In short, human autonomy—the ability of individual persons to make and to act upon their own ethical decisions—derives from the freedom that God has given persons. The affirmation of human autonomy is not the product of Enlightenment thought. Rather, it receives a divine, religious warrant.[2]

In this approach, the rabbi, while certainly a resource for the patient, family, and health care personnel, is not the ultimate arbiter of what is moral in any given case; the individual patient is. As a result, if the patient so chooses, quality-of-life considerations can enter directly into medical decisions, contrary to the bulk of rabbinic opinion to date.

I understand the allure of this approach; as Ellenson says, it "empowers" individuals to make their own decisions, and who does not want to do that? Moreover, the realities of contemporary medicine are indeed very different from those of our ancestors—so much so that one (sometimes) wonders whether *any* reading of the sources can properly give guidance to our decisions. Greenberg also claims that the Holocaust has shown us what terrible things can happen when individuals do *not* take control and responsibility for their own decisions. All of these factors make this suggestion not only innovative, but serious.

Nevertheless, I think that it is wrongheaded. My view ultimately rests upon three factors: (a) my appreciation of the *strengths* of a legal approach to the moral issues in life, and the corresponding weaknesses of the suggested alternative; (b) my conviction that personal responsibility *can* be retained in a properly understood *halakhic* system; and (c) my confidence that, *when properly understood and applied,* legal methods can enable Jewish law to treat realities as new as contemporary medical phenomena. I shall explain the first two assertions in this section, and the third in the next.

Over the course of history, human beings have decided moral issues in a variety of ways, each with its strengths and weaknesses. Some religions and secular systems, for example, depend upon the decision of a specific person, chosen for a variety of reasons (e.g., Catholicism). Others ask the individual to exercise his or her own conscience to resolve moral dilemmas (e.g., Protestantism). Some secular systems decide these matters by majority vote, at least in theory. Judaism, however, has historically depended upon a judical mode, blending exegeses of the Torah and later rabbinic literature, precedents, and customs to arrive at a decision. No method is a foolproof path to moral sensitivity and wisdom, and each one can be abused. Nevertheless, the features inherent in these various procedures give us grounds for analyzing and predicting their respective strengths and weaknesses.

In comparison to the other methods mentioned, the judicial way of deciding moral issues, used by Judaism, has the distinct advantage of continuity, for the determinative parties in the other procedures—a specific person, each individual, or a majority of a society—can switch gears at any moment. A judge may innovate as well, but he or she must justify the innovation in terms of the past tradition. This does not assure a good decision, and it does not even guarantee that the present decision will be a clear-cut copy of past policies; but it does ensure that the tradition will be taken seriously into account and that a thoughtful rationale may be demanded of a judge who deviates from it. Jews have historically adopted this method because they believed that this was the only way to preserve the divine authority of the tradition, but such continuity is also crucial to preserve the identity of a people as widely scattered as Jews are. Moreover, the inherent conservatism of the judicial mode enables it to bring to bear the wisdom of the past without being enslaved to it—at least if judges are adept at judicial methods of stretching the law when necessary. Judgment calls are clearly central to this method, and not everyone will agree with any given decision; but the continuity, authority, and coherence which this method produces, together with its ability to balance the past with the needs of the present, are clear advantages which should not be lightly discarded.

In contrast, a method which seeks to determine morality on the basis of each individual's interaction with God poses a severe danger of anarchy, for each person will be on his or her own in determining what is right and good. One wonders how community is supposed to be maintained under such a system. Reform ideologues like Rabbi Eugene Borowitz have claimed that Jews are identified by their common commitment to the Covenant, but I, for one, doubt whether that has any meaning in practice without specification of authoritative norms under that Covenant.

Moreover, this "covenantal" method ironically robs individuals of precisely what they seek when they turn to religion for guidance in these matters, for it tells them to seek God and decide for themselves! The Reform movement, committed to this kind of autonomy, has even produced a body of responsa in an attempt to inform people of how some rabbis, at least, understand the tradition, but ultimately these responsa cannot relieve individuals of any of the responsibility of such decisions, for on this model, everyone bears the full weight of moral culpability for the decisions they make.

In one sense, of course, individuals should take responsibility for decisions which affect their lives so deeply, and this brings me to my second point. For Rabbi Irving Greenberg, one lesson of the Holocaust is that people should not depend upon the law to tell them what is right and proper, for the legal mode carries with it the ultimate danger of legitimating morally atrocious acts. He is clearly right in his warning, but certainly even he must admit that the Nazis' use of law constitued an *abuse* of it. The correct lesson to learn from that event, I would say, is *not* that, because of this danger, the law should be abandoned as a way of determining moral decisions, but rather that individuals retain the obligation to examine any law or ruling for its morality and to disobey all laws and rulings which are immoral on their face.

This, of course, is not an easy criterion to use, especially in morally complex matters such as those posed by contemporary medicine, for one person's judgment about these issues may well differ from another's. If a legal system is working properly, however, those adhering to it *should* be able to depend on it to guide them through morally murky waters, and they would need to disobey the law only in cases of obvious and gross moral perversion. Jewish law clearly assumes both elements of this methodology: it asserts that God's law is just and good, and it bids us obey the rabbis' interpretation of that law in each generation; but it also requires that we go beyond the letter of the law and even disobey it when it—or a given interpretation of it—is mean-spirited or downright immoral.[3] Thus personal responsibility *can* and *would* be retained in a properly understood *halakhic* system, but the burden of moral responsibility would not fully and exclusively devolve upon the individual.

Weighing the Applicability of Precedents

How, though, should we apply Jewish law to contemporary medical questions?

In the long interaction between Judaism and medicine, Jews have not flinched from exploring and applying whatever could help people overcome illness, seeing this process not as an infringement upon God's prerogatives, but as aiding God in the process of creation. In doing this, they have been remarkably open to seeking and using new discoveries. Medieval rabbis-physicians, in fact, largely ignored express talmudic passages detailing specific cures which they found to be ineffective.[4] They saw their overarching duty in this area to be the healing of the sick, even when that required deviating from precedents encased in legal sources.

Our situation is similar. When we turn to many of the issues in contemporary bioethics, we are confronted with the fact that precedents within the tradition assume a context radically different from our own. Those dealing with extending the life of the dying, for instance, number very few and, more significantly, assume far less human ability than we now have to affect the condition of the dying.

Orthodox rabbis, by and large, have nevertheless taken their customary, literalist approach. Some have indeed been ingenious in making the few precedents available seem to determine the outcome of contemporary questions; Basil Herring's *Jewish Ethics and Halakhah for Our Time* is an especially thorough and fair presentation of their various attempts to do this on many issues. This procedure, however, ignores the historical context of past medical decisions and the crucial differences between medical conditions then and now. In Arthur Danto's felicitous phrase, such responses to the issues are paradigm examples of "misplaced slyness." The sources simply did not contemplate the realities of modern medicine; for that matter, American legal sources from as late as the 1940s did not do so either.

Consequently, reading such laws and precedents closely to arrive at decisions about contemporary medical therapies all too often amounts to sheer sophistry. The texts themselves in such attempts are not providing clear guidance but are rather being twisted to mean whatever a particular rabbi or judge wants them to mean.

In a different form, in truth, this is simply legal method. To bring new situations under the umbrella of the law, judges in any legal system must often stretch precedents to make them relevant to new circumstances. Indeed, for a legal system to retain continuity and authority in current decisions, this *must* be done. Thus, in our case, if a decision is going to be *Jewish* in some recognizable way, it *must* invoke the tradition in a serious, and not a perfunctory, way. One *can* do this without being devious or anachronistic *if one does not pretend that one's own interpretation is its originally intended meaning* (*its* peshat) *or its only possible reading.* The Conservative objection to many Orthodox readings of texts is thus both to tone and method: not only do many Orthodox responsa make such pretensions, often with an air of dogmatic certainty, but they do so with blatant disregard for the effects of historical and literary context on the meaning of texts and for the multitude of meanings that writings can often legitimately have.

Even if we set aside such matters of intellectual honesty, on a sheerly practical basis literalist efforts to arrive at contemporary medical decisions seem to me to be misguided. Even if we presume that our ancestors were consummately wise and perhaps even divinely inspired in making the decisions they did, there is no reason to suppose that their decisions would bear those qualities in our own setting. On the contrary, I am sure that they themselves would have insisted, as the Talmud did, that each rabbi now take a good look at "what his eyes see"[5] to be sure that his or her application of the tradition is deserving of the godly qualities of wisdom and kindness which we ascribe to Jewish law.

In our topic, this means, in my view, what it meant for medieval Jewish physicians and rabbis. Specifically, we should apply the general theological and legal concepts which emerge out of our heritage to the conditions at hand, even if this means deviating from the specific directions given in a specific precedent. We want to root our decisions as strongly as possible in the tradition, but not at the cost of ignoring the significant differences between the medical circumstances of our own time and those of the past. To carry out this program, we must first determine whether or not medicine has changed significantly in the area of medicine we are considering; that itself is a judgment which depends on a substantial understanding of the history of medicine, among other factors. If medicine in this area is more or less the same as it was in times past, we can proceed in a fairly straightforward, legal manner. If, on the other hand, we judge that innovations in medical practice have made conditions relevantly different from what they had previously been, we will have to stretch some *halakhic* and aggadic sources beyond their original meanings. We *should* do this in order to retain clear connections to the tradition not only in spirit and concept, but even in expression. At the same time, we should openly state what we are doing—namely, that we are choosing both the texts to apply and the interpretations of those texts in order to develop a Jewish medical ethic which carries traditional, Jewish concerns effectively into the contemporary setting.

In insisting that we retain the legal form and substance of past Jewish law, I am disagreeing with Reform positions such as that articulated by Matthew Maibaum. He claims that the radical individualism and secularism of contemporary American

Jews mean that "to an increasing degree, trying to talk about Jewish medical ethics from a traditionalist point of view will impress no one."[6] He objects to using not only the precedents of the past, but even many of the concepts which underlie those precedents—concepts such as God's ownership of our bodies.

It seems to me that this makes one's claim to articulate a *Jewish* position all too tenuous. With such an approach, for example, how does one *rule out* anything as being contrary to Judaism? Why, indeed, would one be interested in developing a specifically Jewish approach to medical matters in the first place?

From one perspective, then, there is a methodological spectrum, in which positions are differentiated according to the *degree* to which individual Jewish sources are held to be determinative of specific, contemporary medical practices. For most Orthodox rabbis, who read the classical texts of the Jewish tradition in a literalist way, such texts are totally determinative, and so the only substantive question is how you are going to read your decision out of, or into, those sources. For at least a segment of the Reform movement, the goal, as Maibaum says, is to show secular Jews that a given Jewish position "also happens to be immediately and centrally good for them." If this cannot be shown, then the whole tradition is "like a fine fossil or an elegant piece of cracked statuary; it is venerable, but is not relevant today."[7] In a more muted form, this is also the position taken by Reform rabbis like David Ellenson and even the right-wing Reform rabbi Solomon Freehof, for all of whom individual autonomy is a key desideratum. I am taking a methodological position somewhere in between these two poles, affirming the necessity to root a contemporary Jewish medical ethic in the Jewish conceptual and legal structure of the past, but recognizing that to do so honestly and wisely we will have to make difficult judgments as to when and how to apply that material to substantially new settings.

The position I am affirming, however—largely identified with the Conservative movement in American Judaism—in these matters, as in all others, is not defined solely by what it denies or by its comparison to others. On the contrary, central to its identity is its positive convictions about the proper way to understand and apply Jewish sources. In brief, it affirms that an accurate assessment of Jewish conceptual and legal sources—both early texts and their later interpolations throughout history—requires studying them in their historical contexts. Once one has done that, one can identify the relevant similarities and differences between previous settings and our own. Only then can one hope to apply traditional sources authentically and perhaps even wisely to contemporary conditions. In many cases, this will involve not only legal reasoning, but theological deliberations concerning our nature as human beings created by, and in the image of, God. Even in these more extended applications of the tradition, though, the more a rabbi can connect a decision to classical Jewish legal and theological texts, the better, for then continuity and the other advantages of a legal approach are more confidently assured.

Rules versus Principles and Policies

Ronald Dworkin, an eminent legal philosopher of our time, has made a distinction which will be important for our purposes. He points out that some standards which judges invoke are rules, which "are applicable in an all-or-nothing fashion." If the rule describes facts which exist, then either the rule is "valid" (the term we use for rules which we have agreed upon as governing this situation), in which case the answer the rule supplies must be accepted, or the rule is not valid, in which case it contributes nothing to the decision. Rules play a central role in domains like games, military procedure, and diplomatic protocol much more than they do in legal decisions, and so the use of rules is probably best illustrated in one of the former settings. To use Dworkin's example, in baseball an umpire cannot consistently acknowledge that a batter who has had three strikes is nevertheless not out. There may be exceptions to the rule (e.g., if the catcher drops the third strike), but then an accurate statement of the rule would stipulate that exception. Once the conditions of the rule have been met, however—in this case, three strikes which the catcher has caught—the result that the batter is out follows inexorably.

In contrast, principles and policies do not automatically determine consequences when the conditions stipulated are met. Dworkin defines principles and policies as follows:

> Most often I shall use the term "principle" generically, to refer to the whole set of . . . standards other than rules; occasionally, however, I shall be more precise, and distinguish between principles and policies. . . . I call a "policy" that kind of standard that sets out a goal to be reached, generally an improvement in some economic, political, or social feature of the community (though some goals are negative, in that they stipulate that some present feature is to be protected from adverse change). I call a "principle" a standard that is to be observed, not because it will advance or secure an economic, political, or social situation deemed desirable, but because it is a requirement of justice or fairness or some other dimension of morality.[8]

Legal decisions use principles and policies extensively, but the latter never totally determine the outcome of a case. One principle of American law, for example, is that people should not profit from their legal wrongs, but there are clear cases in which the law allows them to do just that. For example, the law recognizes that adverse possession (that is, when I trespass on your land unchallenged long enough) ultimately establishes my right to cross whenever I please, and, while it may punish my breach of contract with civil damages, I can still break my contract to take one which is much more lucrative. In these instances, we do not say that the principle needs to be amended to stipulate exceptions to it because we cannot hope to capture all of the situations in which we would want judges to decide contrary to the principle. They are not treated, as rules are, in an "all-or-nothing" fashion. Instead, we ask judges to *weigh* principles and policies against each other in every case to which they reasonably apply. In that way principles and policies establish important considerations which courts must address in cases to which they are relevant, but they do not determine outcomes without exception. (There is no weighing of one rule against another; when rules conflict, some second-order rule must stipulate which takes precedence—for example, a second-order rule which prefers a rule enacted by a higher authority, or a rule enacted later, or the more specific rule).

In law, though, it is not always clear whether a standard is to function as a rule or a principle (or policy). Does the First Amendment to the United States Constitution ban Congress from *any* impediment to freedom of speech (that is, is it a rule), or does it establish a policy that Congress may not ban freedom of speech *unless* there is some important social reason to do so? The amendment is not clear on its face as to that issue; only later court decisions determine how the law is going to be construed and used.[9]

It is precisely this issue which applies to much of what we will have to say about end-of-life issues. Orthodox responsa generally treat the sanctity of human life and the consequent need to preserve even small moments of it (*hayye sha'ah*), whatever its quality, as an overarching axiom—a rule, in Dworkin's terminology. In an immensely insightful book, however, Daniel Sinclair has pointed out that, while Judaism certainly cherishes human life, it does *not* include a duty to preserve all human life under all circumstances at whatever cost. On the contrary, in some situations we are actually commanded to *take* a human life (e.g., when execution is mandated by law, or when killing another is required to defend oneself), and in other cases we are obligated to give up our own human life (specifically, when the alternative is that we ourselves must commit murder, idolatry, or incest).[10] Although Sinclair does not mention this, it is important to point out, along these lines, that the biblical phrase, "and you shall live by them" (Lev. 18:5) is a divine *promise* in the Torah, not a command, and in Jewish law it functions as the ground to justify overriding other commandments in order to save a life; it is *not* meant, either in the Bible or in later rabbinic literature, as a general command to save all human life in all cases. Instead, Jewish law, based upon that verse and others, establishes a general *policy* to preserve life, but, like all other policies, this one is open to being supplanted in given circumstances by specific considerations.

It was Maimonides, Sinclair suggests, who quintessentially manifested the method of creating rules to derive specific laws deductively from them. This followed from Maimonides' general distrust of analogical, legal reasoning. One of the principle criticisms leveled against his code, in fact, was that if Jewish law amounted to a series of unexceptional rules, there was no need for rabbinic adjudication. *The overwhelming preponderance of rabbis, however, did not follow Maimonides in articulating general rules and deducing specific rulings from them; most rabbis instead reasoned analogically from individual precedents.* The latter method might admit of generalizing commonly held *policies* with regard to a given matter, but *not* of creating inviolable rules.[11]

Whether one agrees with Sinclair's ascription of this method to Maimonides or not, it can certainly be said that historically some rabbis have tried to establish rules and to deduce their rulings in specific cases from them, while others—the vast majority—have understood generalizations in the law as summaries of some decisions but not as determinative instructions for others. The former, deductive approach was undoubtedly influenced by the medieval penchant for systematics in both thought and law, and it produced the genre of codes; the latter, casuistic method has its roots in the Bible and the Babylonian Talmud, and it has led to the genre of responsa.[12] While many rabbis in the last millennium have used both methods at various times, some have tried as much as possible to fit their decisions under the rubric of a well-defined rule, while most have preferred to reason analogically from a variety of precedents.

In any case, this distinction in method is crucial in the ever-changing world of bioethics for two reasons. First, a rule that seems unexceptional in one era may be subject to serious criticism in another when circumstances have changed. The use of rules to determine law would then require the wrenching task of either discarding the long-standing rule, radically reconceptualizing its meaning and application, or bearing the guilt of making exceptions to it. Any of those alternatives would amount to a disorienting departure in what one had assumed to be a fixed rule. Normal, legal reasoning, however, simply sets one on a search for other precedents within the law which seem to be more appropriate to the case at hand. One may not always find such precedents—and then some serious revision of the law may be necessary even when using this approach—but the chances of extending the law aptly by using this method are considerably greater than when invoking hard-and-fast rules. Moreover, arguing analogically from precedents is the *standard* method in Jewish law, and so following it is actually adhering to the more traditional approach![13]

Balancing General Rules and Individual Cases

The point needs to be taken yet further. Contemporary physicians and ethicists underscore the *complexity* of each case. Even when the medical diagnosis and prognosis of two people may be identical, there may well be differences in temperament, values, family support, financial resources, and the like. These may not be relevant to the analysis of the physical status of the patient, but they are most important in designing appropriate medical and nonmedical responses to these facts. Some have therefore urged that all concerned pay attention not only to what Harvard psychologist Carol Gilligan has called the "masculine voice" in ethics— that voice concerned primarily with abstract principles—but also to what she calls the "feminine voice," which pays more attention to the specific human situation in which the decision is made, the relationships of the people involved, and the question of how a course of action will help or hurt the people *in this case*.[14] A more internally Jewish model which is sometimes invoked is that of the Hasidim, who, at least by reputation, followed their emotions in dealing with specific cases which cried for compassion, in contrast to the Mitnaggedim, who relied excessively on the rules framed by intellect.

In large measure, I agree with this call for increased attention to the details and nuances of specific cases. I must say, though, that this approach is neither distinctly feminine nor distinctly Hasidic. The first story I heard about Jewish law, in fact, came from my father. My grandparents and their children lived across the street from a large, Orthodox synagogue, of which they were members. Because of the proximity, my grandparents often hosted guests of the congregation for Shabbat. One Friday afternoon my grandmother sent my father, then a lad of fifteen or so, to ask Rabbi Solomon Scheinfeld when the guests for that week were expected. Rabbi Scheinfeld served that congregation from 1902 to 1943, and, according to the *Encyclopedia Judaica,* he "was the recognized head of the city's Orthodox congregations during his tenure."[15] The encyclopedia clearly refers to the camp of the Mitnaggedim, for the Twersky family was firmly in charge of Milwaukee's Hasidim. When my father entered the rabbi's office, he was literally in the process of deciding whether a chicken was kosher. As Rabbi Scheinfeld turned the chicken over in his hands, he asked the woman who had brought it many questions about the physical and economic health of her husband and family. After he pronounced the chicken kosher and the woman left the room, my father asked him why he had asked so many questions about her family.

The rabbi turned to my father and said, "If you think that the kosher status of chickens depends only on their physical state, you understand nothing about Jewish law!" If this is true of chickens, how much more so for human beings.

This, of course, attests only to the attitude of one rabbi in one instance, but it does bespeak the Jewish tradition's insistence that law and morality are, and must be, intertwined.[16] Moreover, this does not eliminate the importance of articulating general standards—that is, commonly used policies; one must just know when and how to use them. In the technical terms of contemporary ethicists, I am arguing neither for an exclusively situational ethic nor for a solely rule-based one (regardless of whether the rules are seen as deontological or consequentialist); I am suggesting instead a character-based ethic, in which both rules and contexts play a part, along with moral moorings in philosophical-religious perspectives and narratives, and moral education to produce moral sensitivity in the first place.[17] This is a much richer—and, I think, a much more realistic—view of how moral norms evolve and operate than is the traditional attention exclusively to rules and specific decisions taken under them.

The Impact of the Reader

We must not only pay attention to the unique qualities of the case before us; we must also recognize the individualism inherent in the process of interpreting the law. That is, the complexity of making decisions in medical ethics is not only a function of the varying, multiple factors in the specific instances to which rules or policies are applied; it is also a matter of the differing experiences and sensitivities of the legal experts who are asked to define and apply the law itself.

Recent theorists of literature and law have increasingly pointed out the role of the reader in identifying the meaning of a text. Radical deconstructionists have even suggested that a text does not control meaning at all, that the meaning of a text is totally and exclusively what the reader wants it to mean. More moderate—and, I think, more correct—understandings of this process draw attention to the crucial impact of the reader's background and goals in his or her understanding of a text, but also acknowledge the role of the text in evoking and limiting that meaning. Thus any given literary interpretation is generally and properly subject to critical evaluation based upon the degree to which any given interpretation preserves the language, context, thrust, and apparent purpose of the text.

Legal texts are no different. Karl Llewellyn was probably the first to indicate the elasticity of legal texts and the corresponding effect of the reader in determining their meaning, and Ronald Dworkin and others have expanded on this point in recent times.[18] Ultimately, in legal texts, as in others, what readers bring to the text is crucial in defining its meaning for them—at least as crucial as the text itself.

In a recent article, Louis Newman has astutely and correctly applied these considerations to Jewish medical ethics. On the basis of this awareness of the role of the reader, he argues for semantic, methodological, and conceptual adjustments in contemporary Jewish bioethics. Semantically, we should not talk about what "Judaism" teaches on these matters, but rather, what we, given our particular interpretive assumptions and our particular way of constructing the coherence of the tradition as a whole, find within the traditional sources. That is, each rabbi would be

explicitly offering *a* Jewish position, not *the* Jewish stance. Methodologically, proponents of a Jewish position must not simply state their reading of the tradition, but
argue for it against other possible readings and, more broadly, describe how their
ruling on a given issue fits into their view of the tradition as a whole. They must, in
the language of American jurisprudence, present "a *reasoned* opinion," not just an
opinion. And conceptually, Jewish bioethicists who adopt a legal mode must reflect
greater knowledge and understanding of contemporary theories of legal reasoning
and judicial interpretation, and those who do choose another methodology should
explain why, should demonstrate awareness of other modes in medical ethics, and, I
would add, should articulate how their approach is identifiably Jewish.[19]

When these elements of any decision in Jewish medical ethics are made manifest, one can better understand the role that moral sensitivities can and should play
in arriving at a ruling. Reform writers often speak as if contemporary moral sensitivities should replace traditional Jewish legal sources in shaping current policy. At
best, classical texts should be cited to reinforce what the writer thinks best anyway
on independent grounds. Orthodox rabbis, on the other hand, generally refuse to
admit contemporary moral sensitivities as an independent source of authority; only
that which somehow can be deduced from the classical texts counts as authoritative.
Even those few Orthodox writers who openly speak about a moral component in
halakhic decision making do so defensively, trying to justify why such components
are legitimately considered.[20] Authors affiliated with the Conservative movement
have been much more aggressive than their Orthodox colleagues in asserting a
major role for ethical concerns, but, unlike their Reform compatriots, Conservative
rabbis see morals as an integral part of the Jewish *legal* process by which contemporary decisions should be made.[21]

As a Conservative rabbi, I suppose it is no accident that I embrace this last
approach,[22] but I think that contemporary literary and legal theory needs to
augment the usual arguments for it. It is not only that rabbis over the centuries
have shaped the tradition with a conscious eye toward making it meet the highest
moral standards; it is also that *any* reading of a text will involve the values and
concerns of the reader, and thus moral considerations are quite properly part of
the process of making decisions in contemporary Jewish law. We as the interpreters of our tradition have been taught by it to strive for the right and the good, and
our understanding of that, although surely shaped by it, is not exclusively so.
Moreover, we bring our own contexts, with their inherent complexities, to our
understanding of classical Jewish texts, and so our interpretation of those texts will
inevitably—and properly—reflect those contexts and thus possibly differ from the
readings of our ancestors. The point is that in reading our own concerns and our
own moral sensitivities into the texts, we are no different from our ancestors; this
is how texts must and should be read.

A Traditional, but Dynamic Ethic for Our Time

The methodological principles I have described—that we must retain a legal
method with its inherent discipline in making our decisions; that we must recognize
that Jewish law most often prescribes policies and principles, not inviolable rules,
and we must interpret and apply Jewish law accordingly; that even general policies

must be implemented with sensitivity to the context of a specific case; that we must be aware of the inevitable and proper impact of the reader and his or her context, goals, and values in interpreting and employing a text; and that this awareness does not vitiate the authority of the text, but it does open the door, with appropriate arrgumentation, for contemporary moral sensitivities—must all, in my view, shape the way in which we approach issues of bioethics in our time. Only then can our methodology be sufficiently dynamic to accommodate the revolutionary changes occurring in the world of medicine on almost a daily basis and yet be unmistakably Jewish. Only then can we responsibly and wisely carry on the vital and religiously rooted tradition of medical care and adaptability which we have inherited.

Notes

I have used sections of this article as part of a long responsum on issues at the end of life for the Conservative Movement's Committee on Jewish Law and Standards. That responsum is published in the Spring 1991 issue of *Conservative Judaism,* and those sections are reprinted here with permission of the editor, for which I am grateful. This article, however, like my presentation at the conference of the Jewish Law Association in July 1990, includes methodological points not included in the responsum.

In all of the following notes, M. = Mishnah; T. = Tosefta; B. = Babylonian Talmud; J. = Jerusalem Talmud; M.T. = Maimonides' *Mishneh Torah;* and S.A. = Joseph Karo's *Shulḥan Arukh.*

1. For a good overview of how biomedical decisions have been made historically in other religions, both in theory and in practice, cf. Ronald L. Numbers and Darrel W. Amundsen, eds., *Caring and Curing: Health and Medicine in the Western Religious Traditions* (New York: Macmillan, 1986). For greater detail, see the series of books published by Crossroad (New York), in conjunction with the Park Ridge Center in Illinois, entitled *Health and Medicine in the XXX Tradition,* with volumes on the bioethics principles and practices of the Anglican, Catholic, Islamic, Jewish, Lutheran, Methodist, and Reformed traditions. There is a plethora of books on secular approaches to medical ethics; two good ones, of many, are Tom L. Beauchamp and James F. Childress, *Principles of Biomedical Ethics* (New York and Oxford: Oxford University Press, 1979), and William J. Winslade and Judith Wilson Ross, *Choosing Life or Death: A Guide for Patients, Families, and Professionals* (New York: Free Press, 1986). On the topic of our example, euthanasia, see, for example, Marvin Kohl, ed., *Beneficent Euthanasia* (Buffalo, NY: Prometheus Press, 1975); and John Ladd, ed., *Ethical Issues Relating to Life and Death* (New York and Oxford: Oxford University Press, 1979).

2. David Ellenson, "Religious Approaches to Mortal Choices: How to Draw Guidance from a Heritage", in Barry S. Kogan, ed., *A Time to Be Born, A Time to Die: The Ethics of Choice* (New York: Aldine de Gruyter, 1990), pp. 228–29 [reprinted in this volume as chapter 9]. The articles he cites as articulating one form or another of this approach are these: Daniel H. Gordis [a Conservative rabbi], "Wanted–The Ethical in Jewish Bio-Ethics," *Judaism* 38/1 (Winter 1989), 28–40; Irving Greenberg [an Orthodox rabbi], "Toward a Covenantal Ethic of Medicine," in Levi Meier, ed., *Jewish Values in Bioethics* (New York: Human Sciences Press, 1986), 124–49; David Hartman [an Orthodox rabbi], "Moral Uncertainties in the Practice of Medicine," *The Journal of Medicine and Philosophy* 4 (1979), 100ff.; and Eugene B. Borowitz [a Reform rabbi], *Choices in Modern Jewish Thought* (New York: Behrman House, 1983), esp. 367–68, and "The Autonomous Self and the Commanding Community," *Theological Studies* 45 (1984), 48–49.

3. See my article "The Interaction of Jewish Law with Morality," *Judaism* 26/4 (Fall 1977), 455–66.

4. Tosafot, B. *Mo'ed Katan* 11a; Jacob ben Moses Mollin, *Yalḳutai Maharil* (Segal), cited in Fred Rosner, *Medicine in the Bible and the Talmud* (New York: KTAV, 1977), 21; Solomon Luria, *Yam Shel Shelomo*, "Kol Basar," Section 12; Joseph Caro, *Keṣef Mishneh* commentary to M.T. *Hilkhot De'ot (Laws of Ethics)* 4:18; Abraham Gombiner, *Magen Avraham* commentary to S.A. *Oraḥ Ḥayyim* 173.

5. *B. Bava Batra* 131a. To see how this text and others like it were used in the Middle Ages, cf. Elliot N. Dorff and Arthur Rosett, *A Living Tree: The Roots and Growth of Jewish Law* (Albany: State University of New York Press, and New York: Jewish Theological Seminary of America, 1988), 383–95.

6. Matthew (Menachem) Maibaum, "A 'Progressive' Jewish Medical Ethics: Notes for an Agenda," *Journal of Reform Judaism* 33/3 (Summer 1986), 29. He is definitely right, though, in his call for Conservative, Reconstructionist, and Reform rabbis to articulate their respective views on medical matters in writtten form and to cull them into easily accessible collections so that lay Jews do not mistakenly think that the only Jewish views on these matters are those of the Orthodox simply because they are the only ones in print. (The Orthodox, who publish books with titles like "Jewish Bioethics," certainly do not let on that there are other possible Jewish approaches!)

7. Ibid., 29.

8. Ronald Dworkin, *Taking Rights Seriously* (Cambridge, MA: Harvard University Press, 1977), 22. His characterization of the distinctions among rules, principles, and policies appears on pp. 22–31. (This chapter of his book originally appeared in the *University of Chicago Law Review,* 1967.)

9. As Dworkin points out, sometimes courts muddy the waters yet further by interpreting rules with words like *reasonable, significant, just,* and the like, which invoke the principles or policies that led the legislature to enact the rule in the first place. "But they do not quite turn the rule into a principle, because even the least confining of these terms restricts the *kind* of other principles and policies on which the rule depends." Ibid., 28.

10. The Torah mandates executing people for a long list of offenses; largely through specifying stringent evidentiary rules, the rabbis narrowed the scope of this punishment considerably (cf. *M. Makkot* 1:10), but they retain it, at least in theory. The Talmud (if not the Bible) requires that, even at the cost of killing the attacker, we defend both ourselves (Exod. 22:1; *B. Berakhot* 58a; *Yoma* 85b; *Sanhedrin* 72a) and even others (the law of *rodef, B. Sanhedrin* 72b–73a; *M.T. Laws of Murder* 1:6–7; *S.A. Ḥoshen Mishpaṭ* 425:1). The duty to give up one's own life when the alternative is to commit murder, idolatry, or incest is specified in *B. Sanhedrin* 74a.

11. Daniel B. Sinclair, *Tradition and the Biological Revolution: The Application of Jewish Law to the Treatment of the Critically Ill* (Edinburgh: Edinburgh University Press, 1989), 80–81, 88–89. This distinction is parallel to one commonly cited in Anglo-American law between absolute and rebuttable assumptions of the law.

12. Umberto Cassuto has made this point with reference to biblical law codes, which, he says, "should not be regarded as a code of laws, or even as a number of codes, but only as separate instructions on given matters." See his *A Commentary on the Book of Exodus* (Jerusalem: Magnes Press [Hebrew University], 1967), 260–64. The Babylonian Talmud in *Eruvin* 27a and *Kiddushin* 34a expressly objects to treating the Mishnah's general rules as inviolable principles; moreover, in practice it routinely interprets general principles announced in the Mishnah (with phrases like *zeh ha-klal*) not as generalizations at all but rather as additions of further specific cases. See Jacob Eliyahu Efrati, *Teḳufat Hasaboraim V'Ṣifrutah* (Petaḥ Tiḳvah: Agudat Benai Asher [New York and Jerusalem: Philipp Feldheim, distributors], 1973), pt. 2, 157–278 (Hebrew), who demonstrates this with regard to the eighty-five unrepeated instances in the Mishnah where this expression occurs and who claims that these discussions, limited to the Babylonian Talmud, are Saboraic in origin (i.e., from 500 to 689 C.E.). (I want to thank my colleague at the University of Judaism, Dr. Elieser

Slomovic, for this reference.) With regard to the genre of Jewish codes, its methodological pros and cons, and its origins in medieval systematics, see Dorff and Rosett, *A Living Tree* (*supra* n. 5), 366–401.

13. The more radical option of instituting revisions in the law (*taḳanot*) is also an available alternative within the methods of classical Jewish law, and, given the radically new realities of contemporary medical practice, one might reasonably argue that such revisions can be more easily justified in this area than in most others. I would agree, but I share the tradition's reticence to employ this method unless absolutely necessary (cf. Dorff and Rosett, ibid., 402–20). We do not have much experience in dealing with many of the morally excruciating questions posed by modern medicine, and so at this point we have not yet had time to see if instituting revisions is required. I, for one, think that the classical methods of legal exegesis and analogizing, if used creatively and sensitively, are fully capable of producing appropriate guidelines to modern Jewish medical decisions, and I certainly think that we owe it to the tradition to try to use these more conservative methods for a period of time before resorting to *taḳanot*.

14. Carol Gilligan, *In a Different Voice* (Cambridge, MA: Harvard University Press, 1982).

15. "Milwaukee," *Encyclopedia Judaica* 11 (1590).

16. Cf. *supra* n. 3.

17. Stanley Hauerwas has probably been the preeminent exponent of this in the Christian world; cf. his *Character and the Christian Life: A Study in Theological Ethics* (San Antonio: Trinity University Press, 1975); *Vision and Virtue* (Notre Dame, IN: Fides Publishers, 1974); *Truthfulness and Tragedy* (Notre Dame, IN: University of Notre Dame Press, 1977); and *A Community of Character: Towards a Constructive Christian Social Ethic* (Notre Dame, IN: University of Notre Dame Press, 1981). Cf. also Alasdair MacIntyre, *After Virtue* (Notre Dame, IN: University of Notre Dame Press, 1981); James William McClendon, Jr., *Ethics* (Nashville, TN: Abingdon, 1987); and Paul Lauritzen, "Emotions and Religious Ethics," *The Journal of Religious Ethics* 16/2 (Fall 1988), 307–24. (I am indebted to Professor Louis Newman for this last reference.)

18. Karl Llewellyn, "Remarks on the Theory of Appellate Decision and the Rules or Canons about How Statutes Are to Be Construed," *Vanderbilt Law Review* 3 (1950), 395; *The Common Law Tradition* (Boston: Little, Brown, and Company, 1960), Appendix C; *The Bramble Bush* (New York: Oceana Publications, 1930, 1960), 76. Excerpts from the first two of these are reprinted in Dorff and Rosett, *A Living Tree,* pp. 204–13. Ronald Dworkin, *A Matter of Principle* (Cambridge, MA: Harvard University Press, 1985), 159–77. For a good exposition of the deconstructionist position, cf. Stanley Fish, *Is There a Text in This Class?* (Cambridge, MA: Harvard University Press, 1980). For a critical review of the Fish and Dworkin controversy, see R. V. Young, "Constitutional Interpretation and Literary Theory," *The Intercollegiate Review* 23/1 (1987), 49–60.

19. Louis E. Newman, "Woodchoppers and Respirators: The Problem of Interpretation in Contemporary Jewish Ethics," *Modern Judaism* 10/1 (February 1990), 17–42 (reprinted in this volume as Chapter 10).

20. For example, Eliezer Berkovits, *Not in Heaven: The Nature and Function of Halakha* (New York: KTAV, 1983), 82–84; Shubert Spero, *Morality, Halakha, and the Jewish Tradition* (New York: KTAV and Yeshiva, 1983), esp. 166–200; David Hartman, *A Living Covenant: The Innovative Spirit in Traditional Judaism* (New York: Free Press, 1985), esp. 89–108.

21. For example, Robert Gordis, *The Dynamics of Judaism* (Bloomington: Indiana University Press, 1990), esp. 50–68; Simon Greenberg, *The Ethical in the Jewish and American Heritage* (New York: Jewish Theological Seminary of America, 1977), esp. 157–218; and Seymour Siegel, "Ethics and Halakhah," *Conservative Judaism* 25/3 (Spring 1971), 33–40, and "Reaction to the Modern Moral Crises," *Conservative Judaism* 34/1 (September/October 1980), 17–27.

22. I think, though, that conflicts between ritual and ethics, however those terms are defined, are far fewer and therefore far less important than they are often touted to be. Moreover, I would claim that *both* rituals and ethics are authoritative within Judaism, neither necessarily always taking precedence over the other. Cf. my *Mitzvah Means Commandment* (New York: United Synagogue of America, 1989), 7–9, 223–29.

12

Cases and Principles in Jewish Bioethics: Toward a Holistic Model

AARON L. MACKLER

In recent years a number of writers have argued for a greater focus on theory and principles in Jewish ethics, and in particular Jewish bioethics. Classical approaches of *halakhah* (Jewish law), which are marked by attention to precedents and reliance on analogy, are portrayed as too limited to address problems found in such areas as biomedical ethics. They are criticized also as lacking the focus on theory and formal elegance that we have come to expect from ethics. One author argues that instead of looking to particular cases as precedents, we should focus our attention on fundamental beliefs and principles, and seek a broad theological view of what it is to be human.[1] Another asserts that contemporary approaches in Jewish ethics rise or fall on the basis of their methodological assumptions: "If interpretation is meant to be more than ad hoc decision-making, it must rest upon a theoretical foundation," which must be "stated explicitly and defended."[2]

The attractiveness of theory and foundation principles cuts across denominational lines. David Ellenson in the Reform movement argues that the case-based approach fails to give adequate weight to individual self-determination as a basic principle.[3] Some Orthodox thinkers instead portray the sanctity of life as a decisive fundamental principle that should trump competing considerations. While the substantive differences between these views are profound, both would agree that the enterprise of Jewish bioethics appropriately focuses on general theory and foundational principles.

At the same time that these Jewish ethicists have argued for a need to turn from cases to theory and general principles, many in philosophical bioethics and clinical ethics have argued for the need to move in the opposite direction. They have criticized foundationalism, an approach which seeks to establish with certainty one basic principle (or at most a few such principles), and to deduce rules and resolve particular cases on the basis of this foundation.[4] Critics have pointed to the difficulty of establishing broad principles that provide meaningful guidance in particular cases. "Applied ethics" models that focus on theory and foundationalist principles have been condemned as making inflated claims regarding their principles, and as producing simplistic and inequitable decisions or failing to provide guidance in actual cases. These concerns have led to arguments for a return to cases and casuistic approaches in bioethics, focusing on the details of cases and looking to analogical reasoning and case judgments.[5]

In this paper I will advance a holistic model for Jewish ethics and bioethics. My holistic model includes attention to both particular and general concerns. It holds that there need be no absolute and invariable order of priority among particular judgments, rules and laws, and general principles and values. Neither grand principles expressing the essence of Judaism nor rigid formal criteria need be foundational. In addressing a specific issue (a local level of justification), a particular claim may be supported by a more general norm, or vice versa. A variety of approaches to a problem can each shed light, serve as correctives to other approaches, and contribute to a resolution. At the global level, justification is (to use John Rawls's phrase) "a matter of the mutual support of many considerations, of everything fitting together into one coherent view."[6] The term *holistic* is meant to designate an approach to reasoning and deliberation, and not a metaphysical thesis. The holistic model is compatible with a variety of metaethical positions, including a view that assertions in Jewish ethics correspond to a higher reality or are objectively true.[7] By combining criteria of input and coherence, the holistic model allows for the testing, reshaping, and justification (or vindication) not only of particular beliefs but also of the system of Jewish ethical beliefs as a whole.

I first will present the outlines of the holistic model and suggest its affinities to classical approaches in Jewish ethics.[8] I then will argue that my holistic model best accounts for the significance of general principles and particular rules and precedents in Jewish bioethics. The model also offers an understanding of the contribution of insights of conscience or judgment relative to established norms and provides a basis for the interaction of elements identified as Jewish with other sources of ethical insight such as philosophical ethics. I will conclude by sketching briefly an example of how the model would operate in approaching a particular issue, that of access to health care.

Coherence Reasoning in the Holistic Model

My approach, with its reliance on back-and-forth reasoning and the accompanying rejection of foundationalism, corresponds with the model of reflective equilibrium, developed by John Rawls and others. Rawls describes the process of reflective equilibrium, crucial for the development and justification of moral theory, as beginning with a set of considered judgments, including case judgments as well as more general norms and theoretical concerns. We postulate those principles that would best account for such judgments, and revise principles and more particular judgments in a process of mutual adjustment, with the result (as well as the process) referred to as reflective equilibrium. Wide reflective equilibrium includes consideration of all available theoretical views and reasonable arguments.[9]

Coherence is central to a holistic understanding of the acquisition and justification of beliefs, as found in my model and that of Rawls. Following Laurence BonJour in his discussion of empirical knowledge, I understand coherence as a rich concept that includes more than mere consistency. As BonJour observes:

Intuitively, coherence is a matter of how well a body of beliefs "hangs together": how well its component beliefs fit together, agree or dovetail with each other, so as to produce an organized, tightly structured system of beliefs, rather than either a helter-skelter collection or a set of conflicting subsystems. It is reasonably clear that this "hanging together" depends on the various sorts of inferential, evidential, and explanatory relations which obtain among the various members of a system of beliefs, and especially on the more holistic and systematic of these.[10]

A coherent system of beliefs must avoid logical inconsistencies, but positive connections between beliefs are also required. The coherence of a system is increased in proportion to the number and strength of inferential connections between component beliefs, with explanatory connections central but other inferential connections contributing as well.[11] Coherence is pursued step-by-step in a process of mutual adjustment, as connections of explanation, inference, and analogy are drawn and their implications explored.[12]

In the context of a particular case, a holistic approach to reasoning would investigate detailed circumstances, explore analogies with other known cases, and consider the implications of general rules, values, and principles. An example of this approach is provided by Martin Luther King Jr.'s "Letter from Birmingham City Jail." In this essay King weaves together considerations large and small, general norms and particular case judgments, in order to create a coherent and compelling argument for a particular course of action. He addresses broad issues, including general criteria of when a law is unjust, and articulates a grand vision of the United States and of the church (and religious institutions in general).[13] At a general level King's letter seeks to reconcile broad norms. King is committed to respecting the law, and acknowledges that simple defiance of the law unacceptably would lead to anarchy. At the same time his commitments to justice and human flourishing lead him to oppose laws mandating segregation. King seeks to respect both principles to the extent possible: he would break the law only when no other alternative is available that is consistent with compelling demands of justice, and when the law is broken so as to cause least harm to the principle of lawfulness.[14]

King's letter not only invokes general principles but also appeals to particular case judgments in arguing against segregation. He describes his daughter crying at being told that blacks are not admitted at the Funtown amusement park and a black man was sleeping in his automobile because no hotel would accept him. The judgment of these cases as wrong and intolerable corroborates the need to act against segregation.[15] Further, King does not only use cases to support the pursuit of justice and opposition to desegregation in general terms. He argues for a particular type of action in a particular place at a particular time.[16]

King's holistic deliberation (as sketched earlier) illustrates the interplay of considerations of a variety of levels of generality in reshaping beliefs so as to strengthen coherence. In this process a rule of obedience to the law is revised. A broader principle of respect for the law is also tested, and emerges as vindicated. Even from his cell, King warns of the dangers of lawlessness and accepts the breaking of the law only by those who (among other qualifications) are willing to join him in jail, so as to remain faithful to the broader principle. The process of holistic deliberation not only leads to a decision for the case at hand but contributes to the testing and reshaping of more general norms, which emerge as strengthened in being more clearly articulated, substantively improved, and more fully vindicated.

Holism in Classical Jewish Ethics

I believe that a holistic model provides the best construction of much work in Jewish ethics in all areas, including those involving health and medicine. A holistic approach clearly characterizes ethical reasoning of a traditional Jew in everyday life, in the absence of dramatic conflict. One seeking to follow Jewish ethics would be aware of detailed norms of *halakhah* governing his or her interaction with other people. He or she also would be conscious of traditional sources and popular culture offering paradigmatic examples of ethical behavior, stories of saints and moral heroes, maxims, and admonitions to develop ethical virtues. For example, the Bible provides detailed laws governing ethical behavior, prudent maxims in the Book of Proverbs, narratives of heroes and villains, psalms describing the characteristics of the person of integrity worthy of standing in God's presence. Rabbinic literature as it developed over the centuries would provide a physician, for example, with laws concerning responsibilities toward patients, admonitions to humility and virtue, stories of Abba the therapeutic bleeder and other models to emulate, a prayer attributed to Maimonides expressing the physician's devotion to the patient and humility before God, and so forth. Out of these rich and varied sources one would weave the pattern of a Jewish ethical life.

The holistic model would be followed in the academy as well. The Talmud, for example, does not follow the abstract logical schema of a work of geometry. Rather, a talmudic tractate is a *masechet,* a webbing or weaving together of material. The sages of the Talmud found themselves in a sea of texts and beliefs, including the various books of the Bible, statements attributed to earlier sages, and their own reason and experience. They would construct arguments and utilize exegetical tools in order to reconcile earlier rabbinic statements or biblical verses. Small and large generalizations would be built, step-by-step, to provide guidance in new cases and construct a richer whole. These methods would serve to maximize coherence, using the rich sense of coherence noted earlier, while retaining as much as possible of the original input.

A holistic approach also characterizes the reasoning of later generations of rabbis addressing complex or dilemmatic problems in *teshuvot,* or *halakhic* responsa. Like Martin Luther King Jr. in his essay (ceteris paribus) they would pursue a holistic pattern of reasoning. Typically writers of responsa survey previous sources, analyze fact patterns, elucidate analogies and disanalogies with paradigmatic cases, formulate generalizations, and balance competing concerns. Their argument does not take the form of a foundationalist deduction from first principles, but rather a process of cumulative reasoning yields a judgment in the particular case vindicated relative to alternatives.

Principles and Cases

The classical Jewish approach to ethical issues, then, is similar to that found in case law. Attention focuses on the evaluation of particular cases and consideration of potential analogies to precedents. Daniel Gordis, among other thinkers, has urged greater attention to fundamental principles and broad generalizations. He argues that concentrating on particular cases often forces analogies, and at best distracts attention from the real issues under consideration. Thus, for example, attempts to define criteria for the determination of death should not focus on particular precedent cases or rules; rather, such issues should be explored at the level of our "implicit conceptions of the value of human life and personhood." Guidance for when life-sustaining treatment may be stopped should be sought through consideration of "the fundamental beliefs motivating us" rather than the details of paradigmatic cases or legal codes. In general, "If the Jewish community hopes to be able to articulate sophisticated analyses of these issues, the immediate challenge is to begin a philosophical/theological conversation which can lead to a Jewish conception of personhood or some other fundamental principle which can then be applied in a normative manner."[17]

I would grant Gordis that precedent cases and rules often seem distant from contemporary health care decision making, and their implications may be unclear. For example, the sixteenth-century Shulhan Arukh sets forth a set of rules for a *goses,* one who is imminently dying, with death likely within three days.[18] Basing itself on earlier sources, the Shulhan Arukh states that one cannot cause the patient to die more quickly, for example, by removing a pillow from under his head. On the other hand, if someone is chopping wood outside the patient's window, preventing peaceful acceptance of death, one can ask him to stop. If the patient's tongue is covered with salt, understood to delay the dying process, that too can be removed. These particular judgments have been taken to support a general norm that one cannot cause death, but one may remove an obstacle that is impeding death. Even so, differences between removing a pillow on the one hand and removing salt or silencing a woodchopper on the other are far from clear and have been construed in various ways by different writers. The implications of these precedents at best underdetermine the array of contemporary treatment decisions that may arise, such as those involving respirators, artificial nutrition and hydration, antibiotics, or vasopressors.[19]

One can readily understand why authors such as Gordis and others have wanted to turn to general principles for more definitive guidance. However, recent works in philosophical ethics and bioethics have noted limitations in reliance on fundamental principles as well. While many principles are attractive and strike us as plausible, none has the absolute certainty and exclusive authority to provide definitive foundations for our system of ethical beliefs. Broad theories tend to pursue an elegant simplicity at the expense of evading the complexities of morality, forcing various duties and sources of value into the Procrustean bed of a single (or few) ultimate principle(s). Even if foundationalist principles could somehow be established, they would provide too insubstantial a basis for ethical reasoning about particular issues and cases. An exclusive focus on broad and abstract norms fails to provide the sensitive and prudent guidance needed, and leads instead to speculative irrelevance or overly blunt imposition of generalizations.[20]

All of these considerations mandate caution in asserting fundamental principles in any system. Attempts to establish such principles in Jewish ethics face additional problems. The claim would need to be that one principle (or perhaps a hierarchically arranged set) represents the essence of Judaism in a definitive way. Attempts to define such an essence have produced multiple and differing plausible candidates. Such a claim, it would seem, would need to be based on sources such as the Bible, rabbinics, Jewish philosophy, or Jewish history. Each of these sources is complex and variegated, with values and perspectives that are incommensurable and coexist in tension with each other. Jewish texts and thought are too complex to allow for the establishment of one principle as fundamental to the exclusion of all others.[21]

For example, in deciding about care for a dying patient, many principles seem plausible. Principles might assert that one must seek to benefit the patient, or respect the patient who is created in God's image. It is less clear, though, exactly what these principles would imply for the formulation of rules or resolution of a case. What benefits the patient? Should the preservation of life in the midst of suffering be considered a benefit, or should certain measures be deemed optional and forgone in order to serve the patient's good? What are the implications of the patient being created in God's image? Some have argued that we therefore must sustain every moment of life, for each moment has infinite value. Or perhaps we are called on to have compassion for our fellow creature, whose suffering pains God and whose loss of dignity, as it were, lessens the divine image. Or perhaps the most crucial implication of being created in the divine image is that each person has free will, and so we must respect the autonomous choices of each person. On reflection, each of these claims seems plausible, each resonates with sources in the Bible, in rabbinic literature, in Jewish philosophy. If each is right, though, none can be right in a simple way. The basic beliefs in Judaism provide some general considerations, but these may conflict, and require careful interpretation and evaluation in particular cases.

No clear foundation is available. General principles may conflict and underdetermine the result in particular cases. Precedents may be distant from the case at hand and themselves have implications that are unclear. Jewish ethical evaluation would need to look at both sorts of elements for guidance. I will sketch in the following an example illustrating how such a model might proceed.

Conscience and Particular Judgments

Some might suggest a different response to the lack of definitive guidance from particular precedents or general principles. They might assert that this limitation simply shows that the decision rests with the judgment of each individual, following his or her own conscience. Appeals to moral intuitions may be found in a variety of philosophical approaches, and reliance on individual conscience has played a respected role in classical liberal thought, including much of modern Jewish ethics. Developments in fields such as psychology, as well as philosophy, have made it difficult to believe in a faculty of conscience as infallible and foundational, or a Kantian anthropology of the pure noumenal self legislating universal law in a manner identical to any other self.[22] Other approaches in philosophical ethics that are based on particular judgments as foundational, and attempt to resolve all cases with such intuitions or to build unidirectionally from particular to general, have faced problems as well. Classical intuitionists have failed to establish the validity or even the plausibility of intuitive cognition, and especially to provide an account of a special cognitive faculty.[23] Further, as Henry Sidgwick argues, individuals who seek to rely solely on immediate intuitions do not always find themselves "conscious of clear immediate insight" when confronting a challenging case and face difficulties in making their judgments consistent.[24]

Moreover, even if an infallible cognitive or conscientious faculty could be established, this would tend to dissipate rather than provide a foundation for Jewish ethics. The findings of a Kantian noumenal self, or the perceptions of a special intuitive faculty, would seem to apply for all persons, abstracting from any religious commitment or any other characteristics. This is certainly how the process was understood by thinkers such as Kant and the British intuitionists. Most writers in contemporary Jewish bioethics, however, would acknowledge some central role for Jewish sources and beliefs. As such views reject the classical liberal understanding of conscience, they can no longer assume the power accorded to particular conscientious judgments in that model. They stand in need of a new account of conscience and its relationship to Jewish beliefs and experiences.

I would suggest that judgments play a crucial role in Jewish ethics, as they do in all systems of legal and ethical reasoning. Judgments are best understood not as infallible cognitive insights but as similar to trained judgments in other fields, such as science and medicine.

This approach follows Richard Boyd's suggestion that trained judgments and intuitions may play the same role in ethics as they do in science. Through theoretical study, professional training, and practical experience, an individual "acquires a 'feel' for the issues" of the field and gains proficiency in making informal judgments. These judgments are in part intuitive, in that they go beyond that which can be accounted for by explicit inferences; nevertheless, they are informed by experience and training, and generated as part of an epistemic package that includes theories and practices. The status of these trained judgments is not crucially different from that of judgments for which more explicit reasons are available.[25] Similarly, Boyd argues, "Moral intuitions, like physical intuitions, play a limited but legitimate role in empirical inquiry *precisely because* they are linked to theory *and* to observations in a generally reliable process."[26]

Many fields of deliberation have a role for such trained judgments which complement rather than replace general norms. These judgments provide guidance that may be helpful in some cases in which explicit justification is insufficient to specify a course of action. In medicine, for example, clinical judgment is often needed to formulate a diagnosis, prognosis, or treatment recommendation. The need for clinical judgment does not reduce the importance of physical findings and laboratory tests of the particular patient, or knowledge of general norms and familiarity with analogous cases. Moreover, the intuitive judgment is not a mystical insight but builds on the training of the physician in the general norms and methodologies of medicine, and experience with many cases.

This model explains how the judgments of a Jewish ethicist or other individual can be Jewish. Such judgment is not akin to perception in the sense of raw feels and sensations, but rather the perceptiveness of the trained and experienced person of wisdom. In Jewish ethics as in other fields, perceptive judgments are influenced by experience and reflect the total of one's training, commitments, and beliefs.

As a first and minimal claim, judgments in bioethics can fill in gaps and provide nuanced resolutions. Like the clinical judgments of a physician, they can offer guidance when explicit justification is insufficient to specify a course of action. This role corresponds to the significance of judgment acknowledged by Aharon Lichtenstein, for example. For Lichtenstein, an individual's "moral sense" may be relied on within the realm of *lifnim mishurat hadin,* or within the boundaries of the law. So long as an individual is acting in accord with all general norms, that person's ethical insight may further specify the contours of ethically appropriate action.[27]

My model allows for a more ambitious claim as well. Particular conscientious judgments may represent new input that challenges and enriches the system of beliefs, leading to its growth. The insights of conscience could at least play a heuristic role, like a lead for a journalist or the glimmer of an idea for a medical researcher. Even those who see the *halakhic* process as definitive will generally acknowledge that legal authorities will be concerned with ethical implications of positions, and will make some degree of effort to try to shape a *halakhic* decision in accord with their judgment regarding "the right and the good," the equities of the case at hand. When the insight of conscience disagrees with the established judgments of the system, there is at least reason to reconsider the situation. At the same time, conscientious judgments neither are infallible nor should they automatically trump other considerations. Like paradigmatic cases, rules, and values, they represent an important though fallible indicator of the correct judgment for Jewish bioethics.

Jewish and Universal Elements

The holistic model also provides a framework for incorporating insights gained from non-Jewish sources such as philosophical ethics, in addition to elements deriving from Jewish sources. The relationship of ethical reasoning within the Jewish tradition and intersocietal or universal standards has been a central issue for Jewish thought, especially throughout the modern period. As I argue elsewhere, Jewish thinkers such as Eugene Borowitz have wanted to rely on both types of sources.[28] Borowitz is committed to "a universal sense of ethics, one which every human being ought to acknowledge and obey." "Only if we affirm that there is a universal ethical order, one whose commands everyone can know, can we rightly demand . . . that people resist 'unjust orders' despite fearsome pressure." At the same time, Borowitz is committed to avoid losing all distinctive elements in Jewish ethics by reducing it to a universal standard. He depicts himself as one of those "who know that the universalistic path is unreliable without the corrective guide of Torah." "Asserting the dominance of human reason makes Judaism a hostage to whatever version of rationalism the thinker finds convincing."[29] Retaining commitments to particularly Jewish and universal elements is attractive but difficult. I believe that my holistic model can assist in the work needed to synthesize and adjust these competing elements of Jewish ethics.

Sophisticated liberal thinkers such as Borowitz may acknowledge that the Jewish tradition defines ethical duties within the boundaries of universal ethics. Conversely, as seen earlier, Orthodox thinkers such as Lichtenstein may acknowledge that ethical concerns define duties within the boundaries of *halakhah.* Each thus would accord with my holistic model to a significant extent in acknowledging multiple sources of guidance. However, not only would these two approaches differ in emphasis, but each would insist that its chosen criterion should always be given priority. Greatest controversy ensues when conflict arises between elements within the Jewish ethical tradition and claims seen to represent universal ethics. Often deliberation about this complex issue takes on a polemical cast. Some would claim that *halakhah* (as they understand it) represents God's word, which is by definition decisive over any insight arising from human ethics. Borowitz, in contrast, acknowledges *halakhah* as representing duties to fellow Jews but claims that ethics (as he understands it) represents his duty to God, which must be decisive in case of conflict.[30]

I would argue that there is no gold standard in ethics that is accessible to us, no cognitive faculty or other pipeline to ethical truth. Similarly, God's will is not known infallibly, and the Talmud indicates that even a heavenly voice would not obviate the need for complex and fallible deliberation.[31] Jewish bioethics appropriately gains guidance from a variety of powerful but imperfect indicators of the way in which the enterprise should proceed. These include Jewish values and concepts as well as particular rules and cases in Jewish law, and also ethical claims found compelling on the basis of general ethical considerations. None of these is known with sufficient certainty and precision to enjoy absolute or lexical priority.[32] In the face of conflict among these factors, those engaged in Jewish bioethics should undertake a process of back-and-forth reasoning. They should reexamine and seek to readjust elements. The goal, consistent with input from the wealth of the Jewish tradition as well as other sources, is to maximize coherence of beliefs.

Perspectives from philosophical ethics, and even from other cultures and religions, represent a powerful if volatile source of input for the holistic model. Elements within the system of Jewish ethics could be legitimate even when they diverge from norms in other systems. As Stuart Hampshire argues, one cannot simply pick and choose elements of different cultures, for they may be incompatible with each other and fail to support a coherent way of life; Hampshire terms this claim the "noshopping principle."[33] Still, conscious consideration of the insights of differing ethical traditions, including various approaches in philosophical ethics, can afford a perspective that leads to the tradition being challenged and enriched. In some cases this could include modification in the tradition, or at least in the way that the tradition is understood, articulated, and applied.[34]

The holistic model also provides a basis for considering the implications of Jewish bioethics for others, as I will discuss subsequently. Dialogue between Judaism and other approaches in ethics does not depend on the establishment of common foundations. Consensus at any level of generality strengthens the warrant of the beliefs in question.

Example: Access to Health Care

The issue of justice and access to health care illustrates some of the ways in which the holistic model functions.[35] This issue reflects revolutionary developments in medical technology and social structure, and finds little direct precedent in the source of Jewish bioethics. In developing a response to this issue, both broad values and principles, and particular cases and rules, would play a role. Biblical narrative and law affirm the value of each individual human life, the obligation to meet the requirements of justice, and God's concern for the weak and poor.[36] Rabbinic

Judaism developed the Hebrew Bible's values of justice and support for the poor into an approach of *tzedakah,* literally meaning justice.[37]

These general concepts and values frame the broad contours of a Jewish ethical position but underdetermine such a view. These norms might be seen as compatible with radical egalitarianism, reliance on voluntary charity, or any of a spectrum of intermediate positions. They also fail to provide guidance about the level of health care that should be provided. Detailed rules found in Jewish sources add to the process. For example, *halakhic* sources indicate that "each individual is obligated to give *tzedakah.* . . . If one gives less than is appropriate, the courts may administer lashes until he gives according to the assessment, and the courts may go to his property in his presence and take the amount that it is appropriate for him to give."[38] The obligation for *tzedakah* in Judaism is binding, analogous to the obligation to pay income taxes in the United States. More generally, rabbinic Judaism developed a detailed system of enforceable obligations and careful allocation to achieve foundational justice.[39]

Further guidance is provided by drawing analogies with related issues. Cases involving lifesaving action represent a category of acute needs that are traditionally seen to take precedence even over general obligations of *tzedakah.* Most prominent is the redemption of captives, those captured by slave traders or unjustly held prisoner. Maimonides, for example, states that "the redemption of captives takes precedence over the support of the poor, and there is no greater obligatory precept than the redemption of captives." He offers the explanation that "a captive falls in the category of the hungry and the thirsty and the naked, and stands in danger of his life."[40] Accordingly, funds collected or allocated for any other purpose may be diverted to securing the release of captives when necessary. The redemption of captives provides a precedent analogous to at least some types of medical care. Both concern individuals who are suffering and may be in immediate danger, with special needs that vary greatly among individuals. Jewish ethics understands society to have a fundamental obligation to save lives whenever possible, diverting funds from other projects as required.[41]

A crucial issue remains of specifying the level of health care to be provided, especially when threats to life are not direct. In general, Jewish sources understand society to be responsible to assure provision of the needs of persons. The Talmud sets parameters in its exegesis of the verse in Deut. (15:8): "You shall surely open your hand to him, and shall surely lend him sufficient for his need/lack [*dei mahsoro*], according as he needs/lacks." The Talmud cites an earlier rabbinic interpretation: " 'Sufficient for his lack'—you are commanded to support him, and you are not commanded to enrich him; 'according as he lacks'—even a horse on which to ride, and a servant to run in front of him."[42] Later sources provide a list of paradigmatic examples. "If it is appropriate to give him bread, they give him bread; if dough, they give him dough; . . . if to feed him, they feed him. If he is not married and wants to take a wife, they enable him to marry; they rent a house for him, and provide a bed and furnishings. . . ."[43] However, traditional Jewish sources devote little attention to specifying the levels of food, shelter, or medical care required by justice. The key to the understanding of need seems to be the idea of lack, or that which is missing.[44] While individualized cases of persons coming to lack that which they had previously possessed are considered in the codes, the general standard against which lacks are evaluated is largely implicit and difficult to formulate with precision. These precedents, in conjunction with the general values noted earlier, provide significant but incomplete guidance in defining a societal responsibility to provide for health care needs. Extrapolating from these cases to modern health care concerns remains uncertain at best.

Here I believe that philosophical insights can add to the deliberative process by contributing to a clearer and more complete articulation of a Jewish ethical position. Philosophical ethicists such as Norman Daniels have developed a concept of needs in terms of "species-typical functioning." For Daniels, basic or

> course-of-life needs, would include food, shelter, clothing, exercise, rest, companionship, a mate. . . . [A] deficiency with respect to them "endangers the normal functioning of the subject of need considered as a member of a natural species. . . ." Health care needs will be those things we need in order to maintain, restore, or provide functional equivalents (where possible) to normal species functioning.[45]

Both Daniel's understanding of need in terms of lack, and his list of paradigmatic needs, correspond with the positions found in *halakhic* sources. This understanding contributes to a construction of Jewish sources that identifies a general principle, which in turn assists in discerning the implications of the traditional model for new cases.

More generally, ethical insights, deriving in part from philosophical ethics, subtly shape the deliberative process throughout. For example, I believe that drawing an analogy from redeeming captives to supplying health care for those in need is supported by a number of factors, which are not limited to but include ethical concerns. In contrast, I would be more reticent to draw analogies from some discussions in traditional sources about priorities of rescue. The Mishnah states that a Cohen (or priest) takes precedence over a Levite, who takes precedence over an Israelite, and so forth through lower castes.[46] Even if one is reluctant to condemn this passage, ethical concerns would be one factor counting against extending this ruling to contemporary cases. Throughout the process of deliberation, explicitly Jewish sources are central, but general ethical insights contribute to a process of reshaping and vindicating beliefs.

Conversely, Jewish sources in turn could lead to the reshaping and vindicating of general ethical positions on these matters. The Jewish model of *tzedakah* provides a set of understandings and practices, developed to be both principled and pragmatic, for the achievement of social justice over a fairly broad-based community. At the least, this model can be heuristically useful as a source of insights and guidelines which might be appropriately translated to the contemporary United States. For committed Jews the translation of Jewish views of justice to American society is supported by the traditional injunction to support poor non-Jews along with poor Jews, "for the sake of the paths of peace."[47] For the general reader the relevance of Jewish insights on justice and health care depends on their intuitive appeal, their resonance with accepted American values, and their coherence with the perspectives of other groups and individuals in United States society.

The values of Judaism represent one important perspective within the United States' pluralistic society, to be compared with the perspectives of other groups and individuals as part of a process of developing a consensus. Aside from any value this may have in terms of politics or feasibility,[48] the consensus may have a deeper philosophical significance, although the scope of this paper allows only a brief sketching of this possibility.

In surveying the philosophical studies prepared for the President's Commission on Biomedical Ethics, Daniel Wikler finds significance in an overlapping consensus of various philosophical approaches. He notes that rival theories agree that "[e]very person ought to be assured of access to some decent minimum of health care service," and agues:

> This conclusion cannot be said to have been "proved" by this collection of arguments, but the fact that a recommendation of universal access to (at least some) health care follows from such disparate sets of premises suggests that the recommendation is "insensitive" to choice of moral theory. Even if we do not know which moral theory is correct, then, and thus cannot provide a ground-level-up proof that all should have access to a minimum of health care, such a belief has been rendered reasonable and perhaps even compelling.

The inclusion of Judaism (and other religious traditions) in this consensus bolsters the claim that the recommendation is theory-insensitive and thus strengthens the warranted status of the belief that access to health care ought to be provided.[49]

Finally, judgment is needed throughout the process. My holistic model does not provide any simple formula for decision making but rather depends on consideration of a wealth of factors. Often the final resolution, and certainly its details, depend on the prudent judgment of the decision maker. As described previously, intuitive judgment is neither a mystical insight nor an arbitrary choice, but rather expert judgment reflects the system of Jewish ethics as a whole. The need for such judgment becomes especially apparent as one attempts to move from the considerations noted earlier to specific policy choices, the articulation of clinical guidelines, and decision making in particular cases.

Conclusion

In this essay I have sketched the outlines of a holistic model for Jewish ethics and bioethics and have offered considerations that I believe support this model. I have shown how my holistic model accounts for the significance of general principles and particular rules and precedents; for the role of particular insights of conscience or judgment; and for the interaction of elements identified as Jewish with other sources of ethical insight such as philosophical ethics. Each of these elements contributes to the enterprise of Jewish bioethics; conversely, no one factor is definitive of Jewish bioethics, or takes priority over all competing concerns. In the event of conflict or uncertainty, a process of careful deliberation is required.

My approach thus differs from those of some other thinkers both methodologically, in rejecting foundationalism, and substantively, in arguing that their favored element (whether precedent, principle, or conscientious insight) will not always be decisive. The holistic model for Jewish bioethics is an old-new approach, one that I believe both corresponds with approaches in the Jewish tradition and recommends itself for contemporary work in Jewish ethics, including bioethics. The model is compatible with realism, with certain actions being objectively required as God's will or rationally compelling, but does not require foundationalism. Rather, the combination of input and coherence serves to reshape and vindicate beliefs in Jewish bioethics.

The current state of knowledge is imperfect in this as in all fields. While the importance and profundity of the issues in Jewish bioethics make claims of certainty attractive, they also emphasize the importance of humility, intellectual honesty, and responsibility. Traditionally, the greatest of judges in difficult cases would use phrases such as *l'fi aniyut dati*, "according to the modesty of my understanding," and *tzarich iyyun*, "the matter requires further attention." Uncertainty would be acknowledged, and the process would be open to new considerations. A process of careful deliberation would yield guidance that is substantive and valuable but not absolute. The work of the holistic process of study, deliberation, and ethical action will not yield simple and definitive answers. The process, like Rawls' reflective equilibrium, is always ongoing.

Notes

I would like to thank Elliot Dorff and Neil Gillman for their insightful comments, and Tom Beauchamp, Henry Richardson, and LeRoy Walters for their help in an earlier work in which I developed the philosophical model on which I drew in preparing this paper. The remaining faults are, of course, my own.

1. Daniel Gordis, "Wanted—The Ethical in Jewish Bio-Ethics," *Judaism* 38 (1989): 28–40.
2. Louis E. Newman, "Woodchoppers and Respirators: The Problem of Interpretation in Contemporary Jewish Ethics," *Modern Judaism* 10 (1990): 17–42 (reprinted in this volume as Chapter 10).
3. David H. Ellenson, "How to Draw Guidance from a Heritage: Jewish Approaches to Mortal Choices," in *A Time to Be Born and a Time to Die: The Ethics of Choice*, ed. Barry S. Kogan (New York: Aldine de Gruyter, 1991), 219–32 (reprinted in this volume as Chapter 9).
4. An approach that relied on a definition or methodological criterion as absolutely definitive, or that attempted to base itself on infallible particular judgments and reason solely from the more specific to the more general, would also exhibit a foundationalist structure.
5. See, e.g., Baruch A. Brody, *Life and Death Decision Making* (New York: Oxford University Press, 1988); Albert R. Jonsen and Stephen Toulmin, *The Abuse of Casuistry: A History of Moral Reasoning* (Berkeley: University of California Press, 1988); and Aaron L. Mackler, "Cases and Judgments in Ethical Reasoning: An Appraisal of Contemporary Causistry and Holistic Model for the Mutual Support of Norms and Case Judgments," Ph.D. diss., Georgetown University, 1992, esp. 66–72.
6. John Rawls, *A Theory of Justice* (Cambridge, Mass.: Belknap Press, Harvard University Press, 1971), 21, 579.
7. The holistic model is akin to a coherence approach to justification, not a coherence understanding of truth. On this difference, see, e.g., Laurence BonJour, *The Structure of Empirical Knowledge* (Cambridge, Mass: Harvard University Press, 1985), 157–58. The model is compatible with a variety of metaethical views. I argue elsewhere for the compatibility of a holistic approach to justification with a correspondence understanding of truth, with our coherently justified beliefs providing evidence of moral validity or truth. The approach is one of indirect realism and draws on models developed for empirical knowledge and natural science as well as in ethics. See Mackler, "Cases."
8. I do not claim that my holistic model is unprecedented in Jewish thought. Rather, I take it as a merit of my approach that it accords with much of the most profound and compelling work in Jewish ethics, including consideration of ethical issues in *halakhah*. My

explicitly holistic model should clarify the approach implicit in such works. By explicitly raising the need for a variety of input, it also will serve to broaden the range of factors feeding into the deliberative process, enriching the process and contributing to its vindication. Articulating a holistic methodology also will help to guard against oversimplification and impoverishment in Jewish ethical thought, whether motivated by religious ideology or a belief that narrow foundations must be accepted as the price of philosophical respectability.

I believe that the holistic model would apply for Jewish ethics, as informed by *halakhah,* or for *halakhah* (construed broadly) as it addresses ethical issues. To the extent that these two areas can be distinguished, different elements within the model may be emphasized for one or the other. On the relationship of Jewish law and ethics, see, e.g., Elliot N. Dorff, "The Interaction of Jewish Law and Morality," *Judaism* 26 (1977): 455–66; Louis E. Newman, "Ethics as Law, Law as Religion: Reflections on the Problem of Law and Ethics in Judaism," *Shofar* 9 (1990): 13–31; and the sources cited on p. 13 of the latter article [reprinted in this volume as Chapter Two].

9. John Rawls, *A Theory of Justice,* 195–201, 19–22, 46–53, 577–87; idem, "The Independence of Moral Theory," *Proceedings and Addresses of the American Philosophical Association* 48 (1974–75): 7–8; Norman Daniels, "Wide Reflective Equilibrium and Theory Acceptance in Ethics," *Journal of Philosophy* 76 (1979): 257 n. See also Rawls, "Outline of a Decision Procedure for Ethics," *Philosophicaal Review* 60 (1951): 178–82.

10. BonJour, *The Structure of Empirical Knowledge,* 93.

11. BonJour, *The Structure of Empirical Knowledge,* 91–100. BonJour's account of coherence fits well with Rawl's model of reflective equilibrium and approach to justification, and helps to tie together what may appear to be disparate elements of Rawls's discussion in *A Theory of Justice.* If reflective equilibrium is understood simply to seek a consistent set of judgments and principles, then theoretical concerns and inferential arguments (which are clearly important to Rawls) would play a separate and supplemental role in Rawls's holistic justification. With coherence understood in BonJour's strong sense, the pursuit of coherence in wide reflective equilibrium incorporates such concerns. Cf. the differing approach of Daniels, "Wide Reflective Equilibrium," 258–61.

12. As noted earlier, the holistic model allows reasoning to proceed from the general to the particular or the particular to the general in local contexts of justification. Global justification incorporates both sorts of arguments in the pursuit of coherence, properly understood. The pursuit of coherence may well lead not only to revisions of particular judgments but also to significant change in concepts and general principles. See Mackler, "Cases and Judgments in Ethical Reasoning," 253 n.

13. Martin Luther King Jr., *A Testament of Hope: The Essential Writings and Speeches of Martin Luther King, Jr.,* ed. James Melvin Washington (New York: HarperCollins, 1986), 289–302, esp. 293–94, 298–302; 217. Substantively, a law is unjust when it degrades human personality; formally, a law is unjust when it is not universal and binding on all; procedurally, a law is unjust when a minority is excluded from the process of its creation.

14. One recontruction of King's argument would pose obeying the law and opposing segregation as conflicting prima facie obligations. On prima facie duties, see W. D. Ross, *The Right and the Good* (Oxford: Clarendon Press, Oxford University Press, 1930); Tom L. Beauchamp and James F. Childress, *Principles of Biomedical Ethics,* 3d ed. (New York: Oxford University Press, 1989), 51–55. James D. Wallace's (compatible) reconstruction focuses on an appeal to the values undergirding the conflicting principles, in particular to the basic value or point of lawfulness. In King's words: "I submit that an individual who breaks a law that conscience tells him is unjust, and willingly accepts the penalty by staying in jail to arouse the conscience of the community over its injustice, is in reality expressing the very highest respect for the law" (King, *A Testament of Hope,* 294; James D. Wallace, *Moral Relevance and Moral Conflict* [Ithaca, N.Y.: Cornell University Press, 1988], 87–93.

15. King, *A Testament of Hope,* 290–98. King also invokes cultural paradigms, ranging

from Amos to Thomas Jefferson, in arguing by analogy for the legitimacy of his "extremism" in pursuit of justice.

16. Consistent with the maxim that good ethics begins with good facts, King stresses the need for "collection of the facts" as the first step of a nonviolent campaign of civil disobedience. King describes the organizational structure of the Southern Christian Leadership Conference and summarizes a variety of economic and political considerations contributing to the choice of a particular day on which to begin demonstrations. He emphasizes as well that the proper ethical response in Birmingham in March 1963 cannot be reduced to a set of actions but requires specific intentions and the cultivation of qualities of character as well. "One who breaks an unjust law must do it openly, lovingly"; tone and intention are here integral parts of the action of civil disobedience (ibid., 294, 289–91).

King shows that detailed claims and arguments of the sort associated with casuistry are fully compatible with claims and arguments made at a general level, such as those concerning the criteria determining the justice of a law. His essay exemplifies the key elements of casuistry as presented by Jonsen and Toulmin, *The Abuse of Casuistry,* esp. 251–57. King relies on paradigms and analogies, and invokes maxims. He analyzes circumstances, giving attention to the traditional list of "who, what, where, when, why, how, and by what means." King also develops a cumulative set of arguments, leading to a resolution, a forceful statement of the proper action in the case at hand. King's essay shows both that commitment to a moral imperative is compatible with careful deliberation and attention to detail and that a casuistic method is compatible with certainty and forceful commitment. While King devotes little attention to issues of ethical theory in his essay, this does not reflect an incompatibility between theory and the ethical considerations he does addresses but rather a choice of focus and emphasis. Rawls (*A Theory of Justice,* 364 n) notes the compatibility and complementarity of his more theoretical approach and that of King.

17. Gordis, "Wanted—The Ethical in Jewish Bio-Ethics," 32, 34, 38.

18. Shulhan Arukh, Y.D. 339.

19. Varying interpretations of the *goses* precedent are surveyed by Newman, "Woodchoppers and Respirators," 22–26; Immanuel Jakobovits, *Jewish Medical Ethics,* 2d ed. (New York: Bloch, 1975), 121–25, 275–76; Avram Israel Reisner, "A Halakhic Ethic of Care for the Terminally Ill," *Conservative Judaism* 43, no. 3 (1991): 52–89; Fred Rosner, "Euthanasia," in his *Modern Medicine and Jewish Ethics,* 2d ed. (Hoboken, N.J.: KTAV, and New York: Yeshiva University Press, 1991), 197–215; Eliezer Yehudah Waldenberg, *Tzitz Eliezer* (Jerusalem: Mosad Harav Kook, 1985), 13, no. 89. An approach to this issue based on a differing set of precedents may be found in Elliot N. Dorff, "A Jewish Approach to End-Stage Medical Care," *Conservative Judaism* 43, no. 3 (1991): 3–51.

20. See, e.g., Annette Baier, *Postures of the Mind* (Minneapolis: University of Minnesota Press, 1985), 230; Rawls, *A Theory of Justice,* 51, 577–79. For further discussion of these concerns, see Mackler, "Cases and Judgments in Ethical Reasoning." Writers argue that we may have greater knowledge and confidence at the more specific than at the theoretically more fundamental level; the methodology of natural science suggests that justification and claims to knowledge begin with the more specific and slowly work through intermediate levels of generalization, rather than rush to first principles and grand theory (Ross, *The Right and the Good,* 19ff.; Stephen E. Toulmin, *The Place of Reason in Ethics* [Chicago: University of Chicago Press, 1986]; repr. of *An Examination of the Place of Reason in Ethics* [Cambridge: Cambridge University Press, 1950], 172–76; Rawls, *A Theory of Justice,* e.g., 19–21, 579–86; Brody, *Life and Death Decision Making,* 13–14).

21. Similarly, both Jewish ethics and Jewish thought in general have proven too complex to allow the statement of a definitive set of principles, despite the attempts of Maimonides and others in the Middle Ages, as well as thinkers in the modern era.

22. While Eugene Borowitz posits the individual's conscientious understanding as the ultimate touchstone of ethical decision making, he acknowledges the limitations of classical

liberalism. "The vision of humankind as rational and rationality itself implying a Kant-like ethics lost its old compelling power. . . . What remained of Kantian ethics faded as psychoanalysis from within and anthropology and Marxism from without demonstrated that, realistically, 'conscience' mostly meant the introjected parent or group interest." Or as Boroowitz more bluntly quotes from the book of Jeremiah, "The heart is the most devious of all things—and desperately sick. Who can understand it?" Eugene B. Borowitz, *Exploring Jewish Ethics* (Detroit: Wayne State University Press, 1990), 182, 131, 85, citing Jer. 17:9.

23. See Bernard Williams, *Ethics and the Limits of Philosophy* (Cambridge, Mass.: Harvard University Press, 1985), 93–94. Baruch A. Brody attempts to revive such cognitive intuitionism in *Life and Death Decision Making* and in "Intuitions and Objective Moral Knowledge," *Monist* 62 (1977): 446–56.

24. Henry Sidgwick, *The Methods of Ethics*, 7th ed. (London: Macmillan, 1907; repr., Indianapolis: Hackett Publishing Company, 1981), 98–100 (bk. 1, chap. 8).

25. Richard N. Boyd, "How to Be a Moral Realist," in *Essays on Moral Realism*, ed. Geoffrey Sayre-McCord (Ithaca, N.Y.: Cornell University Press, 1988), 192–93, 200. Likewise in medicine, clinical judgment is often needed to formulate a diagnosis, prognosis, or treatment recommendation. The need for clinical judgment does not reduce the importance of physical findings and laboratory tests of the particular patient, or knowledge of general norms and familiarity with analogous cases. Moreover, the intuitive judgment is not a mystical insight but builds on the training of the physician in the general norms and methodologies of medicine, and experience with many cases. See also Mackler, "Cases and Judgments in Ethical Reasoning," esp. 282–85.

26. Ibid., 207–8. Boyd characterizes the process as one of reflective equilibrium.

27. Aharon Lichtenstein, "Does Jewish Tradition Recognize an Ethic Independent of Halakha?" in *Contemporary Jewish Ethics*, ed. Menachem Marc Kellner (New York: Sanhedrin Press, 1978), 114–17.

28. In my review of Eugene Borowitz's *Exploring Jewish Ethics*, *CCAR Journal* 40 (Spring 1993): 89–91.

29. Borowitz, *Exploring Jewish Ethics*, 34, 202; idem, *Renewing the Covenant* (Philadelphia: Jewish Publication Society, 1991), 64.

30. Borowitz, *Exploring Jewish Ethics*, 190.

31. Babylonian Talmud [B.] *Bava Metzia* 59b.

32. As Rawls (*A Theory of Justice*, 42–43) explains the concept, lexical ordering "is an order which requires us to satisfy the first principle in the ordering before we can move on to the second, the second before we consider the third, and so on. A principle does not come into play until those previous to it are either fully met or do not apply."

33. Stuart Hampshire, *Morality and Conflict* (Cambridge, Mass.: Harvard University Press, 1983), 148. Hampshire argues for the essential differentiation of various ways of life in choosing among not fully compatible values. He allows that some norms, such as justice and utility, represent ethical criteria that hold across societies.

34. A commitment to reasoning within the context of a tradition and belief in the primacy of one's own tradition are compatible with the modification of the tradition in response to outside input. See Alasdair MacIntyre, *After Virtue*, 2d ed. (Notre Dame, Ind.: University of Notre Dame Press, 1984), 270, 276; David Novak, *Jewish Social Ethics* (New York: Oxford University Press, 1992), 3–4; Mackler, "Cases and Judgments in Ethical Reasoning," 294–304. My model would agree with David Hartman's view that a "religious culture has greater opportunities for inner purification and depth when it widens its range of perception through exposures to modes of thought and experiences that stem from other cultural frameworks." *A Living Covenant: The Innovative Spirit in Traditional Judaism* (New York: The Free Press, Macmillan, 1985), 103.

35. I consider this issue in greater depth in Aaron L. Mackler, "Judaism, Justice, and Access to Health Care," *Kennedy Institute of Ethics Journal* 1 (1991): 143–61.

36. See, e.g., Gen. 1–4, 2:15; Deut. 10:17–18.

37. The Talmud (B. *Bava Batra* 9a–10a) states that *tzedakah* is as important as all other commandments put together, that it redeems from death and hastens the redemption of the world, and makes one worthy of receiving the divine presence. Traditional sources mandate personal consideration and respect for the poor; see Shulhan Arukh, Y.D. 249:3.

38. Shulhan Arukh, Y.D. 248:1.

39. See Shulhan Arukh, Y.D. 249, 256–57.

40. *Mattenot Aniyyim* 8:10. See similarly Shulhan Arukh, Y.D. 252:1.

41. Shulhan Arukh, Y.D. 252:4; B. *Gittin* 45a. The Talmud and later codes consider the possibility of a limit on extraordinary expenditures in order to avoid onerous societal burdens. While legal authorities do not explicitly reject such a concern, they accord it relatively little weight. The responsibility to provide for the redemption of captives may also be limited when the captive is responsible for his own predicament, though only in the most extreme cases. The Shulhan Arukh considers the case of one who sells himself into captivity, or is held prisoner as a result of defaulting on a loan. The community must pay to free the captive if this is the first or second time that he has brought about his own captivity, but the community need not make such payments after the third such occurrence. In case of immediate threat to the captive's life, though, even the captive responsible for his own captivity must be rescued. (Shulhan Arukh, Y.D. 252:6). By analogy, those who make choices (in lifestyle or health care) that turn out to be unfortunate or irresponsible thereby attenuate their claims to societal support but do not forfeit all such claims. Society must continue to provide some care even for those responsible for their own misfortune, especially in cases involving threats to life.

42. B. *Ketubbot* 67b.

43. Shulhan Arukh, Y.D. 250:1.

44. Thus the talmudic exegesis noted earlier. In his legal code Maimonides (*Mattenot Aniyyim* 7:3) paraphrases the guideline, "according to that which is lacking for the poor person, you are commanded to give him. . . . You are commanded to fill in for his lack, and you are not commanded to enrich him."

45. Norman Daniels, *Just Health Care* (Cambridge: Cambridge University Press, 1985), 26–32.

46. *Horayot* 3:7–8.

47. Shulhan Arukh, Y.D. 251:1.

48. Cf. John Rawls, "The Domain of the Political and Overlapping Consensus," *New York University Law Review* 64 (May 1989): 233–50.

49. Daniel Wikler "Philosophical Perspectives on Access to Health Care: An Introduction," in *Securing Access to Health Care: President's Commission for the Study of Ethical Problems in Medicine and Biomedical and Behavioral Research,* vol. 2 (Washington, D.C.: U.S. Government Printing Office, 1983). Wikler's argument fits well with my holistic model and with Norman Daniels's ("Wide Reflective Equilibrium" 275–78) account of wide reflective equilibrium, in particular with his discussion of intersubjective agreement and convergence as providing evidence of moral truth. When the widening of reflective equilibrium by including views of Judaism and other traditions results in convergence with results obtained on philosophical and secular grounds, it would seem that the evidence for moral truth is strengthened. On overlapping consensus, see also Rawls, "The Domain of the the Political." A yet more ambitious claim for the significance of Jewish views for United States policy is advanced in Elliot N. Dorff, "Jewish Tradition and National Policy," to be published by State University of New York Press in a volume edited by Daniel Frank.

E. Alternative Visions of Jewish Ethics

13

Jewish Ethics after the Holocaust

MICHAEL L. MORGAN

Situation and Criteria

In his collected responsa (*teshuvot*), Rabbi Ephraim Oshry records *halakhic* decisions, made in the Kovno ghetto during the Nazi Holocaust, that adjust the Jewish legal tradition in order to oppose the deepest purposes of the Nazi state. In a rare case, for example, in which the permission to commit suicide is sought before the fact, Oshry overturns the dominant *halakhic* prohibition (Rosenbaum, 1976: 35–40). He permits the act. But to advocate suicide is to encourage a lack of trust in God and thereby to encourage the Nazis in their attempt to eradicate the Jewish soul together with the Jewish body. So he nonetheless forbids the publication of his decision, and his grounds are at once profound and moving. There is a subtle dialectic in R. Oshry's judgment, for a once-secure trust and hope in God, negated by the decision to permit the suicide, is reaffirmed in the refusal to allow a Nazi victory. A self-reliant acceptance of human initiative and need, affirmed by Oshry's permission, is negated by the reason for that permission, the uncompromising opposition to Nazi purposes. Finally, the religious conviction, recorded in the will to confide in *halakhah* and compromised by the intrusion of an utterly historical purpose, is ultimately reaffirmed by the nature of that purpose, to oppose evil by embracing its object, by clinging to God, a tradition, trust, and hope.

Jewish law and Jewish integrity should characterize any serious, authentic foundation for Jewish moral thinking today, but they will not be its starting point. Rather its beginnings will be the intellectual and historical situation of contemporary Jews and Judaism. This is one of the lessons of R. Oshry's experiences in Kovno. To be sure, there is an initial, almost intuitive presumption in favor of recovering the past, and in the domain of Jewish moral thinking that means, among other things, examining the tradition of Jewish law or *halakhah* and taking it seriously. In fact, however, even that presumption must itself be ratified, and that ratification must be historically situated. Furthermore, once it is agreed that it is necessary to recover the Jewish legal tradition for the present, that recovery—whether it is by an Orthodox *posek* in New York, a member judge of the Israeli supreme court, or a Reform rabbi in Chicago—is determined by the historical and intellectual world of the contemporary Jew. History, on this account, intrudes itself both at the fundamental level where the obligation to recover the past is ultimately moored and the derivative level of interpretation and appropriation. Contemporary Jewish thought as a whole should begin with that history and a sense of which events in it are determinative or orienting (Fackenheim, 1970:8–9). I would like to propose that by starting with the Holocaust we can formulate an account of Jewish obligation and particularly of Jewish moral obligation that responds in a profound way to the deepest Jewish intuitions and to the most serious criteria for Jewish thinking today.[1]

Among modern discussions of Jewish ethics, there is an overriding uniformity. Natural law theories, Kantian-style rationalisms, and traditional divine-command moral theories—all rest on the convictions that the heart of a moral theory is its principles or obligations and that these principles ought to be universal and unconditional (for example, see Fox, 1975, 1979; Kellner, 1978). From Mendelssohn to Cohen, from Luzatto to Marvin Fox, Jewish moral thinkers have viewed ethical imperatives as immune to historical considerations. In this I take issue with this fundamental assumption. What is developed here is the foundation of a historically situated moral theory that in its own way attempts to mediate the extremes of relativism and absolutism.[2]

In a preliminary way this mediation can be characterized as follows. Like every divine-command theory, the ethical theory I shall sketch holds that moral imperatives derive their obligatory status from their source, God and the divine will. (For discussion of the logic of such theories, see Quinn, 1978.) It is because this source is an ultimate authority that obligations which express his will are themselves authoritative. But while the *status* of moral principles is fixed by their source, the *content* of such principles is determined by their formulation and articulation. And, on the view of revelation presupposed by the theory, that articulation is wholly human. (For the basis of this theory of revelation, see Buber, 1970, 1958: 75–77; Rosenzweig, 1970: 156–204; Glatzer, 1953: 208–9, 242–47, 285; Fackenheim, 1968: 13–17, 1967, 1970: chaps. 1 and 2, 1980: chap. 3; Haberman, 1969.) This content is human interpretation that arises out of the historical situation of people who respond verbally and nonverbally to the divine presence. Hence, for the theory I shall outline, the ground of obligation is absolute, but the specific obligations are historical, conditional, revisable, and relative. Language, like action, does not constitute the revelation of the divine presence; the latter is given to man in itself and immediately.[3] Rather, language emerges as a human response or interpretation which articulates the meaning of the event of revelation for those who receive and accept it.

The more distant one is in time from an event of revelation, the more complex is the network of action and interpretation that serves as the bridge between those who directly and originally encountered the presence and those who seek to respond at a later time. For one who comes after a religious tradition has grown up, then, the problems of appropriating the event and receiving the tradition are complex. In part, the moral theory here developed tries to explore how that appropriation and reception work in a particular case, the moral case. From this point of view, the study of Jewish ethics is a study of the continuity of the Jewish legal tradition insofar as it is a tradition that crucially depends on its reception and the conditions for that reception. At the same time, it is a tradition that shapes and determines, to one extent or another, the situation out of which that reception occurs and the character of those who receive it. In short, the study of Jewish ethics is in part a study of the nature and development of Jewish tradition.

What criteria must our moral theory satisfy? How shall we know if the theory is acceptable and authentically Jewish? These are very difficult questions to answer. Only a fully developed account of the nature of Jewish tradition and the character and conditions for its change, with a special eye to its deontic component, could begin to provide such answers.[4] Still, insofar as the theory arises out of a historical situation, it ought to encounter and successfully meet the needs of that situation. It cannot ignore modern challenges to God and revelation; nor can it neglect claims about human freedom, motivation, and purpose. In short, it cannot reject, without thorough examination, modern philosophy and thought. At the same time, it cannot ignore those events and situations that have shaped the experience of Jews today—Jewish history, literature, and practice; the Holocaust; the rebirth and defense of the Jewish state; and the changing character of Jewish life in America and of Western culture generally. All of these factors must be engaged and understood and either accepted or rejected, in part or as a whole. While we cannot perform these tasks here, we can, however, offer a pragmatic alternative. Our theory ought to satisfy certain intuitions that contemporary Jews might be expected to have about any acceptable Jewish moral theory and without which such a theory would simply not be compelling at all.[5] These intuitions might be captured in the following criteria:

1. An authentic Jewish moral theory must ignore neither the past nor the present. For to ignore the past is to cut oneself off from the historically developing destiny of the Jewish people, and to ignore the present is to court irrelevancy and anachronism.

2. An authentic Jewish moral theory must neglect neither God nor man. For Jewish ethics is by its very nature rooted in a divine command that is imposed and yet freely accepted.[6] To ignore or deny God is to cater to a thoroughgoing relativism that is pernicious or to pander to our failings and frailties rather than to take a stand in opposition to them. And to ignore man is to show disrespect for a liberal truth that Judaism itself has always endorsed, the Torah, at once divinely given, must be freely received in order to enrich and not stifle human living.

3. An authentic Jewish moral theory must ignore neither the Jewish people nor the needs of humankind. For to do the former is to lapse into an abstract universalism that is as insufficient in theory as its effects have been painful in fact. (See, on Judaism and the liberal democrat, Sartre, 1948: 55–58; Fackenheim, 1973: 203–13, 1978: chaps. 11, 14.) And to neglect the latter is to deny to others the concern and respect one wants and expects for oneself and thereby to lapse into a parochialism at least as intolerable as the univeralism it opposes.

4. An authentic Jewish moral theory must be a part of a larger theory of Jewish existence and Jewish destiny today. For the moral ideals and imperatives that fall upon Jews should take their place among the variety of obligations and opportunities that shape and structure contemporary Jewish life.

5. An authentic Jewish moral theory must provide both an account of what

Jewish obligations are—how they emerge, what their sources are, and how they are affected by history—and a strategy for identifying, interpreting, and communicating those obligations.

A Jewish moral theory that satisfied these conditions would be rich and fruitful. It would recognize the dramatic importance of the Holocaust for Jewish self-understanding today. It would, furthermore, appreciate the significance of Israel to that self-understanding and would, at the same time, confront with a proper sense of realism the moral sense of Jews outside of Israel. Such a theory would be continuous with the past, drawing on the riches of biblical, *halakhic,* and midrashic literature, and yet it would recognize a central role for both Divine Command and human freedom. It would be a distinctly, unapologetically Jewish theory for which the contemporary historical situation of the Jewish people is essentially determinative. Hence, such a theory would sacrifice the security of moral absolutes and the comfort of an easy universalism to its own essential historicity, opening up honest access to others by shutting off the routes of a disingenuous brotherhood. This theory, in short, would found a Judaism that had learned to live with itself because it will have ceased avoiding its own flesh-and-blood reality.[7]

The Program for the Theory

The framework for such a theory is available. (See Fackenheim, 1968: 17–20; 1970: chap. 3.) The Holocaust and the historical situation of Jews in the modern world are its starting points, and they define the terms and method whereby the past is to be appropriated for the present and future. The Holocaust as part of the theory's historical center authorizes that very appropriation and gives it shape, for by its very character the Holocaust has altered our views about human nature, moral psychology, religious purpose, hope, trust, and resolve. The theory I have in mind develops from its core with due caution, a reserve that suits all too well the horror, the trauma, and the irredeemable evil that surely shatter the serenity of any sane person (see Améry, 1980; Des Pres, 1976). But once the theory finds its way beyond the Holocaust, not by negating it nor by diminishing its priority but rather by acknowledging its depth in a profoundly honest way, it emerges as a strategy for Jewish life today and in the future.[8] Jewish moral thinking finds its place within such a theory and develops as an attempt to provide an account of how moral imperatives arise for Jews, on what basis their moral force is founded, and how they are determined.

The reasoning in support of the theory begins with an initial desire to understand or comprehend the meaning of the Holocaust. What shape does the reasoning take? To be sure, it is neither deductive nor inductive in any standard sense. Rather it begins with an attempt to explain the Holocaust and, once that attempt breaks down, proceeds to ask what significance the event might still have for subsequent Jewish history and Jewish life. The strategy will be to invite the possibility that there *is* such a significance for subsequent Jewish life, to interpret Jewish conduct in terms of this significance, and finally to elaborate that significance by means of a "transcendental deduction" of the conditions within Jewish life and within the Holocaust without which this interpreted significance could not exist. This latter stage, moreover, develops as a series of responses to four questions: What are Jews now doing?

Can Jewish conduct be interpreted as responsive to the Holocaust? What is the precise character of that responsiveness? And what is the ground of that action as so interpreted and understood? This procedure is an example, in a sense, of the kind of interpretive enterprise one might engage in at any time in order to try to understand the role of a compelling event in its historical setting. Presumably it is reasoning initially motivated by a sense that the event *is* compelling and pursued when its significance becomes elusive and problematic. The reasoning proceeds as follows.

1. The Holocaust is *unique*.[9] This statement is neither trivial nor absurd. It is not trivial because it means more than that the Holocaust differs from all other historical events. And it is not absurd because it does not make the Holocaust sui generis in every respect, unlike every other event in every way. What the statement of uniqueness does mean is that the Holocaust is sufficiently different from all *preceding* events—in terms of ideological purpose, technological manipulation, calculated administration, the character of the criminals, the dehumanization of the victims, and so on—to identify the time thereafter as a new stage in history.[10] Its claim on us, moreover, depends not on the event's uniqueness per se but rather on the particular features or constellation of features that make it unique.

2. These features are so horrifying, so traumatic that they paralyze our capacity to explain them. To be sure, this paralysis is not going to be obvious or applicable to all. Surely our attempts to explain and understand the Holocaust will have to be examined and assessed. But for those who accept this judgment of paralysis, no matter how much we come to understand about the Holocaust's antecedent conditions, about the events that follow it, about human nature, or religious doctrine, the Holocaust defies comprehension. No philosophical, theological, psychological, or historical theory adequately explains a sufficient number of its central features to leave us with a confident sense that we have understood this event or have grasped its meaning (Fackenheim, 1970: 69–84; 1973: 192–95; 1980: chaps. 1 and 4). The Holocaust, in short, is as recalcitrant to intellectual as it is to emotional satisfaction. It permits no complacency of thought.

3. But explanatory meaning, comprehending why events occur, does not exhaust all meaning. A failure to locate an event within a theory, be it theological, historical, or whatever, does not entail that the event has no meaning at all for any or all of us.[11]

4. Indeed, all Jewish life subsequent to the Holocaust can be understood with respect to it. Some Jews have acted and do act in conscious response to the Holocaust. Others do not respond consciously or intentionally, but their conduct, too, can be interpreted as responses to it. The meaning that an event has for an agent differs from, and may be independent of, the meaning of the event as understood by a third party with respect to that agent. The former depends on the agent's beliefs and intentions, while the latter is the result of an independent interpreter's reflective comprehension. Indeed, actions can be described and interpreted in many ways; when actions are interpreted as responsive to a given event, whether or not the thought of that event is a conscious component in the agent's intentions, we can say that the event in question has a meaning with respect to that action.[12] This is the case with the Holocaust. Having no *explanatory meaning* for it, we nonetheless have discovered its *interpreted meaning* for subsequent Jewish life. And since all description is situated, determined by the presuppositions, prejudices, and condi-

tions of a time and a place, our description of Jewish conduct and Jewish life as responsive is not discredited by our reasons for so doing. Indeed, our reasons authorize and authenticate that description.[13]

5. These responses reflect an uncompromising opposition to the destructive goals of the Nazi regime. This is the answer to the third of the series of four questions that we listed earlier and now must proceed to answer. First, we notice that Jews today cling to Jewish survival and identification; they underwrite Jewish hope; they show guarded optimism in human goodness, or at least in human capacity, but an optimism nonetheless (Fackenheim, 1968: 19; 1973: 166–67). This conduct can be interpreted as responsive to the Holocaust in the way we have just described (4). All in all, then, the very strength of this responsive and responsible opposition to Nazi purposes makes one wonder about the *basis* for such stubbornness. It is not whimsical or arbitrary to understand this uncompromising opposition as a response to an obligation that is itself uncompromising, unconditional, and absolute. Indeed, in order to understand this action seriously, nothing weaker than such imperative force will do.[14]

6. Absolute imperatives come only from absolute sources, and in Judaism there is only one such source, the divine presence of the commanding God who spoke at Sinai and who speaks still.[15] This is the answer to our fourth question. Now, to be sure, positing such a source, we resist seeing the Jewish responsiveness as conditional. We resist, too, identifying a human or natural source for the obligation, be it qualified or unqualified. (For arguments against such "humanly created ideals," see Fackenheim, 1970: 83.) Our resistance, however, while it may be premature, is not wholly unjustified. Indeed, as we shall see, it can be understood as an example of the very opposition which, in a sense, it grounds.

To this point, then, our account had identified the source of post-Holocaust Jewish imperatives as a divine commanding presence situated within the Holocaust itelf. However, for those interested, as we are, in understanding how Jewish moral thinking develops its imperatives in response to such a presence, we have not proceeded far enough. How, then, does this program for a "transcendental deduction" of the divine commanding presence at Auschwitz lead to a mode of Jewish responsiveness that is structured by moral imperatives of the commanding God?

7. If we couple our conclusion with a concept of revelation as an immediate relation between God and man, and if the content of such a relation takes the form of a *command* and a *response,* both conceived not as divine contributions but rather as human interpretations of the *meaning* of the divine-human encounter, we can begin to see how particular obligations emerge from that encounter. (For this concept of revelation, see Fackenheim, 1976, and other works cited above.) Jewish moral obligations, like all obligations understood to emanate from that presence, are, in one sense, absolute in their source but, in another, relative, human, and historical in their determinate content. The force or impact that founds them is divine; the interpretive responsiveness that articulates them is human. The latter is a finite receptivity that is revisable and provisional, the former an infinite presence that unconditionally demands that *some* response be made. Hence, because the response is imperative, it cannot be a response to the *mere* event, which, even though unique, is still but an event in the world, but must be a response to a divine voice. And because the response and the Voice are related only in terms of the event itself, the Voice must be present *there.*

8. For those who seek to identify the moral obligations of contemporary Jews, one must proceed to interpret what it is that the commanding presence at Auschwitz commands of us. This is no easy task. Since the articulation of such commands is a matter of human interpretation where the individuals, the situations, and the moments of revelation differ, there are no uniform formulae for how to proceed. Still, one needs some guidance, and our theory would be seriously wanting if it did not attempt to provide it.

Objection, Revision, and Guidance

In a sense, we have already begun to articulate the commands in step 5 of our reasoning (Fackenheim, 1970: 84–92). There we describe the responses of Jews subsequent to the Holocaust not as responses to the event itself but rather as responses to an imperative or set of imperatives. We proceeded with such a description on the grounds that the uncompromising character of the responsiveness was only properly understood if we posited an obligation to mediate, as it were, the relation between the Holocaust and the Jews of today. If this were satisfactory and of the kinds of responses we had in mind—acts of opposition, whether conscious and intentional or not—were acceptable, then indeed we would already have begun to define Jewish obligation even prior to arriving at its source.

There are, however, questions about steps 4 and 5, and only when these questions are noted and answered can we actually begin to see how the imperatives of contemporary Jewish life properly emerge.

Step 5 arises after we turn to Jewish life subsequent to the Holocaust and, having understood that life as responsive to the Holocaust, try to discern the imperatives that ground that responsiveness. Clearly, however, even a casual consideration shows that contemporary Jewish life only poorly supports such a judgment. To be sure, it is *our decision* to interpret or describe Jewish experience as responsive that is at issue here and not a matter of empirical fact. Hence, one looks not for proof or evidence but rather for encouragement, support, or reason sufficient to justify such a choice and interpretation. But even this eludes us. Increased intermarriage, weakened formal affiliation with the Jewish community, and population depletion hardly encourage an interpretation of Jewish life as being in dramatic opposition to Nazi purposes, nor do they reflect an uncompromising will to survive. Even a distinction between actions intended as responses and those only interpreted as responses does not save steps 4 and 5 as they are currently stated. For while any action or inaction could conceivably be interpreted as a response to the radical evil of Auschwitz, it is hardly satisfying or comforting to be restricted to interpreting actions or trends that so obviously seem to capitulate to that evil. Furthermore, such a strategy, if it did not fail for these reasons, would surely fail if the responses were *largely* unintentional. Some small justification, beyond our own aborted quest for meaning in the Holocaust, ought to recommend treating Jewish life as responsive to that event. This justification can only come with *international response* and, as we suggested earlier, with intentional, dedicated response that is as well intentional, dedicated opposition. As we look around us, however, too few models, if any, of such opposition come into view. Thought, paralyzed by the Holocaust, cannot seek refuge outside of that event. Perhaps, then, we are at a loss because we are looking in the wrong direction.[16]

These worries about steps 4 and 5 extend to step 6. Having derived and located a divine commanding presence—even if somewhat prematurely—we confront a bewildering dilemma. A divine presence is present to persons in history. If *we* are those who hear, then the presence must be present now, and one wonders what links it to the events of the 1940s. On the other hand, however, if the commanding voice we have identified speaks at Auschwitz, as we have argued, then how can we, now, hear that voice? If the presence was there, then the event was there and the divine-human encounter as well. But how then can we, here and now, be participants in that encounter? How, indeed, can that voice speak to us?

A moment ago we looked for paradigms of dedicated, intentional opposition to Nazi purposes and were disappointed. Now we find ourselves alienated from the very presence whose force is to be the ground of our imperatives. What we seek is a solution to both our difficulties, and that solution must be a bridge between now and then and also between us and the voice of the commanding God. We seek a model of opposition whose actions are listening to that Voice and a speaking to us; we seek a link between us and the divine presence at Auschwitz, a mediator who encounters God in the immediacy of the moment and, at the same time, makes possible our own mediated appropriation of that Voice today.

The stories of such mediators are being told and retold with increasing frequency (Bauer, 1979: 26–40; Des Pres, 1976; Berkovits, 1979; Fackenheim, 1973: 166–68, 1978: chap. 13). They include the tale of Yossel Rosensaft and his fellow inmates in Auschwitz, who, in December of 1944, celebrated Hanukkah with a wooden menorah, carved with spoons, and with candles made of old cartons. Together they sang the traditional Hunakkah song, "Maoz Tsur Yeshuati," a song of praise for God's salvation, for the redemption from Egypt, for the relief from exile in Babylonia, for the foiling of Haman's plot, and finally for the miraculous victory that Hannukah itself celebrates. A traditional song, to be sure, but a setting that is so untraditional as to make the singing of that song an act of transcending opposition to the masters of Auschwitz and their purposes. There is, too, the frequent repeating of the injunction of Rabbi Yizhak Nissenbaum, who, in the Warsaw ghetto of 1940–41, acknowledged that the tradition of Kiddush Ha-Shem, martyrdom as a sanctification of God's name, had been replaced by an imperative to sanctify not death but life. "In former times," he said, "when the enemy demanded the soul of the Jew, the Jews sacrificed their bodies 'for the sanctification of God's Name'; now, however, the oppressor wants the body of the Jew; it is therefore one's duty to protect it, to guard one's life" (quoted by Berkovits, 1979: 99–100). The true Jewish vengeance, a Holocaust victim once wrote, is the power of the Jewish soul and its faith, an abiding trust that cries out "Hear, O Israel" in the face of guns and gallows and that cultivates dignity in the face of every imaginable assault on it (Berkovits, 1979: 110–11). The cases are myriad, cases of dedicated, intentional opposition, but for our purposes it is their common core and not their number that matters. Indeed, in the midst of such hell even one such act would be sufficient encouragement for us. (See Rosenbaum, 1976; Bauer, 1979; Berkovits, 1979; Des Pres, 1976).

When we look around ourselves for a paradigmatic opposition that is a responsive listening to the divine voice, we look in the wrong place. The right place is not here but there; the paradigmatic opposition is during and not after. We should look not at ourselves but rather at R. Oshry and all those who wrestled dignity and nobility from chaos itself. If anyone heard the voice, it was they, and if anyone's response ought to guide and direct our own, it is theirs. Indeed, it is only because of them that we can respond at all, and only through them that we can begin to see how to interpret the meaning of the divine presence for ourselves.

How utterly unsurprising and unremarkable this is. It is the lesson of reception, tradition, and transmission, a lesson so integral to Judaism that it seems hardly necessary to draw attention to it. But because the reception must occur after a determinative event such as the Holocaust, it is indeed necessary to do so. Consider Sinai. The encounter between God and man was and always will be direct, but for Moses it was an origin, for those who followed him both an *origin* and a *goal.* For him it was once and for all an immediacy that resulted in responsive action and speech; for others, that encounter incorporates an impact to be felt only as it is appropriated through a tradition initiated by Moses and for which a new responsiveness is required to build on the old. And what is true for Sinai is true, in a more complex way, for every subsequent encounter between man and God within Judaism. Hence it is true for the divine presence at Auschwitz. The bridge between us and Sinai includes the vast, ramified, intercommentative network of prophetic, rabbinic, and philosophical reflection that is called "Jewish tradition." But that link is rooted in Moses, in him who alone confronted the presence *panim el panim,* face to face, and whose original response, whose words and actions, constituted the earliest Jewish life. That bridge includes as well as those epoch-making events when the same voice was again heard and when new responses confronted and transformed the old. (On epoch-making events, see Fackenheim, 1970: 8–9; on reidentification of the divine voice, see Buber, 1965: 14–15). The utterly momentous Presence during the Holocaust was Itself encountered, and those who experienced that encounter are the vital link, bringing together our imperatives, the event itself, and all of Jewish experience prior to it. Only through the actions and words of people like R. Oshry do we hear the voice that spoke at Auschwitz, and beyond that do we hear the dim but certain echo of that same Voice in its original encounter with the Jewish people.

The Imperatives of the Moral Theory

For articulating contemporary Jewish imperatives, then, there are no ready formulae, but there are models and mediators. R. Oshry is one; there are many others, exemplars and advocates of an overriding imperative, a principle of opposition to Nazi purposes and of resistance to those purposes.[17]

R. Oshry himself is especially remarkable, for he enunciates that principle, celebrates it, and gives it quasi-legal status (Rosenbaum, 1976: 65–68). On November 3, 1941, the Jews of the Kovno ghetto (in Lithuania) had recently survived Nazi actions against the inhabitants in which ten thousand were killed. Those who remained asked Ephraim Oshry whether they were permitted to thank God for their deliverance by reciting the blessing *Ha-gomel* (the Bestower). The Talmud explains the *Ha-gomel* is said by the sick who recovered, the prisoner who was released, the seafarer who landed, and one who crossed the desert. But Maimonides and Joseph Karo, in the *Mishneh Torah* and *Shulhan Arukh,* together with later commentators, disagree about exactly *when* the blessing should be recited. Some permit it even when the deliverance is only temporary; others require that it be complete and permanent. This is R. Oshry's conclusion:

> It it quite possible that the cruel murderers had already condemned these who had escaped that particular *aktion* to death. The reason they let them remain alive was because they deliberately conducted their murderous operation in "cat and mouse" fashion, always allowing some Jews to remain alive for a time. They did this in order to delude them with false hopes so that their despair might be all the greater when the truth became known to them.
>
> Time after time they would lead the ghetto residents astray with all sorts of false rumors of salvation and deliverance in order to instill in them the vain hope that the destroyer's hand had finally been stayed. So, too, when they took them out to be killed, the Germans would lead them to believe that they were simply being transported from one point to another so the Jews should not try to escape or resist.
>
> Therefore, one certainly ought not to instruct those who escaped to recite *Ha-gomel* after having been saved from destruction in this one *aktion*. For these unfortunate ones may begin to imagine that the threat of death is truly over and that salvation is at hand. *In this fashion we would be helping the cursed murderers in their foul plot and would simply be making it easier for them to destroy our sisters and brothers.* Therefore, I ruled that they must not recite *Ha-gomel*. (emphasis added)

Based on a meticulous consideration of Jewish legal texts and precedent cases, Oshry's decision suggests a principle of opposition that is remarkably present and indeed dominant in his mind. And that principle recurs in other of his *halakhic* judgments (cf. Rosenbaum, 1976: 17–21, 24–31, 50–51, 64–65, 92–95). When, for example, a group of students from a nearby rabbinic seminary are threatened with execution, R. Oshry encourages a Jewish official to risk his own life to intercede in their behalf. These students, he says, are the bearers of the Jewish spirit and the Jewish soul. To try to save them—even at the risk of one's own life—is especially meritorious, for to do so is to oppose the Nazi plot to destroy not only Jews but Judaism itself. Recall, too, Oshry's unusual decision to permit a suicide with the proviso that his authorization not be publicized. Together these decisions reveal a conviction that *halakhah* must be served but only when it is made to satisfy a fundamental obligation to oppose what Hitler sought to accomplish—to satisfy, that is, an imperative to keep Judaism alive, to maintain trust and hope, dignity and honor.[18] The spectrum of cases of resistance during the Holocaust, widely and increasingly documented and recalled, here finds both an explicit formulation and, more importantly for us, a role within *halakhic* reasoning itself. Moral-legal decisions, on which permissions and obligations are based, themselves incorporate the principle of opposition to Nazi purposes and indeed give it priority.

The role of R. Oshry's *halakhic* decisions in our practical reasoning as Jews—indeed, the role of the vast, rich reservoir of observations, judgments, insights, and decisions by victims and survivors in general—is a complex one. On the one hand, this testimony helps us to appropriate the urgency and impact of an encounter, at least a sense of obligation and necessity, which we can only appropriate through such mediation. In addition, however, these decisons and comments become a guide for us as we try to identify the imperatives of Jewish life today and a component in such interpretative articulation as well.

Oshry's sensitivity to the Nazi objectives, for example, reveals itself in the obligation to preserve the tradition of law and lore and the imperative not to endorse the abandonment of an otherworldly hope and trust. In the very act of studying the legal literature, carefully collecting precedents from the literature available to him, and interpreting their sense and applicability, Oshry attempts to satisfy this obligation. To confront the complexity of moral-legal dilemmas without recourse to the *halakhic* tradition is to serve the Nazis and not to oppose them. As is clear from Oshry's own reasoning, this is not an obligation to adopt the *halakhah* as it presents itself, even if a specific obligation is uniformly endorsed. It is rather an obligation to consider this tradition, to study it and incorporate its judgments and reflections as components in one's own deliberation. To appropriate the *halakhic* tradition so far as one is able, then, is part of what it means to accept the obligation to keep Judaism alive, to maintain the continuity of a historical tradition of moral and legal reasoning that stretches between the Jew of today and the voice that spoke to Moses himself. And that obligation is a fragment of an imperative of opposition to the Nazi plot (Fackenheim, 1968: 20; 1970: 84–92). That imperative here expresses itself in a particular way by the conviction that the survival of Judaism is jeopardized if the deliberations and decisions of the past are not given due respect in the deliberations and decisions of the present. This is the weight of the obligation to take the *halakhic* tradition seriously; it is an intermediate position between neglect and complete submission. Indeed, I think that R. Oshry himself, whatever his *formal* commitment to the authority of the *halakhah,* in those years in the ghetto felt the weight of just this obligation.[19]

One role of Oshry's decisions and testimony akin to them is to show us the way to an understanding of the primary obligation that arises out of the Holocaust. A further role is to help us elaborate its ramifications, that is, to clarify what opposition to Nazi purposes means and how one might set out to enact that opposition. But there is a further role still and one of profound, immediate importance. For since we, confronting the complexities of Jewish life today, seek to act, having considered the *halakhic* tradition as a component in our deliberations, we must realize, too, that we can only appropriate that tradition as it existed prior to the Holocaust *in terms of* the way its content was, on the one hand, appropriated during the Holocaust and, on the other, transformed at times by the event itself. Not only do Oshry's *halakhic* reflections and decisions guide our interpretation of the general obligations of Jewish existence; they also contribute to the specific ways in which we can and should appropriate that tradition in order to arrive at the precise imperatives for our own lives. The meaning of the *halakhic* tradition is mediated for us by Oshry's understanding of it and even by the very situations which Oshry had to confront.

Among contemporary moral problems that have generated widespread discussion both in scholarly journals and in popular publications and forums, the problem of abortion holds a special place (see Feinberg, 1973). Notwithstanding its controversial nature, however, the abortion question is agreed to turn on two issues: the status of the fetus as a moral person and the boundaries of justifiable homicide. The discussion of both these matters in the *halakhic* literature is complex and provocative; yet out of this variety emerges a dominant view and several minority views (see Feldman, 1968: chaps. 14–15; Bleich 1968). According to the former, the fetus is a person at birth and indeed, for certain legal purposes, only thereafter. Nonetheless, taking its life, the act of feticide, is serious enough to require substantial justification. The dominant view is that only mortal threat to the mother will provide that justification, but minority views allow greater leniency, even to the point of permitting abortions in order to save the mother mental anguish and social disgrace. Throughout the *halakhic* literature, then, attention is focused on the mother and her needs and thereby on the needs of the present.

If, however, we are to take with utter seriousness the obligation to sustain the Jewish people and, in so doing, to oppose a fundamental Nazi purpose, we ought to consider with equal concern the welfare of the fetus and its future, a future that represents the future of the Jewish people itself. To be sure, such a requirement by itself can produce no precise picture; no simple resolution of cases is forthcoming. But appreciating the primacy of the obligation to oppose Hitler and his designs, we notice that certain considerations relevant to a moral decision play a more important role than they might otherwise have. This is starkly highlighted by the following incident.

On May 7, 1942, the Nazis passed a decree prohibiting pregnancy among the Jews in the Kovno ghetto. It was a law aimed at killing hope and joy among the Jews of Kovno and a law aimed at cutting off the Jewish future as well. Punishment was to be immediate and absolute; any Jewish woman found pregnant was to be executed on the spot. On August 9 of that year R. Oshry was confronted with the following problem: given the Nazi decree, could a Jewish woman who found herself pregnant abort the fetus in order to save her own life? Oshry's response is a moving testimony to the power of law to preserve dignity and order where chaos threatens. Carefully examining the legal literature, he chooses to permit the abortion, for to forbid it would be to accept the deaths of both mother and fetus as a virtual certainty. The point to notice here, however, is not Oshry's decision but rather the diabolical purpose served by the Nazi decree. In effect it forced the Jews of Kovno to cancel in advance their own future and hence the future of the Jewish people. And for those women unfortunate enough to become pregnant, it forced them to cut off their own future in order to save the present. In short, the Nazi cunning was not satisfied to annihilate the Jewish future, to instill fear and remove joy; it enrolled the Jews, the victims themselves, in its terrible plot. And more awful still, in cases where pregnancy did occur, it enlisted Jewish women as the assassins of their own hopes, joys, indeed of their future. The effect of this realization on those who took seriously the obligation to oppose Nazi purposes must be profound. Who now can fail to consider the future as well as the present? Who can neglect the importance of the fetus together with the needs of the mother? To be sure, there is no ready formula that will tell us how this important consideration will or should influence particular decisions. What is nonetheless clear, however, is that no facile appropriation of the lenient Jewish tradition is any longer possible. To abort without serious threat to the mother may very well be to betray that woman whose case Oshry was asked to consider and to betray, too, all the Jews of Kovno (see Fackenheim, 1980: 216–17).

Comments and Problems

Having said this much in sketching a theory of moral obligation for contemporary Jewish life, we have not yet said enough. The reasoning that supports this theory and the procedure for its application are not without difficulties.

First, the derivation of the obligation to recover the *halakhic* tradition as a component of moral deliberation for the contemporary Jew depends on one's understanding of the connection between *Jewish survival,* in particular the survival of Judaism, and *the recovery of the tradition.* Some may take that connection to be accidental and arbitrary; they may see no obstacle to a Judaism completely severed from the traditional round of Jewish conduct and the laws that define it. Indeed, to some the interpretation of this connection may seem to be a factual matter and one not easily decided. It is, of course, not a factual matter; nor is it a matter of simply defining Judaism in such a way that traditional Jewish law, even if not authoritative, is essential to Judaism. Rather the justification of the imperative to secure Judaism by recovering Jewish legal literature rests in the paradigmatic opposition to Nazi purposes expressed self-consciously in the actions of R. Oshry and many other *halakhic* authorities and in the respect given those authorities and their decisions by those who solicited them. To ignore that literature is to impugn these individuals as our only link to the divine commanding presence and hence to cut ourselves off from any authentic response to that Presence. Indeed, it would be to cut ourselves off from any *need* to respond at all, at any rate from a sense of the uncompromising imperative that issues from the Holocaust itself. In short, then, we are bound to accept R. Oshry's respect for the *halakhic* tradition unless something decisive supersedes it, that is, unless we have some good reason for thinking that Judaism today can survive without any respect for *halakhic* decisions and the legal tradition.

Secondly, we ought to notice that since specific Jewish obligations derive from a single principle or, perhaps more accurately, are nonhierarchical determinations of this principle, conflicts are bound to arise.[20] One can easily imagine being bound to oppose injustice or to advance the achievement of human dignity in a situation where the necessary action would compromise the Jewish people. In such cases, there can be no neat resolution of the conflict.[21] Contemporary Jewish ethics does not try to avoid the reality of genuine moral conflict or, indeed, of conflict between any pair of Jewish obligations. Nor does it venerate such conflicts. Rather, Jewish ethics acknowledges the authenticity of such paradoxes when they occur and respects the courage and the anguish that mark our encounter with them (see Buber, 1970: 144; Fackenheim, 1970: 89–93; 1978: 252–72).

Thirdly, insofar as the real substance of Jewish obligation reveals itself only when the principle of opposition to Nazi purposes is ramified and given its precise interpretation, it is manifest that this ramification produces a collection of moral, religious, and prudential commands that all have a common source. There is a sense, then, in which the moral and prudential obligations are themselves religious and the religious obligations at least prudential, if not moral as well. Thus for reasons deeper than those we can point to here, our account of Jewish ethics rejects any sharp distinctions between religion and morality and between religious imperatives and prudential, political, secular necessities (see Fackenheim, 1973: 166–67, 1978: chaps. 13, 17; Greenberg, 1977: 45–52). While we can only notice this feature of our theory here, it is a feature well worth careful scrutiny. By appreciating the ways that the Holocaust has markedly altered our very conceptual tools, we reinforce our original conviction of its momentous importance.

Fourthly, the Jewish ethical theory I have sketched takes the interpretation of Jewish moral commands to be the result of the historically situated deliberation of individuals, appropriating the Jewish legal tradition as they consider the needs and requirements of their own situation. These commands, therefore, are always in principle revisable, although in fact they are, when accepted, treated as unconditional. But, one might ask, by treating them as absolute, are we not just deceiving ourselves? Why not simply accept the historicism of our theory? Why indulge in counterfeit absoluteness when an honest relativism waits in the wings?

Perhaps no hasty resolution to this objection will satisfy. But we can certainly caution against accepting it too uncritically. For the objection assumes that no moral obligation can be both divine in origin and human in formulation and hence that none could be both unconditional and revisable at once. But the Jewish moral theory I have sketched is founded on a conception of divine-human encounter that permits, indeed invites just that cooperation of wills. For this reason, the status of the obligations we have been discussing can only be understood when that conception of revelation is critically considered. Others have done this, and we can only hope that their treatment begins to cope with at least some of the reservations noted here (Fackenheim, 1973: chap. 2). It is nonetheless worth observing that the historicism and relativism of our theory are not self-liquidating. For we view the articulated commands as human interpretations of what is in itself a presence that no words or concepts can capture. It is hardly surprising, then, that such interpretations, historically particularized both in source and in application, are in fact taken to be unconditional even when they are in principle subject to modification and even rejection.

Fifthly, our theory must pay the price of historical situatedness in yet another way. Consider once again the reasoning that supports the theory and especially step 2 of that reasoning. It is crucial to the account as a whole and to that step in particular that explanation of the Holocaust fail and that explanatory failure eventually lead to a different kind of meaning. But explanation is contextual; given a certain phenomenon, an explanation of it is satisfactory or not relative to a given person in a particular situation at a certain time and for a certain purpose. This relativity of explanation infects the argument at least in steps 2 and 3, and this means that the move to step 4 and beyond is justified only for individuals who accept 2 and 3. The purpose of the reasoning, however, is to identify the source of a general obligation for all Jews and then to show how that obligation can be formulated and articulated. In short, the argument wants to derive a general obligation, but, as it stands, it simply cannot do so.

This objection rests on a deep misunderstanding. To be sure, the argument is subjective in the sense that the dissatisfaction that leads from explanatory failure to descriptive meaning is relative to subjective needs. But the result is nonetheless general and objective, for the obligation's ontological status is not impugned by the method through which we come to perceive it. What is impugned is the recognition of the generality of the obligation: for some a much weaker explanation will account for the character of resistance both during and after the Holocaust. Not everyone, that is, will agree with R. Oshry that opposition is an obligation, especially one based on divine command. To expect a generally recognized obligation, however, seems far too ambitious to me. It is one thing to claim that an obligation is objective; it is quite another to require that everyone acknowledge and accept it. Indeed, since the proof for the obligation, and for its specific articulation or interpretation, is admittedly human, historically influenced, it is not reasonable to expect that everyone will recognize such an obligation or, indeed, any obligation holding for all Jews. What is reasonable, however, and also possible is to know that there is such an obligation, and this knowledge our reasoning provides.

Conclusion

The Jewish moral theory which we have sketched does, I think, satisfy the intuitive criteria we set down earlier. It is responsive to the past and to the present, to God and to man, to the Jewish people and to all humankind.[22] As a theory that issues in particular moral imperatives, it is part of a larger theory of the imperatives that define Jewish existence today. In short, this is a moral theory that a post-Holocaust Jew, immersed in Western culture yet sensitive to the needs of the Jewish people, of the Jewish state, and of their faith, could endorse.[23]

In the modern treatment of religious ethics there is sometimes a tendency to want the same universality and objectivity for religious ethics that many have found in popular rationalist moral theories. This chapter doubts that in the case of an authentic Jewish ethics such unanimity can be discovered. Many will surely find this result unsettling, if not simply wrong. They would prefer a moral theory that begins with a transhistorical Torah and imposes itself uniformly on Jews of all times and all places and indeed on all people as well.[24] This is not the place to debate their preference. What I have done instead is to offer an alternative with the hope that its virtues will impress the discerning reader.

Notes

1. It is one of the assumptions of this paper that Jewish moral obligations are a subset of Jewish obligations in general and that though moral, these obligations are also *Jewish* in important ways.

2. There are many examples of both relativist and absolutist moral theories. As an instance of an absolutist theory, one might look at Alan Donagan's natural law theory (1977). On the side of relativism, there is J. L. Mackie's *Ethics: Inventing Right and Wrong* (1977). The theory of Jewish ethics in this chapter claims that Jewish moral obligations are objective and unconditional in status but relative and conditional in content.

3. The role of language in the modern Jewish account of revelation has not been thoroughly discussed. Gershom Scholem, however, has treated the linguistic character of the kabbalistic theory of revelation (1972).

4. The justification of a moral theory is an enormously complex matter. Such theories are normally assessed and criticized in a piecemeal fashion and then in terms of their simplicity, consistency, utility, satisfaction of our moral intuitions, compatibility with our understanding of human nature, rationality, and so on. By far the most elaborate recent attempt to develop and justify a moral theory can be found in John Rawls, *A Theory of Justice* (1971).

5. This is a pragmatic alternative in the sense that the theory is being tested not against fully developed views on human nature, etc., but rather against our conception of an ideal moral agent and his or her beliefs, intuitions, etc., on these matters. In the present case, the ideal agent will be characterized by a keen moral sensibility and shaped by the Jewish and non-Jewish worlds in which he or she lives.

6. The relation between divine power and human freedom is articulated within the

theory of revelation on which the moral theory is based. Buber comments that the philosophical antinomy of necessity and freedom here finds its real nemesis in the "lived" paradox of "the reality of [a person's] standing before God" (1970, 144; cf. Fackenheim, 1970: 15–16).

7. Such a Judaism, then, would be quite different from the "eternal people" derived and described by Rosenzweig in *The Star of Redemption* (1970), a people *in* but not *of* history.

8. Jewish thought that confronts the Holocaust as an event determinative for our time is often castigated as wholly negative. This paper is an attempt to belie that criticism. To begin with history is a philosophical necessity; the unavoidable evil of the event which constitutes that historical beginning need not corrupt the thinking that reflects on it or the life that follows it.

9. This claim must not be misunderstood, as I try to explain. Rather than the more accurate term "unprecedented," I use the term "unique" intentionally, in part so that my explanation may serve to place its extensive use in perspective (see Fackenheim, 1978: 244–51, 278–81, 1982: passim; Arendt, 1951: 437–59).

10. The key to the Holocaust's uniqueness, then, is its historical location together with its character. Fackenheim, in the passages cited above (note 9), calls the Nazi Empire "a *novum* in human history" (1978: 245). Time is of the essence.

11. Philosophers of language distinguish between language and speech, and between the meaning of a word in a language and its meaning for a person in a particular situation. This distinction I am drawing in the text is akin to this one. For a celebrated discussion of the meaning of "meaning," see H. P. Grice (1957).

12. Examples are not difficult to give. John is fired because he is untidy, cantankerous, and always late for work. But he is also the union organizer in his shop. The press and his supporters take the firing to be an attack on the union.

13. Later we shall see what finally authenticates the description and our interpretation of the meaning of the Holocaust for subsequent Jewish life and thought is an exposure of our thinking to the event itself via the diaries, memoirs, and accounts of its victims and survivors.

14. I.e., those who oppose Nazi purposes do not do so conditionally or on a whim (see Fackenheim, 1970: 83).

15. In fact, this is surely too bold and anticipatory a claim to make at this point. What one can legitimately say is that there is a need for *some unconditional* ground for the obligation. It is at this stage unwarranted to identify this ground as the commanding God. Until one articulates an obligation to maintain continuity with Jewish tradition, to identify *this* voice as the *same* voice that spoke at Sinai is premature. Buber discusses the question "Who Speaks?" and this problem of reidentification of the divine presence, though without reference to this precise situation, in "Dialogue" (1965: 14–15).

16. Action in defense of Israel is an important exception (see Fackenheim, 1978: chaps. 13, 17).

17. This is not, of course, to say that R. Oshry himself took this principle as the commandment of a God present to him then. Rather he is evidence for us as we seek to interpret what our obligations are. The identification of the divine presence is part of our response to the event and need not have been part of his.

18. The effect of these decisions is to *qualify* the authority of *halakhah* in two ways: (1) it is binding *only because* it is *now* obligatory to appropriate it, and (2) it is binding *only as* interpreted in the new situation.

19. R. Oshry and others doubtless sought relevant precedents that would enable them to comply with and obey explicit *halakhic* commandments rather than merely respect them and give what look like contrary judgments. The effect of the principle of opposition, when treated as itself a divine command, is that even these seemingly contrary judgments become authoritative—and not merely because an authorized decisor made them.

20. It is important to notice that the subsidiary principles derived from this one initial

principle are nonhierarchical. This is unlike the application procedure for the principle of utility, say, where every application to a specific case (whether it be to an action or practice) must result in an exclusive ordinal ranking of the possible alternatives. If avoidance of moral conflicts is an advantage to a moral theory, which I doubt, then it is an advantage that our theory does not have (see Williams, 1973; Nagel, 1972).

21. In *Fear and Trembling,* Kierkegaard maintained the distinction between moral and religious obligations and then, in his famous formulation, advocated the "teleological suspension of the ethical." Insofar as our theory treats moral obligations as a species of religious ones, the Kierkegaardian strategy is undercut.

22. The way in which opposition to Nazi purpose involves a fidelity to humanity has not been developed in the current essay. But that the principle of opposition should result in a vigorous defense of human rights and dignity follows naturally from any responsible assessment of the nature of the concentration camps. Hannah Arendt (1951), for example, speaks of the camps as the central institutions of Nazi totalitarianism, laboratories for an assault on human nature. Améry (1980) sees the camps as destructive of human dignity and as institutionalized attempts to annihilate any sense of human trust and solidarity.

23. It is not necessary to belabor the details. The theory respects the Jewish past (historical and *halakhic* precedents) and present (the contemporary Jewish situation), divine command and human freedom, the needs of the Jewish people and the struggle for human dignity. It identifies a central obligation and requires interpretation of it by an exposure of our thinking to the Holocaust and the experiences of its victims and survivors.

24. Modern liberal Jewish thinkers, like Moses Mendelssohn and Hermann Cohen, take the moral principles of Judaism to be identical with rational ethical obligations and hence binding on all rational agents. Of ritual laws, only those included in the Noahide commandments could possibly be incumbent upon non-Jews. Like traditional thinkers, both Mendelssohn and Cohen treat the Torah as containing a set of timeless commandments. Where they differ between themselves is over the authority of ceremonial law, and where they differ with Orthodox thinkers is over the reasons that might underlie this authority. For Cohen, the core of the biblical teaching is morality. For Mendelssohn, the ritual law is instrumentally tied to the moral law. To Orthodoxy, the entire Torah is authoritative as the divine word (see Morgan, 1981).

References

Améry, Jean, 1980, *At the Mind's Limits.* Bloomington: Indiana University Press.

Arendt, Hannah, 1951, *The Origins of Totalitarianism.* New York: Harcourt, Brace, Jovanovich.

Bauer, Yehuda, 1979, *The Jewish Emergence from Powerlessness.* Toronto: University of Toronto Press.

Berkovits, Eliezer, 1979, *With God in Hell.* New York: Hebrew Publishing Co.

Bleich, J. David, 1968, "Abortion in Halakhic Literature." Pp. 325–71 in J. David Bleich, ed., *Contemporary Halakhic Problems.* New York: KTAV Publishing House, Inc.

Buber, Martin, 1958, *Moses.* New York: Harper & Row.

———, 1965, *Between Man and Man.* New York: Macmillan.

———, 1970, *I and Thou.* New York: Scribner's.

Des Pres, Terrence, 1976, *The Survivor.* Oxford: Oxford University Press.

Donagan, Alan, 1977, *The Theory of Morality.* Chicago: University of Chicago Press.

Fackenheim, Emil L., 1967, "Martin Buber's Concept of Revelation." Pp. 273–96 in Paul A. Schilpp and Maurice Friedman, eds. *The Philosophy of Martin Buber.* LaSalle, Ill.: Open Court Press.

————, 1968, *Quest for Past and Future*. Bloomington: Indiana University Press.

————, 1970, *God's Presence in History*. New York University Press.

————, 1973, *Encounters between Judaism and Modern Philosophy*. New York: Basic Books.

————, 1978, *The Jewish Return into History*. New York: Schocken Books.

————, 1980, *To Mend the World*. New York: Schocken Books.

Feinberg, Joel (ed.), 1973, *The Problem of Abortion*. Belmont, Calif.: Wadsworth Publishing Company.

Feldman, David M., 1968, *Birth Control and Jewish Law*. New York: New York University Press.

Fox, Marvin, 1979, "The Philosophical Foundations of Jewish Ethics: Some Initial Reflections." Feinberg Memorial Lecture, Judaic Studies Program, University of Cincinnati, March 27, 1979.

Fox, Marvin (ed.), 1975, *Modern Jewish Ethics*. Columbus, Ohio: Ohio State University Press.

Glatzer, Nahum N., 1953, *Franz Rosenzweig: His Life and Thought*. New York: Schocken Books.

Greenberg, Irving, 1977, "Cloud of Smoke, Pillar of Fire: Judaism, Christianity, and Modernity after the Holocaust." Pp. 7–55 in Eva Fleischner, ed. *Auschwitz: Beginning of a New Era?* New York: KTAV Publishing House, Inc.

Grice, H. P., 1957, "Meaning." *Philosophical Review* 66: 337–88.

Haberman, Joshua O., 1969, "Franz Rosenzweig's Doctrine of Revelation." *Judaism* 18/3 (Summer): 320–36.

Kellner, Menachem Marc (ed.), 1978, *Contemporary Jewish Ethics*. New York: Hebrew Publishing Co.

Mackie, J. L., 1977, *Ethics: Inventing Right and Wrong*. New York: Penguin Books.

Morgan, Michael L., 1981, "History and Modern Jewish Thought: Spinoza and Mendelssohn on the Ritual Law." *Judaism* 30/4 (Fall): 467–78.

Nagel, Thomas, 1972, "War and Massacre." Pp. 53–74 in Thomas Nagel, *Mortal Questions*. Cambridge: Cambridge University Press, 1979.

Quinn, Philip L., 1978, *Divine Commands and Moral Requirements*. Oxford: Oxford University Press.

Rawls, John, 1971, *A Theory of Justice*. Cambridge, Mass: Harvard University Press.

Rosenbaum, Irving J., 1976, *The Holocaust and Halakhah*. New York: KTAV Publishing House, Inc.

Rosenzweig, Franz, 1970, *The Star of Redemption*. Tr. William Hallo. New York: Holt, Rinehart, and Winston.

Sartre, Jean-Paul, 1948, *Anti-Semite and Jew*. New York: Grove Press.

Scholem, Gershom, 1972, "The Name of God and the Linguistic Theory of the Kabbala." *Digenes* 79 (Fall): 59–80; 80 (Winter): 164–94.

Williams, Bernard, 1973, "Ethical Consistency." Pp. 166–86 in Bernard Williams, *Problems of the Self*. Cambridge: Cambridge University Press.

14

Emmanuel Lévinas's Talmudic Commentaries: The Relation of the Jewish Tradition to the Non-Jewish World

ANNETTE ARONOWICZ

In a way, Emmanuel Lévinas's work represents nothing new in the long tradition of Jewish philosophy. His is another attempt to ponder the relation between the Jewish tradition and that of Western philosophy. The events of World War II, however, have made him depart significantly from his predecessors in the modern period, from Moses Mendelssohn on to the present, who wished to emphasize the coincidence between the great Jewish principles and those of the Enlightenment. Lévinas's work, on the contrary, points to a disjuncture. It is not a disjuncture at the level of ideas but in the very place given to ideas in the two traditions. His life's work has been an elaboration of this different placement, with its myriad of implications, both for Western philosophy and for human beings in general.

Nowhere is this elaboration more accessible than in his talmudic commentaries. Although he himself considers them as an aside to his major philosophical works, they reflect the same preoccupations as the latter, in a much more accessible language. In reading them it becomes clear that the disjuncture Lévinas wishes to delineate between the Jewish tradition and the West or the Jewish tradition and the world at large is far from a turning inward to an exclusively Jewish universe. For at the core of his talmudic commentaries is a peculiar blurring of the lines between what is Jewish and what is not Jewish, made more peculiar by the fact that Lévinas's main goal in these essays is the discovery of the particularity of the Jewish tradition. I would like to give two examples of this peculiar blurring of the lines and then ponder briefly how this blurring yet illustrates the Jewish difference.

The commentary "The Temptation of Temptation,"[1] my first example, seems at first sight an unlikely text to suggest any blurring of lines. From its very title it is intent on *contrasting* the Western and Jewish traditions, on showing the stark difference between them. The "temptation of temptation" is a phrase Lévinas coins to characterize the West. What does it refer to and how does it differ from mere temptation? I will proceed by way of example. It is mine, not Lévinas's, but it should suggest what is at stake better than a generalization: the relation of knowing and doing, of ontology to ethics.

My example distinguishing temptation from temptation of temptation involves marriage. The case of simple temptation would be the following: A person gets married and thus becomes committed to being faithful to his or her spouse. This person may become attracted to someone else and will thus be faced with a decision, whether or not to honor the commitment to faithfulness. Temptation, then, involves being presented with a choice between good and evil, and feeling strongly drawn to the evil. In such a situation, what is good and what is evil have already been determined before the temptation occurs. Otherwise, it would not be a temptation.

In the case of the temptation of temptation, the situation is different. A person, although married, has decided to postpone committing himself or herself to faithfulness to the spouse. This is not because the person is in favor of a free union, committed to complete sexual freedom as the Good. Rather, it is because the person feels he or she needs more knowledge before a commitment to either faithfulness or free union can be made. After all, the person may argue, he or she has never been married before. How can one know beforehand whether faithfulness is the Good? In this case, if a person has an extramarital relation, it cannot really be considered falling into temptation because temptation implies a prior choice for the Good. But here no prior choice has been made. Rather, the choice has been postponed pending further knowledge. Thus, the person who is gathering evidence in view of determining the Good is always a step before temptation, in the temptation of temptation, tempted by the possibility of being tempted but not by temptation itself.

Lévinas's claim that this latter attitude is characteristic of Western spirituality, embodied in all its cultural manifestations, does not mean that the West prides itself on immorality or nihilism, for the pursuit of the Good remains its goal. It just means that the West has always placed knowing before the commitment to the Good, and made knowing a prerequisite for this commitment. Nowhere is this more apparent than in the pursuit of philosophy, for what is philosophy if not the commitment of knowledge as preceding all other commitments, including the ethical. The ethical certainly has been central in many philosophical inquiries, but it is never there first, before philosophy, as a given which puts knowledge in second place. Lévinas argues that this priority of knowing, while praiseworthy if one opposes knowing to mere opinion or naïveté, is nonetheless not adequate to the human condition. This inadequacy is not merely a failure to describe what is. It is a failure to respond properly to the other human being, in that, for the sake of knowing, one eliminates his otherness. The failure on the ethical plane is primary and leads to a distortion of knowledge itself.

It is at this juncture that Lévinas turns to the rabbinic sources. The particularity of the Jewish tradition, he will claim, lies in its reversal of the relation between knowing and doing, giving the priority to doing. To understand what is at stake, he insists on paying very close attention to the details of the text, sniffing out the continuity in its apparent meanderings. The different emphasis characterizing the Jewish tradition can only be brought to light through this struggle with the concrete, seemingly irrelevant detail.

The text he turns to in this commentary is from the Tractate Shabbat (pp. 88a–88b). I will follow only the first half of his interpretation, which I think will be sufficient to indicate both his method and what he sees as the rabbis' focus. The talmudic passage begins with a quotation from Exod. 19:17: "And they stopped at the foot of the mountain . . ." This verse refers to the Israelites just before they receive the Torah at Mount Sinai. The entire text will be about this reception of the Torah. The first rabbinic commentary reads as follows:

> Rav Abdimi bar Hama bar Hasa said: This teaches us that the Holy One, Blessed Be He, inclined the mountain over them like a tilted tub and that he said: If you accept the Torah, all is well, if not here will be your grave.

Where did Rav Abdimi get the idea that God held up the mountain in such a manner? Lévinas explains. It has to do with the Hebrew preposition meaning under, "b tahtit," translated in the verse from Exodus just quoted as "at the foot of." Rav Abdimi takes the preposition to mean "under" in a physical sense, not merely in the sense of "at the foot of" or "besides." But why would he be taking the text so literally? Because, Lévinas tells us, he wants to raise a question regarding the nature of revelation. Revelation would be a kind of knowledge that forces itself on us, as opposed to the kind of knowledge we arrive at through reason, through the weighing of sides. In the case of revelation, we have no choice but to accept it. Its mode of presentation leaves us no time to weigh sides. It takes us by violence, as the image of the inverted mountain about to crush the Israelites suggests. Thus, in Rav Abdimi's understanding, the commitment to Torah precedes reasoning and, therefore, excludes a choice made in freedom.

The next passage of the Gemara comments on this:

> Rav Aha bar Jacob said: That is a great warning concerning the Torah. Raba said: They nonetheless accepted it in the time of Ahasuerus for it is written (Esther 9:22): "The Jews acknowledged and accepted." They acknowledged what they accepted.

Rav Aha bar Jacob is making an observation, according to Lévinas, about the consequences of a commitment made under threat of violence. If one accepts an obligation because forced to do so, is one truly obligated? The commitment to Torah seems to stand on perilous ground. But Lévinas interprets Raba's answer, in the following sentence, to mean that acceptance based on reason can follow a commitment that was originally imposed by force. Reason can go back and affirm a choice from which it was excluded in the first place, thus blocking the flight into irresponsibility.

But Raba's specific reference to the Book of Esther also points out that even here acceptance does not quite mean intellectual acknowledgment by itself, as in an assent to a proposition. Lévinas notes that the Hebrew word for acknowledged, *kymu,* also means to fulfill. Thus the Jews fulfilled and accepted. Their way of accepting Torah had to do with fulfilling it. In the story of Esther this would mean that Mordechai's act of resistance to Haman and Ahasuerus, his "no" to the powers that be, was the "yes" to the Torah, now accepted not because death would ensue if he did not but because he chose to remain loyal to Torah despite all possible enticements to the contrary. The form of acceptance, however, is once again a doing, not a knowing in itself.

The Gemara then seems to shift direction by turning to Psalm 76.

> Hezekiah said: It is written (Ps. 76:9): "From the heavens thou didst utter judgment: the earth feared and stood still (calm)." If it was frightened, why did it stay

calm? If it remained calm, why did it get frightened? Answer: First it was frightened, and toward the end it became calm.

Lévinas points out that the shift of direction is really no shift at all since Hezekiah's inclusion of it here means that, for him, the psalm refers to revelation. Thus, in verse 9 (when "the earth feared," etc.), it is because of the revelation of the Torah that it gets into such a state.

But why did the earth get into such a state? That is indeed the next commentator's question.

> And why did the earth become afraid? The answer is provided by the doctrine of Resh Lakish. For Resh Lakish taught: What does the verse (Gen. 7:31) mean: "Evening came, then morning, it was the sixth day"? The definite article is not necessary. Answer: God had established a covenant with the works of the Beginning: If Israel accepts the Torah, you will continue to exist; if not, I will bring you back to chaos.

Lévinas unpacks Resh Lakish's answer. His focus on the Hebrew definite article (*ha*) comes from the fact that in the Genesis 1 account of creation, *ha* figures only in the description of the sixth day. The other days, when mentioned, are not modified by a definite article. Resh Lakish sees the reference to the *ha* on the sixth day as an allusion to the giving of the Torah, which, according to tradition, occurred on the sixth day of the month of Sivan. Thus, Resh Lakish is signaling that revelation was already alluded to at the moment of creation. God had a purpose when he created the world. In fact, his sole purpose in creating the world was "the fulfillment of Torah." If the Israelites were not to accept the Torah, all of creation would revert back to chaos. This, then, is the reason the earth was afraid. Its fate was dependent upon the creation of man and, more specifically, upon the Israelites' acceptance of the mitzvot, prefigured in the creation of man. Once again we see that the normal order is inverted. We are used to thinking that the doing of goods depends upon the existence of the world. Here, the existence of the world depends upon the doing of good.

This reversal is going to find its consummate expression in the following passage:

> Rav Simai has taught: When the Israelites committed themselves to doing before hearing, 600,000 angels came down and attached two crowns to each Israelite, one for the doing, the other for the hearing. As soon as Israel sinned, 1,200,000 destroying angels came down and took away the crowns, for it is said (Exod. 33:6): "The children of Israel gave up their ornaments at the time of Mount Horeb."

Rav Simai is referring to a strange detail in the Book of Exodus. When the Israelites told Moses to tell God that they would accept the Torah, they said: "*naaseh v nishmah*," we will do and we will hear. This sounds very strange to our ears, as no one would obligate himself without knowing what he is obligating himself to. But, here, the Israelites commit themselves to fulfilling the mitzvot—to doing—without first hearing what the mitzvot are. This would seem worthy of censure. But Rav Simai regards it, on the contrary, as a mark of distinction. Each Israelite receives two crowns as a result. In fact, Lévinas cites a tradition which claims that the reward was even bigger than Rav Simai claimed. The crowns each Israelite got were three: one for the doing, one for the hearing, and one for the reversal of the order. The rabbis, then, not only notice the reversal but glory in it.

Why? The reason, according to Lévinas, is that the reversal signals the rejection of the temptation of temptation. To accept the Torah without first reasoning about its value is to accept that the commitment to the Good is never freely chosen, never the end result of knowing. The Good, the rabbis are saying in this apparently disparate series of exchanges, is of such a nature that it takes possession of a person before the person has time to evaluate it. To receive it as such means to acknowledge that all knowing takes its direction from it, rather than the other way around.

Lévinas, in a later section of the commentary, specifies the nature of this Good. The Torah, he reminds his reader, is given in the light of a face. This means that to be seized by the Good is to be seized by the other person. We respond to the other without ever having chosen to respond. In our relation to the other person, his presence redirects our attention, even if we have made no prior choice to focus our attention on him. Any simple experience of someone entering a room testifies to that. But this attention is not merely visual. It signals our responsibility, our obligation to respond. We are put at his command, again, without having chosen to be at his command. Lévinas calls this a being hostage to the other. This is not a matter of good intentions on our part but a description of what actually prevails in the most ordinary human interactions, when they do not become obstructed. Thus, in accepting the Torah, the Jews are accepting the binding of the self to the other, as something that precedes all reflection, as the Good one is committed to, which no subsequent knowledge or experience can put in doubt.

But this does not mean, as Lévinas is quick to point out, that the Jews never fall away from the Good. The paragraph quoted earlier indicates that no sooner had the Israelites been crowned than the crowns were removed because of their sin. But the sin, here, in Lévinas's reading, would be a giving in to temptation, as opposed to a giving in to the temptation of temptation. The text specifies that "the children of Israel *gave up* their ornaments." Shortly thereafter, it will say that "they renounced them." For Lévinas, this choice of words indicates that the Israelites acknowledged their sin. If one acknowledges one has done wrong, one is acknowledging a prior commitment to the Good, and trying to return to a correct relation with it. This is quite different from glorifying the sin, that is, refusing to see it as sin but proclaiming it instead as courageous act or as royal road to knowledge. Then the commitment to the Good is forever postponed. The priority of the Good is denied.

Neither the Gemara nor Lévinas's commentary upon it stops here. But this summary should give some indication of what he sees as the difference between the Jewish and Western traditions. Yet, *at the same time as he elaborates this difference, an opposite movement is also taking place.* He is inserting the Jewish tradition *within* the Western tradition. This becomes evident if we name the terms he uses to explicate the talmudic text: ethics, ontology, and, as we shall see in the following quotation from the same commentary, self and intelligibility:

> Intelligibility does not begin in self-certainty, in the coincidence with oneself from which one can give oneself time and a provisional morality, try everything, and let oneself be tempted by everything. Intelligibility is a fidelity to the true; it is incorruptible and prior to any human enterprise; it protects this enterprise like the cloud which, according to the Talmud, covered the Israelites in the desert. Consciousness is the urgency of a destination leading to the other person and not an eternal return to self.[2]

As much as Lévinas is contrasting the Western notion of self, as return to the same, with the Jewish notion of self, as a movement toward the other, the very terms *intelligibility* and *self* are Western. The Jewish content is poured into Western vessels.

But in doing this is Lévinas not Westernizing the talmudic text? He himself would undoubtedly say that he is. But for him this Westernization of the Jewish text is also a Judaization of the West, twisting its concepts into paths hitherto unknown to them. The end product is Western Jewish, Jewish Western. At a crucial point, the line between the two traditions blurs.

In my second example, this blurring of the line no longer involves a confrontation between the Western and Jewish traditions. Rather, it involves a certain ongoing tension between the particularity of the Jewish tradition, its noncoincidence with any other, and its universality, its coincidence with the fundamentally human. To illustrate, I will focus on a small portion of "Judaism and Revolution," which bases itself on Tractate Baba Metsia (pp. 83a–83b). The lines which interest us deal with the relation of employer to worker.

> One day, Rabbi Johanan ben Mathia said to his son: Go hire some workers. The son included food among the conditions. When he came back, the father said: My son, even if you prepare a meal for them equal to the one King Solomon served, you would not have fulfilled your obligation toward them for they are the descendants of Abraham, Isaac and Jacob. As long as they have not begun to work, go and specify: You are only entitled to bread and dry vegetables.[3]

The problematic phrase is, of course, "descendants of Abraham, Isaac and Jacob." Would the infinite obligation to feed the worker hold only when the workers are Jews? Lévinas cautions against such a reading:

> I have it from an eminent master: each time Israel is mentioned in the Talmud one is certainly free to understand by it a particular ethnic group which is probably fulfilling an incomparable destiny. But to interpret in this manner would be to reduce the general principle in the idea enunciated in the Talmudic passage, to forget that Israel means a people who has received the Law and, as a result, a human nature which has reached the fulness of its responsibilities and its self-consciousness.[4]

Lévinas then goes on to illustrate what this fullness of responsibilities means through the example of Abraham. After all, Abraham is the man who received the three angels. But how did these angels appear to him? As hungry and tired human beings, Bedouins in the desert. He runs toward them, offers them water, food, shelter. To respond to another human being in such a manner is to be completely self-conscious about one's responsibilities:

> The heirs of Abraham—men to whom their ancestor bequeathed a difficult tradition of duties toward the other man, which one is never done with, an order in which one is never free. In this order, above all else, duty takes the form of obligation toward the body, the obligation of feeding and sheltering. So defined the heirs of Abraham are of all nations: *any man truly man is no doubt of the line of Abraham* (my emphasis).[5]

The last line is very important because it is precisely where the blurring between the Jewish and the non-Jewish occurs. Any human being who treats the other as Abraham treated his guests is a descendant of Abraham. In fact, in this quotation we may have the opposite problem from the one we might have when reading "The Temptation of Temptation." In that latter commentary the contrast between the Jewish tradition and the non-Jewish, in that case, the Western one, was so stark that it took a bit of an effort to see where and how the lines blurred. In "Judaism and

Revolution" the lines seem so blurred from the start that we may well ask wherein lies the particularity of the Jewish tradition.

But is it not the Jewish tradition that has selected out the image of Abraham as exemplifying the human? Without it could we recognize the plain humanity of the person facing us in need, or the plain humanity of the one who feeds the guest? The particularity of the Jewish tradition—its teachings and its practices—remains the avenue through which the significance of what all human beings already do comes to light, allowing responsibility to rise to self-consciousness and choice. Without it, these gestures of feeding and clothing would be like moves in the dark, unseen for what they are, in danger of not standing out as truly human acts, in danger of losing their centrality or never acquiring it in the first place. Jewish particularity becomes a prerequisite, then, for recognizing the other as neither Jewish nor non-Jewish but simply as human.

In both examples provided above, we can see Lévinas's insistence on Jewish particularity and yet his blurring of the line between what is Jewish and non-Jewish. I would like to suggest that this blurring allows for the very embodiment of the teaching Lévinas discovers in the Jewish sources. That is, we are left with certain key images—for example, the Israelites' acceptance of Torah before knowing its contents, Abraham feeding and sheltering his guests. These are Jewish images and yet, because they require contact with Western categories to release their universal meaning, and because they describe the human being in his humanness, not just in his Jewishness (the two being equivalent here), we never know under what guise we might find them. This leaves room for that response to the other which takes precedence over prior knowing. It allows for the responsibility of the host-guest relation in which we do not categorize the guest into Jew and non-Jew but recognize only the human. In the end, Lévinas, in his talmudic commentaries, does not give us a neat package separating "us" from "them" but rather guides us into a certain relation with both Jewish and non-Jewish traditions. That this relation is itself based on the Jewish tradition only emphasizes that the blurring of the lines occurs only if there are lines to begin with. The universality of the Jewish tradition depends on its particularity.

The previous examples far from exhaust Lévinas's way of relating the particularity of the Jewish tradition to its universality. He never tires of examining this problematic, from a seemingly endless variety of angles. In so doing he leaves the Enlightenment tradition—and its impatience of particulars—far behind. But he does not land into postmodernism—with its impatience of universals—as a result. It is in forging another relation between the two that his thought is most significant, for both the Jewish and the non-Jewish tradition.

Notes

1. My references to this commentary are on the basis of the English translation, *Nine Talmudic Readings by Emmanuel Lévinas,* translated and with an introduction by Annette Aronowicz (Bloomington: Indiana University Press, 1990, pp. 30–50).

2. Ibid., p. 48.

3. Ibid., p. 98.

4. Ibid.

5. Ibid., p. 99.

15

An Ethics of Encounter: Public Choices and Private Acts

LAURIE ZOLOTH-DORFMAN

The first years of modern feminist scholarship have offered an extraordinary wealth of literature reinterpreting the Jewish tradition. Feminist scholarship has uncovered voices lost to the canon, has validated alternative ways of hearing and speaking in the discourse, has uncovered and recreated women's prayer, has offered both sharp critique of the issue of praxis and suggested renewed ways of spiritual return. What this essay seeks to accomplish is something different: the development of a new feminist Jewish ethics. Such development must begin with new language and new theory, different ways to hear and speak of the project of social justice than the current claims of individual rights and individual entitlements. I argue that it is by the application of Jewish texts read through a feminist lens that such a language can be constructed. Such a task is, of course, very large and this essay is only a beginning, an outline of the first principles which can make possible such an ethics, which I call "an ethics of encounter." It is a setting of the philosophical and theological context for the implications of actual justice considerations.

I will begin with a brief note on methodology, why *how* we speak of ethics is important to the resultant theory of justice; describe a text to illustrate this method, the Book of Ruth; and detail a specific application in the debate on the allocation of social goods such as health care.

Methodology

Three things are assumed in this essay. The first is that the insights of feminism are to be assumed as a part of the scholarly tools of the discourse, not discovered or defended. That has been the work of many other capable scholars. Second, and sometimes in tension with the first assumption, is that the Jewish textual and legal tradition, the *halakhah,* is a valid place to begin the search for ethical response. Finally, central to this work is the premise that what is at stake in all ethical discourse, including the discourse of feminist ethics, is the radical encounter with the other, the apprehension of her claims in the collective conversation about justice.[1] Justice is, at its heart, relational, and relationship implies social discourse.

Halakhah

One way to develop a collective discourse of justice is through the lens of the traditional text itself. If the way to the truth of an action and the cut to the core in ethical decision making is via the shared narrative, then the text is the first place to begin when rethinking moral language (and certainly alternate moral language) in the discourse of justice and public policy. This is the traditional starting place in the *halakhic* method. It is by use of such a method that normative scholarship begins the reflection on justice: case by case, arguing by analog to the present problem. It is the discursive and argumentative *halakhic* method itself that suggests to us that a richer, deeper account can be given of the problem of allocating scarce resources. If we are to develop new language beyond individual entitlements, it must be language rooted in story and community that draws from a method that is *itself* dialogical and communal. It is the talmudic method itself, larger than any specific text, that describes the relationship between the individual and the collective that creates the social and shared ground for justice. This methodology is the place[2] that is the vantage point within the tradition from which I evaluate and reason. However, the suggestion, the insistence, that other texts are needed to explore an argument is well within the traditional method itself, namely, the search for other accounts on which to base law, morality, and public policy.

Feminism

But for feminist analysis the ethical texts of distributive justice that are usually described by the *halakhah* offer only a partial answer. It is partial, first, because simply stated, the language is taken from textual experiences that are not fully attentive to the reality of the lived experience of women's lives. Furthermore, as many have noted, the Jewish textual tradition is replete with the notion of women as other, as dangerous, or as simply less valued than men. A feminist stance stakes the claim that these considerations are neither petty, nor foolish, nor relatively minor debates over justice at the public policy level. Traditional *halakhic* method would have us take the variety of these texts (and surely there are enough variants when speaking of social justice and the allocation of a scarce resource) and quote them as the central and strongly argued sources of the collective and community-based moral language I am seeking. Surely, we are told, the textual casuistry can be meant to apply to all persons, not only to men! Yet even if the value of women as diminished[3] and the persistent address to the male are historically explainable, they are unacceptable in the modern application of *halakhah* for our ethical purposes.

But the specific search for the female voice in moral reflection is only the first reason to seek further texts. The second reason is that in looking carefully at other justice texts, I found that in some way each of the texts is unsatisfactory. Each addresses only one part of the problem of allocation. Each leaves me with some disquiet: can ownership really account for the right of survival, as in the familiar texts of the two travelers and the one flask in the desert? Can a community rank order human value based on power, status, or gender, as in the texts that address the redemption of captives? Many of the classic texts on distributive justice are derived from extreme situations: war, hostage crisis, siege, the Shoah itself.[4] What is missing in the *halakhic* debate is not simply a nonhierarchical ranking system but more about the fullness of what makes a society function as it addresses the daily struggles of justice.

Feminism insists that the political is at its heart personal, that intimacy, the encounter with the other, is central in the world of social discourse and public policy.[5] Such a consideration leads me directly to two sources for a feminist ethics that inform any text we examine. The first is the philosophy of Emmanuel Levinas,[6] which demands as the first act of philosophy the regard of the "naked face" of the other. The second is the lived experience of the women's movement itself, which begins with the small group encounter, with the story of the other. Both of these sources act as the theoretical ground for a distributive justice based in ordinary friendship, the dailiness of a life that is noticed as a series of choice-gestures among the competing needs of many.

The Necessity of Language

This is cautionary work. Ethical analysis is not a sermon. The text is heterogeneous, told in different voices, heard in different ways, and speaking with different points of view; the gaps in the text signal that the text is in this way interactive. The work of the analytic reader is to honor all of the readings, noting what in the tradition makes certain ones "traditional" and others "variant." Attention to other voices or other stories (even within the textual account itself) suggests both the legitimacy of these voices and the relative arbitrariness of the version that was understood as singular.[7] Analyzing the text closely, listening to the words and the sense of the story, will not "answer" the problem of justice. It will push us toward a view that is newly possible if attention is paid to the particulars. And it will be subject to the argument of commentary.

Finding issues of justice and scarcity in the textual world of the ancient Near East was no problem. The history of the community of Hebrew people is marked by two major famines that shaped the Genesis story and acted as mirrors for one another in the Torah. The first, the famine of Abraham, sends the newly chosen Abram and Sarai to Egypt out of the land that is promised.[8] The next is the great famine of Joseph and his brothers.[9] These famines of the patriarchal story were recalled by all other tellings of famine in the biblical text.[10]

The famine in the Book of Ruth is an echo of these earlier famines. It is *intertextual* because it evokes famine linked with covenant and generativity. All three famines have the same elements: all are desperate moments of scarcity, all mention leaving the land, and all three pose the choice (and this is the first choice in justice considerations) to stand with the community or to abandon it.

The Book of Ruth's mirrored famines and their associated behaviors are considered in rabbinic commentary of the midrash. What marks this *aggadah*, like all rabbinic texts, is the assumption that normative daily rules of action ought to be required despite crisis. It is the commanded acts of justice, *tzedakah*, that ought to guide the behavior of the moral agents in the world of the text. Hence, this text addresses the tension between the extraordinary crisis and the normative problem of just allocation as a fact of daily life. It is the logical consequence of living in the human world of the finite.[11]

The Text Itself: "The Marginal as Central"[12]

In the Book of Ruth, the centerpiece event is a (rare) inside look at an intimate relationship between women. In contrast to some of the problematic female interior relationships in Torah (e.g., Sarah and Hagar, Rachel and Leah) where women are seen competing for the scarce prize of a relationship with a man, the decisive ethical gesture in Ruth actually has little to do with a male figure. It speaks instead of a responsibility to a larger community. In most stories in the Torah the women stand outside, in the peripheral vision of the teller. In the Book of Ruth, the story of women is central; and Elimelech, Mahlon, Chilion, and even Boaz are either dead or nearly silent to the central passion of the story about loyalty to each other outside the safety of a relationship to a man. The details, the verbal action of the story, is women's work of the time. It is this work—eating, gleaning, fecundity, homemaking, and nursing babies; not war making, sacrificing, marching, or destruction— that is honored.

We are to imagine it: two women alone in the desert, shawls in the wind, thirsty, mourning, and walking in silence to Bethlehem. The city of bread is "all astir" when they enter. They are at the point of utter despair, having nothing: without men, without children, without land, without community. Yet their coming is a public event, not simply some private tragedy, which will be taken account of by the public community, for which the community will bear responsibility.

Ruth's ethical gesture, the gesture that makes all that follows possible, is to embrace the angry old woman not out of love or compassion—it is certainly not that simple—but out of a sense of recognition that she and Naomi are fundamentally bound. In Levinas's language, Ruth recognizes the self in the other and, as such, recognizes her responsibility not to turn from the vulnerable face of her former mother-in-law. She is not compelled to stay: the death of her husband has unbound her as it has unbound Orpah. And yet she sees herself as Naomi, as paired as surely as Adam and Eve were paired, a coupling of similar selves in the darkness of the world.

The *halakhic* details that follow the details of harvest and widowhood, and the exchanges of commodity for commodity, are recognized by the larger community as Ruth's choice, the Rutharian alternative of relation over self-actualization, the recognition that self-becoming is not possible in isolation from obligation. My life, says this Rutharian gesture, cannot continue with you, other, lost in the darkness of the desert Moab. The rain would not fall and the grain would not grow if it were so. It is proven by our text, by the bursting fecundity of the barley harvest, and by the fecundity of the widow Ruth in the next year.

The language of the story is critical. It is about going from isolation—no family and no community—to a specific place, to a specific listening to the voice of the most vulnerable, in the context of an actual relationship. The ritual act of the release of obligation (the shoe ritual) is making the connections public (face-to-face).

After the birth of her son, who is linked to the future and to the largest vision of community, Ruth maintains the strongest possible relationship to Naomi: she gives her the child. Naomi thus becomes parent in relationship to the child via the female rather than through the male kinship bonds. These female bonds are spiritual rather than hereditary.

In other words, *t*he Rutharian choice is to understand that one's personal story is part of the collective story of movement of a people in history. It is also a choice at every moment about gesture as intimate, as fragile, and as ordinary as a child passed between women. It is a prophetic act that suggests, "Look, the world can be like this." But it is a prophetic act wrapped in the context of the daily, difficult world—as if to say, "The prophetic act is obtainable, it can be yours."

That is the outline of the story. Embedded within it are seven moments or scenes on which I will focus. It is by a close examination of these moments, the lacunae in the text, the narrative, the commentary, and the language itself that an ethical challenge can be most clearly drawn.

1. To leave the community at a time of scarcity or danger is wrong. There is no personal escape from collective scarcity.

> And it came to pass
> in the days of the judging of the judges,
> that there was a famine in the land.

The text begins oddly, in paradox. It will be a text about justice. Plain words tell the reader where to place the text historically, in a time prior to kingship rule of the Jewish people. What is the justice of the Judges, however? The midrash and commentary say that it was chaotic, capricious, and the opposite of justice. *"The judging of the judges"* (a wordplay in both Hebrew and English) is taken to refer to the era of lawlessness, when the judges ought to have been judged themselves.[13] The troubles were not only physical, linked to the scarcity, but spiritual as well. This was apparent because famines were understood to be linked to God's own judgment of the failings of a people,[14] and apparent because of the historical moment described in the text.[15]

It is in this generalized chaos that the famine occurred, in a society so driven by individual greed,[16] say the rabbis, that it was unable even to regulate the systems of agriculture or to forestall ecological havoc.[17]

From this disaster the leadership flees, abandoning the community. In the *Midrash Rabbah* the compilation of the midrashim that surround the scriptural texts, the rabbinic commentary is extensive on this spare verse. Why does such disaster fall upon this family? Who is this Elimelech? The rabbinic response is that he must have been a man of substance, who abandoned Bethlehem at the first sign of trouble.[18]

> *And the name of the man was Elimelech.* When trouble came, thou hast departed and left them. [This is the meaning of the verse] *"And a certain man of Bethlehem in Judah went."*[19]

What troubles the rabbis that comment in these midrashim is how a man of substance and position, a man capable of undertaking a significant journey in the midst of a cataclysmic famine, could have so thoroughly misunderstood the meaning of his obligation.[20] Another midrash continues the theme of the rabbinic condemnation of leadership that protects itself by denying essential obligation:

> *And a certain man . . . went.* Like a mere stump! See how the Holy One, blessed be he, favors the entry into Eretz Israel over the departure therefrom! In the former case it is written, Their horses . . . their mules . . . their camels, etc. (Ezra 2:66) but in this case it is written, *and a certain man went* like a mere stump![21]

This midrash is sensitive to the judgment of the text. Since the verse does not speak of Elimelech taking anything with him, the plain meaning is that he left Israel and went to Moab empty-handed: "like a mere stump."[22] The midrash contrasts this to the return of the Hebrew people as they enter the Land from their exile in Babylon. Here "The sum of the entire community was 42,360 . . ." and they not only travel as a community, they travel heavily laden with each horse, and mule, and camel, and household object, elaborately inventoried.[23]

The text may be silent on motive, but the names of Elimelech's and Naomi's sons translate as "sickness" (Mahlon) and "vanishing" (Kilyon), hardly neutral signifiers. Further, the land they leave for is the land of Moab, the land that is associated with idol worship, licentiousness, whose people are enemies of the Israelites, and with whom marriages are prohibited. In fact, the midrash supposes that the reason the text says the family lived in the fields was that the cities of Moab were too sordid even for these exiles.

The text that will address the responsibility for the others begins with the negative example. Elimelech is the prudent libertarian. Possessing what is his, he uses what means he has to craft an individual solution. One does not need to position him as the leader or even as a man of extraordinary duty to suggest that the text sees his flight as problematic. A crisis emerges. The individual chooses his individual solution, the Land and the community are left, and disaster strikes. Rather than turn his face to the face of the other, he turns away and heads in the opposite direction.

2. *To resume responsibility, even if one is powerless, is the just course for every citizen.*

> Elimelech, Naomi's husband died,
> and she was left.

Where is Naomi in the moral moment of the first chapter of Ruth? She is without voice and without name, anonymous in Judah until the flight to Moab is begun.[24] Yet she does not protest; she goes without question to the disaster ahead.[25]

Even after Elimelech dies, Naomi does not suggest a return to the Land, nor does she speak a word in the story when first one, then another of her sons marries the prohibited Moabite strangers. She lives in the silence of the text for ten years, and it is only when her sons die that she finds language, and with it, both moral imperative and action in the center stage of the public arena.[26]

> . . . She had heard
> in the field of Moab
> how that the Lord had remembered His people
> in giving them bread.

She arose because she *remembered* that God's remembering has a meaning for her. It is the first time in the narrative that God is mentioned. The text, despite the midrashic embellishments attributing great wealth to Elimelech, now portrays Naomi as the ultimate widow. Stripped of all social standing and surrounded by death, she is not only without land but without support. There is no mention of any community that either surrounds her or takes account of her worth or responsibility for her plight. There is also no social provision made for her destitution. A pagan land, a place of stark individualism, offers no social welfare for the needy.

In the Moabite culture, the only solution for widows is to return to the family of origin.[27] The act of return is not only the righting of an old wrong,[28] it is an echo of earlier biblical decisions: of Abraham, Jacob, and the Israelite people themselves back from depravation, enslavement, and the pagan world of exile. The return to the world of justice begins with the recognition that each person is responsible for the commitment to community. It does not matter how poor or how disempowered one's gender is; each person is a subject, not an object, of another's gaze. The textual language makes this point clearly: Naomi, the anonymous, speechless one, the generic widow of the *mitzvot*, the other that one is to account for, moves to the center stage and sets the opening for all dialogue that is to occur in the text. It is of note that Naomi's language is theological: it is a prayer.

> The Lord grant you that you may find rest,
> each of you
> in the house of her husband.

In Emmanuel Levinas's terms, the gaze between the self and the other is a mutual one requiring a recognition (a remembering) that the other is also self. It is Naomi's radical claim of self that makes possible Ruth's response to her. Naomi assumes that she will be traveling alone. The midrash compares her to the "remnants of the remnants" (of a meal offering: waste, scraps and ashes).[29] Yet, as empty as she is, she is complete, certain of where she is headed. She is not begging. She is with God, with the movement of history.

In Levinas's terms this moment recalls for us the "asymmetry of the interpersonal relations that marks the commencement of moral consciousness." Ruth encounters, in this moral moment, one who is both:

> higher and lower than I am: higher in the sense that she summons me to conscience and judges the arbitrariness of my freedom; lower in the sense that she approaches me not with power to coerce, but in destitution and supplication, offering no resistence other than a moral one.[30]

3. To have a face-to-face encounter makes generations and redemption possible: it is the encounter with the face of the other that makes possible the ethical choice.

> . . . And they lifted up their voice, and wept again;
> and Orpah kissed her mother-in-law;
> but Ruth cleaved unto her.

The movement of this critical scene is as follows: Naomi describes the reality of their situation. They are not actually kin, they are free to go home.[31] Naomi is clear about the limits of their responsibilities. She cannot physically be connected to them because her use value, in a social sense, is now ended. What makes a woman valuable? It is her husband, her ability to bear children, and her ability to organize a household. All features that define personhood and role are gone. Even, as Naomi fantasizes briefly, were she able to start again, bearing sons, with her body restored, it would be of no use. For the work that her daughters-in-law must give their bodies to is immediate. If they are to have identity and value, they must marry quickly and bear children of their own. To wait for Naomi's new sons would be to wait beyond the uses of their bodies, both sexual and procreative.

Orpah sees the tragedy in this: her response is to weep, to grieve, and add not a word to the discourse. Interestingly, most translations add the words "*and she left*" to Orpah's reaction. But it is not in the text.[32] Orpah is a loving and faithful daughter-in-law. She has already done much: married outside of convention, lived for ten years in childlessness, held fast against death and death and death. She does not abandon her chosen family but she "goes nowhere." In staying home in Moab, she falls out of our text and, thus, out of the ethical moment itself. She does the normal and generous act, and it is not enough. Naomi is offering a repeat of Elimelech's original choice: here there is nothing; abandon loyalty and go your way into the singularity of your own life.

Orpah is like most of us most of the time.[33] Radical monotheism and all that it implies is an enormous concept. What Naomi is really asking is easy to turn from and deny in the dailiness of existence. Orpah is faithful within the rules we live by— family, birth, and death. Orpah is sympathetic, alive to the pain of homelessness, poverty, and desperation, and she has cared for Naomi within the limits of the law and the boundaries of her rights.[34]

More is being asked. The text is subtle here, issuing a call covertly and without comment. It is a cloaked call but Ruth hears clearly, and it evokes the extraordinary language of Ruth's reply. The narrator calls the women "daughters-in-law" (*khaloteha*). But Naomi repeatedly calls them her daughters (*b'notai*) in her actual speech. In the Hebrew text she is both pushing them away and binding them at the same time. Orpah is "gone" because she is not present to Naomi's real, embodied situation, not to her actual ethical call. Ruth hears differently. It is this tension in the language, to the opening of the discourse, to which Ruth responds. Ruth hears the prayer behind the speaking and understands the magnitude of the spiritual choice embedded in the social. To hear in this way is to "hear" ethically. It is to understand the language behind the language.

But Ruth cleaved to her.

And she said:
"Behold, your sister-in-law is gone
back to her people and unto her god;
return after your sister-in-law."

Ruth cleaves (*dbq*) to Naomi. (This is the same word used to describe the coming together, both the physical and the spiritual clinging, in Gen. 2:24 of Adam and Eve.)[35] What cleaving represents is the radical encounter with the face of the other. Far beyond civic friendship, it is the "going with" that Naomi is actually demanding by the mere presence of her actual human face. In Levinas's terms, it is the very vulnerability and actuality of the face of the other that commands us. It is the skin of the face that stays the most naked, the most upright, and without defense: "the face is meaning all by itself."[36]

Ruth comes to understand that she is whoever she may be, but she is also the "first person," the one who must find the resources to respond to the utter need of the face of Naomi. It is this ethical premise that is the precursor to what is described as the theme of female bonding in the text. What makes the bond possible and, hence, moral and meaningful is that Ruth has recognized Naomi as a self, taken on the responsibility of the entire capacity of her being and in that moment truly has been able to be a self in the text. It is only after this recognition, or by way of this recognition, that Ruth finds her voice in the text. Levinas posited that full confirmation of self emerges only in radical transcendence of all of our concern for self, including rights. The moral encounter involves a decentering of being, an opening up to plurality and, indeed, to the infinity of possibility in the presence of the other.[37]

This encounter is the responsibility of the subject; the mutuality of response is not the concern of the self. Naomi, in fact, does not respond. The text has Ruth and Naomi continue afterward in silence, calling attention to this silence between them. Naomi will not respond for several more verses. When, then, she acknowledges her responsibility toward Ruth, she takes an extraordinarily active role in the plot, advising Ruth what to wear, how to anoint herself, and what to say to seduce her protector. But this moment will come later, and it is the healing embedded in the text that allows for that doubling of the moral encounter to occur. At this juncture, it is a moment of pure *remembering* on the part of Ruth.

> The readiness to learn from the other, to be a disciple, is thus a crucial moment in the ethical relation to the other. It is the moment by means of which the moral imperative gains its material content. Levinas sums up his analysis by saying that justice is prior to truth, or better, justice is the essential precondition for gaining the truth. In the commencement of moral experience the other is not only higher than I. He is also in important respects lower, the destitute one who entreats me to have regard for his condition. In this dimension the prototype for the other is the widow, the orphan, the poor, the stranger at the gate. . . . In this modality the other is manifest as the one who is in no position to bargain or negotiate fair exchange, as one who has no power to coerce me to give him his due.[38]

What is critical about this text is that both Ruth and Naomi are destitute. Ruth has nothing to give but the infinity of self—infinite responsibility. She recognizes the inalienable responsiblity of subject: no one can substitute for self in this responsibility toward the other. Even while the reader is at all times aware of her destitution, her widowhood, her orphanhood, her poverty, and her estrangement, we can see her acting as subject. While the hearer of the text is aware that none can be more the stranger than this Ruth, at the moment that Naomi is telling Ruth to go home to her own, the Ruth in the text is at that moment beginning the moral recognition that makes her human, voiced, a free moral agent, and a commanded Jew. The rabbis, in clear recognition of this nuanced interplay in the text, explain *midrashically* that Ruth's conversion occurs at that instant, on the spot, and on the road.[39]

> . . . For where you go, I will go,
> And where you lodge, I will lodge;
> your people will be my people,
> and your God my God;
> where you die, will I die,
> and there will I be buried;
> . . . And when she saw that she was steadfastly minded
> to go with her,
> she left off speaking unto her.
> So they two went until they came to Bethlehem.

The two walk out of exile, wilderness, and hunger; out of the starkness and silence of the road, through the desert and into Bethlehem, whose Hebrew name means city of bread; to the Promised Land, into the yellow, ripening, and abundant harvest. In the year of the story in the text, it is just after Passover.

As Levinas asserted, at issue is the death of the other. The nakedness of the face and the totality of the command always underlie the simple presentation of the mortality of the other. The embodied other confronts the embodied self with the reality of their shared mortality and vulnerability. It is the human fragile body that demands the not-killing, demands that the actions of the self not involve the death of the other. Ruth cannot be indifferent to this demand once she has gone beyond Orpah's choice, the legal gesture, and into the ethical moment of her own choice.

Ruth asserts in this language that the face of the other is her responsibility and, moreover, that the body of the other is in some way *her* body.[40] It is this theme of doubling of self that Levinas would claim *is* the ethical itself. In the truth of the later text (and "ethics is prior to truth") Naomi will share the fate, first, of Ruth's body via the pretelling and elaborate planning of the seduction scene on the threshing-room floor; second, of Ruth's fecundity ("to Naomi a child is born" is the cry of the village chorus of women); and, lastly, will suckle her child, utterly merging the most intimate tasks of the body itself with Ruth.[41] All of this intimacy, all of the language of the intense embodiment (the double embodiment) of pregnancy, is heightened by the extraordinary extremity of Ruth's position as the quintessential stranger. Ruth is more than estranged by Naomi's statement delivering her back into Moab. She is textually unbound from the moment of her entrance into the text. She is a Moabite. In the intertextual world of the tradition, she signifies the enemy, the pagan, and the forbidden sexual liaison.[42] The intent of Moab is to destroy, to attack the hungry, homeless Israelites on the road back to the Land. The way of arms, the way of speech, and finally the way of seduction are used to defeat the Israelites on their journey.[43] It is the seduction of the Hebrew men by the Moabite women that does, finally, nearly undermine the entire enterprise of return.[44]

Ruth offers a retelling of the encounter with the Moabites. In a private way the Jew and the Moabite reencounter on the road back to the Land.[45] However, this time the exiled one will be helped; this time the pagan will come to see the holy in the other. This private act must take place before the public acts to follow. Once it is completed, they can be on their way to Bethlehem, where they will encounter the public chorus. Since the text echoes with the depth, both in history and in culture, of the stranger, it calls us to hear the call of the stranger with greater attention. If this moral encounter can be had with a stranger, an enemy, then this must be available to all.

4. To count on social order for a decent basic minimum is a given.

The return to Bethlehem of the textual couple begins the emergence of the problem of scarcity and the allocation of resources not only as a private moral question but also as a public act. Here the text asks: can the private commitment of the face-to-face encounter have meaning in the wider world of social policy amid a city of faces?

Bethlehem, the city of bread, is now the literal symbol of abundance (far removed from the empty Bethlehem of chapter 1). It is the moral order of this commanded community that will provide the concrete, redemptive scaffolding for the poor. The problem of allocation now shifts—how to allocate justly the resource at hand? A city will provide moral order. A chorus greets Naomi, who publicly proclaims her need.[46]

And as soon as her need is publicly acknowledged, Naomi, seemingly newly energized by her public *naming,* sets about the task of justice. She knows she is owed a basic, decent minimum; she understands and remembers the rules of agriculture that provide for *tzedakah.* In essence, the mitzvah of *tzedakah* is to allow to the poor all that is lost through error, all that is left behind, all that is lost by the human design of the harvest itself, and all that is grown in the corners of the field. It is a direct gift from God, from whom all is being given on this Land, to the poor, who do not own the means of production. It is, as it were, God's righting of the inequalities that exists in human and, hence, limited societies, that is enabled through the hand of the reapers. It is not charity; it is the part of the harvest that actually belongs to the poor by right and obligation. If properly given and not expropriated by the landowners, it is enough to feed all widows and orphans, not lavishly but sufficiently. The basic, decent minimum is reparations. It acknowledges that not all are equal, that some are weaker, others stronger. And what is given is out of responsibility for this difference. The text assumes that all know of and will act on the laws. Further, the private choices made by each participant will be part of the public acts of recovery of the vulnerable. Ruth's gesture toward Naomi will become part of the public discourse, the language that defines the narrative of this problem.

5. *Intimacy/family is seen as an obligation beyond justice/the law.*

Yet the measure of this justice is far beyond the dictates of the law. Standing among the crowd, the landowner Boaz sees Ruth and he names her, calling her "*bitti*" ("my daughter") and acknowledging her history. Her daughterliness is acknowledgment of this chosen role. Boaz allows Ruth not only to glean in his field as a stranger with entitlement but to eat at his table as a member of his household. It is this act of sitting at the table, the acknowledgment of kinship, that allows all that is to follow. The language that responds to Ruth's call in the wilderness to be kin to Naomi is linked to this, the first meal in the text after the accounts of famine, hunger, and loss.[47]

Boaz will give Ruth not only what is her basic decent minimum, the gleaning from his harvest, but will reach into his own portion and give from this as well.

> And also pull out for her some of purpose
> from the bundles, and leave it,
> and let her glean,
> and rebuke her not.

This is beyond the basic requirement of the *halakhic* system. His acceptance of Ruth, the stranger, as family, offers a model of justice language in the same way that the text makes plain in Ruth's speech. In fact, Boaz's action is a playing out of Ruth's pledge: "I will give fairly to you, not because I am contracted to but out of bonds of the community, out of familial love."[48]

6. *Reprise: To trust that friendship/family will make generations/redemption possible (again) and that this action is mutually a duty and a right.*

At last, Ruth is acknowledged, and the text describes a burst of activity on Naomi's part. No further laments about her status or loss will appear in the text. From now on she purposefully directs Ruth toward what she understands is her just portion. The text now depicts Naomi as face-to-face with Ruth. It is a moment of reprise.

> And Naomi, her mother-in-law,
> said to her: My daughter
> shall I not seek rest for you,
> that it be well with you?

Whereas before Naomi had implored God to find rest for Ruth, here Naomi takes responsibility for this work. It is surely not a turning away from God. Naomi does not speak in this text without God-reference lacing her syntax. Rather, it is acknowledgment or recognition of responsibility for responsibility. It is at this moment, when Ruth has returned to feed Naomi, her skirt full with ripened barley (the literal image of fertility restored), that Naomi pledges herself to concrete action. A new turn is taken in the text, and the story moves to conclusion in a rush of swiftly told scenes. It is when Naomi can actually return the gaze of the stranger, when she can "see" her, and name her daughter, and know her as kin, that a curious thing occurs in the text. It is at this moment that the reader first hears of a field in the possession of Naomi, an inheritance that, when sold, could certainly relieve the destitution of the women. It is as though this inheritance is somehow evoked by the recognition of the kinship, as though metaphorically the "inheritance" is, in fact, the commitment of kin to kin made tangible. Nowhere in the text up to this point is there language to suggest that Naomi has inherited anything. She is portrayed as unrelentingly bereft. Clearly, this field could have been claimed and sold much earlier so that Naomi and Ruth would not be reduced to gleaning. What seems to bring the physical inheritance into the language of the story is the understanding that it has real meaning, that Ruth, the stranger, is *bitti*. It is an odd moment when scarcity simply drops away: here, there is enough; the poorest have their own resources. It occurs only when all seem to trust that it is possible to *redeem* again land, self, and vision after tragedy.

The intimate, solitary encounter between Ruth and Boaz in the darkness of the threshing room at the end of a long harvest season is an encounter involving a woman who can claim her full personhood. In the language of this speech, she is no longer the stranger. She offers (quite literally) her entire self, and asks for the entire self from Boaz.[49] In tems of the moral encounter, Levinas would argue, this is what is being asked at all times. These are the stakes of all recognition and relationship, and the encounter in the text is merely this enormity made tangible.

> "Who are you?"
> And she answered:
> "I am Ruth, your *amah*.[50]
> Spread therefore your cloak
> over your *amah*
> for you are a near kinsman."[51]

Ruth is asking for more than the obvious straightforward sexual encounter here. She is asking for Boaz to "spread his cloak over her." Spreading the cloak is a metaphor for the act of marriage itself, comparable to spreading the *huppah* over the bride in the traditional Jewish wedding ceremony.[52]

7. *To trust in community and the language of community to name and define the future.*

The text ends with a recommitment to the health and well-being of each as intrinsically tied to the health of the community and citizenship. After the intense, powerful, and startling intimacy of the private encounter, everything—every act, every gesture—in the conclusion of the story happens in the public realm. All of the acts occur in the broad daylight of the city, in the gates of the city, with the community as witness, with the community taking responsibility for the framing and naming of the final acts of justice. Justice is done by public acts in full view of all at the gate, but these acts are echoes of promises made in private human encounter. In both the (repeating) scenes of Ruth-Naomi and Boaz-Ruth, the private face-to-face encounter is made whole and actual by moving the text, language, and, hence, commitment to the public discourse.

Finally, we hear of the swift conception and arrival of the child Oved, named in public by a chorus of women neighbors of the village and nursed in public. Once again, men fall out of the story. In fact, one midrash has Boaz conceiving the child on the wedding night and dying shortly thereafter to explain his curious lack of presence in the text.

Naming and nursing are the ultimate signifiers of parentage, yet the language is clear. These are public acts. The doing of justice, the restoration of Naomi, is a matter of public discourse. It is also crucial to history and foundational for the founding of the Davidic kingship.

> And Naomi took the child
> and laid him on her bosom
> and became nurse to him.
> And the women, her neighbors,
> gave it a name,
> saying:
> "There is a son born to Naomi."

The convention of the midrash is that Ruth and Naomi enter the community from their exile prior to Passover. The barley harvest has begun; the winter has passed. Ruth stays in the fields with Boaz for the full harvest, into the wheat harvest, about two lunar months.[53] The convention continues that Ruth marries Boaz at Shavuot, the Feast of Weeks. She immediately conceives her son, Oved (*ovd*) (meaning "one who serves"), and he is born about nine months later, close to Passover.[54] The name he is given cannot help but reinvoke the image of Passover, the theme of service and freedom being a central motif of the Exodus story.

The name Oved alone might be a slender thread on which to hang this intertextual allusion if the connection and conundrum expressed by the word were not so strong, and if the Ruth narrative of return from the land of exile, a land fled to in famine, were not so parallel to the Exodus narrative. We were slaves, *avadim*, in Egypt, but now we are free. Free to do what? Free to be servants, *avadim* to God. The word is the very same, one of the interior puns of the Passover liturgy, one that trembles with meaning. To be free is to be able to be commanded, to accept and accede to a life of justice and command, acknowledge an order of responsibility, and to understand the responsibility of Exodus itself—that each of us is a stranger in a strange land and that the challenge is to remember to act as though each were herself a recently freed slave (*ovd*), each one of us, Oved.[55]

The rabbinic structure is subtle and unfolds after the close, as it were, of the story. The Ruth story is read aloud yearly in the liturgy cycle at Shavout, both for the agricultural relationship to the story and for the theme of marriage and for the taking on of the Torah, given to the Jewish people at the time of Shavuot. The hearer is meant to remember not only the faithfulness of Ruth and the generosity of spirit of Boaz but the self/servant/slave, who is to come as a result of this story. It links the messianic with the personal and makes the covert but radical claim that it is the face-to-face encounter of the poorest and the most outcast, the female stranger, that makes possible the continuance of the Jewish people and each self.

Hence, the story ends with a reflection on the text after the telling. Justice and reparations are about the move not only from famine to feast but also from enslavement to service and from exile and displacement to community and place.

The Implications of the Theory: The World of the Encounter

Of what use is this text? If the language of the text offers a radical shift in worldview, then we must be able to look to the insights and the call embedded within it to be of use in the actual, difficult world. Such a narrative raises the question of the relationship of justice to public policy. This narrative makes plain that the question of what is "just" is at once both deeply political and intensely personal, that the sense of justice, of rightness of our actions is shaped by a variety of encounters and discourses. An early insight of the feminist movement stands: the personal is political in the deepest moral sense. The contentious debate that surrounds the allocation of resources in the real famines that surround our modern sensibilities—the scarcity of resources in health care, education, and social welfare—must be the terrain of the discourse, the place of real use of this language. It must be of use in the world to real strangers, widows, orphans, the vulnerable, and the homeless on the road. Ethical theory is only as true as its application, and a feminist Jewish ethics must make meaning and good sense as a realpolitik.

For example, we face a health care system that is increasingly competitive, costly, and chaotic. The real struggle for health care reform is going on daily, hourly, in the American clinical encounter. There is not a gesture, not an order, not a touch, that is not painfully rationed. When one by one by one American families come to face their deaths and their losses, they come to know this. Health care could stand in for any problem of distributive justice. But the necessary fundamental and transformational justification for radical moral choices and paradigmatic changes must be addressed prior to the mechanics of access, delivery, or payment. It is with the problem of encounter that justice must begin, and in the insistence on justice that health care reform must be rooted.

The text of Ruth allows us a metaphor for how this might happen. It is a Jewish metaphor, but not exclusively so. In placing a language that is Jewish and feminist as the centerpiece of the framing discourse I risk the perception that I propose a marginalized, particularized response to the problems held in common. Precisely the opposite is the case. I am proposing an "ethics of encounter" that has a clear expression in the Ruth text but whose application, when insisted upon, can be the moral notation that undergirds public policy. The Rutharian encounter on the road, the portrayal of the self and the stranger, provides a pattern of interpretation which allows one to locate the gesture within a larger framework.[56] It allows us to create a template for justice that is at once intimate, possible, and personal, a first location for our actions of conscience.

First, bringing the pattern and language offered by the Ruth text into the debate challenges the discourse of health care reform, and the allocation of scarce resources in general, in several ways. The text of Ruth, not interpreted as a general "religious inclusion" but viewed through the particular lens of the methodology of Jewish textual tradition, asserts that significantly new insights can be brought into the discussion from language and faith principles that are distinct. Further, the Ruth narrative is rooted in the assumption not only of faith but of a particular faith, and a faith that asserts itself not as ethnic color, or anonymous blessing, but of practical and tangible use in the setting of policy.

Further, reflection on both the content of the story and the Jewish and feminist hermeneutics of Ruth means focusing attention from "the female gaze." This gaze is not only rare in any canonical or authoritative texts but rare in the debate on public policy, where the stories of women are allowed admission primarily as objects: objects of pity, illustrations of injustice, barometers of need. The Ruth narrative teaches not from the position of victim but from the position of woman as subject, as central player. She is enmeshed in a successful community event of encounter, obligation, and response that changes the facticity of what appears to be historical inevitability. To allow for this is to allow for the entirely radical notion that the centrality of the view of the other is possible. This method both uses and demonstrates the possibility of an ethics of discourse, where the ability to "reverse" is the gesture at the heart of justice itself.

This is not unique to Ruth, but is a methodological reality of the form itself. The quality of an alternative reading is present in all midrashic interpretation. Midrash is exegesis that by its very nature fills in the lacunae in the textual account. It is a reflection of the story and assumes that the reality of human conversation, that glance, that nuance, that interiority of reflection, are also relevant to an account of full moral action. Rabbinic midrash often brings a quality of attention to the voice of the excluded. It is common to find glimpses or overt references to rabbinic discontent with standard texts or to find troubling questions in the mouths of midrashic characters.

Additionally, applying textual narrative is a method of applied theology that is at the heart of the *halakhic* method. Embellishment of the aggadic source to achieve a template for action is central to Jewish method. What is distinctive about my use of the text is a persistent insistence that the theological pattern has a pertinence to the actual contemporary public policy debate. This example of an alternative feminist gaze is interesting in its own right, in the "room" of Jewish studies and academic reflection. But it is imperative that the possibility of the pattern, in all of its quirky and idiosyncratic Jewish particularity, is seen as requisite to the reordering of the philosophical stance. Without this view of the other, the ground of justice will be impoverished. There is not only poverty in the assumption that the public discourse is Christian and male; there is the certainty of error in describing the very terms of encounter for public debate.

Looking at the established debate via another lens creates the possibility for many alternate readings and many contributions to the common language. This is of particular importance when the multicultural, multiclass, and multiethnic setting of clinical medicine and public distribution is addressed. Hearing the language of a particular discourse from such a particular tradition allows for the radical apprehension of the discourse itself. The entrance into the room of public debate requires that the actors must turn from the ongoing nature of the conversation to notice, to admit the incoming of the other. Before the content of the story, the presence of an alternative narrative changes the terms of the discussion.

Let us see concretely how the text can be used in the health care justice debate. The seven moments I have identified in the text can be specifically lifted up and reflected upon as the critical gestures of choice and justice.

1. To leave the community at a time of scarcity or danger is wrong. There is no personal escape from collective scarcity. The text of Ruth reminds us that there is no personal escape from collective scarcity. The health care debate is quickened by this reality. Unless one is prepared to build a fully equipped hospital with a separate blood product supply on one's own premises, there is no escape from the collective fate that crisis and scarcity imposes on all of American society. To live in New York City in the 1970s was to draw from the very blood of the poorest and most desperate. To travel on the freeway across Los Angeles in the 1990s is to share in the risk that an accident could bring you to the doors of the nearest emergency rooms, the ones that serve as outpatient clinics to the poorest and the uninsured. They will be closed, full beyond capacity, no matter how exquisite your car or provident your health care coverage. To walk in the subway or shop at your supermarket means that your child will share the very air with the homeless one and her child beside you. There is no escape to Moab.

2. To resume responsibility, even if one is powerless, is the just course for every citizen. Hence, it falls to each to resume responsibility, even if one is powerless. It is the just course for every citizen. Even the one who has been silenced, Naomi who had never been trained to speak, each must become a part of the discourse. Each citizen must be asked the question: "What is the most just plan?" And each answer must be taken into account.

3. To have a face-to-face encounter makes generations and redemption possible: it is the encounter with the face of the other that makes possible the ethical choice. Any reform must begin with face-to-face encounter. The selective survey will not do, the advice of many experts will not be enough. It is the radical recognition that what I choose for the body of another will happen also to my body, it is the physicality and the *dbq* character of the encounter, it is the encounter itself that must be insisted upon.

4. To count on social order for a decent basic minimum is a given. But the initial recognition will be of little meaning unless there is a concurrent commitment that allows each to count on the resultant social order for a decent basic minimum. It must be given that certain basic protections, analogous to the minimum standards for the poor in the Ruth story, are respected. A world in which health care access is defined by a market metaphor is inevitably unstable, to say nothing of immoral. Access that is universal must be first assured. The question of the justification of such a basic decent minimum and the content of such a basic minimum share can be answered, in part, by the response of the community to the vulnerable in the Ruth text. In the story, the provision for the poor can be assumed: by Ruth, by Naomi, and by the community. Unlike the society of Moab, where there is nothing and no one in the field, the fields in the Ruth story have a mandated portion, a corner in each that is reserved for the poor in the text of Leviticus. It is not out of pity that Ruth is allowed to glean; it is out of the *halakhic* requirement that a fixed percentage of the crop belongs to the poor, given from God's hand, via the work of Boaz. The access is universally available and guaranteed to all, the citizen and the resident alien. And, in part, the response pattern between the women in the story, the language itself, and the tradition of discourse supports a principle of respect for community that must be adhered to if we are to be faithful to the centrality of the encounter that is prior to all justice. Once there is a commitment both to universal access to scarce social goods and to a process of decision making that involves each, there must be a conversation that centers around the ends and goals of shared resources. What is it that works, what is the outcome, what do we think is fair: the question must be geared to the establishment of the standards to which each will be entitled.[57]

5. *Intimacy is seen as an obligation beyond justice and the law.* Structuring justice debates in this way allows for the setting of limits on a coherent package of social goods to be intimate, to involve the personal reflection of conscience in a collective setting. It allows small moral communities to recognize the stranger as sister, as daughter, to inescapably see the stranger who sits across from you as the fellow traveler on the road. The impulse for a system of justice, and the language of justice itself, must be to see justice as intimate and familial, as an obligation beyond the law and a formal equality, to include relational ties to the specific other.

6. *To trust that friendship/family will make generations/redemption possible (again) and that this action is mutually a duty and a right.* In fact, as was patterned for the reader in Ruth, it is only the mutuality of friendship and relationality that makes even simple continuance possible.

7. *To trust in community and the language of community to name and define the future.* Finally, the language of Ruth teaches that the child of the most vulnerable and excluded really is the salvation of each one of us. The child will be called "one who serves," and thus he will be born into an obligation of his own, his name will define the work of a free person: to respond with faithful action, to pick up the task that is unfinished and that is sacred, the task that is mundane and thus deeply human. It is our mutual responsibility, as citizens of this moral community that is our own America, to name that child, to call him ours. To trust in community and the language of community, to name and define the future means that we must begin with the name of a single child.

An Ethics of Encounter

The policies of social justice must emerge from what I have come to call an "ethics of encounter." What I mean by this term is described in part by the insights of Levinas, in part by the notion of communicative ethics, in part by the acknowledgment of a specific other asserted in feminist philosophy, and in part by calls for "community" and "responsibility" from the communitarians.[58] The ethics of encounter implies a process, however, a process that is most elegantly illustrated in the Ruth story of encounter. In this story it is the Hebrew term *dbq*, meaning to cling or to cleave, that most fully expresses the first principle of the ethics of encounter.

Cleaving to another, recognizing that the other is the bone of the bone and the flesh of the flesh that is given in common, locating the mutual body as the site of the moral gesture, is fundamental to ethical reflection. First, because it pulls the discourse to the specific, the limited and the mortal self, insisting on mortality as the inescapable frame for all moral gesture. Next, because it requires a radical rethinking of all that occurs to the other: all the yearning is my yearning, the loss is in fact my loss. This responsibility for the narratives great and small, for the dreams of the other, for the temptations of the other, for the responsibility of the other, creates a mutual commandedness. The death of the other, the illness of the other, her vulnerability, is your own ("and where you will die I will die"). *Dbq* is a requirement of intensity that precedes and deepens the language of "citizenship." It insists that citizenship, even with the stranger most foreign, could be, ought to be, experienced with the intensity of family. Unlike citizenship, the term *dbq* suggests to us that human beings are, by absolute definition and design, relational. Justice is then personal: it calls for no less than the totality of re-membering, of re-call, of the woman who walks at your side.

The ethics of encounter has a second defining vocabulary. It is the language of community. I am certain that the principle of autonomy, so dominant in the field of bioethics yet so painfully limited in the clinical encounter, is also of limited use in addressing the allocation of resources. It is true that despite the theoretical constructs of the field, human persons are not simply or even primarily autonomous. Rather than living in a world described and defined by the necessity of autonomous choice, freely made, most actual people live in the relational, obligatory, and interconnected world, a world far messier and heavily freighted, far more passionately loving and passionately hating than that described in philosophical texts. I am claiming here a principle that would counterbalance autonomy: the principle of "community" in ethics. It is this term that expresses the next step in the "ethics of encounter" that I suggest. It is the response and recognition of the community that contextualizes the choice for *dbq* that would otherwise simply be an act of personal conscience, a good act, but a limited one.[59]

What Ruth teaches is that citizenship is solidarity, that meaningful discourse starts with the recognition of the other, and that justice is prior to any human freedom. The text insists on the radical recognition that the primary responsibility is calling into being a community that is both prior to and responsible for the just flourishing of any human self. Ruth comes to *conscience* by the moment described in the text as her "cleaving" (*dbq*). It is this moment that makes conscience possible. The conscience can be said, then, not to be the speaking of the voice within but rather the hearing of the quiet voice of the other. It is this voice that must precede any claim in the distribution of the scarce resource. This voice, just as clearly as one's "own," must remind us to see each child as our own, each journey and each need as fundamentally shared.

This is the first gesture of human community. Ruth's story is central because it is her language, at the instant of her human recognition, that frames relationality as primary to ethical choice. The second gesture is, of course, the response of the commanded community that surrounds this gesture. For while recognition and cleaving are essential, they are not enough. It is a foolish and solitary gesture in the arena of public policy if it is not embedded in the community that sequences and interprets ethical gestures. It is the community that gives public voice, that names, and that itself recognizes and insists on the human connection that is the context for language of an allocation based in relationality. There is not atomized self that hears only its own voice and its cause. The entire possibility of internal, reflective dialogue of a self that is capable of response assumes a relational being. Such a self then struggles with the problem of the effect her choice actually has on tangible, identified others. The sense of temporality is present in the reflective sense of integrity that depends on such dialogue and such narrative, and on the human propensity to experience a life as a story told to a circle of others. Narrative assumes community, the listening presence and reciprocity of the other.

Ethics has a prophetic responsibility that is inescapable.[60] Describing the "is" cannot be the entire task of ethics. It is the role of the ethicist to point out what ought to be the case, how a world ought to look (rather than how to achieve only the pragmatic). This is never to depreciate the first step toward the future. But it is also why it is imperative never to lose sight of the vision in light of the possible political achievement. Focusing on the issue of conscience allows a language to develop that is accountable to justice. It is a language that takes account of the yearning toward the good.

It is in light of this language, of a differently apprehended understanding of justice, that all health care reform policies must be apprehended. There is no simple answer to the problem of American health care reform. The application of the language of justice and the delineation of the philosophical ground that must undergird such efforts will be extraordinarily difficult. The focus of this work is not to craft public policy in detail but to reflect on the aspects of the language of the discourse both as it emerges and as I believe it ought to emerge in this debate.

Conclusion: Daily Practice

Ultimately, this would be simply promising philosophy if I could not argue that what I propose about the necessity for small group discourse is true and tangible in actual practice. Thus it must be shown that even in large, pluralistic, anonymous societies like America, long prior to a Utopian conclusion, these small models not only can thrive but can affect social reality. Even in a society of strangers, amid other indices of despair and anomie, this has occurred. And this can be shown: in the women's movement, and importantly, in the reform efforts of citizens' groups around the country, this has happened in ordinary life despite little or no encouragement from the state or popular ideology, an ideology which, in fact, argues for the primacy of the individual and the unrelenting fear of the stranger. This phenomenon of the possible is what gives encouragement to the discourse of the prophetic. The confidence that discourse itself has a power cannot be overstated: it is a different way to view the limited world. The social optimism of the women's movement parallels the textual optimism of the Ruth narrative in the Jewish theological and textual tradition. The women's chorus of naming in the Ruth narrative provides a textual parallel to the face-to-face development of the actual moral communities.

The point of the detailed search in the text just described is to recount with care the texture of the actual gesture in Ruth, to claim the prophetic in the act, and to claim the possible. This is the language that I argue is the best for the application of justice. It argues for the association of justice with encounter, with response: in short with friendship, a deep and enmeshed friendship, *dbq* that characterizes both this text and the actuality of the human experience. Using this language as a starting pattern for a public response to scarcity allows a reframing of the basic pattern of isolation and self-regarding action that now is the dominant tone of contemporary policy discourse.

The lessons of the relationship embedded in the Ruth story are not unique to this one text in the Jewish tradition. The Ruth text adds to Jewish ethics, however, in significant ways. It provides a basis for talk about justice as a social, daily experience that will define the nature of community. While it acknowledges scarcity, it transforms its power: scarcity, the famine that lurks beneath every abundance, does not threaten the fabric of human community if the demand of relationship is consistently heard. It is not a text about violence; it is a text about the lived experience of aging, vulnerability, and solidarity in the face of death. The Ruth text deals with the most difficult issue of agency, that of the limits set between the self and the *ger,* the other, the stranger in the land.

The Book of Ruth adds another voice to the rich and complex tradition of Jewish ethical response to the rationing of the scarce resource. It is a text that is firmly rooted in the story of women as central actors and insists on the primacy and power of women's choices to remake the world. The *halakhah* is not the only way the tradition admits new framing language into the ethical discourse. The method of the telling of the Ruth story is midrashic, lyrical, narrative. It is suggestive rather than directive, rich in detail and context, and thus opens us in a dramatically new way to the ability to see what seemed to be given, fixed, immutable about legal and political relationships. It is language that assumes community, assumes the listening presence and reciprocity of the other. In this way the discourse of justice is reframed by the presence of the other, located in a human community, rich with the collective and naming stories of each. The chorus of women who greet the travelers Ruth and Naomi on the road, and who name the child that is born to them, create such a community. And the text creates a pattern for us to respond to: the existence of such a pattern allows us to imagine that it is possible here as well. The story forces us into the apprehension of the self as always self-in-relationship, self-in-obligation, a child born from a woman into the waiting hands of another. Community is prior to autonomy: we know this is true from the most common details of an ordinary woman's life made luminous by such obligation. It is from these details that our reclaimed language of feminist justice must emerge.

It is the encounter on the road to Bethlehem, city of bread, that the Jewish textual tradition surrounds and defines. The model of the Ruth narrative, and the very method of its telling, honor the discursive relationship, the ethic of encounter and principled community response. It is on these methodological grounds that policy can be resolved: through the actual case story, the actual face of the other, the return to the collective that will surround every gesture. The moral discourse modeled in the language, content, and method of telling that I have described here allows for a renewed certainty that the truest public policy, and the best vision of justice, will be created by the development of collective conscience. This conscience can only be made actual in the moral communities of citizenship, of obligation and discourse. It will only come into being in the full and public encounter between our most private and vulnerable human selves, and the extraordinary and actual human face of the other.

Notes

1. I was interested in the debates around health care reform and rationing: this essay is a part of a longer work on health care justice, but the ethics that I am suggesting is meant to apply in all situations of distributive justice.

2. Jeffrey Stout, *Ethics after Babel: The Language of Morals and Their Discontents* (Boston: Beacon Press, 1988). Stout argues in his book that there is no such thing as a "neutral vantage" and "a universal language for ethics" and that each speaks from the distinctive vantage of their own tradition.

3. As in the texts of rescue, which describe how to save a caravan of people under threat of brigands: in such texts all men are to be saved before all women, unless the threat is to the sexuality of the travelers. In that case female virgins take precedence, but, since forced male sex is assumed to be more painful than female rape, men take precedence.

4. The texts of the pursuit of the *rodef* also seem impartial, as do the seige texts that describe differing justice appeals in hostage settings. In critical ways illness is both like and unlike a "brigand band," and the *rodef* that seeks out a victim is like and unlike death itself. The methodology of casuistry requires attention to what is morally relevant about the case situation. Illness and accident are not caused by human evil, and death cannot be bargained with or outwitted. The texts of pursuit and recovery are fundamentally about the uses of power. Illness and death require an understanding of the essentially uncontrollable, uncertain nature of the world. Further, is the provision of health care services morally distinctive from the more general "giving of assistance"? Are cases and metaphors of war the most useful in the adjudication of healing? Further, the texts about the Holocaust, remarkable in their power, raise the question of the difference between emergency and normative status. Gerald Winslow, in *Triage and Justice,* (Berkeley: University of California Press, 1982) made the point that societies cannot function always in crisis; they must have rules that apply in extraordinary situations that would not necessarily apply in daily life. The texts about the requirements of a just city are closest to this model, but in this text the actual roles and status of the categories of the persons needed and the contours of city life are quite altered by the modern world, and this understanding must temper the use of such texts. Each text cited gives us a measure of an answer, but ultimately none is completely satisfying.

5. This insight is not unique to feminists, of course: "Friendship also seems to hold states together" is an Aristotelian claim. In the *Nicomachean Ethics* Aristotle has a chapter on friendship, an oddity in a book about the ethical relations needed within the polis. A central topic in the discourse of civic structure, however, is civic friendship. Others have referenced the importance of civic friendship and the centrality of relationships among the citizens as solidifying the state itself. What the Aristotelian formulation suggests is the understanding that the personal is political.

6. Whose work is richly described in the essay by Aronowicz in this volume.

7. Ilana Pardes, *Countertraditions in the Bible* (Cambridge, Mass.: Harvard University Press, 1992), p. 2.

8. "There was a famine in the land, and Abram went down to Egypt to sojourn there, for the famine was severe in the land" Gen. 12:10, as translated in *The Tanakh* (Philadelphia: The Jewish Publication Society, 1989), p. 95. The next lines of the account are as follows: "As he was about to enter Egypt, he said to his wife Sarai, 'I know what a beautiful woman you

are. If the Egyptians see you and think 'She is his wife' they will kill me and let you live. Please let me say that you are my sister, that it may go well with me because of you, and that I may remain alive thanks to you.' When Abram entered Egypt, the Egyptians saw how beautiful the woman was. Pharaoh's courtier saw her and praised her to Pharaoh, and the woman was taken into Pharaoh's palace."

Even Pharaoh is appalled at this, asking six verses later, "Why did you not tell me that she was your wife!?" What has been done here is to allow the material enrichment of Abram: he acquires "sheep, oxen, asses, male and female slaves and camels" because Sarai is raped and enslaved by Pharaoh. It is a horrific break in the narrative when Sarai becomes "enthinged" and, for a time, loses even her name ('how beautiful the woman was").

This famine story will resonate against the Ruth story, as it deals with similar themes: power, sexuality, the stranger, and a backdrop of desperation.

9. "The famine, however, spread over the whole world. So all the world came to Joseph in Egypt to procure rations, for the famine had become severe throughout the world. "When Jacob saw that there were food rations to be had in Egypt, he said to his sons, 'Why do you keep looking at one another?' 'Now I hear,' he went on, 'that there are rations to be had in Egypt. Go and procure rations for us there that we may live and not die' " Gen. 42:1. Here note that Jacob, son of the blind Isaac, admonishes his sons *not* to look at each other. The Hebrew verb implies reciprocity. Note the contrast, of course, with the Levinasian insistence to look at the face of the other.

10. In a larger and more telling way, however, the entire biblical text is enclosed in a drama of scarcity, more specifically, in a tension between scarcity and blessing. The expulsion from the Garden is to a world of work and the messianic hope is for the last moment of human abundance.

11. I began this research with no definitive defense about my use of the Ruth text as another source for the language of justice: it was an intuition about the "fitness" of the narrative and an attachment to the story—hardly defensible hermeneutics. It was the research for the prooftext of the talmudic argumentation between Rabbi Akiba and Ben Petura in the pivotal text of the two travelers in the desert and the one flask of water (Bava Metzia 62a) that led me back to Ruth via Lev. 25:35. This link to the Bava Metzia text occurs because the problem of how one lives with the neighbor, the issue of distributive justice, and the tension between the marketplace economy, human desperation, and compassion are the organizing issues behind the call for the Jubilee in Leviticus. But the rabbinic text asks, short of the Jubilee what can we do? How does one *live on the road,* in the interim generation, in the meantime? The text of Ruth is one answer to this question, and the Bava Metzia text is another. Of course, Rabbi Akiba and Ben Petura know the story of the women who traveled on the road alone in famine and scarcity greeted by kin who knew the laws of redemption. And, of course, the literate reader of the talmudic debate ought to know the story, too: the very words, "two travelers on the road," evoke the Ruth text. It is my contention that the story around the story—the reference back to the Jubilee as the prophetic answer to the problem of distributive justice—and the details of the *halakhah* as the practical answer to the same problem link the two texts. I contend also that that story is meant by the author of the text to be held in tension with the other narratives, and that this tension is part of the methodology of temporal simultaneity of the system itself.

12. Pardes, *Countertraditions in the Bible,* p. 99.

13. The following rabbinic midrash makes this point: "*And it came to pass, in the days of the judging of the judges.* Woe unto that generation which judges its judges, and woe unto that generation whose judges are in need of being judged! As it is said, *And yet they harkened not to their judges*" (Judges 2:17).

This is wordplay in the Hebrew as well as in the English. The eighteenth-century Yiddish-language commentary on the biblical text, the *Tz'enah Ur'enah,* explains this midrash further:

The verse lets us know two things. The episode of Ruth and Boaz took place at a time when there was not yet a king over Israel, only judges who led Israel. The verse says *shfot hashoftim* (lit., "the judgment of the judges"), which can be interpreted to mean that the judges themselves were judged. The judges were wicked, and they, too, needed to be judged and rebuked. Or, it may mean that the people were very wicked and did not want to heed the judges. When a judge found them guilty, they would mock him and say: "You punish us? Punish yourself." The word *vayehi* ("it was" [in the days] . . .) hints that Israel shouted *(Oi) Vay!* ("woe"). They had many troubles, because they did not want to heed the judges.

14. As Jack Sasson argues: "Time is at once specific and diffuse ('When the Judges used to judge'), conveying more than the actual words imply, since during that period—as any Hebrew would know—people were constantly losing God's grace before earning it again." Jack M. Sasson, "Ruth," in *The Literary Guide to the Hebrew Bible*, ed. Robert Alter and Frank Kermode (Harvard, Mass.: Belknap Press, 1987). pp. 321–22.

15. Ibid.

16. *Tz'enah Ur'enah.*

17. *Midrash Rabbah*, vol. 8, trans. L. Rabinowitz (New York: Soucino Press, 1983).

18. Note how the following selected midrashim (there are two chapters of midrashim in *Midrash Rabbah* on this first *paragraph* of the story) uses the verse in Psalms to locate the text morally and explains the meaning of the tragedy that is to come. Concerning Elimelech, the commentary reads:

> "*And the name of the man was Elimelech*" (1, 20). Because trouble has come to thee, thou hast forsaken them? *And a certain man of Bethlehem in Judah went*" (1, 1). That is the meaning of the verse "Whose leaders are borne with. There is no breach and no going forth." (Ps. 144:14)
>
> R. Johanan said: It is not written "who bear," but "who are borne." When the young bear with the old, there is no breach, i.e., there is no breaking out of the plague, as it is said, "And no going forth . . ."
>
> R. Lakish transposes the verse (as though it read "Our leaders bear"). When the great bear with the small "there is no breach of exile", as it is written, "And ye shall go out at the breaches" (Amos 4:3) "and there is no going forth into exile, as it is written, "Cast them out of My sight and let them go forth." (Jer. 15) . . .
>
> R. Lulianus said: When the small hearken to the great, but the great do not bear the burden of the small upon them, then the verse applies, "And the Lord shall enter into Judgment." (Isa. 3:14)

19. *Midrash Rabbah*, p. 9.

20. Note how the Psalm used as a prooftext is a text about the mutuality of dependency between leaders and people. The rabbis ask, what causes the disruption of the social fabric of the exilic community, the disaster and the plague? Is it the refusal of the people to "bear with" the elders, the small to listen to the great, asked R. Johanan? No, the contrary is true, responds R. Lakish, it is when the great do not bear with the small. R. Lulianus concurs: it is when the most vulnerable depend on the leadership and the leadership flee from this obligation that the judgment of Isaiah applies: "The Lord will bring this charge against the elders and officers of His people: 'It is you who ravaged the vineyard; That which was robbed from the poor is in your houses, How dare you crush my people, and grind the faces of the poor (in the dust)?' " The verse from Isaiah links the cause of desperation and poverty to the exploitation of the poor by the ruling class. Famine is a direct result of this sort of social plunder. The *midrash* connects the Ruth text, by means of the multiple layering of text, to this judgment.

21. The reason is that in the latter case, since they were leaving the country for another land, Scripture makes no mention of their property but states simply "And a certain man went"—as though empty handed. (*Midrash Rabbah*, pp. 8, 21)

22. Cynthia Ozick, commenting on this verse, was even harsher. She, too, filled in the text with interpretation that is supported by the midrashic material.

Elimelech turns his back on the destitute conditions of hungry Bethlehem, picks up his family, and because he is rich enough to afford the journey, sets out for where food is. He looks to his own skin and means to grab his own grub. . . . This is the Rabbis' view. They are symbolists and metaphor seekers; it goes without saying that they are moralists. Punishment is truthful; punishment is the consequence of reality, it instructs in what happens. . . . The man who throws away the country of aspiration, especially in a lamentable hour when failure overruns it—the man who promotes egotism, elevates the material, and deprives his children of idealism—this fellow, this Elimelech, vexes the rabbis and afflicts them with shame. Of course there is not a grain of any of this in the text itself—not a word about Elimelech's character or motives or even his position in Bethlehem. (Cynthia Ozick, "Ruth," in *Congregation,* ed. David Rosenberg [San Diego: Harcourt Brace Jovanovich, 1987], p. 369)

23. Ezra 1:9–11; 2:64–66.
24. Sasson, "Ruth," p. 322.
25. As Cynthia Ozick notes:

Until Elimelech's death, Naomi has been an exemplum of the normal. She has followed her husband and made no decisions or choices of her own. What we nowadays call feminism is, of course, as old as the oldest society imaginable; there have always been feminists: women (including the unsung) who will allow no element of themselves—gift, capacity, natural authority—to go unexpressed, whatever the weight of the mores. Naomi has not been one of these. Until the death of her husband, we know nothing of her but her compliance, and it would be foolish to suppose that in Naomi's world a wife's obedience is not a fundamental social virtue. (Ozick, "Ruth," p. 370)

26. Pardes, *Countertraditions in the Bible,* p. 100.
27. That this was a Republican campaign theme in the 1992 election was no casual choice. The ideology of autonomy is linked to the theme of traditional, idealized family values since to suggest otherwise would be to assert that perhaps a community might have responsibility for the most vulnerable, not a popular election-year theme.
28. Ozick, "Ruth," p. 371.
29. *Midrash Rabbah,* p. 33. Ozick made this point as well: "detritus and ash."
30. Thomas W. Ogletree, *Hospitality to the Stranger* (Philadelphia: Fortress Press, 1985), p. 48.
31. For an interesting commentary on this scene one can examine its treatment in the *Tz'enah Ur'enah,* the compilation of the commentary in Yiddish that was meant to serve as the guide to women of the Scripture studied in the synagogue. It contains an explanation of how the life of the women of the household could have been conducted for ten years. The explanation is that while they did not convert to Judaism, they practiced "a little" Jewishly; otherwise what could Naomi have meant by "return"? The conversion of Ruth, explains this commentary further, following the midrash, is done by Naomi and is what is not said by Naomi and not in the text during the statement by Ruth of her acceptance of their shared fate.
32. Cynthia Ozick described this moment clearly. Ozick, "Ruth," p. 372.
33. Again, this insight is found in Ozick.
34. There is a parallel text. In Jonah, the sailors on the boat act in much the same way. They are like regular religious people; they pray, they offer sacrifice, they know that God acts in the world, and they are reluctant to hurt anybody, but they will do as they are told.
35. The Book of Ruth is the only biblical text in which the word *love* is used to define a relationship between two women. And once such love is represented, an intriguing rewriting of Genesis takes place. From the very beginning of the Book of Ruth, "clinging" between women determines the movement of the plot. Rejecting the option of returning to Moab to seek a new husband, Ruth chooses to "cling" to her mother-in-law. The verb *dbq* first appears in Genesis in the etiological comment which follows the depiction of a woman's creation out of Adam's body: "Therefore shall a man leave his father and mother,

and shall cleave (*dbq*) unto his wife: and they shall be as one flesh." "To cling" in this case means to recapture a primal unity, to return to a time when men and women were literally "one flesh"; "to leave one's mother and father" is the recurrent phrase that links the two texts. Yet while in Genesis such leaving and cleaving define the institution of marriage, in the Book of Ruth they depict female bonding, a hitherto unrecognized tie. Pardes, *Counter-traditions in the Bible*, p. 102.

36.

> There is first the very uprightness of the face, its upright exposure, without defense. The skin of the face is that which stays the most naked, most destitute. It is the most naked, though with a decent nudity. It is the most destitute also: there is an essential poverty in the face; the proof of this is that one tries to make the poverty by putting on poses, by taking on a contenance. The face is exposed, menaced, as if inviting us to an act of violence. At the same time, the face is what forbids us to kill. The face is signification and signification without context. I mean the Other, in the rectitude of his face, is not a character within a context. . . . Here, to the contrary, the face is meaning all by itself. (Emmanuel Levinas, *Ethics and Infinity*, trans. Richard A. Cohen [Pittsburgh: Duquesne University Press, 1985], p. 86)

37. Ogletree, *Hospitality to the Stranger*, pp. 48, 52.

38. Levinas, *Ethics and Infinity*, p. 50.

39. *Midrash Rabbah*, p. 38. Also noted in *Tz'enah Ur'enah*, p. 834, as follows: "The Sages learn from the story of Ruth how our forefathers used to conduct themselves with one who approached for conversion. The word 'return' is written three times to show that when a person wished to convert he was first told three times to leave. . . . Ruth said: 'If you will not convert me, I will go to another Jew to convert me, but I wish to become a convert through your hands.' When Naomi heard that she truly desired to convert, she first told her some of the commandments to see if she would heed them."

40. A theme that Pardes also recognized.

41. In the spirit of Boyarin, I want to note here that as a mother nursing a child as I write these words, I can scarcely imagine an act more intimate and privileged.

42. Pardes noted another way that the text is itself a comment on the themes of shared fertility in the intertextuality between this story and the story of Rachel and Leah. Pardes's point was that the parallels between the two stories are intentional. The Ruth story, with its themes of barrenness and uprootedness (they are the same word in Hebrew, *aqara*), bitterness, harvest and sexual seduction, of exile and return to the land, acts as both a mirror and a reconciled version of female competition for the matriarchal position in the history of Judaism. As Rachel and Leah, the younger and the older women, come to "share" Jacob, Ruth and Naomi come to "share" Boaz, albeit with a noncompetitive and loving relationality. Pardes, *Countertraditions in the Bible*, p. 105.

43. In Numbers, Balak, the king of Moab recruits Bil'am, his own wizard and prophet, to curse the Israelites and so diminish them. The text assumes the power of the word to create social policy. But Bil'am the Moabite cannot curse: his speech is taken from him, and the animal he rides becomes empowered with speech and, by extension, with rational will. Bil'am is filled only with the word of God: he cannot hurl curses; he must hurl only blessings at the Hebrews.

44. This footnote is inspired by Lebacqz. The text in question, Numbers, Parshah Balak, is read in synagogue each year in connection with a *haftorah* which is a selection from Micah. The Torah text asks the question, as it were, of how to live in a manner that is holy: here the people are blessed, and next the People are whoring. The answer of the rabbis who placed the two texts together can be found in the conclusion of the passage in Micah. It is the same passage that Lebacqz found to be critical to an understanding of health care ethics. See Karen Lebacqz, "Humility in Health Care," *Journal of Medicine and Philosophy* 17 (1992): 291.

45. The Moabite again speaking in the prophet's voice.

46. It is notable that Ruth speaks not a word here, and no one comments specifically on her presence. Despite the eloquence of her gesture of recognition, neither Naomi nor the text acknowledge it.

47.

> Ruth actually wants permission to gather the grain from among the sheaves, a privilege (we learn from v. 15) reserved for members of the clan, which only a landowner can grant. Boaz notices the woman as she stands waiting for his reply. . . . Boaz asks no question from this underprivileged soul but readily offers advice: stay in my field, stick to my girls; even drink a little water if you care to. However, he does not respond to her original request. Ruth is not ready to give up. With a gesture of exaggerated servility—usually only kings and gods receive such prostrations—Ruth gently cloaks her expectations: "Why is it that I pleased you enough to notice me? I am but a foreigner (*nokhriyah*)" (v. 10). Boaz responds with another speech but is now more personal: you are wonderfully loyal and brave; God will surely reward you for seeking his protection. . . . Finally grasping Ruth's intent, Boaz waits until lunchtime to make up his mind. Then, in full view of his workers (an act which may have a legal implication), he seats her among them, personally fills her bowl with grain and mash, and gives her the permission he has not granted previously. (Sasson, "Ruth," p. 322)

48. Further, the female relationships continue to deepen at this moment in the story. Here is the rare example in the biblical story where seduction is not a competitive struggle but a cooperative venture. Here again, it will be the recognition of family that makes generation of the Jewish people possible. The antithetical completion of female bonding and initiative turns out to be unexpectedly essential to the prosperity of the House of Israel. Pardes, *Countertraditions in the Bible,* p. 117.

49. Mieke Bal regards this moment in the text as, in part, being an allusion to Boaz's impotence and Ruth's effort to help. Mieke Bal, *Lethal Love: Feminist Literary Interpretations of Biblical Love Stories* (Bloomington: Indiana University Press, 1987).

50. The word in Hebrew has the connotation of maidservant-who-may be a concubine (Hagar was referred to as *amah*). Ruth is saying that she could be considered his concubine, but she is explicitly asking for more than that. She is asking to be his wife.

51. A word which means a woman that can be taken by a freeman as either a wife or a concubine. See Sasson, "Ruth," p. 323.

52. This is simply a canopy held aloft over the couple, which represents the home they will then make. The *chuppah* is commonly a prayer shawl, thus the connection here to cloak.

53. A period of three months, corresponding to the time that must elapse before a female proselyte is permitted to marry. Judah J. Slotki, "Ruth, Introduction and Commentary," in *The Five Megillith,* ed. A. Cohen (London: The Soncino Press. 1975), p. 6.

54. I cannot find reference to this in any of the midrashim. But surely the rabbis can (and did) count! Perhaps this is the female difference in close textual reading?

55. This point is made by Michael Walzer, *Exodus and Revolution* (New York: Basic Books, 1984), pp. 73–98.

56. Stanley Hauerwas, "Reflections on Suffering, Death, and Medicine," in his *Suffering Presence: Theological Reflections on Medicine, the Medically Handicapped and the Chruch* (Notre Dame, Ind.: University of Notre Dame Press, 1986), p. 31.

57. In the case of the reform in the state of Oregon, the standards were hardheaded yet rich: more generous than what was currently provided, except in cases of procedures that were experimental, or in cases where the risk-benefit burden was very poor, or in cases where the outcome of the illness was self-limiting in any case.

58. The notion of the "specific other" is most clearly grounded in the critical work of Carol Gilligan (Gilligan, *Mapping the Moral Terrain,* edited with Ward and Taylor, Cambridge, Mass.: Harvard University Press, 1988.) The school of communicative ethics is most fully articulated in the work of Seyla Benhabib, *Situating the Self,* New York: Routledge, 1992.

59. In the clinical world one sees this principle in action at all times. Persons speak in the collective voice of tragedies that seem to be individually embodied. Although often their work in invisible to clinicians, families are counted on to mediate and rename the indignities of medicine. It is a powerful clinical truth that, despite the forbidding and sterile world constructed around illness, despite the clinical efforts to make the hospital look as close to a laboratory as possible, families make efforts to personalize and deconstruct the "text of scientific management." Even the tiniest neonate in the most modern intensive care unit, where, arguably the machines far outweigh and outnumber the actual patient, is bedecked with little ribbons, cards, and stuffed animals. Even when the parents of such infants are not present at the bedside, these decorations stand as mute testimony to the power of relationality, of naming, of the signifiers of inclusion in human community.

60. My thanks to Dr. Dina Siden for this point. In her doctoral dissertation, ethicist Siden notes that it is in fact the prophetic voice that makes bioethicists, who stand outside the debate at the bedside, unique.

II

JEWISH MORALITY

Living ethically is not fundamentally a theoretical enterprise. It involves making choices, day by day, throughout one's life, between different courses of action which are judged to be "good" or "bad," "better" or "worse," "right" or "wrong." Sometimes, as when matters of life and death are at stake, these choices can be agonizing for those who must make them. At other times, the proper choice may seem natural, so much so that there scarcely appears to be a real choice at all. But whether they are easy or hard, moral choices are inevitable. Since human life is intrinsically social, we are repeatedly faced with wide ranging and perplexing questions: How should we treat others? How should we balance legitimate self interest with concern for the good of society as a whole? How should we relate to other national and political groups which are in conflict with our own?

But over and above concrete guidance about how to act in specific situations, Jewish morality provides a perspective from which to view ourselves and our relationships with others, an attitude about what is most worthwhile in life and how to be a good person. As many ethicists have recognized, living morally involves attending to the nature and quality of our relationships with others, and to the feelings and attitudes that we must cultivate in order to produce positive human interactions and healthy communities. We misrepresent the moral life when we focus only on dramatic choices and overlook the many attitudes and values that express themselves in everyday life and which shape our sense of ourselves. Given the scope of Jewish moral life—indeed, of all moral life—it is impossible to convey it fully in any simple, logical fashion. And given the scope of this volume, it has been necessary to choose only a few issues that can be explored in some depth and from varying perspectives.

This section of the book thus includes essays of two types. Some address those highly dramatic moral decisions involving life and death which are widely discussed in our time, such as abortion and euthanasia. Others take up moral issues involving familial and social relationships that arise in many different ways throughout our lives. By including both sorts of moral questions we attempt at least to sketch the broad outlines of Jewish morality. It is our hope that the views presented here, especially when contrasted with secular and other religious perspectives on the same issues, will highlight the distinctive aspects of Jewish moral life.

In this context the importance of the theoretical concerns addressed in the previous section of this volume should again be mentioned. As we will see, many disagreements about practical questions arise among Jewish ethicists precisely because they do not share the same ideological or theoretical starting point. How Jewish ethicists understand the relationships between law and ethics, between individuals and communities, between tradition and modernity—all these abstract questions influence (explicitly or implicitly) how they determine what Judaism teaches us about living morally. In addition, the accumulated wisdom of Jewish tradition is vast, including within it multiple points of view and conflicting legal precedents. There is significant latitude, therefore, for equally learned Jewish ethicists to emphasize different strains within their tradition. Finally, Jewish ethicists sometimes differ in their practical judgments because they read the evidence of the tradition differently. As several authors noted above with reference to biomedical issues, the same traditional texts can be cited in support of vastly different stances on a contemporary issue. Throughout this section, we have attempted to juxtapose examples of just such differences.

The opening essays in this section are meant to introduce readers to some of the basic values and virtues imbedded in Jewish morality. Alfred Jospe focuses on a few central theological concepts—chosenness, covenant, messianism—and elucidates their moral implications. Jews are called upon to serve as God's partners who, by living righteously, help to bring about God's kingdom on earth. Sol Roth's analysis of the virtue of humility emphasizes the ways in which the Jew's relationship to others is infused with religious meaning. Humility in relationship to others is the corollary of a properly humble relationship to God.

In the next section, we take up those moral questions—concerning sexuality and family relationships—that are most personal in nature. David Novak finds within *halakhah* a view of the natural order which determines the role of human sexuality in relation to society. Proper sexual behavior is thus determined by the nature of human beings as divinely created and by the purposes of human society as divinely ordained. Arthur Waskow, working outside an *halakhic* framework, sees God's presence within the natural expressions of human affection and sexuality. The limits on proper sexual behavior concern treating others respectfully, while also affirming the spiritual possibilities of fulfilling sexual relationships. Martha Ackelsberg likewise takes as her point of departure a concern for spiritually fulfilling relationships within the family. Jewish responses to non-traditional family structures should be based on the recognition that God can be found whenever and wherever real meeting takes place between people. Blu Greenberg also recognizes the need for traditional roles within the family to change and affirms the ability of *halakhah* to adapt to these changes. In her view, challenging the inequality of traditional Jewish gender roles is thoroughly consistent with the deeper values of the tradition.

The authors in the following section attempt to lay out the theological and legal bases within Judaism for moral positions on several social issues. Robert Gordis discusses how the belief that "the earth is the Lord's" implies a moral responsibility to use natural resources wisely. Seymour Siegel utilizes traditional Jewish teachings about the value of human activity and the nature of innate human inclinations as bases for an economic ethic. The responsibility of people to complete God's creation is the motivation behind economic activity, while the responsibility to provide for the needs of everyone in society sets the moral limits on that activity. Elie Spitz's article indicates the Jewish tradition's tendency to limit the applicability of capital punishment and extends these principles to contemporary issues.

We have devoted a separate section to issues of medical ethics—abortion and euthanasia—because these perplexing questions are so often the subject of heated debate in our society. Fred Rosner and Byron Sherwin offer sharply contrasting readings of Jewish sources pertinent to euthanasia. While both acknowledge the overriding emphasis of Judaism on preserving life and also on alleviating suffering, they weigh these principles differently when faced with the hardest sort of case—a patient suffering from an incurable condition whose death is imminent. Similarly, David Feldman and Sandra Lubarsky offer alternative assessments of Jewish tradition's attitude toward abortion. Feldman summarizes the *halakhic* sources that dictate a generally conservative attitude toward the taking of fetal life except in instances where the mother's health is threatened. Lubarsky approaches the issue by exposing the philosophical and theological assumptions behind the *halakhah*. She then challenges these assumptions and argues that other Jewish views of the relationship between God and humankind could support a more lenient attitude toward abortion.

In the concluding section of essays, we turn to one of the most contemporary and unprecedented of Jewish moral issues. Through the establishment of the state of Israel in 1948 the centuries-old dream of Jewish self-rule was realized. Simultaneously, Jews faced for the first time the political and moral problems of ruling a large non-Jewish minority, and doing so, moreover, in the context of a modern, democratic society. The authors represented here struggle to apply the resources of the Jewish tradition in addressing this enormous moral challenge. Irving Greenberg is acutely aware of the moral risks entailed in the exercise of political power, especially by Jews whose historical experience has been one of political powerlessness. He attempts to chart a middle course between the unacceptable alternatives of Jewish passivity and Jewish dominance. Judith Plaskow approaches the question of Jewish political power as a feminist who sees all hierarchical relationships—whether between Israelis and Palestinians or between Jewish men and women—as closely related and equally unacceptable. For David Hartman the challenge for modern Israeli Jews is to reassess their own vision of Jewish history. Zionism must reappropriate a view of creation that affirms the equal significance of all people without at the same time abandoning the notion that Jewish destiny is uniquely tied to the land of Israel. Finally, Einat Ramon proposes to reconfigure the relationship between the secular authority of the Jewish state and the *halakhah*. Drawing from both classical Jewish sources and the work of the early Zionist thinker A. D. Gordon, she suggests that a marriage of democratic values and traditional Jewish values is both philosophically possible and politically necessary if Israelis and Palestinians are to co-exist in peace.

The essays in this section of the volume confirm, at very least, the vitality of Jewish moral thinking. As new moral challenges arise with developing technology and rapidly changing social conditions, Jewish ethicists continue to find within Judaism a substantial resource for fruitful reflection on the issues. And, as many of these essays testify, they also continue to engage each other, to argue as rabbis have for centuries about the principles that should shape our lives and about the applications of old rules to new situations. Both their persistent efforts and their continuing disagreements attest to a shared conviction that in the late twentieth century, discerning the requirements of Jewish moral living remains a worthwhile, if challenging, enterprise.

A. Traditional Jewish Values and Virtues

16

The Meaning of Jewish Existence

ALFRED JOSPE

Countless attempts have been made to define the meaning of Jewish existence. To John, in the fourth Gospel, the Jews are of the devil, while to the Talmud they are as indispensable to the survival of the world as the winds. To the German historian Heinrich von Treitschke, who lived around the turn of the century, the Jews are the ferment of decomposition, an element of unrest and change in civilization, while for Judah Halevi, Israel is the heart of mankind by its special propensity for religious insight.

To Max Weber, the sociologist, the Jews, because of their lack of power and their persistent insecurity, had to be classified as a pariah group, while even so rational a thinker as Abraham Geiger claimed that Jews have a special genius for religion. And to Arnold Toynbee the Jews are merely a fossilized relic of an ancient Syriac civilization, while to the philosopher Alfred North Whitehead the Jews are very much alive and their survival is largely the result of their being in his view probably the most able people of any in existence.

A bewildering maze of contradictory definitions and claims! Perhaps the best way to arrive at an understanding of the meaning of Jewish distinctiveness is to familiarize ourselves with the historic image Jews had of themselves. What has been their vision of themselves, their view of the meaning of their existence, and their role in history?

The Jewish image of the Jew is embodied, first, in what Arthur Lelyveld has called a *value stance,* a specific attitude toward life and the world.

Man, basically, has only two possibilities of establishing a relationship to the world. He can accept it, or he can reject it. Judaism accepts and affirms life and the world. As Leo Baeck has put it in his *Essence of Judaism,* Judaism demands the moral affirmation of man's relation to the world by will and deed and declares the world to be the field of life's tasks.

Judaism is the expression of the command to work and create; it works for the kingdom of God in which all men may be included. It calls for ascent, development, growth, the long march toward the future. It seeks to reconcile the world with God. Judaism is, therefore, ultimately, the affirmation of an active, creative relationship to the world in which man's life finds meaning and fulfillment.

But there are various ways in which life and the world can be affirmed. In which way does Judaism differ from other affirmations?

The Greeks, for instance, also affirmed life and the world but in a way that was wholly different from the value stance of the Jews. Socrates accepted death even though he was innocent by his own definition of justice. He refused to escape when his friends wanted to make it possible because he accepted and affirmed the higher authority of the state. The state cannot exist when law is set aside. Defiance would result in chaos.

Compare this attitude with that of the Prophet Nathan, who castigates David's defiance of justice in his affair with Bathsheba; of Elijah, who denounces Ahab for his murder of Naboth; of Isaiah, who denounces the religious and political leaders of Jerusalem because of their corruption; of Jeremiah, fearless and flaming in his indictment of the religious hypocrisy and moral depravity of his generation and government. While Socrates was a detached thinker who gave passive assent to the existing social order even though it might have been evil, the Prophets challenged the social order precisely because it was evil.

For the Greek, government embodies laws which cannot be challenged. For the Hebrew, government itself stands under the judgment of the law and can be challenged in God's name. For Socrates, the highest virtue and achievement are that man *think* correctly; for the Prophets, the highest virtue and achievement are that he *act* correctly.

For this reason, the value stance of Judaism is also profoundly different from the worldview of Christianity, which insists that the highest virtue is that man *believe* correctly. Though works are important, the indispensable condition of salvation is faith in Jesus as the Christ; salvation is achieved not by the merit of one's deeds but by the acceptance of the officially formulated correct form of belief. For Judaism, however, it ultimately is man's acts which matter and not his notions or thoughts, which may well be erroneous or mistaken. God's nature and thoughts are beyond our grasp. But his commandments are "neither hidden nor far off."

The Jewish value stance toward life and the world is the context, the frame of the picture, as it were. Within that frame, there emerge the details of the image the Jews had of themselves as Jews.

This image has several dominant features. One is what is usually called the concept of Israel's "election," or the "chosen people." The world is created by God, and man's place in the world is part of a divine plan. At a particular time in this cosmic drama and at a particular place, on Mount Sinai, God revealed himself and his will in a particular document, the Torah. This document reveals not only the will of God, but the instrument through which God has chosen to make his will known to the world. This instrument is the people known as Israel; Israel is therefore God's "chosen people."

The concept of the "chosen people" permeates much of Jewish literature, folklore, prayers, and liturgy. When a Jewish man is called to the Torah, he recites the traditional blessing, *"Asher bahar banu mi'kol ha-amim,"* praising God, who has chosen us from all other nations. When we recite our daily morning prayer, we say the benediction, *"She'lo assani goy,"* thanking God that he has not made us Gentiles. When we pronounce the benediction over the Sabbath wine, we declare that God has chosen and sanctified us from among all other peoples, in the same way in which he has distinguished between Sabbath and weekday. When we make *Havdalah* on Saturday nights, we recite the traditional *Hamavdil,* glorifying God for setting us apart from all other peoples just as he has set apart the sacred from the profane and light from darkness.

Few of Judaism's teachings have been so misunderstood as this concept of the "chosen people." George Bernard Shaw compared it to the *Herrenvolk* concept of the Nazis; H. G. Wells considered it a hindrance to world unity; Protestant theologians persist in speaking of the God of Judaism as a tribal deity, interested only in protecting his own people and not a God who is concerned with the whole of mankind; and avowed anti-Semites cite this idea as proof for their claim that there is a Jewish conspiracy to seek to dominate the Christian world. The concept has even been rejected by Jewish thinkers, especially by Mordecai Kaplan and the Reconstructionist movement as incompatible with the dignity of man and the mandates of democracy.

What then did the Jews mean when they spoke of themselves as "chosen people"? How did they understand the meaning of their election?

The Jewish concept of the "chosen people" does not imply a feeling of racial or political superiority. It does not represent a claim that Jews are superior to the rest of mankind by reason of birth, blood, or racial endowment. Anyone can become a Jew by embracing Judaism. A person who converts to Judaism is called a *"ben Avraham,"* a son of Abraham, which he becomes by the *"b'rit Avraham,"* by entering into Abraham's covenant. Rabbi Meir said that man—Adam—had been created from dust which had been collected from all corners of the earth so that no nation could claim the distinction of being better or having cradled mankind. Some of the greatest rabbis are said to have been descended from converts to Judaism, and, according to Jewish tradition, King David, from whose house the Messiah would come, was a direct descendant of Ruth, the Moabite, a foreigner who married Boaz, a Jew.

The concept of election does not imply the injection of the rest of mankind as inferior. In fact, Judaism clearly acknowledges that men can be blessed with salvation even though they are outside the Sinaitic covenant. Traditional Judaism proclaims that the righteous of all nations have a share in the world-to-come and that man should first lead a good life and then ask God for religious truth. As Morris Joseph put it, "Israel's election does not give him a monopoly of the divine love." For Judaism, all human beings are God's children and have an equal claim upon his care and solicitude. There is no magic passport to the divine favor either here or hereafter. The divine test of a man's worth is not his theology but his life.

In the same way, the protection of the law was extended to every inhabitant of the country, Jew and non-Jew alike. In the words of Leviticus, "Thou shalt have one manner of law for the stranger as well as for the homeborn." The Jew certainly did not need a Supreme Court to decide whether or not minority members had a right to attend the high schools and universities of southern Israel without being segregated. Jews have always been particularly sensitive to these problems for, as the Bible and Jewish observances constantly remind them, they had been strangers in Egypt themselves, and the memory of that experience had burned itself with acid into their consciousness. Because they knew what oppression of minorities meant and what it could do to the soul of the oppressed, they hated oppression and wanted to make sure they would never succumb to its practices.

What the concept of election has meant in Jewish life, in positive terms, is illustrated by a story of the rabbis. The ancient sages once asked: Why did God choose Israel? Because all other nations refused to accept the Torah. Originally, God had offered it to all nations of the world. But the children of Esau rejected it because they could not reconcile themselves to the commandment "Thou shalt not kill." The Moabites declined the offer because they felt they could not accept the commandment "Thou shalt not commit adultery." The Ishmaelites refused because they could not square their habits with the commandment "Thou shalt not steal." All of them rejected the Torah; finally only Israel was left and prepared to accept the Torah.

The story makes a crucial point. Ancient Israel was an insignificant little people in the vast spaces of the Near East. It could have been like all other peoples of the area, content to live, working, procreating, building houses, struggling with nature to wrest a living from it, and gradually fading away from the arena of history.

And yet, in this very people, there suddenly blazed forth the conviction that it is not enough just to exist, to live, but that man must live for something, and that, therefore, this people is different from the peoples in whose midst it had been living; that there is something that gives meaning to life and through which it becomes articulate about the purpose of its existence. For the first time in the history of mankind, national difference becomes transformed into moral and spiritual distinctiveness.

Here we can grasp the meaning of "election." It is in the idea of his "election" that the Jew becomes conscious and articulate about what he conceives his task and role to be. He becomes conscious that he possesses a truth which makes him different from other groups. Hence, election is the "living certainty of a religious community that it possesses a knowledge of the truth which distinguishes it from all other peoples or nations" (Baeck), which is a unique and vital possession and gives its existence a sense of purpose and direction.

That truth which distinguishes the Jew from all other people and gives his life a sense of purpose and direction is embodied in the idea of the "covenant," the second feature in the image which Jews had of themselves. The Hebrew term for covenant is *b'rit,* as in B'nai B'rith. It is an agreement between God and Israel by which Israel accepted the Torah. This acceptance implies two fundamental notions. First, the agreement between God and Israel is bilateral; if God selected Israel, Israel consented to be elected. If God chose Israel, Israel, in turn, chose God. As Israel Zangwill once put it, a chosen people is at bottom a choosing people. Secondly, if the concept of *election* means the consciousness of the fact that one possesses a truth which sets one apart from others, the concept of the *covenant* means the consciousness of what this truth is. It is Torah, the Law of Sinai, the acceptance and affirmation of God's design for man's life. It is the consciousness of what the Torah in its widest sense demands of man—of what we must do to make this truth alive regardless of the hardships or obligations it may entail. The covenant is man's response: "*Hineni*"—"Here I am"—to the voice that calls; it is the acceptance of the obligation inherent in election.

The concept of the covenant has numerous connotations in Jewish tradition and literature. After the flood, God enters into a compact with mankind through Noah, in which God pledges that he will never again engage in destructive violence against the human race, and by which man, in turn, pledges that he will abide by the fundamental moral laws in dealing with his fellow men. The term is used again when God enters into a covenant with Abraham. Abraham is called to train his children and those of his descendants after him to keep the ways of the Lord, that is, to do what is good and right, while God pledges himself to bless Abraham and his descendants.

The prophet Hosea defined the covenant as an act of love between God and Israel, symbolizing their bond of partnership in which man is given a share in the never-ending process of creation and the redemption of mankind through love and faithfulness:

> I shall betroth thee unto Me forever.
> I shall betroth thee unto Me with right and
>   justice, with love and mercy.
> I shall betroth thee unto Me in truth, and
>   thou shalt know the Lord. (Hos. 2:19–20)

The most significant expression of the covenant can, however, be found in Exodus: "Now then, if ye will obey My voice and keep My covenant, then ye shall be a peculiar treasure unto Me above all other people. For all the earth is Mine. And ye shall be unto Me a kingdom of priests, and a holy nation" (19:5–6). Election is not a divine favor extended to a people, but a task imposed upon it. It is not a prerogative but an ethical charge, not a divine title for rights but a divine mandate for duties. And the duties are to live in accordance with the word and spirit of Sinai, to serve God in thought and act, to sanctify life, to diminish evil, to be the prophet and servant and, frequently, the suffering servant of the Lord. The obligation is upon Jews to be heirs and perpetuators of the spirit of the men who entered the arena of history as prophets of the ideal society, as legislators of the priestly and sanctified life, as visionaries of justice and human reconciliation, as challengers of evil and the singers of hope.

More, not less, is expected of Israel by virtue of the covenant. People who are ignorant of God and his will, men who have never been taught or told what truth and justice are, may be forgiven impieties and sin. But Jews cannot be forgiven so easily—Israel has a special commitment to God. When Israel fails, it commits a *hillul hashem,* a desecration of the divine name. Thus Amos warns the people in God's name, "only you have I known of all the families of the earth. Therefore I will visit upon you all your iniquities" (Amos 3:2). To overcome evil and realize the good is man's never-ending task, a normal task for all.

This conception of life as a moral task and never-ending quest for perfection is the third and perhaps most characteristic feature of the Jewish image of the Jew. It finds its highest expression in the concept of the Messiah.

Messianic thinking is rooted in one of man's most profound needs and concerns, his concern with the future. While some nations of antiquity, living through eras of crisis and catastrophe, despaired of the future and turned their vision to the Golden

Age when men lived happily in the past, the Jew did not evade the problem posed by the future. He never placed perfection in the past but instead projected it into the future.

Of course, the Bible starts with perfection too. The first man, Adam, must necessarily have been happy and perfect until his fall. Yet this idea has never played a significant part in Jewish thought. What is important is not man's descent but his ascent, not his origin but his goal, not his past but his future. Jewish thinking looks for happiness, virtue, and perfection not to a past Golden Age but to the future, to "the end of days," a favorite phrase of the Prophets.

This projection of perfection into the future is an integral part of Jewish thinking. It has been called the most striking and characteristic feature of the religion of Israel, originating in the Bible and best summarized in a single word—Messiah.

There are two views of the Messiah in Jewish tradition. The one has come to be called the *man,* the personal Messiah. The other is called the *time* Messiah, or the messianic era. The one is a man, the other an age. The one is a son of the House of David, the other an epoch in the history of Israel and the world. The one is a Jew, the other a time yet to come.

The concept of a personal Messiah has its inception in the historical experiences of the Jewish people and the political conditions in ancient Israel. The events recorded in the pages of our ancient history reveal no rosy picture. There were no glorious conquests, no triumphant victories. The patriarchs had to leave their native countries and wander in foreign lands. Then followed the Egyptian slavery with its memories of oppression. And even after the people had entered the Promised Land, they were constantly attacked by the tribes among whom they lived. They suffered the humiliation of frequent defeats and ultimately the loss of national independence.

It was only natural that a people with a past and such a present should long for a future when there would be an end to their suffering. They hoped for a political redeemer who would unite the people and establish a strong nation able to withstand the foreign enemies. It was not until after the appointment of David that the popular longing for such a redeemer was satisfied. Under David's leadership, the people grew powerful, establishing a kingdom reaching from the borders of Egypt to the gates of Damascus. The glory of this kingdom and of the man who had wrought this miracle caught the imagination of the masses. David became the ideal of the Jewish king, the great national hero and redeemer. He had inaugurated a state of national glory. People hoped it would last forever—a hope that was strengthened by Nathan's prophecy that David's throne would be established forever.

Originally, the Messiah was a national savior, a compensatory ideal conceived in times of national distress, a symbol of the indomitable will of the people to survive and to survive as a people. But at this time, a second ingredient was added to the messianic concept. The Messiah now also began to personify the spiritual values and religious ideals to which the people should be dedicated. Gradually, the Messiah was conceived not only as the king but as the ideal king, the perfect ruler who would establish not only a stable government but a government based on righteousness and justice.

This hope runs through the fabric of all prophetic books and the Psalms. Isaiah crystallized this thought and expectation in immortal language when he spoke of a new king who, endowed with the divine spirit, would arise from the House of David and establish peace and equity in the land, who would usher in the time when tyranny and violence will no longer be practiced on God's holy mountain, and when the land will be full of the knowledge of God as the waters cover the earth.

The messianic idea, at this stage of its development, was still particularistic, not universalistic. When the prophets spoke of the Messiah king, they did not refer to a king who would redeem the world. They meant a king who was to rule over Israel. When they spoke of the need for justice and perfection, they did not envision any utopian world based on justice and perfection. They demanded that the people of Israel practice justice in the land of Israel. The Messiah was still a national concept. He was a redeemer of Israel, not the redeemer of the world.

It is obvious that the development of the messianic concept could not stop at this point. The prophets had proclaimed the one God who created man and the world and who demands righteousness. But if there is only one God, can he be merely the God of one people, of Israel? Is he not also the God of all peoples, of mankind? The prophets had preached that Israel had been appointed by God to practice righteousness, stamp out evil, establish the good society. But should not evil be eradicated and righteousness be practiced wherever men live? The prophets had proclaimed the moral law. But is there one moral code for one people, a different moral code for another people, and still another moral code for a third people? The moral law is universal law. Justice and righteousness are indivisible, valid for all people. God's demands are directed alike toward all men. Driven by its own inner logic, messianism widens from particularism into genuine universalism. It is at this point that the concept of mankind emerges in Jewish thought and, indeed, in Western thought, for the first time. If there is one God who created the world and fashioned man in his image, all men are his children. If there is one God, there must be one mankind. And if there is one mankind, there can be only one truth, one justice, one religion—to which not merely Israel but all men are called—and which cannot find its historic fulfillment until all men are united in it.

Deutero-Isaiah, Micah and other Prophets no longer speak of the personal Messiah of the House of David, the individual who will become the king and establish a reign of righteousness and peace for Zion. They speak of the new life which is to arise upon earth. The concept of the *one man* retreats more and more behind the concept of the *one time*. The personal Messiah gives way to the "days of the Messiah," in which universal peace and brotherhood will be established and all mankind will be united in the service of the one God.

The people of Israel, however, has a special task in helping to fashion the messianic age. It is the people of Israel that has conceived of the one God for the one mankind. And it is the specific task of Israel to be the bearer and guardian of this truth until it will be accepted by all the nations of the earth. As Deutero-Isaiah puts it, "I, the Lord, have called thee in righteousness, and will hold thine hand and will keep thee for a covenant of the people, for a light of the nations, to open the blind eyes, to bring out the prisoners from the prisons, and them that sit in darkness out of the prison house."

Thus the prophets proclaimed the messianic role of Israel in world history. They speak to Israel, but they speak of the world and the nations. Israel is to be the servant of the Lord. As God's servant Israel will suffer. It will be persecuted because injustice, oppression, and evil will continue to exist. But Israel's suffering will not be meaningless or in vain. By its very existence Israel will be the symbol of the protest against oppression, injustice, idolatry, darkness, and evil. Ultimately, Israel will be vindicated, and the world will know that "from the rising of the sun and from the West there is none beside Me"; men will mend their ways, evil will disappear and a new heaven and a new earth will be established—a day "when the Lord shall be king over all the earth, when the Lord shall be one and His name be one for all peoples."

Jewish messianic thinking has a number of fundamental implications. First, the messianic age will not come solely through the grace of God. It requires the labors of man. It does not signify an announcement of something which will ultimately descend to the earth from some other world. It will have to be earned by man.

Second, the messianic age is of this world, not of another world, a world-to-come. It is a historic task and a historic possibility. It is to happen here on earth and not in apocalyptic times, after the end of time. It is the great goal toward which mankind must work and move here on this earth.

Third, messianic thinking implies that man is not merely an object of history. He is also the subject of history. He is not merely driven by a blind fate. He can shape his future.

Hence the central core of the messianic concept is the conviction that history is not blind. History has direction, it has a goal. The future is not what *will* be, but that which *should* be. It is a task entrusted to man, a command to shape his life and make the historic process the instrument of the realization of that which is good.

It is in these thoughts that the messianic ideal reveals its deepest meaning and significance as the central feature of the image which Jews have of themselves and of the meaning of their existence. Man's life on earth is not a blind groping in darkness. It is not a succession of unrelated accidents, devoid of point and purpose, or, as Macbeth put it, "a veritable tale told by an idiot, full of sound and fury, signifying nothing."

Life has meaning. History has direction. There is a goal and purpose to man's endeavors. And this purpose can be lived by the man who learns to listen to the voice that calls him—*election;* who responds by saying *"Hineni"*—"Here I am"— *covenant;* and who, accepting his role in the messianic drama, becomes God's partner in the never-ending task of creation.

17

Toward a Definition of Humility

SOL ROTH

Judaism requires humility on both religious and human grounds. It is a necessary ingredient in the religious perspective and is indispensable in social relations. The importance assigned to this character trait is considerable. In the Torah—the written and the oral—humility is associated prominently with Judaism's most outstanding representatives. No one was ever as humble as Moses. One shall strive to be as humble as Hillel.[1] Rabbi Judah the Prince, redactor of the Mishnah, was so proficient in this virtue that, by comparison, none of his survivors were to be regarded as humble. As the Talmud put it, "When Rebbe died, humility disappeared."[2]

The idea of humility is rich in content and inextricably bound to other principles and precepts included in the complex system of Jewish ethics. In this essay, its wealth of meaning will be explored and its centrality in that system will be exhibited. This essay is offered as a proposal for the characterization of the Jewish conception of humility.

I

A careful analysis reveals two independent conceptions of humility expounded in talmudic literature: (1) The religious conception—the humble person is one who believes that his achievements and acquisitions are the result of divine benevolence rather than personal power or merit. (2) The moral conception—the humble person is one who believes that his personal achievements and acquisitions, whatever they may be, provide no grounds for the judgment that he is superior to his fellow men.[3]

The first conception is formulated in the *Semag* (*Sefer Mitzvot Gadol*, by Rabbi Moses ben Jacob of Coucy, thirteenth century). He explains the verse "Take heed lest you forget the Lord your God"[4] as a warning that "the children of Israel shall not feel pride when the Holy One, blessed be He, brings them blessing and they shall not say that they accumulated these blessings through their own effort and thus fail to acknowledge the good which they received from the Holy One, blessed be He, because of their pride."[5] Rabbeinu Yonah, on the other hand, on the verse which commands the king that "his heart be not lifted up above his brethren"[6] declares, "We are warned in this command to remove from our souls the quality of

259

pride and that the big man shall not behave with arrogance towards the small man but that he shall always be of humble spirit."[7] This statement is an expression of the moral conception. Both conceptions are formulated as prohibitions against pride but humility admits of degrees and, at its lowest, it is simply the negation of pride.

The claim that these formulations represent two conceptions rather than one is based, first, on the fact that they are factually and logically independent. One may, in behavior, exhibit the religious attitude without the moral and vice versa. One may recognize his attainments and possessions as the products of divine grace and display humility in relation to God and yet treat men with contempt if, in his judgment, their successes fall short of his. On the other hand, it is possible that a person does not believe his attainments to be in any way superior and yet, meager though they are, to identify himself as their sole and exclusive cause—in which case he is religiously arrogant and morally humble. Both types are numerous and abundantly available to human experience.

But, secondly, it should be noted that humility is a relational conception, that is to say, it does not denote a *quality* that may be affirmed or denied of an individual but a *relation* into which an individual enters merely as a term. For, it is evident that, from the philosophical point of view, the declaration of the humble, namely "I am unimportant," does not assert that he possesses a certain quality as is the case, for example, with the statement "I am white." Rather does it assert a relation in the same way as the declaration "I am tall." Tallness is not an intrinsic property of an individual. It designates a relation that obtains between the individual and some standard or some other individual. Analogously, unimportance denotes a relation to some standard or to some entity. The humble person may therefore assert unimportance either in relation to God or in comparison with man. But in the two cases the meaning of unimportance differs. In one it means dependence on God; in the other it signifies that success is no basis for the judgment of superiority. These two conceptions are independent. It should also be noted, in passing, that this relational aspect of humility makes it logically possible for a person to experience simultaneously the polar sentiments of importance and unimportance. But more of this later.

By way of further clarification, it should be added that the claim that there are two conceptions of humility should not be construed as the suggestion that there are differences of opinion among the interpreters of Torah as to which of these two is an imperative of *halakhah*. The dispute among the sages focuses exclusively on the question as to which of the two should be assigned primacy. Some include the prohibition on one form of arrogance among the 613 commandments and some include the other in that list;[8] none removes from his conception of the *humble personality* the element stressed by the other. Thus, Ramban [Rabbi Moses ben Nahman (1194–1270)—"Nahmanides"], whose emphasis coincides with that of Rabbeinu Yonah and who maintains that the biblical root of the prohibition on arrogance deals with human relations, writes, "I will therefore explain how you shall conduct yourself as a humble man. . . . Every man shall be greater than you in your eyes. . . . In all your speaking, acting and thinking regard yourself as though you were in the presence of God."[9] A full characterization of the humble personality must therefore, according to Ramban, take into account man's relation to God as well.

Further, arrogance and humility, at their lowest level, are correlative notions. A person is arrogant if he regards himself as the cause of his achievements or if he believes them to be the ground of his superiority. One who avoids these attitudes is humble.

The arrogant person is intellectually in error. One who exemplifies the religious conception of arrogance may declare either "My power and the might of my hand hath gotten me this wealth"[10] or "For my righteousness the Lord hath brought me to possess this land,"[11] that is, he asserts that his achievements are due to his own power or personal merit. In the first case he errs in that he fails to recognize the Almighty as at least a part cause of his success—one may plant the seeds but he cannot produce the rain—and even as the ultimate source of all the powers he is able to activate. In the second case, he errs in that he overemphasizes the good of which he is the source and underestimates the evil of which he is also the origin.

The morally arrogant person contends that he is better than others. This claim presupposes a standard by which he may be compared with others. It may be a standard of physical strength, material accumulation, intellectual achievement, social status, and so forth. But whatever may be the standard that impresses him as most important, the arrogant individual believes that he ranks higher on the scale than those by whom he is surrounded and that consequently he is the better man. His error, in this case, may be rooted in any of three misconceptions. He may be mistaken in his value system. If, for example, he regards material accumulation to be of highest value, he errs in the standard he selects. He may also stray from the truth in his judgment. If piety and morality should be his choice of the ultimate standard, his estimate of his own attainments in relation to those of others may not be accurate. Finally, if human life is of unlimited value, one may, if his standard is good and his judgment right, maintain "My deeds are better than his" but he is not generally justified in declaring "I am better than he." He simply has no way of estimating the value of his life in comparison with the life of another in order to make the invidious comparison.

Two important conclusions which contribute to the understanding of the idea of humility follow from this discussion. First, humility is a function of two things: attainments and attitudes. If one who has lived a life filled with failures refrains from attributing whatever meager success he has accumulated to his own competence or avoids the sentiment that he is superior to others, his attitude, while praiseworthy, cannot be identified as one of great humility—no matter how small the value he assigns to himself. To be outstanding in humility, one must first be outstanding in achievements. "Now the man Moses was very meek, above all men that were upon the face of the earth."[12] To match the humility of Moses, one must first reach his greatness.

Second, the sense of humility is not the same as the psychological sense of inferiority. If a person suffers from the latter sentiment, he feels incapable and incompetent. His very feeling may interfere with his performance. The humble person believes himself to be—not incompetent—but unimportant. He recognizes the successes he has achieved; he is even aware of their value; he simply avoids attaching great importance to himself because of these successes. When Moses declared, "Who am I that I should go unto Pharaoh and that I should bring forth the children of Israel out of Egypt,"[13] he was expressing humility; when he insisted, "For I am slow of speech and of a slow tongue"[14] he was declaring incompetence. The humble person, notwithstanding his humility, is capable of great achievement.

II

The *beliefs* described above however, do not exhaust the meaning of humility. Humility is exhibited in *feeling* as well. It is clear that the sentiment that should be experienced by the personality who exemplifies the religious conception of humility is gratitude. If I must credit God with my success, if I am obligated to acknowledge him as the ultimate source of all the powers I am able to activate, then I should be grateful for all the blesssings that he has seen fit to bestow upon me. On the other hand, the individual who exemplifies the moral conception of humility should experience what we may call the sentiment of equality. If no matter what his attainments may be, he is not to judge himself superior—and, according to the definition offered in the preceding section, there is no requirement to assign to himself a value that will reduce them to a level that is inferior—he should experience himself to be the equal of others.

These two attitudes, namely, gratitude to God and equality in relation to man are in fact mandatory. Rambam [Rabbi Moses ben Maimon (1135–1204)— "Maimonides"] declares that, as part of prayer, we are obligated "to give praise and thanksgiving to the Almighty for the good that he bestowed upon us."[15] The demand that we cultivate a sense of equality was put in the Talmud in the form of a suggestion. "A favorite saying of the Rabbis of Yavneh was: I am God's creature and my fellow is God's creature. My work is in town and his work is in the country. I rise early for my work and he rises early for his work. Just as he does not presume to do my work so I do not presume to do his work. Will you say that I do much and he does little? We have learned: One may do much or one may do little, it is all one provided he directs his heart to heaven."[16]

But, an examination of biblical and rabbinic declarations reveals that more is required than the sentiments that are the concomitants of the beliefs here described. Thus the *Semag,* in elaborating upon the religious conception of humility, applauds the attitude exhibited by King David, who declared, "But I am a worm and no man"[17] and adds "I am obligated to view myself as a worm who hides beneath the dust in shame."[18] We may also recall the patriarch's expression when he was appealing to God in behalf of the people of Sodom, "But I am dust and ashes."[19] It is characteristic of the religious personality when contemplating or addressing Deity to regard himself as of an infinitesimal quantity, as a speck of dust in a vast ocean of unlimited space, as a thoroughly insignificant entity. A philosopher expressed this well. "Returning to himself, let man consider what he is in comparison with all existence; let him regard himself as lost in a remote corner of nature; and from the little cell in which he finds himself lodged, I mean the universe, let him estimate at their true value the earth, kingdoms, cities, and himself. What is man in the Infinite?"[20] Now this attitude seems to be the counterpart of another belief altogether, not that God is the source of all my blessings but that in relation to God I am an infinitesimal and wholly meaningless entity.

Under the heading of the moral conception of humility, it appears that more is required than the feeling of equality. Ramban, for example, demands of the humble personality that he direct attention to his own failings and that he stress the achievements of others. "Every man should be great in your eyes. If he is wise or wealthy, it is your duty to honor him. If he is poor and you are richer or wiser than he, consider that you are more guilty than he and he more innocent than you."[21] The posture seems to involve, not so much an objective belief as the deliberate adoption of an attitude. The humble personality does not prepare a balance sheet of assets and liabilities which are evaluated and weighted in order to arrive at a total which may be compared with that of somebody else. He deliberately underscores his own weaknesses while emphasizing the strengths of others. He adopts an attitude which is both subjective and selfless.

We must conclude that each of the two conceptions—the religious and the moral—may be exemplified in the humble personality in various degrees. Humility is a quantitative conception. In the preceding section attention was directed to the lowest levels at which the concept of humility may be exemplified. We are now concerned with the ultimate in humble behavior. Under the heading of the religious conception, the individual who has attained to the first level believes that God is, at least, a partial cause of his achievements, while the one who has reached the highest level declares that he is totally insignificant in comparison with God. In the category of the moral, the humble personality, on the lower level, believes that his successes do not justify the judgment of superiority, while on the higher level, he is determined to demonstrate that he is inferior. Each of these beliefs is accompanied by the appropriate feelings—the feelings of gratitude and insignificance in relation to God, and the sentiments of equality and inferiority in relation to man.

It seems appropriate, in each of the two conceptions, to distinguish between the *anav* and the *shefal ruach*. The *anav* is grateful and accepts the idea of equality. The *shefal ruach* goes beyond the *anav* by insisting on his own insignificance and on his weaknesses in relation to others. Rambam directed attention to these extremes in humble behavior in the following passage: "It is not good that a man shall be humble (*anav*) alone but that he shall be meek (*shefal ruach*) and that his spirit shall be very low."[22]

III

The concept of humility requires further clarification. It has been said that the humble person entertains certain beliefs and experiences certain feelings. But these, in the genuinely humble personality, must be translated into actions. How then shall we define humility behaviorally? To what kind of actions do these beliefs and feelings give rise?

It is not possible within the limited scope of this essay to give an exhaustive account of all the behavioral patterns that should be associated with the posture of humility. A few illustrations, however, will suffice for the purpose of elucidation.

One who is humble (*anav*) in the religious sense would, among other things, be satisfied with his portion in the world (*sameach bechalko*). If to God belongs the credit of human achievement, man may not claim or demand anything he does not possess as a matter of right. Humility then sets the boundary to human ambition in the material domain. Thus Baachya declares that one who is humble "should be contented with whatever means of livelihood present themselves and with whatever he finds."[23] The *shefal ruach*, however, in addition to behavior of the type just described must also be prepared to act in a manner that would express his sense of personal insignificance when relating to the Almighty. Thus Baachya [ibn Paquda (second half of the eleventh century)] cites, in order to illustrate, the act of Aaron the High Priest who performed the menial task of collecting the ashes of the burnt offering which the fire had consumed, and the leaping and dancing of King David, behavior unbecoming to a man of his stature, when he was expressing gratitude to God.[24]

One who is *anav* in a moral sense, that is, he does not believe that his achievements justify the judgment that he is superior, does not wish to exercise authority over others. Thus, Shmaya urged us to "hate lordship."[25] But the *shfal ruach* who emphasizes his own weakness and the strengths of others is one who is patient with human failings. He accepts their foibles and their insults. The Talmud recommends that we shall be as humble as Hillel. The essence of the entire tale which follows the precept and which is intended to illustrate the humility of Hillel is that he refused to respond with anger to deliberate provocation.[26] He was patient. The Talmud also praises those "who are put to shame and do not put others to shame, hear themselves reviled and do not retort; do everything out of love and rejoice in their own suffering."[27] The patience of the humble leads to forgiveness.

In sum, the humble person entertains certain beliefs, experiences certain feelings, and performs certain actions. In the characterization of humility in this essay, all three—beliefs, feelings, and actions—have been taken into account.

IV

The feeling of self-importance which is, under certain conditions, a manifestation of pride is not entirely proscribed. According to one view in a talmudic debate, a minimal quantity of pride is required for a specified group of people. In a passage of the Mishnah, a variety of the sense of self-importance is declared to be mandatory for all.

In a well-known passage of the Talmud we are told.

> R. Hiyya b. Ashi said in the name of Rab: A disciple of the sages should possess an eighth (of pride). R. Huna the son of R. Joshua said: (This small amount of pride) crowns him like the awn of the grain. Raba said: (a disciple of the sages) who possesses (haughtiness of spirit) deserves excommunication, and if he does not possess it he deserves excommunication. R. Nahman b. Isaac said: He should not possess it or part of it."[28]

Setting aside the question as to how this debate fares in the *halakhah,* the following observations are relevant. First, it is the *talmid chacham* who is permitted to display the minimum amount of pride even according to those sages cited in the passage who condone it. Second, *Rashi* [Rabbi Shelomo bar Yitzhak, 1040–1105] views the grounds of justification for such pride as entirely practical. He declares in his commentary that the *talmid chacham* must have a little arrogance in order that the simpleminded will accept his authority. It would be appropriate to suggest that, under the circumstances, it is only the *act* of pride that should be deemed necessary, not the corresponding feeling or belief.

This last point is stressed by the Meiri [Rabbi Menachem ben Solomon Meiri (1249–1316)], who discussed at great length the suggestion that certain individuals must exhibit pride on practical grounds. In addition to the class of *talmidei chachamim* he recognizes the importance of pride for that smaller group of people who carry on their shoulders the burden of political authority. They too must arouse, even to a greater degree than the *talmid chacham,* reverence and respect. In support of this contention he cites the advice given by Rabbi Judah the Prince (himself outstanding in humility) to his son who was to be his successor, "conduct your patriarchate with pride"[29] and the Meiri explains that this quality was not to become part of his nature; he was merely urged to act in a manner required by his position.[30]

Another form of proud behavior was urged by the Meiri, and also for practical reasons, for the average person. It is the type of pride that prompts an individual to dissociate himself from those in society whose behavior is deficient by moral and religious standards. To verify the legitimacy of this category of practical pride, he cites the talmudic passage, "The fair minded of the people in Jerusalem used to act thus: They would not sign a deed without knowing who would sign with them; they would not sit in judgment unless they knew who was to sit with them: and they would not sit at a table without knowing their fellow diners."[31]

By way of further clarification of the permissible forms of pride, the following observations are in order. First, these forms describe exceptions to the requirements of the moral variety of humility, not the religious variety. They describe circumstances in which one may act with pride in relation to his fellow man, not in relation to God.

Second, the sanction for these exceptions to humble behavior derives from the necessity to enforce moral and religious values upon society and to preserve such values in one's personal behavior. The *talmid chacham* and the *Nasi* are obligated to inspire and enforce obedience to laws that express the values of Torah. The individual must refrain from exposing himself to environmental conditions, for example, the company of scoundrels, that would weaken his inclination to moral and religious behavior. Proud actions that are approved are therefore motivated by *commitment* rather than by the *sense of self-importance.*

It follows that if proud behavior is irrelevant to the enforcement or preservation of value it cannot be countenanced. This will perhaps explain Maimonides' endorsement of an extreme instance of humility in which a man of deep piety traveling on a ship responded with joy in a situation in which he experienced great humiliation.[32]

The Mishnah, however, in another well-known passage, declares that the feeling of self-importance is a necessity for all. "Therefore, every single person is obliged to say: The world was created for my sake."[33] And Rashi explains this declaration to mean "I am as important as the entire world. I will not therefore banish myself from the world even with a single transgression."

It should be noted, in the first place, that this feeling of self-importance is required universally, for all. Further, it is not a minimal quantity of self-importance that is urged but a maximum amount. According to Rashi, each man shall regard himself as equal in value to the entire natural world. Finally it is not merely the *act* which expresses self-importance that is demanded but the correlative feeling and belief as well.

It is also noteworthy that the words which mean pride or arrogance do not occur at all in the Mishnah's formulation of the precept. The Mishnah, then, does not appear to regard this judgment as at all relevant to the question of pride. On the contrary, the very same circumstance which is cited by the Mishnah in justification of the demand that everyone experience a sense of self-importance is also described as the basis for a sentiment which belongs among the experiences of humility. The circumstance is that man was created alone. This is taken by the Mishnah to imply many things—among them that "one might not say to his fellow, 'my father was greater than thine' " (i.e., he shall be humble about his ancestry) and that each person shall believe himself to be of highest value (an experience which apparently belongs to the category of pride).

This merely apparent inconsistency may be easily resolved. Its resolution turns on the fact that humility is a relational conception. The humble individual experiences himself as unimportant in relation to God (the religious conception) and to man (the moral conception). But there is no objection to a feeling of self-importance, even to a maximum degree, by any standard and in relation to any object, which is consistent with the experience of unimportance in relation to God and man. In one relation it is even required.

Consider a standard according to which the animate is assigned greater value than the inanimate, the rational is considered superior to the merely animate, and so forth. This criterion would clearly assign to man, a being created in the image of God, a very high rank on the scale of value. An individual cannot, in virtue of the possession of this quality, regard himself as important in relation to God who is its ultimate source, or to his fellow man who is endowed with the identical quality. On the contrary, it is possible—it is even required—that he deem himself unworthy in these relations because man is nothing in the infinite and because he should always seek excellence in others while diverting attention to his own weaknesses. Nevertheless, by the standard here described, he is obligated to experience a profound sense of self-importance in virtue of his location in the scheme of creation. Thus King David who, in addressing God, compared himself to a worm groveling in the dust, in comparison to the rest of creation, judged himself (and others) to be but a little less than angels.[34]

This sense of self-importance is required. Rashi, in his comment in the Mishnah cited above, stated that a man's sense of self-esteem will help him to avoid sin. We may generalize this view. Man's behavior will depend, to a large extent, on the image he projects of himself. It makes a great deal of difference in terms of human action—if we may use some ancient disinctions—whether man regards himself as a rational animal or as a two-legged animal without feathers. There is a vast difference in the individual and social behavior patterns of those who believe themselves to be the bearers of the *Tzelem E-lokim* (the image of God) and those who regard themselves as structured bits of matter, complex though they may be, or as brothers to the apes.

The human being logically and psychologically can and morally must view himself as of unlimited value in one relation though he believes himself unworthy and insignificant in relation to the divine source of all being.

V

In rabbinic literature, humility is not counted as merely one of a number of virtues—each with equal status. Rather is it judged to be a central virtue[35]—and for several reasons. First, its centrality is due to its moral status. Again, we turn to a discussion on arrogance to shed light on its correlative, humility. The Talmud declares[36] that, on one view, arrogance is the moral equivalent of adultery and incest. According to another opinion, it is equivalent to idolatry or atheism. As the Talmud puts it, the arrogant person is to be viewed "as though" (*K'ilu*) he enjoyed illicit relations with those who are forbidden to him; "as though" he served the gods of the heathens, "as though" he denied the existence of God. On these conceptions, a true estimate of the character of arrogance compels the conclusion that it belongs in the same category as adultery, incest, idolatry, and atheism. If we take into account the moral standard formulated in the literature of the Talmud, we arrive at the result that arrogance is among the most serious violations of the precepts of Torah. It belongs in the category of those precepts which we are not permitted to violate even when threatened with death.

If humility is as much a virtue as arrogance is vice, we may infer that, by the same moral standard, humility ranks among those virtues that are highest on the scale. This is what Ramban intended when he wrote that "humility" is the best of all the virtues."[37] Baachya echoed the same sentiments when he wrote, "It follows that all virtues are secondary to humility which is head and front of them all."[38]

But, secondly, humility is judged to be central in the Jewish system of ethics because of its practical consequences. Ramban regards the virtue of humility as sufficient for the exemplification of the attitude of reverence which in turn leads to fear of God and avoidance of sin. "Through humility there will emerge in your heart the virtue of reverence for you will consider always from whence you came and where you are going . . . and when you will think of all this, you will fear your Maker and you will avoid sin."[39]

The Talmud, furthermore, cites the view that arrogance *leads* to adultery. "Anyone who is arrogant will ultimately stumble with another man's wife."[40] The attitude of arrogance is thus declared to be psychologically adequate to the commission of a serious crime. Another major consequence of arrogance is cited in the Torah. "Your heart will be lifted up and you will forget the Lord your God,"[41] a circumstance which, in turn, may lead to a denial of his existence. All qualities of character involve behavioral consequences but arrogance leads to results which, by the Jewish standard of morality, are the most serious of all, namely, atheism and adultery.

These two grounds of the centrality of humility are, however, not independent of each other. A distinction that is relevant to this discussion will serve to clarify their relationship. We must separate virtues (or traits of character) from the actions that illustrate the virtues. A person may be said to possess a certain moral quality if the habit to act in accordance with the related moral rule has become part of his psychological anatomy. Such a person is expected to exhibit the quality in question, in *most* instances, when the occasion arises. A just man acts justly out of habit, out of an acquired inclination. An action, on the other hand, need not be motivated by a corresponding moral habit, that is, by a quality of character. It may reflect a passing impulse. An unjust individual does, on occasion, act justly.

Now a moral theory may include the formulation of a standard by which both actions and habits may be evaluated. Or, the moral theory may concern itself exclusively with action. While the primary interest of *halakhah* is the specification of rules for action, habits which give rise to behavior in conformity with these rules are endorsed and those that result in violations of the precepts are rejected. In the case of arrogance, that rejection may take the form of assigning to the habit the identical moral status that belongs to the actions to which it gives rise. This is the view of those who declare that the person with whom arrogance is a habit is to be viewed "as though" he had committed the cardinal crimes of adultery, idolatry, and so forth.[42] Or, the rejection may take the form of pointing out the consequences of this trait and encouraging its avoidance. Thus, according to another interpretation, arrogance *leads* to adultery. Analogously, humility may be assigned the moral status identical to that possessed by the actions to which it gives rise; or it may be encouraged on the grounds that it leads to these actions.

In one sense, therefore, humility is central because it results in actions to which Judaism has assigned the highest moral status, and, on one view, because it also belongs to the same moral category. Baachya, however, suggested another ground for its centrality.

Baachya identifies humility as a necessary condition for the possession of any of the other values, that is to say, a person cannot exemplify in his behavior any other virtue if he does not possess humility. "It also follows that no virtue can exist in anyone whose heart is devoid of humility before God."[43] According to Baachya, therefore, though, for example, not every humble person is penitent, no one can be penitent if he is not humble.

Baachya's claim, however, is not clear. Two questions are relevant. First, did Baachya insist on "humility before God" as a necessary condition for the exercise of all virtues, including those that are characteristic of human relations, or did he have in mind only those that belong under the heading of piety? The virtue that he used to illustrate his point is penitence, which surely belongs to the category of piety. But of even greater significance is the second question—which incidentally is not unrelated to the first. When Baachya demands humility as a necessary ingredient of all virtues, is he making a factual claim or proposing a definition? Is he declaring that, on the Jewish view, humility enters into the definition of each virtue?—in which case, no quality of character that is not accompanied by humility could be a virtue by definition. Or, are the various virtues sufficiently defined without the inclusion of the element of humility?—in which case the statement that humility is a necessary condition of all virtues, that is, that wherever one *finds* virtue, there one *finds* humility, is a factual generalization in regard to human nature.

It would appear, from factual considerations, that Baachya's claim can be defended only if it formulates a generalization about the definition of the virtues in the context of Jewish ethical theory. Consider the illustration that Baachya employed, namely, repentance. Suppose repentance meant no more than regret for past transgressions accompanied by a resolution to avoid similar violations in the future. Experience provides illustrations of those who are not endowed with the virtue of humility before God (atheists, for example), but who recognize and acknowledge the sanction of certain moral rules, are guilt stricken when they violate them, experience a sense of regret on those occasions, and affirm the appropriate resolutions. If Baachya's claim is correct, however, this sequence would not be a genuine example of repentance. This conclusion could be maintained only if Judaism were held to define the virtues in such a way that nothing can be a virtue if it does not include the sense of "humility before God."[44]

On this interpretation, it is probable that Baachya regards "humility before God" as an ingredient, not merely of the virtues in the category of piety, but of all virtues. For Baachya is not engaged in the task of psychological analysis of moral conceptions but in their religious definitions. Accordingly, by way of illustration, one may on the basis of purely social considerations extend the hand of generosity to the poor. But it would not be *tzedakah* unless the act was also motivated or, at least, accompanied by "humility before God."

VI

This essay is not offered as a detailed account of the entire domain of human behavior to which the qualities of pride and humility are relevant, but as a brief survey of its landmarks and major approaches. It is a preface to humility.

Notes

1. Num. 12:3; *Shabbat*, 30b.
2. *Sotah*, 49a.
3. In *Sefer Hamaspik* (Jerusalem: Alpha, 1965), p. 53, Avraham ben Ha Rambam distinguishes between what I have designated the religious and moral conceptions of humility.
4. Deut. 8:11.
5. *Sefer Mitzvot Gadol*, negative commandment 64.
6. Deut. 17:20.
7. *Sharei Teshuva*, gate 3, letter 34.
8. Some, Rambam, for example, exclude both conceptions from the list of 613 commandments.
9. *Kitvei Ramban* (Jerusalem: Mosad Harav Kook, 1963), bk. 1, p. 374. While the concept of humility formulated here belongs under a heading that will be characterized in the next section of this essay, it is clear that Ramban regards the humble personality as exemplifying both the religious and the moral conceptions.
10. Deut. 8:17.
11. Ibid., 19:4.
12. Num. 12:3.
13. Exod. 3:11.
14. Ibid., 4:10.
15. *Yad*, Hilkhot Tefillah I, 2.
16. *Berakhot*, 17a.
17. Ps. 22:7.
18. Op. cit., negative commandment 64.
19. Gen. 18:27.
20. Pascal, *Pensees*, par. 72.
21. Ramban, op. cit.
22. *Yad.*, Hilkhot Deot. II. 3.
23. *Chovet Halevovot*, Sixth Treatise, ch. VI.
24. Ibid.
25. *Avot* I, II.
26. *Shabbat*, 31a.
27. *Pesachim*, 88b.
28. *Sotah*, 5a.
29. *Ketubot*, 103b.
30. *Chibur Hateshuvah* (Talpiot: Yeshiva University, 1963), p. 121ff.
31. *Sanhedrin*, 23a.
32. Maimonides' Comments on *Ethics of the Fathers*, chap. IV, par. 4.

33. *Sanhedrin*, 37a.

34. Ps. 8:6.

35. There is a talmudic debate (*Avodah Zorah* 20b) as to whether *chasidut* or *anavah* is the greatest of all virtues. Even if one chooses in favor of *chasidut*, humility may still be regarded as central.

Note too that the distinction drawn in the body of this essay between two conceptions of humility will not be applied in this section. In the sources that will be quoted that distinction is not explicitly made (with the exception of the passage taken from the *Chovot Holevovot*). Further, the talmudic passages to which reference will be made speak—not of the concepts of arrogance and humility—but of the arrogant and humble *personalities*. It may be assumed that the typical arrogant or humble personality exemplifies both conceptions.

36. *Sotah* 4b ff.

37. Ramban, op. cit.

38. Baachya, op. cit., chap. 8.

39. Ramban, op. cit.

40. *Sotah* 4b.

41. Deut. 8:14.

42. The talmudic passage in question speaks of *mi she-yesh lo gassie haruach*. Two interpretations of this phrase, as it is employed here, are, in fact, possible.

1. It refers to a person who is *actually* experiencing the feeling of arrogance.
2. It refers to a person who has cultivated the *habit* of arrogance, though he may not at the moment be experiencing the relevant sentiments. The severity of the pronouncements, however, lends support to the interpretation that it is the habit rather than an individual act that is the subject of the judgment.

43. Baachya, op. cit.

44. This conclusion seems to be suggested by the passage in Baachya as well. After making the point that "no moral quality can possibly exist in any one whose heart is devoid of humility before God," he writes, "Thus also the beginning of repentance is loneliness, submissiveness and humility, as Scripture saith 'If my people which are called by my name, shall humble themselves and pray and seek my face' (2 Chron. 7:14). Further it is said, 'They have humbled themselves: I will not destroy them' (ibid., 12:7)."

In this passage, as Baachya apparently interpreted it, Divine forgiveness which is a response to repentance is described as following on humility. Humility is then at the core of the act of repentance; it is not something that stands at the periphery of penitence and with which it is merely invariably connected.

B. Jewish Perspectives on Sex and Family

18

Some Aspects of Sex, Society, and God in Judaism

DAVID NOVAK

The Thesis about the Relation of Sex, Society, and God

In this chapter I propose a thesis about the relation of sex, society, and God in Judaism, and then I pose two questions that arise directly out of this thesis. In exploring how the questions are dealt with in Jewish tradition, I hope that helpful insights will emerge, for the questions call for rational reflection on the part of all moral and religious persons. The thesis I propose: Judaism teaches that the human person is essentially (1) a sexual being; (2) a social being; and (3) the image of God. From this thesis I now ask two questions: (1) What is the relation between human sexuality and human sociality? and (2) How are human sexuality and human sociality related to God?

Human Sexuality

The first part of the thesis stated that the human person is an essentially sexual being. This is brought out in the following Mishnah:

> One who was half-slave and half-free is to serve his master one day and himself the other—in the opinion of the School of Hillel. The School of Shammai said to them . . . he may not marry a slave woman because he is already half-free; and he may not marry a free woman because he is still half-slave. Shall he do nothing [yibbatel]?! Was not the world created [nivra h'olam] for procreation? For Scripture states, "He did not create it as a void, but formed it for dwelling" [Isa. 45:18]. . . .

271

> And the School of Hillel reversed themselves to rule according to the opinion of the School of Shammai.[1]

The case here seems to involve a slave owned by two partners after only one of them emancipated him.[2] The solution to the sexual dilemma of the slave in the above-quoted text is that he be fully emancipated and that he sign a note for his emancipation price. By being emancipated, he then became a full member of the community.[3]

Concerning this text, my late revered teacher Professor Boaz Cohen wrote:

> The phrase *nibra' ha'olam* [the world was created] is the nearest the rabbis came to the term *Natura,* which literally means to be born. Since the Beth Shammai invoke natural law as their reason, they cite Isa. 45:18, and not Gen. 1:28 which lays down the religious law from which the slave was exempt.[4]

Sex is considered a natural right precisely because its legitimacy is based on a recognition of the normative order of creation rather than on a specific precept. This also comes out in a later talmudic treatment of the dispute between the School of Hillel and the School of Shammai concerning how one fulfills the commandment "Be fruitful and multiply" (Gen. 1:28; 9:1). The Shammaites require that one have at least two sons; the Hillelites require that one have a son and a daughter, as Scripture states, "Male and female He created them" (Gen. 5:2). The Talmud states that the reasoning of the Hillelites is based on "the creation of the world" (*me-briyyato shel olam*).[5] This is important because the seeming admonition "Be fruitful and multiply" is taken as a recognition of the normative order of creation rather than as a specific prescription. The scriptural text, then, confirms the norm rather than establishing it *de nova.*

It should be emphasized, too, that this text does not deal with specifically Jewish sexuality but, rather, with human sexuality. The theory behind it is a reflection on the essential character of human life. The question here is that a legal difficulty has prevented a human being from exercising his or her sexuality. Sexuality is rooted in the natural order created by God. Although the Law itself is also a creation of God, legal difficulties come from the social order created by humans.[6] Here the *halakhah* is indicating that the social order may not obliterate the created natural order, that society is to fulfill created human needs, not deny them. This is why celibacy is so roundly condemned.[7] Along the same lines, the rabbis went to unusual lengths to alleviate the plight of the *agunah,* a woman who, because it is uncertain whether her husband is dead, is unable to live with any other man as his wife.[8] Moreover, in the Aggadah, the denial of sexuality is considered destructive of human life.[9] Human sexuality is not to be suppressed but channeled.[10]

Human Sociality

The indispensability of sociality in human life is seen, for example, in the legal plight of the *mamzer.* According to scriptural law, as traditionally expanded, a person born of an adulterous or an incestuous union "may not enter the congregation of the Lord" (Deut. 23:3), which precludes marriage with any fully pedigreed member of the community.[11] The problem of *mamzers* is social, not sexual. They may marry virtually any member of the community who is less than fully pedigreed—and there seem to have been many of them in talmudic times.[12] The *mamzers'* frustration is the social stigma they carry, a stigma that prevents full participation in society and that is perpetuated in their descendants. The following Mishnah shows a solution to this problem: "R. Tarfon says that *mamzerim* are able to be cleared [*leetaher*]. How so? Let a [male] *mamzer* marry a female slave [*shifha*] and the offspring will then have the status of a slave [*eved*]. Let the offspring be emancipated and have the status of a freeman [*ben horeen*]."[13]

The ingenious legal solution of R. Tarfon is accepted as valid by later authorities.[14] Also, there was a tendency among the rabbis not to delve very carefully into family pedigree.[15] Furthermore, the offspring of a union between a Jewish woman, even a married one, and either a gentile or a slave was not a *mamzer*.[16] This may well have been an attempt to remove any social stigma from rape victims and their offspring.[17] Finally, an aggadic text reports a complaint against the Jewish legal authorities who have it in their power to alleviate the social stigma of the *mamzer* totally and yet do not act as boldly as they could.[18] All of this reflects the notion that no innocent person is to be denied fulfillment of his or her sociality. The plight of Honi Ha-Me'agel, the rabbinic forerunner of Rip Van Winkle, as expressed in aggadic language, shows the motivating idea behind the attempts to remove legal barriers to full sociality. Honi says, "Either fellowship [*haveruta*] or death."[19] Even a criminal sentenced to death, and thereby permanently severed from human society (even denied burial in a regular cemetery), is allowed to repent of his crime publicly so as not to lose the fellowship of the world-to-come.[20]

The Socialization of Sexuality

We have seen how both sexuality and sociality are considered to be natural needs that society as an institution is to help fulfill. Accordingly, they assume the status of "natural rights," namely, society's recognition that the fulfillment of the needs of its human participants is its authentic task.[21] However, because sociality is the immediate source of society's raison d'être and its guiding goal, society in its law and institutions channels sexuality in socially acceptable directions, thereby limiting its intentional range. As Maimonides succinctly put it, "What is natural is left to nature, but measures are taken against excess."[22]

The following legal exegesis shows this social process of sexual limitation at work. Commenting on the scriptural verse "And a man shall leave his father and mother and cleave to his wife and they shall be one flesh" (Gen. 2:24), R. Akibah states:

> "His father" means his father's wife; "his mother" literally means his mother; "he shall cleave" means not with a male; "with his wife" means not with his neighbor's wife. "And they shall be one flesh" means with those whom he is capable of becoming one flesh, thus excluding an animal or beast with whom he cannot become one flesh.[23]

This text is the basis of the elimination of incestuous, homosexual, and nonhuman objects from socially legitimate sexuality. The socialization of sexuality is the constitution of the family. The family, then, is the institution that directs natural sexuality toward personalistic goals. As Hegel insightfully noted, the family is "a *natural ethical community*" and "the *immediate* being of the ethical order."[24] That is, it relates the biological order to the larger society. Both the attempt to solve the sexual problem of the person half-slave and half-free and the attempt to solve the social problem of the *mamzer* involve removing the legal barriers to their living in a normal family/social situation.

In their aggadic speculations about human sexuality, the rabbis see its primordial manifestation as incestuous. Incest is seen as the natural human state, which is overcome only in the interest of sociality. Note the following rabbinic text:

> Scripture states, "If a man takes his sister, the daughter of his father, or the daughter of his mother, and she sees his nakedness, it is a reproach" [*hesed*—Lev. 20:17]. R. Avin said that one should not say that Cain's marrying his own sister and Abel's marrying his own sister are a reproach. Rather, "I [God] said that the world is built by kindness [*hesed*—Ps. 89:3]."[25]

Here in the passage from Leviticus we see the word *hesed*, which usually means "kindness," used in its opposite sense of "reproach."[26] The text plays on this disparate double meaning and states that what is now a reproach was at the dawn of humanity a social necessity, namely, the outward extension of the human race, beginning with siblings. Thus, in a parallel text we read:

> If you say, "Why did not Adam marry his own daughter?" The answer is, in order that Cain might marry his sister so that "the world be built by kindness" [Ps. 89:3].[27]

These discussions are based on the older legend that Cain and Abel were each born with a twin sister, which explains how Scripture can all of a sudden say, "And Cain knew his wife" (Gen. 4:17).[28] The assumption behind all of these discussions seems to be that sibling incest at a very primitive level might well be motivated by a desire to build a world—a society—a motive considered good.[29]

The same aggadic reasoning comes out in this discussion of the incest between Lot and his daughters:

> R. Yohanan said that what does Scripture mean when it states, "The ways of the Lord are straight, and the righteous walk in them, but the wicked stumble in them" [Hos. 14:10]? . . . [F]or example, this refers to Lot and his two daughters. They, whose intent was good [*le-shem mitsvah*] are "the righteous [who] walk in them." He, whose intent was evil [*le-shem averah*], is "the wicked [who] stumble in them."[30]

It will be recalled from the scriptural story of Lot and his daughters that they justify their incest by stating, "There is no man on earth to come upon us according to the way of all the earth. Come, let us give our father wine to drink, and we will live with him, and we will then continue life from our father" (*u-nehayeh me'avinu zara*— Gen. 19:31). But about Lot it is stated, "he was unaware [*ve-lo yada*] when she lay down and when she rose up" (Gen. 19:32, 35). Thus, Lot acted out of immediate physical desire, unaware of the personal identities of the objects of his desire, much less justifying it by any human purpose.[31] It is this socialization that effects the sublimation of sexuality's most immediate objects.[32]

Philo of Alexandria, the first-century Hellenistic Jewish sage, sees the rationale for the prohibition of incest as follows:

Why hamper the fellow-feeling [*koinōnias*] and intercommunion of humans with other humans [*pros tous allous anthrōpous*] by compressing within the narrow space of each separate house the great and goodly plant which might extend and spread itself over continents and islands and the whole inhabited world [*oikoumenen*]? For marriages with outsiders [*othneious*] create new kinships.

On this principle he [Moses] prohibits many other unions. . . .[33]

Philo is advocating that each generation break out of the consanguineous circle of the immediate family when marrying.

The *halakhah* recognizes the universal ban of incest.[34] It also eliminates a loophole in Jewish law that would, in effect, allow de facto incest, for according to the law a convert is "born again" (*ke-qatan she-nolad dami*). If this juridical notion is carried to its furthest logical conclusion, a convert could even marry his own mother (who had also converted to Judaism, she also being "born again"). De jure, they are no longer consanguineously related. Nevertheless, direct incest of this type was prohibited so that the converts might not say, "We have come from a higher level of sanctity to a lower one."[35] Incest is considered to be radically disruptive of society because it introduces regressive sexuality rather than sublimation. Thus, the ninth-century theologian R. Saadyah Gaon sees the prohibition of incest as required by the integrity of the familial relationship. In presenting his rationale for the commandment of filial piety, he writes:

. . . in order that men might not become like the beasts with the result that no one would know his father so as to show him reverence in return for having raised him. . . . A further reason was that a human being might know the rest of his relations . . . and show them whatever tenderness he was capable of.[36]

The rationale for the prohibition of homosexuality is closely connected to the prohibition of incest. Homosexuality is considered to be counterfamilial and, also, counterprocreative. Its intentionality is purely sensual.[37]

In the Aggadah, heterosexuality is seen as rooted in the essentially bisexual nature of human beings. "R. Jeremiah ben Eleazar said that the first man has two faces [*du partzuf panim*] . . . as it is written, 'Male and female He created them [Gen. 5:2].' "[38] This theme appears in a number of rabbinic texts. Another aggadic text expresses it as follows: "R. Eliezer said that they were created as a hermaphrodite (*androgynos*). . . . R. Samuel said that He created him with two faces, front and back, and split him and sawed him in two."[39] This notion of the original bisexuality of man, which has been confirmed by modern embryology, was prevalent in the ancient world.[40] Its most famous enunciation was by Plato.[41] The idea here is that a man's experience of himself as lacking his "missing other half" is the source of heterosexual desire.[42] Thus homosexuality is considered a regression in that it does not seek its true "other." Only the successful consummation of this desire for the human other leads to the recognizable family unit and the possibility of procreation.

The biblical idea that true humanness is rooted in the indispensable connection between man and woman was profoundly seen by the Protestant theologian Karl Barth (d. 1968), who wrote:

The real perversion takes place, the original decadence and disintegration begins, when man will not see his partner of the opposite sex and therefore the primal form of fellow-man (*die Urgestalt des Mitmenschen*) . . . but trying to be human in himself sovereign man or woman. . . . For in this supposed discovery of the genuinely human man and woman give themselves up to the worship of a false god.[43]

Sexuality, then, presents a dialectic between self-possession and relatedness. In Barth's words, "Male and female being is the prototype of all I and Thou, of all individuality in which man [*Mensch*] and man differ from and yet belong to one another."[44] When human beings attempt to construct their autonomous self-sufficiency collectively, *hetero*sexuality asserts their fundamental differentiation as separate bodies. And when human beings attempt to construct their autonomous self-sufficiency individually, hetero*sexuality* asserts their fundamental relatedness to the other side of their humanness.

Another aggadic text interprets homosexuality per se as a fundamental human error.

> Bar Kappara said to R. Judah the Prince, "What does 'abomination' [*to'evah*—in the prohibition of homosexuality in Lev. 20:13] mean?" . . . R. Judah the Prince said God meant 'abomination' means 'something in which you err [*to'eh attah*].'"[45]

Homosexuality is based on a fundamental lie. There can be no good (the object of ethics) that is not based on truth (the object of ontology).[46] In a homosexual relationship between men, one of them assumes a female role; in a homosexual relationship between two women, one of them assumes a male role. Furthermore, even the masculine man in a male homosexual relationship is not relating to a real woman but, rather, to his male alter ego. Even the feminine woman in a female homosexual relationship is not relating to a real man but, rather, to her female alter ego. And even if each participant in a male homosexual relationship asserts he is wholly masculine to the other, and even if each participant in a female homosexual asserts she is wholly feminine to the other, this celebration of absolute masculinity or absolute femininity belies the very biological truth of the essentially intersexual relatedness attested by the fact that the sexual organs and the organs of procreation are the same.

Homosexuality is considered inconsistent with authentic human sociality, that is, it is considered inconsistent with human nature.[47] In the Aggadah it is seen as part of the overall degradation of human life and society in Sodom: "And they called to Lot and they said to him, 'Where are the men who came to you; bring them out to us that we might know them [*ve-ned'ah otam*]' " (Gen. 19:5). In one rabbinic source the last phrase is interpreted to mean "that we might have intercourse with them [*u-neshamesh imehon*]."[48] The point is made elsewhere too.[49] Obviously, the aggadists took the verb "to know" [*yado'a*] in the sense of "carnal knowledge" as in "And the man knew [*yada*] Eve his wife and she conceived (Gen. 4:1). Because Scripture designated the Sodomites as "exceedingly wicked and sinful unto the Lord" (Gen. 13:13), homosexual rape is seen as one of their foremost sins.[50] The rabbis were clearly aware of the prevalence of homosexuality in the Greco-Roman world. Various *halakhic* rulings reflect this awareness.[51] Indeed, their ostensible reflections about the sins of Sodom probably had a more contemporary situation in mind.[52] Furthermore, the concern of this aggadic source with homosexual rape might very well be the rabbis' reflection about the presence of sadistic elements in many homosexual acts, a view found in the *halakhah*.[53] However, even fully consensual homosexuality is forbidden. Female homosexuality, too, is considered by the rabbis as "lewdness" (*peritsuta b'alma*) because there is no explicit scriptural prohibition of it, as there is of male homosexuality.[54]

The rabbis were especially critical of any society that would formally legitimize homosexual unions, undoubtedly because they are considered to be fundamentally antisocial in that they are a burlesque of heterosexual family life. Thus, an aggadic text reads:

> R. Hiyya taught why is "I am the Lord" repeated twice [Lev. 18:3 and 4]?—I am he who punished the generation of the Flood and Sodom and Egypt; I will in the future punish whoever does according to their deeds. The generation of the Flood was blotted out from the world because they were steeped in immorality [*shetufin be-zenuf*]. . . . R. Huna said in the name of R. Yose that the generation of the Flood was blotted out from the world only because they wrote marriage contracts [*gomasiyot*] for male unions and for female unions.[55]

The rabbis seem to be making a distinction between a society in which homosexuality is prevalent and one in which there is an official sanction and recognition of it. This text might well be based on a report that the Roman emperor Nero went so far as to write a marriage contract for one of his favorite male lovers.[56] Perhaps even in the Greco-Roman world, where individual homosexuality was quite common, Nero's elevating a homosexual relationship to the level of a "marriage" was considered shocking and a sign of extreme social decadence. It is something more serious than individual decadence because of its public moral approval.

The prohibition of bestiality was also used by the rabbis to speculate about the development of human sexuality. The rabbis seemed to have recognized that at the level of what psychoanalysts call "primary process," bestiality, or at least the motif of bestiality, is a human possibility. Thus, when Scripture states about animals, "He [God] brought them unto man to see what he would call them" (Gen. 2:19), an aggadist speculated as follows:

> R. Eleazar said that why did Scripture state [that is, the first man's words], "This time it is bone from my bone and flesh from my flesh" [Gen. 2:23]?—It teaches that Adam had sexual relations with every animal and beast, but he was not satisfied [*ve-lo nitqarerah da'ato*] until he had sexual relations with Eve.[57]

Eve satisfied him because with her he could once again—following the motif of primordial bisexuality—"become one flesh." Furthermore, it is emphasized that with Eve alone could Adam speak.[58] Whereas speech is not required by sexuality, it is required by sociality.[59] Thus heterosexuality between human partners is a restriction of biological primary process by human sociality. Satisfaction in the personal sense is even more social than it is physical.

The Socialization of Sexuality and the Status of Women

The socialization of human sexuality in Judaism can be seen in the way the legal status of women in the marital relationship developed into one of true mutuality, for if one reflects on heterosexuality as a physical phenomenon, it clearly requires male initiation and suggests male dominance. This is assumed by the *halakhah* where marriage and divorce are initiated by the man.[60] Reflecting on this legal fact, the Talmud records the following aggadic speculation:

> R. Simon says that why did the Torah state, "When a man takes [a woman]" [Deut. 24:1, but does not state, "When a woman takes a man"? This is because it is the way [*darko*] of a man to go after a woman, but it is not the way of a woman to go after a man. It is like one who lost something. Who goes after whom? The owner [*ba'al*] of the lost article goes after the lost article.[61]

Thus at this level, we see that the desire for the primordial bisexual union, which we discussed before, is *initially* male.

Nevertheless, the Talmud notes that in a key rabbinic text, the woman, not the man, is made the subject of the initiation of marriage.[62] From this, among other texts, it is inferred that a woman may not be married against her will, that is, be acquired like chattel.[63] Furthermore, even though according to scriptural law a female child may be married off by her father without her consent, and even rabbinic law had to accept the validity of such a marriage as valid ex post facto, this practice was subsequently prohibited ab initio, that is, a father is to wait until his daughter is mature enough to say, "It is he whom I want."[64] The following aggadic text shows how the lack of mutual consent in marriage was seen as socially disadvantageous:

> A Roman lady asked R. Yose bar Halafta, "Everyone agrees that God created the world in six days. From the sixth day on what has he been doing?" . . . R. Berakhyah said . . . he said to her that He arranges marriages in his world. . . . She said that she could make a thousand such marriages in one day . . . so she brought a thousand male slaves and a thousand female slaves and paired them off. . . . However, when night came, fighting broke out among them.[65]

The point that emerges from this is that slavery, that is, the subjugation of one human person by another, is inimical to human fulfillment, including human sexual fulfillment. One can see the entire development of Jewish matrimonial law as the steady emancipation of women from anything even resembling slavery.[66]

Along these same lines, even though according to scriptural law only a man could divorce his wife, rabbinic law subsequently enabled a woman to sue for divorce based on certain objective conditions that make true marital mutuality impossible.[67] Moreover, in rabbinic law a woman is to be provided with a marriage contract (*ketubah*), which stipulates that in the event of a divorce (or the death of her husband) she is to be paid a considerable sum of money. The reason for this is given as being "so that she not be easy [*qalah*] to be sent away."[68] Later authorities ruled that under any circumstances a woman could not be divorced against her will.[69] Thus the mutuality that was eventually recognized as being required at the initiation of marriage was finally required at its termination as well.[70] Also, as early as the first century C.E., Rabban Yohanan ben Zakkai eliminated the ordeal of the woman suspected of adultery (*sotah*). He argued that it presupposed mutual standards of virtue, something that could no longer be assumed.[71] And as late as the sixteenth century, R. Moses Isserles made male unfaithfulness grounds for divorce, just as female unfaithfulness had always been the grounds for divorce in the past.[72]

The social requirement of true mutuality can be achieved only in monogamy. The introduction of monogamy as the only acceptable heterosexual union in Judaism ultimately required the elimination of concubinage as well as polygamy (polyandry never having been permitted).[73] It should be noted that concubinage and polygamy were taken for granted in Scripture as perfectly acceptable practices.[74]

It was Maimonides in the twelfth century who banned concubinage. He gave a historical context to the ruling as follows:

> Before the giving of the Torah it was that a man would meet a woman in the marketplace and, if they mutually agreed, then he would give her her price, having relations with her along the way, and would then go on his way. Such a woman is what is called a *qedeshah*. When the Torah was given, the *qedeshah* was outlawed . . . therefore, anyone who has relations with a woman for purposes of fornication [*le-shem zenut*] without marriage [*be-lo qiddushin*] is to be lashed according to scriptural law because he has had relations with a *qedeshah*.[75]

Maimonides' scriptural proof-text is "There shall not be any *qedeshah* among the daughters of Israel, nor any *qadesh* among the sons of Israel" (Deut. 23:18). Even though one might think that *qedeshah/qadesh,* coming as they do from the root *qadosh* ("sacred"), refer only to prostitutes (female or male) connected with pagan shrines, Maimonides makes no distinction between "sacred" and "secular" prostitution.[76] As one of the commentators on Maimonides notes, his reference concerning pre-Torah conditions is the story of Judah and Tamar recorded in Genesis 38.[77] There, Tamar, posing as a prostitute in a clearly noncultic setting, is called a *qedeshah* (38:21). The term is used there interchangeably with the term *zonah* (38:15), an ordinary prostitute. In other words, anything less than a full wife is, for Maimonides, in essence a prostitute, and the Torah outlawed *all* prostitution.

Now a number of subsequent *halakhists*, although in basic sympathy with Maimonides' high moral standards and aspirations for the Jewish people, nevertheless argued that concubinage, as distinct from full marriage, is permitted by both Scripture and the Talmud.[78] It seems, then, that Maimonides was making an explicit innovation in Jewish law, something he did in other areas as well.[79] He might very well have been repulsed by the use of women as concubines (and as prostitutes) in the upper-class Muslim circles in which he worked as a physician. Indeed, the concubine is in essence woman as sexual object alone.[80]

It was the eleventh-century German *halakhist* Rabbenu Gershom of Mainz who banned polygamy. Here, too, there is clearly no explicit precedent in either Scripture or the Talmud. Indeed, we do not even have the original text of this ban, much less Rabbenu Gershom's reasoning for it.[81] Nevertheless, one can see its effect at least as being one more step in the process of making true mutuality in the personal relationship of marriage a social reality. It is interesting to note the following aggadic speculation concerning the first polygamous marriage recorded in Scripture, namely, that of Lamech and his two wives Ada and Zillah (Gen. 4:19):

> R. Azariah said in the name of R. Judah that this was what the men of the generation of the Flood were doing. One would take two wives, one for procreation and one for sex [*le-tashmish*]. The one for procreation would be sitting like a widow during her lifetime; the one for sex would be given a sterilizing potion to drink, and she would sit before him like a prostitute.[82]

The important thing to note about this speculation is that neither woman is treated as a person. Both are used by the man. Now, of course, one could say that this speculation only concerns the generation of the Flood. However, it should be recalled that polygamy is often described in Scripture as a cause of human unhappiness.[83] Indeed, in Scripture the first marriage between Eve and Adam, which according to the Aggadah God himself celebrated, was monogamous.[84] In any polygamous marriage the man is necessarily divided in his heterosexual affection, whereas the woman becomes a particular functionary rather than a whole person relating to another whole person. It is only in a monogamous union that in effect *both* the man and the woman are exclusively sanctified to each other.[85]

Sexuality and God

In classical Jewish teaching all aspects of human life are ultimately related to God. Therefore, we should now examine how the human person as a sexual/social being is the image of God.

At the beginning of the talmudic tractate *Kiddushin,* which primarily deals with Jewish marriage, the Palestinian version records the following statement:

> For we learn that the gentiles do not have religious marriage [*qiddushin*], so how can they possibly have religious divorce [*gerushin*]? R. Judah ben Pazzi and R. Hanin said in the name of R. Honeh, elder of Sepphoris, that either they do not have religious divorce or they divorce each other.[86]

Undoubtedly basing his discussion of Jewish marriage law on this text, Maimonides begins as follows:

> Before the giving of the Torah a man would meet a woman in the marketplace. If they mutually agreed he would marry her, then he would bring her into his house and would have sexual relations with her privately and she would become his wife. When the Torah was given, Israel was commanded that if a man marry a woman, he would take her [*yiqah otah*] initially in the presence of two witnesses and afterward she would become his wife, as Scripture states, "When a man takes a woman and comes to her" (Deut. 24:1).[87]

Now, at first glance these texts seem to indicate that the Torah removed an original mutuality from the initiation of marriage. Nevertheless, the subsequent factor of the woman's required consent clearly indicates that even when marriage is a state initiated by the man, it surely requires mutuality to be valid.[88] Therefore, one must see the point being made that Jewish marriage is more than a civil contract; rather, it is a covenant rooted in the covenant between God and his people Israel. This explains why Maimonides emphasizes the presence of witnesses. Obviously, the initiation of pre-Toraitic marriage, taking place as it does "in the marketplace," is also a public matter. However, whereas this marriage is *consummated as a private sexual matter* between the man and the woman, Jewish marriage is consummated as a public nonsexual matter.[89] The witnesses represent the minimal presence of the sacred community, and as such, they do not simply confirm a legal fact but actually constitute its essential meaning.[90] Indeed, in order for the liturgical rite of marriage to be fully celebrated (with the full invocation of God's name), a minimum quorum of ten is required.[91]

The presence of God in Jewish marriage is the subject of profound aggadic speculation, as for example:

> He [R. Simlai] said to them [his students] that originally Adam was created "from the dust of the earth" [Gen. 2:7], and Eve was created from the man. After Adam they [men and women] were created "in Our image after Our likeness" [Gen. 1:26]. It is impossible for man to live without woman; it is impossible for woman to live without man; and it is impossible for both to live without God's presence [*Shekhinah*].[92]

This idea is further reflected in the talmudic statement that "there are three partners in the formation of a human being: God and the father and the mother."[93] In other words, God is present in Jewish marriage and its fruits.

We have seen how human sexuality and human sociality are correlated in marriage. The idea of marriage as a sacred covenent correlates this relation with the status of the human person as the image of God. Now we must ask: Does this acknowledgment of marriage as a sacred covenant add anything significantly new? Or, is the sacred dimension simply the deification of society as a whole greater than the mere sum of its individual parts, as Émile Durkheim, one of the founders of modern sociology, so consistently and powerfully argued.[94]

In answering this question, I call attention to the analogy between marriage as the male-female relationship and God's relationship with his people Israel, so often made in Scripture and the rabbinic writings. The analogy is based on the idea of faithfulness (*emunah*), which is to be the foundation of both relationships.

> And it shall come to pass on that day, the Lord says, that you will call me "my husband" [*ishi*] and you will no longer call Me "my master" [*ba'ali*]. . . . And I will make a covenant [*berit*] with them on that day. . . . [A]nd I will betroth you unto to Me forever, and I will betroth you unto me rightly and with justice and with kindness and with compassion. And I will betroth you unto Me in faithfulness [*b'emunah*], and you will know the Lord. (Hos. 2:18–21)

> And this second thing you do to cover the altar of the Lord with weeping and wailing. . . . And you say, "why?"—Because the Lord witnesses between you and the wife of your youth against whom you have been unfaithful [*bagadata*], and she is your companion, your covenanted wife [*eshet beritekha*].[95] (Mal. 2:13–14)

In rabbinic literature the most outstanding example of this line of thought is the interpretation of Song of Songs, which uses the image of a male-female love relationship to express God's love for the people of Israel allegorically.[96]

This analogy is usually explained as being a comparison of God's love for his people with the relationship of a man and a woman in a loving marriage.[97] But I find such an interpretation to be wide open to the critiques of religion made by Ludwig Feuerbach and Sigmund Freud, namely, that religion projects onto an idealized realm what is a purely human reality.[98] It seems to me to be more accurate and theologically more cogent to explain the analogy the other way around, namely, it is a comparison of male-female love with God's love of his people. In other words, God's love is the primary reality in which human love becomes a participation. This can mean one of two things.

For the kabbalists, male-female union is a symbolic participation in the union of the male-female aspects of the Godhead itself. As the ZOHAR puts it:

> Come and see that the desire of a male for a female and the desire of a female for a male and their union [*v'itdavquta*] produces a soul . . . and this earthly desire is included in heavenly desire [*be-t'euvtah de-l'ela*].[99]

The problem with this line of interpretation is that it is, as is all kabbalistic theology, a compromise with strict monotheism—a point made by Jewish traditional critics of Kabbalah.[100] Furthermore, by making human sexuality only a symbol of a truly divine reality, it eclipses the factor of finite human embodiment, which seems to be such an essential factor in this human reality. As such, it can be seen as countersexual.[101] Finally, it is a serious departure from the essential aspect of divine love emphasized in Scripture and the rabbinic writings, namely, love as an act of God's self-transcendence, his recognition of a truly nondivine *other*. In Kabbalah, all divine love is essentially a self-enclosed love *into which* creatures are ultimately incorporated.

I would rather emphasize that sexual love in the sacred covenant of marriage is a participation in a higher relationship, that of God's everlasting love for his people. At its best, it reflects that everlasting love. Deutero-Isaiah perhaps best expressed this foundation of all covenantal love when he wrote:

> . . . with everlasting kindness I have loved you, says the Lord your redeemer. . . .
> For the mountains will depart and the hills be moved, but my covenant of peace will
> not be moved, says the Lord who loves you.[102] (Isa. 54:8–10)

This connection comes out more clearly if we consider the phenomenology of sexual love. It is mistaken, it seems to me, to consider the essence of sexual love to be pleasure, although it is certainly a sine qua non of it, for in all other bodily pleasures, such as eating, drinking, bathing, we seek a heightened sense of awareness of our own bodies. Our pleasure is essentially a taking-in, that is, our desire is to make our world around us an extension of our own bodies. In heterosexual love, on the other hand, we seek ecstasy, which comes from two Greek words, *ex histēmi*, meaning "to stand out." In other words, our sexuality intends transendence. Eros seeks spirit.[103] It seems that in true eros we seek *to go beyond our bodies through them*. For a moment we experience a going beyond the body, which is ordinarily the limit of the soul.[104] Nevertheless, sexual love in itself lasts only for a moment before the body, the ever-present, finite, mortal vessel, claims the soul once again. This is pointed out in the following aggadah:

> David said before God, "My father Jesse did not intend to sire me, but intended
> only his own pleasure. You know that this is so because after the parents satisfied
> themselves, he turned his face away and she turned her face away and You joined
> the drops."[105]

Eros is not a function of the body but, rather, the eroticized body ultimately intends that which is beyond limit, that which is beyond death. As embodied souls,[106] we can experience this only by moving through the body beyond it. It cannot be done through any ascetic shortcuts; we cannot pretend to be angels when we are only flesh and blood.[107] And this is why the periodic monthly separation (*niddah*) enjoined by *halakhah* on husband and wife at the time of the menses is seen as a cultivation of eros that is more than bodily.[108] Indeed, even the most banal love lyrics sung today almost inevitably long for "undying love." The intention of what is everlasting seems to be essential to even the most crudely expressed sexual desire.

In Judaism such desire is seen as being grounded in God's everlasting love for his people. This grounding alone enables sexual love to be an expression of creative energy and the ultimate antithesis of all narcissism.[109] This comes out in the rabbinic interpretation of the most erotic of all Scripture, Song of Songs. In conclusion let me cite one outstanding example. Scripture states, "For love is strong as death [*azah ke-mavet*]; jealousy is harsh as the grave; its flashes are fiery flashes, the very torch of God" (Canticles 8:6). From the text it seems as though "death" is used as a superlative, namely, it is the strongest thing we experience, beyond which we know nothing. Love is considered equally strong and equally final. However, the rabbis seem to want to make love stronger than death. Thus, they revocalized the word *ke-mavet* ("like death") and read it as *ke-mot,* "it is like." It is like what?

> For love is strong as [*ke-mot*] the love which God has for you, as Scripture states, "I have loved you, says the Lord" [Mal. 1:2]. "Jealousy is harsh as the grave"—this refers to the times they made Him jealous with their idolatry [*avodah zarah*], as it says, "They made Him jealous with strange gods" [*zarim*—Deut. 32:16]. . . . Another interpretation: "For love is strong as death"—this is the love of a man for his wife, as it says, "experience life with a woman you love" [Eccles. 9:9]. . . . "Its flashes are fiery flashes, the very torch of God"—R. Berakhyah said it is like the heavenly fire which does not consume the water not does the water extinguish it.[110]

In Judaism human sexuality, socialized and sanctified in the covenant of marriage, becomes the way two mortal creatures together existentially affirm God's love, which alone never dies.

Notes

1. M. Gittin 4.5 and M. Eduyot 1.13. See B. Gittin 43b; Y. Gittin 4.5/46a; Maimonides, *Hilkhot Avadim,* 7.7. But cf. M. Kiddushin 4.3; B. Kiddushin 75a; R. Vidal of Tolosa, *Maggid Mishneh* on Maimonides, *Hilkhot Isuray Bi'ah* 15.21; *Tur: Even Ha'Ezer,* 4(end). Also see B. Gittin 41b, Tos., s.v. "kofin" re ibid., 38b, which suggests that this is permitted because of *mitsvah de-rabbim,* which can well be seen as a rabbinic term for the common good (see B. Berakhot 47b; B. Baba Batra 13a and Tos., s.v. "shene'emar;" B. Shabbat 4a and Tos., s.v. "ve-khi"). See *supra,* 38; *infra,* 165f.

2. B. Gittin 42a.

3. See B. Shabbat 135b and B. Berakhot 47b. This full integration into the community was seen as entailing a limitation of the licentiousness formerly enjoyed by the slave. See B. Gittin 12b; B. Baba Metsia 19a and Rashi, s.v. "zekhut;" Maimonides, *Hilkhot Avadim,* 5.2 and 6.1; *Vayiqra Rabbah* 8.1.

4. *Jewish and Roman Law,* 2 vols. (New York, 1966), 1:28 n. 97.

5. B. Yevamot 61b–62a.

6. See Maimonides, *Moreh Nevukhim,* 1.65 and 2.40. Re the human source of legal difficulties, see T. Sotah 14.9; B. Sanhedrin 88b.

7. M. Yevamot 6.6 and B. Yevamot 63b. For the fulfilling status of female sexuality, see B. Sanhedrin 22b re Isa. 54:5.

8. See M. Yevamot 16.7; M. Eduyot 6.1 and 8.5; B. Gittin 3a and parallels; also B. Kiddushin 7a and parallels; David Novak, *Law and Theology in Judaism,* 2 vols. (New York, 1974), 1:31ff.; David Novak, *Halakhah in a Theological Dimension* (Chico, Calif., 1985), 29ff.

9. B. Yoma 69b and B. Sanhedrin 64a. Cf. B. Sotah 47a and B. Kiddushin 81b. See D. M. Feldman, *Birth Control in Jewish Law* (New York, 1968), 88. The celibacy of the first-century C.E. sage Ben Azzai is considered his personal peculiarity. See B. Yevamot 63b; cf.,

however, Maimonides, *Hilkhot Ishut,* 15.3. For Ben Azzai's unhappy end, see B. Hagigah 14b. Also see *Tanhuma: Aharay Mot,* ed. Buber, 31b–32a, for the notion of celibacy as arrogance. The dangers of denying sexuality are brought out by the ancient Greek dramatist Euripides, who in his play *Hippolytus* has Aphrodite say, "Hippolytus, alone among the inhabitants of Troezen, calls me the most pernicious of the heavenly powers; he abhors the bed of love; marriage he renounces. . . . But Hippolytus has insulted me and shall suffer for it." *Euripides: Three Plays,* trans. P. Vellacott (Baltimore, 1953), 28. Cf. Sigmund Freud, *The Origin and Development of Psychoanalysis* (Chicago, 1955), 67–68.

10. For rabbinic recognition of sublimation, see B. Shabbat 156a.

11. M. Yevamot 4.13; M. Kiddushin 3.12.

12. See M. Kiddushin 4.1ff. For a discussion of this whole ethical problem of *mamzerut,* see Novak, *Halakhah in a Theological Dimension,* 11ff.

13. M. Kiddushin 3.13. Upon manumission a gentile slave became a full Jew. See B. Berakhot 47b.

14. B. Kiddushin 69a.

15. Ibid., 71a.

16. B. Yevamot 45b and parallels.

17. See, e.g., M. Ketubot 2.5 and B. Ketubot 23a; Isserles, *Darkhay Mosheh* on *Tur: Even Ha'Ezer,* 7, n. 13.

18. *Vayiqra Rabbah* 32.7. See B. Berkakhot 7a re Exod. 34:7 and Deut. 24:16. Cf. B. Gittin 33a and Tos., s.v. "v'afqa'inu." For attempts to play down pedigree, see, e.g., B. Horayot 3.8 and Y. Horayot 3.5/48c; B. Nazir 23b re Prov. 18:1; M. Yadayim 4.4.

19. B. Ta'anit 23a. For separation from the discursive community as a cause of depression, see Menahot 29b. For sympathy for those separated from the community because of disease, see B. Mo'ed Qatan 5a; *infra,* 108.

20. M. Sanhedrin 6.2 and B. Sanhedrin 47a.

21. See R. Joseph Albo, *Iqqarim,* 1.5.

22. *Guide of the Perplexed,* 3.49, trans. S. Pines (Chicago, 1963), 611.

23. B. Sanhedrin 58a. Freud saw this verse as describing the normal course of psychosexual development. See "The Most Prevalent Form of Degradation in Erotic Life" (1912) in *Collected Papers,* 5 vols., trans. J. Strachey (London, 1950–52), 4:205–6.

24. *Phenomenology of Spirit,* no. 450, trans. A. V. Miller (Oxford, 1977), 268. So, also, Aristotle argues against the suggested abolition of the family (at least for the ruling guardians) in Plato's *Republic* (463Dff.) by asserting that without first having an allegiance to one's own biological family, one would not be able to form enduring allegiances to the larger civil community of which it is part (*Politics,* 1262a5ff.). Certainly, part of that familial allegiance is one's desire to continue the family through his or her procreation. Thus it is quite interesting to note the suggestion of Martha C. Nussbaum in *The Fragility of Goodness: Luck and Ethics in Greek Tragedy and Philosophy* (Cambridge and New York, 1986), 370–71, that Aristotle's emphasis of the political necessity of the family (contra Plato) is related to his heterosexuality. See, also, Harry V. Jaffa, *Homosexuality and the Natural Law* (Claremont, Calif., 1991), esp. 25–37.

25. Y. Yevamot 11.1/11d. Cf. Y. Sanhedrin 5.1/22c. For "seeing" as a euphemism for possession, see B. Pesahim 5b re Exod. 13:7.

26. See Rashbam, *Commentary on the Torah:* Lev. 20:17.

27. B. Sanhedrin 58b.

28. *Beresheet Rabbah* 22.1. Re the question of the rabbis supplying missing data about biblical characters, see B. Baba Batra 91a.

29. For a certain tolerance of quasi incest, see B. Yevamot 62b–63a; B. Sanhedrin 76b re Isa. 58:7.

30. B. Horayot 10b re Hos. 14:10.

31. See B. Nazir 23b re Prov. 18:1 and Tos., s.v. "le-ta'avah."

32. See B. Yoma 69b.

33. *De Specialibus Legibus*, 3:25–26, in *Philo*, 9 vols. trans. F. H. Colson (Cambridge, Mass., 1937), 7:488–9. Cf. Augustine, *De Civitate Dei*, 15.16.

34. See Maimonides, *Hilkhot Melakhim*, 9.5.

35. B. Yevamot 22a. See Maimonides, *Hilkhot Isuray Bi'ah*, 14.12.

36. *Book of Beliefs and Opinions*, 3.2, trans. S. Rosenblatt (New Haven, 1948), 141. See Nahmanides, *Commentary on the Torah:* Gen. 2:24.

37. See Maimonides, *Guide for the Perplexed*, 3.49; *supra*, note 22. Cf. Aristotle, *Nicomachean Ethics*, 1174b30ff. Much of the discussion here concerning incest, homosexuality, and so on is taken from my book, *The Image of the Non-Jew in Judaism: An Historical and Constructive Study of the Noahide Laws* (New York and Toronto, 1983), chap. 6.

38. B. Eruvin 18a. See B. Berakhot 61b re Ps. 139:5; B. Megillah 9a; B. Ketubot 8a; B. Sanhedrin 38b; Louis Ginzberg, *Legends of the Jews*, 7 vols. (Philadelphia, 1925), 5:88–89 n. 42.

39. *Midrash Tehillim*, 139.5, ed. Buber, 265a. See *Beresheet Rabbah* 8.1; Ginzberg, *Legends*, 5:90 n. 48.

40. See K. L. Moore, *The Developing Human*, 2d ed. (Philadelphia, 1977), 228ff.

41. *Symposium*, 191D–192B.

42. See *Zohar:* Qedoshim, 3:81a–b re Job 23:13.

43. *Church Dogmatics*, auth. Eng. trans. (Edinburgh, 1961), III/4:166. Re the priority of "the other" (*l'autre*) in ethics, see Emmanuel Levinas, *Existence and Existents*, trans. A. Lingis (The Hague, 1978), 94–96.

44. *Church Dogmatics*, III/4:150. See also Barth's *Ethics*, ed. D. Braun and trans. G. W. Bromiley (New York, 1981), 181. Some of this material is from my article, "Before Revelation: The Rabbis, Paul and Karl Barth," *Journal of Religion* 71 (1991): 59–60.

45. B. Nedarim 51a. See also B. Sanhedrin 82a re Mal. 2:11; Y. Berakhot 9.2/13c re Jer. 25:30.

46. See *supra*, n. 24.

47. See *infra*, 106ff.

48. *Targum Pseudo-Jonathan, ad locum.*

49. See *Beresheet Rabbah* 50.5; *Tanhuma:* Va-yere, printed ed., no. 12; Josephus, *Antiquities*, 1.200.

50. T. Sanhedrin 13.8. See *Mekhilta:* Be-Shalah, ed. Horovitz-Rabin, 177; y. Kiddushin 1.7/61a re II Chron. 24:24.

51. See, e.g., M. Avodah Zarah 2.1 and T. Avodah Zarah 3.2. Cf. M. Kiddushin 4.14; B. Kiddushin 82a; Y. Kiddushin 4.11/66c; also Karo, *Shulhan Arukh: Even Ha'Ezer*, 24.1.

52. See B. Gittin 57b. Thus, e.g., when the rabbis mentioned Edom, they were referring to Rome; see *Vayiqra Rabbah* 13.5.

53. See M. Sanhedrin 8.7.

54. B. Yevamot 76a; B. Sanhedrin 65a, Rashi, s.v. "gena'an;" Maimonides, *Commentary on the Mishnah:* Sanhedrin 7.4; *Hilkhot Isuray Bi'ah*, 21.8.

55. *Vayiqra Rabbah* 23.9 re *Sifra:* Aharay Mot (ed. Weiss), 86a. See B. Sanhedrin 54b re 1 Kings 14:24; Hullin 92a–b. Re the image of the generation of the Flood as a paradigm of future divine punishment, see M. Baba Metsia 4.2.

56. Suetonius, *Lives of the Caesars*, 4.28.

57. B. Yevamot 63a.

58. See *Beresheet Rabbah* 18.4; David Novak, *Law and Theology in Judaism*, 2 vols. (New York, 1976), 2:13–14.

59. See Aristotle, *Politics*, 1253a10. For attempts to qualify the rabbinic maxim "Do not engage in much discourse with a woman, even one's own wife" (M. Avot 1.5), see *Avot de-Rabbi Nathan* A, chap. 7, ed. Schechter, 18a (cf. B, chap. 15; B. Hagigah 5b re Amos 4:13); B. Eruvin 53b.

60. B. Kiddushin 5b; Y. Kiddushin 1.1/58c; B. Gittin 88b.

61. B. Kiddushin 2b. See *Beresheet Rabbah* 17.8. For the use of the noun *derekh* as a euphemism for sexual intercourse, see Gen. 19:31 and Prov. 30:19.

62. M. Kiddushin 1.1.

63. B. Kiddushin 2b. See B. Gittin 85b.

64. B. Kiddushin 41a. Cf. ibid. 3b re Deut. 22:16.

65. *Bemidbar Rabbah* 3.4. See *Vayiqra Rabbah* 8.1, ed. M. Margulies (Jerusalem, 1953), 1:166 n. 4; Novak, *Law and Theology in Judaism,* 2 vols., 1:5–9.

66. See Novak, *Law and Theology in Judaism,* 2:140–42. Indeed, the fourteenth-century Provençal exegete R. Menahem Meiri noted that if Scripture had explicated the originally involuntary initiation of marriage and divorce, "there would not be any daughter left to Abraham our father!" *Bet Ha-Behirah:* Kiddushin, ed. A. Sofer (Jerusalem, 1963), 8 (cf. B. Ketubot 72b), viz., no woman would want to remain a Jewess.

67. M. Ketubot 5.6 and B. Ketubot 77a. See Novak, *Law and Theology in Judaism,* 1:31–33.

68. B. Baba Kama 89a. See B. Ketubot 11a and 57a.

69. Isserles, note on *Shulhan Arukh:* Even Ha'Ezer, 119.6.

70. For the essential analogy between divorce and marriage, see B. Kiddushin 5a and parallels.

71. M. Sotah 9.9 re Hos. 4:14 and B. Sotah 47b re Num. 5:31; Y. Sotah 9.9/24a.

72. Note on *Shulhan Arukh:* Even Ha'Ezer, 154.1. Cf. M. Sotah 6.1; B. Gittin 46a.

73. See B. Kiddushin 2b and Tos., s.v. "d'asur." Cf. B. Me'ilah 18a–b, Tos., s.v. "ayn" and "v'omer;" Y. Kiddushin 3.1/63c.

74. See, e.g., Cant. 6:8.

75. *Hilkhot Ishut,* 1.4 à la *Sifre:* Devarim, no. 260, ed. Finkelstein, 283; *Sifra:* Qedoshim, ed. Weiss, 90d; T. Kiddushin 1.4 re Lev. 20:14. See B. Sanhedrin 82a re Mal. 2:11 and Maimonides, *Moreh Nevukhim,* 3.49, trans. Pines, 603.

76. See J. Reider, *Deuteronomy with Commentary* (Philadelphia, 1948), 217.

77. R. Vidal of Tolosa, *Maggid Mishneh on Maimonides. Hilkhot Ishut,* 1.4.

78. See note of R. Abraham ben David of Posquières (Rabad) on Maimonides, *Hilkhot Ishut,* 1.4; Nahmanides, *Responsa Ha-Ramban,* ed. C. B. Chavel (Jerusalem, 1975), no. 105; R. Solomon ibn Adret, *Responsa Ha-Rashba* (Jerusalem, 1960), 4, no. 314.

79. See Novak, *Law and Theology in Judaism,* 2:121–22.

80. See B. Sanhedrin 21a re 2 Sam. 5:13; Y. Ketubot 5.2/29d. Most concubines were captives taken in war. The Talmud considers the scriptural permission to take a war bride (Deut. 21:10–14) as a compromise with lust (see B. Kiddushin 21b–22a and B. Sanhedrin 59a). Indeed, the initial contact of the Jewish soldier with such a woman was premarital, i.e., her status was that of a concubine. See Maimonides, *Hilkhot Melakhim,* 8.5–6; also B. Kiddushin 22a, Tos. s.v. "she-lo" (cf. Rashi, s.v. "she-lo"); Y. Makkot 2.6/31d.

81. See Feldman, *Birth Control in Jewish Law,* 38ff.

82. *Beresheet Rabbah* 23.2, ed. Theodor-Albeck, 1:222–23.

83. See, e.g., Gen. 16:5; 21:10; 30:15; also M. Sanhedrin 2.4 re Deut. 17:17 and B. Sanhedrin 21b re 1 Kings 11:4.

84. *Beresheet Rabbah* 18.3 re Gen. 2:22.

85. See B. Kiddushin 4b, Tos., s.v. "haykha" and 7a.

86. Y. Kiddushin 1.1/58c. Cf. Y. Baba Batra 8.1/15d–16a; Josephus, *Antiquities,* 15.259.

87. *Hilkhot Ishut,* 1.1. Cf. *Hilkhot Melakhim,* 9.8.

88. *Hilkhot Ishut,* 4.1. See B. Yevamot 110a and B. Baba Batra 48b.

89. Thus the original scriptural permission to initiate marriage by a publicly evident (although not seen—B. Gittin 81b) act of sexual intercourse (M. Kiddushin 1.1; T. Kiddushin 1.3; *Sifre:* Devarim, no. 268; Y. Kiddushin 1.1/58b) was later removed in the interest of public propriety. See B. Kiddushin 12b; also B. Ketubot 56a and Maimonides, *Hilkhot Ishut,* 10.2.

90. This point was brilliantly expounded by S. Atlas, *Netivim Be-Mishpat Ha'Ivri* (New York, 1978), 246–47; also see Novak, *Halakhah in a Theological Dimension*, 34–36.

91. B. Ketubot 7b.

92. Y. Berakhot 9.1/12d.

93. Niddah 31b; B. Kiddushin 30b; Y. Kiddushin 1.7/61b.

94. See his *Elementary Forms of the Religious Life*, trans. J. W. Swain (New York, 1965), 236–37. For a theological critique of the equation of society and transcendence, see Novak, *Law and Theology in Judaism*, 2:19–20.

95. See B. Gittin 90b; Novak, *Law and Theology in Judaism*, 1:12–14.

96. See *Shir Ha-Shirim Rabbah* 1.11; also my late revered teacher Saul Lieberman, appendix to G. Scholem, *Jewish Gnosticism and Merkabah Mysticism* (New York, 1960), 118ff.

97. See, e.g., R. Gordis, *The Song of Songs and Lamentations*, rev. ed. (New York, 1974), 1–3.

98. See Feuerbach, *The Essence of Christianity*, trans. M. Evans (London, 1893), secs. 643–44; Freud, *The Future of an Illusion*, trans. W. D. Robson-Scott (Garden City, N.Y., 1964), 48ff.; *supra*, 57f.

99. *Zohar:* Lekh Lekha, 1:85b. See also *The Holy Letter*, chap. 2, trans. S. J. Cohen (New York, 1970), 48–49, 58–59.

100. See R. Isaac bar Sheshet Parfat, *Responsa Ha-Ribash* (Constantinople, 1574), no. 159.

101. Thus an important scholar of Jewish mysticism, R. J. Z. Werblowsky writes, "The Jewish kabbalist . . . performed his marital duties with mystico-theurgic intentions, but realized that he was not allowed to give himself up either to his partner or to his passion. Transformed, in theory, into a sacramental act, the 'holy union' of husband and wife was in practice an ascetic exercise which admitted of no genuine relationship between the partners because the kabbalist had to identify with the mystical intention of the act and not with its actuality." *Joseph Karo: Lawyer and Mystic* (Oxford, 1962), 137.

102. See Isa. 40:6–8; Job 19:25–26; also 1 Sam. 13:15 and M. Avot 5.16.

103. Thus the late-nineteenth-century English poet Robert Bridges wrote in his poem "Eros":

Why has thou nothing in thy face?
Thou idol of the human race,
Thou tyrant of the human heart,
The flower of lovely youth thou art;
Yea, and thou standest in thy youth
An image of eternal Truth. . . .

Seven Centuries of Verse, 2d rev. ed., ed. A. J. M. Smith (New York, 1957), 543–44.

104. For the inconceivability of unembodied human life, see *Vayiqra Rabbah* 4.5. For embodiment as a limit, see Maimonides, *Hilkhot Yesoday Ha-Torah*, 1.7; *Moreh Nevukhim*, 1.49.

105. *Vayiqra Rabbah* 14.5, ed. Margulies, 2:308.

106. See Maurice Merleau-Ponty, *Phenomenology of Perception*, trans. C. Smith (London, 1962), 148ff.

107. See B. Kiddushin 54a and parallels; *Shir Ha-Shirim Rabbah* 8.13 re Num. 19:14.

108. See R. Moses Cordovero, *Tomer Devorah*, chap. 9. Cf. Plato, *Symposium*, 202E.

109. Freud writes, "But towards the outer world at any rate the ego seems to keep itself clearly outlined and delimited. There is only one state of mind in which it fails to do this. . . . At its height the state of being in love threatens to obliterate the boundaries between the ego and object." (*Civilization and Its Discontents*, trans. J. Riviere [Garden City, N.Y., 1958], 3.) He then goes on, "Originally the ego includes everything, later it detaches from itself the external world. The ego feeling we are aware of now is thus only a shrunken vestige of a far

more extensive feeling—a feeling which embraced the universe and expressed an inseparable connection of the ego with the external world" (p. 6). For Freud, sexual love is the experience of the strongest pleasure. Even more than other pleasures it is a *taking-in* of the external world, a narcissistic reduction of sorts. But the phenomenology of sexual love seems to indicate that it is essentially the intention of the *other,* irreducible to the embodied ego or any of its functions. As such, sexual love is transcendent in essence; it is not enclosed in an immediately human (and, for Freud, individual) circle. In other words, there is an essential difference between sexual love and all other "pleasures." The difference between sexual love and all other pleasures is generic, not just specific, as it is for Freud.

110. *Shir Ha-Shirim Rabbah* 8.6. It might be useful to compare this ancient Jewish statement about the essence of love with a modern one. In his 1927 novel *The Bridge of San Luis Rey* (2d ed. [New York, 1955], 148), Thornton Wilder concludes with these words: "But soon we shall die and all memory . . . will have left, and we ourselves shall be loved for a while and forgotten. But the love will have been enough; all those impulses of love return to the love that made them. Even memory is not necessary for love. There is a land of the living and a land of the dead and the bridge is love, the only survival, the only meaning." If love, as Wilder seems to be saying, is a *state of being* (as we would say today, "I am in love"), then it is conceivable that it can transcend individual persons and individual memories. But if love is an act, then it is only a person who can consciously *do* it. If, then, we can love with an undying love, it is only because we have been loved by God.

19

Down-To-Earth Judaism: Sexuality

ARTHUR WASKOW

What about the issues of sexual ethics that for many Jews today pose extraordinarily puzzling and painful dilemmas in their daily lives? Few progressive Jews—indeed, rather few Jews of almost any political and religious hue—turn to the traditional Jewish code of sexual behavior as an authoritative or practical guide to their own actual behavior. Most of us feel strongly that the tradition as it was conveyed to us does not resonate with our own values and that indeed, for us, hardly any collective or communal ethical code could apply, because sexual ethics depends so much on unique individual situations. So an approach paralleling what we have suggested about food—a sort of "Commission on Practical Jewish Sexual Ethics"—seems laughable and neither possible nor desirable.

But many of us do not feel we are doing so well when we try to act totally on our own, either. Indeed, the problems many liberal and progressive Jews now face in shaping their sexual ethics is one of the strongest pieces of evidence that a wholly individualistic ethic, not in some sense shaped by interaction between communal and individual needs, is destructive to individuals as well as to communities. So even here it may be useful to see whether aspects of Jewish practice might help many of us sort out deep doubts and confusion in our sexual lives.[1]

What is it in the tradition that we reject or profoundly question?

There are several areas in which a great deal of doubt is expressed, whether in quiet practice or in public questioning. Among these areas of doubt are:

- sexual activity by unmarried people;
- sexual activity between people of the same gender;
- sexual monogamy in marriage;
- the breadth of acceptable sexual practice in whatever kind of relationship.

We will look at each of these areas in some detail; but first let us explore why the traditional sexual ethics in these areas seems out of tune, or questionable.

For most of Jewish tradition, the link between sex and procreation was very strong—though not absolute. This connection strongly influenced rabbinic attitudes about masturbation, homosexuality, contraception, abortion, and marriage. The rabbis paid great attention to the first of all the commandments: "Be fruitful and multiply, and fill up the earth."

In our generation, however, it is possible to argue that the commandment has been so thoroughly fulfilled by the human race as a whole that it no longer needs to be obeyed by all human beings. The earth is filled up; we have done Your bidding; what comes next?

Since "Be fruitful and multiply" is the command that comes at the outset of the Garden of Eden story, perhaps what comes next is Eden for grown-ups: the garden of the Song of Songs. The sexual ethic of the Song of Songs focuses not on children, marriage, or commitment, but on sensual pleasure and loving companionship. What if we were to take this as a teaching for our epoch? What if we were to look at the human race as a whole as if it had entered that period of maturity that a happily married couple enters when they no longer can (or want to) have children? They continue to connect sexually for the sake of pleasure and love—and so could the human race and the Jewish people. Without denigrating the forms of sexuality that focus on children and family, we might find the forms of sexuality that focus on pleasure more legitimate at this moment of human and Jewish history than ever before.

With this broader understanding in mind, let us turn to the specific areas in which ethical doubts and questions have arisen.

First, in regard to sexual activity by unmarried people: most Jews reject in their own practice and in theory the traditional adherence to early marriage and the traditional opposition to sexual activity by unmarried people. The two sentiments are connected. Few American Jews believe that early marriages are wise in our complex society, where personalities, careers, and life paths almost never jell in the teens and often not until the mid-thirties, sometimes come unjelled during the forties and fifties, and usually change again with long-lived retirements beginning in the sixties or seventies. It is hard enough to make stable lifelong marriages when one partner is changing in this way; when both are changing, it becomes extremely difficult.

There are several different conceivable responses to this situation:

1. Reverse the basic situation and restore the kind of society in which life patterns are set close to the onset of puberty and do not change much. Few American Jews believe this can be, or should be, done. The Hasidic communities, however, may be showing that for a subcommunity such a society can be created.

2. Accept the notions that first marriages will occur many years after sexual awakening and that most marriages will end while the partners are sexually active and alert—and practice celibacy for long periods of unmarried time. This is the solution that almost all American Jews have rejected. It is also, however, the solution that they identify as the "official" position of Jewish tradition and religious authority. There are few public assertions by religious authorities or communities that this is *not* the "correct" Jewish view, and almost no public Jewish way of honoring or celebrating sexual relationships other than marriage exists.

This chasm between the practice and the understanding of the Jewish tradition may be one of the most powerful elements driving most Jews in their premarried, sexually active years—from sixteen to thirty-one—and in their "postmarried" sexually active years away from Jewish life. Who wants to be part of an institution that looks with hostility or contempt on the source of much of one's most intense pleasure, joy, and fulfillment? ;

3. Accept the fact that life patterns will change several times in any person's

lifetime and that marriages will change accordingly, and greatly change our expectation of "marriage" so that it carries fewer burdens of financial, emotional, and other involvement. In other words, make it easy for sexually active people from puberty on to enter and leave marriages—make marriage a much "lighter" contract unless children result from it. But to make marriages "light" enough so that sixteen-year-olds or eighteen-year-olds easily could enter them, expecting to exit from them at twenty—and to enter and exit again at twenty-one, twenty-five, twenty-eight, thirty-two—would make that kind of "marriage" so different from one that provides an adequate context for child rearing that it is hard to imagine the two sharing the same name. (Note that many American marriages are dissolving even during the child-rearing years. Should leaving marriages be "light" then too? Or is the distinction one that most Jews would want to keep?)

For those Jews who try to abide by *halakhah,* it might be easier to use the traditional labels and forms of marriage and redefine the content than to follow the paths listed above or those listed below. The Talmud, for example (*Yebamot* 37b), mentions that a few of the rabbis, when they went on what we would call lecture tours, would marry a woman one night and divorce her the next morning. In that period, of course, men were permitted to practice polygamy—so such a practice of "light" marriage did not undermine simultaneous "heavy" marriage—at least not in law.

4. Accept and publicly honor the fact that many unmarried people are sexually active and that there are likely to be periods of "fluidity" in sexuality during any life path—without creating standards of ethical behavior for unmarried sexual relationships or creating ceremonial or legal definitions of them. This is basically the pattern followed by the burgeoning *havurot* (participatory and relatively informal congregations of prayer and study). In many of them, married couples and unmarried people who are fluidly coupled and uncoupled share the same communal space. Acceptance of unmarried sexual activity has been high and public, with little effort to set standards or to deal with painful experiences except among close friends or with the help of psychotherapists who themselves use only such "Jewish" sources as Freud, Reich, Fromm, and Perls.

This solution is not as opposed to Jewish tradition as many of us suppose, for there are many references in the traditional literature that legitimate sex between unmarried people. (See, for example, in the thirteenth-century Nachmanides—#2 in Responsa—and in the eighteenth-century Rabbi Jacob Emden, cited in Gershon Winkler, "Sex and Religion: Friend or Foe?" in *New Menorah,* second series, no. 7, pp. 1–3.) But the main definitive statements of traditional law in the last four centuries—particularly in the popular Jewish consciousness in Eastern Europe whence most of our grandparents came—ignored these permissive authorities.

5. Redefine marriage and create new Jewishly affirmed forms of sexual relationships that are to be publicly defined with certain standards and are to be ceremonially honored. Certain vestiges of ancient tradition might even be drawn upon for such new forms—the *pilegesh* relationship, for example, which is usually translated "concubine" but has great openness to legal, practical, and ceremonial definition.

We could imagine three different basic forms of sexual relationship: Times of great fluidity, when the community might affirm only such basic norms as honesty and the avoidance of coercion, without expecting monogamy or emotional intimacy;

Times of commitment without great permanence, when notice of a *pilegesh* relationship is given to a face-to-face Jewish community—not to the state—and is defined by the people entering it (explicitly monogamous or not, explicitly living together or not, explicitly sharing some financial arrangements or not, etc.). In this pattern, the community joins in honoring, acting in accord with, and celebrating such arrangements, and there is an easy public form by which either of the parties may dissolve the relationship.

Times of marriage, which may also be partly defined by the couple through the *ketuba,* but which are expected to be more long-lasting, to be essential for child rearing (though used also by couples who do not expect to have children), and to be dissolved only by joint agreement of the couple and by serious participation of the Jewish community as well as the civil order in arranging the terms of separation.

This last approach, it seems to me, takes the complexity of our present situation and the resources of Jewish tradition most fully into account. But it would take more than a piece of paper announcing *pilegesh* for this approach to begin functioning. Let us come back to the necessary institutional processes after we have looked at the other areas of doubt that exist in our practice of sexual ethics.

There is much less agreement about sexual relationships between men, or between women, in the Jewish world than about heterosexual relationships between unmarried people. Many American Jews—probably a majority—support guarantees for the civil and employment rights of gays and lesbians. What seems to be a growing minority is ready to assert that a gay or lesbian life path can be a fully and authentically Jewish life path. Somewhat fewer are ready to act in such ways that would allow publicly gay and lesbian Jews to become rabbis, communal Jewish leaders, members of broad-spectrum congregations, and celebrants of life-cycle transformations such as weddings.

The written texts of Jewish tradition and most of the actual practices of the majority of Jewish communities are more heavily weighted against the public acceptance of gay and lesbian life paths than they are against the acceptance of sexual relationships between unmarried heterosexuals. When we look at the most ancient texts, however, some of them may turn out to be slightly more ambiguous than we are used to assuming. For example, what are we to make of the fact that the Bible gives us no obvious prohibition against lesbian relationships? What are we to make of the Bible's celebration of David's love for Jonathan—whose "love was more pleasing than the love of women"?

There can be no doubt that during the rabbinic era of Jewish history most communities and rabbis were strongly hostile to homosexuality on the part of men or women. Yet even in the rabbinic era, Jewish practice may not have been so single-valued as we usually assume. During the Golden Age of Jewish culture in Spain, more than one of the greatest liturgical poets of the period, whose poems grace our traditional Siddur, also wrote poetry of homosexual love. Did these poems rise out of life experience, or only out of literary convention? Even if the latter, what does that say about our assumptions regarding Torah-true Jews and Judaism?

For us to think intelligently about these questions today, we must go beyond biblical texts and rabbinic rulings—even beyond our own midrashic understanding of the texts—to try to hear what may have been the hopes and fears that were at stake; to take them seriously; and then to see where we ourselves come out, trying to hold together all the values that are bespoken by Torah and Jewish life.

Two of the strongest strands of Torah are the hostility to idolatry and the importance of having children. Indeed, one of the deepest traumas of the Jewish psyche seems to have been the fear of not being able to have children—as expressed in the stories of Abraham and Sarah, Isaac and Rebekah, Jacob and Leah and Rachel. The story of slavery in Egypt focuses on the danger that children would be murdered. So do the attacks on Canaanite religion—claiming that in it, children were "passed through the fire to Moloch." Whether or not these descriptions are accurate, they bespeak a deep Israelite concern for producing the next generation.

In such a culture, homosexuality might have seemed a dangerous diversion from fecundity. If, as seems likely, the practice of sacred homosexuality was also part of the worship of the surrounding "idolatrous" cultures of Canaan, then the hostility of the Israelites to homosexuality would have been doubled. As the rabbis encountered Hellenism, with its nontheistic or polytheistic philosophies, its emphasis on the body as an end in itself, and its approval of homosexuality, the Jewish hostility to homosexuality might have been intensified even further.

If these are the concerns that underlie the traditional view, then we may see the issue differently today—perhaps in a manner closer to that of the Golden Age in Spain. We too, in the era of the H-bomb, are concerned about whether there will be a next generation. But we also live in an era of a population explosion. It is clear that the human race as a whole has much more to fear from violence and environmental destruction as threats to its children than from the failure to reproduce. It is true that the Jewish people are not experiencing a population explosion, but in an era when conversion to Judaism is at an extraordinarily high level, the actual need to procreate is not so extreme, even for Jews. What is more, gay and lesbian Jews have been exploring the possibility of having children and rearing them as Jews. So the reproduction issue is not nearly so problematic for openness to homosexual practice as it once was.

As I have already suggested, we may live in an era when the sexual ethic celebrated by the Song of Songs—an ethic of sexual pleasure and love—comes into its own alongside the sexual ethic of family. It may seem ironic that the Song of Songs, one of the greatest celebrations of heterosexual sexuality in all of literature, might be taken to affirm the homosexual community's bent toward sex as pleasurable and loving rather than as procreative. But sometimes ironies bear truth. If any community of Jews in our epoch embodies the values of the Song of Songs (taken at its literal meaning, not allegorically), it is the community of gay and lesbian Jews. Perhaps in our epoch, then, the despised and rejected gay subcommunity may turn out to be the unexpected bearer of a newly important teaching. As the tradition teaches, sometimes the stone that the builders rejected becomes the cornerstone of the Temple.

In this light, it is especially poignant that the sexual ethics of commitment and family have taken on new seriousness within the gay community as a result of the impact of AIDS. It is as if the two ethics, ghettoized from each other and embodied in separate communities, have now formed a more holistic sexual ethic that can incorporate the values of family, commitment, procreation, sensual pleasure, and loving companionship.

If another of the ancient Jewish objections to homosexuality was the belief that it was connected with idolatry or Hellenistic philosophy—today it seems clear that homosexual practice accords with the same range of dedication to and rejection of honesty, modesty, fidelity, intimacy, spiritual searching, holiness, and God as does heterosexual practice. If multiple sexual partnerships, as reportedly practiced in certain specific gay male subcultures, seem incompatible with most Jewish values, then care must be taken both to avoid categorizing all homosexuality in that subculture and to note that there exist similar heterosexual subcultures in our society as well. In other words, if the basic value at stake is some level of stability and focus in sexual relationships, then that value ought to be affirmed without regard to the sexual orientation of the partners; and it is also importannt to be clear about whether we will respect a "time of fluidity" in sexual practice of the kind that we already have sketched.

Two other factors recently have come into play that have their own connections to values of Torah. One is the discovery that for some large proportion of gay men and some (perhaps smaller) proportion of lesbians, homosexuality is not a matter of choice—but of identity set either genetically or very early in life. For those who continue to accept the traditional understandings of *halakhah,* this discovery has brought into discussion the *halakhic* principle that absolves of "sin" those who act under compulsion. At a more Aggadic level, this relatively new discovery raises the question of whether a community that has celebrated the Song of Songs as "the Holy of Holies," imagined its own relationship with God as that of spouse and lover, and refused to make a virtue of heterosexual celibacy ought to be insisting that someone whose deepest sexual identity is homosexual and who cannot experience sexual pleasure with a partner of the other gender should choose a life of celibacy or of privatized, closeted, stifled sexuality rather than one of publicly affirmed homosexuality.

The other new factor is an increasing sense that gay men and lesbians are an oppressed community, "strangers in the land" as we were strangers in the land of Egypt, fellow victims (though not in the same way) of the Nazi Holocaust, and therefore to be treated as the Torah commands that "strangers," the excluded and oppressed, be treated: with love, respect, and equality.

Once we have noted the Torah's demand that the stranger be treated with justice and love, we should also note that it may be precisely the "strangeness" of homosexuality that is at the root of the fear and hatred that has been expressed toward it. Perhaps it is not the desire for children nor the hatred of idolatry that has been the root of the rejection of homosexuals—but rather the fear of what is different, strange, queer. ("What do they *do* in bed, anyway?") Especially the fear that "I myself" am somewhat different, strange, queer—different from the person I have advertised myself to be. The deep fear that when I take a close look at the strange face of the stranger, it will turn out to look a great deal like the strange face in my mirror. The Torah repeats the command to love and respect the stranger thirty-six times—a hint that this command is not easy to obey. We could honestly face its difficulty, and then persevere in our perennially difficult task of embodying Torah. So in our generation it may be necessary for the Jewish community as a whole, in the light of *all* of these values, to reexamine its attitudes toward gay, lesbian, and heterosexual Jews. Is there a way to reaffirm the importance of raising the next generation of Jewish children without denigrating homosexual practice—indeed by affirming the right, the ability, and the duty of *all* Jews to join in that work? Is there a way to develop an ethic of sexual relationships that takes into account the experience of gay and lesbian as well as heterosexual relationships, while the ethic itself addresses the quality of the relationship—not the gender of the partners? Is there a way of celebrating God as Lover and Spouse with images that work for Jews of all sexual orientations?

In my judgment it is possible and desirable to move in these directions—to reexamine ways in which all the values of Torah can be upheld, rather than upholding some (such as fecundity) while shattering others (such as free and equal participation in the community) for part of the Jewish people. On such a path, the values that seem to have been the reasons for celebrating heterosexuality do not need to be discarded. On such a path the choices do not need to be Either/Or—but Both/And-What-Is-More.

If this is the path that a new Jewish sexual ethic is to take, we will need to work out ways for congregations and communities to open up prayer, life-cycle celebration, *tzedakah, shalom bayit,* and other aspects of Jewish life to full and public participation by gay, lesbian, bisexual, and heterosexual Jews. No matter what sexual ethic we develop about the nature, techniques, and celebration of different forms of sexual relationships, it could be applied equally to sexual partnerships regardless of the gender of the partners. Homosexual marriages, homosexual *pilegesh* relationships, and homosexual "fluid" time could all be treated in the same way as their heterosexual equivalents.

The question of what sexual ethic should operate within a marriage is another area of doubt. The asserted norm, for most Jews, continues to be sexual monogamy and fidelity for married people. But a sizable number violate this norm in practice, and the community is certainly unclear what sanctions to apply. Should known adulterers be expelled from congregations? Denied leadership offices? Denied honors such as being called up to read Torah? Admonished privately? Treated as if their sexual behavior were irrelevant?

The question becomes more complicated when some argue that the norm is disobeyed in practice not because people are perverse, but because the norm is untenable—at least for many couples. Should couples then make their own decisions whether their particular *ketubah* requires monogamy? Are sexual relationships outside marriage "adultery" only if the partners entered a commitment to monogamy, and one then betrays that commitment? Or does the community as a whole have a stake in affirming that a "marriage" should be monogamous?

A very few voices have suggested approaching the question by drawing on one of the oldest strands of Jewish sexual ethics—the openness to certain forms of polygamy. Until one thousand years ago among Western Jews, and until a few years ago among Eastern Jews, it was legitimate, though unusual, for men to have more than one wife. Was there any wisdom in allowing this possibility? Because one of the main reasons it was abandoned was the protection of women, who were deeply unequal in status, does the reason for the prohibition of polygamy still stand, or do changes in the status of women suggest that instead the prohibition be ended and men and women both be allowed to take several mates? (For those who would like to avoid a radical break from traditional *halakhah,* the latter decision would be a great deal harder to accomplish.) Or, since the other main reason that polygamy was forbidden to Western Jews was that it exposed them to contempt in Christian eyes, does the incredulity or ridicule that the notion provokes in many people suggest that polygamy is still viewed with contempt in the West and should still be avoided—that de facto adultery is less dangerous than de jure polygamy?

To point out how hard some of the questions about "adultery" are, consider the following hypothetical case: A well-known leader of the Jewish community approaches his rabbi and the lay leaders of his synagogue. He has been lovingly married for many years. His wife has for several years been institutionalized with a debilitating and disabling but not fatal illness. He has cared for her with love and devoted attentiveness. Her illness has now been diagnosed as incurable. He does not wish to divorce her, for that would damage her both financially and emotionally: Yet he cannot bear to live forever lonely. He has come to love another woman, and wants her to live with him and be his sexual and emotional partner. What is the view of the congregation?

Should the Jewish community force this leader to retire rather than let him carry on such a relationship, considering his high visibility in Jewish and public life? Or should he be retired simply on the ground that adultery is forbidden? Should the community tolerate his life path, provided he leads it in secret? Should it insist that he divorce his wife? Should it affirm his choices as being in accordance with Judaism under the circumstances? Or should it perhaps refuse to decide at all, and leave the whole matter to individual conscience?

Even in less agonizing situations, some who assert that they do in fact live by the monogamous norm and some who assert that they have agreed to "open," nonmonogamous marriages both report enormous social pressure against their decisions. Among the monogamous, some report that in a society suffused with sexual attractions, even close-knit Jewish communities do not act fully supportive of their commitment to monogamy, but that some members of the community act both sexually seductive and politically contemptuous, as if such a commitment were old-fashioned and repressive. Some also report that when they seek emotional intimacy outside marriage, not intending to include a sexual relationship as part of the intimacy, both they and their friends find it hard to draw the lines.

As for those who assert that their marriages are "open" and nonmonogamous, some also report that their communities treat them with derision or fear, and some report that they experience intense jealousy and fear of loss. In both groups, some say ruefully that hypocrisy turns out to be more comfortable to live with than either a clear commitment to monogamy or nonmonogamy in theory as well as practice.

Finally, there is the area of doubt about specific sexual practices in any relationship, without regard to who the partner is. Here again, the tradition is more permissive in some areas than some modern Jews assume—though in other areas a great deal more restrictive than most modern Jews would accept in their life practice. For example, some of the rabbis for centuries have approved of both oral and anal sex where the partners find these the source of greatest pleasure. (See, for example, Maimonides, *Mishnah Torah, Hilkhos Issurei Biah,* 21:9, cited in Winkler, *New Menorah,* second series, no. 7.) On the other hand, the rules of *niddah,* prohibiting sexual relations during the menstrual period (and a good many days afterward) have been a clear biblical-rabbinic tradition. Most liberal and progressive Jews see *niddah* as a regressive rejection of femaleness in that it rejects menstruation as an "unclean" time and process; but in our generation it has been explained by Rachel Adler as a way of honoring the uncanny edge of life-and-death that is involved in menstruation's casting off of a viable egg cell, and by others as a way of creating a rhythm of separation and renewal between two sexual partners. Similarly, the opposition of much of Jewish tradition to the use of some forms of contraception has been rejected by most liberal and progressive Jews.

Discussions of *niddah,* however, have turned up suggestions of ways to affirm some of the values that may be at stake without denigrating women. When one couple who were in disagreement about the question asked for help from a feminist leader of the movement for Jewish renewal, she suggested that they explore separating sexually for the days of Rosh Chodesh—the new moon—rather than at the time of menstruation. In this way they could experience the rhythm of separation and return without focusing on menstruation. Others have suggested refraining from sex for just a day or two of the menstrual cycle, thus honoring its occurrence without defining it as unclean.

The more basic possibility underlying these responses is that they come not from law or judgmental sentiments, but from nurturing wisdom, seeking to reconcile deeply held values that did not need to be seen as contradictory and drawing on Jewish tradition in new ways without rigidly obeying strictures that have risen in the past. In a sense, the feminist whom the couple consulted acted as a rabbi not judging as part of a *beit din* (house of legal judgment) but as part of a *beit rachamim* or *beit chesed* (house of nurturing love) or perhaps a *beit seichel* (house of prudence). Pursuing this approach on matters of sexual ethics could be one of the most important steps that Jewish communities and congregations could take. Imagine how different attitudes toward the rich fabric of Jewish thought and practice might become, and how unnecessary the desperate loneliness of people now faced with decisions they see as utterly individual, if every synagogue and *havurah* were to create a panel of women and men noted for their practical *chesed* and *seichel* from whom a person or a couple in an agony of doubt and pain over sexual issues could choose one or a few people with whom to counsel.

We might even consider making it a matter of communal ethical agreement and obligation that before undertaking a major change in sexual relationships, congregants were required—not simply encouraged—to consult with such a *beit chesed.* Whether they followed its recommendations would be up to them. The legal obligation would go not to the content but to the process of consultation. Such an understanding suggests one way to resolve the tug between individual and communal desires.

The decision to create such *b'tei chesed* might begin in any congregation—and if it worked, would spread. Some of the other decisions I have suggested—for instance, a clear and public affirmation that there are three different "times" or kinds of legitimate and holy sexual relationships, the clarification of *pilegesh* relationships, the clear legitimation of homosexual relationships—would require statements by authoritative individuals or groups in Jewish life. Even the clarification of the process of ending a Jewish marriage would require not only a new decision by the Reform movement to insist that a *get* or Jewish divorce is necessary along with a civil divorce to end a Jewish marriage—but a decision by *all* branches of Jewish life to issue a *get* not simply as a formula, but after serious consultation with the couple on the conditions of the end of the marriage.

How do we get these processes of change going, at both the grass-roots and institutional levels? These, like the similar questions about a commission on ethical *Kashrut* and about a network of *tzedekah* activists, we are now ready to address.

In the three down-to-earth areas we have examined in this two-part article, we have suggested both a philosophical outlook on how to apply Jewish tradition in creative rather than rigid ways and some practical suggestions on how to get the process going. There remains, however, a key question: Who shall organize the organizers? When *Moment* magazine put forward the brilliantly simple proposal that Jews should add 3 percent of the cost of their celebratory meals to a fund for feeding the world's hungry, the resulting wave of popular approval from the Jewish community was almost enough to make the pieces of institution-building come together into the organization Mazon.[2] But the proposals we are making will take more time and sweat than that, because the religiopolitical nature of the proposals is more complex and more arguable—just as it took years to get the New Israel Fund off the ground. (And even the New Israel Fund was careful to avoid challenging the secular *"halakhah"* of the UJA, let alone the traditional *halakhah* on issues as hot as sexuality.)

Who will organize the organizers? Who will bring into being a Commission on Ethical Kashrut, a network of wise and loving *b'tei chesed* and *b'tei seichel,* a network of *tzedakah* collectives? I think we need to have what might be called a "Center for Down-to-Earth Judaism"—a center for infusing the daily nitty-gritty of the lives of Jews with Jewish content drawn from a creative response to Torah.

Such a center would pull together the information, the mailing lists, the newsletters, the practical "sh'elahs and tshuvahs" (questions and answers in a new version of the rabbinic mode) that could help weave a fabric of Jewish lving in the workaday time that is not Shabbat or festival, not wedding day or funeral. If this weaving is done in the way and with the openness and experimental outlook we have suggested, there should be few among us who end up feeling trapped in the narrowness and rigidity that we may remember of the tradition. Indeed, we may discover once again that Judaism need not be an inwardly focused system of answers that are already known, answers given to questions that concern only Jews. Judaism can become instead a path for exploring new questions, questions that arise for all human beings as we remake our world—and a path on which the answers themselves can be fluid and creative.

The particularities of the Jewish path will then be seen as "shareable insights." As we draw on our own special history, life experience, and tradition to answer these universal questions, we can both learn from the experiences of others and share our own with them.

As we have looked at specific issues and specific new approaches, we have kept noting that an atmosphere of Both/And-What-Is-More might emerge, quite different from the atmosphere of Either/Or that for many of us seems linked to the traditional Jewish life path. If indeed there is some way to "institutionalize" this atmosphere, then the demons and nightmares of a generation of Jews who fled from narrowness and "command" might be exorcised. For in this atmosphere there is neither rigid command nor utter fluidity; neither utter antinomianism nor utter individuality. There is structure, there are boundaries, there are communal institutions to give communal guidance—*not* command.

In this new atmosphere, the new *kashrut* is understood to come not from a "commander" outside and above us, but from a sense of loving connection between humans and the earth, among those who do the work of growing, moving, shaping, and cooking food, among those who sit to eat it and between them and all these others. In this new atmosphere, the new sexual ethics are seen to emerge not from a "commander" outside and above us, but from the need to make worthy, honest, decent, and stable loving connections among ourselves. So too with a new financial ethic.

These new approaches may lead us toward a redirection of our spiritual searchings, a relocation or re-imaging of what is God and godly—indeed a reconnection of our sense of spiritual wholeness with our sense of social justice. For here the sense of justice, of ethical behavior, springs precisely *not* from rules but from the yearning for wholeness, for harmonious connection between the different parts of a whole that is yearning to be whole, to be *Shalem*.

This *is* a new approach, but there are ancient seeds of it. As we walk this path, we can remind ourselves that Judaism does see the mundane, the down-to-earth, suffused with a sense of community, a sense of intellect, and a sense of the spirit. Perhaps a down-to-earth Judaism should root itself in what is probably the earthiest passage in all of Torah:

> You shall have a place outside the camp, and there you shall go forth—outside. And you shall have a spade among your tools and weapons so that when you squat outside there, you shall dig with it and turn the earth to cover what comes forth from you—your excrement. For the Breath of Life is your God, moving within your camp to sustain you and deliver you from enemies; let your camp be holy, so that I see nothing unseemly in you and turn away from you. (Deut. 23:13–15)

Let us take delight in a Torah so earthy as to see in the health of the person, the health of the community, and the health of the land, the presence of the God Who is the Breath of Life. And let us see this Torah as a holy spade to dig with—to remove outside our living space those ways of being that are unseemly: the waste products of exploitation, division, and oppression that come forth from a society that is dealing badly with food, sex, and money. If we can eliminate these hostile ways of being, turn them under and cover them over with the spade of Torah, the very act of doing so can enrich the soil that gives birth to the next generation—can make fertile our sense of community with each other and with the earth.

Notes

1. In developing the ideas below, I have drawn on conversations with Rabbi Zalman Schachter-Shalomi, founder and chair of the P'nai Or Religious Fellowship, and Phyllis Berman, president of the P'nai Or board. In addition, some of the ideas come from a pioneering article on Jewish sexual ethics in the *Second Jewish Catalog,* by Rabbi Arthur Green, now president of the Reconstructionist Rabbinical College.

2. Information about Mazon can be acquired by writing: Mazon, 2940 Westwood Blvd., Suite 7, Los Angeles, CA 90064.

20

Jewish Family Ethics in a
Post-*halakhic* Age

MARTHA A. ACKELSBERG

My vision of the Jewish future is centered in a revitalized and inclusive Jewish community, the members of which are engaged in a continuing struggle to realize the presence of God in their midst. Such a community would value and support those characteristics we have come to associate with families: making it possible for people to achieve and sustain relationships of intimacy, solidarity, and nurturance; fostering mutual support and interdependence; and providing opportunities to express generativity. It would be a community that recognizes that people may express or experience those characteristics, needs, and potentials in a variety of contexts and constellations; a community that would not limit its members to expressing them, or having them met, only within the structures that have traditionally been defined as "family." In fact, structures that have worked in the past are no longer dominant (whether in the Jewish community or outside it) and are often no longer functioning well. If our communities are fully to meet the needs of their members, we must be open to changing forms that have traditionally addressed those needs.

The title of this essay bespeaks the assumptions that underlie our conversations, the questions we confront, the tools and approaches we have at our disposal. First, the term *post-halakhic:* The term takes for granted that we find ourselves in, at best, a complicated relationship to *halakhah* (Jewish law)—possibly even a relationship that can only be described in the past tense. It implies that what has been handed down to us is not necessarily adequate for our situation, that we are in a time of transition and redefinition. At the same time, to use the term "*post-halakhic*," rather than, say "*non- halakhic*," is to assume a continuing presence of halakhah in our lives and communities, even while acknowledging a lack of unanimity as to its interpretation or its binding nature.

A second term calling for attention is *ethics*. To couple that term with "post-*halakhic*" is to presume that it is possible to develop codes of ethics and criteria for behavior even in the absence of unanimity on what constitutes the right path. To be in a state of transition is not necessarily to be without guideposts, though the guides we come to depend on may well be other than the traditional ones.

Finally, the term *family* seems to assume that there is an entity that we know and recognize as such—or, more specifically, as a Jewish family—and that we share (or at least might come to share) an agreement as to what that entity is. Further, the title treats "Jewish family" as a modifier of "ethics"; it assumes that we can develop an ethics that is specifically appropriate to Jewish families—presumably, both in their internal relations and in relations with other families, individuals, and institutions in the community and in the larger society.

I share many, but not all, of the assumptions and presuppositions reflected in this title. I begin with Jewish tradition, but also with a recognition that tradition has changed, and must continue to change, if it is to meet the challenges of the contemporary world. My reading of Jewish history, and my understanding of the world around me, leads me to believe that there never was, nor is there now, any one entity that we can label and define as "the Jewish family." To the extent that we are part of the larger society in which we live, our family forms are necessarily affected by the world around us; they have been many, varied, and changing, and they will continue to be so. For example, in the early stages of Jewish history, the basic unit was the tribe or clan, consisting of many families as we now know them. Later, the extended family became dominant, frequently including adult siblings in the same household. Members of that family often worked closely together for business purposes and in fact may well have understood their relationships more in economic than in emotional terms. The shift away from the extended family to the nuclear family (of mother, father, and their biological children) occurred gradually with industrialization. Further, as trends in recent years indicate, the classic one-marriage nuclear family no longer reflects the experience of the majority of families. We cannot assume, then, that we all mean the same thing by "family."[1] Finally, although I do believe that ethics is possible—and necessary—I am not convinced that there is such a thing as a uniquely Jewish family ethics. Once again, as our lives and communities change, we are called upon to change with them—and not only as Jews. Yet resources for a response to these changes can be found within Jewish tradition. Furthermore, both the community as a whole and families in particular will be strengthened by the changes I advocate here.

Ours is surely a time of major transformations, within both the secular and the Jewish communities of which we are a part. As Jews in the United States, we are hardly sealed off from the changes going on about us; we confront daily the challenges posed to everyone in a society often characterized by a series of "post-" adjectives; postcapitalist, postfeminist, postindustrial, and so on. Much that we once took for granted is now open to repeated examination and questioning. Such moments of transition are trying—they evoke both fear and excitement; fear of what we have lost and might become, excitement about the possibilities of developing new, albeit preliminary, visions of the future. My own perspective is to welcome this moment, and to aim at maximizing the opportunities for growth it offers—both to us as individuals and to the Jewish community as a whole.

The changes and challenges we experience as Jewish citizens of the United States manifest themselves in specific ways when we look at families. Jews have not escaped the trends affecting the society around us; more people are marrying later, or not at all; divorce rates are high; many children are growing up in other than two-parent households (or, at least, in households headed by adults who are not necessarily their biological parents); poverty is on the increase, especially among children and in families headed by women; ever-higher percentages of women are in the work force, making the traditional nuclear family of father who works outside the home and mother who stays home with the children largely a phenomenon of the past. Debates within the Jewish community have targeted many of these changes as potentially disruptive not only to families but to the future of the community itself. Thus, although divorce rates are somewhat lower among Jews than among non-Jews, rates are higher in the Jewish community than they were twenty to thirty years ago; Jewish families tend to form later and to contain fewer children than do non-Jewish families; and an increasing proportion of Jewish young people are choosing to marry non-Jews.[2] For a community that has typically defined "family"—in particular, the traditional nuclear family—as its central building block, these changes can be experienced as threatening, indeed. Any new Jewish family ethics must confront and address these trends.

The Communal Context of Families and Ethics

My own efforts to define a Jewish family ethics begin from the position powerfully articulated by Martin Buber eighty years ago—that it is not family, but community, which is the locus for the realization of God in the world:

> The Divine may come to life in individual man [*sic*], may reveal itself from within individual man; but it attains its earthly fullness only where, having awakened to an awareness of their universal being, individual beings open themselves to one another, disclose themselves to one another, help one another; where immediacy is established between one human being and another; where the sublime stronghold of the individual is unbolted, and man breaks free to meet other men. Where this takes place, where the eternal rises in the Between, the seemingly empty space: that true place of realization is community, and true community is that relationship in which the Divine comes to its realization between man and man.[3]

To understand the community, and relations within it, in this way is to recognize that contemporary Jewish concerns over the breakdown of traditional families may well be misplaced. What matters, I would argue, is not the particular form that our "intimacy constellations"[4] take, but rather whether they provide the between spaces in which we can realize and experience the divine. To the extent that traditional family structures provide such spaces—contexts in which members relate to one another with honesty and openness, mutual respect, and dignity—traditional family structures contribute to the creation and maintenance of a vital Jewish community. Similarly, to the extent that "alternative families," other intimacy constellations, provide contexts in which their members meet one another in relations of honesty and openness, mutual respect, and dignity, they too can be contexts in which we experience the divine, relationships that are essential building blocks of a revitalized Jewish community. The ethical imperative for Jewish communities, then, is to support and sustain all those family forms, regardless of their particular configurations, that provide contexts for striving toward the realization of the divine.

To put it another way, this perspective on the nature and purpose of Jewish community highlights the importance of the quality rather than the form of relationships. It highlights the value and importance of diversity, of the multiplicity of ways we may experience or meet God in our lives, and in our relations with one another.

And it generates a wariness about defining any one pattern of relationship, or of family, as the uniquely acceptable one. As God is one, even as God's faces are manifold and unnameable, so if our community is one, its unity too must incorporate the diversity of its membership. Therefore, the Jewish family ethics I propose to address and develop here refers as much, if not more, to our community's relationship to families (in all their variety) as it does to the quality of relationships within those families.

Why a new Jewish family ethics now? Because, as I have suggested, family structures are changing and the traditional prescriptions no longer seem to fit. Efforts by the Jewish community to arrest change—to increase the Jewish birth rate, to stop the rising numbers of divorces and intermarriages, to increase rates of marriage—have proven largely unsuccessful. Further, to the extent that the community continues to conceive of traditional nuclear families as the best, if not the only, building blocks of a Jewish future, current trends must surely make it fearful about that future. Increasingly, of course, alternative voices are suggesting that we need not be so fearful, that we can imagine a strong and positive Jewish future constructed around much broader understandings of families and of their relationship to the community. But to do this we need to develop and articulate precepts appropriate to the new structures—precepts both for those who would participate in the structures, and for the Jewish community in relationship to them.

Families do not exist in isolation; they are products of the society and communities of which they are a part. If we are to understand recent changes and be able to respond effectively to them, we must recognize the ways in which families are social constructs.

Too much of the existing discussion and debate about changing families and Jewish communal responses has failed to take that context into account. It tends to treat family structures strictly as the products of individual, self-interested choice, and those who choose to live in alternative structures (whether they be childless couples, those living together without being married, singles, widows, roommates, divorced families, intermarrieds, gay or lesbian families) as having put their "personal" concerns above those of the "community." The community, in such formulations, presumably does not make choices; it simply exists. Many of the common prescriptions for action—for example, increasing communal incentives and/or disincentives in an effort to entice, cajole, or encourage individuals to choose so-called traditional families, or, conversely, to punish or marginalize those who do not—are based on a presumed opposition between what the individual wants and what is good for the community. As a result, such suggestions tend to reinforce an adversarial sense of the relationship between the community and its nonconforming members, and contribute to the alienation and marginalization they are presumably designed to overcome.[5] They force out of the community many who are capable of contributing both creativity and energy to the Jewish community.

This adversarial understanding of the relationship between individuals and communities is both false and misleading. As Jews living in the United States, we ought to have learned only too well that individuals are not so easily separable from their communities. Most Jews have rejected full assimilation as a goal and have come increasingly to recognize and insist that our particularist, communal ties are crucial to our individuality, and that our Jewish identities are inseparable from our American identities. A healthy society, liberal Jews have argued, requires not just tolerance for, but active welcoming of, diversity. Thus, as Jews, we have come to value true pluralism; we strive to create a society in which all of us can participate and contribute in the fullness of our identities as Jewish Americans—a society where we do not have to leave that identity behind at home or in the synagogue. In such a society, not only are Jews and other minorities more secure; the freedoms we enjoy allow us all to contribute more fully and effectively to the community at large.

However, although we have learned this lesson well in the context of American politics and culture, we have only rarely taken it back into our own community. Instead, we as a Jewish community have come to believe not only that there is just one set of norms, but also that there is only one way to meet and fulfill them. Instead of seeing individuals and communities as involved in dynamic, mutual relationships, we freeze our idea of community, define it in terms of certain acceptable patterns of behavior (in this case, family constitution), and then marginalize the individuals who do not meet those norms, while at the same time worrying about Jewish survival and a shrinking Jewish population.

There is another way. We must recognize that we live our lives, including our Jewish lives, in a context. The rugged individualism that dominates American culture is a misleading description of reality: no one "chooses" in the absence of community. Communities affect what we choose, our sense of the choices, as well as our feelings about ourselves and others. Further, communities are themselves human creations. Communities do not exist in some unchanging realm outside of history, but change as people and circumstances change. Consequently, communities are subject to some conscious human control. Those of us who understand ourselves to be living in a post-*halakhic* age should be particularly aware that, through our constructions, we *create* our communities and the values they incorporate at the same time that we are products of them.

The Jewish communities in which we live reflect and participate in many aspects of the larger society. While American society has not always lived up to its pluralistic democratic promise, that vision has exerted considerable influence over the institutions and practices of the Jewish community. The Jewish community has become both more permeable to the world around it and more internally democratic than it was in the past. Such changes have significant implications for the development of a new Jewish family ethics.

To be more specific, Jews in the rabbinic, medieval, and early modern periods lived in communities that were, if not isolated from the world around them, at least semiautonomous entities. They were governed internally by Jewish law and overseen by Jewish communal/legal bodies (always, of course, within constraints set out by the rulers of the surrounding non-Jewish community.) It was not until Emancipation that Jews were accepted into the surrounding political communities as more or less full and equal members, subject no longer to Jewish law but to the secular law of the polity. Although the Jewish community was never hermetically sealed from the communities around it, the processes of emancipation and modernization have broken down its monolithic character. We are left with a variety of Jewish communities possessing various standards of behavior and with growing numbers of unaffiliated Jews who live their lives totally outside of any organized Jewish community. Existing Jewish communal structures have become more permeable to the influences and trends of surrounding communities and steadily less able to set standards for their membership that differ from those of the world "outside."

Related to this increased permeability of Jewish life is its growing democratization. Traditional Jewish communities were hierarchically organized and strictly controlled by Jewish communal authorities. Contemporary American Jews, as a result of the democratization that has accompanied modernization, tend to define community in increasingly open and egalitarian terms. In the traditional Jewish community, upper-class, educated (and usually wealthy) males were granted the right and the authority to set the rules and guidelines by which everyone was to live. Contemporary Jewish communities are both more diverse and, in theory, more inclusive and egalitarian. We insist, for example, that women as well as men be fully participating members of the community in both religious and secular contexts. In addition, we have little ability to enforce standards of ritual or moral behavior. With few exceptions, those who declare themselves Jews—regardless of whether they observe Shabbat or kashrut, and regardless of the standards of behavior they follow in their professional or personal lives—can claim membership in the Jewish community. We as a community have no sanctions to use against them; nor would many of us want to use them if we did! Moreover, many of us are striving to create a community that is egalitarian in an even broader sense, one that challenges the barriers and hierarchies associated with class as well as with gender. We want a community that values and validates the contributions of as wide a range of our membership as possible. In short we live in a world where community membership is defined more broadly than in the past.

Moreover, as community boundaries shift and we develop new understandings of who and what constitutes the community, patterns of power and authority present themselves for reexamination. In a society that takes gender and class hierarchies for granted, power and authority are "naturally" expected to reside in upper-class males (in the Jewish context, in Jewishly educated males). But that expectation leaves unasked, let alone unanswered, questions about the implications of policies that take those assumptions for granted. Let us take, for example, the case of *shelom bayit* (peace in the home), a long-standing precept expressing the belief that the whole (the family) is more than the sum of its parts (the individuals who make it up), calling on those who constitute the family as a whole.

Shelom bayit offers the ideal of a unified and peaceful family whose members work in close cooperation toward goals about which all are in agreement. At its best, the value of *shelom bayit* promotes harmony within each family member as well as among them. Importantly, it assumes a family that is also governed by other characteristics, such as fairness and open communication. When those characteristics are absent, pressure to conform to *shelom bayit* can mask oppression.

If we look at *shelom bayit* from the point of view of those dominant in the community (and in the institution of the family), the suppression of discontent is generally a good thing. Those who are in positions of relative power and authority are by definition those who benefit from the status quo. Given the formal power relations within traditional Jewish families, men who were dissatisfied with their lot could leave and/or divorce their wives; women were left to grin and bear it, or to risk the humiliation and shame of turning to rabbinic courts for relief. But if we look at it from the point of view of the traditionally subordinate member of the community (and the family)—the wife—the admonition to suppress one's concerns in the name of *shelom bayit* takes on very different dimensions. As both Faith Solela and Marcia Cohn Spiegel have argued, even in our own day all too many battered women are sent back to their husbands and households by the rabbis and Jewish communal workers to whom they turn for support, and told to hold their peace in the name of *shelom bayit*. For those women, such advice has often meant resigning themselves to continued abuse, hardly what *shelom bayit* might mean if understood from their perspective![6]

In short, an accurate rendering of the meaning of *shelom bayit*—or of any other communal-ethical precept—must take into account real differences in power as they exist within the community. In fact, in such cases we might well adopt the perspective of liberation theologians and argue that in the face of existing power differentials, the only way to assure truly ethical and egalitarian treatment is to ally ourselves with the weak—in this case, women and children. A Jewish family ethics for an egalitarian community must develop standards and principles of conduct that empower the weak and/or dependent, even as they attempt to contribute to the continuity of the community. The supposed well-being of the family or the community cannot be given priority over the physical and spiritual health of its constituents.

How, then, does a changing community, characterized by new patterns of power, authority, and leadership, define standards of behavior? What are the parameters of acceptable and unacceptable action? What criteria may we use for judging? Where traditional rules and regulations do not serve us, we must rely on the injunction to be a holy people, to attempt to realize God's presence in our midst.

In a truly egalitarian, inclusive community, standards of behavior must be defined in terms of concrete relations in and through which people live. To return to Buber's formulation, we realize God in our midst not simply by following abstract dictates of action, but by interacting with our fellows in ways that recognize the presence of God in each other and in the relationships we create among ourselves. We cannot draw a blueprint for a community by mapping out abstract precepts, but we can articulate as goals the ways in which we want to interact with one another. It is in this context that I believe we must attempt to develop a new Jewish family ethics.

Families: Old and New

Surely much of our communal attachment to traditional family forms—and our fears of what will happen if those forms are no longer normative—derives from a belief that families meet important human and social needs. We think of families, in fact, as the prime contexts in which people meet their needs for companionship and emotional intimacy, for mutual economic support, for generativity (childbearing and child rearing), and, particularly within the Jewish context, for preserving tradition and contributing to the continuity of the community. The Jewish community has tended to view "singleness" as a state of alienation and isolation to be overcome through marriage; economic interdependence as one of the core benefits of family life (rarely, if ever, achieved outside of it); traditional families as the only reasonable contexts for raising children; and bearing and raising children as the primary way of transmitting tradition and ensuring communal continuity. Such beliefs result in the fear that as traditional families change, and as more and more people live in alternative, or nontraditional, structures, individuals will become isolated, community weakened, and the Jewish future threatened.

As I have argued elsewhere, however, families cannot always meet these needs effectively, and in many cases nontraditional arrangements meet them as well or better.[7] Families exist and function within a social context that greatly influences their effectivness. Both historical and contemporary evidence clearly show that a significant proportion of heterosexual nuclear families are unable to meet the needs of their members for emotional, physical, and economic support. Consider the existence of *hevrei kadishah* (burial societies), *hachnasat kallah* (dowry societies), and *maot hittin* (Passover food groups), for example, and the myriad of other charitable Jewish communal organizations that flourished in the shtetls of Eastern Europe and among immigrants to the United States. They serve as evidence of the Jewish community's recognition that families cannot always support their members. And they attest to the assumption of a communal responsibility to meet the needs of individual Jews.

In our own day, reports of wife battering, child abuse, homelessness, and abandonment make clear once again that families at all levels of the social and economic scale often find it difficult to create and sustain the nurturing, loving environment we have come to expect of them. Further, as feminist critics have noted, families often restrain, limit, and disempower the women and children within them, while masking the inequalities of power under the name of love. This is not to say that all families are abusive, or that people have no need for interdependent relationships. It is to suggest, however, that what is ideologically defined as a system of love and care is often lacking in true mutuality, to the particular detriment of women and children.

Treating the nuclear family as the only normative family model also fails to take into consideration how many people are excluded—singles, the divorced and widowed, "blended" families, and single parents, to name but a few. Giving the nuclear family first-class status makes everyone else second-class. The truth is that only a minority of American Jews live in intact traditional nuclear families. Unless we face that fact and move beyond a myopic focus on mother, father, and their biological children as the only normal family, we will be unable to address the needs and problems of the majority of Jews.

Beyond recognizing that traditional families do not always do all they are supposed to do, it is important to realize that clinging to the ideal of the traditional family blinds us to the ways that other relationships may meet many of the same needs as effectively or better—particularly if they are given the appropriate communal recognition and support. Thus, many people find satisfying emotional relationships outside of marriage—either in unmarried heterosexual relationships, in gay or lesbian relationships, in circles of close friends, or in collective living arrangements. Friends and/or communal groups may well help to sustain such relationships economically. Many people raise children without a legal spouse, or in the context of a gay or lesbian family. And many people, both married and unmarried, have found ways other than parenting to express their commitment to raising Jewish children and to contributing to the vitality and continuity of the Jewish community—as teachers, social workers, rabbis, or community service workers, to name just a few.

In short, many of the values we associate with families can be, and have been, met in contexts other than the traditional nuclear family. If we as a community are concerned with having certain needs met in a Jewish context, then it is surely in our interest to assure that those who live in alternative family structures be included in the community, welcome to join in communal activities, and to take advantage of communally offered support services. Those who live in nontraditional ways have all too often reported feeling like pariahs—feared, perhaps, as examples of what might happen to others, or seen as threats to the supposed sanctity of the traditional families everyone finds increasingly difficult to maintain.

But those whose intimacy constellations differ from the norm need not be on the margins of organized Jewish communities. Most are eager for full inclusion as long as the price of inclusion is not the abandonment of their uniqueness. From our vantage points as a Jewish minority in American culture, we can see that the strength of the larger community depends on recognition and support for our particularity. So, too, we should recognize that, within the Jewish communal context, strength and unity depend on recognizing, welcoming, and supporting all those who would wish to contribute to our common project.

New Families, New Challenges

By including those now marginalized, we increase the size and strength of the community. In addition, I believe there are specific resources that those whose intimacy constellations differ from the norm have to offer to the community at large.

Many elderly people, for example, now live alone; their isolation makes it difficult for them to cope with illness, the death of loved ones, and the responsibilities of household management. Group living for heathly older people not only improves the quality of their lives; it reduces the demand placed on their extended families and often on community resources. Perhaps more important, many older people find this way of living more secure and satisfying. It provides opportunities for giving to others, both at home and in the broader community.

Group living arrangements of this sort might well prove more generally valuable; they could be important to single people of whatever age, providing a context for breaking down isolation and loneliness. And they might also offer an alternative for traditional families at various stages of life, who find it difficult if not impossible to sustain an independent life; there is no reason why, for example, a group living arrangement might not include one or two young families with children, some single people, and some elderly people (whether or not related to the younger ones). Such a household could offer substantial benefits to all. To date, Jewish communal organizations have given little attention to such alternatives, perhaps because they do not seem to reinforce the traditional nuclear family.

Gays and lesbians represent another group whose living arrangements have been similarly marginalized by the Jewish community. What would it mean for the community to make gay and lesbian Jews, and members of our intimacy constellations, fully equal members of the Jewish community?[8]

Gay and lesbian families come in all shapes and sizes. Some are constructed along the lines of heterosexual nuclear families—two adults in a committed relationship, and their associated children—except that the two adults are of the same sex. Some may consist of an adult parent and her or his children, without an adult lover present. In other cases, because so many lesbians and gays have been married, have had children in those marriages, and now "share" them with an ex-spouse in some form of joint custody, lesbian or gay households will sometimes have children present and sometimes not. In their variety, gay and lesbian families do not differ significantly from heterosexual families. Nevertheless, some significant differences open new possibilities for the Jewish community at the same time that they seem to challenge deeply held values and commitments.

Challenging Homophobia

Gay and lesbian families do not share in heterosexual privilege, and family members are subject to societal homophobia. On the surface, one might argue that homophobia is not of great consequence to those already in relationships: if we have our love for one another, what difference does it make if that love is validated by others? But if that were so, if we could all live without social validation and recognition, why would anyone go through the formalities of (heterosexual) marriage?

Of course, marriage confers immediate benefits that are denied to gays and lesbians, as well as to others who may be living together outside of legal marriage.[9] Many of these are fairly obvious: the inability to claim and publicly celebrate those relationships most central to one's being; denial of "family memberships," whether in a museum or a synagogue; denial of visiting privileges with a partner if he or she is hospitalized; invisibility and lack of support (or even awarness of the loss) when a relationship ends or a lover dies; fear of losing one's children in a custody battle, or of not being able to continue a relationship with the children of a lover should the lover die.

Many of the consequences of living in a society oriented around the conventional nuclear family are much less obvious. Most significant, perhaps, is that the expectations and social supports that help sustain heterosexual families through the vagaries of interpersonal conflict and familial tension are largely denied to others. In many areas of the country—and in most Jewish communities, in particular—few resources are available if a lesbian or gay couple (or even an unmarried heterosexual couple) runs into trouble and wishes to seek counseling. While most Jewish communal organizations have a clear commitment to helping families sustain themselves, that commitment has rarely been explicitly extended to gay and lesbian families. When we are victims of homophobia on the streets, at work, in school, or in the synagogue, there are, in most cases, no Jewish communal organizations to come to our aid. And when our children have to confront homophobia—whether from their peers or other adults—there are no resources in the Jewish community to which they can turn.

Taking account of that difference in the experience of different family types and fully including gay and lesbian families within the Jewish community would mean acknowledging and addressing homophobia, heterosexism, and their manifestations in the Jewish community. Homophobia and heterosexism affect hererosexuals as well as lesbians and gays, locking us all into confining sex roles and behaviors out of fear that we might be labeled "queer." Addressing those issues directly within our communities would free all of us to live in ways more expressive of our full selves. Moreover, it would mean making counseling and other support services available not only to those in gay or lesbian families, but also to others attempting to cope with new family structures (for example, as a result of divorce, widowhood, single parenthood, or childlessness), and to those struggling with issues concerning sexual orientation—thus overcoming the isolation of many individuals and families and opening the community to many who now avoid it for fear of rejection. Heterosexual families as well as gay and lesbian families would benefit from the infusion of energy that attention to such issues could entail.

Sexual Equality

One largely unresolved issue facing families is that of sexual equality and the dignity of every family member. We live in a male-dominant society, which means that even with the best of egalitarian intentions the average nuclear family must continually struggle against male dominance and conventional sex-role definitions and expectations. It is the rare heterosexual family, for example, in which the woman does not feel some greater responsibility for child rearing or for the administration of the home.

One of the main feminist criticisms of traditional families has been the way in which they participate in, and reinforce, the societal dominance of men over women. Much of the contemporary debate over families focuses precisely on this issue of equality/inequality, and of what happens when women insist on full equality with men in all aspects of familial life. The conservative position, of course, is that families will not be able to sustain the strain, that someone must be at the head, and that given the organization of our society, it makes sense for that someone to be the male. The spate of recent books on "women who love too much" suggests even more specifically that intimacy between men and women is possible only in a context of inequality (where the man does the economic work and the woman does the emotional work).

The absence of a full commitment to women's equality in the Jewish community can be seen in its silence about wife battering and child abuse, and the consequent lack of financial support for counseling and shelters. It can be seen in the failure of the community openly to confront sexual abuse. And it can be seen in our failure to promote models of equality in schools and communal organizations, as well as in synagogues. More thought is needed as to what it would take as a community to sustain all families on a truly egalitarian basis.

As I have suggested, Jewish feminists have criticized the presumption that Judaism is based not just on families, but on families constructed on the basis of sexual inequality. Jewish feminists have demanded of the community that it provide what is necessary to support and sustain more egalitarian family constellations—for example, communally sponsored day care, child care at synagogues, and flex-time schedules—and have challenged communal definitions of *shelom bayit,* which give primacy to maintaining the family even at the cost of the health and safety of the women and children within it. If Jewish communities begin to question and explode the myth of Jewish family, to recognize the variety of actual family types, and to meet the needs of real members of families on a broad scale, the benefits will accrue to a very wide range of people, including women of whatever familial constellation, single parents, and lesbian and gay families. Attention to these needs would, in turn, remove some of the major obstacles that have prevented women from full participation in the work force and the community.

Integenerational Continuity

Later marriage, high divorce rates, and increasing rates of intermarriage among Jewish men have combined to produce large numbers of single Jewish women in their late thirties. They are faced with the difficult choice of never bearing children or becoming single mothers. Despite rhetoric about the need for more Jewish children, there has been little discussion of whether, or how, to support women in their decisions to bear children outside the context of a traditional nuclear family. Little has been done to provide for the special needs of single mothers, whether divorced, widowed, never married, or involved in lesbian relationships. This makes the community's message about the need for more Jewish children problematic at best. Commitment to increasing the Jewish birth rate must mean recognizing the potential for (and actuality of) childbearing for those not conventionally married.

Of course, bearing and raising children is *not* the only way to contribute to the Jewish future. Judaism has long recognized that generativity comes in many forms and guises. Susan Handelman has noted that Jewish tradition holds that one who teaches another's child is as if she or he gave birth to that child. Teachers, community leaders, those who care for the young, the old, the sick, all make their contribution to the vitality and continuity of the community. Single people, the elderly, gays and lesbians have all made major contributions to culture and religious life as teachers, social service workers, community supporters, rabbis, songwriters, poets, writers, critics. Expanding our notion of what constitutes generativity can relieve many childless Jews—whether married or unmarried, heterosexual, lesbian or gay—of the shame and guilt of childlessness while at the same time freeing them to develop and recognize the variety of ways in which they do contribute to the future of the community. Such a shift in perspective can benefit us all.

Sexual Ethics and Family Stability

These same factors of later age at marriage, high divorce rates, and the so- called sexual revolution have posed other significant challenges to traditional Jewish ethics concerning family and sexuality. Jewish attitudes toward sexuality have in some ways been enlightened: Judaism acknowledged that sexuality is an important and valued aspect of our humanity. At the same time, however, the traditional view has been that heterosexual marriage is the only appropriate context for the full expression of sexuality. That view, of course, is now much more honored in the breach than in the observance: the majority of Jews today do have sexual relations before marriage, and many also have sexual relations outside of marriage. Of course, to deny the possibility of sexual intimacy and connection to those who are not married would seem only to compound the frustrations of their existing marginalization from the community.

We are, in short, in desperate need of communal discussion about an appropriate sexual ethics for our post-*halakhic* age. Some such discussion has already begun.[10] I would only emphasize here the value Judaism has traditionally placed on mutuality and respect in sexual relationships. Thus, as in each of the areas I have discussed so far, what is needed is a commitment on the part of the community to retain that emphasis on mutuality and respect while at the same time recognizing that mutual and respectful sexual relationships can take place between young people before they are married, elderly people who are no longer married, and among others who are not married, whether heterosexual or homosexual. What is crucial is the quality of the relationship, rather than the legal relational status of those who constitute it.

Further, as I suggested earlier, the community must actively address the consequences of changes in family constitution (whether these result from divorce, death, or other reasons). Few synagogues or Jewish communal organizations provide counseling or other services for children or other family members struggling with issues of family dissolution or recombination. Rabbis and other communal leaders have been notably silent on the financial hardship most women and their children experience after divorce. As there is little sign that divorce rates (and rates of family reconstitution and recombination) will diminish, hand-wringing on the part of the community is insufficient. What we need—in addition to ethical standards for ending and beginning relationships—is a wide range of supports and services for people experiencing these changes.

Families, Community, and Spirituality: Toward a New Communal Ethic

I want to end by returning, once again, to Buber, and to the vision I articulated of a Jewish community characterized by joint striving to realize the presence of God in our midst. I have argued that if we are to create such a community, it must be based on a recognition of mutual respect and dignity, and that a community cannot be built and maintained at the expense of its weaker members. I have also argued that as a community we have much to gain from the full incorporation of those whose intimacy constellations or family types now make them somewhat marginal. In our struggle to incorporate difference and diversity, our community as a whole can grow much richer.

The spiritual dimension underlying many of these arguments has been stated mostly by implication. I wish to conclude by addressing it more directly, and to argue for the recognition of an important interconnection between spiritual fulfillment and the social-political and familial context in which we live. I believe that a recognition of this connection (encapsulated in the notion of *tikkun olam* [repairing the world]) generates a further demand for the active engagement of the community in struggles to make both Jewish organizations and communities, and our society at large, places where people can live out their differences and realize the full range of their personhood.[11]

If we meet God in Between spaces, then the institutions and relationships which define the Between are essential components of our spiritual lives. A community that strives to realize the presence of God in its midst therefore cannot limit its concerns to the narrowly "spiritual" realm (whatever that might mean). It must, instead, engage in the business of *tikkun olam*, by which I mean that it must commit itself to building, sustaining, and enriching the day-to-day relationships in which people live and work. Those relationships provide the contexts in which we experience the divine. Since relationships of intimacy and commitment are one context in which we experience the presence of God, those relationships must have the support of our communities on a variety of levels.

More basic, of course, is economic survival. At a minimum, meeting our day-to-day physical needs and those of our loved ones is an expression of loving commitment. Provision of basic levels of physical and economic security for all families and intimacy constellations is, consequently, a spiritual, as well as a political, imperative. A contemporary Jewish family ethics must include a communal imperative to struggle for adequate physical and economic supports for all families, whatever their form.

Second, there must be a recognition of the variety of ways intimacy can be (and is) experienced, and families constituted. Traditional families are surely one context for intimacy, but many experience intimacy elsewhere—outside of formal marriage, or in relationships with people of their own sex.

If we are truly committed to everyone's spiritual growth, we must also welcome and validate (both within our own community and within the larger society) the varied contexts in which people experience that growth. Intimacy is too important, and unfortunately too rarely achieved, to limit the acceptable contexts in which people strive to achieve it. To treat married, heterosexual families as the only legitimate context for intimacy, and to deny the legitimacy (and the spiritual nature) of other intimacy constellations grounded in mutual respect, is to deny an important aspect of that humanity which our tradition should foster. Further, it prevents a range of people—unmarried heterosexual couples, singles, the divorced, widows, gays and lesbians—from experiencing foundational aspects of themselves in the context of spiritual-religious community.[12]

Finally, regardless of the form that our intimacy constellations take, our efforts to contribute to the Jewish future must be welcomed. Our community must support all its members in their decisions to raise and nurture children. Those who choose not to have children, or are unable to do so, also deserve respect and understanding. They should have opportunities to develop relationships with others' children and/or ways to contribute to the continuity of our communities and traditions.

Each of these imperatives is related to the tradition of *tikkun olam,* which recognizes a spiritual component to engagement in the world. Just as families do not exist in a vacuum, neither do our spiritual lives. They have a social and political—a communal—context. If, as members of a Jewish community, we are committed to people being able to express and fulfill themselves spiritually, then we must work to create the conditions that will make that fulfillment possible.

What this approach offers us is the image of an inclusive community. Such a community is, of course, one of the goals of our democratic political system, which we, as Jews, have adopted. Inclusiveness should also be the goal of a community committed to meeting the spiritual needs of its members, and, therefore, the essence of a Jewish family ethics for our post-*halakhic* age.

Notes

Acknowledgment: Conversations with many people have contributed to the development of the ideas in my essay. I wish especially to acknowledge the help of Judith Plaskow and Denni Liebowitz and my ongoing discussions and struggles with the women of B'not Esh.

1. On the history and development of Jewish families see Steven M. Cohen and Paula Hyman, eds., *The Evolving Jewish Family* (New York: Holmes and Meier, 1986); also Charlotte Baum, Paula Hyman, and Sonya Michel, *The Jewish Woman in America* (New York: Dial Press, 1976).

2. On changes within Jewish families and communities, and for interpretations of their significance, see Steven M. Cohen, *American Modernity and Jewish Identity* (New York: Tavistock, 1983), especially chap. 6; and Andrew Cherlin and Carin Celebuski, "Are Jewish Families Different?" *Journal of Marriage and the Family* (November 1983), pp. 903–10. I am grateful to Steven Cohen for calling the latter article to my attention.

3. Martin Buber, "The Holy Way: A Word to the Jews and to the Nations," chap. 7 of *On Judaism,* Nahum N. Glatzer, ed. (New York: Schocken, 1967), pp. 110, 112.

4. This term was introduced by Barbara Breitman and Barbara Johnson at a workshop they coordinated at a B'not Esh gathering in May 1986.

5. Note, for example, the title of a February 1986 symposium at the 92nd Street Y in New York: "Lifestyles and Sexual Norms: Personal Choices and Communal Imperatives." Susan Handelman's article, "Family, a Religiously Mandated Ideal," *Sh'ma,* March 20, 1987, suffers from some of these perspectives. See also Anne Roiphe's article, "The Jewish Family: A Feminist Perspective," *Tikkun,* vol. 1, no. 2, 1986, pp.70–76, and my letter in response to it, *Tikkun,* vol. 2, no. 2, 1987, p. 4.

6. Marcia Cohn Spiegel, "Breaking the Silence," plenary address, New Jewish Agenda National Conference, July 1987; reprinted in *Genesis 2.* See also *Lilith,* No. 20, Summer 1988; Faith Solela, "Family Violence: Silence Isn't Golden Anymore,' *Response,* Spring 1985, pp. 101–6.

7. I develop other aspects of this argument in "Sisters or Comrades? The Politics of Friends and Families," in *Families, Politics, and Public Policies,* I. Diamond, ed. (New York: Longman, 1983), pp. 339–56; in "Families and the Jewish Community: A Feminist Perspective," *Response,* Spring 1985, pp 5–19; and in "Redefining Family: Models for a Jewish Future," in *Twice Blessed,* Christie Balka and Andy Rose, eds. (Boston: Beacon Press, 1989).

8. Much of the discussion that follows is taken from my "Redefining Family: Models for the Jewish Future."

9. The "Family Partnership Act" in San Francisco, for example, would extend a variety of benefits to unmarried heterosexual couples (whether elderly or young) as well as to gay or lesbian partners.

10. See, for example, Arthur Waskow, "Down-to-Earth Judaism: Sexuality," pp. 46–49, 88–91, and Bradley Sharvit Artson, "Judaism and Homosexuality," pp. 52–54, 92–93, both in *Tikkun,* March/April 1988; David Teutsch, "Rethinking Jewish Sexual Ethics," pp. 6–11, and Sharon Cohen, "Homosexuality and a Jewish Sex Ethic," pp. 12–16, both in *Reconstructionist,* July–August 1989; Judith Plaskow, *Standing Again at Sinai: Judaism from a Feminist Perspective* (San Francisco; Harper and Row, 1990), chap. 5.

11. I have explored some aspects of this question in "Rabbis Are People Too: Politics, Spirituality, and the Jewish Community," *Reconstructionist,* September 1986, pp. 19–24, 32.

12. Discussions with Denni Liebowitz and the women of B'not Esh have greatly enriched my thinking about these issues.

21

The Theoretical Basis of Women's Equality in Judaism

BLU GREENBERG

We who are committed to traditional Judaism are standing today at the crossroads on the question of women. Feminism disturbs our previous equilibrium, for it makes a fundamental claim about women contrary to the model generated by *halakhah*.

The feminist ideology can be summed up as follows:

1. Women have the same innate potential, capability, and needs as men, whether in the realm of the spirit, the word, or the deed.
2. Women have a similar capacity for interpretation and concomitant decision making.
3. Women can function fully as "outside" persons, in broader areas of society beyond the home.
4. Women can and should have some control over their own destinies, to the extent that such mastery is possible for anyone.

Let us reduce these broad statements from the level of generalization to a theology of woman as Jew:

1. A woman of faith has the same innate vision and existential longing for a redemptive-covenantal reality as a man of faith.[1] She has the same ability and need to be in the presence of God alone and within the context of the community. Such a woman is sufficiently mature to accept the responsibilities for this relationship and the rights that flow from these responsibilities. If these spiritual gifts do not flow naturally from her soul, she can be educated and uplifted in them in much the same fashion that Jewish men are.
2. Jewish women, as much as men, have the mental and emotional capacities to deal directly with the most sacred Jewish texts and primary sources. Jewish women are capable of interpreting tradition based on the sources. They can be involved in the decision-making process that grows out of the blending of inherited tradition with contemporary needs.
3. Some women, as some men, are capable of functioning in the positions of authority related to the religious and physical survival of the Jewish people.

4. Women as a class should not find themselves in discriminatory positions in personal situations. In such matters as marriage and divorce, a woman should have no less control or personal freedom than a man, nor should she be subject to abuse resulting from the constriction of freedom.

These, then, are the basic claims that a woman, sensitized to the new, broader, cultural value system, can carry over into her life as a Jew. I am not arguing here whether *halakhic* Judaism deems a woman inferior, although there are more than a few sources in the tradition that lend themselves to such a conclusion;[2] nor will I accept at face value those statements that place women on a separate but higher pedestal. What I am saying is that *halakhah,* contrary to the feminist values I have described above, continues to delimit women. In some very real ways, *halakhic* parameters inhibit women's growth, both as Jews and as human beings.

I do not speak here of all *halakhah.* One must be careful not to generalize from certain critical comments and apply them to the system as a whole. In fact, my critique could grow only out of a profound appreciation for the system in its entirety—its ability to preserve the essence of an ancient revelation as a fresh experience each day; its power to generate an abiding sense of kinship, past and present; its intimate relatedness to concerns both immediate and otherwordly; its psychological soundness; its ethical and moral integrity. On the whole, I believe that a Jew has a better chance of living a worthwhile life if he or she lives a life according to *halakhah.* Therefore, I do not feel threatened when addressing the question of the new needs of women in Judaism nor in admitting the limitations of *halakhah* in this area. Indeed, it is my very faith in *halakhic* Judaism that makes me believe we can search within it for a new level of perfection, as Jews have been doing for three thousand years.

From this understanding one is moved perforce to ask the next question: If the new feminist categories are perceived to be of a higher order of definition of woman than those that limit her, how are we to explain the gap between the feminist model and the *halakhic* model? This becomes even more problematic when one considers the sheer abundance of ethical and moral constructs in Judaism (e.g., the injunctions not to insult another, to lift up one's brother before he falls, not to lead another into temptation, not to judge unless one has been faced with the same situation). How is it possible that a tradition with so highly developed a sensitivity to human beings could allow even one law or value judgment that demeans women, much less a host of such laws?

There are certain external and internal factors that explain the insufficiency of the tradition with regard to women. The stratification of men and women in Judaism simply reflects the male-female hierarchical states in all previous societies in human history.[3] Moreover, in light of the primary model of Jewish woman as domestic creature—as wife, mother, dependent, auxiliary—all other roles and responsibilities that seemed to conflict with the primary model simply were eliminated.[4]

I do not wish to imply that Jewish women are oppressed. This is far from the truth. Given the historically universal stratification of the sexes, plus the model of the Jewish woman as enabler and the exclusive male (rabbinic) option of interpreting the law, there could have been widespread abuse of the powerless. But this did not happen. In fact, the reverse is true; throughout rabbinic history, one observes a remarkably benign and caring attitude toward women.

Nevertheless, there is a need today to redefine the status of women in certain areas of Jewish law. First, a benign and caring stance is not discernible in every last instance of rabbinic legislation.[5] Second, paternalism is not what women are seeking nowadays, not even the women of the traditional Jewish community. Increasingly, such women are beginning to ask questions about equality, about a more mature sharing of responsibility, about divesting the power of *halakhic* interpretation and legislation of its singular maleness.

I

I have referred to the crossroads at which we stand. A crossroad implies choices. There are three ways in which *halakhic* Jews may proceed with regard to the question of women:

1. We can revert to the fundamentalist pole, where hierarchy of male and female remains unchallenged in most areas of human life.
2. We can allow the new value system to penetrate our civil lives but not our religious lives. In other words, women may be encouraged to see themselves as equals in social, economic, and political spheres. This is the current stance of modern Orthodoxy.
3. We can find ways within *halakhah* to allow for growth and greater equality in the ritual and spiritual realms, despite the fact that there are no guarantees where this will lead us.

It is my firm belief that the third path is the one we now must begin to follow. Admittedly, I have been propelled in that direction by the contemporary Western humanist liberation philosophy of the secular women's movement; those who would hurl at me the charge of "foreign-body contamination" therefore are absolutely right. But is there any religion in history, including Judaism, that has not borrowed from the surrounding culture? The real questions are, What do we do with what we borrow? What are the unique Jewish ways in which we can appropriate positive ideas, customs, and values? How can we enhance our system by these new accretions? And most important, in what ways can they become continuous with the essence of Judaism?

True, the original impulse for all of this, as I have said, derives from feminism, but even if such a movement hadn't evolved, I still would like to think that a creative pondering of the ideals of Torah Judaism might lead to the same conclusions. Thus, the central concern of these observations has to do with organic, internal changes, changes in our private Jewish lives, unmediated by society, quotas, affirmative action, and the like—changes based on intrinsic Jewish values and brought about because the *halakhic* way of life calls them forth.

II

Let us examine briefly some working principles of *halakhah*. *Halakhah* is not simply a collection of laws. It is a way of life or, more correctly, a way of living. For a Jew, a life directed by halakhah is as near perfect a way of life as possible. The sum of its parts—observing the Sabbath, kashruth, giving to charity, having a family, being part of a community, teaching children, studying Torah, loving God—is infinitely greater than each of the parts. All things great and small—reciting a blessing over new clothes, or after elimination, or over different varieties of foods; cutting the toenails, or breaking an egg the Jewish way—each minute act further distills that Jewish core.

Why do I say "near perfect"? *Halakhah* is a system that is being perfected continually. Indeed, the rabbinic tradition stresses humanity's role as a partner in the task of perfecting an imperfect world. One cannot but perceive *halakhah* as a fluid, dynamic system. Fluidity on specific laws about women is itself an example of that dynamism.

Halakhah interprets and reflects reality, not just tradition. *Halakhah* never operated in a totally closed system. There always has been a healthy consideration of immediate circumstances and broader societal forces. Even when rabbinic learders enacted circumscribing legislation, that too was a form of interaction with broader society. The whole body of responsa literature reflects those influences. So do such rabbinic concepts as *gezerah she-ayn ha-tzibur yakhol la-amod bah* ("restrictions imposed upon the populace that the majority cannot endure are not be be levied") and *dina de-malkhuta dina* ("the civil law of the land is the law").

The techniques of reinterpretation are built right into the system. It was proper use of these techniques that enabled rabbinic Judaism to be continuous with the past, even as it redefined and redirected the present and future. The techniques also allowed for diversity, for allowances based on local usage, for a certain kind of pluralism. After all, in a normative system how can you have two ways of doing something without each side's reading the other out of the community? Hence, the acceptance of various *minhagim* (customs). Once a particular *minhag* withstood the test of time, it became an integral part of *halakhah*.

An even more striking example of the technique of *halakhic* accommodation is the use of *asmakhta,* a scriptural passage or word on which a novel transition is pegged. An *asmakhta* often seems illogical, far-fetched, arbitrary. Yet the logic is in the technique itself. Through the use of *asmakhta* one never loses sight of the original revelation at Sinai, even though the new interpretation may go far beyond the old. Other *halakhic* techniques to accomplish similar ends are *takkanot* (directives enacted by *halakhic* scholars enjoying the force of law), *gezerot* (precautionary rulings), and *hora'ot sha'ah* (emergency rulings); even pilpulistic interpretations were used to develop and refine legal rulings further.

A central theme seems to emerge: where there was a rabbinic will, there was a *halakhic* way. This is not to say that talmudic and posttalmudic literature is not "the law of Moses at Sinai." It is that, but it is also the substance of rabbinic will finding a *halakhic* way. What shall we call it? Continuing revelation? Wise, interpretive judgment based on inherited tradition? An understanding, divinely given or intuited, of the appropriate moment for greater restraint, or relaxation of the rules, or heightened responsibility? Surely the rabbinic decision to accept the testimony of a wife or a single witness—as sufficient evidence to establish the fact of death of the husband and thereby free her to remarry—is a sign of rabbinic compassion that somehow found *halakhic* expression. Surely Rabbenu Gershom, the tenth-century authority, used his power and position to enact a *takkanah* (ordinance) that disallowed forcible divorce.

A good deal of leeway in interpretation was given to individual scholars. The lack of centralization of authority from the Second Temple period and onward was not perceived as a weakness in rabbinic tradition. The concept of *moreh de-atra* (following the ruling of the local rabbinic authority), the full disclosure of disputes between scholars, the transmission of minority ruling along with the majority ones—these are as fundamental to the workings of Torah as Torah itself.

There is a heavy emphasis of ethical content in biblical and rabbinic literature. Ethical principles are at least as important as ritual ones.[6] The concept of equality in both ethical and ritual spheres emerges not only as principle but as process—a gradual movement from a society where slavery was permitted to the de facto abolishment of slavery; the jubilee year as a means of avoiding concentration of wealth in the hands of a few; the developing structure of a convenantal community rather than a hierarchical one; authority based on merit (the rabbis) rather than birth or wealth (priests, Levites, and landowners). Clearly, this trend in Jewish history—hierarchial to convenantal, birth to merit—has far-reaching implications for women in Judaism.

III

In light of these working principles of *halakhah,* one must ask some pointed questions: Does *halakhic* stratification of the sexes explicitly serve a theological purpose, that is, relatedness to God? For example, is inequity in divorce law or exclusion from court testimony or insufficiency to be counted for a quorum of some ultimate value in Judaism? Is there any way that the release of women from the obligation to study Torah, or praying at the prescribed times, can be understood in the sense of *kedushah,* holiness, a "setting aside"? We are offered no reasons for observing kashrut, yet we clearly understand it as an act of holiness, a special calling, a symbol of the unique relationship between God and the Jewish people. Is that how we must understand the stratification of male and female in Jewish ritual? Must we say that God's eternal plan for the sexes was a hierarchy, one dominant and one subordinate sex as law and ritual define us? Could it be that God, who loves all of his creatures, prefers and esteems the devotion of one whole class more than the other? Or can we say perhaps that the inequity is reflective of an undisputed socioreligious stance of ancient times?

Intuitively, and with a new awareness of the ethics of male-female equality, I find it hard to accept any notion that assigns to God a plan for hierarchy of the sexes: role division, yes to some extent; but superiority, no. That could be only a time-bound, human interpretation of God's will, from which women ought now to be exempt. If the male-female stratification is sociological rather than theological, are we bound to it forever? Does the fact that this long-standing sociological truth has been codified into *halakhah* oblige us to make an eternal principle out of an accident of history? For that answer we must turn to other characteristics of the *halakhah,* as I have indicated above: its proven ability to undergo reinterpretation in specific areas, particularly on women's issues; its pattern of equalizing unequals;

its allowance for human subjectivity; its process of self-perfection over the long course of its unfolding; its emphasis on ethical sensitivity so that no class of people feels disadvantaged; its movement from ascribed to earned status, with authority flowing from merit, not birth or sex.

It would seem, then, that full equalization of women in Judaism should be consistent with the wider principles of Torah. In fact, we ought to go one step further. If the hierarchy of the sexes serves no religious function, if *halakhah* has the capacity for reinterpretation, if equality is a basic positive value in Judaism, then it behooves the community and its leaders to take the initiative; together they must search for new ways to upgrade religious expression and new means by which to generate equality for women in tradition. No longer shall we hear the argument that women are demanding this or that of the *halakhah*. Rather, the issue should be set forth in the following terms: *halakhah*, the Jewish way, cries out for reinterpretation in the light of the new awareness of feminine equality, feminine potential.

IV

Let us apply this theoretical structure to specific situations. Given the unmistakable pattern toward equalization in Jewish divorce law—that is, the gradual limitation of the male's absolute rights and the gradual expansion of protections for women—the rabbis of today can no longer plead an inability to rectify the inequality. To say that their hands are tied or that they can resolve an individual case but cannot find a comprehensive solution is to admit that they are unworthy of the authority vested in them. Worse, it bespeaks a lack of rabbinic will to find a *halakhic* way. How else is one to explain the reluctance of certain *gedolim* (rabbinic authorities) to build upon the *halakhic* groundwork laid out by such contemporary scholars as Emanuel Rackman, Eliezer Berkovits, and Ze'ev Falk, who have come forth with alternative solutions in the form of respectable *halakhic* precedents? What these *gedolim,* the principal religious decision makers of contemporary Orthodoxy, are really saying is that they feel a need to preserve the original male prerogative in matters of divorce, for they know well that the only person whose hands are tied is the woman, who is often fair game for blackmail.

Similarly, we can apply the theoretical model to education and religious leadership. If Torah study and its teaching is something of high value, surpassing all other mitzvot, what could possibly justify closing off parts of the activity to one-half of our people? Is it ethical to say that women are unequal to the task, especially when exceptional models have indicated otherwise? Moreover, here is a clear instance whereby the system continuously perfects itself. What is accepted now in the way of Torah study for women was absolutely out of bounds three generations ago. Sara Schneier, the founder of the Bais Yaakov movement of education for girls, faced severe opposition in her time, but every young Jewish woman who has received a Jewish education from that day on is the beneficiary of her vision and persistence. Once she accomplished what she did, those who watched it happen and those who understood it as a more perfect expression of a woman's Jewishness somehow found a *halakhic* way to make Jewish education for women legitimate, even desirable.

Let us press the perfection model one step further and confront the dilemma head-on. If the study of Torah and Mishnah is not forbidden to women, why does

Talmud remain off-limits? And if certain study is permitted to women, why is it not encouraged? The answer is clear: because direct access to learning is the key to religious leadership in the traditional Jewish community. Without it, there is no way a woman can qualify as a scholar, a *halakhic* decision maker, or a rabbi. With equal access, women will begin to raise disturbing questions. A woman with a sense of her innate potential will begin to ask, "Why shouldn't I, too, strive to be learned?" A woman the match in learning of any rabbinic student will sooner or later ask, "Why can't I, too, be ordained?" Ultimately, a new generation of parents who place high value on Torah study will ask, "Why not expect the same from our daughters as from our sons?"

To deny fulfillment of these expectations is to assume that women never can be equal to men in spirit and intellect and therefore to demean and shame the class of women; it is also to deny *halakhah* its power to interpret reality—and live. If it is none of these things, then it can be only a means of reserving power and authority as an exclusively male prerogative. Otherwise, who would not share Torah with all who seek it?

Finally, we come to a consideration of the place of women in Jewish liturgy. If prayer is a form of Jewish commitment, if women as Jews are nourished by the same covenantal-redemptive vision, how can we justify excluding them from the unity of the spiritual congregation? Some would advance the familiar set of hoary arguments—that the honor of the community is diminished by women's participation, that women are not capable of making a sustained commitment to the fixed times of prayer, that women are unable to handle the tension between this pull and that. But are these real descriptions of a whole class of women? Were they ever inherent truths, or simply convenient excuses to preserve the privileges of a male fraternity whose business, admirably enough, was God-centered?

If one perceives that change of any sort goes against the grain of the *halakhah,* then there can be no shared universe of discourse above the level of form. If, on the other hand, we being with the idea of *halakhah* as the divine way to perfection, then we can proceed to examine form and essence independently. If prayer (essence) is primary in the Jewish system and fraternity (form) secondary, the next stage would be to acknowledge women as equals in the spiritual community and allow men to find other expression for their fraternal impulses.

A sense of community emanates not so much from shared physical presence as from shared memory and obligation. Thus, a Jew experiences feelings of kinship even when praying in the privacy of his home. The inclusion of women in liturgy—public and private—becomes, then, a building up of tradition and community, not a breaking down. If young boys can grow biologically into Jewish responsibilities, perhaps it is not too much to expect that women can grow historically.

V

So much for an idealized rendering of Jewish feminism. Despite the fact that the theory seems to fit—internally consistent, organically linked, and *halakhically* coherent—there remains nevertheless much fear and resistance, the kind that goes far beyond learned considerations.

The antagonists' charges take many forms: tampering with *halakhah,* changing the unchangeable, watering down Judaism, undermining the family, destroying virtues of female modesty, blurring sexual roles, mixing religion with sexual politics. And finally the veiled and distant threat that while these specific emendations in *halakhah* in and of themselves may be fine, all this tinkering ultimately will undermine Torah, tradition, mitzvot, *halakhah,* norms, faith, stability, rootedness; in short, everything we hold so dear.

This is indeed a heavy load for Jewish feminists to bear. Surely some of the voiced fears serve to prevent those with new ideas from veering too widely off course. Nevertheless, these fears must be addressed directly, for they have a way of escalating, of feeding on themselves, of losing touch with reality.

One aspect of that reality is that the status quo, as we have inherited it, has not been totally static. Surely there are risks involved whenever tradition undergoes change. But *halakhah* is not to be treated as a *goses,* a rapidly failing body that one cannot move lest it give out its final death rattle. *Halakhah* was intended to be preserved, and there is a healthy difference between preserving and freezing solid. "Preserving" does not preclude bringing to the system human responses that will enhance and expand Torah values. Those who counter this claim with labels of Conservative and Reform are simply playing the name game, an easy way to avoid confronting the issues.

Taking the risk at its very worst, if giving religious equality to women should turn out to be a dreadful mistake for ritual life, there ought to be that recognition and assurance that *halakhic* Judaism will outlast the folly of any single generation. To think otherwise bespeaks a lack of faith in the divinity, as well as the eternality, of revelation and the Covenant. It also bespeaks an overwhelming pride and cosmic immodesty to assume that the entire religious enterprise depends wholly on human action or inaction.

Let us now turn to the accusation that these adaptations constitute a watering down of Judaism. I find myself thoroughly confused by this equation, even more so when I hear its paraphrase: "Strike a blow for Yiddishkeit, keep a woman from learning Torah." Does the encouragement of women's learning or the inclusion of women in the prayer structure actually sap the strength of Judaism?

If the religious community operates by the criteria that guided us throughout rabbinic history, then this accusation must fly out the window. We must ask the proper questions: Do the changes enable us to grow as Jews? Do they enlarge our commitment in some way? Are they serious and sustained additions to the religious life? Certainly an increase of obligations and rights for women cannot be equated to adding a fifth fringe on the tzitzit or a fifth variety to the lulav.[7]

The charge that Jewish feminists are mixing religion with sexual politics must be examined, not denied. Those who say it is unthinkable, unwise, unholy, or untraditional to speak of *halakhah* and political pressure in the same breath are simply hiding historical facts. Politics and pressure—the substance as well as the art— certainly have affected *halakhic* decisions throughout our history. How could leaders know the needs of individuals and special interest groups if not through politics, pressure, power plays, protest, and pleading. These actions enabled those with knowledge and authority to bring a different subjectivity to their task of interpreting the law.

The issue of *tzniut* has often been invoked in discussions of such matters. (*Tzniut* is the concept that embraces privacy, modesty, restraint, decency, and chasteness.) Is there a loss of this virtue as women take on public and private roles previously assigned only to men? Yes, if we define *tzniut* to mean women as "inside" persons with no public presence in ritual or liturgy and subject to circumscribed actions and areas of control; breaking all these taboos, in this view, constitutes a flagrant violation of the norms of *tzniut*. But it is necessary to define *tzniut* of women more broadly, that is, in terms of its characteristics, not its role limits. *Tzniut* is both absolute and relative; absolute in modes of behavior, dress, speech, and relative in all those things as well. In certain communities at certain times, a woman did not initiate actions, speak until spoken to, or venture forth into public places (a man's domain); she did not uncover her ankles, elbows, neck, eyes. What is today perfectly acceptable behavior in the modern Orthodox community in speech, thought, dress, and action was unheard of a generation ago. Furthermore, what is permissible in one community is not permitted in another.

At a recent conference in Israel, held at a religious kibbutz, not a single Israeli woman, not even the *shaitl*-covered wives of some of the yeshiva rabbis, wore nylon stockings at the Sabbath synagogue services. Sandal-covered feet were considered modest enough; not so the American women present, who wouldn't think of showing up in shul with bare toes. And at a recent *sheva berakhot*—a celebration in honor of the newly married couple—the young bride, a graduate of the strict Orthodox Bais Yaakov school, delivered a *d'var Torah* (homily) in the mixed audience. This would have been considered *peritzut* (licentious behavior) a mere generation ago.

Even in the most closed sectors of the Jewish community, women are no longer inside persons. They are moved inexorably in the other direction, into jobs, careers, higher education, communal roles. A woman who assumes a public presence in secular society without overstepping the bounds of an internal modesty will do no less in the religious sector. To enable a woman to become a *bat Torah* is hardly likely to lead her to immorality; to consider a woman part of the holy congregation will not lead to profligacy. Initially, the newness of it all may jar the sensibilities, but soon much of it will be taken for granted. With hindsight, we shall say how inadequate our double standards were.

All of this is not to discard *tzniut* as a criterion of behavior for men as well as women, in secular as well as religious life. Surely there is too little of it today; Western social mores have run amok, scrambling all existing codes and outdistancing even the most liberal imagination. How to maintain an economy of *tzniut* in a free society is a problem of immense general concern to which religious leaders ought to put their energies. It should not, however, be confused with keeping a woman in her place.

There is, in addition, the fear that there will be a blurring of the sex roles as a woman increasingly does a "man's thing. " This again is based on the premise that authority, leadership, initiative, and matters of the spirit (prayer) and the mind (study) are exclusive male prerogatives. (Oddly enough, matters of the spirit and the mind seem somehow feminine; but never mind, we now know that these stereotypes do justice to neither sex.)

To be sure, Judaism places very heavy emphasis on separation. We are always separating things into their categories, spaces, time slots, and so forth: Sabbath from weekday, milk from meat, wool from linen, leaven from unleaven, and yes, men from women. In doing so, the uniqueness of each thing or each being is

enhanced; a sense of holiness is miraculously established through the commandments of setting apart.

One cannot deny that Judaism has succeeded in generating a healthy sense of
sexual identity, and we must be on guard to preserve this. But it cannot be done in
ways which keep women suppressed, nor by means of which women are perceived
as less holy or more limited. Moreover, the specific repair that Jewish women are
suggesting need not—indeed, will not—break up healthy categories of male and
female. How do we know this? From what we see all around us. We once had
imagined that women as executives and priests and men as househusbands and
kindergarten teachers inevitably would become either masculinized, feminized, or
neutered in the process. Not so. Nor have women rabbis become sirens or manlike.
Somehow, there must be other, perhaps finer, ways to keep human sexuality intact
than the broad, sweeping functions we have inherited.

Finally, we must respond to the oft-expressed fear that equality in Judaism will
undermine family life. Whether it is their disaffection with family life that drives
some women to feminism or the new knowledge that there is an unstigmatized
alternative (divorce) to a marriage of unequals or the heavy feminist emphasis on
self-actualization that somehow generates an impatience with the difficulties of
building a relationship, the fact is that an exceedingly high proportion of women
with feminist leanings have been or are now being divorced. A Jew committed to
the idea of family stability is rightly scared.

Yet we must take the issue apart. Every splintered marriage cannot be laid at
the doorstep of the women's movement; the attempt to repair circumstances of
abuse or powerlessness in a marriage should not be lumped together with, say, a
predisposition to creating a tunnel vision about the female self. The shortfalls of
women's liberation are used too easily as a cover for maintaining the status quo in
Orthodoxy. A healthy family life and feminist values certainly are not mutually
exclusive. Similarly, full status for women in the religious life of the community
need not of necessity compete with marital bliss. On the contrary, it can enhance
the relationship in many subtle ways.

For a marriage to succeed today, there must be a general equation of partners.
There may not be perfect equality at every given moment; in fact, there may be
large periods of unevenness. One character and personality may dominate; sometimes one partner needs and takes much more than the other. In a good marriage,
however, there must be a basic minimum perception of each other as equals. It is
to this center that the relationship returns after the inevitable rough spots; it is this
cognitive equality that lends stability to marriage.

Such a psychological valence of equals is not generated currently by *halakhah*,
neither in its assignment of primary mitzvot to men nor in the legal asymmetry of
the marriage relationship, as divorce law retrospectively defines it. Those who
persist in interpreting *halakhah* along the lines of male-female hierarchy truly miss a
great leadership opportunity; if only they would use their positions of authority to
strengthen a cognitive equality, without which contemporary marriages seem
doomed to failure.

On a practical level, extending religious obligations and rights to women does not
preclude a healthy family life. Just because a Torah scholar opens up her mind does
not mean that she must shut up her womb. Women will not abandon their babies
wholesale in order to attend the morning minyan. Those few women who will choose

the rabbinate, with its open-ended demands, it is hoped will choose and be chosen by husbands willing to take up the family slack (as countless rebbetzins have done all these years). And a woman who learns how to say kiddush or havdalah or read the Torah with correct cantillations is not destroying the fabric of family life unless we willfully define it that way. The truth is that the rigors of law school or a nine-to-five job or a demanding career represent far greater intrusions into family life than the religious responsibilities that will fall to a woman under a true equality in Judaism. If anything, the participation of women will strengthen ritual and religious institutions, which are themselves major support systems of family life.

These are times for learning new combinations. A young woman, an only child, wanted to say kaddish for her beloved late father. (Kaddish, the daily prayer by mourners during the eleven months following the death of an immediate relative, can be recited only in the presence of a quorum of ten). It didn't matter to her whether she was counted in the minyan (she wasn't); all she wanted was to recite the ancient memorial prayer, at the appropriate time, in the appropriate setting—in this instance, at the early morning synagogue service. But she had a two-year-old daughter. Her husband, a sociology professor, found it perfectly natural to take full responsibility for the early-morning parenting. When queried by a suspicious friend as to his own liturgical responsibilities, the young father responded with candor: yes, at first it did interrupt his own prayer, but quickly he learned to adjust the schedule to his little daughter's needs, at no loss to his own morning-prayer routine.

I do not want to sound glib on this issue. Family stability is a variable that the community must monitor continually and carefully with each new change. I know that even as we appropriate feminist values to enhance the position of women in Judaism, we must take care to maintain a dialectical stance. Without yielding its legitimate claims to justice and quality, we have to be able to separate ourselves from those elements that can be destructive of Jewish family values, such as an excessive emphasis on self-actualization that can erode human relationships, and we must maintain a commitment to family and the need for continuity in a community. But we also must refrain from using family stability as a blanket slogan in the name of which women will continue to be read out of the fullness of the tradition.

What I envision, then, when the theory of Jewish feminism is carried to its practical conclusion, is an adaptation of tradition that will allow for the maturation of woman as Jew—learned, responsible, observant of *halakhah*, able to exercise her fullest potential—a woman so committed to the Jewish people that she will incorporate its values and needs as she begins to make the personal choices society now holds out to her.

Notes

1. See Joseph B. Soloveitchik, "The Lonely Man of Faith," *Tradition* 7 (Summer 1965): 5–67. Rabbi Soloveitchik writes of the "democratization of the God-man confrontation" to all men; it seems that the author also is describing the condition of women.

2. See Leonard Swidler, *Women in Judaism* (Metuchen, N.J.: The Scarecrow Press, 1976).

3. Simone de Beauvoir, *The Second Sex* (New York: Bantam Books, 1953); Rosemary R. Ruether, ed., *Religion and Sexism* (New York: Simon and Schuster, 1974); Michelle Z.

Rosaldo and Louise Lamphere, eds., *Women, Culture, and Society* (Palo Alto, Calif.: Stanford University Press, 1974).

4. Regarding the elimination of conflicting responsibilities, see *Sefer Abudraham hashalem* (Jerusalem: Usha, 1959), Order of the Weekday Prayers, the Morning Blessings.

5. Moshe Meiselman, *Jewish Women and Jewish Law* (New York: KTAV, 1978), chap. 16.

6. See, for example, the commentaries on *ve-haya ekev tishma'un*, Deut. 7:12; *naval bireshut ha-Torah*, Lev. 12:2, particularly Nachmanides' comments; *shiluah ha-kan*, Deut. 22:6, and commentaries.

7. These are the examples found in the Sifre on Deut. 13:1, explicating the law neither to add to nor subtract from the mitzvot in the Torah. On this verse see also the comments of B. H. Epstein, ed., *Torah temimah* (Jerusalem: Hotza'at Sefer, 1970).

C. Jewish Perspectives on Social Problems

22

Ecology and the Judaic Tradition

ROBERT GORDIS

The ecological threat, indicated by the mounting evidence of the contamination of our environment, is perhaps the newest problem to affect the human race. Pollution, of course, is not new; technological progress has been with us for many decades. But only recently has pollution of air, water, and food been recognized as a major hazard.

In view of the importance of the issues involved, it should be of interest to explore the insights and attitudes on ecology in the biblical and postbiblical tradition. This is particularly true since Hebraic teachings on the subject are not merely unknown, they are often misunderstood even by those who should know better. Thus at a conference on the theology of survival held a few years ago, virtually all the scholars agreed that the traditional Christian attitude toward nature had actually "given sanction" to the exploitation and spoliation of our natural resources. Moreover, the source of this destructive attitude, they declared, is the Hebrew Bible, specifically, Gen. 1:28:

> God blessed them; and God said to them: "Be fruitful and multiply, and replenish
> the earth, and subdue it; and have dominion over the fish of the sea, and over the
> fowl of the air, and over every living thing that moves on the earth."

They solemnly pointed to this verse, and particularly to the phrase "and subdue it," as giving men the license to use and abuse the natural world and its resources as they see fit, without limitation or restriction.

The well-meaning theologians who passed these devastating judgments did not stop to notice that the same opening chapter of Genesis, in which man is given the right to "subdue" the earth and to "have dominion" over all living things does not even permit him to use animals for food. For the very next verse—Gen. 1:29—declares: ". . . I have given you every plant yielding seed which is upon the face of

all the earth, and every tree with seed in its fruits; you shall have them for food."
This is surely a drastic limitation upon man's rights. Not until many centuries later,
after the Flood, is man (in the person of Noah and his family) permitted to eat meat
(Gen. 9:3–4). And even then, all men are forbidden to eat the blood of the creatures they have used for food, because the blood is the seat of life. Reverence for
life dictates that the blood be poured out and not consumed. This ritual is a
symbolic recognition that all life is sacred—all life, even the life of animals that men
kill for the sake of sustenance.

Actually the paradigm of man's relationship to his environment is expressed in
the task assigned to Adam in the Garden of Eden before the Fall: "He placed him
in the Garden of Eden to till it and to guard it" (Gen. 2:15).

What is the meaning of the Hebrew phrase in the opening chapter of Genesis,
"and subdue it"? The truth is that the passage in Genesis was never used to establish a principle of aggressive action by man vis-à-vis the environment. In fact, the
Talmud relates the phrase to the first part of the verse, "Be fruitful and multiply." It
then declares that since subduing enemies in war is primarily a male undertaking,
the verb "subdue" must refer to a male obligation. Hence the duty to propagate the
human race falls upon the male rather than upon the female (*B. Yebamot* 65b). It
may be added, in view of the agitation revolving around planned parenthood, that
the obligation to "be fruitful and multiply" is fulfilled in rabbinic law when two
children are born to a family. The only point at issue is the sex of the children; while
the School of Shammai requires that there be two sons, the School of Hillel requires
one son and one daughter (*M. Yebamot* 6:6; *Yoreh Deah* 1:5).

This obligation, the first commandment in the Bible, underwent a complex development in postbiblical life and law.[1] Its application should obviously be different in
the highly industrialized nations of the West and in the starving, vastly overpopulated
countries of Asia and Africa. The Jewish community today constitutes a special case.
It has undergone a 40 percent *negative* "population growth" as the result of the
Holocaust and is exposed to the inroads of assimilation and a minuscule birthrate in
Europe and the Americas. In fact, it may be argued that modern Jews are too zealous
in maintaining the rabbinic limitations on the commandment!

In any event, the Talmud relates the verb "and subdue it" to the propagation of
the race. Medieval Jewish commentators saw in it a reference to the biological and
ecological fact that man is the dominant species on this planet, able to exercise his
will upon other creatures (with the possible exception of insects and some rodents)
and to modify the environment as he chooses. Nahmanides explained the passage as
follows: "He gave them law and dominion on the earth to act according to their
wish with the animals and creeping things and to build and uproot plants and to
mine copper out of the hills and carry on other similar activities." The Italian
commentator Obadiah Sforno gave the phrase a more restricted meaning: "And
subdue it—that you protect yourself with your reason and prevent the animals from
entering within your boundaries and you rule over them."[2]

The fundamental Jewish teaching on man's relationship to his environment is explicitly contained in two very broad and far-reaching ethical principles that are written
large in biblical and postbiblical literature. The first principle governs man's treatment of the so-called lower animals; the second expresses man's proper attitude
toward inanimate nature. Taken together, these basic principles, with their corollar-

ies, have considerable relevance for directing and shaping man's proper attitudes and actions toward his fellow creatures and his environment on earth.

Judaic thought generally prefers to avoid abstractions. Nevertheless, the first principle relating to the treatment of "lower" animals carries a poignant name in rabbinic literature: *za'ar ba'alei hayim,* "the pain of living creatures." This concept, deeply rooted in the Bible, has been extensively elaborated upon in rabbinic law and ethics. Unique in its sympathy for what has been called "brute creation," the Fourth Commandment in the Decalogue enjoins rest for one's ox, donkey, and every creature on the Sabbath day (Exod. 20:11; Deut. 5:14; see also Exod. 23:12). Deuteronomy forbids the farmer to plow with an ox and a donkey yoked together, because the practice would obviously impose great hardship upon the weaker animal. Nor was the farmer permitted to muzzle an ox during the threshing period to prevent its eating any of the grain (Deut. 22:10; 25:4).

Equally significant was the desire of the Torah to spare the feelings of living creatures and simultaneously inculcate the spirit of mercy in man. Thus, it is forbidden to slaughter a cow or a ewe together with its offspring in the same day (Lev. 22:28). This twofold concern finds exquisite expression in the law in Deuteronomy:

> If you chance to come upon a bird's nest, in any tree or on the ground, with young ones or eggs, and the mother sitting upon the young or upon the eggs, you shall not take the mother with the young. You shall let the mother go, but the young you may take to yourself, that it may go well with you, and that you may live long. (Deut. 22:6–7)

The traditional laws of kosher slaughtering (*shehitah*) are designed to keep alive the sense of reverence for life by forbidding the eating of blood and by minimizing the pain of the animal when it is slaughtered.

In all societies, hunting has been highly regarded as a sport. Whatever the practice of the ancient Hebrews may have been, only two biblical figures are described as hunters and they were not Hebrews, Nimrod and Esau. Both were regarded very negatively in the postbiblical tradition and were taken to symbolize the anti-Jewish spirit.

Rabbinic law permitted hunting for practical purposes, such as food, commerce, or the removal of animal pests, but hunting for sport was strongly condemned in all periods as not being "the way of the children of Abraham, Isaac, and Jacob."[3] Albert Einstein cites a report, possibly apocryphal, that Walter Rathenau said, "When a Jew says that he hunts for pleasure, he lies."

The contemporary concern with "endangered species" would seem to be adumbrated in a comment by the medieval legist and exegete Moses Nahmanides. We have already referred to the biblical prohibitions against slaughtering a cow and her calf on the same day and the taking of a bird with her young as emanating from the wish to spare the mother as much anguish as possible. In his commentary on the latter passage Nahmanides declares: "Scripture will not permit a destructive act that will bring about the extinction of a species, even though it has permitted the ritual slaughtering of that species for food. He who kills the mother and offspring on one day is considered as if he destroyed the species."[4]

Perhaps the most eloquent affirmation of preoccupation with the welfare of all living things—eloquent precisely because it is indirect and seemingly unintentional—occurs in the unforgettable climax of the Book of Jonah. The prophet Jonah feels himself aggrieved because his forecast that the sinful city of Nineveh will be destroyed has been averted—the people having repented. Jonah then finds a measure of comfort in a gourd, a large-leafed plant which the Lord has created especially to shield him against the sun. The next night God destroys the gourd and Jonah becomes very angry. A colloquy then ensues, which ends, be it noted, in characteristic Jewish fashion—with a question!

> God said to Jonah, "Are you very angry for the gourd?" And Jonah said, "I am very angry, angry enough to die." And the Lord said, "You pity the gourd, for which you did not labor, nor did you make it grow, which came into being in a night, and perished in a night. And should I not have pity for Nineveh, that great city, in which there are more than a hundred and twenty thousand persons who do not know their right hand from their left, and also much cattle?" (Jon. 4:9–11)

Love and pity for innocent children are equated with mercy for animals.

The biblical ordinances regarding the treatment of animals laid down in the Torah are tolerably well known. In the Prophets, the eloquent climax in the Book of Jonah is deservedly famous. The biblical prophets, sages, and psalmists vie with one another in describing the harmony between man and nature as a fundamental element of life in the ideal future, which later generations described as the messianic age (Hos. 2:20–24; Amos 9:13–15; Isa. 11:1–9; Joel 2:21–26; Ps. 91; Job 5:23).

A profound theological basis for ecology, including the right of animals in the world, is to be found in a biblical source that to my knowledge has hitherto never been invoked in this connection. The Book of Job is unique in its conception of the purpose of Creation, which is adumbrated in its climax in the Speeches of the Lord Out of the Whirlwind. After the debate of Job and his friends has ended and the brash young Elihu, though uninvited, has made his contribution to the heart-rending problem of human suffering, the Lord, speaking out of the whirlwind, confronts Job in two speeches.[5] He offers no facile answer to the mystery of evil; instead he raises the discussion to an altogether higher level. With exultant joy, the Lord has the world that he has created pass in review before Job, and he challenges him to understand, let alone share in, the task of creation. In powerful lines, the wonders of inanimate nature are described. The creation of heaven and earth, stars and seas, morning and night, light and darkness is pictured. The snow and the hail, the flood and the lightning, the rain, the dew, the frost, and the clouds—all are revelations of God as Creator. But we do not have here a cold "scientific" catalogue of natural phenomena, such as is to be found in the Egyptian *Onomasticon* of Amenemope.[6] What is significant is not the explicit listing of the items, but the implication the poet draws from them—like the rain in the uninhabited desert, they were all called into being without man as their purpose and they remain beyond his power and control (Job 38:1–38). This significant implication will be underscored more strongly as the speech proceeds.

 The Lord now turns to the world of animate nature and glowingly describes seven creatures: the lion, the mountain goat, the wild ass, the buffalo, the ostrich, the wild horse, and the hawk. What they have in common, apart from being beautiful manifestations of God's creative power, is that they have not been created for man's use; they have their own independent reason for being, known only to their Creator.

This theme is powerfully reenforced in the second Speech of the Lord Out of the Whirlwind. He now pictures two massive creatures, Behemoth the hippopotamus, and Leviathan, the crocodile (40:15–24; 40:25–41:26). It is not merely that they are not under human control, like the animals already described; they are positively repulsive and even dangerous to man. Yet they too reveal the power of the Creator in a universe which is not anthropocentric but theocentric, with purposes known only to God, which man cannot fathom. The world is both a mystery and a miracle; what man cannot understand of the mystery he can sustain because of its beauty. Man is not the goal of creation and therefore not the master of the cosmos.

The basic theme, that the universe is a mystery to man, is of course overtly expressed in the God speeches. There are, however, two other significant implications. In accordance with characteristic Semitic usage they need to be inferred by the reader.

The first is theological: since the universe was not created with man as its center, neither the Creator nor the cosmos can be judged from man's vantage point. The second is ecological. Though the poet was not concerned with presenting a religio-ethical basis for ecology, he has in effect done so. Man takes his place among the other living creatures, who are likewise the handiwork of God. Therefore he has no inherent right to abuse or exploit the living creatures or the natural resources to be found in a world not of his making, nor intended for his exclusive use.

If we have read the meaning of the Speeches of the Lord aright, we now have a sound conceptual basis for one of the more beneficent aspects of twentieth-century civilization—the growing concern for the humane treatment of animals. This sensitivity expresses itself both practically and theoretically.[7]

On the practical side, a far-flung and highly varied network of organizations has arisen in Western Europe and America designed to protest the cruel treatment and undue suffering to which animals are often exposed in industry and even in scientific research. Many concrete proposals have been advanced for laws to protect animals against abuse and needless pain. The rising tide of protest against contemporary practices in these areas takes on many forms, some perhaps ill-considered and at times even bizarre and violent. On balance, however, the essentially positive character of the movement for animal rights is undeniable.[8]

Aside from a deepening involvement with concrete measures in this area, there has also been an increased interest in a philosophical basis for the rights of animals, with a growing literature on the subject as a branch of secular ethics.

The Book of Job offers a religious foundation for the inherent rights of animals as coinhabitants of the earth, adumbrated two millennia earlier than the emergence of secular ethics in this area.[9]

By insisting on a God-centered world, to which man has only a conditional title, the Book of Job presents a basis in religion for opposing and ultimately eliminating the needless destruction of life and the pollution of the natural resources in the world.

As important as the biblical and postbiblical teaching on man's treatment of his fellow tenants on the planet is the attitude toward the natural environment inculcated by the Jewish tradition. It is referred to in talmudic and posttalmudic literature as *bal tashit,* "do not destroy." The phrase is borrowed from a striking passage in Deuteronomy which, strange as it may seem, deals with the laws of warfare.

> When you besiege a city for a long time, making war against it in order to take it, you shall not destroy [*tashit*] its trees by wielding an axe against them. You may eat from them, but must not cut them down, for are the trees in the field human beings, that they should be besieged by you? Only the trees which you know are not fruit-bearing you may destroy and cut down, in order to build siege-works against the city that makes war with you, until it falls. (Deut. 20:19–20)

This injunction ran counter to accepted procedures in ancient war practiced, for example, by the Assyrians, who were particularly known for their cruelty. In modern times, *Schrecklichkeit,* "frightfulness," was an accepted canon of German military tactics. It has continued as a prime method in war to this day. The "scorched-earth" policy was widely used in the Vietnam conflict, developing new technological efficiency in the use of poisonous chemicals. The term "defoliation" was a euphemism to cover up the horror of total destruction of the countryside by American forces and by the Communist enemy, who was not more merciful.

The biblical laws of warfare clearly forbade wanton destruction. But the rabbis went far beyond the law in Deuteromomy. With their genius for discerning a general principle in a specific law, they enunciated a universal doctrine under the rubric of *bal tashit.* They then proceeded to develop a comprehensive code on ecology by extending the biblical law in three directions:

1. The biblical passage forbade wielding an axe against a tree during a siege. The rabbis extended the prohibition to any other means of wanton destruction in war, direct or indirect, including shifting the course of a stream so that the tree would dry up (*Sifrei, Shofetim,* sec. 203). They condemned the stopping of wells, a tactic King Hezekiah had adopted in wartime (2 Chron. 32:2–4, *B. Pesahim* 56a). They forbade the killing of animals or giving them possibly polluted water to drink (*B. Hullin* 7b; *Tosafot B. Baba Kamma* 115 b, based on *B. Abodah Zarah* 30b).

2. Even more far-reaching was the extension of these prohibitions to apply not only to war tactics but to all situations, including the more usual conditions of peace. Under all circumstances, the wanton or thoughtless destruction of natural objects was prohibited. In addition, the pollution of the air by various enterprises, like a threshing floor operation, or the establishment of tanneries, furnaces, or cemeteries in proximity to cities was forbidden (*M. Baba Batra* 2:8–9, B. Baba Kamma 82b).

3. Going beyond ecological concerns was the extension of the doctrine "You shall not destroy" from objects of nature to human artifacts. The biblical passage deals with a tree, which is a product of nature. The rabbis of the Talmud applied the principle to all the artifacts of man: "Whoever breaks vessels, or tears garments, or destroys a building, or clogs up a fountain, or does away with food in a destructive manner, violates the prohibition of *bal tashit*" (*B. Kiddushin* 32a).

The general principle was clearly formulated: "It is forbidden to destroy or to injure [*hamekalkel*] anything capable of being useful to men [*lehanot bo bnei 'adam*]."[10]

There are, to be sure, variations among the posttalmudic authorities with regard to the exact legal status of the prohibition. Maimonides declares that only cutting down of a tree is biblically forbidden, and all the other extensions are only rabbinic in character.[11] Curiously, the *Shulḥan Arukh* of Rabbi Joseph Karo omits the entire subject, including the explicit biblical prohibition. Various efforts to explain this fact have been made. However, there are other instances of similar omissions in this code. But the binding power of the commandment "You shall not destroy," with its extensions to conditions of peace and its application to human artifacts as well as to natural objects, was never in doubt. Over centuries the horror of vandalism became part of the psyche of the Jew.

The full dimensions of this profound ethical principle need to be appreciated. *Bal tashit* has nothing in common with the sanctity of private property. One is forbidden to destroy not only the property of others, but also one's own. This principle derives in part from the recognition that what we are wont to call "our" property is really not our own, but God's. It is this principle that is invoked to validate the two great laws of the *Sabbatical year* and the *Jubilee year*.

The Torah ordained that the farmer was permitted to plow, sow, and reap his harvest for six years. Each seventh year, however, was to be observed as "a Sabbath to the Lord." Neither the field nor the vineyard might be tended, and what grew was public property to be used equally by freemen and slaves, natives and strangers (Lev. 25:5–6).

The Sabbatical year served several purposes. The first was *ecological* in character. In the days before crop rotation or the availability of chemical nutrients for the soil, the practice of letting the land lie fallow enabled it to regain its fertility.

The second was *social* and *ethical*. Only the poor and the stranger had the right to eat the produce that grew by itself during the seventh year, just as they had the right to the gleanings, the forgotten sheaves and the after-growth in the corners of the field in other years. This was an important element in the far-flung system of social legislation for the underprivileged in ancient Israel.

Finally, even more fundamental than the agricultural and social functions, biblical law reaffirmed a *deep religious principle;* God was dramatically reasserting his ownership of the land, of which man is only a temporary custodian.

After seven Sabbatical years had passed, the fiftieth year was ushered in as the Jubilee year (Lev. 25:8–24). The law ordains that on the Jubilee all property that has been sold during the preceding half century be returned to its original owner without compensation. This radical step is justified by the basic legal principle: "The land shall not be sold in perpetuity, for the land is Mine; for you are strangers and sojourners with Me" (Lev. 25:23). Psalm 24 gives this same principle poetic expression in cosmic terms: "The earth is the Lord's in all its fullness, the world and those who dwell therein."

The biblical laws of the Sabbatical and the Jubilee years were long regarded as utopian legislation never put into practice. The Talmud itself declares that the Sabbatical year ceased to function a decade before the destruction of the Northern Kingdom of Israel, which took place in 722 B.C.E. However, the agricultural and ritual provisions of the Sabbatical year are observed even today by ultrapious Jewish groups: they eat no produce grown in the soil by Jewish farmers in the Holy Land during the seventh year. Some also transfer any outstanding debts due them in the seventh year to the rabbinic court for collection, in accordance with a rabbinic ordinance by Hillel called the *prosbul*. By means of this legal fiction, the obligation may be collected by the creditor after the seventh year. Admittedly, these practices preserved today are external rites, but they point to an earlier period when these laws were basic to Israelite life. Moreover, in recent years, archaeological evidence has accumulated to indicate that the socioeconomic aspects of the Sabbatical year have analogues in ancient Mesopotamia, making it a reasonable assumption that the biblical regulations had a basis in reality.

Both the Sabbatical and the Jubilee Years have left their impress on modern society. In New York City's Rockefeller Plaza there is a short street running between Fifth and Sixth Avenues. Embedded in the pavement is a small metal tablet stating that this thoroughfare was the private property of Columbia University. Every year the street was closed off to traffic for one day, to reassert and thus maintain the university's title to the land—a modern variation of the same technique as that of the Sabbatical year!

Basing itself explicitly on the biblical law, the Jewish National Fund, the Zionist land-purchasing agency in Israel, leases its property to individuals and groups, but does not sell it in perpetuity.

From this basic concept of God's ownership of the earth and all of its natural resources, it follows that any act of destruction is an offense against the property of God.

The principle of *bal tashit* contains still another religious insight. As we have seen, the Book of Job gives magnificent expression to the recognition that every natural object is an embodiment of the creative power of God and is therefore sacred. The law of *bal tashit* goes further. Whatever has been fashioned by *man,* the product of his energies and talents, is equally a manifestation of God's creative power one step removed, since man is himself the handiwork of God. Vandalism is, therefore, far more than a violation of private property or the destruction of potentially useful objects; it is rebellion against the cosmic order of the universe, which human beings are commanded to enjoy and forbidden to destroy, "For the earth is the Lord's in all its fullness, the world and all who inhabit it" (Ps. 24:1).

Notes

1. It is traced in R. Gordis, " 'Be Fruitful and Multiply': Biography of Mitzvah," *Midstream,* August–September 1982, pp. 21–29.

2. See their respective commentaries on the passage.

3. R. Ezekiel Landau, *Noda Biyehudah, Responsa, Yore De'ah* II, 10.

4. Naḥmanides, *Commentary on the Torah,* vol. 5, ed. Ch. B. Chavel (New York: Shilo, 1976), p. 265.

5. The debate of Job and his friends (chaps. 3–31); Elihu's speeches (chaps. 32–36); the Lord's two speeches (38:1–40:2 and 40:6–41:26).

6. This Egyptian text and several similar ones were edited by A. H. Gardiner, *Ancient Egyptian Onomastica* (London: Oxford University Press, 1947). G. von Rad, who calls attention to the Egyptian and the Hebrew text, does not recognize the vast difference between them in literary character. See A. H. Rad, "Job XXXVIII and "Ancient Egyptian Wisdom," in J. L. Crenshaw, ed., *Studies in Ancient Israelite Wisdom* (New York, KTAV 1976), pp. 267–77.

7. For a recent comprehensive survey of the current literature on the subject by a strongly committed advocate, see Peter Singer, "Ten Years of Animal Liberation," *New York Review of Books,* vol. 31, nos. 21–22 (January 17, 1985), pp. 46–52. His essay, "Animal Liberation," published in the *New York Review of Books* on April 5, 1973, followed by a

book with the same title, was one of the earliest presentations of the case for the rights of animals in our society.

8. See e.g. Andrew Rowan, *Of Mice, Models and Men: A Critical Evaluation of Animal Research* (Albany: State University of New York Press, 1983).

9. The first treatment of the question of the ethical status of animals by an academic philosopher, according to Singer (op. cit., p. 47) was Roslind Godlovitch's pioneering article, "Animals and Morals" published in *Philosophy* in 1971. For a bibliography of subsequent publications on the ethics of animal rights, see Singer, op. cit. Notes 6.

10. See *Shulḥan Arukh of the Rav, Hilkhot Shemirat Guf Vanefesh,* sec. 14.

11. *Tosafot* on *Abodah Zarah* 11a; *B. Baba Metzia* 32a.

23

A Jewish View of Economic Justice

SEYMOUR SIEGEL

When a person is brought before the Heavenly Court, they first ask him, "Were you honest in business?"

Talmud, Shabbat, 33b

In analyzing Jewish economic theory it is necessary to point out that throughout the more than three-thousand-year history of the Jewish people, national sovereignty was achieved only during a relatively short time. Most of the history of the Jews was lived under foreign rule and in the status of a minority. The major period of national independence was during biblical times when economic structures were relatively primitive. It is, therefore, difficult to make direct applications of biblical or talmudic principles to the complicated and intricate economies of our time. Yet it is instructive to analyze the principles of economic justice emerging from Jewish tradition, if for no other reason than that these principles, as frequently misunderstood, have so often been utilized to justify socialism and other noncapitalist systems.

In the biblical picture, the Garden of Eden story represents *original rightness;* that is, the state of things that *ought* to be. This is in contrast to historical time when things are obviously the way they are—which is different from the normative state depicted in the Garden. Only in the End of Days will the state of affairs return to its original rightness. Therefore consideration of the first chapters of Genesis yields a picture of the normative state of existence, according to the biblical mind.

Even when Adam was in the Garden of Eden he was admonished "to work it and guard it." The talmudic rabbis, noting this fact, taught that "Even Adam tasted nothing before he worked, as it is said, 'and He put him into the Garden of Eden to till it and to keep it'; only then is it written: 'Of every tree of the garden thou mayest eat freely.' " Rabbi Tarfon adds, "The Holy One, praised be He, likewise did not cause His Schechinah (divine presence) to rest upon Israel before they did work, as it is said, 'and let them make Me a sanctuary, then shall I dwell among them.' "

It is assumed, therefore, that the human being was to labor in the world. This was the divine intent. Creation is not perfect, finished, all ready for human consumption. Human effort, the creation of new resources and the guarding of those that already exist, is indispensable to make life livable. In the Garden of Eden there is, of course, no problem of justice, exploitation of workers, or a just wage. In the Garden there is perfect harmony. The human pair is in harmony with itself; both are in harmony with nature, which produces all that is necessary (with the aid of man's toil).

In the biblical story, this idyllic harmony is upset by human sin, which is the misuse of human freedom to defy the divine. Paradise is then lost. Historical time begins. The workplace is the place where the means of life are produced—now, however, the primordial harmony is lost. Work yields results. It also yields strife and discomfort: "By the sweat of thy brow shalt thou eat bread." There will be weeds and thistles. Nature will not always be cooperative. Sin—that is, greed and the drive for ego-enhancement at the expense of others—makes the whole economic life fraught with paradoxes and ambiguities. The realistic situation is that the notion of uncoerced harmony motivated by love is utopian—an impossible dream. In reality, economic life is a struggle that includes the inevitable human drive for gain at the expense of others. This fact must be accepted as a tragic necessity of life. It also makes it mandatory that there be restraints and laws applied to economic activity.

Left to their own devices, men would, as the saying goes, "swallow each other up alive." We need some coercion—laws—to restrain and inhibit the inevitable sins that humans commit against each other, for pure love in human affairs is only rarely possible, if ever. Because there is sin, it is necessary to institute a system of *justice,* which is the institutionalization of love, and the best possible arrangement given the human condition. Justice approximates the ideal. Justice is not the ideal. It is the concretization of the ideal—the rule of love—within the ambiguities of existence. To demand the ideal or to think we have it is utopian. It is to pretend that we can regain paradise. It is an illusion because Paradise will be regained only in the End of Days—not now, in historical time.

In the entire history of Judaism, beginning with the Bible and continuing through the various epochs of Jewish history, it was taken for granted that the economic life of man would involve agriculture, manufacturing, and buying and selling for profit. There is no indication that the profit system is in any way evil or that it will yield to something "higher." Material wealth itself was seen as a blessing. The patriarchs blessed their children that they might possess economic goods. The Prophets of Israel, the most eloquent spokesmen for social justice, did not advocate revolution or the socialization of the means of production and distribution. They opposed and condemned in the name of the God of Justice the use of false weights and measures; the exploitation of the poor by the rich; and the buying off of judges and the cornering of markets so as to raise prices. Overturning of society was not demanded, but repentance—that is, a return to the moral law and the end of the perversion of the laws of justice and compassion that ought to govern the lives of men and women—was required. The rich are condemned not because they are rich but because they use their wealth to wield unjust power over those who are weaker, by bribing judges and raising prices through monopolies. They are also admonished to be compassionate and help those who are in need by loans and gifts of charity.

God's Work on Earth

Thus we see a system that looks favorably on the creation of new wealth, and recognizes the need for coercion in human affairs to curb the tendency within man to exploit whatever he has to deprive others of their rights and freedoms. Yet to analyze the Jewish view on social justice more deeply, it is necessary to dwell on three aspects of the problem. First, what is the general view of the world that is proposed as undergirding the activity of buying, selling, producing, and inventing? This leads to what might be called the *theology* of economics. Second, what is the view of man reflected in the processes that are promoted to order the economic life? This might be called an *anthropology* of economics. Third, what ethical guidelines are imposed upon the economic life? This might be called the *ethics* of economics.

The Theology of Economics

In the normative Judeo-Christian viewpoint, creation is open, not limited, not yet completely finished. God has not created the world "ready-made," to remain the way it came forth from his hand. The human being—in the splendid rabbinic phrase—is a partner with God in the work of creation. The human being's place in creation is to preserve the world but also to transform it. *The greatest of all natural resources for the creation of economic goods is the mind and energy of man.* Manufacturing, inventing new things, thrusting into the unknown, and breaking with encrusted methods of distribution and production are not, as the Greeks thought of it, *hubris*. It is rather the fulfillment of the human estate; it is doing God's work on earth.

Indeed, the rabbis of the Talmud, knowing the Promethean myth, deliberately retell it to change its thrust. They teach that when Adam was expelled from the Garden of Eden, he spent his first night in fear—for it was dark and full of dread. God, seeing his plight, sent him two sticks and told him to rub them together that fire could be created. In the light and warmth generated by the flame, Adam and Eve found comfort and challenge. Fire, the symbol of civilization, industry, and modification of nature, is not, as in the Promethean myth, *stolen* from the gods; rather it is a gift given to Adam to make it possible for him to fulfill his mission in the world.

This leads to a positive approach to the goods of the world. The material things are not evil, filthy, to be shunned and disdained. Because creation belongs to God, the material is good. Furthermore, man's task is to so modify, use, and transform Creation so that it will yield more material goods: to increase food, shelter, clothing, and convenience. Man must not only guard Creation—but also make it yield more to increase the comfort of human beings. It is important to create wealth so that there can be more to be put at the disposal of humankind.

The Anthropology of Economics

Jewish teachers stress the necessity of seeing the human being as he is—with his faults and weaknesses, and his holy dimension. They were neither cynical about human possibilities, nor utopian about failings.

The rabbinic psychology is based on the idea that the human being is made up of two *yetser*s (coming from a root meaning to create)—that is, two drives that are part of the human makeup. One of these is called *yetser hatov,* the good inclination. This is the source of the power of human beings to transcend their own self-interest. It makes it possible for humans to obey God's laws, even when it means giving up their own freedom and desires. It makes it possible for men to perform deeds of loving kindness and compassion; to perform sacrificially for the sake of others. The other, much stronger, inclination is called the *yetser hara,* the evil inclination. It comprises the drive toward ego enhancement, selfishness, greed, and idolatry (that is, putting oneself in the center, instead of God). Life is a battle waged continually between the two *yetsers.* The *yetser hara* will be completely uprooted only in the End of Days when all things will be redeemed. Until that time, we must deal with it; try to modify it; and be on guard against it.

There is a striking rabbinic statement concerning the *yetser hara* that has a direct bearing on our discussion.

> The evil inclination is sometimes called good. How can this be? Were it not for the evil inclination a man would not marry, build a house, or engage in commerce.

It is true that business and economic ventures, toil, and labor are the outcome of the baser motives of human nature. The drive to create and accumulate wealth is pushed by the desire to have more and to be above others. From this point of view it is the result of the *yetser hara.* Yet when people channel this drive for ego enhancement into hard work, daring, invention, risk, and dedication, which are indispensable for successful outcomes, the sum total of the world's goods is increased. In this view, the evil inclination is entitled to be called good. The evil inclination is not good; but it can lead to good. Since we are dealing with ambiguous forces, we are in need of regulation, obedience to law—in other words, the influence of the good inclination. Left to itself, the drive for more material wealth will lead to much good, but it will also use the power thus created to seize illegitimate power.

It is important to point out again that the Judaic tradition is antiutopian. It does not foresee, except in the end of time, the total elimination of the *yetser hara.* Therefore, *all* human structures—political, social, and economic—are flawed. *None* produces perfect harmony. *All* can be transformed into instruments of evil. The tradition is likewise aware of the capacity of the human being to obey a transcendent source of value. We have the power to give up some of our own goods for the sake of others or for the sake of the whole. This is the outcome of the workings of the good inclination. The good inclination is the drive that makes possible hard work and self-sacrifice for the good of the community. It is also the source of the human capacity for *tsedaka,* philanthropy, which is the extension of a helping hand to those who are poor, unfortunate, sick, aged, or destitute.

Yet even in this there is a dialectical tension. Ideally from the moral point of view, philanthropy should be freely given, uncoerced—as men frequently do give. This provides philanthropy with its moral tone. However, Judaic thought is not that sanguine. It does not believe that those who are needy should depend *totally* on the *yetser hatov* of others. In the view of Judaism, the community can enforce philanthropy, or at least the minimum amount necessary. This makes *tsedaka* a combination of coercion and free will; forced compassion may not be morally laudable—however, it does increase the sum total of good to others. Thus the anthropology of economics characteristic of Judaism is very similar to the classical free-market outlook. Human desire for ego enhancement works to create more and more wealth. Adam Smith's "invisible hand" recognizes the same irony: that evil—perhaps against its own will—thus serves the good. And as Smith knew, this ambiguity requires laws and safeguards as well as a certain amount of "forced philanthropy."

The Ethics of Economics

From the Judaic viewpoint competition is good, for it lowers the price and increases the quality of the product. The community is, therefore, obliged to ensure, as much as possible, a situation where competition can be secured. This meant that rabbinic authorities were particularly concerned about monopolies because they can lead to price-fixing, thus making the lot of the poor more difficult. One example from rabbinic literature—which seems quaint to modern ears—illustrates the viewpoint of the rabbis.

Jewish women were required to offer two doves as a sacrifice after each birth, based on the Levitical legislation. Since many lived far from Jerusalem, they waited to offer the doves when they made the pilgrimage to the Temple on festivals. This sometimes meant that they could not bring their sacrifices for intervals of several years. When they did get to Jerusalem they therefore often had to offer several pairs of doves—a pair for each confinement. Thus the seasonal demand for doves was high. At one time they reached the very high price of two dinarii. Rabbi Simeon b. Gamaliel, the leader of the religious Council, proclaimed:

> By the Temple, I shall not sleep this night until they cost one silver dinar (one twenty-fifth of a golden dinar). He went to the House of Study and taught: If a woman has five miscarriages or five births she need bring but one offering. . . . By the end of the day a pair of doves cost one-quarter of a silver dinar each.

Price-gouging by monopolists can be combated even by changing cherished ritual laws. But *profit* is justified. It serves as a motive for the creation of wealth, and therefore, helps to progress the affairs of the world.

The profit system inevitably results in differences of income. There are some who are rich, others who are poor. There are those who because of age, health, or circumstance cannot compete with those more fortunate. The community has a responsibility to maintain those individuals who cannot earn enough to maintain themselves. This was expressed in the great and important mitzvah (commandment) of philanthropy.

When I was a child, I was told over and over again that one either gives charity or receives it. But would it not be more equitable to equalize incomes? This is the subject of an interesting conversation that is recorded in rabbinic literature:

> It has been taught: Rabbi Meir used to say: The critic of Judaism may bring against you the argument, "If your God loves the poor, why does he not support them?" If so, answer him, "So that through them we may be merited for the rewards of the World to Come."

Turnus Rufus, who was a Roman and who frequently engaged in dialogues with the talmudic rabbis, upon hearing of this argument complained, citing a parable.

> Once a king was angry with his son. He put him in prison and ordered that he be given no food or drink. And a man went and gave him food and drink. If the king heard would he not be angry?

Rabbi Akiva (the most prominent of the rabbis) answered him:

> I will illustrate by another parable. Suppose an earthly king was angry with his son, and put him in prison, and ordered that no food or drink should be given to him,

and someone went and gave him food and drink. If the king heard of it, would he not send him a present?

This strange conversation illustrates two basic approaches to the question of why there are poor and rich in the society. Turnus Rufus (perhaps representing the pagan approach) views those who are poor as being punished and cursed by the gods. Therefore, to alleviate the lot of the poor is to go against fate, the will of the gods. Rabbi Akiva (representing the Judaic view) seems to be saying that those who are poor lack some of the gifts given to the richer citizens. Inequality is the result of differences of luck, endowment, effort, talent (most of these are, after all, God's gift). Providence allows this situation as a reward for those who labor to achieve and also to present a challenge to the more prosperous to practice philanthropy. The rich and poor are both the children of God.

In this approach there is a polarity. There is a constant interplay between the individual and the community. On the one hand, the central figure is the individual. The commandments are addressed to him. He is commanded to help his fellow man. However, an indispensable and all-inclusive role is given to the community. The community supervises, enforces, and administers *tsedaka*. The individual gives his donation to the community. The community establishes the institutions for the sick, the poor, the disturbed, and the aged. But this leads to a high-powered, mechanized philanthropy, and that is not good. Therefore, coupled with the communal activity, there is a call for *personal* involvement in the assistance of those who need help. A person should himself assist the poor, especially the aged, in filling their personal needs. *The main thing is that the person who needs help gets it.* In the words of one of the great contemporary teachers of Judaism (A. J. Heschel), " . . . we insist on the deed and pray for the intention."

There is another aspect of philanthropy that is relevant to our discussion. Maimonides, the greatest of the Jewish teachers of the medieval period, designates eight degrees of charity. He writes: "The highest degree exceeded by none, is that of the person who assists a poor person by providing him a gift or a loan or by accepting him into a business partnership or by helping him find employment—in a word, by putting him where he can dispense with other people's aid." Philanthropy can demean the recipient. The ultimate aim is to make the recipient self-sufficient so that he does not require assistance from others. This raises his dignity and enhances his humanness.

In sum, the *theology* of economics underlying Judaic thought is based on a concept of the human responsibility to use creation to "complete" it, to create wealth and abundance.

The *anthropology* of economics in Judaism recognizes the dual nature of man. The drive for ego enhancement, though founded in "greed," leads to the creation of wealth and thus can be seen as "good."

The *ethics* of economics requires honesty and justice, a fully competitive system, and care for the poor and the needy through individual giving and "enforced philanthropy" administered by the community. Private property is a basic element. Ultimately, however, the world belongs to God. We are, therefore, obliged to use the world to further the divine purpose, and also to heed his command to make it possible for all his children to have their basic needs fulfilled.

Justice for All

All societies acknowledge the responsibility to establish justice. (Even totalitarian regimes have "ministries of justice.") In Jewish teachings, the duty to establish justice is one of the Seven Noahide Commandments—the duties of which are incumbent upon the whole human race. Justice, in this view, is rooted in the demands of God, Who is the God of Justice.

Justice can be understood in various ways. There are varying definitions. But underlying all the relativities in the understanding of justice is the conception that it involves, at the very least, the unbiased, impartial adjustment of conflicting claims in terms of some determined standard. Partiality or bias in judgment is by definition injustice. The true judge applies the rule according to the evidence. The Bible exhorts the judge not to favor *the rich or the poor* in judgment (Exod. 23:3). The law, in its majesty, applies to all regardless of their status in the society or the community. Of course, if after the judgment you wish to help the poor man pay his debt, it behooves you to do so—out of *philanthropic feelings*. But justice demands the application of the norms of morality to everyone.

Justice is the institutionalization of the law of love in concrete, real society. In love, all others are treated as "thou's." As Buber himself pointed out, in real life this "law" has to be translated into procedures, law, institutions, and legislation. This means that for society to function, a measure of love is sacrificed to make life possible.

Injustice, the perversion of fairness, is usually the result of the undue concentration of power in one source. Those who wield power—without any "check or balance"—are subject to corruption. There has to be constant vigilance and criticism of existing arrangements in order to prevent the injustices that come in the wake of unrestrained power.

This is particularly important in the realm of economic justice. The just economic order, as we have remarked, is a basic requirement of biblical religion. God is the God of justice. He wants his children to imitate him. He has given us the fruits of the earth. He has also given us minds to thrust into the unknown, and the energy to produce. The use of our power to increase the goods of the earth is a fulfillment of a divine command.

There seems to be a natural drive in argumentation and debate to try to seize the middle ground. This is true especially of the classical papal encyclicals. It is clear that unrestricted *liberalism,* as the papal documents use the phrase, is not adequate. It tends to produce too great concentrations of power, which can lead to injustice. This is why the creation of trade unions to make it possible for the worker to bargain on levels of rough equality with his employer is necessary. (It is also necessary to curb the powers of the unions when they become vehicles of injustice). Similarly, *socialism,* which requires centralization and collectivism, is guaranteed to produce tyranny. The reins of economic power cannot be held either by a monopolistic economic conglomerate or by an elitist party bureaucracy. Tyranny, in both cases, is almost inevitable.

What has emerged from the experience of the twentieth century is that the closest approximation of a just economic order is one in which there is freedom to engage in enterprise and the creation of wealth. This freedom has to be tempered by legislation and enforcement of reasonable measures to limit the formation of monopolies and to enforce honesty and fairness. There can be a difference of opinion as to how much regulation is ncessary. But there is no debate that there should be *some* regulation. There also has to be some "enforced philanthropy" so that the community provides a floor under those who cannot fully participate in the economic life. Workers should be able to organize freely so as to bargain collectively with their employers, even as the public must remain vigilant against unbridled union power as against any other concentrated source of power.

If the twentieth century has taught us anything, it has taught that there is nothing as dangerous as a utopian power. Utopianism is the belief that in historical time the ideal society will be produced, an illusion that human beings frequently have been prone to adopt. But no existing or future social order will embody the ideal of love. We must try to improve our society so that it moves *closer to* the ideal. Only at the End of Time will the original rightness be restored. Until then, we trust the Lord of creation to help us overcome the frustrations and challenges of our time. The free-market economy that leads to the production of wealth, the enlargement of freedom, and the stimulation of enterprise is, so far, the best system human beings have found to share in God's work of creation.

24

The Jewish Tradition and
Capital Punishment

ELIE SPITZ

Jewish sacred text is viewed by the traditional Jew like myself as a product of the Jewish people's relationship to God. The laws of our people are a product of that relationship and inform the believer's definition of what is ethical.

The legal writings of our sages through the ages have precedent value for contemporary Jewish courts. Moreover, Jewish literature includes a pyramid of commentary and insight which provides us with the perspective of many lifetimes of experience and a connectedness to the wellspring of our people's past. At the same time, we must approach the wisdom of our sages with bifocals, simultaneously noting their enduring holdings while appreciating the unique variables of our own time.

As a system of criminal jurisprudence the Jewish tradition has much to say with regard to punishment in general and the death penalty in particular. Capital punishment was not an ethical problem for the Bible. Indeed, it was a commanded punishment for a whole range of offenses, from witchcraft to striking a parent to murder. While the rabbis of the Talmud narrowed the procedural and evidentiary requirements for the death penalty, it was never explicitly called immoral. Yet it is precisely these rabbinic safeguards which make the current execution of those on death row morally problematic by the lights of Jewish scriptures and tradition.

The starting point for this analysis is the Bible, the foundation of our tradition. To understand its oft-repeated command to execute, it is important to note that the Bible was seemingly unaware of the option of prison. While anecdotally Joseph and Samson were incarcerated, there is no mention of a sentence of prison in the Bible. Indeed, jails did not exist in the ancient Near East, Greece, or Rome except as a place to await trial. Prisons are a relatively new historical phenomenon. In this context, it is relevant to examine the underlying reasons for the Bible's exhortations for execution and then to examine how those sentencing goals apply to our judicial system today.

There are three overarching objectives for punishment to be found in the Bible: the realignment of God with creation, retribution, and deterrence.

The Bible presents God the Creator as deeply invested in the moral order. Immoral practices are abhorrent to God and cause God to feel angry with a condoning people. Because of immorality, the Bible relates, God rejected the people who lived in Canaan before the Israelites (Lev. 20:23; Deut. 20:18). God commands Israel to execute idolators in order to reverse God's display of anger against Israel (Lev. 25:4). Accordingly, when Pinhas fatally pierces with a sword an Israelite engaged in sex with a Midianite woman, he is rewarded with a covenant. The Bible says of the unusual honor: "It is given to him because he zealously took up God's cause and made atonement for the Israelites" (Num. 25:13).

The execution of moral offenders appeased God because it was a correction of the moral order. It was not just the offender who needed punishment, but the offensive behavior demanded branding and ostracizing as unacceptable. The death penalty, the strongest statement of reproach, reflected God's call "to put away the evil from the midst of thee" (Deut. 17:7, 12; 19:19; 21:21; 22:24).

So integral was morality to creation that the Bible states that even the earth was revolted by the crime of murder. In the Book of Numbers, reflecting the earlier language of the story of Cain and Abel (Gen. 4:10–11), God declares: "You shall not pollute the land in which you live; for blood pollutes the land, and the land can have no expiation for blood that is shed upon it except by the blood of him who shed it" (Num. 35:33).

It is clear from these citations that a moral God demands punishment of wrongdoing. The punishment reasserts the moral order, which is imprinted in creation and thereby realigns God with creation itself.

The Bible is quite explicit as well about the specific need for execution for the sake of retributive justice. Even before Abraham arrived on the biblical scene, God commanded humanity: "Whoever sheds the blood of man, by man shall his blood be shed, for in God's image did God make man" (Gen. 9:6). God later states to the Jewish people: "Do not take ransom for the life of a murderer who is under the death penalty, since he must be put to death" (Num. 35:31).

Talionic language—"fracture for fracture, eye for eye, tooth for tooth" (Lev. 24:20; Exod. 21:23–25)—appears in several places in the Bible. Yet the rabbis had no problem interpreting these words as connoting compensatory damages for maiming, because retribution was inherently inexact and therefore unjust (BT Baba Kama 84a). The rabbis of the Talmud, however, never rejected execution as an inherently unjust punishment. Professor Moshe Greenberg suggests that talion for murder was indeed a moral step forward in the Near East. The death penalty prevented the rich person from buying himself or herself out of the crime.

The last major reason for the death penalty was deterrence, or in the words of the Bible, "people should hear and be afraid" (Deut. 21:21). Toward the goal of publicizing an execution the Bible even commanded that subsequent to the execution the corpse of the offender should be hung for public viewing (Deut. 21:22–23). Although the corpse had to be taken down when it got dark, out of respect for God, the deterrent value of execution was seen as powerful and necessary (Deut. 21:23).

In summary, the death penalty is commanded in the Bible with no moral qualms. It is presented as a just penalty which facilitates a realignment of God with creation, provides retributive justice, and serves as a deterrent.

Actual cases of judicial execution in the Tanakh and in the Second Commonwealth are quite rare. Moreover, the rabbis of the Talmud, who developed a legal system through interpretation of the Bible, imposed an array of restrictions on capital cases.

To obtain a capital conviction two credible eyewitnesses were required, witnesses who had each forewarned the potential offender against committing the crime. Circumstantial evidence, no matter how compelling, could not serve as a substitute for the required second witness. The witnesses were questioned only when separated from each other. Questions of identification were seen as critical, and differences even in such marginal matters as the color of the accused's garment or the number of buttons on a cloak constituted reason for exclusion of a witness's testimony (see M. Sanhedrin 5:1–2; J. David Bleich, "Capital Punishment in a Noachide Code"). A confession by a suspect was inadmissible (BT Sanh. 9b).

These extraordinarily strict demands, meant to prevent mistaken identity, allow for a situation in which execution would have become very rare. We do not know how rare because the Romans eliminated capital punishment at least forty years before the Temple was destroyed and Jewish jurisprudence no longer had standing to impose the death penalty. Yet, in that context, the rabbis of the Talmud created the "rules of evidence" and the famous statement in Mishnah Makkot (1:10):

> A Sanhedrin that puts a man to death once in seven years is called destructive. Rabbi Eliezer ben Azariah says: Or once in seventy years. Rabbi Tarfon and Rabbi Akiva say: Had we been in the Sanhedrin, none would ever have been put to death. Rabbi Shimon ben Gamliel says: They [Rabbi Tarfon and Rabbi Akiva] would have thus multiplied the murderers in Israel.

This debate as to the deterrent effect of capital punishment became moot for Jewish courts with the destruction of the Temple. For according to the agreed rabbinic interpretation of Scripture, the required sentencing court of twenty-three only had capital punishment authority as long as the Sanhedrin Ha-Gadol, comprising seventy-one judges, was meeting within the confines of the Temple Mount (BT Sanh. 37b, Ketubbot 30a).

In our own time, when the modern State of Israel was presented with its first murder trial, the two chief rabbis cabled the minister of justice with a call for the immediate abolition of the death penalty and warned that a capital sentence would be incompatible with and a sin against Jewish law (*Encyclopaedia Judaica*, s.v. "Capital Punishment"; Elon, *The Principle of Jewish Law,* p. 530).

Yet for us in America, Jewish law, which includes the Noachide law for non-Jews, theoretically permits executions. The Noachide law, which binds non-Jews to set up courts, is still in force (BT Sanh. 56–60; Maimonides, Mishneh Torah, Hilkhot Melakhim 8:10, 10:12). Moreover, according to Maimonides, the strict rules of evidence of Jewish courts do not apply to a Noachide court. The Noachide court may impose the death penalty based even on the testimony of a single witness (Maimonides, Melakhim 9:14, based on BT Sanh. 57b). Maimonides also states that a king has the authority to do whatever is necessary, including execution, to establish order and protect his authority (Melakhim 3:10). Thus, the question remains for us as American Jews: should our government begin executions again in earnest?

While not condemned by our tradition as immoral, the death penalty has special safeguards since execution is irreversible. Although rabbinic authorities did not impose the same stringent restrictions on Noachide courts as on their own, there are good reasons why we as U.S. citizens should do so. We live in a time with a punitive option which our tradition lacked, namely, prisons. This new factor plus the following practical considerations constitute a moral challenge to the death penalty in our current U.S. penal system.

First, there is always the problem of mistaken identity. The rabbis of the Talmud imposed the requirement of two eyewitnesses to address this concern. Circumstantial evidence, no matter how persuasive, could not meet this two-witness evidentiary test. This Jewish demand for certainty is morally compelling and as such is appropriate for our secular courts as well.

The second problem is the capriciousness of the death penalty today. Recent statistics clearly indicate that the race of the victim is a critical variable in the imposition of the death penalty (see Cytron and Schwartz, *When Life Is in the Balance,* pp. 185–88). In calling for the death penalty in Leviticus, the text emphasizes: "You shall have one standard for stranger and citizen alike, for I am the Lord thy God" (Lev. 24:21–22). Where racial issues are a factor in sentencing, the death penalty should not be imposed.

The third consideration has to do with the role of the state as a teacher. Law and its enforcement are essential educational tools for the state. Since life is spiritually precious, the state must not utilize the death penalty as simply another form of punishment. A clear line must be drawn to limit the death penalty so as not to allow for an ever-expanding category of execution as the penalty becomes more and more familiar.

The sparing use of the death penalty in the State of Israel is a positive model for us. The death penalty is imposed only in the rare case of treason or genocide, crimes against the entire people. Under those rules only Adolf Eichmann was sentenced to death. His execution made the statement that his crime of genocide demanded retribution of the most extreme kind. In allowing for the execution of Eichmann, Israel is of course drawing a line short of saying that execution is forbidden altogether. It is a line I am comfortable with because there is a moral difference between retribution and the murder of an innocent person, just as there is a difference between imprisonment and kidnapping, a fine and theft. Yet, to keep people sensitive to the awesome nature of execution and to safeguard against the ever-increasing ease of imposing the death penalty, the line should be drawn for the exceptional case, specifically crimes against the entire people.

The last problem with the imposition of the death penalty has to do with the fact that today prisons provide an alternative to execution.

As we noted, imprisonment does not appear as a judicial sentence in the Bible. In the Talmud it is introduced only in a very limited way. *Hakhnasah lekippah,* confinement in a cell, is noted in at least one place as the suitable punishment for the person who committed murder but for whom the stringent procedural rules were not met (M. Sanh. 9:5; Tosefta Sanh. 12:7–8). Such cells were different from modern prisons—people's lives would be shortened because of the difficult conditions under which they were kept. Still, the option of prison perhaps allowed the rabbis of the Talmud to refine the evidentiary rules for capital cases. Since they had no actual power to inflict death, they could only write about the importance of imposing the death penalty with great stringency.

Prisons today do meet the three goals of execution of the Bible. First, they create a realignment of God with creation. The major thrust of this category was the need to punish the offender and to mark the offense as abhorrent. Stiff prison sentences, when imposed swiftly, do make that statement. The rabbis of the Talmud even went so far as to say that even when God had explicitly said in the Bible that a criminal would not be guiltless and escape divine wrath (Exod. 20:7; Deut. 5:11), the court, in imposing a sentence of flogging, was authorized to totally clear the person (BT Shevuot 21a; also see Maimonides, Melakhim 3:15). Hence, God's key concern regarding realignment was the exercise of justice by effective courts, rather than a particular punishment per se.

The second goal is retributive justice. This is the strongest argument for the death penalty. It is based on the idea that we have to take into account the plight of the victim. In cases of murder, for example, since the victim is dead, the murderer should not be given the opportunity to enjoy the daily gifts of life and even gain freedom down the road.

The Bible is clear: *midah keneged midah,* measure should be met with like measure. Yet a lifetime sentence without probation, which is appropriate for murder in the first degree, provides a severe-enough punishment that can be equated with the death penalty. After all, money can never replace an eye either, yet for the sake of justice our rabbis were willing and able to make moral equivalencies.

Deterrence is the third goal of execution in the Bible. There is no evidence that the death penalty is a greater deterrent than a life in prison. There is, however, evidence that quick sentencing does impact significantly on the effectiveness of imprisonment. Moreover, our rabbis emphasized the need for a swift trial and the quick implementation of the sentence. Toward that end the American system is in need of major repair. The solution is quicker and surer sentences rather than executions.

Proponents of the death penalty argue that in these times of rising crime we must do the dramatic and "up the ante" with our punishments, even if only to see whether it makes a difference. The rabbinic response to increased crime was just the opposite. The Talmud in Avodah Zarah (8b) relates that:

> Forty years prior to the destruction of the Second Temple, the Sanhedrin moved from the Temple and met in the marketplace, so as not to judge capital cases. What was the reason? Because they recognized the proliferation of capital crimes which they were unable to judge properly, thus they relocated so as not to pass the death sentence.

This passage of Talmud suggests that when the crime rates increases, far from further implementing the death penalty, the Sanhedrin deliberately chose to suspend it as a judicial response to the "needs of the hour." Under this view, the implementation of the death penalty in a widespread fashion in fact reduces its deterrent effect and thus the justification for its use. The exigencies of our day demand addressing the problem of crime, but capital punishment is the wrong address.

In conclusion, our tradition teaches us that capital punishment is a power which God has given to human courts. Yet the rabbis teach that courts should use their power with the greatest of care, leading to the rarity of its imposition. For all the practical reasons suggested, the death penalty should not be used for the murderers on death row. Today, with a developed prison system, we should tighten sentencing laws and enhance their speed to serve as a deterrent and as a substitute for the death penalty.

References

Bleich, J. David. "Capital Punishment in the Noachide Code," In *Jewish Law in Our Time,* edited by Ruth Link-Salinger. Bloch, 1982.

Cytron, Barry D., and Schwartz, Earl. *When Life Is in the Balance.* United Synagogue, 1986.

Elon, Menachem. *The Principles of Jewish Law.* Encyclopaedia Judaica.

Herring, Basil F. *Jewish Ethics and Halakhah for Our Time,* KTAV, 1984.

Prager, Dennis, "Capital Punishment: A Rorschach Test." *Ultimate Issues* 5, no. 2 (Spring 1989).

D. Jewish Perspectives on Medical Ethics

25

Euthanasia

FRED ROSNER

The word *euthanasia* is derived from the Greek *eu,* meaning "well, good, or pleasant," and *thanatos,* meaning "death." Webster's dictionary defines euthanasia as the mode or act of inducing death painlessly or as a relief from pain. The popular expression for euthanasia is mercy killing. Perusal of the medical literature of the last three decades reveals a host of books, articles, editorials, and letters to editors of journals dealing with this subject. These writings are exclusive of the legal, theological, psychological, and social literatures. Even the lay press is replete with writings on euthanasia, from the withholding of treatment from a handicapped newborn to the withdrawal of life-support systems from a terminally ill patient.

There is thus little doubt as to the tremendous interest in euthanasia. This chapter is an attempt to briefly review the subject by providing classification and terminology, citing selected examples, describing the legal attitude toward euthanasia in various countries, discussing the arguments put forth for and against euthanasia, briefly mentioning the Catholic and Protestant viewpoints on euthanasia, and finally presenting in detail the Jewish attitude toward euthanasia.

Classification and Terminology

A euphemistic term used by euthanasia societies for mercy killing is "merciful release"[1] or "liberating euthanasia."[2] Some people classify euthanasia into three types: eugenic, medical, and preventive.[3] A more meaningful classification speaks of eugenic, active medical, and passive medical euthanasia.[4] Eugenic euthanasia encompasses the "merciful release" of handicapped newborns and socially undesirable individuals, such as the mentally retarded and psychiatrically disturbed. Perhaps an extreme example of this method of extermination was the Nazi killing of all the socially unacceptable or socially unfit, including Jews. To many, this German practice as well as all eugenic euthanasia is considered nothing less than murder; there are very few proponents of this type of euthanasia.

Active medical euthanasia is exemplified by the case where a drug or other treatment is administered, and death is thereby hastened. This type of euthanasia may be voluntary or involuntary, that is, with or without the patient's consent.

Passive medical euthanasia is defined as the situation in which therapy is withheld so that death is hastened by omission of treatment. This type of euthanasia has also been called automathanasia,[5] meaning automatic death, such as without therapeutic heroics. This passive form of euthanasia can also be voluntary or involuntary.

Exemplification of the Problem

Many a physician has had to wrestle with the problem of an incurably ill, suffering patient. Such physicians fully realize that "whereas life is lengthened, man's period of usefulness is not always lengthened."[6] Some are of the opinion that advanced medicine should "serve only to improve the condition of human life as it increases the life span and not the useless prolongation of human suffering."[7] Thus, a general practitioner in Manchester, New Hampshire, ended a cancer patient's suffering by injecting into the patient a substantial quantity of air intravenously. He was acquitted.[8] A Stamford, Connecticut, woman shot and killed her father who was dying of incurable cancer. She was acquitted.[9]

The problem is far from localized to the shores of the United States. Giuseppe F., having settled in France, was struck with an incurable disease. He summoned his brother Luigi and convinced the latter to kill him, which Luigi did. The jury acquitted Luigi.[10]

One of the most famous instances exemplifying many of the problems surrounding euthanasia is the case of the physician son of the founder of the British Euthanasia Society, who told a Rotary meeting: "To keep her from pain . . . I gave her an injection to make her sleep."[11] His objective, as specifically stated, was to relieve pain, not to put an end to the patient's life. An outcry in the British press followed, labeling the incident "a mercy killing." Even the British Euthanasia Society admitted that from a strictly legal sense mercy killing is murder, but it backed the physician by insisting that "every doctor must be guided by his own conscience." Many physicians disagreed, saying euthanasia is legalized murder. Others cited the Hippocratic oath, which states: "I will give no deadly medicine to anyone if asked, nor suggest any such counsel." Still others were of the opinion that the Hippocratic oath refers only to premeditated murder. The medical council refused to act against the physician unless the family of the deceased lodged a formal complaint. However, the family consented to the physician's actions. Thus, all the ingredients to emphasize the problem of euthanasia are present in this case: the incurable patient in great pain, the request for euthanasia by patient and family, and the physician's acquiescence and participation.

The list of examples one could cite is endless. The aforementioned illustrative cases serve as background for the ensuing discussion.

Legal Considerations

Although suicide is not legally a crime in most American jurisdictions, aiding and abetting suicide is a felony, Euthanasia, even at the patient's request, is legally murder in the United States. In England the Suicide Act of 1961 states that it is not a criminal offense for a person, whether in sickness or in health, to take his own life or to attempt to do so. However, any individual who helps him to do so becomes liable to a charge of manslaughter. Euthanasia per se does not exist in the law books of France and Belgium, and in both countries it is considered premeditated homicide. However, a bill to legalize euthanasia for some "damaged" children came before the Belgian government following the famous Liège trial involving parents, relatives, and a physician charged with murdering a thalidomide-damaged child.[12]

In Italy, euthanasia is only a crime if the victim is under eighteen years of age, mentally retarded, or menaced or under the effect of fear. More tolerant attitudes also exist in Denmark, Holland, Yugoslavia, and even Catholic Spain. In Russia euthanasia is considered "murder under extenuating circumstances" and punishable with three to eight years in prison.[13] Switzerland seems to have the most lenient legislation.[14] The Swiss penal code, as revamped in 1951, distinguishes between killing with bad intentions, that is, murder, and killing with good intentions, that is, euthanasia. In addition, in 1964 in Sweden, passive euthanasia was legalized. Even in countries where euthanasia is legally murder, "the sympathies of juries towards mercy killings often cause the law to be circumvented by various methods, making for great inequities of the legal system."[15]

In 1935 the first Euthanasia Society was founded in England for the purpose of promoting legislation which would seek to "make the act of dying more gentle." In 1936, one year after the founding of the society, a bill was introduced into the House of Lords which sought to permit voluntary euthanasia in certain circumstances and with certain safeguards. Following a rather heated debate, it was decided that "in view of the emergence of so many controversial issues, it would be best to leave the matter for the time being to the discretion of individual medical men . . . the bill was rejected by 35 votes to 14."[16]

Three years after the inception of the British group, the Euthanasia Society of America, Inc., was founded. This nonsectarian, voluntary organization, rather than seeking to have legislation enacted to legalize euthanasia, attempts to achieve a more enlightened public understanding of euthanasia through dissemination of information through discussions in medical societies and other professional groups, research studies and opinion polls, dissemination of literature, a speaker's bureau, and other responsible media of communication.

Other euthanasia societies have been founded in other countries. Support for these societies and their work comes from various other groups, such as the American Humanist Association and the Ethical Culture Society. Opposition to euthanasia is also strong, however. The Academy of Moral and Political Sciences of Paris passed a motion completely outlawing, forbidding, and rejecting euthanasia in all its forms.[17] In addition, the Council of the World Medical Association, meeting in Copenhagen in April 1950, recommended that the practice of euthanasia be condemned.

The debate continues. The problem has been well stated by Fibey: "When a tortured man asks: 'For God's sake, doctor, let me die, just put me to sleep,' we have yet to find the answer as to whether to comply is for God's sake, the patient's sake, our own, or possibly all three."[18] Even if the moral issue of euthanasia could be circumvented, other questions of logistics would immediately arise: Who is to initiate euthanasia proceedings? The patient? The family? The physician? Who is to make the final decision? The physician? A group of physicians? The courts? Who is to carry out the decision if it is affirmative? The physician? Others?

Arguments For and Against

The arguments in favor of and against euthanasia are numerous and will only be briefly summarized. Opponents of euthanasia say that if voluntary, it is suicide. Although in British law suicide is no longer a crime, Christian and Jewish religious teachings certainly outlaw suicide. The answer offered to this argument is that martyrdom, a form of suicide, is condoned under certain conditions. However, the martyr primarily seeks not to end his life but to accomplish a goal, death being an undesired side product. Thus martyrdom and suicide do not seem comparable.

It is also said that euthanasia, if voluntary, is murder. Murder, however, usually connotes premeditated evil. The motives of the person administering euthanasia are far from evil. On the contrary, such motives are commendable and praiseworthy, although the methods may be unacceptable. A closely related objection to euthanasia says that it transgresses the biblical injunction *Thou shalt not kill.*[19] To overcome this argument, some modern biblical translators substitute "Thou shalt not commit murder," and, as just mentioned, murder usually represents violent killing for purposes or gain or treachery or vendetta and is dissimilar to the "merciful release" of euthanasia.

That God alone gives and takes life[20] and that one's life span is divinely predetermined is not denied by the proponents of euthanasia. The difficulty with this point seems to be the question of definition as to whether euthanasia represents shortening of life or shortening of the act of dying.

It is also said that suffering is part of the divine plan, with which man has no right to tamper. This phase of faith remains a mystery and is best exemplified by the story of Job.

It is further argued by opponents of euthanasia that since physicians are only human beings, they are liable to error. There is no infallibility in a physician's diagnosis of an incurably ill patient, and mistakes have been made. They may be exceedingly rare, but they do occur. The same is true of spontaneous remission of cancer: it has been reported, but only in very rare instances.

The need for euthanasia today is minimized by some because of the availability of hypnotics, narcotics, anesthetics, and other analgesic means to keep a patient's pain and distress at a tolerable level. This fact, in general, may be true, but occasional patients develop severe pain which is refractory of all drugs and requires surgical interruption of nerve pathways for relief.

The Hippocratic oath or similar vow which physicians take upon graduation from medical school is conflicting. On the one hand, it states that a physician's duty is to relieve suffering, yet on the other hand, it also states that the physician must preserve and protect life. This oath is used as an argument by both proponents and opponents of euthanasia.

A valid point of debate is the suggestion that if euthanasia for incurably ill, suffering cancer patients were legalized, extension of such legislation to handicapped, deformed, psychotic, or senile patients might follow. An editorial states: "If euthanasia is granted to the first class, can it long be denied to the second? . . . Each step is so short; the slope so slippery; our values in this age, so uncertain and unstable . . ."[21]

Further questions are the sincerity of patients and/or family in requesting euthanasia. A patient racked with pain may make an impulsive but ill-considered request for merciful release which he will not be able to retract or regret after the fait accompli. The patient's family may not be completely sincere in its desire to relieve the patient's suffering. The family also wishes to relieve its own suffering. Enemies or heirs of the patient may request hastening of the patient's death for ulterior motives. These and further arguments both for and against euthanasia continue to be discussed and debated.

Catholic Attitude

In at least five places the New Testament contains the biblical admonition *Thou shalt not kill.*[22] Based thereon, the attitude of the Catholic church in this matter is cited as follows:

> The teaching of the Church is unequivocal that God is the supreme master of life and death and that no human being is allowed to usurp His dominion so as deliberately to put an end to life, either his own or any one else's without authorization . . . and the only authorizations the Church recognizes are a nation engaged in war, execution of criminals by a Government, killing in self defense. . . . The Church has never allowed and never will allow the killing of individuals on grounds of private expediency; for instance . . . putting an end to prolonged suffering or hopeless sickness.[23]

Thus we see a blanket condemnation of active euthanasia by the Catholic church as murder and, therefore, a mortal sin. The reasons behind this teaching include the inviolability of human life, or the supreme dominion of God over his creatures, and the purposefulness of human suffering.[24] Man suffers as penance for his sins, perhaps as earthly purgatory; man endures pain for the spiritual good of his fellowman, and suffering teaches humility.

Passive medical euthanasia is treated quite differently. The church distinguishes between "ordinary" and "extraordinary" measures employed by physicians when certain death and suffering lie ahead. In his day of artificial and auxiliary hearts, artificial kidneys, respirators, pacemakers, defibrillators, and similar instruments, the definition of "extraordinary" is unclear. Pope Pius XII issued an encyclical not requiring physicians to use heroic measures in such circumstances.[25] Thus, passive euthanasia seems to be sanctioned by the Catholic church. In an address to the congress of Italian anesthetists on February 24, 1957, the Pope further stated: "Even if narcotics may shorten life while they relieve pain, it is permissible."[26]

Protestant Attitude

In the Protestant churches there are "all possible colors in the spectrum of attitudes toward euthanasia."[27] Some condemn it, some favor it, and many are in between, advocating judgment of each case individually. Perhaps the greatest Protestant advocate of legalized euthanasia is the Anglican minister Joseph Fletcher. His three main reasons are the following: (1) suffering is purposeless, demoralizing, and degrading; (2) human personality is of greater worth than life per se; and (3) the New Testament phrase "Blessed are the merciful, for they shall obtain mercy" is as important as the biblical *Thou shalt not kill.*

Jewish Attitude

Biblical Sources

In the Bible we find: *Whoso sheddeth man's blood, by man shall his blood be shed.*[28] In the second book of the Pentateuch it is stated: *Thou shalt not murder,*[29] and in the next chapter, *And if a man come presumptuously upon his neighbor, to slay him with guile: thou shalt take him from Mine altar, that he may die.*[30] In the next book is the phrase *And he that smiteth any man mortally shall surely be put to death,*[31] and four sentences later, *And he that killeth a man shall be put to death.*[32] In Numbers it states: *Whoso killeth any person, the murderer shall be slain at the mouth of witnesses.*[33] Finally, the Sixth Commandment of the Decalogue is repeated: *Thou shalt not murder.*[34] Thus, in every book of the Pentateuch, we find at least one reference to murder or killing. Accidental death or homicide is dealt with separately in the Bible and represents another subject entirely.

Probably the first recorded instance of euthanasia concerns the death of King Saul in the year 1013 B.C.E. At the end of the First Book of Samuel, we find the following:

> Now the Philistines fought against Israel, and the men of Israel fled from before the Philistines and fell down slain in Mount Gilboa. And the Philistines pursued hard upon Saul and upon his sons; and the Philistines slew Jonathan and Abinadab and Malchishua, the sons of Saul. And the battle went sore against Saul, and the archers overtook him, and he was greatly afraid by reason of the archers. Then said Saul to his armor-bearer: "Draw thy sword, and thrust me through therewith, lest these uncircumcised come and thrust me through and make a mock of me." But his armor-bearer would not; for he was sore afraid. Therefore, Saul took his sword and fell upon it. And when the armor-bearer saw that Saul was dead, he likewise fell upon his sword and died with him. So Saul died and his three sons, and his armor-bearer, and all his men, that same day together.[35]

From this passage it would appear as if Saul committed suicide. However, at the beginning of the Second Book of Samuel, when David is informed of Saul's death, we find the following:

> And David said unto the young man that told him: "How knowest thou that Saul and Jonathan his son are dead?" And the young man that told him said: "As I happened by chance upon Mount Gilboa, behold, Saul leaned upon his spear; and

lo, the chariots and the horsemen pressed hard upon him. And when he looked behind him, he saw me, and called unto me. And I answered: Here am I. And he said unto me: Who art thou? And I answered him: I am an Amalekite. And he said unto me: Stand, I pray thee, beside me, and slay me, for the agony hath taken hold of me; because my life is just yet in me. So I stood beside him, and slew him, because I was sure that he would not live after that he was fallen . . ."[36]

Many commentators consider this a case of euthanasia. Rabbi David Kimchi (*Radak*) specifically states that Saul did not die immediately on falling on his sword but was mortally wounded and in his death throes asked the Amalekite to hasten his death. Rabbi Levi ben Gerson (*Ralbag*), Rabbi Shlomo ben Isaac (*Rashi*), and Rabbi David Altschul (*Metzudat David*) also support this viewpoint. Some modern scholars think that the story of the Amalekite was a complete fabrication.

Talmudic Sources

The Talmud states as follows: "One who is in a dying condition [*goses*] is regarded as a living person in all respects."[37] This rule is reiterated by the codifiers of Jewish law, including Maimonides and Karo, as described below. The Talmud continues:[38]

> One may not bind his jaws, not stop up his openings, nor place a metallic vessel or any cooling object on his navel until such time that he dies, as it is written: *Before the silver cord is snapped asunder.*[39]
> One may not move him, nor may one place him on sand or on salt until he dies.
> One may not close the eyes of the dying person. He who touches them or moves them is shedding blood because Rabbi Meir used to say: This can be compared to a flickering flame. As soon as a person touches it, it becomes extinguished. So too, whosoever closes the eyes of the dying is considered to have taken his soul.

Other laws pertaining to a *goses,* or dying person, such as the preparation of a coffin, inheritance, marriage, and so forth, are then cited.

The Talmud also mentions: "He who closes the eyes of a dying person while the soul is departing is a murderer [lit. he sheds blood]. This may be compared to a lamp that is going out. If a man places his finger upon it, it is immediately extinguished."[40] *Rashi* explains that this small effort of closing the eyes may slightly hasten death.

The most famous talmudic passage concerning euthanasia is the story of Rabbi Chanina ben Teradion, who was wrapped by the Romans in a Scroll of the Law (Torah), with bundles of straw around him which were set on fire.[41] The Romans also put tufts of wool which had been soaked in water over his heart so that he should not die quickly. His disciples pleaded with him to open his mouth "so that the fire enter into thee" and put an end to his agony. He replied: "Let Him who gave me [my soul] take it away" but no one is allowed to injure himself or hasten his death.

Codes of Jewish Law

The twelfth-century code of Maimonides treats our subject matter as follows:

> One who is in a dying condition is regarded as a living person in all respects. It is not permitted to bind his jaws, to stop up the organs of the lower extremities, or to

place metallic or cooling vessels upon his navel in order to prevent swelling. He is not to be rubbed or washed, nor is sand or salt to be put upon him until he expires. He who touches him is guilty of shedding blood. To what may he be compared? To a flickering flame, which is extinguished as soon as one touches it. Whoever closes the eyes of the dying while the soul is about to depart is shedding blood. One should wait a while; perhaps he is only in a swoon.[42]

Thus, we again note the prohibition of doing anything that might hasten death. Maimonides does not specifically forbid moving such a patient, as does the Talmud, but such a prohibition is implied in Maimonides' text. Maimonides also forbids rubbing and washing a dying person, acts which are not mentioned in the Talmud. Finally, Maimonides raises the problem of the recognition of death, a problem becoming more pronounced as scientific medicine improves the methods for supporting respiration and heart function.

The sixteenth-century code of Rabbi Joseph Karo devotes an entire chapter to the laws of the dying patient.[43] The individual in whom death is imminent is referred to as a *goses*. Karo's code begins, as do Maimonides and the Talmud, with the phrase "A *goses* is considered as a living person in all respects," and then Karo enumerates various acts that are prohibited. All the commentaries use the concept "lest they hasten the patient's death" to explain these prohibitions. One of the forbidden acts not mentioned by Maimonides or the Talmud is the removal of the pillow from beneath the patient's head. This act had already been prohibited two centuries earlier by Rabbi Jacob ben Asher, known as *Tur*.[44] Karo's text is nearly identical to that of *Tur*. The latter, however, has the additional general explanation: "The rule in this matter is that any act performed in relation to death should not be carried out until the soul has departed." Thus, not only are physical acts on the patient, such as those described above, forbidden, but one should also not provide a coffin or prepare a grave or make other funeral or related arrangements lest the patient hear of this and his death be hastened. Even psychological stress is prohibited.

On the other hand, thirteenth-century Rabbi Judah ben Samuel the Pious states: "If a person is dying and someone near his house is chopping wood, so that the soul cannot depart, then one should remove the [wood] chopper from there."[45]

Based on this ruling, Rabbi Moses Isserles, known as *Rema*, in his famous gloss on Karo's code, asserts:

If there is anything which causes a hindrance to the departure of the soul, such as the presence near the patient's house of a knocking noise, such as wood chopping, or if there is salt on the patient's tongue, and these hinder the soul's departure, it is permissible to remove them from there because there is no act involved in this at all but only the removal of the impediment.[46]

Furthermore, Rabbi Solomon Eger, in his commentary on Karo's code,[47] quotes another rabbinic authority, who states "it is forbidden to hinder the departure of the soul by the use of medicines."[48] Other rabbinic authorities, however, disagree with the latter view.[49] Rabbi Joshua Boaz Baruch, known as *Shiltei Gibborim*, pleads for the abolition of the custom of those who remove the pillow from beneath the dying person's head, following the popular belief that the bird feathers contained in the pillow prevent the soul from departing.[50] He further states that Rabbi Nathan of Igra specifically permitted this act. *Shiltei Gibborim* continues: "After many years I found in the *Sefer Chasidim* support for my contentions, as it is written there that if a person is dying but cannot die until he is put in a different place, he should not be moved."[51] This law is not contradictory to the earlier statement in the *Sefer Chasidim,* as both *Shiltei Gibborim* and *Rema* explain: To do an act which prevents easy death, such as chopping wood, is forbidden, and on the contrary, such impediments to death should be removed. On the other hand, it is definitely forbidden to perform any act which hastens death, such as moving the dying person from one place to another.

Recent Rabbinic Rulings

This discussion of the Jewish attitude toward euthanasia is summarized by Jakobovits, who states that

> any form of active euthanasia is strictly prohibited and condemned as plain murder . . . anyone who kills a dying person is liable to the death penalty as a common murderer. At the same time, Jewish law sanctions the withdrawal of any factor— whether extraneous to the patient himself or not—which may artificially delay his demise in the final phase.[52]

Jakobovits is quick to point out, however, that all the Jewish sources refer to an individual called a *goses* in whom death is imminent, three days or less in rabbinic references. Thus, passive euthanasia in a patient who may yet live for weeks or months is not condoned. Furthermore, in the case of an incurably ill person in severe pain, agony, or distress, the removal of an impediment which hinders his soul's departure, although permitted in Jewish law, as stated by *Rema,* may not be analogous to the withholding of medical therapy that is perhaps sustaining the patient's life unnaturally. The impediments spoken of in the codes of Jewish law, whether far removed from the patient, as exemplified by the noise of wood chopping, or in physical contact with him, such as the case of salt on the patient's tongue, do not constitute any part of the therapeutic armamentarium employed in the medical management of the patient. For this reason, such impediments may be removed. However, the discontinuation of life-support systems which are specifically designed and utilized in the treatment of incurably ill patients might only be permissible if one is certain that in doing so one is shortening the act of dying and not interrupting life.

Rabbi Eliezer Yehudah Waldenberg reiterates that physicians and others are obligated to do everything possible to save the life of a dying patient, even if the patient will only live for a brief period, and even if the patient is suffering greatly.[53] Any action that results in hastening of the death of a dying patient is forbidden and considered an act of murder. Even if the patient is beyond cure and is suffering greatly and requests that his death be hastened, one may not do so or advise the patient to do so.[54] A terminally ill incurable patient, continues Waldenberg, may be given oral or parenteral narcotics or other powerful analgesics to relieve his pain and suffering, even at the risk of depressing his respiratory center and hastening his death, provided the medications are prescribed solely for pain relief and not to hasten death.[55] Waldenberg also states that it is not considered interference with the divine will to place a patient on a respirator or other life-support system.[56] On the contrary, all attempts must be made to prolong and preserve the life of a patient who has a potentially curable disease or reversible condition.[57] Thus, one must attempt resuscitation on a drowning victim who has no spontaneous respiration or heartbeat because of the possibility of resuscitation and reversibility.[58] One is not obligated or even permitted, however, to initiate artificial life-support and/or other resuscitative efforts if it is obvious that the patient is terminally and incurably and irreversibly ill with no chance of recovery. One is also allowed to disconnect and discontinued life-support instrumentation, according to Waldenberg[59] and others, if one can establish that the patient is dead according to Jewish legal criteria,[60] that is, if the patient has no independent brain function or spontaneous cardiorespiratory activity. If it is not clear whether the respirator is keeping the patient alive or only ventilating a corpse, the respirator must be maintained. It may not be turned off to test whether the patient has spontaneous respiratory activity because that small act may be the one that causes the patient's death, similar to the flickering lamp which may be extinguished if someone touches it (see above). Therefore, from a practical standpoint, Waldenberg advises that one use respirators with automatic time clocks set for a twelve- or twenty-four-hour period.[61] When the respirator shuts itself off, one can observe the patient for signs of spontaneous respiration. If none are present and if the heart is not beating and the brain is irreversibly damaged, one does not reconnect the respirator. Finally, Rabbi Waldenberg asserts that blood transfusions, oxygen, antibiotics, intravenous fluids, oral and parenteral nutrition, and pain-relief medications must be maintained for a terminally ill patient till the very end.[62]

Rabbi Shlomo Zalman Auerbach also states that a terminally ill patient must be given food and oxygen even against his will.[63] However, one may withhold, at the patient's request, medications and treatments which might cause him great pain and discomfort. Rabbi Gedaliah Aharon Rabinowitz reviews the laws pertaining to the care of the terminally ill and the criteria for defining the moment of death.[64] He also states that experimental chemotherapy for cancer patients is permissible but not obligatory.[65] Such therapy must have a rational scientific basis and be administered by expert physicians. Untested and unproven remedies may not be used on human beings. Dr. A. Sofer Abraham quotes Rabbi Auerbach as distinguishing between routine and nonroutine treatments for the terminally ill.[66] For example, a dying cancer patient must be given food, oxygen, antibiotics, insulin, and the like, but does not have to be given painful and toxic chemotherapy which offers no chance of cure but a best temporary palliation. Such a patient may be given morphine for pain even if it depresses his respiration. An irreversibly ill terminal patient whose spontaneous heartbeat and breathing stop does not have to be resuscitated.

Rabbi Moshe Hershler opines that withholding food or medication from a terminally ill patient so that he dies is murder.[67] Withholding respiratory support is equivalent to withholding food, since it will shorten the patient's life. Every moment of life is precious, and all measures must be taken to preserve even a few moments of life. However, if the physicians feel that a comatose patient's situation is hopeless, they are not obligated to institute life-prolonging or resuscitative treatments.

Hershler also states that if only one respirator is available and two or more patients need it, the physicians should decide which patient has the best chance of recovery. However, a respirator may not be removed from a patient who is connected thereto for another, even more needy patient, since one is prohibited from sacrificing one life to save another. Only if the patient has no spontaneous movement, reflexes, heartbeat, and respiration can the respirator be removed.

Rabbi Zalman Nechemiah Goldberg discusses the question of whether or not a physician may leave a dying patient to attend another patient.[68] Rabbi Avigdor Nebenzahl describes the permissible use of narcotics for terminally ill patients.[69] The treatment of the terminally ill and the definition of a *goses* are reviewed by Levy and Abraham.[70] Rabbi Nathan Friedman reiterates that euthanasia in any form is prohibited as an act of murder even if the patient asks for it.[72] A person is prohibited from taking his own life even if he is in severe pain and suffering greatly.[72] Even if the patient cries out, "Leave me be and do not help me because I prefer death," everything possible must be done for the support and comfort of the patient, including the use of large doses of pain-relief medications.[73]

Rabbi J. David Bleich affirms that although euthanasia in any form is forbidden, and the hastening of death, even by a matter of moments, is regarded as tantamount to murder, there is one situation in which treatment may be withheld from the moribund patient in order to provide for an unimpeded death.[74] While the death of a *goses* may not be hastened, there is no obligation to perform any action which might lengthen the life of such a patient. Bleich emphasizes, however, that "the distinction between an active and a passive act applies to a *goses* and a *goses* only." Among the criteria which indicate that the patient has become terminally ill and can be classified as a *goses* is the observation that he has the death rattle in his throat, probably representing "secretions in his throat on account of the narrowing of his chest."[75] Bleich cites some authorities who not only sanction withholding of treatment but prohibit any action which may prolong the agony of a *goses*. Other authorities insist that the life of a *goses* may not be shortened even passively by withdrawal of medication. Even the permissive rulings only sanction acts of omission for a *goses* in whom death is expected in less than seventy-two hours but not for a terminally ill patient who may yet survive weeks or months.

Conclusion

Bleich has succinctly summarized the Jewish attitude toward euthanasia.

> The practice of euthanasia—whether active or passive—is contrary to the teachings of Judaism. Any positive act designed to hasten the death of the patient is equated with murder in Jewish law, even if the death is hastened only by the matter of moments. No matter how laudable the intentions of the person performing an act of mercy-killing may be, his deed constitutes an act of homicide. . . .
>
> In discharging his responsibility with regard to prolongation of life, the physician must make use of any medical resources which are available. However, he is not obligated to employ procedures which are themselves hazardous in nature and may potentially foreshorten the life of the patient. Nor is either the physician or the patient obligated to employ a therapy which is experimental in nature.
>
> . . . The attempt to sustain life, by whatever means, is naught but the expression of the highest regard for the precious nature of the gift of life and of the dignity in which it is held.
>
> . . . Only the Creator, who bestows the gift of life, may relieve man of that life, even when it has become a burden rather than a blessing.[76]

Since the decisions about withholding specific therapy for a terminally ill patient, about the discontinuation of life-support systems, about whether or not to employ resuscitative measures in a given situation are complex and not free of family and/or physician personal and emotional involvement and even bias, it seems advisable to consult with a competent rabbinic authority for adjudication on a case-by-case basis.

Notes

1. E. E. Fibey, "Some Overtones of Euthanasia," *Hospital Topics* 43 (1965): 55ff.
2. C. P. Delhaye, "Euthanasie ou mort par pitié," *Union Médicale de Canada* 90 (1961): 613ff.
3. J. Crinquette, "L'euthanasie," *Journale de Sciences Médicales de Lille* 81 (1963): 522ff.
4. Fibey, op. cit.
5. F. Monnerot-Dumaine, "Les notions d'euthanasie et d'automathanasie," *Presse Médicale* 72 (1964): 1458.
6. A. A. Levisohn, "Voluntary Mercy Deaths: Sociolegal Aspects of Euthanasia," *Journal of Forensic Medicine* 8 (1961): 57ff.
7. Ibid.
8. Delhaye, op. cit.
9. Ibid.
10. P. R. Archambault, "Le problème d'euthanasie considerée par un médecin Catholique," *Union Médicale de Canada* 91 (1962): 543ff.
11. Levisohn, op. cit.
12. L. Colebrook, "The Liège Trial and the Problem of Voluntary Euthanasia," *Lancet* 2 (1962): 1225.
13. Delhaye, op. cit.
14. Crinquette, op. cit.
15. G. A. Friedman, "Suicide, Euthanasia and the Law," *Medical Times* 85 (1957): 681ff.
16. *A Plan for Voluntary Euthanasia* (London: Euthanasia Society, 1962), p. 28.
17. Delhaye, op. cit.
18. Fibey, op. cit.
19. Exod. 20:13 and Deut. 5:17.
20. See Deut. 32:39, *I kill and I make alive,* and Ezek. 18:4, *Behold, all souls are Mine.*
21. Editorial, "Euthanasia," *Lancet* 2 (1961): 351.
22. Matt. 5:21; 19:18; Mark 10:19; Luke 18:20; Rom. 13:9.
23. I. M. Rabinowitch and H. E. McDermot, "Euthanasia," *McGill Medical Journal* 19 (1950): 160ff.
24. E. F. Torrey, "Euthanasia: A Problem in Medical Ethics," *McGill Medical Journal* 30 (1961): 127ff.
25. Archambault, op. cit.; J. H. McClanahan, "The Patient's Right to Die: Moral and Spiritual Aspects of Euthanasia," *Memphis Medical Journal* 38 (1963): 303ff.
26. Archambault, op. cit.
27. Torrey, op. cit.
28. Gen. 9:6.
29. Exod. 20:13.
30. Ibid. 21:14.
31. Lev. 24:17.
32. Ibid. 24:21.
33. Num. 35:30.

34. Deut. 5:17.
35. 1 Sam. 31:1–6.
36. 2 Sam. 1:5–10.
37. Semachot 1:1.
38. Ibid. 1:2–4.
39. Eccles. 12:6. The midrash interprets the silver cord to refer to the spinal cord.
40. Shabbat 151b.
41. Avodah Zarah 18a.
42. Maimonides, *Mishneh Torah, Hilchot Avel* 4:5.
43. Karo, *Shulchan Aruch, Yoreh Deah* 339.
44. *Tur, Yoreh Deah* 339.
45. Judah the Pious, *Sefer Chasidim,* no. 723.
46. *Rema on Shulchan Aruch, Yoreh Deah* 339:1.
47. Eger, Commentary *Gilyon Maharsha* on *Shulchan Aruch, Yoreh Deah* 339:1.
48. Jacob ben Samuel, Responsa *Bet Yaakov,* no. 59.
49. J. Reischer, Responsa *Shevut Yaakov,* pt. 3, no. 13.
50. Baruch, Commentary *Shiltei Gibborim* on Moed Katan, end of chap. 3.
51. See Judah the Pious, op. cit.
52. I. Jakobovits, "The Dying and Their Treatment in Jewish Law: Preparation for Death and Euthanasia," *Hebrew Medical Journal* 2 (1961): 251ff. See also idem, *Jewish Medical Ethics* (New York: Bloch, 1959), pp. 123–25.
53. Waldenberg, Responsa *Tsitz Eliezer,* vol. 5, *Ramat Rachel,* no. 28:5.
54. Ibid., no. 29, and vol. 10, no. 25:6.
55. Ibid., vol. 13, no. 87.
56. Ibid., vol. 15, no. 37.
57. Ibid., vol. 13, no. 89.
58. Ibid., vol. 14, no. 81.
59. Ibid., vol. 13, no. 89.
60. Ibid., vol. 9, no. 46, and vol. 10, no. 25:4.
61. Waldenberg, op. cit., vol. 13, no. 89.
62. Ibid., vol. 14, no. 80.
63. S. Z. Auerbach, in *Halachah Urefuah* 2 (1981): 131.
64. G. A. Rabinowitz, in *Halachah Urefuah* 3 (1983): 102–14.
65. Ibid., pp. 115–18.
66. A. S. Abraham, in *Halachah Urefuah* 2 (1981): 185–90.
67. M. Hershler, in *Halachah Urefuah* 2 (1981): 30–52.
68. Z. N. Goldberg, in *Halachah Urefuah* 2 (1981): 191–95.
69. A. Nebenzahl, "The Use of Narcotics for Terminally Ill Patients," *Assia* 4 (1983): 260–62.
70. Y. Levy, in *Noam* 16 (1973): 53–63; A. S. Abraham, "Treatment of the Terminally Ill (*Goses*) and the Determination of Death," *Assia* 3 (1983): 467–73.
71. N. Friedman, Responsa *Netzer Matta'ai, no. 30.*
72. Asher ben Yechiel, known as *Rosh, Responsa Besamim Rosh,* no. 348; M. Schreiber, Responsa *Chatam Sofer, Even Ha'ezer,* pt. 1, no. 69.
73. Waldenberg, op. cit., vol. 9, no. 47:5.
74. J. D. Bleich, *Judaism and Healing* (New York: KTAV, 1981), pp. 134–45.
75. M. Isserles, Commentary *Rema* on Karo's *Shulchan Aruch, Even Ha'ezer* 121:7 and *Choshen Mishpat* 211:2. Bleich also refers the reader to Maimonides' (*Rambam*) and Yom Tov Lippman Heller's (*Tosafot Yom Tov*) commentaries on Arachin 1:3.
76. Bleich, op. cit.

26

A View of Euthanasia

BYRON SHERWIN

Scripture says: "You should love your neighbor as yourself" [Lev. 19:18]; therefore, choose an easy death for him.

Pesahim 75a

The "miracles" of modern medicine have engendered the complexities of modern
medical ethics. Advances in medical technology have exacerbated moral decision
making in medical settings. One of the most compelling issues confronting contemporary bioethics is euthanasia. The word *euthanasia* derives from the Greek and
means a "good death."

Modern philosophers often distinguish between two kinds of euthanasia: active
and passive. Active euthanasia refers to an action that causes or accelerates death.
Passive euthanasia refers to the withdrawal of life support. In addition, a distinction
is also often made between "voluntary" and "involuntary" euthanasia. In voluntary
euthanasia, the individual whose life is in question takes an action that brings his or
her own life to an end. In involuntary euthanasia, an action to end the patient's life
is taken without his or her explicit consent to end his or her life. Thus, euthanasia
may take a variety of forms: active-voluntary, passive-voluntary, active-involuntary,
and passive-involuntary.

An example of active-voluntary euthanasia would be where the patient wills to
end his or her own life and actively implements this decision. For instance, if a person
with terminal cancer makes a conscious decision to die by swallowing an overdose of
painkilling medicine that, besides alleviating pain, may also accelerate death, this
would be a case of active-voluntary euthanasia.

Passive-voluntary euthanasia would be where the patient chooses to remove the
means that are prolonging his or her life, without which he or she *might* otherwise die.
For example, if a patient who may not be able to breathe normally removes a
respirator or an intravenous unit (IV), which then brings about his or her death, this
would be an example of passive-voluntary euthanasia.

Active-involuntary euthanasia would be when a party *other than the patient* takes
deliberate action to accelerate the patient's death. Passive-involuntary euthanasia
would be when a party other than the patient removes certain life-support systems
without the patient's knowledge or consent—for example, if a patient has a flat
electroencephalogram (EEG) and is in an irreversible coma but the heart and lungs are

operating because of mechanical assistance, then "pulling the plug" would be an example of passive-involuntary euthanasia.

To be sure, the distinction among these four forms of euthanasia is helpful, but it is also often hazy. For instance, is "pulling the plug" passive or active euthanasia; does it remove an action, for example, is it the introduction of "heroic measures," or *is* it an action aimed at accelerating death?

Before looking at some of the responses Jewish sources offer to the complex and multifaceted problem of euthanasia, it might be helpful to try to identify further some of the questions and situations these sources might address.

Voluntary Euthanasia: May a Patient Choose to Take an Action That Would End His or Her Own Life?

Under this general question many more specific questions may be subsumed: Does one have a right to die as well as a right to live? To whom does one's life belong—to oneself, to society, to God? What obligation does one have to preserve one's life? To what extent does this obligation extend?

One who decides to end one's life may do so in a variety of ways. Is killing oneself always suicide? Is suicide justifiable? Would active-voluntary euthanasia (e.g., through self-injection) *or* passive-voluntary euthanasia (e.g., through cessation of administering certain drugs) be any more or less morally problematic than the other?

Would asking someone else to end one's life be voluntary or involuntary euthanasia? Would the person who does the asking or the person who actually performs the action be morally responsible for an act of euthanasia? Is euthanasia murder?

How might the motives of a person who undertakes an act of voluntary euthanasia be considered in evaluating the morality or the immorality of the actions? Suppose a person decides upon voluntary euthanasia to alleviate his or her own pain and suffering; could "pain and suffering" include psychological anguish? What if a patient or a family member of a patient chooses voluntary euthanasia to alleviate the psychological or financial burden or both to his or her family?

Involuntary Euthanasia: May a Party Other than the Patient Choose to Take Action That Would Result in the Ending of the Patient's Life?

In many cases the patient is in no condition, physically or mentally, to make a decision as far as euthanasia is concerned—for example, the patient may be drugged or in a coma. In such a case, it might fall to someone other than the patient—such as a relative—to make a decision about whether to take action that would or might result in the patient's death. Or a patient might decide to take an action of active or passive euthanasia on his or her own. In such a case, the means employed and the motives that lead to this action would have to be morally evaluated. Would a moral distinction be made between active and passive euthanasia in such a case? Would "pulling the plug" be comparable to giving the patient a lethal dose of painkiller? Would deliberately injecting a lethal dose of painkiller be distinguished morally from doing so accidentally? Would shooting the patient to end his or her misery be murder? (Would it be murder if the patient pleaded that it be done?) Would practicing euthanasia on a relative or a friend by murder if the primary motive, rather than mercy, is hatred for the patient? If the family of the patient—either individually or collectively—authorizes medical personnel to practice euthanasia on the patient, would the family members be morally liable for the action since the doctor or nurse would be acting as their agent, or would the medical personnel themselves be morally liable for the action since they actually performed the act itself?

In some hospitals, it is standard procedure for physicians to practice euthanasia without consulting the patient or the patient's family. Some reasons for this include (1) the patient may not be conscious, or the patient may already be "medically dead" and unable to make such a decision;[1] (2) the physician might not want to burden the patient's family with having to make such an extraordinary decision about their loved one; (3) the physician may have to consider the needs of other patients and the availability of personnel and machinery (e.g., heart-lung machines) to treat other patients, who might have a better chance of survival. Physicians treating severely ill or terminal patients have to ask themselves many questions, such as should treatment be rendered, or should the patient be allowed to die naturally without initiating treatment? For example, an elderly patient suffers heart failure. The heart is so weak that resuscitation would only prolong the process of death. Should a do-not-resuscitate (DNR) order be maintained, or should the patient be put on a heart-lung machine? Should the cardiorespiratory functions simply be allowed to cease naturally? Once treatment has been initiated but irreparable life-threatening damage (e.g., brain damage) has been inflicted, should treatment be discontinued that would or might directly lead to the patient's death? Should artificial hydration or nutrition be removed once it had been introduced? Should active or passive euthanasia be practiced on a terminal patient? At what point? Should the physician use his or her best medical judgment as the basis for practicing euthanasia in any or all circumstances? Should the physician practice euthanasia at the request of the patient's family if it is an agreement with the physician's own medical judgment? If it does not so concur? Should the physician take into account local legal options (e.g., a DNR directive), his or her religion's teachings, his or her physician's oath in practicing euthanasia? Should a physician or a nurse practice euthanasia simply because it is ordered by a higher medical authority, or should the moral judgment always be his or her own, independent from that of others? How does Jewish tradition deal with euthanasia?

Though as a rule Judaism condemns murder and suicide, there are exceptions to the rule. For example, martyrdom—killing oneself or others, or allowing oneself and others to be killed—for "the sanctification of God's Name" is not considered murder or suicide by talmudic and subsequent Jewish tradition.[2] Killing in self-defense and other forms of "justified homicide" have been sanctioned as "necessary evils" by rabbinic tradition.[3] Neither were all examples of manslaughter considered murder; rabbinic tradition required conditions such as premeditation and malicious intent before defining an act as murder.[4]

Since martyrdom is one of the exceptions to suicide and murder, it is interesting that posttalmudic Jewish sources found a precedent for euthanasia in a talmudic text that discusses martyrdom:

> It was said that within but a few days Rabbi Jose ben Kisma died and all the great men of Rome went to his burial and made a great lamentation for him. On their return, they found Rabbi Hanina ben Teradion sitting and occupying himself with the Torah, publicly gathering assemblies, and keeping a scroll of the Torah in his bosom. Straightaway they took hold of him, wrapt him in the scroll of the Torah, placed bundles of branches around him and set them on fire. They then brought tuffs of wool, which they had soaked in water, and placed them over his heart, so that he should not expire quickly. His daughter exclaimed, "Father, that I should see you in this state!" He replied, "If it were I alone being burnt, it would have been a thing hard to bear; but now I am burning together with the scroll of the Torah, He who will have regard for the plight of the Torah will also have regard for my plight." His disciples called out, "Rabbi, what seest thou?" He answered them, "The parchments are being burnt but the letters are soaring high." "Open then thy mouth" [said they] "so that the fire enter into thee." He replied: "Let Him who gave me [my soul] take it away, but no one should injure oneself." The executioner then said to him, "Rabbi, if I raise the flame and take away the tufts of wool from over thy heart, will thou cause me to enter into the life to come?" "Yes," he replied. "Then swear unto me" [he urged]. He swore unto him. He thereupon raised the flame and removed the tufts of wool from over his heart, and his soul departed speedily. The executioner then jumped and threw himself into the fire. And a *bat kol* [a heavenly voice] exclaimed: "Rabbi Hanina ben Teradion and the executioner have been assigned to the World to Come." When Rabbi heard it, he wept and said: "One may acquire eternal life in a single hour, another after many years."[5]

This talmudic text was interpreted by later authorities as having established the following principles:

1. Martyrdom is not to be considered self-murder or suicide.
2. An individual's life belongs not to himself or herself but to God.
3. Active-voluntary euthanasia is prohibited, but passive-voluntary euthanasia *may* be permitted. When the rabbi is encouraged to open his mouth so that the fire may enter and end his agony (i.e., active-voluntary euthanasia), he refuses. But, when the executioner offers to remove the soaked tufts of wool artificially prolonging his life (i.e., a life-support system), the rabbi gives him permission (i.e., passive-voluntary euthanasia).

As discussed later in this chapter, the views on euthanasia that are drawn from this talmudic text are reiterated in subsequent Jewish literature.

Active Euthanasia Is Prohibited

The *Sefer Hasidim,* states: "If a person is suffering from extreme pain and he says to another: 'You see that I shall not live [long]; [therefore,] kill me because I cannot bear the pain,' one is forbidden to touch him [the terminal patient]." The text continues and proscribes the terminal patient from taking his or her own life. "If a person is suffering great pain and he knows that he will not live [long], he cannot kill himself. And this principle we learn from Rabbi Hanina ben Teradion who refused to open his mouth [to allow the fire to enter and take his life]."[6]

In one of the "minor tractates" of the Talmud, we read:

> A dying man [*goses*] is regarded as a living entity in respect to all matters in the world. Whosoever touches or moves him is a murderer [if by so doing his death is accelerated]. Rabbi Meir used to say: He may be compared to a lamp which is dripping [going out]; should one touch it, one extinguishes it. Similarly, whoever closes the eyes of a dying man [thereby accelerating his death] is considered as if he had taken his life.[7]

This prohibition against practicing active euthanasia is reiterated by the medieval codes of Jewish law. It extends to the patient, the attending physician, the family and friends of the patient, and to all other individuals.[8] In his legal code, the *Mishneh Torah*, Maimonides wrote:

> One who is in a dying condition is regarded as a living person in all respects . . . He who touches him [thereby accelerating his death] is guilty of shedding blood. To what may he [the dying person] be compared? To a flickering flame, which is extinguished as soon as one touches it. Whoever closes the eyes of a dying person while the soul is about to depart is shedding blood. One should wait a while; perhaps he is just in a swoon.[9]

The fourteenth-century code of Jacob ben Asher is called the *Arba'ah Turim*. In many ways, it served as the model for Joseph Karo's sixteenth-century code, the *Shulhan Arukh*. Echoing earlier texts, Jacob ben Asher wrote: "A dying man is to be considered a living person in all respects . . . [therefore] anyone who hastens the exiting of the person's soul is a shedder of blood."[10] The *Shulhan Arukh* reads, "A patient on his deathbed is considered a living person in every respect . . . and it is forbidden to cause him to die quickly . . . and whosoever closes his eyes with the onset of death is regarded as shedding blood."[11]

The nineteenth-century *Kitzur Shulhan Arukh* by Solomon Ganzfried embellishes a bit on the earlier sources: "Even if one has been dying for a long time, which causes agony to the patient and his family, it is still forbidden to accelerate his death."[12]

The premises upon which classical Jewish views regarding active euthanasia are based include the following:

1. An individual's life is not his or her own "property" but God's, and therefore God has the final disposition over it. In other words, each person serves as God's steward for the life given into his or her care. As Hanina ben Teradion put it, "Let Him who gave me my soul take it away."[13]

2. Jewish law does not dwell on the issue of quality of life. Rather, Jewish law maintains that each moment of life is inherently valuable in and of itself, independent of its quality. Life being sacred—each moment of life being intrinsically valuable—every effort must be made to preserve each moment of life, even to the moment of death. For example, according to Jewish law, "even if they find a person crushed [under a fallen building] so that he can live only for a short time, they must continue to dig," and if this has occurred on the Sabbath, one is *required* to violate the Sabbath even if it means granting the victim only "momentary life."[14]

3. An individual is prohibited from inflicting self-injury, particularly the ultimate self-injury—suicide, which is generally defined as self-homicide.[15]

4. Since "there is no agency for wrongful acts," and since murder is a wrongful act, one may not act as the agent of a person who desires death and bring about or accelerate that person's death, even at that person's explicit request.[16] In this regard, the physician is explicitly enjoined from employing medical intervention for the intention of accelerating death.[17]

Passive Euthanasia May Be Permitted

As noted, the talmudic case of Hanina ben Teradion is used by some posttalmudic sources as a precedent for the permissibility of passive euthanasia. The rabbi permitted the tufts of wool which were "artificially" sustaining his life to be removed. This would seem to permit both voluntary and involuntary passive euthanasia, either on the part of the patient (voluntary) or on the part of another party (voluntary or involuntary), such as a physician. To be sure, Jewish law would not permit the removal of all life-support mechanisms. For example, it generally would not permit withholding insulin from a diabetic.[18] The text of the story of Hanina ben Teradion clearly relates to an individual who has no chance of survival in any case.

In many of the same sources noted above proscribing active euthanasia, one finds material that permits passive euthanasia. The *Sefer Hasidim* observes, "One may not [artificially] prolong the act of dying. If, for example, someone is dying and nearby a woodcutter insists on chopping wood, thereby disturbing the dying person so that he cannot die, we remove the woodcutter from the vicinity of the dying person. Also, one must not place salt in the mouth of a dying person in order to prevent death from overtaking him."[19] This view is adapted and is quoted almost verbatim in subsequent codes of Jewish law. In his gloss to the *Shulhan Arukh,* Moses Isserles observed, "It is forbidden to cause one's death to be accelerated, even in the case of one who has been terminally ill for a long time . . . *however,* if there is some factor which is preventing the exit of the soul such as a nearby woodchopper or salt placed under his tongue—and these things are impeding his death—it is permissible to remove them because in so doing one actively does nothing but remove an obstacle [preventing his natural death]."[20] Again, echoing the *Sefer Hasidim,* the *Shulhan Arukh* states, "One must not scream at the moment at which the soul [of another] departs, lest the soul return and the person suffer great pain. That is to say, it is not simply permitted to remove an obstacle to one's [natural] death, but one cannot lengthen the pain and suffering of the patient."[21]

In this regard, Isserles interpreted the view of the *Sefer Hasidim* as meaning that "it is certain that for one to do anything that stifles the [natural] process of dying [of a dying person] is forbidden."[22] Similarly, the sixteenth-century Italian rabbi Joshua Boaz referred to the *Sefer Hasidim* as being the basis of his own view, "it is permissible to remove any obstacle preventing [death] because so doing is not an action in and of itself."[23] Furthermore, in a seventeenth-century responsum by Jacob ben Samuel, the author takes the controversial view that any medical or pharmacological intervention that impedes the natural process of dying should not be introduced.[24]

Commenting on the phrase in Eccles. 3:2, "There is a time to die," the *Sefer Hasidim* observes that Ecclesiastes does *not* also state that "there is a time to live." The reason for this, according to the *Sefer Hasidim,* is that, when the "time to die" arrives, it is not the time to extend life. Consequently, the *Sefer Hasidim* prohibits efforts to resuscitate a terminal patient on the grounds that extending the process of dying by resuscitation would cause the patient continued unnecessary anguish and pain.[25] This text might serve as the basis for justifying a DNR order for terminal patients whose condition has reached the point of death and whose resuscitation through heroic measures would only prolong their death and extend their agony. Just as some sources consider active euthanasia to be a presumption of God's authority over life and death, the *Sefer Hasidim* insists that extending the process of dying, when the terminal patient is in severe pain, is also a presumption of God's authority over life and death and a presumptive rejection of the scriptural view that "there is a time to die."

It should be noted, though, that the specific removal of natural hydration and food from a terminal patient to hasten death is specifically proscribed, probably because such withdrawal is considered cruel.[26] According to a text in the *Sefer Hasidim,* however, the removal of food and water is required in two kinds of cases. One is in the case in which nutrition or hydration would harm the patient. The second is in the case of a terminal patient where death is imminent. Such a patient must be made comfortable, for example, by keeping his or her lips and mouth moist, but such a patient must not be fed, lest the process of dying be prolonged and painful agony be unduly lengthened.[27]

From the literature reviewed to this point, it would appear that the Jewish view of euthanasia is that active euthanasia is prohibited, but passive euthanasia may be permissible and even desirable; for while classical Jewish sources place great value on saving and prolonging human life, they put no premium on needlessly prolonging the act of dying.[28] However, the sources seem uncompromising in the view that active euthanasia, under any circumstances, is a form of suicide or murder and is therefore prohibited. Indeed, a number of contemporary Jewish scholars, after reviewing the relevant sources, have come to this conclusion. For example, Immanuel Jakobovits, in his significant work *Jewish Medical Ethics,* summarizes the Jewish position on euthanasia as follows:

> It is clear, then, even when the patient is already known to be on his deathbed and close to the end, any form of *active euthanasia* is strictly prohibited. In fact, it is condemned as plain murder. In purely legal terms, this is borne out by the ruling that anyone who kills a dying person is liable to the death penalty as a common murderer. At the same time, Jewish law sanctions, and perhaps even demands, the withdrawal of any factor—whether extraneous to the patient himself or not—which may artificially delay his demise in the final phase.[29]

Despite this apparent consensus on the matter, a number of contemporary scholars have attempted to discover and to formulate a basis for active euthanasia under certain circumstances. This reevaluation of the sources has been prompted by certain contemporary medical and pharmacological developments and by the present proliferation of terminal cancer cases brought about by the lengthening of the average human life span.

Active Euthanasia Reconsidered

There seems to be unanimity of opinion in Judaism that life is intrinsically precious, even "momentary life." This assumption makes moot any discussion regarding life versus the quality of life. This claim also serves as a foundation for the condemnation of murder and suicide, of killing and self-killing. However, as noted above, exceptions to the prohibition against killing and self-killing were condoned by classical Jewish tradition, such as in cases of martyrdom and "justifiable homicide." These exceptions to the rule lead one to conclude that the value of life itself is not *always* considered absolute. The permissibility, even the desirability, of martyrdom assumes that there are occasions where life itself may be set aside because the preservation of life is not always an absolute moral imperative.

While it is true that the dominant view of Jewish tradition is that life itself is of intrinsic value, there exists an alternative view that relates both to cases of martyrdom and to cases of pain and anguish. For example, one talmudic text maintains that a life of unbearable pain, a life coming to an inevitable and an excruciating end, is not a life worth continuing, that such a life is like having no life at all.

A talmudic passage describes an individual who is overcome with a severe physical affliction as one "whose life is no life."[30] Similarly, a nineteenth-century commentary on the Mishnah observes that "great pain is worse than death." And while "a dying person [*goses*] is like a living person in all respects," the Mishnah in effect "devalued" the monetary worth of a dying person who wished to vow the equivalent of his monetary worth as a donation to the sanctuary.[31] The Mishnah reads, "One at the point of death [*goses*] . . . cannot have his worth vowed, nor be subject to valuation." On this text, the Talmud comments, "It is quite right that one at the point of death cannot have his worth vowed, because he has no monetary value; nor can he be made the subject of a valuation because he is not fit to be made subject of a valuation.[32] Thus, the imperative "Choose life" (Deut. 30:19) is not as absolute as is often assumed.

A further examination of classical Jewish sources related to martyrdom reveals that life in and of itself was not always considered of ultimate value. Such an examination also reveals precedents for taking one's own life and allowing oneself to be killed rather than to endure the physical torture that was frequently a martyr's fate. In such cases, taking one's own life was often not considered suicide. What proves intriguing is the pertinence and the applicability that instances in which martyrs chose death to physical suffering, chose to accelerate their own death rather than to withstand physical agony, may have to the problem of euthanasia, in general, and to the problem of active euthanasia, in particular.[33]

Talmudic literature records many instances of martyrdom. One, noted above, was the case of Rabbi Hanina ben Teradion. Another text describes how four hundred Jewish children drowned themselves at sea to avoid submitting to rape at the hands of Romans. In a medieval commentary to the tale of the children, a reference is made to the case of Hanina ben Teradion. The two cases taken together are interpreted by Jacob Tam as meaning that, to avoid sufferings certain to result in death, it is permitted to take one's own life, and in such an instance it is required (not necessarily prohibited) to injure onself by choosing death.[34]

While suicide is proscribed by Jewish law, the prohibition against suicide was clearly set aside in the aforementioned cases of martyrdom. In other sources, suicide was redefined so that killing oneself was not always defined as suicide.[35] One such source is a controversial nineteenth-century responsum by Saul Berlin.

Berlin's responsum maintains that an individual who takes his or her own life because of mental or physical pain and anguish is not to be considered a suicide. According to Berlin, the earlier *halakhic* regulations prohibiting suicide were primarily intended for cases where the act resulted from a pessimistic view of life. However, Berlin asserted, a person who takes his or her own life to avoid continued pain and anguish is not to be considered a suicide.[36]

The controversial and unprecedented nature of Berlin's responsum and the possibly tenuous analogy between cases of martyrdom and cases of euthanasia, while suggestive, still do not adequately defend an option for active within Jewish tradition. Consequently, it is necessary to look further.

In a late midrash on Proverbs, the text tells us,

> It happened that a woman who had aged considerably appeared before Rabbi Yose ben Halafta. She said: "Rabbi, I am much too old, life has become a burden for me. I can no longer taste food or drink, and I wish to die." Rabbi Yose answered her: "To what do you ascribe your longevity?" She answered that it was her habit to pray in the synagogue every morning, and despite occasional more pressing needs she never had missed a service. Rabbi Yose advised her to refrain from attending services for three consecutive days. She heeded his advice and on the third day she took ill and died.[37]

This text may be interpreted as a reinforcement of the view that passive euthanasia is permitted by Jewish law under certain conditions. The woman's withholding of her prayers removed the cause of the extension of her life. Similarly, the removal of life-support systems from a patient to whom—like this woman—life has become a burden, would be permissible.[38] Nevertheless, it may be argued that this case underscores the inability always to make a clear-cut distinction between passive and active. Her discontinuance of her prayers or a physician's or nurse's "pulling the plug" may be considered a deliberate action aimed at precipitating an accelerated death. Once the line between passive and active becomes so blurred, one may attempt to cross the line with care and with caution. For if the woman's withholding of her prayers is a sanctioned action deliberately designed to accelerate her own death, then other actions designed to hasten the death of those to whom life has become an unbearable burden might also be eligible for the sanction of Jewish tradition.

The underlying assumption of this midrashic text is the efficacy of prayer in attaining particular results. Here, the woman effected those results (her own death) by withholding prayer.[39] But, what about a case in which one actively prays for death to avoid enduring pain and suffering? The woman's withholding of her prayers caused her *own* death, but what about a case in which prayer is aimed at bringing about the death of another? It would seem to reason that if the rabbis permitted one actively to pray for one's own death and even for the death of another, rather than have one endure pain and suffering, then a basis of an argument could be made for a rabbinic precedent as far as both voluntary and involuntary active are concerned. In the Talmud one finds such a precedent.

> On the day that Rabbi Judah was dying, the rabbis decreed a public fast and offered prayers for heavenly mercy [so that he would not die]. . . . Rabbi Judah's handmaid ascended to the roof and prayed: "The immortals [the angels] desire

him [to join them] and the mortals desire him [to remain with them]; may it be the will [of God] that the mortals may overpower the immortals [i.e., that he would not die]." When, however, she saw how often he resorted to the privy, painfully removing and replacing his *tefillin* [in terrible agony], she prayed: "May it be the will [of God] that the immortals may over-power the mortals." The rabbis meanwhile continued their prayers for heavenly mercy. She took a jar and threw it down from the roof to the ground. [For a moment,] they stopped praying, and the soul of Rabbi Judah departed.[40]

Some interpret this text to mean that the death of Rabbi Judah was caused by the rabbis' cessation of their prayers when they were startled by the noise of the shattering jar. Others interpret this text to mean that his death was caused by the handmaiden's active prayer aimed at bringing about Rabbi Judah's death in order to alleviate his substantial suffering. It is in this latter sense that the text was interpreted by the fourteenth-century talmudic commentator Rabbenu Nissim (Ran). "Sometimes one must request mercy on behalf of the ill so that he might die, as in the case of a patient who is terminal and who is in great pain."[41]

The question of whether one may pray for the death of a patient in pain is discussed in a lengthy responsum by the nineteenth-century Turkish rabbi Hayyim Palaggi. In this case, a woman has been suffering for many years with a degenerative terminal disease. She has been afforded the best available medical treatment. Her family has provided constant and loving care. Hope for a remission has been abandoned by the patient, by the family, and by the attending physicians. Her condition progressively has deteriorated. Her pain has become constant and unbearable. Her illness has left her an invalid. She has prayed to God to die, preferring death to life as a liberation from pain. She has asked her family to pray for her death, but they have refused. Palaggi has been asked whether there are any grounds for prohibiting prayers that she might find rest in death.

In a long and complicated argument, the details of which need not be restated here, Palaggi ruled that, while family members may not pray for her death, others may do so. In the course of reaching this conclusion, Palaggi quoted a number of earlier sources, including the previously cited statement of Rabbenu Nissim. Thus, Palaggi reaffirmed the earlier view that active prayer for the death of a terminal patient in pain, whose life has become a self-burden, is both permissible and even desirable. It is noteworthy that Palaggi did not even question the woman's right to pray for death on her own behalf.

Among Palaggi's reasons for refusing the patient's family permission to pray for her death was the possibility of their actions being motivated by less than honorable motives. Palaggi specifically considered the possibility of the patient's spouse wishing her death so as to remarry someone already in mind. Palaggi also reflected on the possibility that the members of the patient's family may have desired her death—consciously or subconsciously—to free themselves from the burden of her care and support. This insightful psychological observation should be considered in cases of involuntary euthanasia, where the patient's family is confronted with the decision—even at the patient's request—to bring about the patient's accelerated death either by active or by passive euthanasia. As Palaggi noted, consideration for the patient is the only consideration. The financial or psychological condition of family members must not be the determining factor in such discussions. The establishment of ethics committees in many hospitals has helped to relieve patients' families of the anguish of such decisions and of the future guilt that may be precipitated by the realization that a decision to accelerate death might have been because of conscious or subconscious ulterior motives. As Palaggi noted, "strangers" cannot be held under suspicion of ulterior motives.

What is also significant about Palaggi's responsum is the manner in which he dealt with the endemic conflict of principles embodied in any examination of euthanasia from a Jewish perspective. These conflicting principles are preserving life and relieving agony. Palaggi attempted to obviate this apparently unresolvable conflict by reframing the question. According to Palaggi the question is, to what point is one morally obligated to continue life? By stating the question in this manner, Palaggi found a loophole in the categorical imperative to continue preserving life. He was therefore able to conclude that, in certain instances, such as the one at hand, it is both permissible and even desirable to take positive action that will liberate a terminal patient from agony by accelerating his or her death.

To be sure, Palaggi did not explicitly advocate active euthanasia in the sense of performing concrete medical or other intervention other than prayer to accelerate the death of a terminal patient in agony. Nevertheless, Palaggi established the viability of an attitude that would recommend active euthanasia in particular instances. And, while it was not his intention to do so, his view might be extended a step further to serve as the basis for advocating active euthanasia in cases similar to that of the woman described in his responsum.[42]

A further basis for a possible justification for active euthanasia from classical Jewish sources may be posited by combining related precedent with a form of argument characteristic of Jewish legal discourse. The precedent is the talmudic text in which the term "euthanasia"—an easy, good, or quick death—occurs (Hebrew: *mitah yafah*). The form of argument is a fortiori (Hebrew: *kal va-homer;* literally: "the light and the weighty"). An example of this form of inference would be, "Here is a teetotaler who does not touch cider; he will certainly refuse whiskey." The acceptability of applying this form of argument is stated in the Talmud.[43]

The term *mitah yafah* is used in the course of talmudic discussion concerning the execution of criminals convicted of capital offenses. In one text, the verse "You should love your neighbor as yourself" (Lev. 19:18) is interpreted to mean that the criminal is to be given a *mitah yafah;* the pain usually inflicted by the various types of death sentences is to be reduced both in time and in degree by administering a painkilling drug.[44] At this point, one may argue either from one comparable case to another or from the "weighty" to the "light" case.

1. The terminal patient is compared by the Talmud to a criminal condemned to death in that his or her case is hopeless.[45] From this equation one might argue that the terminal patient ought to be given at least the same consideration as a criminal about to be executed for having committed a capital offense.

2. One may also argue that if a criminal, guilty of having committed a capital offense, is shown such consideration, how much more should be shown the terminal patient, innocent of any capital offense?

3. One may extend these lines of argument to a further consideration of how cases of martyrdom, that is, cases of "justified" self-homicide, might be extended to cases of active euthanasia. As noted earlier in this chapter, some sources maintain that it is permissible in cases of martyrdom to allow oneself to be killed quickly or to take one's own life rather than to endure prolonged suffering and anguish.[46] One

may maintain that, if such cases of martyrdom are not to be considered suicide or self-homicide, so cases in which an individual suffering agony takes his or her own life are similarly not to be condemned as suicide, and that certain cases of accelerating one's own death, to be free of excruciating pain, may be justifiable.

4. Jewish law forbids self-harm. Jewish law further prohibits an individual from intentionally placing himself or herself in a harmful or a potentially harmful or dangerous situation. Yet, even though Jewish legal authorities recognize the potentially hazardous nature of various types of medical, pharmacological, and surgical intervention, they nevertheless sanction such intervention. Therefore, the rule against potential danger may be set aside where such treatment is concerned. Consideration of the following *halakhic* precedents in this regard leads to further conclusions regarding possible justification of various forms of active euthanasia within the framework of Jewish law.

According to some *halakhic* authorities, when conventional therapies have been exhausted, experimental therapy may be introduced by a competent physician. This approach is sanctioned even if death were to result from such experimental therapy, especially where a terminal patient is involved. As long as even the most remote possibility of remission exists, hazardous therapy, even life-threatening therapy, may be employed. Using such therapy, though it is known in advance that it might immediately end the patient's life, would be a form of active euthanasia that would not be proscribed by Jewish law.

The prohibition against placing oneself in danger is also set aside when a medical or surgical procedure potentially endangers the life of a patient whose life is not clearly endangered by his or her medical condition. Specifically, if the purpose of the procedure is to reduce or eliminate substantial pain, such a procedure is permitted, despite its potential threat to the life of the patient.[47] From this perspective, as from that of Palaggi, the imperative to reduce or to eliminate pain is given precedence over the obligation to sustain life at all costs. One may extend this argument to a conclusion that would sanction the administering of painkilling drugs or procedures, even if it is known in advance that the patient might die as a result of such action. Hence, active euthanasia employed with the specific primary intention of alleviating unbearable pain would be an acceptable moral option, even if, in the act of alleviating pain, the death of the patient resulted.

In this case, as in those previously discussed, an a fortiori argument can be made: if administering a painkilling drug or undertaking a pain-alleviating procedure that may accelerate the patient's death can be done in cases in which death is not imminent, then it should be permissible to administer a painkilling drug or a painkilling procedure that may accelerate the patient's death in cases in which death is certainly imminent. From this basis, one may argue that, if there is a choice between prolonging the process of dying, where death seems imminent and certain, and taking action that will alleviate pain but that will also accelerate the process of death, where death is imminent and certain, then the later option is both morally viable and legally permissible.

Not only may one make a case for active euthanasia in Jewish law, one may also argue that in certain circumstances the killer is not to be considered a murderer. To consider an act as murder, according to Jewish law, two of the conditions that must be satisfied are premeditation and malice (see Exod. 21:14). Rabbinic literature specifically exonerates a physician who kills his patient, even if he acted with willfulness, when malice is not also present. Though the medieval codes link pre-meditation with malice, there is no logical or psychological reason to do so. The rabbinic precedent may stand on its own.[48] Thus, under certain circumstances, according to this minority view, the physician may be legally (but not necessarily morally) blameless for practicing active euthanasia.

One specific case in which active euthanasia by patient, agent, or physician may be more justifiable than others, according to some of the literature, would be that in which the patient is afflicted with a terminal disease, such as cancer.

Talmudic law distinguishes between *goses,* that is, one terminally ill, and *tereifah* (literally, torn), that is, one terminally ill, for instance, as the result of irreparable organic damage. Apparently, in the former case, recovery is at least theoretically possible, whereas in the latter case, recovery is altogether impossible. One who kills a *goses* is considered a murderer by the Talmud and the codes. But one who kills a *tereifah* is not guilty of murder.[49]

Though the majority view found in classical and contemporary Jewish literature condemns active euthanasia, this chapter's discussion and the sources noted herein indicate the viability and the defensibility of a minority view supporting voluntary euthanasia when the primary motive is to alleviate pain and suffering. Indeed, a number of contemporary rabbinic decisions and views affirm this position. For example, David Shohet, writing in *Conservative Judaism* as early as 1952, came to this conclusion after a review of the classical Jewish sources on the matter. His article states that an adequate defense can be made to "support the contention that to bring a merciful end to intolerable suffering to a patient who has no longer any hope of recovery and his death is imminent is an act which may be considered lawful and ethical in Jewish law."[50]

Conclusion

Continued developments in medical technology, increased life expectancy, and the rapid "graying" of the American people all point to an inevitable collision of events that have made, and will continue to make, the problem of euthanasia evermore severe in the foreseeable future. For the American Jewish community, with its median age already substantially higher than that of the American population as a whole, the problem of euthanasia is of particular and immediate pertinence.

It is only reasonable for Jewish patients, families, medical professionals, social workers, clergy, and those involved with the Jewish hospice movement to look to Jewish tradition—particularly to Jewish law and bioethics—for direction and for guidance in dealing with life's challenges and crises, especially those that come at life's end, such as the process of dying and the problem of euthanasia.

Jewish sources have developed a variety of concrete attitudes and views regarding the attempt to resolve the inevitable conflict between a commitment to valuing life and a commitment to mitigating pain and suffering during the process of dying. What emerges from a consideration of a vast number of classical sources is that Jewish tradition puts a high premium on extending life, but it recognizes that prolonging the process of painful death is not necessarily desirable. Therefore, it endorses passive euthanasia in most cases where death is imminent and inevitable and where the process of dying is accompanied by considerable and unbearable suffering and anguish. This attitude, as noted above, also relates to the introduction of heroic measures. In some instances, when death is near and certain and where considerable pain will ensue, heroic measures, or resuscitation, are not encouraged and, according to some authorities, are proscribed.

The preceding discussion outlines the dominant view in Jewish sources prohibiting active euthanasia of any kind. However, in view of contemporary realities, I have felt it necessary to defend a position within the framework of classical Jewish sources that would justify active euthanasia in at least certain circumstances. I believe that patients, families of patients, physicians, health care workers, and social service professionals, who deal with the death and dying of individuals, whose last days are overwhelmed with unbearable agony, should be able to advocate and to practice active euthanasia without feeling that they are criminals, without being burdened with great guilt for actions that they sincerely consider merciful, without feeling that they have transgressed divine and human laws, and without feeling that they have rejected the teachings of Jewish tradition. To be sure, Judaism instructs us to "choose life" (Deut. 30:19), but Judaism also recognizes that "there is a time to die" (Eccles. 3:2). In each case in which the problem of euthanasia presents itself, each person involved must decide which verse applies and how the fulfillment of that verse may best be implemented.

Notes

1. On definitions of death and "brain death" in Jewish law, see Fred Rosner and J. David Bleich, eds., *Jewish Bioethics* (New York: Hebrew Publishing Co., 1969), pp. 277–317, and Gedaliah Rabinowitz's and Mordecai Konigsberg's Hebrew essay "The Definition of Death and the Time of Death according to Jewish Law" in *Ha-Darom* 32 (1970): 59–76. In a resolution, the (Conservative) Rabbinical Assembly has opted for a definition of death related to the "cessation of spontaneous brain function." It should be noted that death is increasingly being understood as a process rather than as an event, thus making the exact moment of death difficult to determine precisely.

2. On the requirement to sacrifice one's own life rather than transgress, see, e.g., *Sanhedrin* 74a, *Yoma* 82a; Karo, *Shulhan Arukh—Yoreh Deah,* para. 357. Because martyrdom represented the ultimate expression of self-sacrifice for God (*Kiddush ha-Shem*), it has been considered the highest virtue—transcending the obligation to preserve life—by many prominent rabbinic figures and Jewish religious movements throughout history. In early postbiblical Jewish literature, see, e.g., 2 Macc. 14:37–46; *Berakhot* 61b (the martyrdom of Rabbi Akiba); *Sanhedrin* 110b; *Sifra* (Vienna: Shlossberg, 1862), *"Emor"* no. 9, p. 9; *Mekhilta de-Rabbi Ishmael,* ed. Lauterbach, *"Ba-Hodesh,"* chap. 6 end, p. 247; *Midrash Song of Songs* 2:7. Emulating Rabbi Akiba, the medieval German Hasidim extolled and followed his example. For example, commenting on the verse, "For He is our God, and we are the people in His care" (Ps. 95:7), the *Sefer Hasidim,* ed. J. Wistinetzki and J. Freimann (Frankfurt: Wahrmann Verlag, 1924), no. 256, p. 84, comments, "When do we acknowledge that He is our God? When we are slaughtered like sheep for the sanctification of His Name, He is our God." Also, see the discussion and sources collected in Shalom Spiegel, *The Last Trial* (New York: Pantheon, 1967). On Hasidic attitudes to martyrdom during the Holocaust, see Pesach Shindler, "The Holocaust and Kiddush Ha-Shem in Hasidic Thought," *Tradition* 13/14 (1973): 88–105, where the idea of martyrdom as a privilege is discussed. See also Charles W. Reines, "The Jewish Attitude toward Suicide," *Judaism* 10 (1961): 161–70.

3. Jewish tradition recognizes certain categories of "justifiable homicide." One such

category is killing in self-defense; see, e.g., Exod. 22:1, *Sanhedrin* 72a–b. Another such category relates to killing a potential murderer to ensure the safety of his or her intended victim; see, e.g., *Sanhedrin* 73a; Maimonides, *Mishneh Torah—Sefer Nezikin*, "Laws of Murderers," 1:9. *The Book of Torts*, Eng. trans. Hyman Klein (New Haven: Yale University Press, 1954), pp. 196–97. Other examples include killing in certain types of "just wars" and capital punishment.

4. *Encyclopedia Judaica, s.v.* "Homicide" by Haim H. Cohen. See also the discussion within this chapter on this issue. Note, e.g., Rashi on Exod. 21:4, *Mekhilta d'Rabbi Ishmael*, ed. Horovitz and Rabin, "*Mishpatim*," no. 4, p. 263.

5. *Abodah Zarah* 18a.

6. *Sefer Hasidim*, ed. Wistinetzki, no. 315, p. 100.

7. *Semahot* 1:1, 1:4. *The Tractate Mourning*, Eng. trans. Dov Zlotnick (New Haven: Yale University Press, 1966), p. 30. For definitions and discussion of *goses*, see *Encyclopedia Talmudit*, vol. 5, 393–403. See especially Isserles on Karo, *Shulhan Arukh—Even ha-Ezer*, para. 121:7, and *Shulhan Arukh—Hoshen Mishpat*, para. 211:2; Yom Tov Lipmann Heller's sixteenth-century commentary *Tosfot Yom Tov* on M. *Arakhin* 1:3, in standard editions of the Mishnah.

8. For additional sources that prohibit active euthanasia, note the following: *Shabbat* 151b and Rashi there. The Mishnaic text there reads, "He who closes the eyes [of a dying person] at the point of death [thereby accelerating death] is a murderer." In his commentary to *Baba Kamma* 85a, Solomon Luria observed that it is not permissible to accelerate death to relieve suffering; the patient is forced to "choose life." See Luria, *Yam Shel Shelomo*, "*Perek ha-Hovel*," no. 59. Similarly, Moses Schreiber maintained that even a suffering individual who actively ends his or her life "is a murderer and dies in guilt." See his *Responsa Hatam Sofer—Yoreh Deah*, no. 326. "To do anything that causes death to be accelerated is forbidden," wrote Moses Isserles, *Darkhei Moshe* to Jacob ben Asher, *Arba'ah Turim—Yoreh Deah*, para. 339:1, in standard editions of *Arba'ah Turim*.

9. Maimonides, *Mishneh Torah—Sefer Shofetim*, "Laws of Mourning," 4:5. Eng. trans., p. 174.

10. Jacob ben Asher, *Arba'ah Turim—Yoreh Deah*, para. 339.

11. Karo, *Shulhan Arukh—Yoreh Deah*, para. 339:1.

12. Solomon Ganzfried, *Kitzur Shulhan Arukh* (Lwow, 1860), *Yoreh Deah*, para. 194:1.

13. *Abodah Zarah* 18a. Also see Ezek. 18:4; Maimonides, *Mishneh Torah—Sefer Nezikim*, "Laws of Murder," 1:4 Eng. trans., p. 195. David ibn Zimra's commentary to Maimonides, *Mishneh Torah—Sefer Shofetim*, "Laws of the Sanhedrin," 18:6; Shneur Zalman of Liady, *Shulhan Arukh ha-Rav* (Zhitomir, 1856), *Yoreh Deah*, "Laws of Injuring the Body," para. 4.

14. See *Yoma* 84–85; Karo, *Shulhan Arukh—Orah Hayyim*, para. 329:4.

15. *Baba Kamma* 91b; *Abodah Zarah* 18a; *Midrash Genesis Rabbah* 34:13; Maimonides, *Mishneh Torah—Sefer Nezikin*, "Laws of Murderers," 2:3. Eng. trans., p. 199. Note *Midrash Pesikta Rabbati*, ed. Friedmann, 24:1, p. 134b. See also *Sefer Hasidim*, ed. Margaliot, nos. 675–76, pp. 428–29, where neglecting one's own physical and spiritual health is considered a form of self-injury, and even of suicide. On self-injury, see also *Tosefta*, ed. Zuckermandel, *Baba Kamma*, chap. 9, p. 366, and *Yalkut Shimoni* on Gen. 9:5 "Noah," no. 60. In the medieval codes, see Maimonides, *Mishneh Torah—Sefer Nezikin*, "Laws of Wounding and Damaging," 5:1. Eng. trans., pp. 176–77; and Karo, *Shulhan Arukh—Hoshen Mishpat*, para. 420:31. Also Solomon Luria, *Yam Shel Shelomo on Baba Kamma* 91a, no. 59.

16. *Kiddushin* 42b; *Midrash Genesis Rabbah* 34:14. Note Peretz Segal, "No Agency for an Illegal Act," *Annual of the Institute for Research in Jewish Law* 9/10 (1982–83): 73–95.

17. See the gloss of Shabbatai ben Meir, *Siftei Kohein* on Karo, *Shulhan Arukh—Yoreh Deah*, para. 336:1, in standard editions of the *Shulhan Arukh*.

18. On the specific issue of withdrawal of insulin treatment from a diabetic, see Nissan

Telushkin's Hebrew essay, "*Ha-Nimuk ha-Musari she-ba-Mitzvot ha-Teluyot ba-Aretz,*" *Orha-Mitzrah* 2 (1961): 20–24, and Abraham Steinberg's Hebrew essay, "Mercy Killing" in *Assia* 5, no. 3 (Jan. 1978): 30–31. See also Fred Rosner, "Rabbi Moses Feinstein on the Treatment of the Terminally Ill," *Judaism* 37 (Spring 1988): 188–99.

19. *Sefer Hasidim,* ed. Wistinetzki, no. 315, p. 100.

20. See Isserles's gloss on Karo, *Shulhan Arukh—Yoreh Deah,* para. 339:1.

21. *Sefer Hasidim,* ed. Wistinetzki, no. 316, p. 100; Karo, *Shulhan Arukh—Yoreh Deah,* para. 339:1.

22. Isserles's commentary *Darkhei Moshe* to Jacob ben Asher, *Arba'ah Turim—Yoreh Deah,* para. 339:1.

23. *Sefer Hasidim,* ed. Wistinetzki, no. 316, p. 100; ed. Margaliot, no. 723, p. 443; see Joshua Boaz on Isaac Alfasi's commentary to *Mo'ed Katan* 16b, in standard editions of the Talmud.

While most of the sources agree that the removal of external impediments to the process of dying is permitted, there is disagreement regarding the removal of treatment that has already begun. The classic reference in the *Sefer Hasidim* refers to the removal of things like the sound of wood being chopped, which would disturb a patient in a death swoon. This precedent, however, would not justify the removal of already employed heroic measures. Consequently, many contemporary orthodox authorities sanction a decision not to introduce artificial life-support systems but prohibit the removal of such once introduced.

The *Sefer Hasidim,* in the same text, i.e., ed. Wistinetzki, no. 315, p. 100, prohibits "placing salt in the mouth of a dying person to prevent death from overtaking him or her." In a case in which salt already has been placed, most authorities prohibit its removal. Such action is proscribed as an act of active euthanasia, which would cause the patient to be touched or moved, i.e., an action that would actively accelerate death. See, e.g., Karo, *Shulhan Arukh—Yoreh Deah,* para. 339:1, commentaries of Isserles, Shabbatai ben Meir, and David ben Samuel. However, in his note on this text, Zevi ben Azriel of Vilna, *Beit Lehem Yehudah* (Zulka, 1733), maintained that removal of the salt is an example of passive euthanasia in keeping with the principle that the removal of any impediment to the process of dying is not an action at all and hence permissible. In so doing, he cautioned, the patient must not be moved. He, therefore, interpreted the prohibition of the earlier authorities as being related to the apprehension of moving the patient and not to an absolute prohibition against the removal of the salt. According to this view, if translated to contemporary parlance, the introduction of heroic measures to a terminal patient is not encouraged and may be prohibited. However, if heroic measures have been introduced, they may be removed. See also C. D. Halevi, "Disconnecting a Terminal Patient from an Artificial Respirator," in *Crossroads* (Jerusalem: Zomet, 1987), pp. 147–55.

24. Jacob ben Samuel, *Beit Ya'akov* (Dyrenfureth, 1696), no. 59. In this responsum, the author also maintained that one may not violate the Sabbath to save a dying patient. These views are rebutted by the eighteenth-century *halakhist* Jacob Reischer in *Shevut Ya'akov* (Lwow, 1860), 3:13. For a review of these arguments, see Solomon Eiger, *Gilyonei Maharshah* to Karo, *Shulhan Arukh—Yoreh Deah,* para. 339:1, in standard editions of the *Shulhan Arukh.*

25. *Sefer Hasidim,* ed. Margoliot, no. 234, p. 208.

26. See, e.g., *Sanhedrin* 77a; Maimonides, *Mishneh Torah—Sefer Nezikin,* "Laws of Murderers," 3:10. Eng. trans. p. 204. Leopold Greenwald, *Kol Bo al-Aveilut* (New York: Moriah Printing Co., 1947), 1:10, p. 21.

27. *Sefer Hasidim,* ed. Margaliot, no. 234, p. 208.

28. See, e.g., Moses Feinstein, *Iggrot Moshe—Yoreh Deah,* 2 vols. (New York: Balshon, 1963), vol. 2, p. 174, where the view is that it is forbidden to prolong the agony of a *goses* unnecessarily.

29. Jakobovits, pp. 123–24. See also Simon Federbush, "The Problems of Euthanasia in

Jewish Tradition," *Judaism* 1 (1952): 64–68; G. B. Haliburd, "Euthanasia," *Jewish Law Annual* 1 (1978): 196–99; Fred Rosner and J. David Bleich, eds., *Jewish Bioethics*, pp. 33, 253–331; Steven Saltzman, "The Sanctity of Life in Jewish Law" (D.H.L. diss., Jewish Theological Seminary, 1982), pp. 227–312. Note Immanuel Jakobovits's Hebrew essay on euthanasia in *Ha-Pardes* 31:1, 3 (1956): 16–19, 28–31.

30. *Beitzah* 32b.

31. Israel Lipschutz, *Tiferet Israel* (Hanover, 1830) on *M. Yoma* 8:3; *Semahot* 1:1.

32. *M. Arakhin* 1:3; *Arakhin* 6b. However, on suffering as being preferable to death, see, e.g., Ps. 118:18; Yom Tov Lippmann Heller, *Tosafot Yom Tov* on *M. Sota* 1:9; Solomon Luria, *Yam Shel Shelomo* on *Baba Kamma* 91a, no. 59. Note Eliezer Waldenberg, *Tzitz Eliezer*, 10 vols. (Jerusalem: n.p., 1954–), vol. 9, 47, 5.

33. The case of King Saul's death provoked considerable discussion in classical Jewish literature that concerned itself with suicide. Wounded in battle, Saul asked to be killed rather than to be handed over to his enemies. According to one version, Saul killed himself by falling on his sword (1 Sam. 31:1–6). According to a second version, he asked a youth to kill him: "Stand over me and finish me off, for I am in agony and barely alive" (2 Sam. 1:9), and the Amalekite youth complied. David consequently had this youth executed for killing God's "anointed" (2 Sam. 1:13–17). Commentators debate whether the youth was justified in killing Saul, whether David was justified in killing the youth, and if so, on what grounds? The text suggests that David had the youth executed not because he put Saul out of agony but because he presumed to slay God's anointed king. In any case, Saul was found justified in his action by some rabbinic authorities because he chose death, martyrdom, rather than to be abused by the enemies of Israel, a precedent followed throughout Jewish history. What is particularly relevant to euthanasia is the comment of the twelfth-century biblical commentator David Kimhi (Radak) on this episode. Kimhi commented (to 2 Sam. 1:9) that Saul's statement means: "I suffer so severely from my wound, and my soul is yet in me; therefore, I want you to accelerate my death." Thus, according to Kimhi, Saul's motive was to choose death rather than to continue to suffer, rather than to choose death to escape being abused by his enemies. If both Saul's action and his motive (according to Kimhi) are considered justifiable, then this text would serve as a precedent for active euthanasia. Kimhi's commentary is found in standard editions of Hebrew Scripture with commentaries. On Saul's action see the lengthy discussion of Joel Sirkes's *Bayit Hadash* and Karo's *Beit Yosef* on Jacob ben Asher, *Arba'ah Turim—Yoreh Deah*, para. 157, and Israel Lipschutz's *Tiferet Yisrael* on *M. Yoma* chap. 8, where he proscribes Saul's action. Sirkes's commentary is found in standard editions of *Arba'ah Turim*.

34. *Tosafot* on *Gittin* 57b and *Abodah Zarah* 18a. Some primary texts and some commentaries stress the notion that one can take one's own life to avoid sufferings certain to result in death while others stress the idea that death is only preferable when that suffering will lead to such sins: as sexual sins (as in the case of the children) or to apostasy (see, e.g., *Ketubbot* 33b). Others claim that these instances are not applicable to euthanasia since here the affliction is the result of human oppression whereas in cases of euthanasia, the affliction is from illness which may be the will of God; see, e.g., Jakobovits in *Ha-Pardes*, 31, no. 1:29. Nevertheless, it is noteworthy that the language of the deathbed confessional of a dying person is remarkably reminiscent of that of a martyr. In one version of the confessional, the patient says, "I surrender my life, my body and my soul for the unification of the Divine Name." Here there is a clear parallel between the martyr and the dying person.

35. One finds the view in the Talmud, e.g., *Abodah Zarah* 27b; and in the medieval codes, e.g., Karo, *Shulhan Arukh—Yoreh Deah*, para. 155:5–7, and Abraham Zevi Eisenstadt's commentary *Pithei Teshuvah* there that it is sometimes preferable, particularly in the case of a terminal patient, to choose death rather than to be treated by a Gentile physician who may try to entice the Jewish patient to apostasy or who may use "idolatrous" practices to effect a cure. In such instances extending "momentary life is not considered." This clearly

indicates that the preservation of life in itself was not always of paramount importance or consideration.

36. Saul Berlin, *Responsa Besomim Rosh* [Hebrew] (Berlin, 1793). In some subsequent editions, this responsum has been eliminated by the printer. No doubt the reason is because Berlin's view, which, in effect, redefines "suicide," is without precedent in *halakhic* literature.

Berlin was a protoreformer and a distinguished talmudist who associated with the "enlightened" circle of Moses Mendelssohn. Interestingly, Berlin's collection of responsa, *Besomim Rosh,* is a pseudepigraphal work. Berlin claimed that this collection of responsa was written, not by himself, but by the famous fourteenth-century *halakhic* authority. Asher ben Yehiel, known by the acronym Rosh. Actually, these responsa were written by Berlin himself. The book was attacked as a forgery soon after its first publication. On this whole matter, see discussion and sources noted in Jacobs, *Theology in the Responsa,* Appendix 1, pp. 347–52; M. Siemet, "The *Besamim Rosh* of Rabbi Saul Berliner," *Kiryat Sefer* 48 (1972/ 1973): 509–23. On the initial question of whether mourning for a suicide is prohibited, see the uncharacteristically "liberal" view of Moses Schreiber, *Responsa Hatam Sofer,* no. 326. Schreiber holds that relatives of a suicide should indeed observe mourning rites. Also, see the lengthy discussion in Eisenstadt's *Pithei Teshuvah* to Karo, *Shulhan Arukh—Yoreh Deah,* para. 345:2, where suicide is virtually defined out of existence; note the reference there to the *Besomim Rosh.* See also in this regard the lengthy discussion and sources noted in Greenwald, pp. 319–20.

37. *Yalkut Shimoni,* "Proverbs," no. 943.

38. Contemporary *halakhists* are divided on the question of whether "pulling the plug" is a form of withholding treatment (i.e., passive euthanasia), and therefore permitted, or an overt act of intervention designed to shorten life (i.e., active euthanasia), and therefore prohibited. See discussion and sources in J. D. Bleich, "The Quinlan Case: A Jewish Perspective," in *Jewish Bioethics,* ed. Rosner and Bleich, p. 275 n. 2.

39. For praying or not praying for the recovery of a sick individual actually *causing* life or death, see the statement of Rav Dimi and the commentaries on that statement in *Nedarim* 40a.

40. *Ketubot* 104a. On praying for one's own death, see, e.g., 1 Kings 19:4, Jon. 4:3, *Ta'anit* 23a. On praying for the death of another person, see *Baba Metzia* 84a. However, see an opposite view in Waldenberg, 9:47, 5. Steinberg, p. 36, refers to a specific prayer for another to die to free him or her from pain. Without noting a specific source, Steinberg refers to such a prayer in Isaac Lampronti's *Pahad Yitzhak.*

41. Nissim (Rabbenu Nissim) on *Nedarim* 40a, in standard editions of the Talmud. In his nineteenth-century commentary on *M. Yoma* chap. 8, Israel Lipschutz maintained that the case of the handmaiden's praying for the death of Rabbi Judah (*Ketubot* 104a) relates not only to the case of Rabbi Judah but to any individual case because "great suffering is worse than death." Lipschutz, did, however, claim that taking any action other than prayer that accelerates death is forbidden.

42. Hayyim Palaggi's responsum is found in vol. 1 of his collected responsa, *Hikkeke Lev* (Salonika, 1840), no. 50, pp. 90a–91a. I am grateful to the Klau Library of Hebrew Union College for lending me this volume for use. A translation and an extended analysis of this responsum is found in Peter J. Haas, "Toward a Semiotic Study of Jewish Moral Discourse: The Case of Responsa," *Semeia* 34 (1985): 59–85. Also note Greenwald, 1:9, p. 20, no. 14, where Pelaggi's responsum is briefly summarized. See also the reference to Palaggi in Solomon B. Freehof, *Reform Responsa* (Cincinnati: Hebrew Union College Press, 1960), p. 120–21.

43. *Niddah* 19b.

44. *Sanhedrin* 45a, 52a; *Baba Kamma* 51a; *Pesahim* 75a. In his eighteenth-century commentary to the Talmud, *Glosses of Ya'avetz,* in standard editions of the Talmud, Jacob Emden observed that the practice of giving a painkilling drug to a criminal about to be

executed was practiced so that the pain of execution would not hamper the exit of the soul and extend the person's pain and anguish. See gloss to *Sanhedrin* 43a.

45. *Arakhin* 6b.

46. See, e.g., *Midrash Song of Songs Rabbah* 2:7. For a diametrically opposite view, see Solomon Luria, *Yam Shel Shelomo on Baba Kamma*, "*Perek ha-Hovel*," no. 59.

47. If one person kills another by performing a surgical procedure aimed at alleviating pain where the condition is not life-threatening, there may be no legal culpability. See, e.g., Menahem Meiri, *Beit ha-Behirah—Sanhedrin* (Jerusalem: n.p., 1965), p. 85a. See also Nahmanides, *Torat ha-Adam*, vol. 2, pp. 42–43. Also note the discussion and sources quoted by Greenwald, p. 21, no. 16. On endangering the individual with possible death regarding treatment for an ailment or a potential ailment that may or may not be life-threatening, see Lipschutz, *M. Yoma*, chap. 8. See the extensive discussion and sources noted in *Jewish Bioethics*, ed. Rosner and Bleich, pp. 32–34.

48. Rashi on Exod. 21:14. Also see *Mekhilta de-Rabbi Yishmael*, ed. Horovitz and Rabin, "*Mishpatim*," 4, p. 263.

49. *Sanhedrin* 78a; Maimonides, *Mishneh Torah—Sefer Nezikin*, "Laws of Murderers," 2:8. Eng. trans., p. 200. On the definition of a *tereifah: Rashi on Sanhedrin* 78a maintains that the definition of a human *tereifah: Rashi on Sanhedrin* 78a maintains that the definition of a human *tereifah* is the same as that of an animal *tereifah* while Maimonides disagrees and defines a human *tereifah* as one with internal injuries. See Steinberg, pp. 12–13. Note the important responsum by Schreiber, *Hatam Sofer—Yoreh Deah*, no. 52. See also Moses Feinstein, "Medical Responsa," in *Crossroads*, pp. 129–34. Note the significant study by Daniel B. Sinclair, *Tradition and the Biological Revolution* (Edinburgh: Edinburgh University Press, 1989), pp. 19–70.

See also the intriguing argument by Werner in *Torah she-be-al Peh* 18 (1976), no. 40, which states that active euthanasia is not prohibited to Gentiles. This argument is based upon the Amalekite's killing of Saul to end his agony (2 Sam. 1:5–10), and the torturer's actions in the death of Hanina ben Teradion, *Abodah Zarah* 18a.

50. See David M. Shohet, "Mercy Death in Jewish Law," *Conservative Judaism* 8, no. 3 (1952): 1–15.

27

This Matter of Abortion

DAVID M. FELDMAN

The moral and political debate on the subject of this chapter continues unabated after several decades of modern discussion and analyis. Ultimate answers remain elusive, but several issues within the larger discussion can indeed be clarified.

Abortion played a major role in the 1984 political campaigns, as if the Supreme Court decision in January 1973 had resolved nothing at all. The right to take advantage of the Court's permissive ruling is itself the subject of debate, with efforts being launched to remove that right by constitutional amendment.

Six months before that historic Court decision, the legislature of the state of New York was among the first to abolish on its own any legal obstacles to abortion. Six months before that, NOW, the National Organization for Women, not anticipating such a turn of events, took New York State to court to have it enjoined to remove the antiabortion statute from its books. I was called to testify on behalf of NOW, but the exchange took the following unexpected form:

The attorney put the question to me: "Do you agree that the laws against abortion in New York State interfere with your freedom of religion, with your right to practice the rabbinate as you see fit?" Surprised by my reply in the negative, she demanded: "What do you mean, 'no'? I read your book, *Birth Control in Jewish Law,* and I got the distinct impression you would say 'yes.' "

"You must first answer a prior question," I replied. "Namely, is abortion murder? If it is murder, then you cannot talk about freedom of religion. There is no freedom of religion in the face of murder. To take an example, the Bible tells us that the ancient Canaanites used to practice child sacrifice. They would take a born child and sacrifice it on the altar. The Torah calls this an abomination and forbids us to do it. Now, what if these Canaanites or their modern counterparts were to come to America and wish to practice child sacrifice here, in the name of freedom of religion? Would we allow it? Of course not. If we forbid polygamy to the Mormons, we're certainly not going to permit murder to anyone on the grounds of religious freedom. But if abortion is not murder, then we can talk about it. Then I would say, yes, it does interfere with my ministry. Since Jewish law does not equate it with murder, there are circumstances under which Jewish law would permit, or even mandate, an abortion. But I am not at liberty to invoke any lenient rulings of Jewish law as long as the State law forbids it."

The attorney heaved a sign of relief and pressed on to the next question: "Do you not agree that the State's law against abortion is a violation of women's rights, of the right of a woman to do with her body or her reproductive faculties as she sees fit?" Again I said "no," and again she was flustered. "What do you mean 'no'? Your book clearly implies that you would answer 'yes.' "

"Again I must say you have first got to answer the prior question. Is abortion murder? If it is, then you cannot talk about women's rights. There are no rights to murder. May a woman take a gun and shoot a one-year-old child or a ten- or twenty-year-old person, on the grounds that that person is the fruit of her womb? Of course not. But if the antiabortion people are right, then what happens after birth is equal to what happens before birth, and no woman has any more right to end a life then than later. So the right of a woman to her body or reproductive faculties is just not relevant, not applicable. But if abortion is not murder, then we can talk about it. Then I would say that the State's law does infringe on the rights of women. I would go much further and say that it infringes even more than you might think. Because in the Jewish legal-moral tradition on abortion, the woman's welfare plays an even greater role than NOW would claim. A principle in the Jewish view of the matter is *tza'ara d'gufah kadim,* that her welfare, avoidance of her pain, comes first.

"Accordingly," I continued, "maternal indications for abortion do count where fetal indications do not. It's not that the fetus has a right to be born or that the husband has a right to his progeny, but it's the welfare of the mother that is the first, and to some the only, consideration that warrants an abortion." The court trial proceeded as it did, but the points made above need now to be set forth.

Abortion is not murder, vociferous and repeated claims to the contrary notwithstanding. Abortion cannot be murder in Jewish law, because, as indicated above, murder is one of the three "cardinal" sins that require martyrdom. Rather than commit murder of the innocent, public idolatry or gross sexual immorality (adultery-incest), one has to surrender his own life in martyrdom. All the rest of the Torah is under the category of *ya'avor v'al ye-hareg,* "let one transgress rather than die," but not for murder of the innocent. Hence if abortion were declared murder, a mother would not be allowed to have an abortion even to save her life, which is obviously not the case.

There is—need it be stated?—no commandment that reads "Thou shalt not kill." It reads, "Thou shalt not murder." The differences is in the circumstances. Killing is allowed in self-defense, in war, perhaps by a sentencing court, even in the case of a prowler. In these situations the victim is no longer innocent; he has forfeited his protection under the commandment. He must, of course, do so consciously. He must have deliberately placed himself in a position of attack or threat in order to lose his protection. Another such category is that of *rodef,* the aggressor, who may be killed if that is the only way to stop his pursuit or aggression of a third party.

The Talmud considers defining the fetus as a *rodef,* an aggressor against its mother, and making that the reason why abortion to save the mother's life is permitted. (The idea entered the writings of Saint Thomas Aquinas through its citation in the works of Maimonides.) But the Talmud proceeds to reject that reasoning on the obvious grounds that the fetus is not yet of responsible age to deliberately forfeit its protection against being murdered. The only valid grounds for permitting even therapeutic abortion is that murder is not involved because the fetus is not yet a human person.[1] Killing is admittedly involved, but not murder. Killing is the taking of life of, say, an animal or a chicken, or of a human who forfeits his protection by an act of aggression. And the difference between fetal life and human life is not determined by the biologist or the physician but by the metaphysician. It's the determination of the culture or the religion that declares not when life begins but when life begins to be human.

To trace the issues from the start, the abortion question in talmudic law revolves around the legal status of the embryo. For this the Talmud has a phrase, *ubbar yerekh immo,* which phrase is a counterpart of the Latin *pars viscerum matris.* This is, the fetus is deemed a "part of its mother," rather than an independent entity. This designation says nothing about the morality of abortion; rather, it defines ownership, for example, in the case of an embryo found in a purchased animal. As intrinsic to its mother's body, it belongs to the buyer. In the religious conversion of a pregnant woman, her unborn child is automatically included and requires no further ceremony. Nor does it have power of acquisition; gifts made on its behalf are not binding. These and similar points mean only that the fetus has no "juridical personality," but say nothing about the right of abortion. This turns rather on whether feticide is or is not homicide.[2]

The law of homicide in the Torah, in one of its formulations, reads: "*Makkeh ish . . .*" "He who smites a man . . ." (Exod. 21:12). Does this include any man, say a day-old child? Yes, says the Talmud, citing another text: ". . . *ki yakkeh kol nefesh adam*" "If one smite any *nefesh adam*" (Lev. 24:17)—literally, any human person. (Whereas we may not be sure that the newborn babe has completed its term and is a *bar kayyama,* fully viable, until thirty days after birth, he is fully human from the moment of birth. If he dies before his thirtieth day, no funeral or shivah rites are applicable either. But active destruction of a born child of even doubtful viability is here definitely forbidden.[3] The "any" (*kol*) is understood to include the day-old child, but the "*nefesh adam*" is taken to exclude the fetus in the womb. The fetus in the womb, says Rashi, classic commentator on the Bible and Talmud, is *lav nefesh hu,* not a person, until he comes into the world.[4]

Feticide, then, does not constitute homicide, and the basis for denying it capital-crime status in Jewish law—even for those rabbis who may have wanted to rule otherwise—is scriptural. Alongside the above text is another one in Exodus that reads: "If men strive, and wound a pregnant woman so that her fruit be expelled, but no harm befall [her], then shall he be fined as her husband shall assess. . . . But if harm befall [her], then shalt thou give life for life" (21:22). The Talmud makes this verse's teaching explicit: Only monetary compensation is exacted of him who causes a woman to miscarry. Note also that though the abortion spoken of here is accidental, it contrasts with the homicide (of the mother) which is also accidental. Even unintentional homicide cannot be expiated by a monetary fine.[5]

This critical text, to begin with, has an alternative version in the Septuagint, the Greek translation of the Bible produced in Alexandria in the third pre-Christian century. A change of just one word there yields an entirely different statute on the subject. Professor Viktor Aptowitzer's essays analyze the disputed passage: The school of thought it represents he calls the Alexandrian school, as opposed to the Palestinian—that is, the talmudic—view set forth above. The word in question is *ason,* rendered here as "harm"; hence, "if [there be] harm, then shalt thou give life for life." The Greek renders *ason* as "form," yielding something like: "If [there be] form, then shalt thou give life for life." The "life for life" clause is thus applied to fetus instead of mother *and* a distinction is made—as Augustine will formulate it—between *embryo informatus* and *embryo formatus*. For the latter, the text so rendered prescribes the death penalty.[6]

Among the Church Fathers, the consequent doctrine of feticide as murder was preached by Tertullian, in the second century, who accepted the Septuagint, and by Jerome in the fourth, who did not. Jerome's classic Bible translation renders the passage according to the Hebrew text accepted in the church. The Didache, a handbook of basic Christianity for the instruction of converts from paganism, follows the Alexandrian teaching and specifies abortion as a capital crime. Closer to the main body of the Jewish community, we find the doctrine accepted by the Samaritans and Karaites and, more importantly, by Philo, the popular first-century philospher of Alexandria. On the other hand, his younger contemporary Josephus bears witness to the Palestinian (*halakhic*) tradition. Aside from its textual warrant, this tradition is more authentic than the later tendency, "which, in addition, is not genuinely Jewish but must have originated in Alexandria under Egyptian-Greek influence."[7]

In the rabbinic tradition, then, abortion remains a noncapital crime at worst. But a curious factor further complicates the question. One more biblical text, this one in Genesis and hence "before Sinai" and part of the Laws of the Sons of Noah, served as the source for the teaching that feticide is indeed a capital crime—for non-Jews. Gen. 9:6 reads: "He who sheds the blood of man, through man [i.e., through the human court of law] shall his blood be shed." Since the "man, through man" (*shofekh dam ha'adam ba'adam*) can also be rendered "man, in man," the Talmud records the exposition of Rabbi Ishmael: "What is this 'man, in man'? It refers to the fetus in its mother's womb." Being in Genesis—without the qualifying balance of the Exodus (Sinaitic) passage—this verse made feticide a capital crime for non-Jews (those not heir to the covenant at Sinai) in Jewish law. Some hold this exposition to be more sociologically than textually inherent, voicing a reaction against abuses among the heathen. In view of rampant abortion and feticide, they claim, Rabbi Ishmael extracted from the Genesis text this judgment against the Romans.[8]

Regardless of rationale, the doctrine remains part of theoretical Jewish law, as Maimonides, for example, codifies it: "A 'Son of Noah' who killed a person, even a fetus in its mother's womb, is capitally liable. . . ." Therapeutic abortion is not, however, included in this Noahide prohibition; nor is an abortion during the first forty days, according to some. The implications of this anomaly—a different law for the Sons of Noah than for Israel—were addressed in a responsum of the eighteenth century: "It is not to be supposed that the Torah would consider the embryo as a person [*nefesh*] for them [Sons of Noah] but not for us. The fetus is not a person for them either; the Torah was merely more severe in its practical ruling in their regard. Hence, therapeutic abortion would be permissible to them, too."[9]

If abortion is not murder in the rabbinic system, neither is it worse than murder. It is worse than murder in those religious systems concerned with "ensoulment" of the fetus. At a conference some time ago on the subject, I made bold to say that the discussion for the past several sessions of the conference was monumentally irrelevant. They had been debating the time of ensoulment—does the soul enter the fetus at conception, at the end of the first trimester, at birth? From the Jewish standpoint, this must be declared irrelevant. It's not when does the soul enter, it's what kind of a soul enters? Classic Christianity has been saying that a tainted soul enters the fetus which must be cleansed by baptism to save him or her from eternal perdition. In line with the doctrine of original sin, each individual soul inherits the taint of its primordial ancestors. When Saint Fulgentius of the sixth century was asked when that stain attaches to the person, he replied that it begins with conception. Hence the concern with allowing the fetus to be brought to term so that it can be baptized; otherwise it is condemned to death in both worlds, making abortion clearly worse than murder. It must accordingly be said that when Catholics reputedly decide to "let the mother die" rather than allow an abortion, they are not at all being cruel, merely consistent with a logical concern. The mother has been presumably baptized as an infant; let her die and "go to her reward." But let the child be brought to term and baptized and saved from perdition. So sincere is this concern that theologians at the Sorbonne in the nineteenth century invented a baptismal syringe, wherewith to baptize a fetus in utero in the event of a spontaneous abortion, a miscarriage.[10]

But this is surely a concern that the Jewish community cannot share. Having no such concept of original sin, we recite daily in our prayers something that comes directly from the Talmud: "My God, the soul with which thou hast endowed me is pure." We inherit a pure soul, which becomes contaminated only by our own misdeeds. By that token, early abortion would send a fetus to heaven in a state of pristine purity! While the Talmud does discuss the time of ensoulment—is it when the child is conceived, or at the first trimester, at birth or, as one opinion has it, when the child first answers Amen?—but then dismisses the question as both unanswerable and irrelevant to the abortion question.[11]

Abortion, then, is neither murder nor worse than murder, nor an option when the alternative is death to the mother. Since the mother is not allowed to choose suicide, abortion in that extreme case becomes mandatory. This is the sense of the fundamental passage in the Talmud bearing on the subject. The Mishnah (*Oholot* 7,6) puts it this way:

"If a woman has [life-threatening] difficulty in childbirth, the embryo within her must be dismembered limb by limb [if necessary], because her life [*hayyeha*] takes precedence over its life [*hayyav*]. Once its head (or its greater part) has emerged, it may not be touched, for we may not set aside one life [*nefesh*] for another."

The justification for abortion, then, is that before the child emerges we do not yet have a *nefesh*. The life of the fetus is only potential, and that cannot compete with actual human life.

This was relevant to my experience at a conference in Rome. After presenting a Jewish view calling for abortion to avoid a threat to life, a Catholic woman physician challenged the point on the grounds of her own experience, where she had accepted the ruling of her priest against any abortion over the contrary advice of her doctor. But a priest present at the conference explained that while the Catholic faithful must obey the church's teaching against abortion, a Jewish woman was equally duty-bound to follow the tenets of Jewish law. She must abide by the physician's determination that abortion is called for because her life is in danger, even if this later turns out to be mistaken. The priest correctly articulated the Jewish legal-moral position on the question.

Another such clarifying confrontation took place in New York City, when another Catholic woman rose to question the point of view. She began: "Don't you believe in the Bible?" Unsure of what she may have had in mind, I answered with a tentative yes. She said: "Well, the Bible says, 'Therefore, choose life.' Since abortion is the killing of life, how can you allow it?" "Because," I replied, "when you see 'choose life' in the Bible and when we see 'choose life' in the Bible, we are both seeing different things. From a Catholic standpoint, which is essentially other-worldly in orientation, you see 'life' as life in the next world. Otherwise, why would you ever allow the death of the mother? That, too, is taking life. Yet, you feel that the mother, having already been baptized, can 'choose life' in the next world. But when we see those words, we think of life in this world, and that's why we strive to save the mother, to save existing life. How do I know this? Because the Talmud gives the rationale for the principle that 'saving life sets aside all else in the Torah,' that the Sabbath and even Yom Kippur must be violated in order to protect or preserve life or health. The rationale is simple: 'Violate [for the patient] this Sabbath, so that he will be able to keep many Sabbaths.'"[12] In other words, we want to 'choose life' here on earth, and a therapeutic abortion is therefore indicated, even mandated."

As cited at the outset, the Talmud considered basing the justification rather on the fact that the fetus is a *rodef*, an aggressor. Since the law of *rodef* allows us to kill the pursuer in order to save his intended victim, where we cannot stop him otherwise, the fetus may be defined in this way. But, says the Talmud, perhaps the mother is pursuing the child? The life-threatening impasse could be the result of a narrow cervix, or any physiological condition of the mother which makes continuation of the pregnancy a threat to her life. If the condition is the mother's, how is the child the pursuer? Rather, says the Talmud, "she is being pursued from Heaven." That is, the pursuit is an "act of God," desired or intended by neither mother nor child. The argument is therefore inadmissible and, in any case, unnecessary; it's simply that the fetus is not yet a person with equal title to life.

Yet Maimonides, in his great summarizing law code, seems to retrieve the rejected argument. He formulates the talmudic law as follows:

"This, too, is a [negative] Commandment: Not to take pity on the life of a pursuer. Therefore the Sages ruled that when a woman has difficulty in giving birth, one dismembers the fetus in her womb—either with drugs or by surgery—because it is like a pursuer seeking to kill her. Once its head has emerged, it may not be touched, for we may not set aside one life for another; this is the natural course of the world."[13]

Since abortion is not murder, and Maimonides could not have ruled otherwise, the commentators on his code explain that he made figurative use of the pursuer idea in order to buttress the justification for abortion when necessary. Hence his formulation *k'rodef*, that the fetus is "like a pursuer."

Illustrative of the difference, albeit technical, between murder and killing is the following report: Rabbi Issar Unterman, late Chief Rabbi of Israel, is firmly opposed to abortion except under extreme circumstances. He labels it "akin to murder," but preserves the distinction. He tells of a Jewish girl made pregnant by a German soldier during World War I. She asked the soldier for support of the child to be born; he instead took her to a physician to abort. the physician, who was Jewish, declined to perform the abortion, insisting it was against his principles. The soldier then drew his gun and threatened the doctor: Either you abort or I will shoot you. Rabbi Unterman declared that, had he been asked the question by the doctor he would have told him to abort. If abortion were really murder, the doctor would have had to martyr himself, to lay down his life rather than comply. Much as I would like to call it murder, he said in effect, the clear sense of Jewish law is that it is not.

It might also be mentioned in this connection that Rabbi Joseph Rosin of Rogatchov responded, in the early part of this century, to a query as to whether a man may divorce his wife because she brought about an abortion. His answer was "no": although abortion is "akin to homicide," it is not a real enough homicide or offense to make her divorcible against her will.[14]

Rabbi Unterman stood squarely in the tradition of Maimonides and, in fact, all rabbinic teaching on the subject of abortion can be said to align itself either with Maimonides, on the right, or with Rashi, on the left. The "rightist" approach begins with the asumption, formulated by Unterman, that abortion is "akin to murder" and therefore allowable only in cases of corresponding gravity, such as saving the life of the mother. The approach then builds *down* from that strict position to embrace a broader interpretation of lifesaving situations. These include a threat to her health, for example, and perhaps a threat to her sanity in terms of suicidal possibilities, but exclude any lesser reasons.

The more "liberal" approach, based on Rashi's affirmation that the fetus is not a human person, is associated with another former Chief Rabbi of Israel, Ben Zion Uziel.[15] This approach assumes that no real prohibition against abortion exists and builds *up* from that ground to safeguard against indiscriminate or unjustified thwarting of potential life. This school of thought includes the example of Rabbi Yair Bachrach in the seventeenth century, whose classic responsum saw no legal bar to abortion but would not permit it in the case before him.[16] The case was of a pregnancy conceived in adultery; the woman, "in deep remorse," wanted to destroy the fruit of her sin. The responsum concludes by refusing to sanction abortion, not on legal grounds, but on sociological ones, as a safeguard against further immorality.

Other authorities, such as Rabbi Jacob Emden, disagreed on this point, affirming the legal sanction of abortion for the woman's welfare, whether life or health, or even for avoidance of "great pain."

Maternal rather than fetal indications are the rule for both schools of thought. The rightist position certainly considers only the mother, but so does the leftist one. The latter school includes even the mother's less than life-and-death welfare, expressed in the words "great pain," and based on the principle that *tza'ara d'gufah kadim*. Rabbinic rulings on abortion, when collated and distilled, are thus amenable to the following generalization:

If a woman were to come before the rabbi and seek permission for an abortion by saying, "I had German measles, or I took thalidomide during pregnancy, and the possibility is that the child will be born deformed," the rabbi would decline permission on those grounds. "How do you know," he might say, "that the child will be born deformed? Maybe not. And if so, how do you know that such a condition is worse for him than not being born? Why mix into 'the secrets of God'?" But if the same woman under the same circumstances came to the same rabbi and expressed the problem differently; if she said, ". . . the possibility is that the child will be born deformed, and that possibility is giving me extreme mental anguish," then the rabbi would rule otherwise. Now the fetal indication has become a maternal indication, and all the considerations for her welfare are now brought to bear. The fetus is unknown, future, potential, part of the "secrets of God"; the mother is known, present, human and seeking compassion.

One rabbinic authority, writing in Rumania in 1940, responded to the case of an epileptic mother who feared that her unborn child would also be epileptic.[17] He writes: "For fear of possible, remote danger to a future child that maybe, God forbid, he will know sickness—how can it occur to anyone to actively kill the fetus because of such a possible doubt? This seems to me very much like the laws of Lycurgus, King of Sparta, according to which every blemished child was to be put to death. . . . Permission for abortion is to be granted only because of mental anguish for the mother. But for fear of what might be the child's lot?—The secrets of God are not knowable."

He was, in fact, basing his decision on an explicit ruling in 1913 by Rabbi Mordecai Winkler of Hungary: "Mental-health risk has been definitely equated with physical-health risk. This woman, in danger of losing her mental health unless the pregnancy is interrupted, would therefore accordingly qualify."[18]

The emphasis on maternal as opposed to fetal indications caused a dilemma with regard to such tragic, but clearly fetal, afflictions as that of Tay-Sachs. Screening of prospective mates or parents is recommended; but after a pregnancy begins, may amniocentesis be performed in order to determine if the cells of the fetus have been affected? Having limited the warrant for abortion to maternal indications, and no risk to the mother's life or health exists even with the birth of a Tay-Sachs child, the answer would be negative. And since abortion is ruled out, amniocentesis itself would be *halakhically* proscribed as a gratuitous invasive assault, with its own attendant risks, upon the womb. The dilemma, however, is resolved by a perception on the part of the mother that this is really a maternal indication. The present knowledge that the child will deteriorate and die in infancy, although the birth itself will be safer for her, gives her genuine mental anguish now. The fetal indication has become a maternal one. Alternatively, though the majority of *halakhic* positions are as described here, there are at least two eminent authorities who rule that some fetal indications, such as this one, are serious enough in themselves to warrant an abortion. Rabbi Saul Israeli of the Jerusalem Rabbinical Court and Rabbi Eliezer Waldenberg, an expert in medical ethics, have so ruled.[19]

The spectrum of Jewish positions on the matter of abortion, from right to left, stands in sharp contrast to its consensus on neonatal defectives. Here the attitude is starkly illiberal, making the Jewish tradition the real "right-to-life" affirmation. Another look at that passage from the Mishnah proves that all this concern for the welfare of the mother obtains prior to birth. From the moment of birth, the life of the infant is as inviolate as that of the mother. Its right to life is then absolute. Before birth, however, right to life is not the applicable concept; it is "right to be born." The right to be born is not absolute, but relative to the welfare of the mother. There is no right to be born any more than a right to be conceived. Use of the "right-to-life" slogan by antiabortion people is therefore essentially misleading.

But just as the Mishnah makes the fetus secondary to the mother before birth, so it rejects any distinction after birth. This negates another popular slogan, "quality of life." If quality of life were a factor, it would be absurd to say that the newborn babe is equal to its mother. The mother has her achievements and her interconnected dependencies; the infant has none of these yet. Still, we reject any considerations of relative quality; all existing life is equally precious; the operative slogan is rather "sanctity of life." From the moment of its birth, the life of the newborn is sacred, as indivisibly and undifferentially sacred as that of the mother. This is the true "right-to-life" position. Whereas "right to be born" is relative to the welfare of the mother, "right to life" is not relative to the mother's or anyone's welfare. Right to life means that *no person* need apologize for living, neither to parents, to physicians, to society, or to self.

The great pains this chapter takes to prove abortion warrantable under some circumstances should not obscure the fact that abortion retains its stigma and remains a last resort. Procreation is a positive mitzvah, and potential life has the sanctity of its potential. The Talmud, in fact, uses the dreaded word "murder" in a figurative, hyperbolic sense even in connection with not conceiving. Bachelors or the couple who decline to conceive are called "guilty of bloodshed" for their sin of omission. Procreation is a desideratum as well as a mitzvah, and casual abortion is accordingly abhorrent. There may be legal and moral sanction for abortion where necessary, but the attitude remains one of solemn hesitation in the presence of the sanctity of life and of a pronatalist respect for new life.

Accordingly, abortion for "population control" is repugnant to the Jewish mind. Abortion for economic reasons is also not admissible. Taking precaution by abortion or contraception against physical threat to the mother remains a mitzvah, but not so as to forestall financial difficulty. Material considerations or career concerns are simply improper in this connection, especially in view of the readiness of others to adopt or nurture. A degree of brutalization is scarcely avoidable in the destruction of even potential life or in the rejection of a precious gift of God. But when the reasons for considering abortion are nonetheless overwhelming, the right to do so remains hers after all.

In the course of the 1984 presidential campaign, Archbishop John O'Connor of New York made an impassioned plea for people of all religious and political persuasions to join in the struggle against abortion on demand and in support of reverence for life. The Jewish community applauds and shares in that battle, but also in the pluralistic concern for individual liberty. Some contemporary rabbis welcome the strong stand of antiabortion groups, and regard the leniencies of traditional Jewish law as either too subtle or too dangerous for broad consumption. Others see the right of choice as inherent in the Jewish treatment of the subject, and stress the noncapital nature of the offense. Either way, it is important that reverence for life be affirmed as a religious imperative, but that political candidates or parties not be allowed to equate abortion with murder and prochoice people with murderers or outlaws. Murder is a fundamental evil that no civilized society should tolerate, but abortion can be understood in more than one way; the right to it under circumstances consistent with conscience should not be compromised or unduly stigmatized.

Notes

1. *Sanhedrin* 72b; David Feldman, *Birth Control in Jewish Law* (New York: New York University Press (1968), chaps. 14 and 15.

2. Viktor Aptowitzer, "Observations on the Criminal Law of the Jews," *Jewish Quarterly Review* XV (1924), pp. 111ff.; *BCJL*, pp. 253–54.

3. Rashi; *Yad Ramah to Sanhedrin* 72b.

4. *BCJL*, p. 255.

5. *BCJL*, pp. 255–56.

6. *BCJL*, p. 258.

7. Aptowitzer, *JQR*, p. 88.

8. I. H. Weiss, *Dor Dor VeDor'shav* (1924), vol. 2, p. 21.

9. Rabbi Isaac Schorr, Responsa *Koah Shor*, vol. 1, no. 20 (dated 1755).

10. St. Fulgentius, *De Fide* 27, cited by E. Westermarck, *The Origin and Development of the Moral Ideas* (1908), vol. 1, pp. 416–17. On use of the syringe in baptism, see H. W. Haggard, *Devils, Drugs and Doctors* (New York, 1929), p. 4.

11. *Sanhedrin* 110b; *Yalkut* to Psalms, no. 689.

12. See David M. Feldman, *Health and Medicine in the Jewish Tradition* (New York: Crossroads, 1986), chap. 2.

13. *BCJL*, pp. 275ff.

14. Rabbi I. Unterman, *Noam: A Volume for the Clarification of Halakhic Issues* (Hebrew), vol. 6 (1963), p. 5; Rabbi I. Rosin, Responsa *Tzofenat Pa'aneah* (Dvinsk, 1934), no. 56.

15. Responsa *Mishpetei Uziel*, vol. 3, *Hoshen Mishpat*, no. 47.

16. Responsa *Havvot Yair*, no. 31.

17. Responsa *Afarkasta D'Anya*, no. 169.

18. Responsa *Levushei Mordekhai, Hoshen Mishpat*, no. 139.

19. Responsa *Amud Ha Yemini*, no. 32 (1966), and Responsa *Tzitz Eliezer*, vol. 9, no. 51:3:9 (1967).

28

Judaism and the Justification of Abortion for Nonmedical Reasons

SANDRA B. LUBARSKY

All rabbis see the need for justifying abortion, and almost all have found the sole justification in the preservation of the mother's life or health. Yet, there is no clear-cut prohibition against abortion in biblical or talmudic sources and no *halakhic* reason to limit abortion to those circumstances described as "medically indicated." Why, in the absence of any *halakhic* prohibition; do so many rabbis decide against abortion unless it is necessary to a woman's physical well-being? What is the basis of this Jewish stance against abortion other than for medical reasons?

The answer involves a discussion of the status of extra-*halakhic* philosophical and theological principles in rabbinic decision making. In general, the rabbis do not find that the legal action guides given in *halakhic* literature sufficiently address the issue of abortion. The legal status of abortion is clear: the killing of an embryo is not murder. But what of the moral implications of abortion? As R. Jacob Emden put it in his Glosses to the Talmud, "Who would *permit* killing an embryo without reason, even if there be no death penalty for it?"[1] Abortion may not be a capital offense, but it is still morally reprehensible. Within Jewish circles, the discussion about abortion is a discussion about sufficient moral justification for an act that is not legally culpable.

Though agreement among rabbis as to what constitutes *sufficient reason* for abortion falls short of unanimity, it does not fall short by much. In the greatest number of decisions made by members of both the "lenient" and the "stringent" schools, abortion has been permitted on medical grounds only.[2] By "medically advised" abortion I mean the traditional "therapeutic" abortion, that is, abortion for the purpose of preserving the life of the mother, a definition that was often broadened to include any severe threat to the mother's physical health, and less often included a threat to the mother's mental health. By "non-medically advised" abortion I mean abortion that is justified by ecological, sociological, economic, emotional, or intellectual reasons. These reasons may be predicated upon such current concerns as pollution, overpopulation, and male and female liberation. One way to account for the rabbis' conservative attitude—the attitude that permits only medically advised abortion, in the face of a more permissive *halakhah*—is to seek a set of premises that is common to the rabbis and predisposes them to a more restrictive view of abortion. Because the rabbis hold to these premises, they find themselves uncomfortable with the *legal* position on abortion and attempt to mitigate the influence of that position.

In the first section of this essay I will give support for my assertions about the method of rabbinic decision making. The second section will be a very brief overview of the biblical and talmudic passages that address abortion. In the third section, I will consider the six theological and philosophical assumptions which I believe form the implicit foundation for rabbinic decisions on abortion. In the last section, I will argue against the validity of some of these assumptions and for a reinterpretation of others.

Extralegal Elements in Rabbinic Decision Making

The rabbinic decision-making process as it pertains to the issue of abortion is an inductive one, that is, the rabbis enter the discussion with certain preestablished ethical perspectives which they then seek to validate by invoking corroborative texts and rulings. This assertion is in direct opposition to that made by J. David Bleich, who contends that "definitive *pesak* [is] derived from fundamental principles,"[3] rabbinic decisions on abortion are reached through a deductive process. I base my assertion on the debate engendered by Maimonides' discussion of abortion in terms of "pursuer" and "pursued."

Maimonides' discussion is as follows:

> This, too, is a [negative] commandment: Not to take pity on the life of a pursuer. Therefore the Sages ruled that when the woman has difficulty in giving birth, one may dismember the child in her womb—either with drugs or by surgery—*because he is like a pursuer seeking to kill her.* Once his head has emerged, he may not be touched, for we do not set aside one life for another; *this is the natural course of the world.*[4]

Maimonides' postulate that the fetus can be destroyed because it is a pursuer of the mother has been variously interpreted as an additional requirement for abortion, as an independent criterion, as a more specific and hence more rigorous requirement, and as a more specific and hence more lenient requirement for abortion. For example, R. Hayyim Soloveitchik renders the strict reading that *only* when the fetus is a pursuer can its life be forfeited.[5] R. Isaac Lampronti follows this with the notion that dire physical distress arising from nonfetal causes (for example, diabetes), but complicated by pregnancy, is not a valid reason for abortion. Abortion is justifiable only if the "pursuer" fetus is *directly* responsible for the threat to the mother's life.[6] The justification for abortion is made even more rigorous by R. Ezekiel Landau, who maintains that although the status of the fetus is inferior to that of the mother (as established by *halakhah* and upheld by Rashi), the justification for abortion *must be augmented* by Maimonides' "pursuer" argument. That the fetus is inferior to the mother is insufficient; it must also be "like a pursuer seeking to kill her" if abortion is to be authorized.[7] More lenient positions are held by Rabbis Isaac Schorr and Jacob Schorr, who hold that Maimonides' formulation serves to reinforce the right of feticide, and by R. Moshe Zweig of Antwerp, who believes that the pursuer argument changes the status of therapeutic abortion from permitted to required.[8]

There is, in short, no single interpretation of Maimonides' ruling. That the pursuer argument can be used both to justify abortion and to limit it strictly suggests that interpretive decisions are based not on "pertinent sources"[9] but rather on preconceived ethical stances. The underpinnings of these ethical positions are extralegal philosophical and theological ideas.

Overview of Biblical and Talmudic Sources on Abortion

There are no biblical or talmudic statements directly opposed to abortion. Indeed, in the one place in which abortion is explicitly dealt with, one finds outright support for medical abortion:

> If a woman has [life-threatening] difficulty in childbirth, one dismembers the embryo within her, limb by limb, because her life takes precedence over its life. (Mishna, Oholot 7:6)[10]

There are other passages which, although they do not address the matter of abortion per se, suggest that a fetus is not considered to be a person:

> If men strive, and wound a pregnant woman so that her fruit be expelled, but no harm befall [her], then shall he [the assailant] be fined as her husband assesses, and the matter placed before the judges. But if harm befall [her], then "shalt thou give life for life . . ." (Exod. 21:22–23)

> [In the case of] a woman [convicted of a capital crime] who goes forth to be executed [and who, after the verdict was returned, is found to be pregnant], we do not wait for her to give birth. (Mishnah, Arakhin I, 4 [7a])

In the first case, feticide is not murder because the fetus does not have the status of a self-sufficient human being. Capital compensation is not required, only monetary. In the second case, punishment of the woman that results in the fetus's death is not murder because the fetus has no status distinct from any other part of her body. While the fetus is in utero, it is not an independent entity. It is a part of the mother like her thigh or her limb.[11] In both cases it is clear that the death of a fetus is not murder. Prior to being born, the life within a pregnant woman is not a human life.

In the above passages, the fetus is accorded little value because of its status as a dependent and undifferentiated being. There are, however, talmudic statements which presuppose that the fetus has some intrinsic value. For example, it is required that the Sabbath be broken in order to remove a fetus from a woman who has died during labor.[12] Though the fetus's viability is yet doubtful, it is sufficiently valuable that the Sabbath laws must be set aside in order to save it. There is debate between the authorities as to whether the Sabbath should be violated to save a fetus that has not attained the transitional status of a *gufa acharina* (a separate, though not wholly independent, body), that is, a fetus that has not reached the birthing stage. Nevertheless, all authorities agree that at some point in its development, the life of the fetus is of such worth as to require the violation of the Sabbath laws. Though not a person, the embryo participates in life and for this reason is awarded some degree of value.

The assumptions undergirding the legal action guides on abortion may be summarized as follows: (a) Human fetal life has little independent value. It is certainly not "sacred." (b) The value that it has is far inferior to the value of a fully viable human being, so much so that only monetary recompense must be made for the destruction of fetal life, whereas capital recompense is made for the destruction of a person's life. (c) An existing human being has greater worth than a *potential* human being, that is, the mother is of greater value than the fetus, so that "medically advised" abortion—abortion when the mother's life is endangered—is not only permitted, but is required. The question of abortion, then, is not a question of "whose blood is redder," nor is it a matter of "setting one life against another." The legal tradition makes it clear, first, that human fetal life is not equivalent in value to fully formed, self-supportive human life and, second, that "medically advised" abortion is required.

Philosophical and/or Theological Assumptions

There are at least six assumptions that are evident in the thinking of most Jews (and non-Jewish Westerners) who are opposed to a policy of abortion which, like the Supreme Court ruling of 1973, allows for both medically advised abortion and abortion for other than medical reasons within the first three months of a pregnancy. Of course, not all six of the assumptions listed below are held by every Jewish thinker who opposes "nonmedically advised" abortion. Still these six notions have a centrality and popularity that justify our consideration of them. The assumptions are these:

1. With the exception of God, human life is valued over every other kind of life.
2. In almost all cases, an increase in human life amounts to an increase in value.
3. All humans are of equal worth from God's perspective.
4. God is unchanging, or, at least, God's essence is unchanging.
5. The mental or psychological aspect of human life is (somehow) less basic than the physical aspect.
6. Existing human life has precedence over potential human life.

Assumption 1. Except for God, nothing is more valuable than human life. Murder and adultery are sins because they undermine the value of human life, but the greatest sin of all is idolatry because it places something above God. Most Jews do not deny that value can be located outside the divine and human realms—all that God created was called "good"—but only God is more valuable than human life, which was given dominion over the earth. The death of an animal *may* be a genuine loss, the death of a plant, less so, but the death of a human being is always a loss. There is a reverence for all life, but especially for human life.

Assumption 2. If human life is intrinsically valuable, then an increase of human life leads to an increase of value in the world. What requires justification is the taking of a human life or the intentional delay or absence of procreational activity, that is, contraception. There is a sense that abortion and/or neglect of the duty of procreation can be said to "diminish God's image."

Quality of human life is linked to quantity of human life. Except in times of famine, an increase in population has been preferred to an increase in material comfort. Qualitative increase in any other sense that numerical increase is seen as a secondary, though not unimportant, value.

A corollary to the notion that quantitative increase is of primary importance is the idea that the principal activity in life is reproductive activity. And in the post-Holocaust world, the increase of human life, especially Jewish life, takes on new significance. There are few Jews who would doubt that an increase in the Jewish population is an increase of value in the world.

Assumption 3. From God's vantage point, all humans are of equal value. Some are wise, some are foolish, some rich, some poor, some strong, some weak, but none is more valuable in God's eyes than the next. God is just, which means that God discriminates between the good and the bad, but God's judgment of each individual is made in light of the Divine's ideals for humanity and not in light of other individuals.

Assumption 4. God in Godself is changeless. What God has revealed and what God has decided are as true today as they were in the time of Moses. The Jewish God of history—the divine may intervene in the course of human events—but God will not reinvent the terms of history itself. If God said, "Be fruitful and multiply," that command is as appropriate to our time as it is to any other time. The value system of the historical structure stands firm.

Assumption 5. This assumption addresses the implicit belief that the mental or psychological aspect of human existence is dependent upon the physical aspect of human existence and, therefore, that the physical aspect is more fundamental. If a pregnancy threatens the physical existence of a woman, an abortion is always in order; if a pregnancy threatens the psychological well-being of a woman, abortion may be permitted, but is not required. The primary concern is with the woman's continued physical existence, not with her happiness or peace of mind. Mental health is at best secondary to physical health and at worst, epiphenomenal.

Assumption 6. Present life is more valuable than future life. A pregnant woman's life is more valuable than the life of a fetus, because her life is actual and its human life (note the qualification "human") is only potential. Similarly, though less obviously, a woman's life *now,* or the life of any person now, is more valuable than what it potentially might be in the future. At each moment the present is actual, the future only potential. In the case of pregnancy, both types of actual-potential distinctions are relevant, for a pregnant woman is both who she actually is and who she potentially could be, while the fetus within her is actually alive as a fetus and potentially alive as a person.

Reassessment of the Philosophical and/or Theological Assumptions

It is my contention that the biblical and talmudic evaluations of human fetal life—that, at least in the early stages of pregnancy, a fetus is not a *human* life, and that while it has great *potential* value, it has only minimal *actual* value—makes for a position that upholds abortion for both medically advised and other than medically advised reasons. The fact that most rabbis believe that only medically advised abortion is justified (and abortion for economic, sociological, ecological, or intellectual reasons is not justified—even though abortion as presented in authoritative Jewish sources was not restricted to any one set of justifications) is evidence that an extra-*halakhic* conviction set is operating in the decision-making process. It is my belief that the rabbis depend to a large extent on these extra-*halakhic* presuppositions when formulating their position on abortion. The purpose of this final section is to examine some of the ways in which these six philosophical and/or theological assumptions mitigate the justification of non–medically advised abortion and to consider some of the consequences such exclusion has in the contemporary world.[13]

Assumptions 1, 2, and 3

The first three assumptions of the extra-*halakhic* conviction set are so closely interconnected that it is useful to address them jointly. These three assumptions are: (1) With the exception of God, human life is valued over every other kind of life; (2) in almost all cases, an increase in human life amounts to an increase in value; and (3) all humans are of equal worth from God's perspective.

The two questions under consideration are: (a) "How does an interpretation of these notions lead to a justification of only medically advised abortion?" (b) "is this the only legitimate interpretation at which one may arrive within the Jewish tradition?"

The first question can be restated as, "Why are abortions for other than medical reasons not permitted?" Part of the answer lies in the anthropocentrism of the first two assumptions. In Judaism, human life is held to be superior to nonhuman life because only humans are created in God's image and only they are endowed with souls. Nonhuman life has intrinsic value, but in rabbinic tradition its intrinsic value is generally subordinated to its instrumental value, that is, the value it has *for* human beings. There is a reverence for life in general in Judaism, but there is a particular reverence for human life, and often this comes to mean that human life is "absolutely" valuable (subject, of course, to God's will). By "absolutely" valuable the rabbis mean both that human life is superior to nonhuman life (Assumption 1) and that one human life cannot be weighed against another insofar as human life per se is absolutely valuable (Assumption 3). Two consequences of this anthropocentrism are the neither ecological concerns nor (oddly enough) sociological concerns are accepted as legitimate justifications for abortion. The reason that ecological concerns are not treated with any seriousness is because of a philosophy of nature that is anthropocentrically dualistic—humanity is distinct from and superior to nonhuman nature. The reason that sociological considerations are not judged legitimate is because of a philosophy of human nature that is absolutistic.

A worldview that, in fact (if not in principle), separates the human realm from the nonhuman realm is a distorted worldview.[14] We come to see ourselves as related only externally to the nonhuman world so that we think of ourselves as the only real *subjects* in a world of objects. The relationship that subjects and objects have is one-directional—the lower species contribute to the life of the higher species but not vice versa—and the essential mutuality, interdependence, and internal relatedness of all beings is denied. It then makes sense to limit the justifications for abortion to human concerns alone. In such a world, it is only the robbing of potential (and actual) human life that must be justified.

In the statement "Whatever the Holy One created in His universe, He created for His Glory," "His Glory" has been interpreted to mean humanity.[15] Here is conspicuous and unnecessary anthropocentrism; it is quite fair to the text to understand "His Glory" as referring to God, and not to humanity. When it is understood in this way, the intrinsic value of nonhuman life is recalled; it, too, is a direct glorification of God. From an ecological perspective (which includes humanity), life itself is robbery, for the living depend on the dead to sustain them. Because life feeds on life, "the robber requires justification."[16] Human life requires some sort of justification for the sacrifice it demands from other forms of life. The taking of any life, human or nonhuman, must be justified. Abortion, then, becomes an issue that cannot be considered apart from ecological issues.

A philosophy that recognizes that all beings have some degree of intrinsic value is very different from a philosophy in which only human beings have intrinsic value or a philosophy in which all beings are equally valuable. The first worldview requires that some kind of hierarchy of value be established. The rabbinic belief that every individual is of immeasurable worth in God's sight, that is, that human life per se is absolutely valuable, stands against the calculation of life presumed by a hierarchy of value. The rabbis have been unwilling to "set one life against another," to judge the "redness" of one person's blood over another's. In fact, however, there is a hierarchy at work in rabbinic evaluations, most obviously in the qualitative differences made between human and nonhuman life, between humankind and God, and between actual and potential persons. The distinction between humans and nonhumans is discussed above. The second distinction, between humanity and divinity, is made clear in the discussion of those situations in which human life is not worth living. Under conditions that lead to idolatry, adultery, or murder, the absolute value of human life is shattered. By divine command, human life in those instances is to be forfeited. Thirdly, in the discussion of abortion, it is affirmed that the fetus is less than a person; though it is life, it is not at the level of human life and hence is of lesser value.[17] There is, then, a calculus of lie embedded in Jewish tradition so that a discussion of hierarchy of value is not without precedent.

That calculus is, I believe, based on the measure of *experience*—on the unique, purposeful moments of existence that distinguish one form of life from another. There is no equality of value between a fetus and a person because the experiences that define their existences are radically unequal—the fetus's experience lacks the richness, intentionality, and consciousness of a person's experience. We can affirm the intrinsic value of a fetus, an infant, and an adult, without also having to affirm an equality of value for them. And since we can do this, it is unreasonable to limit abortion to those instances in which a threat to the mother's health is present. Abortion may then be justified for other than medical reasons. Abortion may be judged to be beneficial to the mother's experience as a whole, including her intellectual, moral, emotional, and physical health and her sociological and ecological milieu.

Assumption 4

This is the assumption that God is unchanging, or, at least, the divine essence is unchanging. But if experience is worthwhile, if it counts for us, then it must also count for God. The biblical roots of this thesis are exemplified in the concept of a God of History. A God who is truly involved in the world is a God who is felt by others and who feels the experiences of others. To be affected by our relations with others is to be *internally related*. In the model of internal relations, an entity is what it is in relation to the environment. It is an abstraction, then, to talk about an entity without reference to its environment.[18]

What God does is influenced to some degree by what kind of world God participates in. If the world is an unpopulated one, God may work to increase the richness of experience by urging the creation to reproduce at a higher level. If the world is an overpopulated one, God may work to increase the richness of experience by urging the creatures to reduce their rates of reproduction and to increase their enjoyment in other ways. God is a deontologist only insofar as God *always* works to bring about good in the cosmos. God's purpose is to elicit intensity of experience, not to achieve one final experience. And the ways in which God works are never decided independently of the situation. Hence, God may not always act so as to increase the human population, although God will always act in such a way as to encourage richness of experience. To say that abortion always "diminishes God's image" is to undermine God's ability to be responsive.

Assumption 5

Both the mental and physical aspects of human beings are affirmed in Jewish tradition. Indeed, it is because we are not merely material beings that God can influence us in noncoercive ways. But there is an overwhelming tendency in the tradition to emphasize the physical aspects over the mental aspects, so much so that the mental is often understood to be an epiphenomenon of the physical. This tendency is very apparent in rabbinic discussions of abortion.

It is an issue of debate among the rabbis as to whether a threat to mental health is a justifiable cause for abortion. Many agree that it is, but a good many of these hold that it is so only when mental instability is a threat to physical health, for example, when suicide threatens. The permit for abortion is less likely to be granted when the mother's mental instability appears not to be reflected in self-damaging physical behavior.

Even when the mother's mental health is considered in an abortion decision, there is no evidence that "mentality" is understood to include anything other than "emotional health." The intellectual aspect of a woman's mental life is not considered. "Considerations of physical hazard and fundamental welfare of existing children are admissible" as justifications for abortion, and occasionally a woman's emotional well-being alone is admitted. However, a woman's intellectual life is never discussed as a possible reason for abortion, and it can be surmised that such an argument would fall under the category of "self-indulgence or convenience."[19]

Not to take a woman's mental life, in all its aspects, seriously is to deny women what has been permitted to men: the assumption of interiority and, thereby, of individuality. Not to accord significance to the mental aspects of her life—significance that at least equals and ought to surpass the physical aspects of her life—is not to accord her the freedom and creativity that is given to men. In this kind of Judaism, women bear children, not witness. So long as mentality is subservient to physicality in the discussion about abortion, or any issue concerning women, the tendency will be to perceive women as being less than fully human.

Assumption 6

The assumption that existing human life has precedence over potential human life is the basis for many of the more "lenient" rulings on abortion. "The judge can rule only on the evidence before his eye," and in many cases it was ruled that "her pain comes first," that is, that abortion on the basis of her physical and sometimes emotional pain is justified.[20]

This logic is commendable because it recognizes the difference between the value of potential life and the value of actual life; or, to put it differently, it recognizes that a fetus is potentially very valuable, but *actually* only somewhat valuable. When the actual life of the mother is weighed against the actual life of the fetus qua fetus, the mother's concerns (at least her physical and sometimes mental concerns) are given precedence. The health of an actually existing child also is granted precedence, in one responsum, over the life of the actually existing fetus. And finally, greater weight is given to the life of the actual fetus over the life of the future fetus; abortion on the grounds that the fetus is probably developing in a defective way such that the future child's life will be less than normal is not permitted.[21]

However, always to grant precedence to the present over the future—to existing human life over potential life—is to ignore the pull of the future upon the present moment. Our actions and God's actions in the present are partially influenced by our anticipations of the future. The danger in focusing almost exclusively on the present is the danger of becoming almost entirely centered on the momentary self. Shortsightedness and self-centeredness are obstacles in the way of transcendence. Our survival—and beyond that, peace—depends upon our ability to respond to the present in light of the possibilities that may become actualities.

The concept of sacrifice is an important corrective to the view that potential life is always less valuable than actual life. In sacrifice, one gives up a present actuality in order to enable the possible actualization of present potentialities. The possible is given greater weight than the actual. There are cases in which the value of potential life—the intrinsic value of future humans which may be actualized if these future humans become actual humans—is greater than the value of actually existing life. And those cases include not just that potential value the fetus harbors, but that potential which is completely unactualized (i.e., the value of potential fetuses) and that potential which is part of the future life of those who are already persons, for example, the existing mother's future, the existing family's future, the future of the population at large, and so forth.

Conclusion

The purpose of this essay has been to illuminate some of the extra-*halakhic* assumptions that undergird the rabbinic responsa on abortion and to show that these assumptions are not demanded by tradition. There are biblical and talmudic precedents for correcting anthropocentrism with ecocentrism, absolutism with a hierarchy of values, philosophical materialism with dipolarity, conservatism with "sacred discontent,"[22] and sexism with egalitarianism.[23] When these correctives are assumed, Judaism becomes a worldview that recognizes that all life—human, nonhuman, and divine—is interdependent and mutually responsive. Hence, a decision about abortion is a decision that must be made in light of both actual and potential human, nonhuman, and divine life. All decisions involve judgments of values, and if those judgments are to be made with the subtlety that an ecological and dipolar worldview demands, they will be decisions based on concrete units of experience rather than on abstractions of life. When the Jewish sources are thus considered, it becomes clear that Judaism not only permits abortions for medical reasons, but also supports abortion for nonmedical reasons. More importantly, Judaism can uphold such positions without denying either the tragedy of abortion— "What might have been and was not"—or the life affirming aspects of abortion— "What can be."[24]

Notes

1. *Hagahot Ya'avetz* to Nida 44b.

2. See David Feldman, *Birth Control in Jewish Law* (New York: New York University Press, 1968), (chapters 14 and 15, for his thorough discussion of the positions represented on the one hand by R. Untermann and on the other by R. Uziel.

3. J. David Bleich, "Abortion in Halakhic Literature," *Tradition*, vol. 6, no. 4 (Winter 1968), p. 73.

4. *Yad, Hilkhot Rotseach Ushemirat Nefesh*, 1, 9, quoted in Feldman, op. cit., p. 276.

5. R. Hayyim Soloveitchik, *Chiddushei R. Chayim Halevi* (1936), quoted in Feldman, op. cit., pp. 279, 281.

6. R. Isaac Lampronti, *Pachad Yitschak*, s.v. *nefalim*, quoted in Feldman, op. cit., p. 282.

7. R. Ezekiel Landau, Responsa *Noda Biyehuda*, Second Series, H.M., no. 59, quoted in Feldman, op. cit., p. 278.

8. R. Isaac Schorr, Responsa *Koach Shor*, no. 20.; R. Jacob Schorr, Responsa *Ge-onim Batra-ei*, no. 45; R. Moshe Zweig, *No-am*, VII (1964), especially pp. 49–53, quoted in Feldman, op. cit., pp. 277–83.

9. Bleich, op. cit., p. 73.

10. The passage continues: "Once its head (or 'its greater part') has emerged, it may not be touched, for we do not set aside one life for another."

11. E.g., Bab. Talmud, Hulin 58, "The fetus is the thigh of its mother," and Gittin 23b, "The fetus is regarded as one of her limbs."

12. Bab. Talmud, Arakhin 7a.

13. I make the following evaluation from a Whiteheadian-Hartshornean perspective. The Whiteheadian, or process, metaphysics is not, I believe, in conflict with the thrust of our basic Jewish insights and may be used to place these insights within an appropriate ontology. Central to the process schema are such notions as the internality of relations, the primacy of experience, the gradation of values, the dipolar (mental-physical) nature of every experience, and a sympathetic and mutable God. These are notions that are applied in the discussion which follows.

14. This is true from both a biblical and a Whiteheadian perspective.

15. Avot 6:2. This interpretation is given by A. Cohen in *Everyman's Talmud* (New York: Schocken Books, 1978), pp. 67ff.

16. Alfred North Whitehead, *Process and Reality*, corrected edition, ed. David R. Griffin (New York: The Free Press, 1978), p. 105.

17. Also pertinent here is the mishnaic ruling that "A man takes precedence over a woman when it comes to saving a life and to restoring something lost" (M. Horayot 3.7).

18. Formally referred to by Whitehead as "the fallacy of simple location."

19. Feldman, op. cit., p. 53.

20. *Ibid.*, pp. 292, 294.

21. *Ibid.*, p. 292.

22. See Herbert N. Schneidau, *Sacred Discontent* (Baton Rouge: Louisiana State University Press, 1976).

23. See Cynthia Ozick, "Notes toward Finding the Right Question," in *On Being a Jewish Feminist*, ed. Susannah Heschel (New York: Schocken Books, 1983), pp. 120–51.

24. Alfred North Whitehead, *Adventures of Ideas* (New York: The Free Press, 1933), p. 286.

E. Jewish Perspectives on Politics and Power: The State of Israel

29

The Ethics of Jewish Power

IRVING GREENBERG

We are at the beginning of a fundamental change in the Jewish condition: the assumption of power. After almost two millennia, Jews are again exercising sovereignty in their own land. In the Diaspora and in Israel, the Jewish people is taking responsibiliy for its fate in the realm of politics and history. Only now are we beginning to confront the profound challenge to religious understanding and ethical capacity implicit in this revolutionary change.

Many people are devastated when they see Jewish hands dirtied with the inescapable blood and guilt of operating in the world. The classic Jewish self-image—the innocent, sinned-against sufferer—is being shattered. The traditional Jewish conviction of being morally superior which has sustained our self-respect throughout centuries of persecution is being tested. Who imagined the day that to reestablish order, Jewish soldiers would deliberately beat Arabs on the hands? Or smash arms and legs of some civilians, not just terrorists? Who anticipated that such a policy would be morally superior to the alternative in which clashes led to shootings with live ammunition and to deaths? Some recoil and wish Israel away; some lash out and blame particular leaders. Many yearn for an alternative to regain lost innocence. The truth is more painful and must be faced.

Power corrupts. But there is no other morally tolerable choice. The alternative is death. This is the lesson that the Jewish people learned from the Holocaust.

The Holocaust demonstrated that, thanks to concentrations of power created by modern culture and technology, there has been an enormous shift in the balance of power between the victims and the persecutors. The victims were always weaker but there were inherent limits in the power of the dominant groups. Now many of the limits on the aggressors—ranging from moral taboos on killing to technological limitations—have been shattered. The total imbalance of power from 1939 to 1945 corrupted the murderers into ever more destructive behavior. Powerlessness encouraged the indifference of the bystanders. In the face of Jewish political passivity and weakness even great liberals like Franklin D. Roosevelt and Winston Churchill did little or nothing to stop the carnage. The overwhelming force tormented or broke many victims before they were killed. Thereby, Jews learned that power corrupts, absolute power corrupts absolutely, but absolute powerlessness corrupts even more.

Driven by the will to live, survivalist Jews have become overwhelmingly Zionist, even if they have no intention of ever living in Israel. Goaded by the absolute pain of the Holocaust, American public opinion became pro-Zionist and has stood by Israel ever since. All understand that Jews must have access to the kind of power and guaranteed haven that only a government and an army can provide. This lesson has been learned by others as well. Liberation movements have arisen in the former colonial world, as well as among women, blacks, and other minorities worldwide.

Erstwhile victims should not be romanticized. The moral purity of victims is often a function of the fact that they have no power to inflict evil. They are equally, sometimes more, subject to being corrupted by accession to power. Throughout history, when downtrodden classes would arise, they would often turn a murderous fury against the equally victimized neighboring Jews. Many a liberation movement has denied the Jewish right to liberation. It is delusion or self-righteous flattery to believe that Jews can avoid the same tendencies. The historical challenge of power must be taken on with eyes open.

The Bible recounts that when Israel's ancestral father paused in his flight and turned to defend himself against the oncoming armies of Esau, "Jacob feared and was greatly distressed" (Gen. 32:7). Said the rabbis: " 'Jacob feared' that he might be killed, 'and was greatly distressed' that he might kill others." The costs of power are always both human and moral.

The Moral Philosophy of Power

Renouncing Power

For almost two thousand years, Jews and Christians have glorified the renunciation of power. The original moral insight of Judaism was that might does not make right and that power itself must be judged by its results. Over the ages, the original morality principle was steadily extrapolated until it became an idealist code of the powerless. (This is what Nietzsche mocked when he dismissed the two religions as slave morality.) Jews went into exile and a state of powerlessness. Living on sufferance, Jews had to accept the political order as given and seek to accommodate to it or serve it. Christianity interpreted redemption to be a spiritual rather than a political-economic matter and made the exercise of power irrelevant or a distraction from the ultimate goal. The principles "turn the other cheek" and the inherent wickedness of any force or violence replaced the prophetic demand for social justice. Power itself became identified as the source of evil by people who taught that it was better to save one's soul and give up activity in the world.

A good expression of this tendency was incarnate in the growing Jewish culture of passivity. The medieval Jewish Mussar (ethical) literature treated anger in any manifestation as an extreme sin, even as idolatry. Jews, who in biblical times were warriors, now focused on the talmudic idea that God made Israel swear not to revolt against the nations in whose midst it served its term of exile. Jewish actions to redeem the world were turned inward to individual and community concerns or were directed to mystical, cosmic realms. The concept of the Jews as a merciful, compassionate people was extended to the idea that the Jew will not or even cannot shed blood. Gentile persecution seemed all the more evil by comparison with Jewish helplessness.

The idealistic tendency of Western culture was adopted and greatly strengthened by the liberal-progressive-utopian wing within modern culture. Liberal idealization of human nature and repugnance for war or realpolitik sometimes lead uncritical liberals to confuse the dream of worldwide peace and the ultimate victory of ideals with the actual facts. Such ethicists tend to see the use of force as atavistic behavior and the moral ambiguities of statecraft as ethically inferior—both doomed to die out. The views of this wing have been particularly attractive to Jews and other Americans as well.

When, under the influence of modern values, Zionists set out to create a Jewish state, most Jews were neutral if not opposed. Traditionalists said it was impious to take power into one's own hands and that the state was premature (the Messiah not having arrived). Modernists said it was unnecessary to take power into one's own hands and that the state was too late (universal modern culture having arrived). The sledgehammer blow of the Holocaust smashed these constellations of beliefs and changed the course of Jewish history. The Jewish people determined not to yield up hope, but to recreate life and human dignity. The consensus was that Jews must take power into their own hands in order to live. The State of Israel was established. Jews set out to shape a society in which justice and *tzedakah* would govern. Thus, they reaffirmed the ancient Jewish belief in the call to perfect this world and took up the classic Jewish role of modeling a society on the way to that final redemption for all humanity.

Taking Power

The creation of the State of Israel places the power in the hands of Jews to shape their own destiny and to affect and even control the lives of others. This is a revolutionary 180-degree turn in the moral situation. The dilemmas of power are far different from the temptations and problems of powerlessness. Jews have been fond of contrasting Christian persecution of Jews with Jewish innocence. Modern Jews often juxtapose Christianity's failure to lead the fight for social justice in the medieval world with the Hebraic prophetic passion for helping the oppressed. Christian implication in upholding an unjust status quo and abusing Jews is contrasted with Jewish martyrdom, and Judaism's high moral standards. These shorthand images incorporate elements of self-flattery. You need power to do harm as you need power to do good. It remains to be seen whether Jewry's innocence reflects its past powerlessness or some intrinsic higher moral performance. The test will come now in Judaism's relationship to Jewish sovereignty and Jewry's ability to ethically elevate the Jewish exercise of power. The entire issue must be addressed with absolute seriousness. We are dealing with a matter that is a historic turning point. The costs are already staggeringly high; the moral risks are even higher.

The Human Costs of Power

The Jewish people has been paying the costs of the assumption of power for most of the twentieth century. Thousands of *halutzim* (Zionist pioneers) voluntarily declassed themselves, gave up hearth and home to go struggle with hostile authorities, swamps, malaria, and flinty soil to build the infrastructure of the future Israel.

Hundreds of thousands of survivors, after going through hell and losing everything, chose confinement in D.P. camps or internment in Cyprus under primitive conditions for additional years rather than yield their part in building a Jewish homeland. More than half a million Oriental Jews were stripped of their wealth and fled the Arab lands to join in the formation of the Jewish state. Thousands of their families lived in shacks for years and suffered the loss of their native cultural and geographic guideposts until they rebuilt their lives. The price of parental authority lost, of children deracinated, of old people dying in an unfamiliar place, of the normal existential difficulties compounded by uprooting and migration was enormous—but Jews paid it to build a new Jewish society.

When the State of Israel was declared, it was invaded, precipitating the first of the "Wars for Israeli Independence." During this first war, Israel had neither the armaments nor the trained soldiers that it needed. At one battle, near Latrun, hundreds of survivors were rushed from shipside and thrown with inadequate arms and no training into a desperate battle against the Jordanian Legion. Most died. Individually, they were the remnant—one from a family, two from a city. With each one, whole worlds died. They should have been treated like whooping cranes or some other remainder of life so rare that its surviving exemplars must be sheltered from normal history. But the pressure was too great. Jews were too weak and nothing could be held back. When the war ended, Israel's losses stood at six thousand dead—almost 1% of the Jewish population. The equivalent today in the United States would be 2 million people.

Every Israeli has been on permanent service ever since. From 1950 to 1956, there were three thousand armed clashes with Arab regular or irregular forces outside Israeli territory and some six thousand acts of sabotage or theft by infiltrators. Israeli men and women serve in the army, for three or two years, respectively, followed by reserve training up to the age of forty-nine. Behind these deceptively simple statistics is an infinite chain of human cost.

Every year, thousands of students miss examinations and have to rearrange their lives; stores and artists' galleries close for weeks because the sole proprietor is away for *miluim* (reserve duty). How many fathers miss births or birthday parties? How many children do not get put to bed by their fathers? How many wives sleep alone? And all these people are the lucky ones because their lives go on. How many widows lie awake night after night in the isolation of their torn lives?

In every decade, the costs have been paid again. I think of two close friends, American families that went on *aliyah*. Their turn came in the Lebanon war. One lost a twenty-three-year-old son, a student in yeshiva, handsome, full of life, full of plans for the future. The other's son-in-law was one of two pilots who did not survive the downing of his plane on the mission that uncovered the Syrian introduction of Sam-8s into Lebanon. He was a young father, and brilliant, a warm person who had extraordinary promise as a scholar. He put that aside to stay in the professional air force because that was where he was needed. He left behind a young wife, two small children, and grieving parents and in-laws.

These are the people that I, a sheltered American Jew living six thousand miles away, know. Who can chronicle the rest—the Israeli family that lost a father in 1948, a child in 1967, a grandchild in 1982? . . . A relative's brother who was killed by a random terrorist bomb placed on a bus of travelers in Jericho? . . . A friend attended a funeral in which the bereaved father was the only survivor of his family from Europe. The father told the mourners that one son was killed in 1967, another in 1973, and with the loss of his final child in 1982, the family was now permanently cut off.

Of course, in this generation, even paying these terrible costs of power is a betterment. Once we stood in a group, shell-shocked at the final tabulation of more than 2,500 dead in the Yom Kippur war and asked ourselves: will Israel be able to live with such ongoing costs? Edwar Luttwack restored our perspective. Said Luttwack: only thirty years ago, the Nazis killed 10,000 to 15,000 Jews a day with *Einsatzgruppen* (shooting squads) or gas chambers and every death weakened Jewish security, leaving the other Jews more vulnerable to destruction. The Yom Kippur loss was staggering. But with their deaths, the 2,500 reversed a dangerous invasion, secured the lives of their loved ones, and left every Jew in the world safer. And their inheritance went for their children and their people and not to enrich their murderers . . . But this contrast does not stop the pain.

To arrive at a rough appraisal of the human cost of power, one would have to take each of the ten thousand dead from the five Israeli wars and multiply them by the lives cut off, the families left behind, the worlds unbuilt. Then one would have to multiply the total by three or four: for thousands who were wounded or disabled before and after the establishment of Israel in 1948. For every paraplegic, handicapped, or permanently scarred soldier, one would have to add the interminable hours of struggling and living with the physical and psychic costs of going on. Then multiply all this by the countless families sharing or touched by those lives. Who but God can measure the oceans of tears that have been shed in this process?

Despite these terrible costs of assuming power, there has been an overwhelming consensus in the Jewish community that this people must pay the toll and proceed. For one, the alternative to power would be death. Then, too, the consciousness of the rectitude and morality of the Jewish cause sustained the people. Despite a continuing series of wars and a universal draft, the State of Israel, during its history, had very few conscientious objectors; before the Lebanon war, hardly any. (The objections to women serving in the army and the demand for exemptions for religious scholars are connected to issues of modesty and sheltered cultural existence rather than to the ethics of war and violence.) Despite heavy casualties, the morale and willingness to fight of Israeli soldiers have remained high, they feel they are fighting for home, family, and life itself. And as they overcome their initial dependence on maximal acceptance and approval from Gentiles, Diaspora Jews also grow more and more steadfast in support of Israel.

But the issue of the moral costs of power has grown ever more pressing over the past few decades. The widespread sense that Jews must hold themselves to a higher standard of ethics has increasingly come into conflict with the morally compromising situations that Israel has entered. The types of allies that Israel sometimes works with make some uneasy. The links to South Africa during its years of apartheid drew the most attention as the antiapartheid movement grew. But the Somozist connection in Central America also became highly controversial in the 1970s as the Sandinistas drew the support of the world's left. From a moral perspective, the Lebanese war was the most marginal war Israel fought. Unlike the Six Day and Yom Kippur wars, the existence of a clear and present danger to actual Israeli survival was not beyond argument, leaving the moral side effects (such as civilian casualties and destruction of local society) open to severe challenges. Willingness to criticize Israeli policy has grown—especially among American Jewish leadership. This phenomenon has been portrayed as a weakening of the Israel-Diaspora bonds. I believe that criticism properly done represents not a backing away from Israel but an important piece of the Jewish ethic of power currently in creation. Still, many people feel that any criticism is betrayal, so the conflict over the moral costs of power has escalated.

"Moral" delegitimation of Israel has grown in certain radical circles. At the height of the outcry over the Sabra-Shatila massacres, it appeared for a few days that Israel might have been implicated in instigating the massacre. A leading American Jewish theologian, in an anguished cri de coeur, lamented that if this was the cost of the Jewish state, then the cost was too high! My personal reaction was: I do not believe that Israel would do such a thing. But let us assume the worst—what if it had organized the massacre (God forbid). The action should be condemned unequivocally. However, the United States of America was made possible in part by a systematic genocide of the Indians, pursued over the course of centuries. This was shameful and it remains a permanent moral blot on America's record. But did anybody suggest that the cost was too high and it were better that there had never been a United States? Russia has enslaved hundreds of millions, has persecuted Jews, has engaged in a genocidal invasion of Afghanistan. Does anyone seriously propose that it has lost its legitimacy as a state?

It seems clear that without some context of a Jewish ethic of power to guide us along our historical way, we may lose our moral compass. Dangerous alternatives tempt us at every step: undermining Israel or abandoning it through excessive criticism and faulty judgments—or betraying Israel by giving it a moral blank check and uncritical love.

The Moral Costs of Power; or, Toward an Ethical Jewish Power

Reality and Morality

When the vast majority of believers have little say in their own fate, religions legitimately play their classic role of comforting the afflicted by focusing on such teachings as the dignity of the powerless, the preciousness of suffering, the moral heroism of renunciation and asceticism. On balance, Judaism and Christianity moved toward more idealistic moral codes as their power diminished. Morality standards were developed by people with little ability to carry them out. This led to more utopian and absolute standards—standards relatively unchecked by reality. Worldly power was generally left to those who had it. They had fewer qualms about exercising it. This increased inequality and the corrupting effects of power. But the religious community prided itself on its moral purity and blamelessness.

The new rules cannot be identical with the old. Operations in the real world are affected by human error and vested interest. There is no one moral policy carried out but an endless series of judging specific situations and reconciling conflicting claims and shifting facts. This means linking ultimate ends and proximate means in a continual process; it cannot be done without involvement, partial failures, guilt. Since real policy rarely meets the absolute standard of the ideal, those who exercise power are in constant tension with the prophets who denounce their moral failures. The contrast is not always in favor of the prophets. If those in power are responsible people, they must renounce prophetic stances. Prophets can rely on spiritual power and make absolute demands for righteousness. Governments have obligations to protect people. On the other hand, when governments ignore prophets, they usually end up abusing the people they are supposed to protect.

What appears to be moral in the abstract may work poorly in actual practice. An alternative, more compromising approach may achieve its goals brilliantly and come out ahead. This is why reality eventually disciplines moralism. Says the Talmud: Those who are merciful to people who deserve cruelty will end up being cruel to people who deserve mercy. Often the punishment for failure to take reality into account is to do the opposite of what was intended. In the 1930s, an underground religious group considered assassinating Hitler but decided against it on the grounds that there is no moral right to kill a bad ruler. The millions of innocent victims of Hitler's later murderous war on the Jews and others could well claim that the righteousness of the German underground paved the way for the cruel sadistic war on them. Similarly, in 1967, the absolute radical demand for justice of many in the American New Left led them to denounce the all-too-human, bouregois Israel with its social imbalances. As a result, they ended up supporting slaveholding and feudal Arab oil sheiks intent on genocide. Those murderous designs were frustrated by Israel's strength, no thanks to the uncompromising radical moralism that only led its practitioners to de facto collaboration with attempted mass murderers.

Some Principles of Power

The beginning of ethical wisdom is the recognition that in an unredeemed world, one must be able and willing to exercise power to protect or advance the good. Yet, power is not self-validating; giving power that kind of respect is tantamount—or will lead—to idolatry. All exercises of power must be judged by the standard of perfecting the world and the triumph of life that such exercises seek to advance. However, any exercise of power, no matter how well intentioned, will have inescapable "immoral" side effects. Yet, if doing nothing leads to greater evil than doing something, then failure to act is moral default. Those who refuse to use such "immoral" means are guilty of placing their moral image above the suffering of others—which is a form of selfishness.

The truly moral do not avoid stain by not exercising power. They act, but only when necessary and they seek to reduce suffering caused by their actions to the minimum. The firm moral principle is that *given the evil that cannot be avoided, there is still an ideal way of exercising power.* A moral army uses no more force than necessary. If it uses less force than necessary, and fails, it betrays those it seeks to protect or its own soldiers who died in vain. If the amount of force necessary is unclear, then willingness to take losses to avoid causing innocent suffering is the ethical test.

Sometimes, there is a deadlock that can only be broken by an action which has immoral elements (civilian casualties, etc.). But the justification for causing innocent suffering—that greater suffering will be prevented by this action—is not assured. In such cases, only the outcome will decide if the action was morally right (on balance). In other words: If it works, it is moral. If it fails (to yield less suffering on balance), it is immoral. In abstract ethical systems, morality is independent of success; in actual life, it is not. In a perfect world, there will be no gap between reality and principle, which is why Judaism strives to bring the Messiah. In the interim, the good is often advanced by a morally ambiguous process.

Moral acts producing immoral side effects are intermixed with flawed acts yielding good effects. The historical record shows that participation in power often leads to the weakening of conscience unless there is some continual refreshment of judgment through exposure to prophetic norms. Happy is the people which learns to reconcile prophetic demands with the compromising arts of governance and real policies. Those who care inescapably take on guilt—and they know it. Show me a people whose hands are not dirty and I will show you a people which has not been responsible. Show me a people which has stopped washing its hands and admitting its guilt, and I will show you a people which is arrogant and dying morally.

On Being Normal

The exercise of power is unrelenting; in history, one cannot take up one's marbles and go home—this is especially true when, as in the case of Israel, the state is surrounded by a sea of unreconciled enemies. Power is corrupting, and the Jewish people's relative weakness (compared to larger powers) narrows the margins for purely magnanimous, morally idealistic behavior even more. The net effect of constant struggle and involvement in morally ambiguous situations can be readily projected. Over time, the gap between the ideal and reality is reduced; the movement is in the direction of the demands of reality. The behavior of all people in history can be fit within a bell-shaped curve of moral performance. Inevitably, the continuous exercise of sovereignty will narrow the spread between the behavior of Jews and of other people.

This is what classical Zionists meant when they glorified the "normalization" of the Jewish people. They recognized that many pathological social phenomena were absent among Jews because there was no Jewish holistic political society. The price of an organic Jewish community—one not confined to urban ghetto areas or money-lending professions by discrimination, or absent a proletariat because it had no means of production—would be crime and prostitution and a host of ills of modern life. The price was inescapable—but, in light of the greater good, more than worth it.

In dreaming about the future reality, the founding Zionists could romanticize and soften the hard edges of the unborn pathology. Now that we are back in history, we see, up close, the hard edges of social sickness and corruptible power. Jewish military force is not exempt from killing innocents or skewing lives or officers' privileges or attracting camp followers. Only "how much" can be modified by Jewish action and ethical will.

This is a painful admission for most Jews. But to believe otherwise is to commit a "genetic fallacy" and assume that Jews are intrinsically more moral than other people. Such a belief bespeaks a covert racism. After all, Jews are like other people—only more so. The Bible portrays the Jews as no better inherently than other nations. Its picture of Jewish sovereignty shows a deeply flawed record. "Not because of your righteousness does the Lord your God give you the good land to inherit, for you are a morally stubborn, recalcitrant people . . ." (Deut. 9:6). The illusion of ethical perfectionism grows out of the record of millennial powerlessness whose results are projected incorrectly into the new reality. It also happens that in coming out of an extended period of heightened moral consciousness, initial behavior may be more ethically sensitive. The memories of suffering are fresher and the moral energy released by the shift from potential to actual behavior is unusually high. But such releases are temporary phenomena. They are abnormal; they can be utilized once or twice but are not automatically self-renewing.

While this truth is sad, it should not be a cause for depression or moral recoil. In actual history, excellence is contextual—and always possible. Exercising heroic self-control, within the give and take of self-interest and political-military pressures, utilizing ethical restraints of a particularly demanding nature—such as the Jewish convenantal ethic of *tikkun olam* (perfection of the world)—will yield a record that is the highest achievement; one worthy of honor and celebration. Five or 10 percent better than the other nations—that is what it means to be "a light unto the nations." To be perfect is the light that never was on land or sea. The Promised Land is a normal land whose inhabitants are raised to a heightened awareness of God and human ethical responsibility. The chosen people is a normal people called to an intensified commitment to create a moral community as part of a human-divine partnership to perfect this world. Even if it were possible to set up a perfect society, it would have a limited impact. For the most part, it would be so far beyond the capacity of others to imitate that it would be dismissed out of hand. (As it is, the 5-percent-better model has evoked anti-Semitism, the most sinister, protean, and wide-ranging, social pathology in human history. If the Jews really were perfect, they would be insufferable.) Perfection is better than life but nonexistent. In history, less is more.

The Building Blocks of an Ethic of Power

Once it is recognized that an ethic of Jewish power must be established within the parameters of normal politics, it becomes clear that Jews cannot be beyond criticism. It will take a struggle to prevent Jews from lowering their guard and yielding to all the corruption of history. Since moral erosion and/or compromise is inevitable, the key question is: What can be done to uphold an ethical standard? The first answer is a paradox. Sin is inevitable; therefore, the ethical health of a society is judged not so much by its ideal procedures or potential ability to do good but by the excellence of its corrective mechanisms. Every moral person and society will misbehave. "There is no righteous person in the world who will do good and never sin"

(Eccles. 7:21). The truly moral person and society will be willing to admit the error and organize to correct it.

One cannot depend only on goodwill for moral reparation. There must be built-in mechanisms to challenge and test the exercise of power. When the will to do good falters, the structure is there to encourage correction. It follows that the fundamental building block of an ethic of Jewish power is a structure not a principle. The most effective ethical structure in any situation is a balance of power. To put it in classic Jewish theological terms: only God's power should be absolute (and God has waived exercising that degree of power through commitment to operating through covenant).

To relativize human power, one must distribute it widely. One-sided force corrupts both the governors and the governed, the aggressors and the victims. The more one-sided power is, the less likely it is to be challenged on its merits. Countervailing force, exercised independently, checks the tendencies to abuse the other—for the other has the power of self-protection. Being in a situation when one cannot act with impunity (or being forced into better actions by the ability of the other to retaliate) usually brings out the best behavior in people.

The ethical ideal would be a balance of power in the Middle East in which Israel cannot dominate the Arab nations and the Arab nations cannot dream of destroying Israel by force. Ideally, the Palestinian Arabs should have their own state and should treat the Jews living on the West Bank with dignity. They should respect Jews' rights and cultures just as the internal Arab minority in the Jewish state has a vital inner life and real political power to protect itself. Arab sovereignty should check potential Israeli excesses even as Israeli might should check Arab aggressiveness. The interaction of balance of power combined with cultural and religious openness creates the best setting for the flowering of ethical relationships and true brotherhood. (According to the Bible, God gives up absolute power and enters into covenantal self-restrictions for the sake of loving and being loved by humanity.)

There is a serious flaw in this statement of the ideal. Major elements in the Arab world are unreconciled to Jewish sovereignty and would gladly destroy Israel if they could. Under such circumstances, a balance of power is not morally acceptable. A situation of approximate equality of force tempts the aggressors to try for one strategy, one breakthrough, that can tilt the balance in their favor. There should be no equation between one people threatened with extermination and one people fearful, at worst, of expansionism. Therefore, the ethically ideal balance of power must be a dynamic one. As acceptance of Israel goes up, the balance should be adjusted toward greater military and political parity.

In the interim, Israel should seek maximum Arab autonomy in Judea and Samaria by encouraging the emergence of indigenous leadership willing to live in peace with the Jewish state. Let the word go out unequivocally from Israel that Palestinian Arabs can earn autonomy and even a state by seeking peace and taking risks for it. In theory, the PLO also can earn the status of a negotiating partner with Israel. The PLO would have to disavow its call for the destruction of Israel and purge its "rejection front" elements—preferably by military confrontation—to make clear that it really intends to live in peace with Israel. Of course, this will not happen until the Arab nations and the world stop romanticizing and encouraging the murderous elements in PLO leadership.

Internal sources of moral balance of power are equally crucial. Religious pluralism will prevent any one group from seizing control and imposing its unchecked will (in the name of God) on policy. A free press and independent media are major sources of moral criticism and of evaluation of policies from within. Whatever the excesses of media sensationalism, infantile leftism, and so forth, the costs are well worth it. The channels of communication are indispensable to moral regulation and to ensure that prophetic voices are heard throughout the society. Plural sources of values—synagogues and churches, universities, the private sector, wide distribution of economic power, separation of business and unions, mediating agencies and institutions—are all major contributors to a moral and political balance of power.

World Jewry also can play a role in establishing standards of behavior. Since Israel is wielding sovereignty, its moral responses will be skewed toward realism. World Jewry's responses, being those of observers on many issues, will be skewed toward "idealist" models. These tendencies can be mutually corrective. As loving critics, world Jewry can be truly helpful to Israel in its effort to keep on the moral path. However, the key is to avoid stereotypical positions and extreme polarization. A conventional Diaspora idealist critique of Israeli policy will not be very useful. It could undermine Israeli viability, and Israel would be well advised to dismiss it as "armchair generalizing." It would be far more helpful if world Jews showed deep understanding of the pragmatic parameters of policy and offer morally realistic advice and criticism. Similarly, it would be healthier if Israeli society generated internal prophetic criticism side-by-side with a mainstream policy blend of Jewish ideals and Jewish realities. The balance of king, priest, and prophet was the glory of biblical covenantal ethics and politics—when it worked. As the Prophets taught us, loving criticism is the highest loyalty, and failure to make judgments is a betrayal of the covenant and of the policy makers. On the other hand, extreme polarization on policy between kings and prophets led to ethical breakdown and disastrous policies.

Another major source of moral parameters for a Jewish ethic is the internal culture, its paradigms and memory. Jews are committed to the redemption of the world. But the covenantal process mediates this utopianism by encouraging a step-by-step progression toward the ideal goal. The ideal of freedom was achieved by a gradual narrowing and improving of the conditions of slavery. Thus entrenched injustice and vested interests could be dealt with realistically and overcome gradually. A contemporary ethic of Jewish power also should combine moral utopianism with a pragmatic methodology of perfection. The balancing models of the Exodus and the covenant can serve as guiding principles for power when they are yoked to hard-headed analysis and practical steps toward the desired goals. And, as the classic tradition reminds us, the memory of Jewish suffering is supposed to increase empathy for those who are oppressed or those who will suffer because of Jewish exercise of power.

Memories of being a stranger in Egypt, in medieval Europe, in a Muslim *mellah* should be guiding Jews who set policy vis-a-vis the Arab minority in Israel. The memories are specifically intended to create greater concern for the other. Thus Meir Kahane correctly summons Jews to keep the memory of the Holocaust vividly before them in setting policy. But he reverses the ethical direction of the classic tradition in allowing the pain of remembered suffering to deaden Jewish conscience. To encourage Jews to turn Arabs into refugees or into victims of violence is to continue the Holocaust, not oppose it.

. . . . . .

Identifying Anti-Semitism; Another Judgment of Power

In the past, anti-Semitism has been an ever-present factor in others' responses to the Jewish situation, and the phenomenon persists. The very fact the Jews were excluded from power justified the assumption that discrimination was a prima facie factor when Jews were denied their needs. Now that Jews are involved in governmental and political processes on a day-to-day basis, a host of differences and legitimate conflicts of interest and needs are bound to occur. Operating in the realm of power, Jews must resist the tendency to invoke anti-Semitism as the explanation for opponents' behavior.

In going to Bitburg in 1985, Ronald Reagan was guilty of moral insensitivity by equating victims and murderers. He should be faulted for offering premature reconciliation and shallow foregiveness—but not for anti-Semitism. By meeting with Kurt Waldheim in 1987, Pope John Paul II was guilty of tawdry associations and of putting Vatican realpolitik considerations ahead of moral concerns—but not of anti-Semitism. All the more so, those who vote against Jewish interests or specific societal, legislative, or governmental policies should be presumed innocent of anti-Semitic intent unless they prove otherwise. Premature or excessive invocation of the specter of anti-Semitism can cripple Jews' capacity to see their own inevitable errors or pretensions and deaden their sensitivity to inflicting pain on others.

In normal political processes, groups and even good friends disagree intensely on specific policies from time to time. People of goodwill need the assurance that they can disagree with Jews without incurring spiritual "nuclear retaliation," that is, an escalation to the ultimate denunciation that they are guilty of anti-Semitism. Anti-Semitism is still stigmatized by association with past hatred and the Holocaust. When Jews were powerless, this obloquy was a verbal weapon to be hurled at persecutors when there was nothing else to do. Now that Jews have other levers to evoke proper treatment, so grave a moral charge as anti-Semitism is best used with great restraint. Stamping others' behavior with this absolute seal of disapproval blinds judgment; in fact, the other side may have a point. Too quick a resort to the charge of anti-Semitism weakens the future impact of such a finding. It alienates the innocent and overlooks the fact that today's opponents may be tomorrow's supporters.

The most problematic application of this principle is in dealing with opposition to Israel's policies. There is legitimate disagreement with Israel, but it has not been easy to separate it from anti-Semitism.

First of all, many anti-Semites seek to mask and dignify their behavior by defining it as anti-Zionism. Most such haters betray their true colors by their language or actions, as when Russia's anti-Zionist rhetoric turns to libeling the Talmud or when hijackers segregate all Jewish passengers, not just Israelis, or when terrorists open fire on synagogues in France or Turkey. Jews have to be on guard against semantic smokescreens. This makes it even harder to separate out legitimate opposition to Zionist policies. In any event, blanket condemnation of Zionism as against opposition to specific Zionist policies is ipso facto anti-Semitic. Generic anti-Zionism opposes the Jewish right to national self-determination in contrast to the treatment of other nationalisms where people condemn specific acts or policies but do not deny the basic right to peoplehood and sovereign dignity.

However, not every Israeli policy touches upon fundamental existence. As Israel's use of diplomacy and military force becomes more the expression of statecraft than of immediate self-defense or survival, there is more room for legitimate criticism and opposition. Open debate is as important to Israel's moral health as to the development of accurate intelligence and effective policy formation.

On the other hand, since Israel is functioning in the real world, its morality must be exercised and judged in that arena. A normal country—let alone one like Israel that is continually threatened—will not survive if it ties its hands with absolute moral strictures and does not adjust to the pressures of power and the threats posed by its enemies. Using this reasoning, the United States Supreme Court ruled that those dedicated to the overthrow of the system are not entitled to all the constitutional guarantees. To rule otherwise would be to turn constitutional rights into a cover for an assault designed to destroy them. Those who insist that Israel must live by absolute morality are similarly perverting morality, turning it into a battering ram for destruction. If you insist that Israel's right to exist *depends* on its being perfect, then you are making common cause with the anti-Semites. Obviously, there is a difference whether the individual making those absolute judgments is a sworn enemy of the Jewish people or a devoted and spiritual Jew who cannot abide the limits of the flesh. Imposing absolute messianic demands on flesh-and-blood people in an unredeemed world does not bring the Messiah closer; rather it endangers the fragile first blossoms of Jewish redemption.

Why is this moral absolutism deemed to be "anti-Semitic" rather than "immoral"? Because this insistence discriminates against Jews. Israel is the only nation that is expected to always live only by the highest moral standards. Since it is impossible to survive with these standards in today's world, Israel, by its very existence, must inevitably be condemned as a guilty nation. Israel then becomes the only nation whose right to exist is denied on the grounds that it has not lived up to ideal standards. What makes this all so insidious is that some individual moralists who profess a love for Israel as well as committed Jews push these standards, as do overt anti-Semites. The sponsorship makes the judgments harder to resist. Those who weaken respect for Israel through judgments based on these standards of perfection are, de facto, collaborating with those who seek to destroy Israel for less noble motives. Noble fellow-traveling with anti-Semitism may be more dangerous than ignoble anti-Semitism because it is more persuasive. By making total demands, moral absolutists destroy the partial good that is possible. The ultimate immorality is to obliterate the difference between the righteous-but-flawed and the wicked, and by moral exaggeration, pave the way for the destruction of the righteous.

On Being Special

One question remains: Why the continuous insistence that Israel and Jews not be held to an absolute ethical standard? Is not the Jewish covenant that has guided Jewish existence throughout history, that is the great source of Jewish influence on the world, a covenant that imposes special expectations on the Jews? Did not the Prophets hold Israel to this higher standard? "Of all the families of the earth, I have known you singularly, therefore I will call you to account for all your sins" (Amos 3:2). Did not the Torah make it unequivocally clear that failure to live up to the covenant will lead to expulsion from the land of Israel?

The answer to all these questions is: yes. But the prophetic demand operates in a convenantal context. Demands and commandments are not external; they are ethically rooted in the relationship and behavior of their covenantal partners. Otherwise, law is coercion and torment instead of blessing and love. In the biblical period, the prophet could legitimately assure Israel that those who obeyed the Lord's instruction would be saved even from world powers and overwhelming force! (cf. Isa. 37:5–7, 33–38). Correspondingly, those who violated the covenant would be spat out by the land that is uniquely the locus of divine presence. Because the land is in the eye of God, the land's capacity to maintain life is sustained sacramentally (Deut. 11:12–25). In turn, the land responds to Israel's behavior by blessing or cursing, accepting or expelling the Jewish people.

Today we live after the Holocaust. This event is a clear signal that the divine will not intervene to save miraculously. In this tragic event is a divine call to humanity to take up full responsibility for accomplishing the covenant and for stopping the forces of evil. The divine decision not to intervene to save the righteous morally invalidates any divine right to expel a people that does not live up to the covenant fully. There are people whose religious fervor leads them to disregard reality considerations in their actions—including calculation of the balance of power and the effects of policies. There are people who, in the name of God or covenant, make absolute moral judgments on Israel—while ignoring the pragmatics of ethical standards or the impact of their words on support for Israel. In the light of the Holocaust, both types are guilty of irresponsibility and of deafness to divine instruction. Repeating the prophetic dicta that make possession of the land conditional on obedience and a preset standard of perfection constitutes not upholding divine authority but an attempt to hold God to an earlier stage of relationship. Such views are regressive in that they forgo a responsibility now being offered to humans and pass it back to God. This borders on clinging to infantilization or childlike behavior in the face of being called to adulthood. Such clinging is often motivated not by love of the other but love of one's self or the desire to be cared for by others.

But did not Israel's unique quality and higher morality garner special support for its existence from the world, particularly the United States, and, above all, from the Jewish people? The answer to this question also is: yes. Therefore, Israel should not lightly give up the special moral standards that have always guided its actions. It would be foolish to dissipate the enormous fund of goodwill and respect that its moral stature and traditional Jewish norms have given Israel. But what Israel does voluntarily because of its internalized moral values dare not be demanded of it on pain of delegitimation. After the Holocaust, neither humanity nor God has the right to require that Israel justify its existence by a perfect morality.

It was miraculous enough that Jews chose to live and recreate life after experiencing total degradation and death. To speak of Israel's "mere survival" or to dismiss it if it becomes just a "Levantine state" is to miss the incredible significance of its witness to life and redemption just by existing normally. The old Zionist ideal of normalizing the Jews is finally coming true. In a true Jewish twist, the normality is not only challenged and isolated abnormally, but it witnesses to the world in extraordinary fashion. Those who insist on an absolutely spiritually superior Israel and are embarrassed by the moral ambiguities of the actual Jewish body politic show how little they understand spirituality. There must be a body to embody ideals. Even in its cloddish or earthiest moments, this particular body's existence in defiance of the forces of hatred and history is a testimony to the Hidden God's concern and a tribute to the infinite commitment of life of a people. By existing and overcoming death, the survival of Israel's body points to the legitimacy of covenantal hope and the power of the transcendent.

Israel has the right—and thus far it has the record—to act by a higher moral standard in accordance with past norms of Jewish values. But now that it is a flesh-and-blood state, it can only act and be judged in the context of the real world. Israel can be 5 percent better, or 10 percent more restrained, perhaps 20 percent more judgmental of its own behavior than the rest of the world. Achieving such a level would make Israel one of the greatest nations in the world morally—but this begins to approach the limits of survivability. Put it this way: If Israel proves to be 10 percent better ethically than the rest of the world, it will be "a light unto the nations." If it proves to be 25 percent better, it will bring the Messiah. If it is 50 percent better, it will be dead.

No one and no group can survive in this world if they act 50 percent better than the rest of humanity. Therefore, to insist on perfection—that Israel must never fail the highest standard—is to deny its right to exist. Since Israel is practically the only country in the world that is continually delegitimated by armed neighbors and whose legitimacy is continually assaulted by overwhelming majorities at the United Nations, insistence that it act perfectly constitutes incitement to destruction. The double standard applied to Israel constitutes a particularly vicious form of anti-Semitism—collaboration with attempted genocide—in the name of morality! Jews must be particularly alert to resist this double standard because it appeals to a deep-rooted instinct and a two-thousand-year-old conditioned response that was appropriate in a different, that is, powerless, context.

The End of the Double Standard

In the summer of 1982, Senator Joseph Biden was asked why he spoke so critically to Menachem Begin, then Israel's prime minister, when he visited Washington, D.C. Biden explained that predecessor liberals, like Hubert Humphrey, had viscerally supported Israel because they had experienced the Holocaust through firsthand encounter. He was a member of a new generation that judged Israel more by the cooler standards of realpolitik and its congruence with American interests, so he felt no inhibition in criticizing it. Biden failed to grasp the other consequence of his judging Israel by the standards of realpolitik—that is: Israel had the right to use force and strategic considerations to meet those tests. Israel recovered from the debilitating effect of judgments made according to the double standard during the Lebanon war. The recent relentless attacks on Israel in the media and in the university would prove that we must make an end to the double standard before it collaborates with the enemies who seek to make an end of Israel.

If anything, the fading of the absolute taboo power of the Holocaust, which is also manifest in various outbreaks of anti-Semitism worldwide, means that Israel should be granted greater moral leeway. Israel remains a country which, if it loses a war, would be wiped out. The Jewish experience in the Holocaust shows that this is no idle threat. The model of the breaking of the killing taboos vis-à-vis Jews continues to influence behavior. Were this threat removed, more criticism of Israel would be proper. As long as Israel's basic legitimacy is not beyond contest or threat, well-meaning people with impressive moral agendas (or media trying to cheer on the underdog) can be paving the way for a new Holocaust by playing on the double standard and weakening support in its lifeline country, the United States of America.

Israelis continue to judge their own moral performance by a higher standard because the memories of Jewish suffering and of the Holocaust are still vivid and motivating. This is as it should be. The Holocaust should not be invoked just in self-serving ways. Its ethical implications must be used to judge Israel's behavior as well.

One of the deeply disappointing aspects of Menachem Begin's response to the Beirut massacre in 1983 was his failure to see the incident in the light of the Holocaust. He was so busy fending off the hypocritical and dissembling attacks on Israel that he failed to summon up the Holocaust memories of innocents killed while others remained apathetic. To paraphrase Golda Meir, one day we may forgive the anti-Semites for applying the double standard to Israel, but we will not forgive them for turning us into defensive rationalizers when something really went wrong.

In 1983, the overwhelming bulk of the Jewish people reacted as they should have—with anguish at the sight of the bodies of Palestinian men, women, and children mercilessly slaughtered, with shame and anger at those who did it and those who may have been guilty of permitting it. The Israeli population insisted on an inquiry. They refused to allow the hostility of those who seek only to indict Israel to distract the Jewish state from correcting its sins of omission or commission.

It took America, one of the great countries of the world, years to overcome the obstacles to a Watergate inquiry. It took the people of Israel one week to get the government to investigate the slaughter. Not a single general was held accountable for the My Lai massacre, although it was carried out by an American battalion. The Kahan Commission found no involvement by Israelis in planning or executing the Sabra-Shatila massacre. Yet, for the sin of omission, or failing to anticipate, the defense minister was forced to resign his post and three generals—the chief of staff, the director of military intelligence, and the division commander, Beirut area—suffered irreparable damage to their careers. The head of the Mossad, the foreign minister, and the head of the Northern Command of the Army were censured. All this shows the vitality of Jewish conscience and Israel's democracy—which is the opposite of what the anti-Semites and the false prophets claimed.

This same standard of ethical memory suggests that Israel must seek ways of finding room for the Palestinians' dignity and national identity. Whether this takes the form of local autonomy or an Israeli-Jordanian condominium or an independent Palestinian state is a secondary question. The form should grow directly out of historical process, direct negotiations, and the ability of the Palestinians to win the confidence of the Israeli public and world Jews. The Holocaust standard suggests that the Palestinians must earn this trust by getting rid of their murderous leadership and making crystal clear beyond doubt, by actions and words, that they intend to live in peace with Israel.

To ask Israel to allow Palestinian self-expression in return for anything less than ironclad, Israeli-enforced arrangements with new leaders is again to apply a double standard to the Jewish state. No other state in the world whose ruling population is a majority of the inhabitants would be asked to turn over land or power to enemies sworn to destroy it. The tragic clash of Jewish historical destiny and Arab nationalism continues. To incite to suicide in the name of morality or sympathy for the underdog is grotesque.

To Strive Together

There are no easy solutions in sight. Taking power has opened the door to an endless chain of struggles and decisions. Survival of the body and survival of the soul are at risk every step of the way. This is a task that can only be properly undertaken by a partnership of Israel and the Jews of the world, with the United States and with all decent non-Jews of the world.

American and other Diaspora Jews have gotten a relatively free ride on this long march to power. For a long time, Diaspora Jews thought of Israel as their surrogate for the Jewish assumption of power. Now the recognition is growing that they cannot pass the buck. In the last two decades, American Jewish political action has become a major factor in United States policy. And if there were any Diaspora Jews who "imagined to themselves that they would escape to the royal sanctuary from the fate of all the Jews" (Esther 4:13) then they, too, are increasingly disabused of this notion by the dynamics of history.

During the struggles over arms packages for Arab countries, both Presidents Carter and Reagan were not above trying to intimidate American Jewry. Both presidents (or front men for them) dropped open hints that American Jews had a conflict of loyalty in the matter. True, the charges were not followed up and, later, were even repudiated by designated spokesmen. But the Pollard Affair raised the issue all over again. Pollard acted as an individual, and his actions have been repudiated almost universally by American Jews. Still, there have been reports of Jews excluded from certain areas of foreign or defense policy. This is wrong morally and offensive to democracy—but the bottom line remains. Whether tacitly or openly, the legitimacy and acceptance of American Jews in the United States will be on the line in the struggles over American support for Israel.

For decades, Diaspora Jews basked in the sunshine of approval for Israel; with every triumph of the "new Jews" of Israel, Jews all over the world gained standing and respectability. Now, if the Diaspora assumes some of the burden of vulnerability in Jewish history, morally that is only right. The attacks on French Jewry and its synagogues, the murderous assault on the Neve Shalom synagogue in Turkey, the upsurge of anti-Semitism in Italy in the wake of the Gaza–West Bank clashes, show that, in fact, the risks of being Jewish go beyond the shores of the State of Israel. Similarly, Russian Jews who have stood up in solidarity with Israel have been isolated and punished. Inevitably, they opted to return to the body of world Jewry, thereby bringing down on themselves further persecution and a general assault on the loyalty and integrity of all Russian Jews. One fate and one destiny is the logic of Jewish unity and the price of Jewish power.

There are many Jews who will be unnerved by this prospect. Some will distance themselves because of indifference and lack of commitment and seek only to cover themselves. Others will evoke moralistic judgments on Israel to come to the same conclusion. Jewish history shows that the real dividing line will not be drawn by Israel's behavior or even by whether one agrees with that behavior or not, but by a simple principle: whether one is prepared to pay the costs of Jewish destiny.

What, then, can a Jew who has embraced Jewish destiny say? Israel remains the central theater of collective Jewish action. It is *the* place where Jewish religion and Jewish morality are put to the test because there a Jewish majority decides policy. The results can neither be evaded nor denied nor can responsibility be divided and diluted. Nothing can separate me from Israel. It is my people's statement of life and the vehicle to the future of a world perfected. I will be active to assure its safety and will intervene to help it perform as morally and humanely as possible. It is not a matter of "us" and "them." Some of the battles of Jewish power and life will be fought in the Diaspora. Let there be a covenantal partnership between all Jews— and all people who care—to assure that the power is exercised for life and with full respect for the lives of others.

My unqualified support means that I am responsible when Israel's force is misapplied or hurts others. I cannot pass the buck. I will remonstrate and criticize when Israel acts wrongly; I will plead for change, particularly "within the family" and in a manner that will not endanger its existence. I have confidence that Israel will err, but like all democracies, that it will correct itself. I cannot withhold my money, my visits, sending my children, because its travail is my travail, even as its triumphs are my triumphs. Building Israel is not a one-year campaign—or a one-lifetime mission— because the goal is nothing less than redemption, the perfection of life. This is not a onetime pledge because there is no one achievement to resolve the challenge of *tikkum olam* (the transformation of the world). This is a calling to life and power. Ahead lie lifetimes of work for myself, my children, and generations yet unborn.

The bulk of committed Jews have made the challenge of assuming power their premier concern. They have proven their seriousness by their pattern of philanthropic giving and political activity, by the way they express religious loyalties and moral response. They ask only for help in confronting the issue together.

Here, then, are the parameters of the new condition. Jewish powerlessness is absolutely incompatible with Jewish existence. But Jewish power is incompatible with absolute Jewish moral purity.

Moral maturity consists of grasping both these truths without evasion or illusion. Moral responsibility consists of the continuous struggle to contain both truths without letting them paralyze either the will to power or our moral faculties. To take power is to give up innocence and take up greater responsibility. If we understand that we are pledged to the covenant of life for everyone and that we are accountable to a divine covenantal partner who dwells "with the oppressed and the humble in spirit," then we will be more self-critical and humane in the exercise of strength.

By any objective measurement, taken in the context of the real world where Israel operates, Israel is—and is struggling to remain—a model of taking power without abusing neighbors, of resisting assault without turning cruel or yielding democracy, of building a humane and fairly distributed society without tyranny and without uprooting the traditional values of a people. On the other hand, there have been sufficient errors and failure along the way to show the human limitations of Israel and its moral imperfections.

The growth of Palestinian nationalism and of Jewish attachment to the West Bank have generated growing friction, hostility and reaction, suffering, and a sense of clash of destiny. The extended Gaza and West Bank riots and the Israeli efforts to suppress the violence have created a powerful force for hardening of heart on both sides. This means that all those determined to link power and ethics, to reconcile Israeli life and Arab rights should redouble their efforts to make room for the security and dignity of all. Nor is this a time for despair. At some point, Arab rage or fundamentalism will come up against the limits of reality—Jewish power, United States support—and choose the road of peace and life together. At some point, Jewish anger and fundamentalism will shift to acceptance of peace and sacrifices for the sake of living as neighbors—as occurred when Sadat came to Israel in peace.

At one point in history, hatred and loathing were the dominant attitudes of Frenchmen and Germans toward each other. This was the outcome of three consecutive major wars between the two nations. Now stable structures of peace and trade and culture between them have brought a new alliance and widespread mutual regard into being. The geographical and demographic closeness of Israel and the West Bank suggests that the ultimate scenario for peace will be more open borders, more flexible citizenship, more religious pluralism than anywhere else in the world. Isn't that the way the Promised Land should be special? At present, that ultimate situation is further away than in most places in the world, but that is only the measure of the task to be done, of the greatness to be achieved.

With all, Israel has made remarkable progress since 1948. Should Jewish sovereignty be reconciled with social justice and Arab dignity in peace, then the whole world will learn a lesson in taming nationalism and turning it into a blessing. Should Jewish, Muslim, and Christian religious-national needs all find fulfillment in Jerusalem, then this will be a model of how renewal of faith is a blessing to the world. It will show the way that tradition can increase communal love instead of civil strife. This will be a Torah for humanity that goes forth from Zion, a healing word of God that sounds from Jerusalem. The alternatives—genocide or regression to an earlier human passivity, back to the age of acceptance of a status quo of suffering, poverty, and oppression—are not acceptable. We must believe that once the divine word of redemption and perfection goes forth, it will not return in vain. Once humans have taken on the task of freedom their hopes and conflicts must be realized—for good. The task is to persist with hope and realism until the final perfection.

In meeting the challenge of power, the Jewish people again is the embodiment of humanity. In its body and history, the dilemmas of humanity are reflected and illuminated. There is no political security for Israel yet, and there are no moral guarantees, either. Jews are not immune to the errors and corruptions of the human condition. I would venture my life that by its total behavior Israel will be a model and a light unto the nations.

Jewish hands have grasped the wheel of Jewish destiny. Jews will bear the shame and the glory. But the blessing will be for all the nations of the earth.

30

Israel: Toward a New Concept
of Community

JUDITH PLASKOW

For the last twenty years, Jewish feminists in the United States have been calling the American Jewish community to a truly pluralistic egalitarianism. We have demanded of the community not simply equal access for women to all the rights and responsibilities of Jewish life but, more importantly, equality in and through our particularity—a particularity that women ourselves will articulate and define. Jewish texts and Jewish religious and communal institutions have too often taken maleness as normative, dropping women's unique history and spiritual insights, attitudes, and feelings from the long chain of Jewish memory. Jewish feminists declare that this is no longer acceptable. We ask that the Jewish tradition become *wholly* Jewish, that it incorporate the suppressed history and experiences of women into the memory and ongoing life of Judaism and, in doing so, transform the tradition.

The fact that this demand of Jewish feminists is analogous to the demands both of minority feminists and of Jews in the modern West brings into focus the enormous obstacles to creating communities rich in diversity and accountable to different perspectives. The projection of women as Other and the insistence on the part of liberal Jews that Jewish women adapt ourselves to a male tradition echoes the Otherness of the Jew in the larger society and the insistence that Jews "melt" into the prevailing culture as a condition of our citizenship. Similarly, the feminist community, despite its explicit commitment to inclusiveness, has repeatedly offered accounts of women's experience that falsely universalize a white middle-class (race and class) perspective and expected minority women to conform to its generalizations. It seems that in so many contexts, difference is perceived as something to be feared; the recognition of difference is fraught with guilt;[1] and community building is identified with the eradication of difference and the fostering of uniformity.

To this human heritage of difficulty with diversity, Jews bring our own long history of suspicion and ranking of difference. Thinking of itself as a "kingdom of priests and a holy nation," the Jewish people from its beginnings understood its own holiness partly in contradistinction to the beliefs and behavior of the surrounding nations. The key notion of *chosenness,* so central to Jewish self-understanding, expressed itself both in shunning foreign gods and morality and in setting up a host of internal separations that set apart distinct and unequal objects, states, and modes of being. On a religious level, to be a holy people was both to be different from one's neighbors and to distinguish between pure and impure, Sabbath and week, kosher and nonkosher, and male and female. On a social level, the Otherness of women was the first and most persistent among many inequalities that have marked Jewish life. Differences in wealth, learning, and observance; differences in cultural background and customs; differences in religious affiliation and understanding have all provided occasions for certain groups of Jews to define themselves as superior to different and nonnormative Others.

The challenge of overcoming this heritage and creating communities that respect and nurture particularity without hierarchy is the very heart of the feminist project, and it is in light of this project that I approach the question of the State of Israel. Committed though I am to a Diaspora context, I cannot as a late-twentieth-century Jew think about the transformation of Jewish community without taking into account the place in the world where Jews have deliberately and self-consciously sought to create a Jewish society. The persistent human difficulties in dealing with difference, the social implications of traditional Jewish attitudes toward difference, the continuities between the modern Jewish construction of difference and historical Jewish treatment of Others all emerge with a special vividness in the context of the State of Israel. The crucial issues of community and diversity with which feminism is concerned take on new urgency in relation to the national community that Jews have created.

The early Zionist vision of an abundant and self-determined Jewish life in continuity and contention with tradition has much to commend it to the feminist imagination. This vision was rooted in awareness of the importance of community and the desire for a community that could nurture its members. Growing out of the experience of emancipation and its failure to end anti-Semitism, Zionism knew the issue of difference and the importance of particularity. In providing an opportunity to bring renewed life to traditional Jewish values while taking seriously the lessons of the modern world, the establishment of a Jewish homeland challenged Jews to create a culturally rich and diverse society on the basis of a new understanding of difference. The fundamental feminist question concerning the State of Israel is whether it has found fresh ways to accommodate particularity or whether it has instead perpetuated the same hierarchical construction of difference that has hitherto shaped Jewish communal existence.

While the early Zionists imagined an egalitarian community in Palestine formed by Jews from the many lands of dispersion, numerous factors in the development of Israel have conspired against the realization of their vision. The complexities and conflicts of Zionist ideology and history, and the story of the many forces at work in shaping the state are well beyond the scope of this essay.[2] But what is important from a feminist perspective is that the enduring inequalities of the Jewish community have found new and complex embodiment in the laws and structures of a nation-state struggling to secure its existence and survival.

With reference to women, for example, the establishment of a Jewish homeland provided an unparalleled opportunity to "start afresh," building a community and nation in which women would define and shape Jewish history side-by-side with men. Since most early Zionists had little sympathy with the strictures on women's roles delineated by religious teaching, their understanding of Jewish community seemed to promise a new beginning for women who wanted to live full Jewish lives and at the same time free themselves from traditional Jewish restrictions. Yet while the *myth* surrounding Jewish Israeli women is that their aspirations for liberation were realized, in fact sexual equality never was taken seriously in Israel as an important social goal.[3] The image of pioneer women draining swamps, changing the face of the land, fighting enemies alongside male comrades, projects as *reality* the *hopes* of the first Zionist women settlers. These women envisioned a society in which differences would be treated equally, in which they could bring their full physical and intellectual capabilities to all aspects of common life.[4] The Labor Zionist movement with which they identified, however, subordinated women's emancipation to the overriding project of establishing a Jewish home. Just as was the case with many liberal Jewish institutions in the Diaspora, sexual equality was taken for granted in principle and ignored in the concrete. Women found that many male settlers simply could not comprehend or take seriously women's desire to build the land side-by-side with them. Even in the communes that were forerunners of the kibbutz, women were assigned limited, primarily domestic, roles and were considered to work for the men rather than being full members of the collectives.[5] Indeed, on the kibbutzim themselves, while there were women who fought for and won the right to do men's work, no one ever suggested that men ought to be in the kitchen and nursery; the sexual division of labor went unquestioned.[6]

With the establishment of the State of Israel in 1948, important new factors came into play that served to consolidate and intensify sexual inequality. The role of Orthodox parties in the formation and governance of the state guaranteed that, even for the non-Orthodox majority, important areas of women's lives would be shaped by Orthodox patriarchalism. Israel has a declaration of independence granting "equal social and political rights for all citizens, irrespective of religion, race, or sex"—but this declaration functions only as a statement of general principles that does not have the force of law. Lacking a constitution, Israel ensures the rights of its citizens through statutes that are open to ongoing modification. In 1951, Israel passed a Women's Equal Rights Law, but within the law itself severely limited its application by exempting marriage and divorce. When in 1953 the Orthodox establishment was granted complete control of these areas, equal rights for Jewish women were effectively annulled.[7] While secularist compromises with Orthodox parties have had a profound effect on many areas of Israeli life, in the case of women, they have functioned to give institutional and legal sanction to some of the most disabling aspects of *halakhah* (Jewish law).

Another factor that has profoundly shaped women's lives is Israel's ongoing concern for survival and the consequent emergence of its citizens' army as a major institution in the Israeli state. While in this case also, myth would have it that Israel is one of the few countries in the world to include women in the military on equal terms, here too myth obscures a very different reality. Of the 50 percent of women who serve at all in this major socializing institution, the majority do the same kind of office work they perform in the civilian market. Rather than serving alongside men, women replace them in clerical, switchboard, and social services so that men are freed for combat. Women's jobs in the army accord with a traditional understanding of female roles. The name of the women's corps—*Chen,* meaning charm—indicates the expectation that women are to humanize the military, strengthening the morale of male soldiers and making the army a "home away from home." Sexual relationships, formally ignored, are informally encouraged, and women are to provide amenities and forms of support that men are accustomed to in a patriarchal family.[8]

This supposed humanizing and softening effect of women on the armed services signals the presence of a "cult of true womanhood" at work in Israel.[9] In a situation of continuing profound insecurity, women and the home come to be constructed as antidotes to, and havens from, the harsh realities of Israeli life. As the exemption of married and pregnant women from national service indicates, the role of women in the country's defense is less important than their role in the home. Or rather, the crucial role of women in Israel's survival is the role of mother. Living constantly in the fear of war and concerned that a growing Palestinian population threatens the Jewish character of the Israeli state, many in Israel see procreation as women's most important contribution to the Israeli future.[10] Thus the vision of equality in difference that was shared by at least some of Israel's founders has given way to traditional forms of women's subordination, now shaped and colored by the exigencies of an embattled nation-state.

The subordination of women is not the only hierarchical differentiation in Diaspora Jewish life that has found expression in Israel. The relationship between Ashkenazim (Jews of Eastern European origin) and Mizrahim (Jews from Africa, Asia, and the Middle East) is also hierarchically ordered, with the "first" Israel (Ashkenazim) setting itself up as normative and expecting the "second" Israel to adapt to Ashkenazi standards. Like the subordination of women, this hierarchy is also a product of the Diaspora, with the politics of statehood giving new form to older class and ethnic divisions. In the Diaspora, Jews of different cultural and national backgrounds regarded one another as Other! There were hierarchies within the Eastern European Jewish community and also between that community and outsiders. Jews from Lithuania looked down on Jews from Galicia and also the religiously different Mizrahim. Sephardim in turn saw themselves as superior to Jews of Eastern European origin. In addition, each community had its own class structure, based on inequalities in wealth and learning. In Israel, traditional ethnic and cultural differences came to coincide with class differences in a way that realigned and solidified the divisions of the Diaspora community.

Zionist belief in the fundamental unity of the Jewish people was put to the test quite soon after 1948 by the influx of great numbers of oriental immigrants from many Arab lands. Viewed with consternation and contempt by the Ashkenazi founders of the state, these "primitive" people from "backward countries" were expected to modernize and Westernize, acculturating to Israeli society by taking on European customs and values.[11] Since this process was not to be reciprocal—Ashkenazi Israelis were not to learn from or be influenced by the culture of Middle Eastern Jews—Ashkenazim effectively identified their own interests with the interests of the state. The resulting glaring social and economic discrimination against oriental Jews and their exclusion from Israeli leadership have been important items on the Israeli national agenda for many years.[12] While the relationship between Ashkenazim and Mizrahim has shifted and been complicated by the oriental community's important role in the election of Likud (in 1977), this shift has not fundamentally altered the discomfitting role of ethnic pluralism in the Jewish state. In a situation in which many activist oriental Jews have themselves been ambivalent about whether they are claiming equality within an Ashkenazi state or demanding recognition of a separate oriental Jewish identity,[13] Israel has been no more effective in mining the creative possibilities inherent in differences among Jews than have Jews in the Diaspora.

It is the Palestinians, however, rather than the Mizrahi Jews, who pose the most fundamental test of Israel's capacity to deal with difference, and whose situation highlights the connection between the creating of hierarchies within the Jewish community and between that community and others. Palestinian Israelis constitute a segregated and peripheral underclass whose grievances, unlike those of the Mizrahim, seldom capture the attention of the wider society. Formally granted equal rights by the same Declaration of Human Rights that gave equality to women, Palestinians are in fact excluded from the central symbols and institutions of the Jewish state. Both the ordinary operation of Israel's major institutions and specific government programs and policies have fostered the isolation and internal fragmentation of the Arab community and its economic dependence on the Jewish majority.[14] While the operation of these dynamics is complex, massive, and subtle, the barring of Moslem Arabs (the vast majority of the Arab population) from military service can serve as a symbol of the Palestinian population's isolation and lack of access to important resources. The question of Palestinian army service is a difficult one, tied up with broader questions of Jewish Israeli security and self-definition. Yet since the army is a key institution in building a sense of Israeli identity, transmitting a wide range of skills, and providing entrée to jobs and public assistance programs, the exclusion of Palestinians from the army means they are "cut off from the major dynamic processes of social integration and mobility which exists in Israel."[15]

The contradictions of a democracy in which 17 percent of all citizens are suspected as a fifth column and subjected to discrimination are vastly intensified by Israel's direct military rule of over a million and a half Palestinians on the West Bank and in Gaza. In the occupied territories, there is no pretense of democracy. Palestinians have no control over the government that determines the conditions of their existence, no right of appeal against the judgments of military courts, no secure rights to the land on which they live.[16] While these conditions are supposedly temporary, pending a permanent peace settlement, the Palestinian uprising has dramatized the untenability and injustice of such rule and the profound effects of twenty years of it on Jewish Israeli attitudes and values. Those Jews who favor annexing the occupied territories do not imagine offering Palestinians equal rights within a "Greater Israel." An increasingly vocal and militant religious right claims divine sanction for Israeli expansion—expansion that leaves no room for non-Jewish citizens within a Jewish state. As some religious nationalists understand it, equality of rights is at best an alien, that is, European, democratic principle, and at worst, a violation of the biblical commandment to exterminate Amalek. Thus twenty years of military rule has created a situation in which Israeli government policy is to treat occupied Palestinians as intruders in their own land, and in which some Jews are actually advocating expelling or killing Palestinians in the name of chosenness.[17]

While the conflicts and inequalities between Jews and Palestinians, and Eastern European and oriental Jews have their own distinct origins and manifestations, they are also interstructured with the inequalities between women and men. As a few examples can make clear, the fact that many Israeli women are Palestinians or oriental Jews means that the relations between men and women are shaped partly by these other rifts; conversely, the subordination of women means that anti-Arab or Mizrahi discrimination falls differently on women than on men. Thus when Palestinian society was radically disrupted by the creation of Israel in 1948, one reaction of Palestinian men was to maintain cultural stability by increasing their traditional control over Palestinian women. As this control has relaxed and Palestinian women's independence has increased over the last twenty years, Israeli politicians have sought to control Palestinian women's political activism by appealing to the traditional Arab value system in relation to women.[18] Or, if we look at the role of (Jewish) women in the Israeli army, it is striking that of the approximately 25 percent of women exempted from service for lack of basic qualifications (insufficient level of literacy, inability to tolerate discipline), almost all are oriental. Just as most Palestinians are excluded from the important integrative and social functions the army performs, so are large numbers of oriental Jewish women.[19] Or, as Israeli occupation of the West Bank and Gaza has brought the number of Palestinians under Jewish Israeli control to 30 percent of the population, the pressure on Jewish women to bear large numbers of children has increased greatly. The Jewish Israeli woman must serve as a breeder not only to supply future soldiers to the army but also to do her part in the "demographic war" for a continued Jewish majority in the state.[20]

As we look at this picture of interstructured hierarchical differentiations in Israeli society, a striking analogy emerges. The embattled Israeli Jew ignoring the inequities of Israeli society bears a disquieting resemblance to the oppressed ghetto Jew ignoring the internal inequalities in the Jewish community.[21] In the ghetto situation, God was believed both to vindicate Jewish suffering and to define and justify the subordination of women within Judaism. The rage engendered by male powerlessness was projected onto women, who become the doubled Other in a community of Others. In Israel, Israeli Jews wish to see themselves as new and free people, but in fact are as surrounded by enemies as the Jews of the Diaspora. In this situation, they claim a struggle in which they have "no choice" as warrant for oppressive policies toward Palestinians and for diversion of financial and moral resources from the resolution of internal social conflicts to the military budget. As in the Diaspora situation, struggle with the enemy outside also fosters the oppression of women, whose theoretical equality is sacrificed to the needs of a beleaguered state.

It seems that the Jewish experience of oppression has led not to the just exercise of power by Jews in power, but to the Jewish repetition of strategies of domination. The many forms of oppression to which Jews have been subject, from denial of fundamental rights and outright expropriation of resources, to lack of respect for Jewish culture, to discrimination in housing and employment, are recapitulated within and between various groups in Israel. Not only has the Jewish historical experience not served as a lesson and warning, but past oppression has even been used as a justification for the right to oppress others. Past Jewish suffering is presumed to confer a moral purity that covers over and excuses moral weakness and rage.[22]

If this cycle in which oppressed becomes oppressor is psychologically comprehensible and historically familiar, it is, nevertheless, not inevitable. While the Israeli government often has set aside internal debate about the nature of Israel in the name of building and protecting the state, Israel's citizens have shown a persistent and remarkable willingness to discuss and reassess the purpose of Is-rael's existence and to question the values that informed its actions.[23] Books and articles examining and criticizing various aspects of the state are widely read and vigorously debated, and numerous organizations have been formed to deal with the inequalities of Israeli society. Thus alongside discrimination against women and Mizrahim, there exist battered women's shelters, the Israeli feminist move-ment, numerous self-help organizations for Mizrahim, and groups working to facilitate Mizrahi and Ashkenazi cultural integration.[24] Alongside the multifaceted discrimination against Israel's Arab citizens and governmental unwillingness to consider the existence of a Palestinian state, there exist literally dozens of organi-zations working for peace and Arab-Jewish reconciliation, trying to create a future in which Jews and Palestinians can peacefully and respectfully coexist.[25] Moreover, just as the various forms of discrimination in Israel are interstructured, so efforts toward ending discrimination seek to form coalitions across various structural lines. In numerous woman-to-woman dialogue groups, for example, Jewish and Arab women attempt to speak to one another directly of the conflicts between them and the pain and complexity of their lives. At the UN Decade for Women conference in Nairobi, Jewish and Palestinian women from Israel and the Dias-pora sponsored a public workshop on the Arab-Israeli struggle attended by four hundred women from around the world.[26]

These groups and organizations working toward a new vision of community shift the boundaries of community, creating out of the multiple allegiances and identities that define the modern experience communities committed to a common purpose, able to address the issues that unite and divide them. Rather than leaving Ashke-nazim and Mizrahim, Jews and Palestinians confronting each other across an abyss, projects for justice, peace, and dialogue forge—however temporarily—a shared Israeli, or woman's, or Middle Eastern identity that, without denying differences, places these groups in a new context. Projects like these enact the conviction that difference need not be expressed in dominance or strife. If people work to make it so, shared oppression and resistance to oppression can be a bridge to mutual understanding and joint action. There may be no guarantee that the oppressed will not become oppressors, but it is nonetheless possible to forge links between oppres-sion and the commitment to justice by careful and conscious insistence on remem-bering and using one's experience precisely for that purpose.

While the impulse toward self-questioning that characterizes many in Israel has sometimes been connected to the notion of chosenness, it is more appropriately linked to particular values central to Jewish memory and to the historical experi-ence of oppression. The recent history of the religious right in Israel would seem to suggest that belief in chosenness can go hand in hand with the worst idolatry of the state and the willingness to justify any sort of abuse of the non-Jewish Other.[27] Over against this willingness lies the pain of oppression experienced in one's own flesh and the injunction of memory: "You shall not wrong or oppress a stranger, for you were strangers in the land of Egypt" (Exod. 22:20, altered). The multiform wrongs that the Jews have experienced, the commitment to remembering these wrongs as part of the struggle against them, and the continuing quest for integrity and self-definition as a community fuel questions about what kind of society the state is fighting to protect and whether there are forms of self-defense that undermine what supposedly is being defended.

If the State of Israel is to find modes of self-preservation compatible with and productive of a just society, it must learn from the whole Jewish experience what makes a society just. Surely, a just society is one in which the rights of minorities are not simply promised but guaranteed in law and in practice, in which the resources of the society are available to and shared by all its members, in which citizens are free from religious coercion, even if it be the coercion of their own tradition. It is a society that recognizes not simply the individual citizens who dwell within it but also the diverse communities, that acknowledges the different needs and traditions of these communities and expects that all will contribute to shaping the character of the nation as a whole. Such internal justice is not possible, moreover, unless a society recognizes the rights of its neighbors and has done its utmost to live in peace with them. The economic, social, and moral costs of military occupation make it incompatible with equity within one's own boundaries. The rightful claim of Palestinians to a land of their own renders occupation profoundly unjust.

Sometimes it seems that the realities of the Israeli occupation are only marginally related to the central agenda of Jewish feminists. Yet if we recognize that different forms of hierarchy and oppression intersect with and reinforce one another, then we must know that none will be abolished until all are addressed. Jewish feminists must apply the vision of community in which difference is nurtured and respected to all communities and all differences with which Jewish feminists are involved. When one group in a community has had the power to rule or speak for all within it, acceptance of difference entails dislodging long-fixed patterns of dominance. Such transformations are never easy, but they promise much, and not simply to those whose experience is obscured or denied by the reigning order. An Israel that honored diversity might transform itself from a fortress state into a country enjoying the energy and resources of a remarkably rich and varied multicultural citizenry, just as Diaspora communities respecting particularity might find themselves with both a broadened and enlivened Jewish memory and present spiritual resources of unexpected depth. If difference is threatening, it also holds power. The struggle to find new models for relating to difference is a struggle to bring the manifold riches of a complex human heritage to the careful nurturing of communal and individual life.

Notes

1. Audre Lorde, *Sister Outsider* (Trumansburg, NY: Crossing Press, 1984).

2. Hertzberg's *The Zionist Idea: A Historical Analysis and Reader* (New York: Doubleday and Herzl Press, 1959) provides an excellent discussion of and sourcebook on the important ideological differences among Zionist thinkers. See also Ben Halpern, *The Idea of the Jewish State,* 2d ed. (Cambridge, MA: Harvard University Press, 1969), chap. 2.

3. Dafna Izraeli, "The Zionist Women's Movement in Palestine, 1911–1927: A Sociological Analysis," *Signs: Journal of Women in Culture and Society* 7 (Autumn 1981): 89; Deborah Bernstein, *The Struggle for Equality: Urban Women Workers in Prestate Israeli Society* (New York: Praeger, 1987), 4–5; Lesley Hazelton, *Israeli Women: The Reality behind the Myths* (New York: Simon and Schuster, 1977), chap. 1; Natalie Rein, *Daughters of Rachel: Women in Israel* (Harmondsworth, Engl.: Penguin Books, 1979), 27–29.

4. Bernstein, *The Struggle for Equality,* 1, 2, 5.

5. Izraeli, "The Zionist Women's Movement in Palestine," 90–95; Bernstein, *The Struggle for Equality,* 16–20; Hazleton, *Israeli Women,* 15–17.

6. Vivian Silver, "Sexual Equality on Kibbutz—Where Did We Go Wrong?" (unpublished paper delivered at the International Conference "Kibbutz and Communes—Past and Future," May 21, 1985); Naomi Fulop, "Women in the Kibbutz: A Jewish Feminist Utopia?" *Shifra* 3 and 4 (Dec. 1986): 33–35; Paula Rayman, *The Kibbutz Community and Nation Building* (Princeton, NJ: Princeton University Press, 1981), 53–54.

7. Tom Segev, *1949: The First Israelis* (New York: The Free Press, 1986), 249–52; Frances Raday, "Equality of Women under Israeli Law," *The Jerusalem Quarterly* 27 (Spring 1983): 81–83; Hazleton, *Israeli Women,* 22–23.

8. Hazleton, *Israeli Women,* 137–51; Nira Yval-Davis, "The Israeli Example," *Loaded Questions: Women in the Military,* ed. W. Chapkis (Amsterdam: Transnational Institute, n.d.), 73–77.

9. This term was used by Barbara Welter to describe the nineteenth-century American image of women's nature and role; *Dimity Convictions: The American Woman in the Nineteenth Century* (Athens, Ohio: Ohio University Press, 1976), chap. 2.

10. Yuval-Davis, "The Israeli Example," 76–77; Nira Yval-Davis, "The Jewish Collectivity and National Reproduction in Israel," *Khamsin* 13 (July 1987): 86–87.

11. Segev, *1949,* 155–61.

12. Sammy Smooha and Yochanan Pere, "The Dynamics of Ethnic Inequalities: The Case of Israel," *Studies of Israeli Society,* vol. 1, *Migration, Ethnicity and Community* (New Brunswick, NJ: Transaction Books, 1980), 167–73; Erik Cohen, "The Black Panthers and Israeli Society," ibid., 147, 149–50.

13. Cohen, "The Black Panthers and Israeli Society," 610–61.

14. Ian Lustick, in *Arabs in the Jewish State: Israel's Control of a National Minority* (Austin: University of Texas Press, 1980), thoroughly analyzes these dynamics. See chap. 3 for discussion of his analytic framework.

15. Ibid., 93–94. Cf. Anton Shammas, "The Morning After," *The New York Review of Books* (September 29, 1988): 49.

16. Abba Eban, "The Central Question," *Tikkun* 1 (1987): 21.

17. Ibid; Amnon Rubenstein, *The Zionist Dream Revisited: From Herzl to Gush Emunim and Back* (New York: Schocken Books, 1984), chap. 7; Uriel Tal, "Foundations of a Political Messianic Trend in Israel," *The Jerusalem Quarterly* 35 (Spring 1985): 42–45.

18. Mariam M. Mar'i and Sami Kh. Mar'i, "The Role of Woman as Change Agents in Arab Society in Israel," in *Women's Worlds,* ed. Marilyn Sahr, Martha Mednick, Dafna Israeli, Jessie Bernard (New York: Praeger Special Studies, 1985), 251–58.

19. Hazleton, *Israeli Women,* 143; Yuval-Davis, "The Israeli Example," 76. Only 10 percent of Jewish Israeli men are exempted from military service.

20. Yuval-Davis, "The Jewish Collectivity and National Reproduction in Israel," 60–90, esp. 85.

21. This analogy became clear to me in the course of a conversation with Paula Rayman on July 20, 1987. I am indebted to Paula both for pushing me to deal with the State of Israel and for helping me to organize my thoughts on many of the issues I discuss.

22. I have in mind here the use of the Holocaust to justify almost everything and anything that Israel does, including the occupation and the aggressive response to the Palestinian uprising.

23. Donna Robinson Divine, "Political Discourse in Israel: Literature," *Books in Israel,* vol. 1, ed. Ian Lustick (Albany, NY: SUNY Press, forthcoming).

24. See, e.g., *The New Israel Fund: Annual Report, November 1987* (New York: New Israel Fund, 1987), 8–11, 20–23; Rein's *Daughters of Rachel,* pt. 2, deals with the emergence of the Israeli women's movement.

25. Good sources of information about such groups are *Shalom: Jewish Peace Letter*

(published quarterly by the Jewish Peace Fellowship, Box 271 Nyack, NY 10960) and Jay Rothman with Sharon Bray and Mark Neustadt, *A Guide to Arab-Jewish Peacemaking Organizations in Israel* (New York: The New Israel Fund, 1988). (This and other publications and reports of the NIF are available from the NIF, 111 West 40th Street, New York, NY 10018). See also Saul Perlmutter, "The Light at the End of the Tunnel" (unpublished paper, 1988) and "The Israel Palestinian Center for Research and Information (IPCRI)" (unpublished letter, May 26, 1988).

26. This workshop took place as part of the Non-Governmental Forum at Nairobi. Christie Balka and Reena Bernards, "Israeli and Palestinian Women in Dialogue: A Model for Nairobi. New Jewish Agenda's Role at the U.N. Decade for Women Conference Forum '85 in Nairobi" (unpublished report to New Jewish Agenda), 2–3.

27. Tal, "Foundations of a Political Messianic Trend in Israel," 36–45.

31

Living with Conflicting Values

DAVID HARTMAN

In the past fifteen years, my thinking and teaching have focused almost exclusively on internal Jewish issues. It is easy to pray for the Ingathering of the Exiles, but can we live with that ingathering? Can we live with the fact that Jews today have no shared normative consensus about how we understand Jewish history and our own character as a nation? The very meaning of Zionism, of the establishment of the State of Israel, was the bold attempt to bring home a people whose members were in disagreement with each other. This was Zionism's fundamental courage—its belief that a national community could be forged although a national consensus was lacking.

The question central to my thinking, as a *halakhic* Jew in the Orthodox tradition, was how to appreciate Judaism in a way that allows for the flourishing of a variety of ideologies. Can I live as a Torah-observant Jew while knowing that there are many other Jews who have totally different views of what Jewish history could and should be?

There are, however, times when a new problem—or an old problem that has been lurking in the background—invades our consciousness in ways which do not allow us to return to everyday normalcy. For me as for many others in Israel, just that has now happened regarding our problem with the Palestinians.

This problem relates not only to the future physical existence of our society in Israel. Everything we value Jewishly, historically, and spiritually, is at stake.

It is of such urgency, of such proportions, that it touches the very soul of the nation. Who we are as a people, what connection we have with our stories and our history—all will be decided by how we deal with the Palestinian question. What is at stake is the significance of our national renewal and our identity as Jews.

This is not only an Israeli issue; it is also world Jewry's concern. Therefore, it is not only people who vote in Israel who must be engaged by it, but all who care about Jewish history, Jewish spirituality, and Israel's vision of the future.

There is a fundamental characteristic of a certain type of apologetic thinking that took place during our exile, in which Jewish theology or Jewish philosophy sought to find room for Jewish existence in non-Jewish environments. Traditionally, the way to find that room was to establish legitimization for Jews in the eyes of others. If Jews decided to be part of the surrounding world, they felt obliged to explain themselves in the other's categories. A German philosopher like Rosenzweig had to explain how Judaism fitted into Christianity. Hermann Cohen had to show that Judaism possesses a universalist ethic. If Jews preferred to live in the ghetto, on the other hand, then they did not have to speak a strange language, and self-legitimization grew out of their own internal experience.

When Jews came home to their own land, one of the most refreshing things about Zionism and its quest for normalcy was that the need for self-justification ceased to be urgent. A Jew could say, "I do not have to justify my right to live and to be a people."

Coming home meant the end of apologetic thinking. It became enough to speak our own language, to have our own history, to read our own Bible. We could build our culture on our own story and allow our elemental passions to exist without justification.

We did not have to win the "Moral Man of the Year Award" by being a light unto the nations. Like any other nation, some of us were noble, some weak. It was so good just to be able to breathe free that in coming home we did not see that someone else was also there.

It is crucial to understand that in the Bible there is only one people's story. Where in the Book of Joshua do we find how the Canaanites or the Jebusites felt when the Children of Israel came into the land? Who ever spoke about what it meant to be a Canaanite? The only time we meet Ishmael or Esau is when they enter or leave the Jewish story. The Bible gives us a story of the world in which the history of the Jews is what excites God. He is like an enormously involved Jewish supreme being, even though in the beginning God was not Jewish. He began to be Jewish only when he met Abraham.

There are some brief passages in the Prophets on other people's history, but it is fundamentally a private story. Coming home to the biblical land, we inherited that biblical sensibility in which there is only one story. Unpreparedness to deal with the other is therefore deeply related to our elemental sense of coming home. It is easy for us to feel that the other is just invading our territory.

In Germany, Samson Raphael Hirsch interpreted "And you shall love your neighbor as yourself" to include the non-Jew as well. In the Exile, neutral space, we could find room for the other without feeling that our own identity and integrity were being violated. The question is whether we can find room for the other within the context of our own intimate, passionate home. Does "my place" mean that he has no place? Does "his place" mean that I have no place? This is the true question, and the passions it unleashes are enormous.

The fact that the other, the Palestinian, also speaks as if there is only one story, and acts as if I am not here, makes it all the more complex and intense. We have a history of two peoples, each one living in its own story, unable to understand what it means for the other to be in this land. In the Bible, only one receives the paternal blessing. One is the blessed son; the other is the rejected son. There is no room for both Ishmael and Isaac. There is no room for both Esau and Jacob. There is only one blessing and only one son gets it.

Can there be any way to resolve this issue? Before we begin to deal with it, we have to appreciate the magnitude of the passions that this land unleashes, and reflect on how it feels for a people so long homeless to come home.

Nahmanides, Judah Halevi, and in our times Rabbi Joseph B. Soloveitchik in *Kol Dodi Dofek*, speak of the desolate land waiting for its lover to return. The land cannot be inhabited by anyone who is not part of Israel, part of the Sinai covenant.

Nahmanides, for instance, bases one of his central concepts on his reading of Lev. 18:25: "the land vomits out its inhabitants." This land cannot tolerate sin because it is the land where the God of the covenant lives. It can only be inhabited by Israel, and only when Israel does not stray in the manner of other nations. It has been desolate for a thousand years, waiting for its lover to return.

These are the passions that this land awakens. Unless they are understood, we cannot deal with the basic problem that Jews in Israel face today. We cannot talk about justice or utter moralisms like "Love you neighbor as yourself" unless we first empathize with the passion of a people who believe they and only they have redeemed this land from its desolation and therefore it is theirs in the deepest elemental sense.

I would like to distinguish between two forms of moral conflict. One is a conflict between good and evil. The question here is, Do we give in to passion, or can we overcome it? In response to the question "Who is the mighty?" the Mishnah says, he who can control his impulse—his *yetzer.* There is *yetzer ha-ra,* the instinct that leads to evil, and *yetzer tov,* the one that leads you to good. Judaism believes that you can win this struggle through an act of will. *Yetzer tov* can conquer the *yetzer ha-ra* through a victory of will.

From a certain perspective, this is a simple conflict. It is a problem that requires determination and personal resources in order to be solved, but it is not confusing in terms of values. It does not touch the core of your value system. The question is merely, Are you weak or not? Can you overcome temptation or not?

However, there is another form of conflict in the Talmud, which is not one between evil and good, but between good and good. Examples of such conflicts are represented by various dilemmas. Does saving a life take precedence over keeping the Sabbath? If you, your father, and your teacher are captives, who has the right to be ransomed first? If you find objects lost by your father and your teacher, to whom do you return his lost object first? A more poignant variation asks, If you see that your father and your rabbi are poor, whom do you help first?

The issue here is not a firm will against eager passion but a conflict between two positive values, obliging us to evaluate the foundations of these values. Establishing priorities in this second kind of conflict requires analysis, reflection, and a sense of clarity, since this type of question touches upon the core of a whole value system.

Our conflict with the Palestinians is not an issue of good versus evil, where there is no uncertainty about the moral choice. The conflict involves two goods, two legitimate claims, which are mistaken in their narcissism but legitimate in their sense of justice and fairness. The first is justice, the dignity one accords to human beings and their collective history and culture. The second is survival, security, and self-preservation. The dilemma can be summarized as follows: How much can I risk survival for the sake of justice and how much am I allowed to give up for the sake of love?

I would like to offer the perspective of two teachers who might guide us in this conflict: Judah Halevi and Maimonides. For Halevi as for Nahmanides, the very meaning of the Jewish people is to bear witness to the concept of miracle in history. In Halevi's book *The Kuzari,* the rabbi is asked by the king, "Whom do you believe in?" The rabbi replies, "I believe in the God of Abraham, Isaac, and Jacob." The king continues, "Why not say, 'I believe in the God who created heaven and earth?' " Basically, the king is asking, "Why not say you believe in the God of nature?" Halevi's answer is that the God of nature is the God of the philosophers. The God of the Jews is the God of history.

In the God of history, Halevi sees a God who is not enchained by the principle of necessity. He is the God who announces revolutions, who can take a slave people and offer them a new future. He is the God who announces that through Israel he bears witness to the notion of radical surprise, radical innovation. Given that this is our God, the past does not restrict what we can expect from the future. Wisdom is not accustoming ourselves to necessity, as in the Greek stoic notion. Wisdom is living with the expectation of radical innovation.

Israel's future is open, an uncharted possibility. Who would have dreamed that a slave people would become the People of the Book? Israel is the bearer of that experience and therefore the major story for Jewish identity is Passover.

What do we love to do when we tell this story? As we dip our finger into the wine on Passover night, we count ten miracles. Then we begin to expand: "No, not ten. There were fifty. Not fifty, two hundered. Even two hundred and fifty." We are a people who love to tell stories like that of the rescue at Entebbe. Our need for miracle is in our very nature. Miracle embodies the notion of surprise, of hope.

In this context, what is God's name, for Halevi? God's name is *Ehyeh asher ehyeh*—"I will be what I will be." Israel's story is the source for revolutionary aspirations in history. Messianism is a Jewish innovation. It did not come from Plato and Aristotle. The Greeks gave us rigor and truth; they gave us the scientific understanding of nature. It was the Prophets who gave us a dream which enabled us to believe that tomorrow could be radically different from yesterday.

For Halevi, this is the fundamental meaning of being a Jew, of Jewish nationhood, of "I am the Lord your God, who brought you out of the Land of Egypt." The Jews are the people that convey to the world the experience of miracle. That is their story and no other; not the story of truth, not the story of necessity. Their story is the parting of the sea—*the* miracle par excellence.

Therefore, the Jewish story requires a beginning. The Jews do not speak, as Aristotle does, of the world as a necessary reflection of the power of God. For Aristotle, the world is the necessary effect of God as the divine cause. The effect lives as long as the cause. Therefore, the world is eternal as the cause is eternal.

For Jews, the starting point is not eternal necessity but Creation. In the beginning was God's will, which produced the world out of chaos. If God's will is what drives the world, then history is an open drama. Herzl's Zionist vision had this attitude in common with the traditional Judaism that classical Zionism sought to supersede. His famous saying was "If you will it, it is no dream." Jews as a people believe in will. To want it all is a deep part of being Jewish.

The Creation story in the Bible is not told solely for its own sake. What is its point? According to Nahmanides, the point is that the cosmos is in order when Israel is in its land. The Creation story is a prolegomenon, a preamble, to the Jewish claim of will. It is the underpinning of the belief in miracle. The Creation story enables us to say that when we live in this land, we live under divine protection. Israel is a people defined by divine and not by human causality.

So also when we consider our coming home today, the category that we use to explain it is miracle. I would say that the interpretative category of Zionism is miracle, but the success of Zionism is reality. We interpret what we do in the category of surprise and wonderment. When we think of Auschwitz, and then think of that decimated people coming home, we think of Ezekiel and the resurrection of the dry bones.

Given that sense of history and national identity, it is understandable that many Israelis should reject realism as a value. They are impervious to the arguments of Abba Eban or Shimon Peres, who are worrying about the demographic time bomb on the West Bank and Gaza. They are likely to agree with Israel Eldad or Hanan Porat, that if we had been realistic we would not have come here in the first place. If we had been realistic, we would not even have built Degania Alef. Who could have thought that the yeshivah boy could turn into a pilot? That is what Zionism brought about.

So, in Israel they use the word "Zionism" to mean "to do the impossible, not the realistic." To be a Jew is to believe in miracles. Forget demography and other difficulties. With willpower, all is in our hands. It means that there is no causal principle outside our own will, that Aristotle's principle of causality has no relationship to Jewish political self-understanding. This land breathes with the power of will. If we give up believing in will, we give up everything, because that is the Jewish story.

That is the legacy of Halevi and Nahmanides. Even Marxist visions of utopia come from this deep perception of will, of a God who says "I will be." That is the passion deep in the soul of the Zionist revolution, both religious and nonreligious.

If this were the only tradition that could unlock our memory, the only interpretative key for Jewish self-understanding, I would be deeply pessimistic. A theology of will creates political narcissism, a private story in which reality becomes the outgrowth of an internal decision. What is, is what I claim must be. Therefore, nature, the other, the external world, do not channel or bridle the inner passion of my own will.

However, there is another voice in our tradition, that of a great teacher who passionately hated dependency on miracles. Every time he read about a miracle in the Bible, he sought a natural explanation. This is the voice of Maimonides. In contrast to Halevi, Maimonides believed that the story of Creation was not meant to teach the principle of will; rather, Creation was only a founding catalytic moment to be absorbed by the principle of necessity.

Maimonides said that Judaism requires only the belief that the world started, whereas we could believe in the eternity of the world after Creation. It may seem strange to discuss medieval metaphysics in the context of our problems in Israel today, but I hope Maimonides' relevance will soon be clear. In his eyes, the causal structure of the ordered patterns of reality does not vitiate, violate, or minimize the passion of his love for God. On the contrary, Maimonides saw the presence of God not in surprises but in principles of order and necessity. For Maimonides, if you lose nature, you lose God.

Maimonides does not teach about miracle, but about the importance of causal necessity, of the natural order, of respecting the given world. In other words, reality is not the product of our will. Reality imposes itself on our consciousness. Who, then, is God?

For Halevi, when God introduced Abraham into the covenant, it is as if he told him, "Forget all you learned about philosophy. Now you are meeting the God of the covenant." For Maimonides, Abraham found God through philosophical reflection on nature. At the age of forty, Abraham found God by understanding the mystery of the cosmos. Abraham is not the announcer of miracle; rather, he announces that God is the principle of order and wisdom and not the principle of will. It is not miracle that tells you that there is a God, but predictability, causal necessity, order. Therefore, the God of Maimonides is also *Ehyeh asher ehyeh,* but understood as "I am that I am: I am the principle of necessity."

The big question for Maimonides was, What are the limits of necessity? How much room is there for freedom in this world? What do the Jewish people bear witness to? What is their task? It is not to announce miracle in the world. Their central task, as Maimonides sees it, is to do battle against every form of idolatry. What infuses the passion of the *Guide of the Perplexed* is Moses announcing to a people, "Your task is to fight the false gods of the world. Your task is to fight against fantasy." The priests of idol worship, what were they? They played on human weakness. They exploited people who were frightened of their children dying. The priests told them, "Do this, and your children will live." All paganism thrives on human vulnerability and fear, on the manipulation of human weakness.

Therefore, Israel's task, for Maimonides, is not to allow human beings to fall prey to their fears, to their longing for cheap solutions. God is not a product to satisfy fantasy, to open up a world in which all is possible, but rather, God ensures that within the principle of necessity, there is room for freedom and creativity. Within the principle of limit, there is ample room for dignity and achievement.

Maimonides' messianism is not utopian but, rather, fundamentally rooted in an appreciation of reality. When asked why the Second Temple was destroyed, he answered in a letter: it was because Jews were reading astrology books and forgetting to learn the art of war. Fantasy is the source of idolatry because fantasy removes the principle of limit. Losing the pinciple of limit, we lose the principle of reality, and when we lose the principle of reality, God becomes a figment of our own imagination and our own needs.

Who is Israel? For Maimonides, Israel is the people that tells the world that dreams must be anchored in what is humanly feasible. For we can dream even though remaining tied to reality.

What does is mean to be a Jewish nation? It does not mean we announce utopia or we say that nothing in the past limits the future. The meaning of being a Jewish nation is to declare war against the distortion of the imagination, against fantasy, against idolatry. We must be the people that bears witness to the futility of the idolatrous quest.

For Maimonides, Creation is not the story of how God gave the Jews the land; Creation is what takes the Jews out of their own story and places them in a cosmic drama. The Bible begins with Creation in order to teach us that God is not Jewish, that there is a world which has a drama and a dignity not defined by the Jewish story. Halevi makes the Creation narrative a Jewish historical story. Maimonides views it instead as a corrective, as a larger cosmic filter placing limits upon our private story.

What does this mean for today? I shall try to clarify how I believe we must approach the conflict between the Palestinians and the Israelis. The events of the *intifada* have forced us to acknowledge a nation in revolt rather than individuals in revolt. Rabbi Druckman argues that the "disturbances" are the work of a few rabble-rousers. This view assumes that on the other side there is not an organized national will because in the Jewish story the land has one nation. People who share Druckman's views can allow individual Palestinians to be here but not a Palestinian nation. The first question for us to face is, Whom do we see facing us—individual Palestinians or a people with a national will seeking political freedom and political sovereignty?

Our first step toward recovering our sense of reality is to recognize that what we see is a nation. The second question is then, Can this home to which we have returned contain another nation? In terms of our own history, the land has one nation, the God of history elects one people. If there is no corrective to this vision of history, then the ultimate resolution is total war. If there is only one way or people that mediates the God of history, then Jerusalem will be a city in flames.

What is the thrust of the idea of Creation, how does it filter our historical memories? Does the God of Creation enable us to understand ours as one possible story, but not the only one? Does the God of revelation announce an exclusive truth or one particular way? Is Israel the bearer of Halevi's principle of miracle, or is it the bearer of the rejection of idolatry and of the claim to the *only* story?

For Maimonides, the details of history are not important. What counts is the integrity of a people who are committed to the principle of reality, committed to wage war on fantasy and on the rejection of the principle of limit. Can this understanding of Creation enter into our story, so that room can be made for the Palestinians to be here as a nation? Can we feel the joy of our story, the joy of being home, knowing that another nation also feels that this is its home?

We have to deal with this problem in the manner of Hillel. Why according to the rabbis, is the *halakhah* according to Hillel? Because whenever he taught, he brought the words of Shammai, his rival, first. Accordingly, those of us who seek to find a way with the Palestinians have first to understand the passion of Gush Emunim and not call them Fascists or Nazis. We must not be seduced by integrity as a validation of a principle. The great mistake of existentialism was to think that if something is sincere, it is right. Sincerity is not a criterion for content.

We shall not attain reconciliation unless we can explain the position of those who disagree with us. We have to understand the elemental passions that feed their love for this land, and only then argue with their position and offer an alternative. We cannot ignore that they are speaking out of a definite strand in the Jewish tradition. We have to understand the passion of those who think that there is only one people in this land. By admitting their passions, we can argue constructively with them. By denying them, we risk being haunted by them. We stop listening to each other and substitute name-calling for dialogue. If we continue to do this, total chaos will ensue.

When there is a conflict of values between a positive and a negative commandment, the Talmud teaches that the positive commandment takes precedence over the negative. Nahmanides explains that a positive commandment is grounded in love, while a negative commandment is ground in fear. Abstention from wrongdoing derives from fear of punishment, fear of God. Doing something good grows out of love. A positive commandment takes precedence over a negative one because love is mightier than fear.

In the conflict with the Palestinians, there is a conflict of two values. Although it may sound romantic, I believe that love can make room for the other in a way that allows us to retain our own identity without feeling threatened by the other.

The meaning of Israel, of Zionism, is the affirmation of Jewish identity. When Jews sought justice in exile, they felt they had to deny their Jewishness. When admitting the other's moral claim, they felt they had to give up their identity.

Given this situation, it is understandable that people in Israel often say, "Liberalism, caring constantly about others, is a *galut* [exile] mentality. If I allow concern for the other too much weight, I commit suicide as a Jew. When Jews become overly moral, they lose their healthy instinct for survival. This was true for German Jews, Russian Jews, and it is true for North American Jews."

The beauty of being in Jerusalem is that we do not have to make this choice. Being at home, we allow elemental passions to surface. That is why we sometimes see violent behavior by people who feel threatened and think they are losing their home. When they think they are losing their home, they act in ways which are often alien to our most cherished values. But must they behave thus, or is there an alternative?

I believe and hope deeply that the instinct of our people in this land can be guided by the spirit of Maimonides. I believe that we neither seek nor require the degradation of a whole nation. We can live as lovers of God and Torah, which means making room for the other without negating our own dignity. In embracing the Palestinians, we show the power of love to allow another story into our reality. It is to show that our story has room for them because it is defined not by fear but by love. It shows that we have not come home because we are frightened by the world, that it is not fear that keeps us here, but the love of our own story, the love of our own history, the joy of recreating our own culture.

It is then not the fear of Hitler that nurtures us. During the war in Lebanon, Prime Minister Begin said, "Nine hundred thousand troops in twenty-four hours. A ghetto people! Look what we have become." We do not need to mass nine hundred thousand troops in order to compensate for the Warsaw ghetto. We do not need to work through the horrors of the Holocaust to find meaning here. If fear and terror control our reality, then ultimately there is no room for the other.

Of course, I do not call for a love that leads to national suicide, as was the case in Russia and Germany, where we did not see the reality of evil. Therefore, we have to make room for the Palestinians on the clear condition that they understand that we will not allow them to jeopardize our security. We will not interpret Arafat sophistically or mystically. We need straight answers when we ask, Do you see me or do you hope I disappear? Not only do you see me, but do you recognize that I never left here?

The nightmare can only be healed by Palestinian voices that will say, with pristine clarity, that they are willing to give up military power for political dignity. If they are prepared to do that, then we can say that there can be room in this land for both our story and theirs. We can make room for the Palestinians when they give up all thoughts of our disappearance. That is the condition, the sine qua non, of our ability to be open to a Palestinian national entity. Security, however, must not be confused with political control.

What if the Palestinians do not say that they are willing to give up military power for political dignity? Then, I am afraid, the viewpoint of our hawks will win. The Palestinians have to understand that if they themselves cannot change, Israel cannot heal its own trauma. We will only be able to find room for love in our story if they, too, make a major change. Monologues among ourselves only create fears.

Therefore, the time has come for another voice, the Palestinian voice, to speak with great clarity and strength. If it does not, then I fear greatly what will be in this society. It will tax all the strength of what is, I believe, the most passionate and vigorous democracy in the world. It is amazing that in our country, which has always been under constant threat of war, there is such public debate and discussion and arguments and disagreements.

There will be no future in the Middle East if we do not have new interpretative keys to help make sense of our past. The past will come back to haunt us and may possibly fall into the hands of a Kahane or a Levinger. There will be no future in our homecoming unless we unlock our memories in a new way.

Gush Emunim echoes a voice in the tradition, but is not the only voice. I have presented a perspective showing that there is room within Jewish theological thinking for multiple voices to be drawn from the tradition. Halevi and Maimonides give us different approaches to Jewish memory. Our past has to be rethought, reevaluated, and not given over to one group.

The keys we use to open up our past and the way in which we make sense of our stories are today life-and-death matters. Unless we reinterpret the Torah, we will choke with each other's dogmatism. Torah is open to creative possibilities and the last chapter has not yet been written. That is the meaning of oral tradition in Judaism. We never live by the literal word alone. We live by a word that is open and reinterpreted and recreated.

As we face the Palestinians, everything that we were in Jewish history calls for reinterpretation. We cannot yield up our past to those who see no way to find room for another people. We must go back into our memory, open up our source books. Only then can we find our way.

The Ethics of Ruling a Jewish State with a Large Non-Jewish Minority

EINAT RAMON

Questions, Challenges, and Presuppositions of Zionist Ethics

During the past few decades Israel as a state and Israelis as individuals have been struggling with ethical questions that touched the heart and the core of our Zionist identity. Most of these questions touch upon our relationship with the Palestinians, our neighbors, and the largest minority in the Jewish state. Our dilemmas concerned boundaries, not only in a geographical sense but also in a moral one. Originally Zionism had set as its goal to secure Jewish physical and spiritual survival in modernity. Escaping the fate of a minority everywhere else in the world, either pressured to assimilate or considered as second-class citizens and persecuted, Jews sought cultural and physical refuge in the land of their ancestors, the land of Israel. Lately, however, many Israelis have begun to wonder if and when we have ceased to be a nation, fighting for our cultural and political independence, and have become instead occupiers and colonizers of another people. Where is the boundary between the murder of people who live under Jewish sovereignty and acts of self defense?[1]

In this essay I show how traditional Jewish ethical terms can be applied to the challenge of ruling a large non-Jewish minority. I discuss the general context of the relationship between Judaism, *halakhah* (Jewish Law), and the Jewish state. I believe that ethical discussions regarding Israel must evolve out of the fruitful dialogue between Judaism and democracy in the Jewish state. In the second part of the essay, I present the ethical thought of an early Zionist thinker, Aharon David Gordon (1856–1922), as a suggestive source for moral thinking on the topic. I then expand his ethical discussion by introducing *halakhic* terms that bear on the morality of being a ruling majority, and refer to the practical applications of those terms.

Israel and Her Minorities

When discussing morality, I follow an important moral principle from the Mishnah (The Ethics of the Fathers, 2:4): "Do not judge your fellow human till you stand in his place." Because ethics is determined in daily life by every single person—at home, in the street, in the army, and in court—I cannot provide accurate ethical prescriptions. Instead I try to provide moral "language" or tools to confront ethical dilemmas, reflect upon them, and act responsibly.

As we apply ethical principles to contemporary political reality, we must keep in mind an important distinction between Israeli Palestinians who are citizens of the state, and Palestinians who live in the West Bank and Gaza who live under military rule. Currently Israel rules over both. However, while Israeli Palestinians are represented at the Knesset and are entitled to many social benefits as citizens of the state, Palestinians who live in the West Bank and Gaza live under occupation. My hope is that ultimately a Palestinian state will be established alongside the Jewish state. Knowing the complexity of Middle East politics, however, the dream of a peaceful partition of the Land may not become a reality for a while. Unless a recognition of the dependency of Jews and Palestinians on one another will infiltrate political consciousness on both sides, we are bound to fight with one another to the bitter end. Yet, even in the case that there will be a Palestinian state that will live peacefully with Israel, there will remain a large percentage of Palestinians (one-sixth of the population) who will continue to live under Jewish rule.

To date, Israeli Palestinians enjoy more freedom and economic stability than Palestinians who live under occupation. Nevertheless, compared with Israeli Jews they suffer from various forms of discrimination. Morally, it is this community that is of greater concern to Jews because even after the establishment of a peace agreement, Israeli Palestinians will continue to live under Jewish sovereignty. My treatment of the principles of *ger toshav* (the stranger in the land) and the concept of *darkhei shalom* (paths of peace) refer only to Israeli Palestinians. My discussion of the category of *Rodef,* the pursuer, and the question of self-defense refer mostly to daily situations of the guerrilla war of independence that takes place in the West Bank and Gaza. I believe that Israel must strive to discontinue her control of these territories. It is impossible to extend the responsibility that Israel has toward her Palestinian citizens to a number of non-Jews almost half the size of Israel's Jewish population. This is precisely the reason why we must do everything we can to bring about the reality of Palestinian self-rule. Nevertheless, as long as we remain occupiers we have the responsibility to respect the basic human dignity of Palestinians who live under our occupation.

The ethical challenge of being a majority is one with which many cultures and nations in today's world struggle, more or less successfuly. While there are many common denominators between Israel and other nations, there are also some characteristics unique to Israelis' particular situation. The common denominators are issues of human, economic, and cultural minority rights.

What distinguishes Israel is the fact that while Jews are a majority within Israel, they are a minority in the Middle East and a persecuted minority in some other parts of the world. The largest minority living under our sovereignty, the Palestinians, is culturally (though not necessarily politically) affiliated with the Arab majority in the Middle East, a world that until now has refused to recognize our legitimate national claims and has threatened to destroy us. This is why moral discussions concerning the challenge of being a Jewish majority cannot be separated from the context of the Israeli-Palestinian question.

There are other minorities who live in Israel, such as the Vietnamese boat people to whom Israel gave refuge in the late 1970s or various groups of non-Arab

Christians who live in Israel for religious reasons. We hardly hear about those minorities because, unlike the Palestinians, they are small communities who do not have any national claims over the territory of the State of Israel.

The fact that relatively recently Jews emerged smaller in numbers and with wounded souls from one of the greatest traumas in our history, the Holocaust, complicates things even more. This vulnerability explains why it is difficult for Israel to emulate progressive policies of other secure majorities in today's democratic states. It also determines that a contextual rather than a structural approach is necessary to create peaceful coexistence between the Jewish state and her large, Palestinian minority.

Coming from a background of powerlessness, Jews have become completely absorbed in our own national and personal pain. Traumatic experiences of persecution have imbedded in all of us a sense of being victimized and have made us insensitive to the pain of others. We tend to forget that while the Holocaust was the most vicious and horrible crime ever committed in human history, Jews do not have a monopoly on human suffering.

Current political voices handle the complexity of the moral condition in Israel poorly. There is a tendency to adopt one-sided opinions and highlight either Jewish power or Jewish powerlessness. Voices on the left portray Israelis as strong, vicious colonizers of another people. Thus they dismiss the Jews' legitimate craving for cultural and political independence, and the real scar that persecutions and endless wars with the Arabs have marked on Jewish national and personal memory. Right-wing politicians manipulate Jewish consciousness of victimhood to the degree of dismissing Jews from any responsibility for the pain of others. In response to these two extreme approaches we must reintroduce some traditional Jewish concepts. To do that, however, we must first articulate a hermeneutic for interpreting and for applying traditional Judaism to the modern world.

Judaism, *Halakhah*, and Ethics in the Jewish State

One Jewish precept that most non-Orthodox modern Jewish ethicists share is that a schism between law and ethics is itself unethical. Their presupposition stems from their understanding of the important role that *halakhah* has played in the shaping of Jewish moral thinking. While Jews always recognized human limits in creating a perfect system of justice, they have never given up the principle that justice must be reflected in human actions, law, and behavior. *Halakhic* logic also taught us that ambiguous situations challenge ethical reasoning. It is easy to say that one must not kill, but if one refuses to defend herself, or worse, defend her relatives, isn't that a murder of those whom she refuses to defend? While introducing the commandment of "Thou shall not murder" to the Western world, Judaism always asserted the importance of self-defense. Acknowledging the principle of seeking peace, it also recognized the danger of paying lip service to noble values and thus endangering the enterprise of peace altogether.

Torn between their critique of rabbinic *halakhic* expressions and their appreciation of the tradition, early Zionist thinkers called for the emergence of a new *halakhah*. The Zionist rebellion of thinkers such as A. D. Gordon, Ahad Ha'Am, Haim Nachman Bialik, and Berl Katznelson against traditional Judaism was not a rebellion against rabbinic tradition per se but against *rabbinic authority.* As students of Spinoza's *Tractatus,* early Zionist intellectuals no longer considered the rabbis (of any generation) the sole authoritative voice of biblical interpretation. The relationship between secular Zionists and rabbinic Judaism was therefore dialectical: the voice of rabbis of all generations became the voice of Zionist aggadah, of their moral thought—not of *halakhah.*[2]

For a variety of reasons early Zionists left the difficult problem of the relationship between traditional Judaism and the Jewish democratic state to the following, perplexed generations of "post-Orthodox[3]" Israeli Jews. Today, more than one hundred years after the emergence of Zionism, most Zionists still face this problem with much confusion and bewilderment. The question "To what extent we should use *halakhah* when we discuss law and morality in a modern, democratic Jewish state?" is still valid.

Most Orthodox Zionists respond to this question by presenting the ideal of theocracy, that is, a Jewish state governed by *halakhah* and *halakhic* decision makers, namely, Orthodox rabbis.[4] Contrary to mainstream Orthodoxy, radical secularists and liberal Orthodox thinkers[5] argue that there should be complete separation between Jewish legal and moral teachings, and the law of the Jewish state. Either one of those positions does not represent the majority of Israelis who want Israel to be both a democracy and a state that reflects cultural and moral Jewish characteristics. Insofar as law and moral teachings are part of our cultural heritage, they too must be included in the Jewish cultural revival that Zionism has set for itself. One of the greatest Israeli law scholars, Supreme Court Justice emeritus Haim Cohen, points out that not to use *halakhic* teachings as legal resources of the laws of the Jewish state is absurd.[6] Thousands of years of Jewish moral and legal wisdom are lost when we refuse to apply this wisdom to everyday reality and leave it in esoteric books. Yet there is no doubt that in order to apply *halakhah* to a democratic reality we must violate several fundamental *halakhic* precepts.

If parts of *halakhah* were to be democratized, we must first assume that all citizens subject to that law ought to share equal rights and civil status regardless of their gender, religion, nationality, race, and physical ability. This presupposition, though stated by the Declaration of Independence of the State of Israel, was not shared by rabbis of previous generations who, although they occasionally had democratic sensibilities, lived in predemocratic societies.

Furthermore, if we wish to democratize *halakhah,* we must also distinguish between the ritual and civil aspects of it. Traditionally Jewish law did not do so, indicating that the sacred and the profane were two faces of the same coin. The State of Israel must make such a distinction in order to avoid religious coercion.

Lastly, the authority to interpret those parts of Jewish law that would become Israeli civil law must become accessible to every citizen who wishes to specialize in the field. That is, we must take the law away from the rabbis and transmit it back to the people, or more accurately, to their democratically elected representatives in the Kenesset and in the Israeli judicial system. Since elected representatives in Israel, women and men, have diverse religious beliefs, the outcome of such a process would be to universalize parts of Jewish law. *Halakhah* would thus become an important legal resource in the same way as, or even more than, Roman, Ottoman, or English law, the current historical sources of law in Israel.

The possibility of reconfiguring the authority[7] of those who determine *halakhah* is perhaps the most radical among my suggestions. It is important to mention that the idea that parts of Jewish law may be disobeyed on certain occasions is a legal concept rooted in the rich *halakhic* literature. In several cases the Talmud mentions rabbis and religious leaders who violated one law in order to maintain the validity of the system.[8] Yet, reconfiguring the authority of *halakhic* decision makers is a product of modern democratic consciousness, a consciousness that brings the dialectical cultural Zionist vision to its fulfillment. It implies that part of the legal training of Israeli lawyers should be in the area of Jewish civil and business law. Since this training must be accessible to all Israeli citizens, we will ultimately face the reality of women, non-Jews, or secular Jews (who were regarded as second-class citizens in the eyes of the traditional *halakhic* system) as authoritative interpreters of *halakhah* on certain matters. The whole body of Jewish ritual law would remain to be determined by religious communities and their leaders according to their own standards of interpretation and authority.[9]

The dialectical attitude toward Jewish law, which is the only viable way to reconcile *halakhah* with democracy, will no doubt face opposition and thus might not take place in our day and age. Until it does, the Jewish state will continue to operate according to the laws of the Jews' different colonizers, the Romans, the Ottomans, and the British, rather than according to Jewish law. People who are aware of that absurdity and who refuse to adopt either the strictly Orthodox or the radical assimilationist positions will continue to introduce *halakhic* teachings into moral discussions of the political and educational agenda in Israel in order to influence Israeli legislators, leaders, and citizens. As long as the refusal to democratize parts of *halakhah* persists, *halakhic* teachings cannot function as law but as aggadah, moral discourse. Even without its official democratization, *halakhah* can serve as the soil upon which new Jewish cultural and legal expressions must grow.

In either case, the role of rabbis in a democratic society changes. While some of them may continue to be legislators concerning ritual law in their own communities, a democratic Jewish state restores the original role of rabbis within the larger society. From now on, rabbis must serve as spiritual leaders and teachers of the Jewish people. In a democratic society rabbis and scholars of Jewish thought no longer function as legislators but as teachers of the people's moral language shaped by the people's traditional cultural heritage. In that sense rabbis and other Jewish scholars become creators of aggadah, out of the *halakhah* of previous generations.

One last hermeneutical note must be mentioned before we turn to the implementation of these principles regarding the ethics of treating a minority. A non-Orthodox, historically conscious interpretation of the Jewish tradition recognizes its pluralistic nature. It realizes that there is a diversity of moral opinions and approaches within the classical sources. When we interpret our moral heritage, we do not pretend that other opinions do not exist. Nor do we wish to fall into the trap of complete relativism and argue that all opinions are equally valid. When we try to walk the middle ground between those two approaches, we engage in the process of what I call "contextual prioritizing." It is a constant process of learning and self-criticism that involves highlighting some opinions of our predecessors and diminishing others. We make such distinctions based on certain moral and hermeneutical convictions that we derive from previous reflections and encounters with our tradition. The more we learn about Jewish moral teachings, the more we are led to reflect upon its priorities. Because our tradition is so rich, we occasionally confront contradictory statements. We then must decide when one statement has an authoritative voice, a higher priority, over another. "Contextual prioritizing" is how I understand the continuous process of interpreting traditional scriptures.

Aharon David Gordon and the Dialectic of Particularism and Universalism

The hermeneutical principle that guides my understanding of Judaism is that of a delicate balance between universalism and particularism. Judaism's message of prophecy was that of liberation, of social commitment to spreading justice in the world among all people. At the same time, the Torah and the *halakhic* system that emerged out of it recognized that a commitment to a universalist vision at the expense of the immediate, namely, at the expense of one's family, community, and nation, is a false commitment to justice.

My own thinking on the dialectic of universalism and particularism was shaped by the works of the modern Jewish thinker Aharon David Gordon. Gordon is considered to be one of the "founding ancestors" of Israel and a person of moral stature among the early Labor Zionists. After immigrating to Israel in 1904 when he was forty-eight, he insisted on becoming a laborer (despite his relative old age) and eventually became a founder of the non-Marxist labor and kibbutz movements. Arthur Hertzberg claimed that "If Herzl was Zionism's president-in-exile and Ahad Ha-Am its secular rabbi, Aaron David Gordon was the movement's secular mystic and saint."[10]

Gordon's ethical doctrine, mostly overlooked and misinterpreted by modern intellectual historians, demonstrates the constructive tension between universalism and particularism in Jewish tradition. Relying heavily on biblical and rabbinic teachings and Kabbalistic theology, Gordon developed an original ethical model symbolized by the metaphor of motherhood.

Gordon criticized Western philosophical and Marxist ideals of universal love because those ethical models were too pretentious and did not take into consideration the complexity of the human condition. Universal ideals of love occasionally demanded acts of altruism at the cost of one's nearest subjects of responsiblity (oneself and one's family and nation). Likewise he pointed out that exclusive commitment to particularistic causes created alienation and narrowness in human life.

According to Gordon the experience of motherhood demonstrates how the universal object of care must not be cared for at the expense of the immediate. He refers to the maternal feature as the "extension" of the ego, indicating the psychological features of real care: that it must never happen at the expense of the caregiver, and that its natural tendency is to extend itself to more and more beings. Recognizing that there were tragic situations when the survival of one costs the life of another, and that it is hard to prescribe how one should act on such tragic occasions, he did not consider actions of self-defense immoral. He acknowledged that for the preservation of one's own life violent measures that break the organic connection of humanity and nature must be taken. Yet he pointed out that a narrow approach to survival, the approach of me-or-the-other must never be adopted as a general moral premise.

Gordon did not explicitly draw a line from his maternal ethic to his opinions on the Israeli-Palestinian conflict; however, a close reading of his corpus leads one to conclude that the principle was implicitly applied to this moral dilemma. Gordon lived at a time when Jews were a minority in the Land of Israel and the Palestinians a majority. At about the time of the killing of one of his closest friends, the writer Yosef Chayim Brenner, by an Arab mob, Gordon wrote the following words:

> We, who were the first ones that said "all nations shall go each in the name of their God"(Mic. 4:5), "Nation shall not lift up sword against nation" (Isa. 2:4) . . .must create a new people, a human nation, a nation that relates humanely and has fraternal relations with other nations. . . . What is our relationship with the Arabs? They are, after all, whether we like it or not, our political and social companions. What do we know about them that is more than what the anti-Semites know about us?[11] . . . One acquires ownership on a Land through living on her, through labor and creativity, and this is how we will return our right to the Land to ourselves. . . . They [the Palestinians] dwell on the Land and we neither have the right to deprive them of this right nor [do we have a right] to drive them away. But they, too, have no right to deprive us from our right over the Land that we toil upon and upon which we live.[12] . . . We must be very careful in our relationship with the Arabs, when we purchase land from them etc. so that we will not hurt their human rights in any way . . . Generally it is our obligation to have humane relationships with the Arabs and not to determine our relationships with them based on the negative aspects of their behavior, like the anti-Semites who treated us based on the negative characteristics [of our behavior]. . . . So long as we strive to be more humane, more alive, we will find the correct relationship to humanity and to other nations in general and to the Arabs in particular."[13]

That same dialectical thinking could be detected in Gordon's reflections about the problem of the use of force. One the one hand, he admitted that self-defense was necessary and thus supported the establishment of Hashomer[14] (an organization for Jewish self-defense established by members of the second Aliyah in prestate Israel). On the other hand, he wrote numerous articles and passages condemning militarism and military thinking and objecting to the Yishuv's (prestate Israel) participation in World War I. Although he understood that self-defense was necessary for the Jews' survival, he wished to minimize Jews' enthusiasm for the use of force and militarism.[15]

Gordon died in 1922, long before crucial historical events had shaped and complicated Jewish-Palestinian relations. During his lifetime Jews were an unwelcomed minority in Palestine, where the Arabs were the majority. He could probably not imagine that the demographic and political balance would dramatically change within a period of less than thirty years. Nevertheless, his comments concerning Jewish attitudes toward Palestinians and his critique of the worship of militarism remain, tragically, relevant.

Extending an Ethic of Organic Responsiblity: *Halakhic* and Moral Terms and Their Practical Implications

In my view Gordon should set the authoritative ethical and hermeneutical premise of how a Jewish majority must treat a large, non-Jewish minority. Judaism begins its universalist endeavor from responsibility to a particular people and attachment to a particular land. Its ultimate goal is to extend that responsiblity to the whole world.

When Jewish particularism refuses to recognize that mission, it becomes paranoid and chauvinistic. When Jewish universalism refuses to acknowledge particular responsibilities and attachments, it becomes hypocritical. Both extremes are self-destructive and dangerous.

Through Gordon's moral foundation other *halakhic* voices are "filtered." Based on his analysis of morality one perceives Palestinians and Jews as organically connected through their attachment to the same land. Given this presupposition, I do not think that the biblical requirement of the killing of all the Canaanite inhabitants of the land is relevant for the present discussion. Therefore, for the purpose of creating a moral vocabulary I select only those sources that flesh out the vision of this organic, though occasionally bloody, connection.

The art of ethical living relies on our ability to apply the principle of "extending" care to others but not at the expense of survival. The difficulty is that of boundaries: how to distinguish between cruelty and self-defense, between care for the immediate and discrimination against outsiders. The *halakhic* terms that are developed in the following provide moral guidelines and expand the dialectical principle of universalist and particularistic commitments.

Ger Toshav: The Stranger Who Dwells in the Land

The moral teaching that Jews must care for non-Jews who live in their land, an imperative which the Prophets of Israel constantly preached, is one of the fundamental teachings of the Torah. Its psychologically sophisticated characteristic stems from the observation that sensitivity to the non-Jew's vulnerability is embedded in the Jew's own memory of vulnerability. If we should forget that we are vulnerable, as the left suggests, how can we respond to the suffering of others? Gordon's call not to treat Palestinians in the same way that the anti-Semites treat us echoes the words of the Torah. The Torah teaches us that our experience as a minority in exile demands from us greater care and concern with non-Jews who live among a Jewish majority. "You shall not oppress a stranger, for you know the feelings of the stranger, having yourselves been strangers in the land of Egypt" (Exod. 22:24). The first golden rule of ruling over a non-Jewish minority is that of empathy with their distress—the distress of the stranger in the land.

The prophet Ezekiel extended the commandment of empathy toward non-Israelites who live in Israel by addressing the non-Jewish residents' connection to the Land, their right to dwell on it and inherit it along with the Israelites.

> This land you shall divide for yourselves among the tribes of Israel. You shall allot it as a heritage for yourselves and for the strangers who reside among you, who have begotten children among you. You shall treat them as Israelite citizens; they shall receive allotments along with you among the tribes of Israel. You shall give the stranger an allotment within the tribe where he resides—declares the Lord God. (Ezek. 47:21–23)

The political situation described by the Prophet Ezekiel in these verses is a messianic reality. Despite its utopian nature, Ezekiel's vision of social justice is relevant to contemporary political reality. It forces us to pay attention to the Palestinians' deep attachment to the land of Israel and to the prophetic commandment to respect that attachment. A sovereign Jewish state should be sensitive to the sore pain of

Palestinian loss of land, should strive to limit expropriations of land from its Jewish and Arab citizens to the absolute minimum, and must compensate the owners of the expropriated piece of land accordingly.

Darkhei Shalom: Paths of Peace

Other *halakhic* concepts that teach us about the morality of ruling over a non-Jewish minority stem from the rabbinic tradition. The rabbis struggled with the dilemma of distribution of social and economic public resources. When the Jews returned to their land to build a national home and absorb Jewish refugees from all over the world, there was a question as to what degree the Jews were also responsible for the improvement of economic, educational, and social conditions of local Palestinians. When we look to *halakhic* guidance on the topic, we confront two teachings that seemingly contradict each other. One tradition teaches that limited resources must always be allocated first to the ones closer to you, your own people and the people of your hometown.

> Rabbi Joseph said: "My people and a gentile—my people comes first. . . . the impoverished of your city and the impoverished of another city, the impoverished of your city come first." (Bava Kama 71)

Another talmudic tradition blurs the dichotomy between close and distant human beings by introducing the concept of *Darkhei Shalom:*

> Our Rabbis taught: We support impoverished gentiles along with impoverished Israelites, we visit sick gentiles along with sick Israelites, and we bury deceased gentiles along with deceased Israelites because of paths of peace. (Gittin 61a)

When we remember the principle of organic dependency, these two moral teachings go well together so long as the atmosphere of peace prevails. We therefore must follow the "principle of paths of peace" when we consider the status of Israeli Arabs, who until now were largely loyal to the state. Perhaps when the State of Israel was overwhelmed with an influx of Jewish refugees from around the world, allocation of resources according to the principle of "paths of peace" was an unrealistic possibility. Yet we have allowed this emergency-oriented thinking of me-or-the-other to last too long, resulting in a narrow, shortsighted political logic. Israeli Arabs are "the impoverished of our city," their fate is intertwined with ours, they live under Jewish sovereignty and are therefore part of the immediate responsibility of Jews. They must therefore be entitled equally to enjoy job opportunities, welfare, and medical and educational benefits from the state, and they should, like every Israeli Jew, serve the society in which they live.

Rodef: The Pursuer

The full equality that should exist for Israel's Jewish and Arab citizens does not apply to Palestinians who live in the West Bank and Gaza. They are fighting their war of independence and do not wish to become citizens of the State of Israel. The moral guidelines that Israel must follow when treating Palestinians who are at war with us are different. As rulers we should guarantee educational freedom and accessibility of good medical care (Israel usually keeps the latter rule better than the former). Nevertheless, admitting that we are in a relationship of war does not mean that no rules of morality apply to such unfortunate conditions. On the contrary, *halakhic* rules are even stricter, more complicated, and require a greater responsibility from each individual when it comes to *diney nefashot,* laws of human lives.

Perhaps the first premise upon which *halakhah* operates is that bloodshed defiles the Land and causes the *Shekhinah* (God's immanence) to depart.[16] The Land of Israel is desanctified as a result of bloodshed and war. This rule is important to remember because in a situation of war an ongoing process of dehumanizing the enemy goes on, a process in which the lost lives of the enemy seem cheap. It is in this kind of situation that we must constantly remind ourselves not to rejoice when our enemy falls (Prov. 24:17) and that "the Holy Blessed One does not rejoice in the defeat of the wicked." The Talmud indicates that as the Egyptians were flailing about in the sea, the angels wanted to sing hallelujah for Israel's redemption, but God rebuked them,[17] saying "My children are drowning in the sea and you are chanting praises"?! (Megillah 10a). All of these concepts must become an integral part of our national political language.

Yet even after we establish the moral principle that any bloodshed is a tragedy, the most difficult dilemma remains: under what circumstances is it moral to use military force? Holding on to the moral principle of condemning bloodshed, the rabbis introduced the concept of a *Rodef,* the pursuer who may be killed when it is self-evident that he or she is about to commit murder. In one instance the Talmud justifies the killing of a *Rodef* on the basis of the right to self-defense: "With regard to a pursuer the Torah says: If he comes to slay you, stop him by slaying him first" (Berakhot 58a, Sanhedrin 72a.) In another instance, however, the rabbis justify the murder of the pursuer on the basis of preventing him or her from committing murder. "If someone pursues his fellow—save him/her [from committing the sin of murder] at the cost of his/her life" (Tosefta Sanhedrin 8).

The rabbinic authors of this precedent were quite aware of possible abuses of legitimating security and self-defense. Thus they provided both an additional layer of reasoning and carefully detailed guidelines for the permission to kill a human being. "How do they save him at the cost of his life? They cut off one of his limbs. And if they cannot stop him (in this way), they go ahead and kill him" (Tosefta, Sanhedrin, 8). There are prescribed stages that one must follow before one takes the life of another human being. The later rabbis of the Talmud carried this logic even further: "For it has been taught: If one was pursuing his fellow to slay him, and he could be saved by maiming a limb [of the pursuer] but [the pursued person] did not thus save himself [and killed him instead], he [the defender who is now a murderer] is executed on his [the original murderer's] account" (Babylonian Talmud Sanhedrin 73b–74a.).

The following midrash conveys a similar message as it portrays Moses' insistence on seeking ways to establish peace before declaring war:

> God told Moses to make war on Sihon (Deut. 2:24), but Israel did not make war: they
> sent messengers of peace (Deut. 2:26). God said, "I ordered you to make war, but
> you made overtures of peace. 'There is no peace,' says the Lord, 'for the wicked' "
> (Isa. 47:22). How great, then, must be words of peace, if Israel disobeyed God for
> peace's sake, and yet God was not wrath with them. (Tanhuma B., Debarim, 3b)[18]

These rabbinic teachings clearly emphasize that while it is not possible to pre-vent violence at all times, one must always try to do so. They teach that peaceful ways ought to be sought first and precede any violent measures. Furthermore, killing may be exercised only after other degrees of violence do not stop the mur-derer from attacking. In either case, they point out the importance of constantly trying to avoid bloodshed even at the risk of disobeying God's words(!).

It is of great concern that those midrashim are unknown to the majority of Israelis. One incident that comes to mind is the medium of Israeli public television that broadcasts every night a biblical or a rabbinic verse. In the case of a terrorist attack or war in Israel the verse regularly broadcast on television is, "He who comes to kill you, get up early and slay him first." I do not intend to minimize the anger and the pain that envelops all Israelis when war or killing occurs. Yet this "educa-tional" response worries me tremendously. It fuels revenge rather than restraint, and, worse: it presents war and hostility as normal living conditions.

Toward True Organic Responsibility

As Jews and Palestinians approach the twenty-first century, Gordon's teachings must be remembered as a rule of thumb. National and religious ties of the two people to the Land of Israel–Palestine necessarily connect us to each other. Our survival will ultimately depend on our ability to coexist without sacrificing the national and cultural independence of either the Jews or the Palestinians. Such a view of Israeli-Palestinian relations requires a revision of national ethos on both sides, and, moreover, a rethinking of the whole concept of security. Moral and *halakhic* sources from biblical to modern times direct us to remember the organic responsibility that humans have toward one another. They remind us not to have short-term and short-sighted conceptions of security.

Finding the delicate balance that could guarantee our survival may be difficult in the face of fundamentalism, yet the other option may be total destruction. Today both sides consider the recognition of the other side's emotions and vulnerabilities as weakness and betrayal of the national and religious cause. In order to create a reality of peaceful coexistence there must be a recognition that Jews and Palestinians are bound to depend on one another. This recognition should be supported by traditional teachings from both sides. The greatest chal-lenge for peace is thus educational. Palestinians would have to find parallel con-cepts in their religious and national traditions. Unless both sides reinterpret their "national narratives" and renew national midrashim that do not dehumanize the other nation, peace will not be secure.

Our responsibility as Jews is to renew the Zionist ethos that has eroded morally over the past few decades. We must do so even before such transformation takes place on the other side. It is our goal to teach that

> The Torah was not given but to sanctify God's great name, as it was said: "You are my servant, Yisrael, in whom I will be glorified" (Isa. 49:3). Therefore they con-cluded: One must stay away from robbing Israelites and Gentiles . . . since anyone who steals from a Gentile ultimately steals from an Israelite, anyone who robs a Gentile ultimately robs an Israelite, anyone who swears at a Gentile ultimately

swears at an Israelite, anyone who lies to the Gentile ultimately lies to an Israelite, and anyone who spills the blood of a Gentile ends up spilling the blood of Israelites. The Torah was not given for this purpose but for the purpose of sanctifying God's great name, as it said, "And I will send a sign among them, and I will send those that escape of them" (Isa. 66:19). What does Scripture say at the end? "And they shall declare thy glory among the nations." (Tana Debi Eliyahu Raba 26)

The purpose of establishing the State of Israel was to secure and to glorify the existence of Judaism and of the Jewish people. As long as we mistreat our largest minority, we fail to comply with this vision.

Notes

1. I wish to thank my husband, Rabbi Arik Ascherman, a man who loves peace and pursues it, who inspired me to learn and explore many of the ideas which I am about to present in this article. For financial assistance I am indebted to the Memorial Foundation for Jewish Culture.

2. I employ the terms *aggadah* and *halakhah* based on previous discussions of those two categories by Haim Nachman Bialik, "Halakhah and Aggadah," in *The Writings of Haim Nachman Bialik* (Hebrew) (Tel Aviv: Dvir, 1939), pp. 207–13; and Abraham Joshua Heschel, *God in Search of Man: A Philosophy of Judaism* (New York: Farrar Straus and Giroux, 1985), pp. 336–40. However, I take their analysis further by assuming that both *halakhah* and *aggadah* are pluralistic in nature.

3. I use the term "post-Orthodox" to describe any Jew who is critical of Orthodox political thinking either within or without the Orthodox. I learned this term myself from a liberal Orthodox woman, Leah Shakdiel, who was the first woman to sit on a religious council in Israel.

4. Today, the only legal area where a theocratic model is implemented is that of family law, the part of Jewish law that requires the most radical reevaluaion. Marital law in Israel is determined and handled exclusively by Orthodox rabbinic courts. It is perhaps the worst possible scenario for a relationship between *halakhah* and a democratic Jewish state. The legal phenomenon of rabbinic courts is the source of the greatest legal discrimination against women in Israeli society and is a tragic example of how democratic civil rights are violated by Israeli law in the name of *halakhah*. Even today, when the Knesset is about to pass an act of civil rights that intends to protect minorities, the fact that women are subject to theocratic discriminations remains untouched. By making this concession, secular politicians have sacrificed women on the alter of the fragile Orthodox-secular coexistence in Israel.

5. Yeshayahu Leibowitz, "The Law of the Torah as a Law for the State of Israel," in his *Judaism, The Jewish People and the State of Israel* (Hebrew) (Tel Aviv: Schocken Books, 1975), pp.192–208.

6. Haim Cohen, "The Secularization of Divine Law," in *Jewish Law in Ancient and Modern Israel* (1971), pp. 1–49.

7. The term "reconfiguring the authority" is based on Arnold Eisen, "Constructing the Usable Past: The Idea of 'Tradition' in Twentieth-Century American Judaism," in *The Uses of Tradition,* Jack Wertheimer (ed.), (New York: Jewish Theological Seminary, 1992).

8. The following rabbinic sources demonstrate cases where a law was violated in order to maintain the integrity of the *halakhic* system. Berakhot 54a, Gittin 60a, Numbers Rabbah 8.4, Exodus Rabbah 5:5, Megillah 9a, Sifrei Deut no. 113, Yeb. 90b, Sanhedrin 90a, Berakhot 19b, Numbers Rabbah 14:1. Eliezer Berkovits, *Not in Heaven: The Nature and the Function of Halakha* (New York: Ktav, 1983), chap. 2. I wish to thank Zak Braiterman for referring me to some of these sources.

9. See Elliot Dorff and Arthur Rosett, *A Living Tree: The Roots and Growth of Jewish Law* (Albany: State University of New York Press, 1988), pp. 564–65.

10. Arthur Hertzberg, *The Zionist Idea* (New York: Macmillan, 1959), p. 369.

11. Aharon David Gordon, "Avodatenu Me'Ata," *Kitvei Aharon David Gordon Be' Chamishah Krakhim* (= Kitvei) vol. 2, pp. 53–54.

12. Ibid., p. 57.

13. Ibid., p. 58.

14. *Lezikaron*, "In Memory" (1918), *Kitvei*, vol. 4, p. 183.

15. Ibid., p. 180–91.

16. *Mekhilta Derabi Yishmael*, Tractate Nezikin, chap. 13 (Exod. 22:1–3).

17. Translation based on Richard Levy, *On Wings of Freedom* (Washington, D.C.: B'nai B'rith Hillel Foundation, 1989), p. 51.

18. Translation taken from C. G. Montefiore and H. A. Loewe, *Rabbinic Anthology* (New York: Schocken Books, 1974), p. 536.

Epilogue: The Future of Jewish Ethics and Morals

Ethics and Morals

This book has included two sections, one on Jewish ethical theories and one on Jewish moral practice. We have divided the topics this way for the sake of clarity and accuracy: only then could it be clear that there are two distinct levels of discussion in these matters, one dealing with concrete, moral problems and the other pertaining to the grounds and methods for making Jewish moral judgments of any kind on any topic.

At the close of the book, then, it is important to remind our readers that these *are distinct* sets of questions which must be treated by the different methods and concepts appropriate to each, and yet these are *interrelated* areas of inquiry. Neither can be done successfully without the other. Discussions of ethical theory which are not rooted in specific moral examples are not only ethereal in tone and substance but often inaccurate, detached as they are from the real world in which moral decisions are made and in which moral education takes place. Conversely, rabbinic responsa and other modes of discussion of particular moral problems which ignore questions of method are at best self-delusive and at worst misleading in that they falsify the tradition by pretending that there is only one way to read it. *Everyone* who derives anything from the Jewish tradition approaches it in a specific way, and that way must be open to analysis and evaluation in comparison with other ways which seek to derive meaning and guidance from the tradition. This is especially important in our time, when Jews of all stripes, and, indeed, non-Jews as well, read Jewish texts, bringing with them their own convictions about life and their own assumptions about the origins and status of the tradition's texts. Only when those underlying beliefs are laid bare can the strengths and weaknesses of a particular mode of interpreting and applying the tradition be evaluated, and only then can one determine the accuracy and authority of a given statement claiming to represent the tradition on a given issue.

This interdependence makes it critical that students of the Jewish tradition, of morality in general, and of their intersection in the realm of Jewish morals and ethics study *both* Jewish ethical theories and at least some examples of current discussion of Jewish moral norms. The organization of this book into its two sections thus flows not only from our educational goal of making the disparate questions involved in these two levels of inquiry clear but also from our shared conviction that both sets of questions must enter into any serious Jewish moral discussion. If separating the discussions into two distinct sections of the book in any way misled readers into thinking that we think these levels of thought are independent or separable, then we hope that these paragraphs will clear up that confusion. Ethics and morals are distinct, but they are both important and are, indeed, interrelated.

All present and future discussions of Jewish moral problems, then, ignore theoretical questions at their peril, for they assume a basis of authority and a methodology which themselves may well be at issue for many of the people the author is trying to convince. Conversely, all present and future Jewish theories of ethics, if they are going to have any relevance to the modern world, must consider how they would apply to concrete moral decision making and moral education in contemporary times, when developments in society and technology almost daily raise new moral problems and old ones in new ways, and when Jews live not only among but in interaction with non-Jews, with all of the complications that that implies in determining the authority and content of Jewish moral judgments.

The Grounds of Authority of Jewish Moral Norms

Many of the readings in the first section of this book, the one on ethics, arise out of concerns which are part of all Western religious approaches to ethics. How, if at all, does the religious character of Jewish ethics affect its methodology and contents? How does it affect the reasons why one should pay attention to Jewish ethics in the first place and maybe even seek to shape one's life according to its dictates and ideals?

The Bible portrays Jewish ethical norms as the commands of God. This means, at least, that God will enforce those commands, and so we should obey to avoid punishment and attain reward. The Bible, though, is already sophisticated enough to indicate a number of other ramifications of the divine origins of its moral (and other) commands. Because a wise and benevolent God is the author of the commands, the commandments themselves are wise and good and should be followed for their own sake (Deut. 4:6–8). Because God has done favors for us in the past and continues to do them now, we owe God obedience in gratitude for that beneficence (e.g., Deut. 4:32–40). That is especially true because we promised to obey God in the Covenant we made with the Eternal One, and so the morality of promise keeping, in addition to that of gratitude, binds us to God's commands. Moreover, the commandments make us holy, and our obedience of them enhances God's reputation on earth. Finally, and perhaps most inclusively, we should obey God's commands out of our love of God.[1]

That all assumes, though, that we believe in God in the first place, and in contemporary times that is anything but a given for many Jews. The question they raise, then, is this: are there reasons to pay attention to Jewish ethics apart from the theological reasons advanced by the Bible? Are they, for example, internally wise, as the Bible itself maintains, and so worthy of attention and even adherence for their own sake? Are there, to take another tack, national or ethnic reasons to comply with the norms of Jewish ethics? Should Jews follow them, for example, in order to identify as Jews, or to enhance the reputation and pride of Jews?

Some Jews have sought answers along such secular lines in an effort to preserve an attachment to the Jewish tradition in making their moral decisions without adopting its theological underpinnings. At the other extreme, some contemporary Jews have adopted one form or another of Orthodoxy, affirming what they construe to be traditional Jewish beliefs about the authority and methods of Jewish moral norms.

Between these polar opposites is a third group, one which has explored a different, intermediate route to explain the authority of Jewish moral norms for them. It has sought to analyze what difference it makes to couch moral discussions in religious terms and then to deal with the extent to which new understandings of religious commitment can embody those distinctly religious elements in Jewish ethics and morals. So, for example, some members of this group have developed nonverbal theories of revelation, such that the maxims of Jewish law are not the direct word of God at Sinai but are not totally detached from God either. Jewish law instead is the product of human beings inspired by God, just as we might be, or it consists of the values and forms of behavior which express the Jewish community's—or the Jewish individual's—aspiration for living a life suffused with an awareness of the divine.[2]

Others in this third group have concentrated not so much on revelation but on the nature of religious language, adapting some of the new understandings in general literary and linguistic theory of the many ways in which language gains meaning. What does it mean, for example, to be in covenant with God? How does that affect the way one thinks about moral norms which are part of that Covenant? How, if at all, does construing Jewish moral norms as part of the Jewish Covenant with God give them authority? Attention to revelation and to theological and moral language, then, are two of the ways—but only two of them—in which this third school seeks to explain the relevance and authority of Jewish moral norms for contemporary, nonfundamentalist Jews.

The articles in the second, third, and last sections of Part I are examples of the approaches of this third, intermediate school. Along the same lines, the articles in the fourth section of Part I are an attempt to explore a proper methodology for arriving at moral norms in one particular area of concern, that of medical ethics, if one assumes a religious, but not a fundamentalist, version of Judaism. Such analyses of the grounds and methods of Jewish ethics in the context of plural understandings of the nature of Jewish faith are, in our view, the wave of the future.

The Definition of Jewish Moral Norms

Those who base the authority of Jewish norms on something other than God must define not only why Jewish norms should hold interest for us and even guide us but also how the content of Jewish norms is to be determined. Should that be done by rabbis, acting individually or collectively in some way? Should it be done by majority rule of all Jews, or of all Jews in a given community? Is each person to determine what the Jewish tradition requires of him or her? If so, in what sense is the norm Jewish?

Defining the content of Jewish moral norms is no easier for those who root the authority of Jewish moral norms in God. Such people may think that they know full well what is right and good, for they may just refer the inquirer to the record of

God's commandments in the Torah—or, if they are somewhat more sophisticated, to the Torah as interpreted by the rabbis throughout the generations.

Such a stance of belief, though, involves at least two problems. First, the problem that Plato stated long ago in the *Euthyphro* still holds: is a given action good because God commands it, or is it good on independent grounds and therefore the good God commands it? Put more broadly, even if a given action is commanded by God, why does that make it right or good?

Most believers sidestep this question by asserting a belief not only in God but in an omniscient and morally good God who, by virtue of his goodness, commands only morally good actions and who, by virtue of her omniscience, knows what indeed is good. In other words, believers get around the problem of the ultimate ground of morality by building more assumptions into their theological beliefs.

Even if that step is accepted, though, another critical problem arises for a theologically based morality: if goodness is what God commands, we need to have firm knowledge of what God wants of us, but how do we know that? The Bible is already aware of this question, for in several places it addresses the problem of determining who is giving an authentic account of God's will—or, in biblical terms, who is a true prophet.[3] The rabbis got around this problem by declaring that true prophecy ended with the fall of the First Temple, and so claims to true prophecy no longer needed to be evaluated for their authenticity as the divine word. That, though, only transformed the problem into a different guise. Specifically, if prophecy was not to be the way God revealed his will and was to be replaced by the interpretations and decisions of the rabbis themselves, why were such rabbinic understandings of God's will to be trusted as accurate renditions of what God wants of us in our own time? The rabbis justified their fidelity as interpreters of God's will primarily on the basis of Deut. 17, from which they derived not only their own authority to make decisions under the law but also their right thereby to limit the range of acceptable interpretations and practices.[4]

The two issues in this and the last section of this epilogue, though—namely, that of the authority of the Jewish tradition to define the right and the good, and that of determining and justifying a method to know what God wants of us—have been exacerbated in our own time by modern developments. Modern biblical scholarship has determined that the record of revelation, the Torah, consists of several documents which were later edited together. Therefore, even if God dictated the laws at Mount Sinai, what we have in hand is, at best, the human records of that event put together, from what we can tell, centuries after the event itself. Therefore, even if God spoke in words at Mount Sinai, and even if Moses was a faithful transmitter of those words, and even if scribes from the time of Moses on did their best to copy the manuscripts given to them accurately, what we have in hand may not be what God said in the first place. Indeed, even with the valiant efforts of the rabbis to reconcile the varying versions of stories and laws in the Torah, the archaeological and cross-cultural evidence available to us now makes most modern Jews ask the Bible's question about true and accurate prophecy with a new urgency: to what extent, we wonder, does the Torah define the word of God at all, or is it simply the understanding of a given human author at a particular time and place of what is moral? Or is it, as we suggested earlier, something in between—perhaps the understanding of a particular person or group of persons of what God wants? Thus the modern developments in biblical scholarship mean that the Torah does not define the right and the good—or even God's will—in anything like the authoritative way our ancestors believed it did.

Moreover, the Jewish community is not nearly as cohesive as it once was, and it does not have the power to enforce its dictates, as it did before the Enlightenment. Consequently, there is no one rabbi or set of rabbis whose interpretation of Jewish norms is recognized by all Jews as authoritative.

There are some communities of Jews who, at least officially, abide by the decisions of a given rabbi or group of rabbis. So, for example, Conservative Jews are supposed to look to their congregational rabbi and, ultimately, to the Conservative movement's Committee on Jewish Law and Standards for authoritative decisions in matters of Jewish law and morals, and, especially in crisis situations like those at the end of life, many do. Similarly, Orthodox Jews variously look to their own congregational rabbi or to one or another of the respected rabbis of our time for definitive rulings, and Reform Jews may do likewise. Because almost all Jews now live in countries governed by Enlightenment principles, however, there is no legal compulsion to follow the decisions of any particular rabbi or rabbinic body, and so their norms, even if couched in the language of authoritative rulings of Jewish law, are, in effect, guidance which individual Jews are free to obey or ignore.

This brings to the fore another question which has become acute in modern times, even for believers in God and in the tradition as the embodiment of the will of God: to what extent do I as an individual have the right to interpret God's will on my own? Traditionally, it was the Jewish community which determined the authoritative way in which God's will was to be understood, whether by official rabbinic ruling or through the ongoing custom of the community committed to God's will. The Enlightenment, however, brought with it a new attention to, and appreciation of, individual autonomy, and virtually all modern Jews are the product of that development. To what extent, then, and how should I bend my own will to that of God—or of the community interpreting God?

This critical methodological question of the individual and communal components in the definition of God's will—and, by extension, in the definition of what is right and good—is one important factor behind the existence of the four movements in North American Judaism. While each, as a religious approach to Jewish identity, seeks to articulate and motivate its constituents to follow the will of God, each movement, in determining what the will of God is on any given issue, blends autonomy and heteronomy in a different mix.

All of this means that now and in the future, scholars of Jewish ethics will need to pay increasing attention to questions of the status and authority of revelation and to issues in general philosophy of law as it is emerging and as it can be applied to Jewish law. The readings in the first section of this volume all come out of this awareness and seek to explain the authority and content of Jewish ethics in terms of contemporary theories of ethics, law, language, and faith. As those articles demonstrate, if the modern world has made the old questions of the authority and definition of God's will much more complicated, it also offers us some new insights into the nature of religious faith, ethics, language, and law, insights which can help us understand the significance, authority, and proper methodology of Jewish ethics in our time.

The Shape of Contemporary Moral Problems

The second part of this book focused on contemporary treatments of specific moral problems. Some of these problems have been around for a long time. People, after all, are born, they live, and they die, and so issues of abortion and euthanasia arise for us as they did for generations past. In our time, though, with the rise of ever-new technologies, old problems like these take on a very new complexion. Since we are now able to affect the medical outcomes of cases which we were helpless to change in the past, we now must ask which of the various things we now can do we should adopt—if we should do anything at all.

In some cases old problems are new not so much because of new technology but because of changing social conditions. Our planet now supports several times the human population that existed just two hundred years ago. This makes questions of poverty all the more critical; it raises the need for sound ecological planning on a scale unheard of just a few decades ago; and it puts the issues surrounding birth control in a whole new light.

The increased numbers of human beings and modern means of communication and transportation both mean that we live in an ever-smaller global village. We thus come into contact with peoples whom we would have barely known about in past generations, let alone seen up close. Sometimes that leads to the dissolution of prejudices and the broadening of perspectives, and then it is to be prized. We come to know more about ourselves as we learn about others, and we test our convictions and shape them anew in the light of new insights from other cultures. That reaction, however, requires both the psychology and the philosophy open to pluralism, and not everyone has both of those. Therefore, sometimes the new exposure to other peoples and cultures instead produces violent reactions against the new, the unfamiliar, and the threatening. The fact that we now live in close proximity with one another thus imposes upon us an ever-greater obligation to learn about other peoples and cultures and to find ways to live together in peace. These are not only pragmatic necessities; they are also moral duties, for the preservation of our very lives depends upon them.

In some ways none of this is new. From time immemorial the trilogy of creation-revelation-redemption has formed the core of Jewish theology and liturgy.[5] As such, this trilogy also forms the basis for Jewish moral thinking, for moral norms always arise out of a view of the world and ourselves. Creation identifies who we are—namely, the creatures of God in a world created by God. Revelation bespeaks the nature of our covenantal relationship to God and the responsibilities and rewards that that entails. Finally, the concept of redemption adumbrates our ultimate hopes, who we aim to be and the world we should try to foster. Many of the new problems can readily be seen as just new applications and adaptations of these themes of creation, revelation, and redemption.

Contemporary circumstances, though, require us to reexamine not only our means to attain our goals but the very goals themselves, together with the conceptions and values which underlie them. The need and the methods to preserve creation in our own time are new as we face overpopulation and ecological disaster. Our understanding of the complex process by which divine revelation takes place is more sophisticated, making it harder to discern God's will. While this may rob us of the confident self-assurance that our ancestors once had that we know what God wants and that others do not, it simultaneously can and should expose us to the moral thinking of others, thus making our own moral discussions and our own discernment of God's will all the sharper. Even our hopes for the future—our image of redemption—may be somewhat different from that of our ancestors, as we look forward to a world not only of peace and prosperity, as they did, but also one of individual freedom and creativity within the context of strong and deeply rooted communities. Only when our new and old images of creation, revelation, and redemption are integrated and articulated can we know how we should try to fix the world.

The New Contexts of Jewish Moral Judgments

Contemporary moral problems are new in some ways, and, on the other hand, they share some of the same themes as the issues of the past. The contexts in which Jews are dealing with those problems, however, are radically new, for now Jews live primarily either in a state of their own or in a democracy which accepts them as full citizens.

The existence of a Jewish state in Israel raises new, perplexing moral problems for Jews, problems with which Jews have not had to deal during nineteen hundered years of dispersion. Aside from the problems which every sovereign nation must face—setting priorities, finding ways to provide for the citizens' welfare, preventing crime, and so forth—Israel must deal with ruling a largely hostile minority within its midst. The moral ambiguities of power have been graphically demonstrated during the decades of Israel's existence as it has sought to defend itself while still maintaining a strong sense of human rights and decency. It is not, and cannot legitimately be expected to be, perfect in balancing these competing claims. If only because Israel is a human society, there have been, and will be, both political and moral mistakes. The new phenomenon of Jews ruling themselves in a Jewish state, however, imposes new obligations upon Jews to deal with the morality of politics out of the resources of their tradition, looking at questions which Jews have not had to face for a very long time, if ever.

The vast majority of the world's Jews now live in countries whose political structure makes them full-fledged citizens, whether in Israel or elsewhere. Anti-Semitism still rears its ugly head at various times and places, but, by and large, Jews are called upon to participate in, and to contribute to, the nations in which they reside. In most cases this includes the obligation to take part in setting social policies, not separately as Jews per se but as individual citizens. In doing so they probably will not be asked to give "the Jewish view" on the topic at hand, for that has no special claim on any modern democracy (except, to some extent, Israel). Still, Jews are inevitably influenced by their Jewish heritage, and that may indeed be salutary as Jews contribute the wisdom of their own long history and tradition to modern problems. To do that intelligently, however, Jews must learn their tradition and how to apply it to issues which may not have a direct precedent in Jewish literature—or may have such a precedent but one decided under different circumstances or when Jewish moral sensitivities were not what they are today. In other words, Jews need to learn not only what their tradition says but how and when to apply it, and that requires not only the lawyer's skills of differentiation and application but the moral and religious sensitivity to discern God's will in our time.

If the musings on Jewish ethics and morals contained in this book do nothing else, then, they should alert us to the limits of human knowledge of the right and the good and the need ever to try to learn more. Contemporary moral problems are, if anything, more complex and more difficult than those faced by our ancestors. The importance of identifying and articulating the theoretical underpinnings of contemporary moral discussions has become ever more evident to us as we seek to do Jewish ethics in the exciting, but confusing, pluralistic setting of the modern world.

None of this means that we are at a total loss to discern the right and the good in our time. We have the resources of our ancestors' experience spanning thousands of years and the awareness of a variety of methods to tap it. Moreover, the need to discern the right and the good is all the more urgent in the crowded, closely knit world in which we live. Thus, even though we have been chastened by our cognizance of the limits of human knowledge, we are goaded on to our moral quest by the critical need to identify moral norms and ideals for our time. In this process the words of Rabbi Tarfon can appropriately be the last ones: "Yours is not to finish the task, but neither are you free to desist from it."[6]

Notes

1. For more detailed discussion of these biblical motives to obey and the ones the rabbis added, see Elliot N. Dorff, *Mitzvah Means Commandment* (New York: United Synagogue of America, 1989), chaps. 1, 3–5.

2. For a description of the theories of revelation currently adopted by the theorists in the modern Jewish movements, see Elliot N. Dorff, *Conservative Judaism: Our Ancestors to Our Descendants* (New York: United Synagogue of America, 1977), pp. 110–57.

3. Deut. 13:2–6; 18:9–22. Jeremiah, in particular, complains bitterly about the "false prophets" of his time; see Jer. 6:13–15; 14:4; 23:23–40; 27:9–18; 28:1–17; 29:21–32. Jeremiah himself, though, predicted an ignominious end for King Jehoiakim (Jer. 22:19), but the historical account in 2 Kings 23:6 indicates that Jehoiakim died a natural and, presumably, honorable death. Such examples of prophecies which did not come to pass delivered by people whom the later tradition considered to be true prophets force us to understand the Jewish tradition's conception of true prophecy not as the ability to predict the future but as a true (and often courageous) call to moral rectitude.

4. E.g., Mishnah *Rosh Hashanah* 2:9; Babylonian Talmud, *Bava Mezia* 59b. For a more extended treatment of these and other sources on this issue of authority, see Dorff, *Mitzvah Means Commandment* (at n. 1), chap. 6; and Elliot N. Dorff and Arthur Rosett, *A Living Tree: The Roots and Growth of Jewish Law* (Albany: State University of New York Press, 1988), pp. 82–123, 187–257.

5. Isaac Arama (c. 1420–1494) in his *Akedat Yitzhak* (55 ed., Bialystok, 1849), pp. 285–89, lists these as the three themes of the Sabbath, and Franz Rosenzweig (1866–1929), in his *Star of Redemption* (New York: Holt, Rinehart and Winston, 1970), pp. 308–15, ties them to the evening, morning, and afternoon services of that day and to the pilgrimage festivals (Passover, Shavuot, and Sukkot), explicating along the way the importance of this trilogy theologically. Neither Arama nor Rosenzweig spells out the moral implications of these themes, but moral norms always derive from one's view of life and its goals, and so the connection is not hard to delineate. Each of these themes individually, of course, plays a role in concrete, Jewish moral decisions, as some of the essays in Part II of this book illustrate; it is the moral significance of the combination of them that yet has to be explicated, a task which we begin to do in the rest of this paragraph of the epilogue.

6. Mishnah, *Avot* (*Ethics of the Fathers*) 2:21.

Contributors

MARTHA A. ACKELSBERG is a professor of government at Smith College in Northampton, Massachusetts, a founding member of Ezrat Nashim and of B'not Esh, and author of *Free Women of Spain: Anarchism and the Struggle for the Emancipation of Women* (1991).

ANNETTE ARONOWICZ is associate professor of religious studies at Franklin and Marshall College, Lancaster, Pa. She is the author of *Freedom from Ideology: Secrecy in Modern Expressions* (1988) and translator of *Nine Talmudic Readings by Emmanuel Lévinas* (1990).

EUGENE BOROWITZ is Sigmund L. Falk Distinguished Professor of Education and Jewish Religious Thought at the Hebrew Union College Jewish Institute of Religion in New York City, where he has taught since 1962. He has authored thirteen books and is the founder of *Sh'ma, A Journal of Jewish Responsibility.*

DANIEL BRESLAUER is professor of religious studies at the University of Kansas, Lawrence, Kans. He has authored numerous articles, including "Judaism and Human Rights in Contemporary Thought: A Bibliographic Survey" (1993) and "Judaism and Civil Religion" (1993).

ELLIOT N. DORFF is rector and Sol and Anne Dorff Professor of Philosophy at the University of Judaism in Los Angeles, Calif. He served on the Ethics Committee of Hillary Rodham Clinton's Task Force on Health Care. He has authored some seventy articles and six books, the last of which is *Knowing God: Jewish Journeys to the Unknowable* (1992).

DAVID H. ELLENSON is I. H. and Anna Grancell Professor of Jewish Religious Thought at Hebrew Union College–Jewish Institute of Religion, in Los Angeles, Calif. He is the author most recently of *Rabbi Esriel Hildesheimer and the Location of a Modern Jewish Orthodoxy* (1990).

DAVID M. FELDMAN is the rabbi of Teaneck Jewish Center in Teaneck, N.J., and is the author of *Birth Control in Jewish Law* (1968) and *Health and Medicine in the Jewish Tradition* (1986).

ROBERT GORDIS was professor of Bible and Rappaport Professor in the Philosophies of Religion at the Jewish Theological Seminary of America, a past president of the Rabbinical Assembly and the Synagogue Council of America, and past editor of the journal, *Judaism.*

BLU GREENBERG writes and lectures on issues of contemporary Jewish interest. Her books include *On Women and Judaism* (1983), *How to Run a Traditional Jewish Household* (1993), and *A Special Kind of Mother* (poetry).

IRVING GREENBERG is president and cofounder of CLAL. A seminal thinker on the theological implications of the Holocaust and the rebirth of Israel, he is the author of *The Jewish Way* (1988).

DAVID HARTMAN is director of the Shalom Hartman Institute in Jerusalem, a professor at Hebrew University there, and the author most recently of *Conflicting Visions: Spiritual Possibilities of Modern Israel* (1990).

RICHARD J. ISRAEL is director of the Campus Rabbi Program at the Reconstructionist Rabbinical College, Philadelphia, Pa.

ALFRED JOSPE was national director of programs and resources of the B'nai B'rith Hillel Foundations and author of *Judaism on the Campus* (1963) and *Religion and Myth in Jewish Philosophy* (1932).

MENACHEM KELLNER is the Wolfson Professor of Jewish Thought at Haifa University and is author most recently of *Maimonides on Judaism and the Jewish People* (1991).

SANDRA LUBARSKY is an instructor of philosophy at Eureka College, Eureka, Ill.

AARON L. MACKLER is assistant professor of theology at Duquesne University in Pittsburgh, Pa. He has served as staff ethicist at New York State Task Force on Life and the Law. Dr. Mackler is a Conservative rabbi and chair of the Subcommittee on Bioethics for the Committee on Jewish Law and Standards.

MICHAEL L. MORGAN is professor of philosophy and Jewish studies at Indiana University in Bloomington, Indiana, and is the author of *Platonic Piety* (1990) and of *Dilemmas in Modern Jewish Thought* (1992). He is editor of *The Jewish Thought of Emil Fackerman* (1987) and of *Classics of Moral and Political Theory* (1992).

LOUIS E. NEWMAN is an associate professor of religion and director of the program in Jewish Studies at Carleton College, Northfield, Minn.

DAVID NOVAK is Edgar M. Bronfman Professor of Modern Judaic Studies, University of Virginia, Charlottesville, Va. His latest book is *Jewish Social Ethics* (1992).

JUDITH PLASKOW is professor of religious studies at Manhattan College, N.Y., and is cofounder and coeditor of *The Journal of Feminist Studies and Religion*.

EINAT RAMON is the first Israeli woman ordained as a rabbi. She has been the circuit rabbi for Congregation Har Shalom, Missoula, Mont., since 1991 and is a doctoral candidate at Stanford University, where she is writing a dissertation on A. D. Gordon.

FRED ROSNER is director of medicine at Mount Sinai Services at Queens Hospital Center, Jamaica, N.Y., and professor of medicine at Mount Sinai School of Medicine in New York.

SOL ROTH is adjunct professor of philosophy and Samson R. Hirsch Professor of Torah and Derekh Eretz at Yeshiva University in New York City.

HAROLD M. SCHULWEIS is rabbi of Valley Beth Shalom, Encino, Calif., and founding chairman of the Jewish Foundation for Christian Rescuers.

BYRON L. SHERWIN is vice president and Verson Professor of Jewish Philosophy and Mysticism at Chicago's Spertus Institute of Jewish Studies. He is the author of seventeen books and over one hundred articles and monographs relating to Jewish theology, philosophy, education, and history.

SEYMOUR SIEGEL was professor of theology and ethics at the Jewish Theological Seminary of America and the chairman of the Committee on Jewish Law and Standards of the Conservative Movement.

ELIE SPITZ is rabbi of Congregation B'nai Israel, Tustin, Calif. He is a graduate of the Jewish Theological Seminary of American and Boston University School of Law. Prior to rabbinic studies he was legal counsel for Brigham and Women's Hospital, Boston, Mass.

ARTHUR WASKOW is a Fellow of ALEPH: Alliance for Jewish Renewal; editor of its journal *New Menorah;* and author of *Godwrestling* (1987), *Seasons of Joy* (1991), and the forthcoming *Down-to-Earth Judaism: Food, Money, Sex, and the Rest of Life.*

LAURIE ZOLOTH-DORFMAN works as a clinical ethicist for a large national HMO and is a lecturer at the Graduate Theological Union in Berkeley, Calif. Her chapter in this book was part of her doctoral dissertation there.

Suggestions for Further Reading

There is an extensive and rapidly expanding literature on Jewish ethics and morality, only a portion of which can be mentioned here.

For useful, if somewhat outdated, annotated bibliographies of materials in this area, see S. Daniel Breslauer, *Contemporary Jewish Ethics* (Greenwood Press, 1985) and *Modern Jewish Morality* (Greenwood Press, 1986). Other collections of essays include Marvin Fox, ed., *Modern Jewish Ethics* (Ohio State University Press, 1975), Menachem Kellner, ed., *Contemporary Jewish Ethics* (Hebrew Publishing Co., 1978), and Milton Konvitz, *Judaism and Human Rights* (W. W. Norton, 1972). Daniel Jeremy Silver, ed., *Judaism and Ethics* (Ktav, 1970) contains some older but still very worthwhile essays drawn from the [Central Conference of American Rabbis] *CCAR Journal*.

Because an understanding of the development of Jewish law is essential for an appreciation of Jewish ethics, some major works on this subject will be of interest: Elliot N. Dorff and Arthur Rosett, *A Living Tree: The Roots and Growth of Jewish Law* (State University of New York Press, 1988), Joel Roth, *The Halakhic Process: A Systemic Analysis* (Jewish Theological Seminary, 1986), and Louis Jacobs, *A Tree of Life: Diversity, Flexibility, and Creativity in Jewish Law* (Oxford University Press, 1984).

Some works dealing with the nature of Jewish ethics and its relationship to law are of note: Shubert Spero, *Morality, Halakha and the Jewish Tradition* (Ktav and Yeshiva University, 1983), Ze'ev W. Falk, *Religious Law and Ethics* (Mesharim Publishers, 1991), and Haim Cohn, *Human Rights in Jewish Law* (Ktav, 1984). See also Elliot N. Dorff, "The Interaction of Jewish Law with Morality," *Judaism* 26(1977):455–66. Jacob Agus, *The Vision and the Way* (Frederick Ungar, 1966) highlights the idealistic and pragmatic aspects of the Jewish ethical tradition.

There are several collections of modern orthodox responsa, or case studies, substantial portions of which deal with questions of morality: J. David Bleich, *Contemporary Halakhic Problems* (Ktav and Yeshiva University Press, 1977; vol. 2, 1983; vol. 3, 1989). Basil F. Herring's books, *Jewish Ethics and Halakhah for Our Time* (Ktav and Yeshiva University Press, 1984; vol. 2, 1990), invite readers to see how Jewish sources can be applied to contemporary moral problems. Solomon Freehof published several collections of Reform responsa: *Current Reform Responsa* (1969), *Modern Reform Responsa* (1971), *Contemporary Reform Responsa* (1974), and *Reform Responsa for Our Time* (1977) [all published by Hebrew Union College Press]. For distinctively Conservative thinkers, see Robert Gordis, *Judaic Ethics for a Lawless World* (Jewish Theological Seminary, 1986), Seymour Siegel, ed., *Conservative*

Judaism and Jewish Law (Rabbinical Assembly, 1977), and Simon Greenberg, *The Ethical in the Jewish and American Heritage* (Jewish Thelogical Seminary, 1977).

We especially wish to draw readers' attention to other major works on Jewish ethics by the authors represented in this volume. David Novak's *Jewish Social Ethics* (Oxford University Press, 1992) represents his most recent collection of essays in this area. Earlier papers, some of them on issues of ethics, can be found in *Law and Theology in Judaism* (Ktav, 1974; vol. 2, 1976). Eugene Borowitz's *Exploring Jewish Ethics* (Wayne State University Press, 1990) is a collection of his essays spanning three decades, while his *Choosing a Jewish Sex Ethic* (Schocken, 1979) represents an earlier attempt to articulate a liberal Jewish position. S. Daniel Breslauer offers another liberal theory of Jewish ethics in *A New Jewish Ethics* (Edwin Mellen Press, 1983). Byron Sherwin has collected a number of important ethical reflections in his *In Partnership with God* (Syracuse University Press, 1990).

In the area of Jewish medical ethics a number of substantial studies and collections have been published, most representing Orthodox perspectives. The earliest major book in this field was Immanuel Jakobovits, *Jewish Medical Ethics* 2d ed. (Bloch Publishing, 1972). More recent studies include Fred Rosner, *Modern Medicine and Jewish Ethics* (Ktav and Yeshiva University, 1986) and J. David Bleich, *Judaism and Healing: Halakhic Perspectives* (Ktav, 1981). Anthologies include Fred Rosner and J. David Bleich, eds., *Jewish Bioethics* (Hebrew Publishing Co., 1979), and two collections by Levi Meier, ed., *Jewish Values in Bioethics* (Human Sciences Press, 1986) and *Jewish Values in Health and Medicine* (University Press of America, 1991). A more liberal but still traditional approach to Jewish medical ethics is presented in David M. Feldman, *Marital Relations, Birth Control and Abortion in Jewish Law* (Schocken, 1974) and *Health and Medicine in the Jewish Tradition* (Crossroad, 1986).

For a more focused study of Jewish law and the treatment of the critically ill, see Daniel B. Sinclair, *Tradition and the Biological Revolution* (Edinburgh University Press, 1989). For an essay critical of the Orthodox drift of much work in this area, see Ronald Green, "Contemporary Jewish Bioethics: A Critical Assessment," in E. E. Shelp, ed., *Theology and Bioethics* (D. Reidel Publishing, 1985), pp. 245–66. Other critical analyses of Jewish bioethics include Louis E. Newman, "Text and Tradition in Contemporary Jewish Bioethics," in P. F. Camenisch, ed., *Religious Methods and Resources in Bioethics* (Kluwer, 1994), pp. 127–43, and "Talking Ethics with Strangers: A View from Jewish Tradition," *Journal of Medicine and Philosophy* 18, no. 5 (1993): 549–67.

The Conservative movement has begun to publish extensively in this area. See the entire Spring 1991 issue of the journal *Conservative Judaism,* devoted to two long responsa on end-of-life issues, i.e., Elliot N. Dorff, "A Jewish Approach to End-Stage Medical Care," and Avram Israel Reisner, "A Halakhic Ethic of Care for the Terminally Ill." Forthcoming essays on issues at the beginning of life and on the distribution of health care are already planned for the Conservative movement's Committee on Jewish Law and Standards and its journal, *Conservative Judaism.*